High Participation Systems of Higher Education

High Participation Systems of Higher Education

edited by

Brendan Cantwell,
Simon Marginson,
and Anna Smolentseva

OXFORD
UNIVERSITY PRESS

OXFORD
UNIVERSITY PRESS

Great Clarendon Street, Oxford, OX2 6DP,
United Kingdom

Oxford University Press is a department of the University of Oxford.
It furthers the University's objective of excellence in research, scholarship,
and education by publishing worldwide. Oxford is a registered trade mark of
Oxford University Press in the UK and in certain other countries

First Edition published in 2018

Impression: 1

Published in the United States of America by Oxford University Press
198 Madison Avenue, New York, NY 10016, United States of America

British Library Cataloguing in Publication Data

Data available

Library of Congress Control Number: 2018945291

ISBN 978-0-19-882887-7

Printed and bound by
CPI Group (UK) Ltd, Croydon, CR0 4YY

PREFACE

As the title suggests, *High Participation Systems of Higher Education* is about systems of higher education with advanced levels of student enrolment: how they work, and what they mean for universities and other institutions, and for the societies in which they are embedded.

Like much in higher education studies it is multi-disciplinary in approach. Between us we see through lenses from political economy, sociology, political science, and policy analysis, and draw on historical sensibility and cultural semiotics; and we conduct quantitative and qualitative social science research. However, *High Participation Systems of Higher Education* is not based on newly collected and analysed data. Rather it is the outcome of an extended process of reflection and synthesis, individual and collective. The chapters integrate and combine a wide body of research and scholarly work in education studies, sociology, political economy, government, and global studies, and draw extensively on both large-scale data sets in the public domain, and the outcomes of individual research projects conducted by the authors and many others. The objective of this combined project is ambitious: to capture what is distinctive and new about the high participation systems (HPS) phase in higher education—the phase that Martin Trow in 1973 called 'universal' higher education—when more than 50 per cent of young people in a society become enrolled at an advanced level of study.

The book seeks to theorize HPS at the world level, building a comprehensive picture by using literature, observation and discussion. The principal findings have been developed in the form of theorization and are distilled to the seventeen propositions about HPS presented on pages xxi–xxii. The propositions are claims to be tested, challenged, and refined rather than final conclusions. The orthodox social science approach would be to explore and test one of the propositions on a comparative basis through large scale data analysis. Because we believe that the HPS era is not well understood, and because generic secular tendencies must run the gauntlet of contextual variation, that approach is not used here. It would have been premature. The threshold need is to at least begin to understand the bigger picture through theorization—to think about how the many changes entailed in the HPS era connect, thereby opening up a richer terrain for future inquiry, while also providing space to explore contextual variations at national level. Hence the seventeen generic propositions, and hence also their critical interrogation in eight national cases.

Part I of the book looks at HPS in world terms and reviews comparative data. Part II looks at HPS in Australia, Canada, Finland, Japan, Norway, Poland, Russia, and the

United States. Each part of the book has been written with an eye on the other and in the light of seventeen propositions, which evolved during the course of the writing of Part I. We see the next phase of the inquiry into HPS as the further and systematic national case-by-case testing and subsequent amendment of these seventeen generic (world-level) propositions; and development of the generic discussion in Chapters 3–7 that underlies them, especially the exciting question opened in Chapter 7: What is high participation society? What is different in an HPS world?

The book is the direct fruit of a collaborative cross-country study, including researchers from nine countries that first met in September 2013 at the invitation of Anna Smolentseva of the Higher School of Economics in Moscow. The project was collectively defined on an evolving collegial basis rather than sanctioned by a research agency after competition and peer-review. It was never funded and has been carried from beginning to end by the voluntary labour of scholar-researcher participants. We met during five academic conferences to plan and develop the work, with much email traffic between meetings. Work in progress was presented at conferences of the Consortium of Higher Education Researchers (CHER) in Europe in Lausanne 2013, Rome 2014, and Lisbon 2015; and the Association for Studies in Higher Education (ASHE) in the United States in Denver 2015. Faced with a choice of whether to proceed with single country chapters—the most usual approach—or with a theme-based approach that would combine insights from the different countries, we opted for the second. Country chapters alone, it was thought, would tell us what we already know, and emphasize differences and parallels without identifying features common to HPS. The subtle play of national and cultural variation in common HPS tendencies and factors shaping variation would be missed. Illustrative national case material had to be included, but it was resolved to develop theme chapters first, and use these to structure and interrogate the national level.

It was decided to include a chapter with comparative data on systems with high participation rates (Chapter 2), and to develop arguments on the changing nature of higher education in relation to four themes as follows: governance (Chapter 3), system diversity (Chapter 4), system stratification (Chapter 5) and social equity (Chapter 6). Chapter 7 is a first look at the larger issue of high participation society. Those involved in the preparation of Chapters 1–7, as authors and/or critical friends, were Dominik Antonowicz, Brendan Cantwell, Patrick Clancy, Isak Froumin, Glen Jones, David Konstantinovskiy, Marek Kwiek, Simon Marginson, Reetta Muhonen, Rómulo Pinheiro, Anna Smolentseva, and Jussi Välimaa. Of the jointly authored chapters in Part I, Chapter 2 was led by Pat Clancy and Chapter 3 by Brendan Cantwell. Chapters 4 and 5 were shared more equally by the authors. Most members of the project group provided feedback on chapters other than those they wrote. For Part II, in addition to most of the above names we were joined by Futao Huang, Misha Lisyutkin, Bjørn Stensaker, and Aki Yonezawa.

Each theme-based chapter devised a synthesis by integrating theoretical concepts with the outcomes of various research studies, data sets, and other observations of national systems. Once chosen, inevitably the four themes shaped what was observed and discussed about HPS—and by the same token, not observed and discussed—through the project. Inevitably, also, both the generic chapters and country studies have been coloured by our individual knowledge and ways of seeing. However, we were always mindful of the need to pool our insights, open ourselves to change, and work towards a common understanding. The discipline of circulating summative drafts between authors from contrasting systems challenged our sense of the familiar and led to more restrained (and perhaps deeper) generalizations. It is hoped that the range of system coverage, from Anglo-American 'market' societies to Nordic, Post-Soviet Eastern European, and East Asian cases, has led to generic statements more robust than could have been developed on the basis of one or two countries alone. No doubt the project would have been stronger in its generic reach if it had included further national-cultural variations, with at least one case from a Latin American HPS, more variations in East Asia, and countries such as Germany, Netherlands, United Kingdom, France, Italy, Spain, and others in Europe. National and cross-border research granting systems may provide future opportunities to explore the development of the propositions about HPS, and further exploration of what constitutes high participation society, and in more countries than the eight included here.

We would like to sincerely thank Adam Swallow at Oxford University Press, for his support and counsel; Jenny King, who guided us through the production process; Catherine Owen who administered the project; and our copyeditor Joy Mellor. We also thank the three anonymous reviewers of the manuscript, whose suggestions generated, among other changes, a new Chapter 16 and the substantial development of Chapter 1. Nathan Johnson helped with formatting of references.

We would also like to thank our fellow authors and each other. Working together has been productive, stimulating, and happy. It has been a long journey to completion. There was much redrafting of the material as we strove to push the analysis to a higher level. Unfunded projects battle for focus amid busy schedules, including matters that, unlike this project, put bread on the table. The seventeen propositions were a challenge to all. We were not always sure that we would make it. But in the end, *High Participation Systems of Higher Education* has reached this point, and it has proven to be a very fruitful experience. Few of our projects have taught us as much about higher education.

Brendan Cantwell, Simon Marginson,
and Anna Smolentseva

March 2018

CONTENTS

■ LIST OF FIGURES

LIST OF TABLES

GLOSSARY OF TERMS

AAU	American Association of Universities in the United States of America
ARWU	Academic Ranking of World Universities (Shanghai Jiao Tong University)
ASEAN	Association of Southeast Asian States
BRICS	Brazil, Russia, India, China, and South Africa
CCE	Central Council for Education (Japan)
DAAD	German Academic Exchange Service
ECTS	European Credit Transfer System
EEA	European Economic Area
EFTS	effective full-time students
EMI	effectively maintained inequality (a sociological concept)
EU	European Union
FTE	full-time equivalent
GDP	gross domestic product
GER	gross enrolment ratio
GPI	Gender Parity Index
GTER	gross tertiary enrolment ratio
HPS	high-participation system(s): National systems of higher or tertiary education that enrol more than 50 per cent of the school leaver age cohort
ISCED	International Standard Classification of Education: A statistical framework for organizing information on education maintained by UNESCO
ISCED tertiary education Type A or Type B	Type A refers to programmes that are largely theoretically based and designed to provide qualifications for entry into advanced research programmes and professions with high skill requirements. Type B programmes are typically of shorter duration, and for the most part are more occupationally oriented and lead to direct labour market access
ICT	information and communication technology
IT	information technology
JASSO	Japan Student Service Organization
KEJN	Komitet Ewaluacji Jednostek Naukowych
MEC	Finnish Ministry of Education and Culture
Mercosur	South American trade bloc
MEXT	Ministry of Education, Culture, Sports, Science and Technology (Japan)
MMI	maximally maintained inequality (a sociological concept)
MOOC	mass open online course
MoSHE	Ministry of Science and Higher Education
NATO	North Atlantic Treaty Organisation

NCBR	Narodowe Centrum Badań i Rozwoju
NCN	Narodowe Centrum Nauki
NGO	non-governmental organization
NOKUT	independent agency for quality assurance (Norway)
NPM	new public management
NTNU	University of Trondheim
OECD	Organisation for Economic Co-operation and Development
PAS	Polish Academy of Sciences
PISA	Programme for International Student Assessment (conducted by OECD)
PKA	Polska Komisja Akredytacyjna
PLN	Polish currency: zloty
PPP	purchasing power parity
R&D	research and development
RMIT	Royal Melbourne Institute of Technology University
SAT	Scholastic Assessment Test
SES	socio-economic status
STEM	science, technology, engineering, and mathematics
UAS	universities of applied sciences
UK	United Kingdom
UNDP	United Nations Development Programme
UNESCO	United Nations Educational and Cultural Organisation
USA	United States of America
USSR	Union of Soviet Socialist Republics
UT	universities of technology
VET	vocational education and training
WB	World Bank
WCU	world-class university

LIST OF CONTRIBUTORS

Dominik Antonowicz (dominik.antonowicz@uni.torun.pl) is an associate professor and policy expert at the Institute of Sociology at the Nicolaus Copernicus University, Poland. His research interests cover higher education policy in transition countries, university governance, and national systems of research evaluation.

Brendan Cantwell (brendanc@msu.edu) is an associate professor of Higher, Adult, and Lifelong Education at Michigan State University, USA, and a coordinating editor for *Higher Education*. He specializes in the political economy of higher education.

Patrick Clancy (patrick.clancy@ucd.ie) is Professor Emeritus in the Department of Sociology at University College Dublin. His research in higher education includes four national studies on participation in higher education published by the Higher Education Authority and a comparative book, *Irish Higher Education: A Comparative Perspective* (Dublin: Institute of Public Administration, 2015).

Isak Froumin (ifroumin@hse.ru) is Head of the Institute of Education at National Research University, Higher School of Economics, in Moscow, the first graduate school of education in Russia. He formerly led the World Bank education programme in Russia. In 2012–16 he was an advisor to the Minister of Education and Science of Russia. He is the author of more than 250 publications.

Futao Huang (futao@hiroshima-u.ac.jp) is Professor at Research Institute for Higher Education, Hiroshima University, Japan. He is mainly concerned with research into internationalization of higher education, academic profession, university and college curriculum, and East Asian higher education.

Glen A. Jones (glen.jones@utoronto.ca) is Professor of Higher Education and Dean of the Ontario Institute for Studies in Education of the University of Toronto. His research focuses on higher education governance, systems, and academic work. Information on his research can be found at <www.glenjones.ca>.

David L. Konstantinovskiy (scan21@mail.ru), Doctor of Sociology, is Chair of Department of Sociology of Education of the Institute of Sociology, Russian Academy of Sciences in Moscow. He earned his PhD degree in Institute of Sociology, Russian Academy of Sciences. His publications are in the areas of sociology of education and youth studies.

Marek Kwiek (kwiekm@amu.edu.pl) is Professor, Founder (2002), and Director of the Center for Public Policy Studies; and UNESCO Chair in Institutional Research and Higher Education Policy at the University of Poznan, Poland. His research interests include higher education governance, funding, and reforms, academic entrepreneurialism, and the academic profession.

Mikhail Lisyutkin (mlisyutkin@hse.ru) is a research fellow at the Institute of Education, National Research University Higher School of Economics. His current research interests include the dynamics of the universities' development and decline, universities' international competitiveness and excellence initiatives in higher education, and the development of the higher education systems.

Simon Marginson (s.marginson67@gmail.com) is Professor of Higher Education at the University of Oxford, UK; Director of the ESRC/OFSRE Centre for Global Higher Education; and Editor-in-Chief of *Higher Education*. He was previously Professor of International Higher education at the UCL Institute of Education. He uses political economy, sociology, history, and political philosophy to investigate higher education in social, national-systemic, and global contexts.

Reetta Muhonen (Reetta.Muhonen@staff.uta.fi) works as Postdoctoral Researcher at the Research Center for Knowledge, Science, Technology, and Innovation Studies, at the University of Tampere, Finland.

Rómulo Pinheiro (romulo.m.pinheiro@uia.no) is Professor in Public Policy and Administration at the University of Agder. His research interests lie at the intersection between public policy and administration, organizational studies, regional science and innovation, and higher education studies.

Anna Smolentseva (asmolentseva@hse.ru) is Senior Researcher at the Institute of Education at National Research University Higher School of Economics, Moscow, Russia. She is a sociologist focusing on the changing role of higher education in societies, issues of globalization, educational inequality, the academic profession, and transformations in post-socialist higher education systems.

Bjørn Stensaker (bjorn.stensaker@iped.uio.no) is a professor of higher education at the University of Oslo. He has a special interest in governance, organization, and management of higher education, and has published widely on these issues in a range of international journals and books.

Jussi Välimaa (jussi.p.valimaa@jyu.fi) is Professor and Director of the Finnish Institute for Educational Research at the University of Jyväskylä, Finland.

Akiyoshi Yonezawa (akiyoshi.yonezawa.a4@tohoku.ac.jp) is Professor and Director of the Office of Institutional Research, Tohoku University. With a background in sociology, he mainly conducts research on comparative higher education policy—especially focusing on world-class universities, internationalization of higher education, and public-private relationships in higher education.

PROPOSITIONS ABOUT HIGH PARTICIPATION SYSTEMS OF HIGHER EDUCATION

General

1. As high participation systems (HPS) spread to an increasing number of countries, equity in world society is enhanced.
2. In HPS there is no intrinsic limit to the spread of family aspirations for participation in higher education until universality is reached; and no intrinsic limit to the level of social position to which families/students may aspire.
3. Once transition from a primarily agricultural economy is achieved, the long-term growth of HPS is independent of political economic factors such as economic growth and patterns of labour market demand; patterns of public and private funding of higher education; the roles of public and private institutions; and system organization and modes of governance.

Governance

4. HPS are governed by multi-level control, coordination, and accountability mechanisms.
5. HPS governance tends to involve the management of horizontal differentiation.
6. HPS complex multi-level accountability and coordination, coupled with system differentiation, result in higher education institutions adopting increasingly corporate forms and robust internal governance and management capacities.

Horizontal Diversity

7. In the HPS era, regardless of the political economy and culture of systems, an increasing proportion of higher education becomes centred on comprehensive multi-discipline and multi-function research universities, or 'multiversities'. The multiversity is increasingly dominant as the paradigmatic form of higher education.
8. Regardless of the political economy and culture of the HPS, when participation expands there is no necessary increase in the overall diversity of institutional form and mission; and this has probably declined, except in relation to online provision.
9. As participation expands the internal diversity of multiversities tends to increase. This affects some or all of the range of missions, business activities, institutional forms and internal structures, the discipline mix, research activities, levels of study and range of credentials, the heterogeneity of the student body, links to stakeholders, cross-border relations, and forms of academic and non-academic labour.

10. All else being equal, the combination of expanding participation and enhanced competition in neoliberal quasi-markets is associated with specific effects in relation to diversity, including (1) increased vertical differentiation of higher education institutions (HEIs) (stratification); (2) reduced horizontal differentiation (diversification); (3) convergence of missions through isomorphistic imitation; and (4) growth in the role of private HEIs, especially for-profit institutions.

Vertical Stratification

11. The expansion of participation towards and beyond the HPS stage is associated with a tendency to bifurcation and stratification (vertical diversification) in the value of higher education, between elite (artisanal) institutions and mass (demand-absorbing) institutions.
12. The tendency to institutional stratification is magnified by features common (though not universal) among HPS including (a) intensified social competition for the most valuable student places; (b) variable tuition charges; and/or (c) intensified competition between institutions.
13. In stratified HPS, a middle layer of institutions tends to form, shaped by the combination of upward aspirations (drift) with systemic scarcity of resources and status.

Equity

14. As participation expands in the HPS phase, equity in the form of social inclusion is enhanced.
15. Because in the HPS phase the growth of participation is associated with enhanced stratification and intensified competition at key transition points, all else being equal (i.e. without compensatory state policy), the expansion of participation is associated with a secular tendency to greater social inequality in educational outcomes and, through that, social outcomes.
16. Within a national system, as participation expands in the HPS phase, all else being equal, the positional structure of the higher education system increasingly resembles that of society (albeit with the caveat of Proposition 15). The HPS is increasingly implicated in the reproduction of existing patterns of social equality/inequality.
17. As the HPS boundary of participation expands it becomes more difficult for the state and/or autonomous educational systems/institutions to secure a redistribution of educational opportunities, and, through that, of social opportunities.

Part I
Worldwide Tendencies

1 High Participation Systems of Higher Education

Simon Marginson

> It seems to me very unlikely that any advanced industrial society can or will be able to stabilize the numbers going on to some form of higher education any time in the near future.
>
> (Trow, 1973: 40)

Introduction

In the vast majority of countries across the world higher education has become one of the central institutions of human society. Higher education systems are continually evolving, and in the last twenty years the sector has been shaped by three broad tendencies that combine in various ways according to national circumstances. The first tendency is mass-scale growth, or 'massification'. The second is the intensification of competition between institutions and the adoption of business-like features, marketization, under the influence of neoliberal policies. The third is the partial global integration and convergence between national systems, or globalization. More is written about globalization and marketization than massification. Yet massification is monumental in scale and the most universal of the three tendencies. Global convergence touches some national systems more than others, though most are part of the global science system and of global comparison and ranking. Marketization has reshaped higher education in English-speaking countries and Eastern Europe, but in many European systems tuition is free and business models play a more modest role. However, nearly all systems of higher education in middle- or high-income countries are undergoing or have undergone sustained and dynamic growth, and some systems located in low-income countries are also undergoing a major expansion.

High Participation Systems of Higher Education is about the dynamics of massification. The large-scale higher education that began in North America, Western Europe, Russia, Japan, and Australia has reached Eastern Europe, East Asia, and Latin America, and is spreading through South and West Asia as well. At the same time, the multi-disciplinary, multi-purpose, comprehensive research university, as an institutional form of higher education, has also radiated across the world. Most of the growth in student numbers and research has occurred in the last twenty years. At the world level, participation in tertiary education is expanding at 1 per cent per year, 20 per cent every twenty years (UNESCO, 2018). More than a third of the world's tertiary education systems enrol more than 50 per cent of young people after they leave secondary school, with roughly a third or so of the age cohort entering degree-level-programmes. The number of these 50 per cent plus systems is growing. In this book, such national education systems are designated as 'high participation systems' (HPS).

High Participation Systems of Higher Education has two starting points. First, the scale and depth of this increase in participation in tertiary and higher education is under-estimated, is not well understood, and needs more explanation and discussion. Second, a massive alteration on this scale, repeated in country after country, involving half the age cohort or more, means higher education is changing—and the societies in which HPS are embedded also must be changing. Those changes need discussion. This book is about the nature of HPS of higher education. Why have they emerged and what kind of society do they imply? What are the social dynamics of HPS? What is it that is new, distinctive, and different about higher education, and society, in the HPS era? What is the relation between higher education, state, family, and society under HPS conditions? What is common to the growing systems of higher education, and what is different, in a convergent but contextually contingent world?

Much research in the field of higher education studies treats higher education as a bounded zone. Though there is awareness of the government role in regulation and funding, society and economy are viewed from a distance through a limited education-centric lens. But higher education has always had larger social meaning and in the HPS era this is more obvious. HPS higher education engages not only with government and its agencies, from finance to welfare to security; but with employers and industries; professions, occupations, and labour markets; cities, municipalities, and regions; communications and cultural institutions; and agents, organizations, and networks that span the world. It is shaped continuously by inward and outward flows of ideas, people, and money. It is implicated in power and social class. The group that prepared this book has primarily interrogated HPS in four domains: governance, diversity, stratification, and equity. Each has an interior dimension, inside higher education institutions, and a broader social dimension. The key questions for *High Participation Systems of Higher Education* are always the social questions. In turn this enables the interior of higher education institutions to be reconsidered.

High Participation Systems of Higher Education is multi-disciplinary in its founda-tions. The inquiry is united not by the methods and topics of one social science discipline but by the need to understand and explain HPS of higher education. This means setting aside the dualistic proposition that there is only one possible kind of truth about social phenomena. No single body of knowledge can suffice to grasp the many-sided problem of HPS, which encompasses domains often understood separately as educational, social, economic, demographic, psychological, cultural, and political that at the level of society become combined in complex ways. The inquiry also must be sufficiently sensitive to national/local specificity and agency, and emerging causal factors, while grasping a complex total picture.

THE SPREAD OF HIGH PARTICIPATION

The worldwide tendency towards HPS began in the United States of America (USA), which by 1971 enrolled 47 per cent of the school-leaver age cohort in programmes of two-year full-time equivalent or more, designated as 'higher education' in the USA and as 'tertiary education' by the United Nations Educational, Scientific and Cultural Organization (UNESCO) and the Organisation for Economic Co-operation and Development (OECD). (For the higher/tertiary distinction, see the next section of the chapter.) In 1973, Berkeley sociologist Martin Trow published *Problems in the Transition from Elite to Mass Higher Education*. He found a 'broad pattern of development of higher education' in 'every advanced society'. Higher education was growing from an 'elite' system with less than 15 per cent of the age group, to a 'mass' system with 15–50 per cent, and then a 'universal' system with over 50 per cent. Higher education was 'universal' at 50 per cent because by then it had become a common necessity.

Trow's distinctions remain useful. However, this book refers to systems with over 50 per cent of the age cohort as HPS, not 'universal', to distinguish between the 50 per cent and 100 per cent levels of participation. First, 100 per cent is the more conventional meaning ascribed to 'universal'. Second, to treat 50 per cent participation as 'universal' in 1973 suggests a certain complacency, in relation to higher education systems in which women, students from poor families, and students from non-white families were substantially under-represented. Some HPS are now approaching the 100 per cent mark.

As a sociologist Trow understood the growing role of higher education institutions as a *social* process and not just an educational one. High participation higher education entailed a new set of relations between the state, education, and society. Though in 1971 only nineteen countries had reached 15 per cent 'mass' higher education, he predicted that all industrial countries would move towards HPS. He was right. In 2013 there were fifty-six world HPS with an enrolment of 50 per cent, and no less than 112 'mass' systems with Trow's 'mass' enrolment level of 15 per cent or more (World Bank, 2016). Fewer than fifty higher education systems, less than one-quarter, were still below the 15 per cent mark. Chapter 2 discusses the statistical tendency towards HPS in most of the world, and the countries yet to experience the surge of participation.

Table 1.1. Eight high participation systems* of higher education and eight lower participation systems from large population countries, 2016

	GER		GDP per head PPP constant $s	Proportion of labour force in agriculture	Proportion of population in urban areas	Internet connectivity of population
	1995 %	2014 %	2013 $US	2017 %	2016 %	2013 %
Australia	70	90	44,414	3	90	85
Finland	67	89	39,523	4	84	92
USA	78	87	53,342	2	82	87
Russia	43	79	24,026	7	74	71
Norway	54	77	64,179	2	81	96
Poland	32	68	26,051	11	61	67
Japan	40	63	38,252	4	94	91
Canada	90	n.a.	43,088	2	82	87
China	4	39	14,399	31	57	49
Indonesia	11	31	10,765	27	54	17
Vietnam	3	30	5,955	42	34	48
Mexico	14	30	16,832	13	30	44
India	6	26	6,093	44	33	18
Bangladesh	5	13	3,319	41	35	10
Pakistan	2	10	4,855	42	39	14
Ethiopia	1	8	1,608	71	20	3

Notes: The eight comparator systems are from the eight largest countries by population that do not house an HPS and for which GER data are available (no GER data are available for Brazil, Nigeria, and the Philippines). n.a. = ata not available. GDP per capita in constant 2011 prices USD. PPP = purchasing power parity. *HPS have GERs of more than 50 per cent.
Source: Compiled by the author from various World Bank (2018) data.

Table 1.1 introduces some characteristics of HPS. The eight HPS in the top half of the table figuring in the case studies in Part II of this book: two Nordic systems (Finland and Norway), three Anglo-American systems (USA, Canada, and Australia), two Post-Soviet Eastern European systems (Russia and Poland) and one East Asian system (Japan). There are distinctions between them. The Gross Enrolment Ratio (GER) varies from 63 to 90 per cent. Poland and Russia are more rural and have a lower Internet connectivity than the others. These differences are dwarfed by the commonalities. Six are high-income countries, with Russia and Poland high-middle-income countries. In all the proportion of labour in agriculture is low and the proportion in non-agricultural occupations in industry and services is high. Three-quarters or more of the population is in cities, except in Poland (61 per cent). Internet connectivity is between 67 and 96 per cent of the population.

These indicators contrast with the large population lower participation countries in the bottom half of the table. These have lesser income per head, more labour in agriculture, lower levels of urbanization, and less Internet connectivity. There are differences within the second group. National income and urbanization are rising rapidly in China and Indonesia. Vietnam has high participation and Internet connectivity relative to per capita national income; Mexico has low participation relative to per capita income and urbanization. Notably, however, five of the second group are well above Trow's 1973 threshold for 'mass' higher education of 15 per cent, and in all countries, regardless of income per capita, the GER is rising sharply though it is still very low in Ethiopia. Many so-called 'developing' (emerging) countries include a modernizing urban social zone, connected to global trade and governmental and information networks, in which higher education grows quickly. That was not the case in previous generations. Higher education is now qualitatively more important, everywhere.

HIGH PARTICIPATION SOCIETY

The guaranteed provision of a growing higher education system has become a core duty of states, like airports and roads, clean water, and a viable banking system. Higher education is becoming as important in forming people and social relations as kin, local communities, temple, church, and mosque, especially where organized religion is fading. This is a different social world to that of two generations ago. It will become more different.

What are the characteristics of this emerging world, with many more graduates than before? An OECD survey of adult skills compares the attributes of graduates from tertiary institutions with leavers at the end of secondary school. In the case study countries, between 5 per cent (Canada) and 13 per cent (USA) more of tertiary graduates were in 'good health' (OECD, 2014: 180–1). Graduates from higher education also do better in managing their finances (McMahon, 2009). Futher, and importantly, in HPS a much larger group of people enters the workforce with advanced generic and vocationally specific knowledge and skills. Whether or not this more advanced graduate capability is reflected in graduate pay packets (if it is not, it is invisible to economists that measure productivity), the potential of graduate work, the use value of graduates, exceeds that of non-graduates. If present trends in the growth of participation continue into the future, in a generation, a majority of the world's working people will enter tertiary education. Perhaps a third will carry degrees or diplomas. This ought to lift the use value of the non-graduate work alongside them—though much depends on whether labour markets evolve so as to differentiate and utilize skills on this scale.

In this and other ways, HPS higher education is altering the relational social environment. Higher education is associated with more advanced competence in social communications both close-up and across distances. The OECD survey shows that compared to people who left education at upper secondary stage, tertiary graduates were between 11 per cent (Russia) and 30 per cent (USA and Poland) more likely to have 'good ICT and problem solving skills' (OECD, 2015: 46–7). Higher education is also associated with greater political capabilities. The scope for political agency depends partly on the character of the polity, but in any HPS country the transparency of government is increased: all else equal, graduates are more capable in holding organizations to account. The OECD survey reports a significantly higher proportion of tertiary graduates believed they had a 'say in government', compared to non-graduates (OECD, 2014: 186–7). At the same time, higher education is associated with increased social solidarity in OECD countries. The survey associates graduation with a higher propensity to 'trust others'—perhaps because education forms people in homogenizing intellectual and professional cultures. Among the book's case study countries this enhancement of trust was highest in Nordic Norway (21 per cent) and Finland (17 per cent) (pp. 184–5). Trust is a pillar of the Nordic social model (see Chapters 6 and 13–14).

The tally of graduate attributes begs the question of the extent to which graduates are shaped by the higher education experience, or by their often socially advantaged backgrounds. Still, it is hard to avoid the conclusion that worldwide HPS are helping to form more capable and confident human agents (Sen, 2000), in common, on a massive scale. Above all, higher education enhances self-efficacy and the potential for self-determination and positive freedom, 'effective freedom' as Sen (1985), and Marginson (2018) call it. Graduates are less tightly gripped by fate than are non-graduates—more at ease with knowledge, information, and other reflexive tools; more lucid and creative in communication and cross-cultural relations; more adept with governments, corporations, and markets; better at planning family, household, and financial management and security; and more proactive, flexible, and productive at work.

Consider the implications of degree holding for mobility. The OECD's (2016) *Perspectives on Global Development 2017: International Migration in a Shifting World* compares the cross-border mobility of people with, and without, university degrees. Among those without degrees the tendency to move across borders is correlated to income. As income rises people had more scope for mobility; that is, capacity for mobility appears as economically determined. However, among those with university degrees there is a different pattern. First, at a given level of income, those with degrees are much more mobile than those without: higher education helps to democratize mobility (provided there is access to higher education). Second, for those with degrees, above a modest threshold of income there is little change in potential mobility. Graduates' propensity to move becomes income inelastic. Strikingly, because higher education helps graduates to achieve greater personal agency, it weakens the limits created by economic determination and class. *It constitutes greater personal agency, freedom, in its own right.*

SOCIAL EXCLUSION

Herein also lies the downside of high participation higher education. This is the growing social exclusion of those without diplomas and degrees, those outside the agency building benefits. As higher education and its credentials become more widely distributed, the polarity between the higher educated and others (given the demographics of educational growth, this is partly a polarity between young and old) is intensified. First, those without higher education are more disadvantaged than before, lacking both the signifying credential and the confidence, cultural capital, and ease of mobility (economic, social, spatial-global) higher education brings. Though HPS social inclusion is broader than before, by definition, once the higher education experience becomes normal the penalties of exclusion are profound. Second, the polarity between the higher educated and others, and the resentment it creates, can be mobilized politically.

In 2016, in both the USA and United Kingdom (UK), there was a surge of political support for nativist ethno-nationalism. This triggered a UK referendum decision to leave the European Union (EU), and propelled an anti-migration protectionist, Donald Trump, into the White House. Both Trump and the Brexit campaign divided the electorate between on the one hand singular ethno-national identity, on the other global openness, cosmopolitanism, and plural identity. As noted, ease with mobility and plurality is strongly associated with higher education. The best overall predictors of how people voted in both countries were not their income or class position, but whether they lived in large cities (for the EU and Clinton), or small towns and rural areas (for Brexit and Trump); and, second, whether they held degrees. These factors are related. Like global connections, degree holders tend to concentrate in cities. In the UK, 26 per cent of degree holders supported Brexit, with 78 per cent of people without qualifications. Young people, the most educated generation and more at ease with mobility and multiple identity, overwhelmingly voted for the UK to stay in Europe (Swales, 2016: 8). Silver (2016) shows that in the fifty least educated American counties, Trump made major gains; in the fifty counties with the highest level of college education, otherwise diverse in income and ethnic composition, Clinton improved on Obama's 2012 Democrat vote by an average of 9 per cent. In effect, both electorates were polarized between the higher educated and the non-educated.

This suggests that if participation in higher education continues to expand, extending to more of society, the political potential of nativist populism shrinks. Yet to the extent that stratified higher education systems are culpable in growing economic and social inequality (Saez, 2013; Piketty, 2014), and in emphasizing World-Class Universities and the private rates of return to graduates, with little regard for the larger common good (Marginson, 2016d), they become more vulnerable to continued nativist positioning of higher education as exclusive and 'elite'.

The future meanings of HPS and high participation society (see Chapter 7) are yet to emerge. It is unclear whether higher education's potential to foster democratization, inclusion, and social solidarity or whether its potential to create social stratification and exclusion will be uppermost. In part it is a nation by nation issue, in part a function of secular tendencies common to all systems. What *is* clear is that HPS means that education and society are undergoing a major transformation.

OVERARCHING PROPOSITIONS ABOUT HPS

The seventeen propositions listed prior to this chapter summarize the generic features of HPS that have emerged from the collective scholarly work for *High Participation Systems of Higher Education*. These propositions are presented in quasi-hypothesis form. Some can be tested in quantitative research, though others encompass ambiguous qualities or too many variables. The propositions relating to governance, diversity, stratification, and equity are discussed in Chapters 3–6. There are also three overarching propositions (discussed in this chapter:

- *As HPS spread to an increasing number of countries, equity in world society is enhanced.*
- *In HPS there is no intrinsic limit to the spread of family aspirations for participation in higher education until universality is reached; and no intrinsic limit to the level of social position to which families/students may aspire.*
- *Once transition from a primarily agricultural economy is achieved, the long-term growth of HPS is independent of political economic factors such as economic growth and patterns of labour market demand; patterns of public and private funding of higher education; the roles of public and private institutions; and system organization and modes of governance.*

The next section of the chapter reviews the definitions of 'tertiary' and 'higher education'. The sections that follow explore the drivers of educational growth, and the relations between varying national factors and common world trends. The final section presents Chapters 2–16.

What is Higher Education?

The meaning of 'higher education' varies from country to country. Some national systems define 'higher education' by type of institutions, others by type of study. In each case, the inclusions vary. In some nations 'higher education' includes just degree granting institutions and/or degree or post-Bachelor's diploma programmes. In others it reaches down to shorter certificates and diplomas. In some countries first degrees of four-year, full-time study are normal, in others three years are standard, with some longer, and there are cases of two-year degrees.

It would be neat if 'higher education' was applied (or not applied) on a consistent basis, across borders, and to professions and occupations. It does not happen. Certain activities are always 'higher education', such as medical training and Doctoral research—in fact nearly all degree-level programmes, everywhere, are seen as constituting 'higher education'—but beyond that, there are a range of national practices. Some national systems include as 'higher education' only course of study in the 'pure' or theoretical knowledge (e.g. science, humanities), plus elite professions (medicine, law, sometimes but not always engineering). Others extend the accolade 'higher' into a wide range of vocational training—and vocational training for different occupations can have variable locations. For example in Australia most (though not all) nurses and accountants are prepared in university programmes at degree level; in the HPS in Russia these occupations are generally trained outside higher education.

In reality, 'higher education' signifies not just cognitive achievement, or occupational and educational complexity, it also stands for social status. Social status markers tend to be flexible over time yet at any one time they touch the interests of many. Though the extent to which the term 'higher education' is socially exclusive, the level where the boundary falls, differs from country to country, efforts to change the definition can be fiercely contested.

UNESCO'S 'TERTIARY EDUCATION'

Despite the difficulties in making comparisons, there is demand across the world for data on participation in post-school education that will do just that. The most authoritative collection is by the UNESCO Institute of Statistics. UNESCO has devised an 'International Standard Classification of Education'. Here forms of education and training more advanced than secondary schooling are mostly classified as 'tertiary education'. Within this large category, UNESCO identifies ISCED Level 6–8 programmes which ascend from Bachelor's degrees to Master's and then to Doctoral education, and ISCED Level 5, 'short-cycle tertiary education'. Nearly all national systems have programmes at ISCED Level 5, but nations differ on how much ISCED they have and how much of ISCED Level 5 is classified 'higher education'.

ISCED level 5 programmes...are often designed to provide participants with professional knowledge, skills and competencies. Typically, they are practically based, occupationally specific and prepare students to enter the labour market....Academic tertiary education programmes below the level of a Bachelor's programme or equivalent are also classified as ISCED level 5. Programmes at ISCED level 5...are shorter and usually less theoretically oriented than ISCED level 6 programmes....Although ISCED level 5 programmes are usually designed to prepare for employment, they may give credit for transfer into ISCED level 6 or 7 programmes. Upon completion of these ISCED Level 5 programmes, individuals may in some education systems continue their education at ISCED level 6 (Bachelor's or equivalent level) or long first degree ISCED level 7 programmes (Master's or equivalent level). Programmes classified at ISCED level 5 may be referred to in many ways, for example: (higher) technical education, community college education, technician or advanced/higher vocational training, associate degree, or bac+2. For

Table 1.2. Inclusion of ISCED 5 programmes in national definitions of 'higher education'

Country	Inclusion of ISCED Level 5 programmes as part of national 'higher education'
Australia	Higher education in national data and Chapter 10 includes everything in designated higher education institutions at ISCED Levels 6–8 and two-year ISCED Level 5. Most two year programmes, and short vocational courses, are in vocational education and training, *not* higher education.
Canada	Higher education includes both universities and colleges, and covers all of ISCED Levels 5–8. Data in Chapter 9 include ISCED Level 5. There are significant provincial variations in the form of provision in the colleges.
Finland	Higher education means ISCED Level 6 Bachelor's degrees in universities of applied sciences, Level 7 (Master's degrees), and Level 8 (Doctoral and Licenciate degrees) in universities. There is almost no Level 5 provision at all, and none in higher education or in Chapter 13.
Japan	Higher education includes all programmes at ISCED Levels 5–8, according to the national government's administrative definition, and Chapter 15. This includes specialized training colleges that have been reclassified from 'post-secondary education' to 'higher education'.
Norway	The official label is 'tertiary education', not higher education, and includes all of ISCED Levels 5–8. The National Qualification Framework states that shorter one- to two-year offerings at ISCED Level 5 are part of tertiary education. They are part of the data in Chapter 14.
Poland	Higher education means ISCED Level 6–8 programmes only. The relatively small number of Level 5 enrolments (see Table 1.3) are *not* included in the definition of higher education in Poland and are excluded from the data in Chapter 12.
Russia	Higher education means ISCED Level 6–8 degrees in institutions of higher education. ISCED Level 5 is *not* included in Chapter 11, though enrolments at Level 5 have increased in higher educational institutions due to structural changes such as cross-sectoral mergers.
USA	Higher education means all programmes in degree-granting institutions. Thus Department of Education statistics, and Chapter 9, include all academic and terminal programmes at colleges and universities, covering most (but not all) enrolments at ISCED Level 5 and above.

Note: For ISCED 5 programmes, see main text citations from UNESCO (2018: 48).

Source: Author, on the basis of data from authors of Part II chapters in this book.

international comparability purposes the term 'short-cycle tertiary education' is used to label ISCED level 5.   (UNESCO, 2018: 48)

Table 1.2 sets out the differences in data coverage among the eight case study countries in this book (see Chapters 8–15). In Russia, Poland, and Finland, ISCED Level 5 enrolments are not seen as 'higher education'. In Australia, a small minority of two-year ISCED 5 programmes in universities are 'higher education'. In contrast, the main part of ISCED 5 programmes are classified 'higher education' in the USA, and in Canada and Japan all ISCED 5 enrolment is treated as in higher education. Norway uses the term 'tertiary education', not 'higher education', and it covers all of ISCED Levels 5–8.

THE GROSS ENROLMENT RATIO

The calculation of the UNESCO 'gross enrolment ratio' (GER) is based on a definition of 'tertiary education' that includes both all degree programmes at ISCED Levels 6–8 and

Table 1.3. Proportion of enrolment in tertiary* education at ISCED Levels 5–8, 2014

Country	ISCED Level 8 (Doctoral) %	ISCED Level 7 (Master's) %	ISCED Level 6 (Bachelor's) %	ISCED Level 5 (2-year) %
Finland	6.8	20.3	73.0	(0.01)
Poland	2.5	30.7	66.5	0.3
Norway	2.8	22.8	70.8	3.7
Australia	3.9	16.0	64.0	16.0
Russia	2.0	37.9	42.8	17.3
Japan	1.9	8.6	69.4	20.0
USA	2.0	12.7	48.0	37.2
Canada	n.a.	n.a.	n.a.	n.a.

Notes: *As defined by UNESCO Institute of Statistics. n.a. = data not available.

Source: Author, based on data from UNESCO (2018).

longer programmes at ISCED Level 5. The latter are 'academic tertiary education programmes below the level of a Bachelor's programme or equivalent', and generally two-year full-time enrolment equivalent (though it must be said that nations that are meant to be collecting exactly these data for UNESCO, and no more, sometimes capture a broader set of ISCED Level 5 activity). This UNESCO notion of 'tertiary education' is close to the US notion of 'higher education'. As Chapter 2 will discuss, UNESCO's definition of 'tertiary' has limitations, but it enables comprehensive global comparison of participation rates.

In this book, which needs a standard indicator for comparisons, *'higher education' is equated with the UNESCO definition of 'tertiary education'*. That is, the UNESCO GER, based on tertiary education, is understood here as a gross higher education enrolment ratio. (The limitations of the GER measure are discussed in Chapter 2.) UNESCO's 'tertiary education' in Table 1.3 fits closely to the national notion of 'higher education' in Table 1.2 in Canda, Finland, Japan, Norway, Poland, and the USA. This is not the case in Russia and Australia where UNESCO's 'tertiary' is more inclusive than is the national idea of what constitutes 'higher education'. In those two countries, the UNESCO definition is used in Chapters 1–2 but the national definition is used in Chapters 10–11.

Despite the good fit between 'tertiary' and 'higher' in six out of eight of the case study countries in this book, in other countries such as the UK the fit is less good. In reading *High Participation Systems of Higher Education* it must be borne always in mind that:

- Tertiary/higher education is not a constant. The proportion of 'tertiary' ('higher education') enrolment that is conducted at ISCED Level 5, below the level of degree provision, varies significantly by nation. For example Table 1.3 shows there are more short programmes, some with a sub-professional vocational flavour, in the USA (especially), Japan, Russia, and Australia, than in Norway and Poland, and almost none in Finland. The Master's level plays a larger role in Russia and Poland than in Japan, there are proportionately more Doctoral degrees in Finland, and so on.

- 'Tertiary education' as indicated by ISCED Levels 5–8 is almost the same as the status category of 'higher education' in all case study countries in the book, except Australia and Russia. Some of the much larger group of nations discussed in Chapter 2 also classify part of ISCED 5 as outside nationally designated 'higher education'.
- Differences in the reliance on ISCED 5 provision can have implications for the extent to which tertiary/higher education takes the form of knowledge-intensive cognitive development. Also, there can be implications for social equity. Students from families with relatively low incomes and parental education levels may congregate in sub-degree programmes, which often have lower completion rates and lower graduate earnings, and in Australia and Russia can lack the status of 'higher education'.

These are the forms of higher education. But how did it become high participation?

Theories and Narratives of HPS

There have been two main sociological theorizations of the growth and massification of higher education, by Martin Trow (1973) and Evan Schofer and John Meyer (2005). Common understandings have been shaped also by explanations from economic policy.

MARTIN TROW

For Martin Trow 'elite', 'mass', and 'universal' higher education were Weberian ideal types. He saw them as historical stages, and also as practices alongside each other in the present. For example, elite higher education continued alongside the newer mass and universal forms.

The transforming effects of massification. As Trow saw it, in the process of massification, the purpose of higher education shifted from 'shaping the mind and character of the ruling class' (elite), to preparing a larger group in professional and technical skills (mass), to preparing the whole population in 'adaptability' to social and technological change (universal) (Trow, 1973: 1–2, 5–20). Higher education took in all of society, 'distinctions between learning and life become attenuated' (p. 8), and university autonomy was diminished. Access shifted from a privilege (elite), to a right (mass), to an obligation (universal) for middle class families and then for all. In some ways higher education scaled up successfully, in other ways it altered, but in each phase higher education-in-society was qualitatively different.

In the elite phase the student enters directly after school. In the mass phase some delay entry 'until after a period of work or travel'. In the universal phase 'there is much postponement of entry' and broken attendance, and vocational training and mixed work/study modes constitute a larger proportion of higher education. 'Emphasis on "lifelong learning" is compatible with a softening of the boundaries between formal education and other forms of life experience' (Trow, 1973: 9–10). The curriculum moves from a 'highly structured' programme based on mandatory intellectual or professional requirements in the elite phase, to a choice-based modular structure in the mass phase, to the breakdown of sequencing, structure, and assessment requirements in the universal phase 'where no single conception of higher education obtains' (p. 8). The pedagogical relationship between student and teacher moves from personal mentoring designed to shape individual development in the elite phase, as in the Oxford college, to formal instruction in large classrooms in the mass phase with emphasis on the transmission of skills and knowledge, to displacement of student-teacher relations in the universal phase amid correspondence programmes, 'video cassettes and TV's', the 'computer and other technological aids' (p. 9). Trow anticipated the attenuation of mass education through diverse reductions in teaching intensity. Student community is also attenuated. Fragmented populations of unlimited size have merely nominal connections, being no longer united by frequent association, values, or identity (pp. 10–13).

In the transition the internal governance of higher education institutions is much changed. Elite institutions are run by small homogenous groups. Part-time amateur academic leaders are served by a handful of administrative staff. In the mass phase, leaders are increasingly affected by interest groups and democratic pressures inside and outside the sector. Academic administrators are full-time and university bureaucracy grows rapidly. In the universal phase financial managers and specialist services flourish. Institutions function within external relations and the public media space: academic values and processes appear archaic and are habitually questioned (Trow, 1973: 13–15). Massification has ambiguous implications for institutional diversity. There is some potential for greater diversity. Elite systems 'tend to be highly homogeneous'. Small institutions resembling each other share strong notions of membership, clear university/society boundaries, and ('at least in their meritocratic phase') high standards. Mass systems are comprehensive and more diverse in functions and standards, with institutions of up to 40,000 students and more fuzzy and permeable external boundaries. Amid universal access, with greater natural diversity and the dissolution of standards and boundaries, there is enhanced administrative standardization of units and functions (p. 16). Trow anticipated corporatization, noting also that the standardizing effects of state regulation and the tendency for imitating behaviour by institutions might combine to reduce diversity of institutional type, mission, and educational approach (pp. 51–2).

Stratification and inequality. For Trow participation was and should be highly stratified. In 1960 California established a Master Plan for higher education that provided access for all students qualified to enter—a notable democratization of opportunity, but with most growth taking place in two-year diplomas in public community colleges. Above them were the state universities, and the campuses of the University of California, led by Berkeley and Los Angeles, open to just the top 12.5 per cent of school leavers (Kerr, 2001). In the USA the Master Plan's combination of access and excellence was widely admired. 'In a mass system, elite institutions may not only survive but flourish' stated Trow (1973: 19).

At the same time, he stated, amid massification issues of social equity are transformed. The primary student selection proceeds from academic merit in the elite phase, to programmes designed to create social equality of opportunity in the mass phase, and then to open access in the universal phase, but 'social inequalities show everywhere a stubbornly persistent effect on educational achievement' (Trow, 1973: 23–4). As the system expands the new goal of equality policy is 'to achieve a social, class, ethnic and racial distribution in higher education reflecting that of the population at large' (p. 45). However, 'the growth in student numbers at university' becomes 'largely made up of an increase in the proportion of middle class students, who almost everywhere are the first to take advantage of increases in educational opportunities of every kind and at every level'. It is very difficult to achieve social equality in relation to entry into elite institutions, because of the association between educational requirements and middle class culture. Social advantage is 'stubbornly persistent' in meritocratic selection (p. 24). But the tension between social mobility and social reproduction could be regulated within a tiered Master Plan type system. Sardonically Trow remarked:

It is hard to imagine a successful move to end the expansion of higher education, although that is certainly talked about in conservative circles in all Western countries. But the establishment of different sectors of higher education, reflecting the status hierarchies in the larger society, is a more effective way of using higher education to buttress rather than undermine the class structure.

(Trow, 1973: 25)

In the USA and other mass-to-universal systems as they emerged, there was (and is) an unresolved struggle between those who saw more democratic participation as social solidarity, along Nordic lines, and believed a classless educational meritocracy was within reach; and those who mobilized educational competition and selection to maintain existing social exclusion and reproduction, reducing the 'universal' in universal higher education.

Trow's explanation for growth. Trow also explained the tendency of higher education systems to grow. Expansion was not primarily driven by economic demand for graduates, but by family aspirations to maintain and improve social position. This led him to two insights.

First, because there is no limit to aspirations for social betterment through education, there will be 'continued popular demand for an increase in the number of places in colleges and universities'. 'It seems to me very unlikely that any advanced industrial society can or will be able to stabilize the numbers' (Trow, 1973: 40). As more people enter higher education, it becomes 'a symbol of rising social status' (p. 41), and non-participation is an individual deficiency. Despite

loose talk about graduate unemployment or of an oversupply . . . it is still clear that people who have gone on to higher education thereby increase their chances for having more secure, more interesting, and better paid work throughout their lives.

In addition, graduate unemployment is not a problem due to the 'educational inflation of occupations'. Graduate jobs move down the occupational scale. Graduates displace those without college, sometimes using educated capabilities to enrich the jobs. 'What mass higher education does is to break the old rigid connection between education and the occupational structure' that prevents graduates from taking what were non-graduate jobs. Graduates can 'seek employment without loss of dignity wherever the jobs may exist' (pp. 42–3).

Trow's second insight was that government policy must follow social demand for higher education, rather than social demand being determined by policy or funding. Government everywhere will be under ongoing pressure, especially from the middle class, to facilitate the growth of higher education until saturation is reached, using expanded supply and financial support for participation (Trow, 1973: 5–6, 40). It was a bold prediction given that in 1973 governments outside the USA were more concerned to foster demand for higher education than follow it. They used 'manpower planning', as it was called, fed by rates of return and employment data, to plot a rational fit between education and the labour markets (or so they hoped). Yet in the long run Trow's idea of government behaviour prevailed.

Though Trow was familiar with differences between countries in educational provision he saw himself describing a universal script, in which American social and educational forms were spreading everywhere. The essay was remarkably perceptive in relation to generic developments but did not get it wholly right, even in relation to the USA.

INSTITUTIONAL THEORY

Unlike Trow, Schofer and Meyer (2005) grounded their account of the 'worldwide expansion of higher education in the twentieth century' in a quantitative analysis. As with Trow the narrative, drawn from institutional theory, saw the growth of participation in terms of a universal Americanizing script. They saw the expansion of higher education as a single global process: 'The postwar shift to a liberal, rationalist, and developmental model of society generated a worldwide pattern of increased higher education expansion'. While growth accelerated almost everywhere after 1960, higher education expanded 'most rapidly in countries linked in organization and identity to world models' (pp. 903–5), entailing:

scientization, democratization and the expansion of human rights, the rise of development planning, and the structuration of the world polity. With these changes, a new model of society became institutionalized globally—one in which schooled knowledge and personnel were seen as appropriate for a wide variety of social positions, and in which many more young people were seen as appropriate candidates for higher education. An older vision of education as contributing to a more closed society and occupational system—with associated fears of 'over-education'—was replaced by an open-system picture of education as useful 'human capital' for unlimited progress.

(Schofer and Meyer, 2005: 898)

They found there was 'a great deal of isomorphism around the world'. Higher education institutions taught similar subjects with 'similar perspectives leading to very similar degrees and to credentials that take on worldwide meaning'. 'Every society has a schooled population and institutions that function as a greatly expanded set of receptor sites collecting ideas and practices from world society'. This led to 'a great deal of global integration' (Schofer and Meyer, 2005: 917). The authors developed a set of indicators said to reflect the 'world model' of society and tested the expansion of enrolment against these indicators. The indicators were the numbers of international human rights organizations, international scientific associations, countries with a national development plan, states classified as democracies, and international non-government organizations (NGOs). The last reflected 'the overall structuration of the world polity' (p. 904): the more ties countries had with international organizations, the closer were these countries to the 'world polity' (pp. 904–7). Statistical test found the advance of the 'world model' as expressed in the indicators had a 'strong and significant effect on higher education enrolments' (p. 910), with enrolments expanding faster 'in countries with strong links to the international system or the "world polity"' (p. 916). They observe an 'essentially global system of higher education' (p. 917) in which 'global institutional and cultural change . . . has paved the way for hyper-expansion of higher education' (p. 900).

This analysis is consistent with work in institutional theory on global convergence in the forms of modern organization, for example *Globalization and Organization* (Drori et al., 2006); and Baker (2011) on the 'greater institutionalization of education' in society (p. 10) through the spread of educational credentialing as the master system of merit-based social differentiation and allocation. Baker referred to the 'schooled society', in which educational opportunity was seen as the source of social justice and the extension of education signified progress (pp. 10–13). Arguing against the notion that changes in education were a function of changes in 'occupations and the economy . . . external to the system of education' (p. 10), Baker asserted that education had direct effects and was primary in social transformation.

Schofer and Meyer (2005), and Baker (2011) are suggestive about the educational dimension of modernity, including the spread of scientific capacity, the ubiquity of credentialling and of educational opportunity policies, and the convergence of institutional forms. Since the 2005 paper there has been further convergence in research universities shaped by global ranking and the World-Class University movement (Hazelkorn, 2015). Yet the idea of 'world society' and 'world polity' driving educational growth, in a sweeping worldwide pattern of imitation sustained by individual institutions, is more problematic. First, the proofs are unconvincing. When modelling the world using multi-variant equations, there can never be enough variables, and they are neither independent of each other nor adequate proxies for each other. Nor are the chosen variables adequate to the larger tendencies they purport to represent. For example, the number of scientific associations is not in itself a convincing illustration of the growing breadth and depth of scientific practices. It may simply reflect greater ease in cross-border communication. Quantitative growth in NGOs does not adequately evidence a 'world polity', any more than growth in multi-national corporations proves that national economic barriers have dissolved into a single world economy. One global development does not automatically lead to another. Second, the notion of a global trend to expansion that is shaped from above at global level (Schofer and Meyer, 2005: 899) downplays the agency of nation-states, the continued potential for not only national-cultural variations but diverse innovations, and most importantly, the agency of families and students.

The authors seem to confuse two kinds of global tendency—externally driven changes triggered by cross-national global systems, such as the world science system or global university rankings; and changes via cross-border policy borrowing and partial organizational imitation. In HPS both kinds of global tendency are in play. Arguably, the second is more important. In cross-border policy borrowing common global forms and tendencies are filtered and nuanced via contextual factors. *High Participation Systems of Higher Education* places more emphasis than do Schofer and Meyer on bottom-up and middle-level drivers of HPS, alongside global commonalities. Though in the long run measured GERs tend to converge at a near universal level, national factors affect the forms and rhythms of expansion. Each national system finds its own pathway to a HPS, within a larger setting in which imitating behaviour is normal but variable and is not driven from a single pivot.

As with Trow (1973), in Schofer and Meyer (2005) perceptive findings on the social character of high participation are unnecessarily framed as a universal model. Institutional theory can be

rather deterministic. It draws much of the power of its analysis from its ability to depict a very limited number of institutional forms to which actors have access, and to show how particular forms are very homogeneous and monotonic.   (Crouch, 2005: 2)

This leaves insufficient space for locality, agency and hence diversity. A further difficulty with Schofer and Meyer (2005) is that their 'new model of society' is grounded in an idealized American polity based on liberalization, democratization and human rights. The rapid expansion of higher education is occurring in all societies and polities, as they in fact note (pp. 898, 908). Their finding that expansion has been greater where 'state control over education is low' (p. 898), which again privileges American forms, is belied by the most recent growth in GERs. Recent expansion has been at least as equally rapid in dynastic single-party China and quasi-single party Russia as in multi-party India and Indonesia. This also shows that the expansion of higher education (though not necessarily its social forms) has become even more universal than when Schofer and Meyer published in 2005.

OTHER NARRATIVES OF EXPANSION

State policy. States, and the global policy agencies that advise states—the World Bank, UNESCO, and OECD—mostly support the expansion of higher education. It is often assumed that HPS size is determined simply by state policy, funding, and regulation. In most systems governments directly regulate enrolment levels, sometimes in private as well as public institutions, and in 2012 governments funded 69 per cent of the costs of public and private tertiary institutions in OECD countries (OECD, 2015: 248). In orthodox public policy narratives, states expand higher education because they routinely facilitate economic development and provide social opportunity. A variation of this narrative is that the right mix of government policy is needed to foster expansion. For example, US's neoliberal policy assumes that competition for student enrolments between mass education providers, the subsidization of the for-profit sector, and state provision to student-consumers of student loans and market information will tend to maximize the growth in numbers.

This narrative of state-driven expansion is replicated in much research and scholarship. For example in *Stratification in Higher Education* (Shavit et al., 2007), Richard Arum and colleagues argue against the notion that HPS normally 'expand in response to growing aggregate demand by individuals for education'. They state that while this may be relevant to the USA, in many other countries 'education is centrally regulated and numerous constraints are imposed on expansion', including formal quotas on admissions, the rationing of elite education, funding constraints, or restrictive requirements in relation to accreditation or curricula (Arum et al., 2007: 6–7). However, *Stratification in Higher Education* was published ten years ago, using data collected in country studies almost twenty years ago, before the tendency towards HPS was fully manifest. Rapid expansion has now extended to higher education systems varying markedly in forms of regulation, financing protocols, and public/private mixes. In addition, in the marketized and competitive US system, with its deregulated (and subsidized) for-profit sector, the GER has stagnated.

As these outcomes suggest, the orthodox narrative about state-driven expansion is questionable. First, it is necessary to distinguish stated policy rationales from the real political imperatives shaping states. Government finds it expedient to present higher education as an opportunity framework. The provision of access broadens its social-political legitimacy, while it also claims economic legitimacy as the maker of productivity-driven growth and global competitiveness. It is easier to create educational opportunities than jobs, and the expansion of education transfers responsibility for social outcomes from the state to universities and families. Second, though states have autonomy they respond to elites and articulate middle class citizens (Jessop, 2007). State agency is variable. If state intervention at times appears purposely driven and based on economic or social agendas, at other times states seem to act more as facilitators. Third, the role of the state in the expansion of higher education varies historically on the basis of the stage the emerging HPS has reached.

The role of states is especially important in the early stage of massification. Without at least some state financing of infrastructure and trained personnel there can be individual institutions, but no system building. For-profit education cannot carry the cost of public goods. Without visible bricks-and-mortar institutions, emerging middle class aspirations are limited. States foster and legitimate aspirations for higher education by subsidizing not only tuition but student living costs, partly compensating families for income forgone, and redirecting individual trajectories on a mass scale. At this stage, social demand appears as a function of state policy. Later, the relationship reverses. Once provision has achieved stable mass, social demand feeds on itself as Trow (1973) explained. The dynamic of continually expanding participation is established. This places increasing pressures on states. State involvement becomes less essential for expansion per se, though government may still intervene selectively to extend the participation of students from particular social groups.

In the progression towards HPS states may continue to influence the pace of expansion; but once systems take in a large minority of the population, and still more at the HPS stage, cuts to regulated student numbers are rare except for demographic reasons—and *nowhere* has any state moved to secure a lasting reversal of an increase in the enrolment ratio. This is despite the cost pressures created by expansion, and the recurring concerns about graduate unemployment and 'over-education' that as Trow noted are endemic to HPS. Regardless of the kind of polity, electorally contested or one-party regime, it is politically too difficult to reverse growth. If impelled to reduce unit public costs or total public costs for fiscal reasons, states reduce unit subsidy rates rather than the volume of funded places. Far from being routinely negated by states, as suggested by Arum and colleagues, the expansionary dynamic has proven politically irreducible, everywhere. This suggests the presence of a generic factor or factors driving growth with compelling power across otherwise different HPS.

In short, state policy is insufficient to explain the HPS phenomenon. Rhetorical links between global competition policy and policy on participation help to explain the forms of neoliberal education policy but not the actual dynamics of growth. However, there is still the question of whether the long-term drivers of expansion are institutional, economic, or social.

Economic development. After the narrative about state policy and often in conjunction with it, the leading explanation for educational expansion is the economic narrative. Most policy economists have little doubt the long-term growth of higher education is driven by economic demand for 'human capital' in the labour markets, signalled by the wage returns to marginal productivity (Becker, 1964). In this narrative, students and their families, or (more often) states operating on their behalf, invest in education in terms of time, income forgone, and tuition, to the point where the lifetime returns to degree holders equal the cost of the investment. In the human capital imaginary the economic drivers, measured with apparent precision, modulate the volumes and rhythms of expansion.

Since the mid-1960s the economic narrative has sustained many thousands of studies of rates of return to investment in education. Longitudinal research mostly finds that as higher education grows, graduate earnings move back towards the social mean, but the 'graduate premium', the difference between returns to graduates and non-graduates, is sustained. This begs the question of causality. Earnings are affected by many factors other than education (Piketty, 2014: 304–21). For example, higher returns to graduates may reflect family background advantages (Marginson, 2016b, c). Nevertheless, in both policy and in popular culture, higher graduate earnings are routinely attributed to higher education. This can lead families to unreasoning optimism about graduate prospects (Hansen, 2011: 80–1; Arum and Roksa, 2014: 85, 105)—suggesting that what supports participation is the *narrative* about the contribution of education to earnings and social position, not systematic calculation of the returns to human capital. The human capital narrative helps to drive educational growth, but the extent to which actual economic outcomes drive growth is not so clear.

Sociologists who review the growth of educational participation often find the human capital explanation to be unpersuasive. As mentioned, Trow (1973) noted that demand for graduate jobs was not fixed but moved down the occupational hierarchy as participation increased, with graduates displacing non-graduates. Teichler (2009: 28) makes a similar point. For Schofer and Meyer (2005),

the rapid expansion of higher education in the 1960s does not coincide with especially large historical changes in occupational structures, job skill requirements, or labour market demands that would create a need for massive expansion of higher education.

Since then, the apparent association between economic demand and participation growth weakened (Schofer and Meyer, 2005: 900, 916). Geiger (2014) remarks that labour markets and education markets are not joined but on 'separate tracks'.

Cross-country comparisons of economic growth and enrolment growth suggest a modest association. This does not mean the expansion of participation is necessarily driven by the economy. The causality could be reversed, or mutual, or a third element (or complex of elements) could be driving both. There are also exceptions, for example countries where participation has surged alongside slow growing economies. Between 2000 and 2012 in Portugal, GDP grew by 0.2 per cent per year while the GER rose from 47.6 to 68.9 per cent, 21.3 per cent in twelve years. There was also high participation growth and low economic growth in Denmark, Netherlands, Hungary, and Croatia (World Bank, 2015; UNESCO, 2016).

National differences in the relation between educational growth and economic development suggest that the relation is not a constant social law but varies by time and place. Economic conditions encourage the evolution of HPS in two ways. First, a threshold level of national wealth is needed to kick-start mass higher education and demand for it as a positional good (see also Chapter 2). Second, all else equal, economies with larger industry, business services, public services, and professional services need more higher education. As Tables 1.1 and 1.4 show, one characteristic of HPS countries is that agricultural work has a modest and reducing role. The large-scale movement of rural populations to city-based work in manufacturing and services is associated with the rapid growth of educational participation, though there may be a lag; and as noted, economic globalization further quickens demand for skilled labour associated with cross-border trade, communications, and government. In fully fledged HPS countries, a high proportion of people work in industry and services. Business services and retail utilize advanced generic skills like communicative competence. Teaching and nursing need sector-specific knowledge and skills. Manufacturing draws on technical training. In HPS the mix between services and manufacturing varies. It is not necessary for countries to be 'post-industrial' services economies to sustain an HPS. For example, South Korea is a high-income country with a large manufacturing sector and a GER at close to 100 per cent. HPS are associated with 'post-Neolithic' economies rather than 'post-industrial' economies.

However, the fact educational growth is (variably) associated with economic modernization does not settle the hard-edged question of what drives the compelling and ubiquitous tendency towards educational expansion—economic demand for labour, social demand for opportunity, the self-driven growth of cities or education itself, or some combination. The economic narrative, at governmental and popular levels, encourages HPS. Higher education is also associated with the labour market take-up of skills, and with social advantage. The question is the extent to which relations between educational growth, popular demand for education, and social outcomes take the form imagined in the economic narrative.

Table 1.4. Employment by industry distribution, eight HPS countries, various years

	GER 2014 %	Proportion of employment in 2017 in:			Proportion of 2013 labour force with completed tertiary qualifications %
		Agriculture %	Industry %	Services %	
Canada	n.a.	2	20	78	52
Norway	77	2	20	78	42
Australia	90	3	21	76	n.a.
Finland	89	4	22	74	41
Japan	63	4	27	70	41
Russia	79	7	27	66	56
Poland	68	11	30	60	31
USA	87	2	17	81	34

Notes: n.a. = data not available. Qualifications of labour force data: 2014 for Finland, USA, Norway, Poland, and Canada; 2012 for Ethiopia; 2011 for Mexico; 2010 for India; 2008 for Japan and Pakistan.
Source: Author, compiled from World Bank (2018).

Credentialism. The credentialism narrative in economic sociology offers an alternative explanation of educational growth to human capital theory using much the same evidence. Here the economic role of education is not to impart useful skills but to be a sorting system for employers (for an early version, see Berg, 1971). Credentialism rightly recognizes the role of higher education in positional competition (Hirsch, 1976). More tendentiously, it sees growth as primarily driven by the self-interest of educational institutions. They use their screening role to elongate the study period, lift qualification levels, and multiply the types of credentials and learning programmes. The credentialism argument assumes that supply drives demand. It overlaps with institutionalist narratives in which educational institutions propel the outward spread of their social differentiating role (Baker, 2011); but the credentialism narrative excludes the positive claim of the human capital narrative. Screening is seen as the source of economic and social barriers, and too much education is seen as wasteful.

However, while many institutions and systems extend their social reach (Chapter 5), there are counter-factuals to the credentialism claim. First, as noted, higher education is not the only determinant of allocation (Marginson, 2016b). Second, occupational licensing and credential structures, and the extent to which they are autonomous, vary greatly between countries that share the common dynamic of growth. There is also the question of proportionality. The credentialism narrative emphasizes the agency of institutions at the expense of the agency of the families and students that use them, who (like employers) are seen as blind followers in a game controlled by educational institutions for their own benefit. This is highly questionable. Self-building universities alone cannot explain a tendency as powerful as HPS. Credentialism is everywhere—but more as the opportunistic follower of expansion than as the leader of the pack.

Urbanization and the middle class. If there is an organizational agent driving HPS the city is a stronger claimant than the institution. The city is both a collective agent in its own right and the incubator of family agency and aspirations on a massive scale. Like higher education it is growing rapidly. Between 1970 and 2010 the world proportion of people in cities rose from 37 to 52 per cent (UNDESA, 2012). It is expected to reach 66 per cent in 2050 (United Nations, 2014). In China, the urban share climbed from 17 per cent in 1970 to 54 per cent in 2013; in Indonesia from 17 to 53 per cent; and in India from 20 to 33 per cent (UNDESA, 2012; World Bank, 2016). When the largest countries are arranged in order of the extent of urbanization and the GERs are graphed, the line of best fit suggests a strong association between urbanization and the GER (Marginson, 2016a). Figure 1.1 displays the reverse correlation. It arranges countries in order of enrolment ratios, and shows that in 2013, except in three small island nations, urbanization exceeded 50 per cent in all nations with HPS; and the line of best fit indicates a moderate association between urbanization and the GER.

Three statistical trends are marching together: growth of the middle class, growth of cities, growth of higher education. Historically, in the 1970s and 1980s urbanization in most countries moved ahead of the rise in educational participation. The urban percentage still exceeds the enrolment percentage in the bulk of systems in Figure 1.1. But in most countries GERs are now increasing more rapidly than the urban share of population. The gap is closing. Why this association between cities and higher

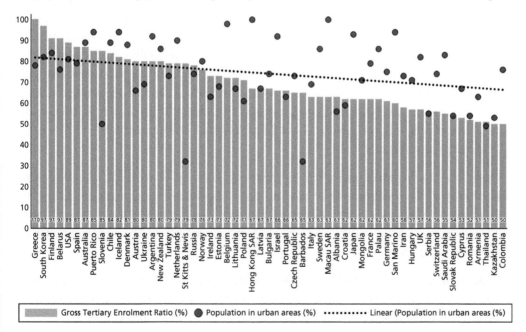

Figure 1.1. Gross enrolment ratio and proportion of the population living in urban areas, all high participation systems, 2013

Source: Author, based on data from World Bank (2016).

education? Large-scale institutions such as universities and full-size colleges are generally sustainable only in cities. Correspondingly, the non-rural middle class families that lead social demand for education are concentrated in cities. The critical mass of upper secondary students in cities concentrates the political pressure for expanded higher education provision while enabling economies of scale. The relation between city and social demand is symbiotic. Growing educational infrastructure itself funnels and magnifies aspirations for education, in turn triggering more institutions. This is not to say all people living in cities are middle class, or that educational aspirations are confined to such families. The location of higher education in cities brings it within sight of the whole urban population, pushing the demand for access to 50 per cent and beyond.

SOCIAL DEMAND FOR POSITION

There is no reason to wholly exclude any one of these narratives from the explanation for HPS—government, the economy, credentials, urbanization. Equally, no one narrative seems sufficient as a universal cause. All are manifest in the expansion of higher education and part of its description. Arguably, none constitute a sufficient motive force. All four explanations are somewhat trapped on the structure side. What is the human agency driving expansion? While state policy and economic development provide enabling conditions for HPS, top-down factors do not consistently predict educational growth. Accumulating social demand, bottom-up agency, has to be added from outside. Yet it is more than an add-on. And while across the world political economies and political cultures are nationally variant, every country sees the same remorseless tendency towards educational expansion, the essence of HPS as a global phenomenon. The growth of cities (especially) and the credentialling moves of institutions are closely associated with growth but, again, do not fully explain social demand.

Proposition 3 states that

> *Once transition from a primarily agricultural economy is achieved, the long-term growth of HPS is independent of political economic factors such as economic growth and patterns of labour market demand; patterns of public and private funding of higher education; the roles of public and private institutions; and system organization and modes of governance.*

Participation also grows regardless of the specific configuration of higher educational institutions, the industry mix in the economy, the forms of government, or the political culture. The question is, why?

There is one explanatory narrative for the expansion of higher education that places human agency at the centre of the picture. That is what Adam Smith in *The Wealth of Nations* called 'the desire of bettering our condition' (Smith, 1776: 441) and Fred Hirsch in *Limits to Growth* (1976) described as social competition for 'positional goods' (Marginson, 2016b, d). Adam Smith argues that the desire for betterment is universal. Once basic needs for subsistence are met, parents turn their minds to lifting their children above themselves. If they are already affluent, they still want to improve the position. For parents schooling and higher education are mediums for advancing the prospects of their children. Likewise, adult students invest in higher education to broaden their vocational and earnings prospects and elevate their status. As higher education accumulates the growing weight of the combined social demand, it expands more rapidly than the volume of 'positional goods', the elevated social outcomes or 'betterings', that can be accessed. At a given time there are only so many positions of social leadership, so many status-generating professional positions, so many middle class incomes. The zero-sum character of positional competition kicks in. At this point, for many families, educational participation is a 'defensive necessity' (Trow, 1973): more a matter of preserving and reproducing social position than of bettering it.

At the same time, once the majority of families enter higher education, families and young people that remain outside it (via non-participation) face growing disadvantages, as Trow (1973) suggested. Higher education becomes associated with advanced personal agency and a common social literacy, and an essential and widely distributed social status essential for full social inclusion. But whether higher education is associated with social betterment, social maintenance, or simply social inclusion, the secular trend at every stage is for growth in participation, until universal participation, 100 per cent inclusion in the HPS, is approached.

Family agency, the drive for social reproduction and betterment, and the tendency for participation to grow on an open-ended basis are found everywhere. Proposition 2 states

> *In HPS there is no intrinsic limit to the spread of family aspirations for participation in higher education until universality is reached; and no intrinsic limit to the level of social position to which families/students may aspire.*

Arguably, also, for many individual students, the drive for 'betterment' pertains to more than parental concerns about social status or income. It takes in a broader range of aspirations for personal development as 'self-formation' via learning, knowledge, and the institutional experience (Marginson, 2014, 2018).

Systems have differing starting points, the secular tendency proceeds in fits and starts, but in the long run participation expands everywhere without limit. This shapes a specific political economy of HPS that evolves along with growth. It seems that as systems expand, and aspirations tend towards the universal, the elasticity of family/ student demand for higher education falls towards zero. One implication is that in countries where tuition fees are paid by families, students, or graduates, as demand elasticity falls, states and/or institutions more readily increase the proportion of the costs of higher education paid from private sources.

Social demand for higher education is not an abstraction. It is rooted in real human agents. It is not equivalent to 'market demand', which is effective demand in the economic sense, differentiated by the price of products and the capacity to pay. Nor is social demand ruled by the logic of economic scarcity. Not only does the desire for betterment have no limit, there is no necessary relationship between costs and status. For higher education, families' and students' occupational status is often as important or more important a goal as earnings (e.g. Arum and Roksa, 2014: 80–1; Triventi, 2013: 55–7; Hu and Vargas, 2015). Status is larger and less bordered than rates of return calculations. Prospects of assuming a managerial role are especially important for graduates from prestige institutions, and those with generic degrees who enter public sector and NGOs, which includes many women (Roksa, 2005: 207). Stating the problem still more generally, for families and students higher education offers prospects of self-formation and self-actualization with many social forms. Families and students aim to maximize their opportunities, working the pre-given structures of schooling and higher education as well as they can for their own advantage and fulfilment. In modernity, agential dreams have no limit, within the social structures in which those dreams are conceived and expressed. Like the money system, HPS provide an institutional structure, combining incremental progression with transformative upward leaps, that nurtures a bounded yet infinite imagination. These are seductive systems.

In the outcome, having established large-scale higher education systems, modern states have little choice but to stand back and allow those systems to channel and concentrate the universal desire for betterment. As noted, the potency of social demand as a political factor is shown by the facts that all states sooner or later respond to ongoing pressure from below for growth in educational opportunities; and that once states have sanctioned growth in higher education they do not unwind it. Some encourage private sectors with a mandate for demand-driven growth. Others, even in neoliberal polities, tolerate rising costs, as in the deregulated growth of state-funded places in Australia from 2012 to 2018 (Kemp and Norton, 2014) and England from 2015. When the GER reaches two-thirds of the age group and most school students aspire to higher education, there is no defensible rationale for keeping anyone out.

In short, social demand is the best available candidate for the role of common driver of the worldwide tendency towards HPS. Advanced social aspirations and participation in higher education have become a common cultural fact still spreading across the world. The filmic metaphor is *Slumdog Millionaire* (2008). There the ladder is a television quiz show not a university, but knowledge is the means of elevation. The social hierarchy continues but the caste world, in which the fate of persons is determined at birth, is being left behind. This augmentation of individual and social agency is a global process of democratization, though not necessarily Americanization: Schofer and Meyer (2005) are only half correct. Even so, the common social tendency is articulated through national-local factors. Social demand for higher education is not identical everywhere, in timing or substance. If in the long-run it looks unstoppable, in each HPS short of universality it is shaped in educational structures and differentiated by social, cultural, political, and economic factors. Research is needed to unpack its constituents on a country-by-country basis. The Part II chapters begin this process.

The variability of national contexts and systems, amid the common worldwide tendency towards the expansion of higher education, raises the question of how to theorize, investigate, and analyse across the global/national conjunction. That is considered next.

Global and National Tendencies

The inquiry into the worldwide tendency towards HPS calls up two contrasting objectives, and the need to integrate those objectives: (1) to understand what drives the evolution of higher education in each specific HPS, and (2) to understand the similarities between cases, without imposing on them a meta-theoretical framework in which only features that appear in the framework are visible. The case studies in Part II of this book focus on objective (1), while Part I explores objective (2). The preparation of this book entailed an oscillation between (1) and (2). Investigation began with discussion of national cases of HPS. It moved to generic findings (the seventeen propositions) across the field of HPS, informed by the research literature and the cases. Then the HPS case studies in Part II were prepared in the light of the generic findings of Part I. In that process the seventeen propositions were tested against the cases.

International comparative research calls up both sameness and difference. To study differences it is essential to adopt a common framework in which they can appear in coherent fashion. Similarity is a necessary condition of difference. That is generally understood.

The tension between generalizing arguments and contextual understanding of the cases makes comparative studies very different from single country or higher education institution case studies, because in comparative research settings there is a real and concrete need to find common categories and concepts to study the cases and to explain differences and similarities between them.   (Välimaa and Nokkala, 2014: 425)

What is not always agreed is that to understand similarity and commonality, the realm of the generic, it is also necessary to explore and understand specificity and difference on the basis of 'contextual understanding of the cases'. Many researcher-scholars use determinist inquiry on the basis of pre-given theories or models. All countries are seen as variations of the master narrative of development. This is deductive top-down inquiry without the balancing item, inductive bottom-up inquiry, grounded in each country context. *High Participation Systems of Higher Education* attempts to find the balance. Meaningful generalizations about the expansion of HPS can only be constructed from a range of cases and their variety-in-context. The two perspectives, the general and the particular, are used to interrogate the findings from each other, revising themselves and each other in a never-ending reciprocation.

Clark (1983) states that: 'Cross-national comparison is particularly advantageous in uncovering the unique features and unconscious assumptions that possess our vision when we study only a single country, generally our own' (p. 2). Yet the deductive determinism of many studies in comparative education is often joined to a second methodological limitation, the tendency towards impose the norms of the researcher's home system, which becomes the basis of the allegedly universal model of development. Välimaa and Nokkala (2014) refer to 'single country myopia' in comparative education. Shahjahan and Kezar (2013) critique 'methodological nationalism', which assumes 'that the nation/state/society is the natural social and political form of the modern world' (Wimmer and Schiller, 2002: 301). Methodological nationalism has two costs for explanation. First, it blocks from view those features of the higher education landscape not part of the master system. Second, it leads to under-estimation of phenomena that cross borders, or pertain to global systems, including such 'marginal' phenomena as the world research system, the spread of neoliberal 'global competition state' (Cerny, 1997) policies in national systems, and the mimetic worldwide spread of aspirations for social position and self-realization through higher education.

All of this raises two questions about the method of understanding HPS: how to engage with the particular while acknowledging but not privileging the general, and how to achieve the general perspective without privileging one's own particulars.

THE NATIONAL ASSEMBLAGE

First, the question of engaging with the particular. Each HPS can be understood as part of a specific social *assemblage* of family/state/education/economy with nationally distinctive features. Each is also a product of its history. However, though the elements affecting national variation are path dependent they are not fixed; they evolve over time. Each HPS is both embedded in national society and culture, and also embedded in the global setting.

What then is the relation between national embeddedness and global embeddedness? The global dimension is increasingly important in higher education, especially in research, global comparison, and cross-border imitation. Tendencies to global homogenization are obvious. However, in relation to HPS global effects are not uniform and should not be overstated. For example, nations vary in the extent to which they have installed the neoliberal competition policy template, or are affected by global systems such as university ranking. Global systems and flows are articulated through differing family-state-economy-education assemblages in each country; in which national agency variously resists and blocks those global effects, reworks them, or operates as their collaborator or instrument. Though nations can no longer ignore or absent themselves from the global it is not the always-already master dimension in higher education, except in scientific research. Higher education is a creature of the nation-building agendas of states (Scott, 2011). National aspects are primary, in policy, regulation, and public and private funding arrangements. Nearly all higher education institutions continue to draw their main funding and status from national sources. Most students and faculty are not mobile across borders, though in a few nations mobility is common. Most higher education institutions are not research-intensive or strongly active in global networks, though they can still be affected by the global, for example if it further elevates the top research universities in their HPS.

In short, each national HPS is both autonomous, *and* part of a larger set of relations, and evolves in a dialectic of sameness and difference with other HPS. Relations between global patterns, effects, and self-forming national systems take many configurations. Some HPS are more globally open, more globalized, and/or more globally shaping than are others.

THE TRANSPOSITIONAL POSITION

Second, how is it possible to develop generalizations about HPS that evade the mental imprint of one's own system habits? One answer is to study HPS within a cross-country research group in which each person takes responsibility not just for their own case study but for the common generalizations, as in this project. This in turn opens the way for closer integration. In *Objectivity and Position* (1992), Amartya Sen suggests that an 'objective inquiry' can be achieved by developing a 'transpositional' view, enabling 'position-independent generalizations'. Necessarily, this starts from the national cases. 'Any attempt at non-positional objectivity has to start with knowledge based on positional observations', despite 'the inescapable fact that what is actually observed may be significantly dependent on the position from which the observation is undertaken' (Sen, 1992: 1, 3). 'Positional specifications tend to be typically incomplete' (p. 5), and there is something to be gained by learning from each other, and integrating the multiple positions.

Transpositional objectivity is not a 'view from nowhere', but a composite of primary information derived in several positional views (Sen, 1992: 1–2) drawn together by 'discriminating aggregation' to reach 'a combined view' (pp. 4–5). Exactly how this is done is less clear to Sen, but he writes variously of the broker between different positions, and the 'impartial spectator' who is in some measure sympathetic to all. No doubt both approaches have affected the composition of *High Participation Systems of Higher Education.*

TYPES OF HPS

Transpositional objectivity lends itself better to a small number of general propositions than to a comprehensive understanding of HPS. Situated HPS case studies within each national assemblage enable a stronger take on the detail but may lose the wood for the trees. This suggests there are gains in developing a meso-level of analysis, in which national studies are grouped together into a small number of contrasted types of HPS with common features, enabling richer mid-range generalizations that in turn can inform the national case studies. The small grouping of middle-level types also can be used to test global-level findings about HPS, restraining the tendency to see the whole world as identical. Crouch comments in relation to comparative studies in economics that when 'national cases are grouped together under a small number of contrasted types... [this] has provided an intellectual counterweight to easy arguments about globalization, which predict an inevitable trend towards similarities among the world's economies' (Crouch, 2005: 25–6).

Esping-Andersen (1990) has developed a typology of welfare states. Amable's (2003) types of capitalism separates Anglophone 'market-based', Nordic 'social democratic', Southern Europe 'Mediterranean', East Asian, and central European, though the last is heterogeneous. In higher education, a case can be made for regional-cultural distinctions between Anglophone, Nordic (Välimaa, 2011), German, French, Southern European, Russian (Smolentseva, 2016), East Asian or Chinese civilizational (Marginson, 2013), and Latin American models. Others could be added. The point is not to allocate empirical cases to one model or another but to determine which models are present in each empirical case, and their proportion, and to map changes taking place. Real cases are always hybrids and open to change. For example, all HPS are influenced to some degree by the Anglo-American model of the research-intensive university, normalized in world science and global ranking.

In HPS, certain features seem to cluster on a meso-level basis in groups of systems with shared cultural roots. These include university-state relations, norms of university autonomy and academic freedom, approaches to social equity, the public/private share of financing, and the extent of systemic stratification. Take the relation between expansion and tuition fees. English-speaking governments assume a tradeoff between free tuition and growth, seeing free higher education as unaffordable. As participation rises, student contributions increase. Some Anglophone scholars see the growth/tuition tradeoff as a quasi-law of high participation (e.g. Johnstone and Marcucci, 2010). The quasi-law was also applied in the post-Soviet zone in the 1990s: after public funding collapsed, fees in public institutions and a deregulated private sector were seen as essential to growth (see Chapters 11 and 12 on Russia and Poland). Yet in other regional groupings, different assumptions prevail. All of the Nordic countries have achieved HPS while maintaining higher education as free at entry for domestic students. In Germany a lower level of participation, and neoliberal financial policy, are joined to free tuition. In East Asia relations between tuition and expansion are different again. There has always been family investment and private funding. Public funding is used selectively to fulfil policy objectives like building leading research universities. However, in the transition to HPS in Japan, Korea, Taiwan, and Singapore, systemic reliance on private funding has not increased; and in China a fast growing GER is joined to fast increasing public funding. There is marketization as competition, but not price regulation. Again, it is striking how countries with variant political economies and cultures exhibit similar patterns of participation.

Regional differences are explored in Chapter 6 and Part II. With three Anglophone country cases, two Nordic, two Post-Soviet, and one East Asian there is scope to explore commonalities between world regions, contrasts between regions, and contrasts within them.

This Book

High Participation Systems of Higher Education is concerned with some but not all aspects of massifying higher education systems. It does not visit Martin Trow's remarks on teaching and learning, and changing academic cultures, though it shares his interest in the trajectories of elite and mass institutions. The book is more interested than Trow was in research. It does not closely explore student learning and technologies, or the third mission of universities, or the knowledge economy in patents, and is marginally interested in the distinctions between fields of study. Jurgen Habermas on communications and the public sphere, Michel Foucault on governmentality, Basil Bernstein's codes, and many other suggestive theorizations do not figure in the account. Rather it focuses on the system-ordering issues of governance, diversity, stratification, and equity: issues that touch the intersections between HPS higher education and national societies, and the related policy, regulation, and politics. Government and politics are never very far way in higher education, but a key contribution of this book is to argue that accumulating social-cultural demand for education is also centrally important.

Nor is *High Participation Systems of Higher Education* a fully global study. It outlines participation in all countries, rich and poor, in Chapter 2. Otherwise it does not discuss emerging systems where participation is well below 50 per cent. It is about the future of higher education in emerging countries rather than the present. To trace that future, the book focuses empirically on the transformative effects of high participation in countries that have already achieved it. In sum, this book sees four meta-tendencies associated with HPS.

1. *Growth*: Driven by ubiquitous social demand, participation grows towards universal levels, as Trow (1973) forecast (Chapter 1).
2. *Convergence with society*: HPS higher education joins with the whole society at many points, for example in its internal architecture (Chapter 3) and its structuring of rewards and outcomes (Chapter 6). Society becomes 'a high participation society' in which higher education shapes people's lives and augments capabilities (Chapter 7).
3. *The multiversity*: The comprehensive multiversity (Kerr, 1963) consolidates as the primary form of higher education, becoming larger and more internally diverse (Chapter 4), more corporate inside (Chapter 3) and often—except in selective institutions—more socially inclusive. Multi-purpose institutions expand up to the research function and down to mass teaching and credentialing, and also drift upwards from sub-degree to degree education. The comprehensive size and reach of the multiversity helps to maximize the value of institutional brand, and retards slippage in the value of middle institutions as participation expands (Chapter 5).
4. *Stratification and inequality*: Following Pierre Bourdieu (1988, 1996), HPS tend towards bifurcation between selective elite higher education institutions and demand-responsive mass higher education institutions, and towards steeper stratification in the value of institutions, all else equal (Chapter 5). Participation in mass higher education tends towards a social average experience, though the gap with non-participation is maintained. Relative to mass education institutions, elite institutions become more elite. They are more contested, more difficult to enter, and more subject to middle class capture. Social inclusion expands but equality of opportunity declines (Chapter 6).

Chapter 2 maps the extent of HPS across the world, and isolates countries yet to achieve Trow's mass participation level of 15 per cent. It then provides a data-based comparison of features of HPS across the OECD countries.

Chapter 3 focuses on governance in HPS. While there is no single model and governance is shaped by system context and policy contingency, greater size and social inclusion trigger common features across the world—such as multiple relationships with external stakeholders, multi-level coordination and accountability, and the growing use of corporate organization.

Chapter 4 reconsiders diversity in higher education. It explores the differing dynamics of horizontal and vertical differentiation in HPS. Horizontal diversity and organizational innovation are more limited than might be expected, though internal diversity increases.

Chapter 5 explores vertical stratification. In expanding and bifurcating systems inter-institutional inequalities in resources and status tend to increase, though stratification is policy sensitive: government can flatten stratification, or foster a middle layer of institutions.

Chapter 6 extends the stratification issues to social equity and inequality. In HPS access to elite institutions is more unequal, and it is harder for states to redistribute opportunity. When there is consensual support for equality, government can modify the secular tendency of equality of opportunity to decline. But quasi-market competition exacerbates inequalities.

Chapter 7 asks but does not finally settle the question 'What is a high participation society?' in which most people engage with higher education. Two interacting domains of inquiry are key to the answer: (1) the self-formation of educated persons in social settings, and (2) how individuals are shaped by social stratification and the occupational structure.

Chapters 8–15 in Part II provide national HPS case studies that discuss, illustrate, and sometimes depart from the seventeen general propositions about HPS in this book. The cases are Australia, Canada, Finland, Japan, Norway, Poland, Russia, and the USA.

Chapter 16 brings the national case studies together, summarizes the overall outcome for the seventeen propositions, compares this study to Trow (1973), and then concludes the book.

▨ REFERENCES

Amable, B. (2003). *The Diversity of Modern Capitalism*. Oxford: Oxford University Press.

Arum, R., Gamoran, A., and Shavit, Y. (2007). More inclusion than diversion: Expansion, differentiation and market structures in higher education. In Y. Shavit, R. Arum and A. Gamoran (eds), *Stratification in Higher Education: A Contemporary Study*. Stanford: Stanford University Press, pp. 1–35.

Arum, R. and Roksa, J. (2014). *Aspiring Adults Adrift: Tentative Transitions of College Graduates*. Chicago: University of Chicago Press.

Baker, D. (2011). Forward and backward, horizontal and vertical: Transformation of occupational credentialing in the schooled society. *Research in Social Stratification and Mobility* (29)1, 5–29.

Becker, G. (1964). *Human Capital: A Theoretical and Empirical Analysis with Special Reference to Education*. Chicago: University of Chicago Press.

Berg, I. (1971). *Education and Jobs: The Great Training Robbery*. Clinton Corners, NY: Eliot Werner Publications.

Blockmans, W. and de Weerdt, H. (2016). The diverging legacies of classical empires in China and Europe. *European Review*, 24(2), 306–24.

Cerny, P. (1997). Paradoxes of the competition state: the dynamics of political globalization. *Government and Opposition*, 32(2), 251–74.

Clark, B. (1983). *The Higher Education System*. Berkeley, CA: University of California Press.

Corak, M. (2006). Do poor children become poor adults? Lessons from a cross country comparison of generational earnings mobility. IZA Discussion Paper No. 1993. Bonn: Institute for the Study of Labor.

Corak, M. (2012). *Inequality from Generation to Generation: The United States in Comparison.* Graduate School of Public and International Affairs, University of Ottawa, Ottawa Canada.

Crouch, C. (2005). *Capitalist Diversity and Change: Recombinant Governance and Institutional Entrepreneurs.* Oxford: Oxford University Press.

Douglass, J. (2000). *The Californian Idea and American Higher Education: 1850 to the 1960 Master Plan.* Stanford, CA: Stanford University Press.

Drori, G., Meyer, J., and Hwang, H. (eds) (2006). *Globalization and Organization: World Society and Organizational Change.* Oxford: Oxford University Press.

Esping-Andersen, G. (1990). *The Three Worlds of Welfare Capitalism.* Princeton, NJ: Princeton University Press.

Geiger, R. (2014). Higher Education in high participation systems. Paper to the conference of Ontario Confederation of University Faculty Associations, Toronto, 27–28 February.

Goodman, D. (2014). *Class in Contemporary China.* Cambridge: Polity.

Gustafsson, B., Shi, L., and Nivorozhkina, L. (2011). Why are household incomes more unequally distributed in China than in Russia? *Cambridge Journal of Economics*, 35(1), 897–920.

Hansen, H. (2011). Rethinking certification theory and the educational development of the United States and Germany. *Research in Social Stratification and Mobility* 29(1), 31–55.

Hazelkorn, E. (2015). *Rankings and the Reshaping of Higher Education: The Battle for World-class Excellence*, 2nd edn. Houndmills: Palgrave Macmillan.

Hirsch, F. (1976). *Social Limits to Growth.* Cambridge, MA: Harvard University Press.

Holcombe, C. (2011). *A History of East Asia: From the Origins of Civilization to the Twenty-first Century.* Cambridge: Cambridge University Press.

Hu, A. and Vargas, N. (2015). Horizontal stratification of higher education in urban China. *Higher Education* (70)3, 337–58.

Jessop, B. (2007). *State Power.* Cambridge: Polity Press.

Johnstone, B. and Marcucci, P. (2010). *Financing Higher Education World-wide: Who Pays? Who Should Pay?* Baltimore, MD: Johns Hopkins University Press.

Kemp, D. and Norton, A. (2014). *Review of the Demand-driven Funding System.* Canberra: Australian Government. https://docs.education.gov.au/system/files/doc/other/review_of_the_demand_driven_funding_system_report_for_the_website.pdf

Kerr, C. (1963). *The Uses of the University*, 1st edn. Cambridge, MA: Harvard University Press, 2001.

Kerr, C. (2001). *The Gold and the Blue: A Personal Memoir of the University of California, 1949–1967.* Volume 1: *Academic Triumphs.* Berkeley, CA: University of California Press.

Marginson, S. (2013). Emerging higher education in the Post-Confucian heritage zone. In D. Araya and P. Marber (eds), *Higher Education in the Global Age.* New York: Routledge, pp. 89–112.

Marginson, S. (2014). Student self-formation in international education. *Journal of Studies in International Education* 18(1), 6–22.

Marginson, S. (2016a). High participation systems of higher education. *The Journal of Higher Education* 87(2), 243–70.

Marginson, S. (2016b). The worldwide trend to high participation higher education: Dynamics of social stratification in inclusive systems. *Higher Education* 72(4), 413–34.

Marginson, S. (2016c). *The Dream is Over: The Crisis of Clark Kerr's Californian Idea of Higher Education*. Berkeley, CA: University of California Press.

Marginson, S. (2016d). *Higher Education and the Common Good*. Melbourne: Melbourne University Publishing.

Marginson, S. (2018). *Higher Education as Self-formation*. London: Institute of Education, University College London. https://www.ucl-ioe-press.com/books/higher-education-and-lifelong-learning/higher-education-as-a-process-of-self-formation/

McMahon, W. (2009). *Higher Learning Greater Good*. Baltimore, MD: Johns Hopkins University Press.

Mettler, S. (2014). *Degrees of Inequality: How the Politics of Higher Education Sabotaged the American Dream*. New York: Basic Books.

Milanovic, B. (2011). *The Haves and the Have Nots: A Brief and Idiosyncratic History of Global Inequality*. New York: Basic Books.

OECD (Organisation for Economic Co-operation and Development) (2014). *Education at a Glance 2014*. Paris: OECD.

OECD (Organisation for Economic Co-operation and Development) (2015). *Education at a Glance 2015*. Paris: OECD.

OECD (Organisation for Economic Co-operation and Development) (2016). *Perspectives on Global Development 2017: International Migration in a Shifting World*. Paris: OECD.

Piketty, T. (2014). *Capital in the Twenty-first Century*. Cambridge, MA: Belknap Harvard University Press.

Roksa, J. (2005). Double disadvantage or blessing in disguise? Understanding the relationship between college major and employment sector. *Sociology of Education* 78(3), 207–32.

Saez, E. (2013). *Striking it Richer: The Evolution of Top Incomes in the United States*. Berkeley, CA: University of California, Berkeley, Department of Economics, Berkeley. http://eml.berkeley.edu//~saez/saez-UStopincomes-2012.pdf

Schofer, E. and Meyer, J. (2005). The worldwide expansion of higher education in the twentieth century. *American Sociological Review* 70(6), 898–920.

Scott, P. (2011). The university as a global institution. In R. King, S. Marginson and R. Naidoo (eds), *Handbook of Higher Education and Globalization*. Cheltenham: Edward Elgar, pp. 59–75.

Sen, A. (1985). Well-being, agency and freedom: The Dewey Lectures 1984. *The Journal of Philosophy* 82, 169–221.

Sen, A. (1992). *Objectivity and Position*. The Lindley Lecture, The University of Kansas. Lawrence, KA: The University of Kansas.

Sen, A. (2000). *Development as Freedom*. New York: Basic Books.

Shahjahan, R. and Kezar, A. (2013). Beyond the 'national container': Addressing methodological nationalism in higher education research. *Educational Researcher* 42(1), 20–9.

Shavit, Y., Arum, R., and Gamoran, A. (eds) (2007). *Stratification in Higher Education: A Comparative Study.* Stanford, CA: Stanford University Press.

Silver, N. (2016). Education, not income, predicted who would vote for Trump. *Five Thirty Eight.* http://fivethirtyeight.com/features/education-not-income-predicted-who-would-vote-for-trump/

Smith, Adam (1776). *The Wealth of Nations.* Harmondsworth: Penguin Books, 1979.

Smolentseva, A. (2016). Universal higher education and positional advantage: Soviet legacies and neoliberal transformations in Russia. *Higher Education* 73(2), 209–26.

Swales, K. (2016). *Understanding the Leave Vote.* London: NatCen and The UK in a Changing Europe. http://natcen.ac.uk/our-reseach/research/understanding-the-leave-vote/

Teichler, U. (2009). *Higher Education and the World of Work: Conceptual Frameworks, Comparative Perspectives, Empirical Findings.* Rotterdam: Sense Publishers.

Treiman, D. (2012). The 'difference between heaven and earth': Urban–rural disparities in well-being in China. *Research in Social Stratification and Mobility* 30(1), 33–47.

Triventi, M. (2013). The role of higher education stratification in the reproduction of social inequality in the labor market. *Research in Social Stratification and Mobility* 32(1), 45–63.

Trow, M. (1973). *Problems in the Transition from Elite to Mass Higher Education.* Berkeley, CA: Carnegie Commission on Higher Education.

United Nations (2014). World's population increasingly urban with more than half living in urban areas. http://www.un.org/en/development/desa/news/population/world-urbanization-prospects-2014.html

UNDESA (United Nations Department of Educational and Social Affairs) (2012). *World Urbanization Prospects: The 2011 Revision.* New York: United Nations.

UNESCO (United Nations Educational, Social and Cultural Organization). (2016). UNESCO Institute for Statistics data on education. http://data.uis.unesco.org/.

UNESCO (United Nations Educational, Social and Cultural Organization). (2018). International Standard Classification of Education, ISCED 2011. http://uis.unesco.org/sites/default/files/documents/international-standard-classification-of-education-isced-2011-en.pdf

Välimaa, J. (2011). The corporatisation of national universities in Finland. In B. Pusser, K. Kempner, S. Marginson, and I. Ordorika (eds), *Universities and the Public Sphere: Knowledge Creation and State Building in the Era of Globalization.* New York: Routledge, pp. 101–19.

Välimaa, J. and Nokkala, T. (2014). The dimensions of social dynamics in comparative studies on higher education. *Higher Education* 67(4), 423–37.

Wimmer, A. and M. Schiller (2002). Methodological nationalism and beyond: Nation–state building, migration and the social sciences. *Global Networks* 4(2), 301–34.

World Bank (2015, 2016, and 2018). Data and statistics. http://data.worldbank.org/indicator/all

2 Comparative Data on High Participation Systems

Patrick Clancy and Simon Marginson

> Global history ... seeks answers to the same questions in multiple sites.
>
> (Belich et al., 2016: 3)

Introduction

The focus of this volume on high participation systems (HPS) of higher education requires systematic consideration of comparative statistical data. While at one level this is unproblematic when focusing only on the vast increase in higher education enrolments which is a feature in the great majority of countries, the significance of enrolment growth needs to be related to the size and age structure of the base population of each country. The needs of comparative research require robust statistical measures of participation. The inexorable growth in the individual and social demand for higher education, discussed in Chapter 1, stems from the perception that advanced education is the key mechanism in the status attainment process. For national governments which have supported this expansion of higher education, the driving force has been the imputed link between higher education, and economic growth and national development. The enhancement of human capital and the cultivation of new knowledge and innovation are viewed as the critical elements in the competitiveness race in a globalized world. It is this realization which has led to a heightened interest in comparative data on participation and achievement in education.

The desire for accurate comparisons, and the ability to 'benchmark' a country's progress against leading countries which are viewed as key competitors, is not matched by the availability of appropriate statistical data. Part of the problem is related to difficulties in defining 'higher education' and the increasing blurred boundaries between degree programmes in higher education and other post-secondary education. Existing comparative work both by supra-national agencies such as UNESCO, the OECD, EUROSTAT, and by individual scholars have tended to use, either singularly or in combination, measures of entry rates, enrolment rates, or output measures such as graduation rates or measures of the educational level of the population. This chapter starts with a review of the principal measures available within each of these categories. One of our conclusions is that there is an inevitable tradeoff between what may be the optimum statistical measure and what is feasible given the limitations of available comparative data. For global comparisons, the chapter relies on *gross enrolment ratios* (GER) which offer a relatively robust measure of international trends in participation in higher education. These trends are summarized in the second section of the chapter. The third section seeks to develop a more nuanced statistical measure of comparative trends in participation and also explores some structural characteristics of HPS. This analysis is necessarily limited to OECD countries which provide more detailed statistical data. In making judgements about comparative participation it is unwise to rely on any single indicator and we recommend the use of a *higher education participation index* which combines indicators on enrolment and output measures.

In addition to providing a robust measure of the scale of participation in higher education, analysis of country scores on the separate indicators highlights distinctive features of each higher education system. This complements the other chapters in this volume. While the different HPS of higher education share the experience of massification, the structural features of the systems still exhibit considerable country variability.

Statistical Measures of Participation

Entry rates into higher education offer the potential for the most unambiguous measure of access and participation. Entry rates measure the inflow to higher education at a particular period rather than the total stock of students enrolled, which is measured by enrolment rates. Traditionally, entry rates were measured as the number of new entrants to higher education in a particular year, expressed as a percentage of the population at the typical age of entry—frequently the average size of the 18–19 or 19–20 age cohort, or the average size of the age cohort from which at least 70 per cent of the entrants belong. This is described as the *gross entry rate*. Although easy to calculate since it does not require very detailed data on the age distribution of entrants, this measure lacks precision because of the lack of correspondence between the age distributions of the numerator and the denominator. More recently the *net entry rate* is more widely used, especially in OECD countries. The net entry rate for a specific age is obtained by dividing the number of first-time (new) entrants of that age by the total population in the corresponding age group, multiplied by a hundred (OECD, 2004: 143). The overall net entry rate is calculated by summing the rates for each single year of age. This *sum of age specific entry rates* is based on a 'synthetic cohort' assumption, according to which the current pattern of entry constitutes the best estimate of the behaviour of today's young adults over their lifetimes (OECD, 2013: 291). While this is a comprehensive measure it does require detailed data on the age composition of entrants.

There are additional complications. One concerns the definition of 'new entrant': a new entrant to a particular college or university may have previously been enrolled in another college or on a different programme in the same college (the same difficulties also arise with the measurement of gross entry rates). Furthermore, since most countries identify different sectors of higher education, the movement of students between sectors can lead to double counting if the same student is classified as a new entrant in each sector.

Prior to 2015 the OECD entry data was reported separately for two different sectors; Tertiary Type A education and Tertiary Type B. The former refers to programmes that are largely theoretically based and designed to provide qualifications for entry into advanced research programmes and professions with high skill requirements, while Type B programmes are typically of shorter duration, and for the most part are more occupationally oriented and lead to direct labour market access. Since some students who enter Type B may enter Type A at a later period, and since it is possible that the same student may be enrolled simultaneously in both, the two entry rates cannot be added together to obtain overall entry rates. The lack of a useable indicator on the rate of entry to higher education has been a serious impediment to comparative analysis. Consequent on the revision of the International Standard Classification of Education (UNESCO, 2012) the OECD in 2015 altered its statistical data on entry rates into higher education. It now prioritizes the distinction between *programme duration* of first degree programmes rather than the *type of programme*. As noted in Chapter 1, it publishes data on entry rates to short-tertiary (of two to three years) and Bachelor's degrees or equivalent.[1] It also publishes an aggregate first-time tertiary entry rate although these data are available for just over half of OECD countries (OECD, 2015). While this very recent development offers the prospect that there soon may be reliable entry statistics which eliminate the issue of double counting, this is not yet the situation.

In the absence of reliable comparative data on entry rates to higher education some analysts have focused on closely related statistics on upper secondary graduation rates, which in most countries represent the immediate pipeline for higher education entry. However, these rates need to be disaggregated to differentiate between general pro-grammes and vocational programmes, since most students from the latter programmes are not eligible for direct entry to higher education. The OECD country average sum of age specific upper secondary graduation rates was 85 per cent in 2013: these rates range from 100 per cent for New Zealand and Portugal to 51 per cent for Mexico. The rates exceed 90 per cent for nine countries while they are less than 75 per cent for only four countries. Of more direct relevance for higher education entry is the greater variability

---

[1] As noted in Chapter 1, the ISCED classification also includes Master's level (ISCED 7) and Doctoral (ISCED 8).

between countries in the relative size of upper secondary rates from general programmes (Clancy, 2010). On average more than 60 per cent of upper secondary graduations are from general programmes with the remainder graduating from vocational programmes. In nine of the twenty-five countries for which this disaggregated data are available[2] the graduation rates from general programmes are less than half of the overall graduation rates while in Austria, Czech Republic, and the Slovak Republic these rates are less than a third of the overall graduation rates (OECD, 2015).

In the absence of satisfactory comparative measures of rates of entry to higher education most analyses have centred on the enrolment data. As with entry rates the statistical measures of enrolment use either gross or net age specific measures. The simplest and for a long time the most widely used measure of enrolments is the GER, which for tertiary education is based on the number of students enrolled, regardless of age, expressed as 'a percentage of the population . . . in the five-year age group following on from the secondary school leaving age' (UNESCO, 2005: 149). This measure is used by UNESCO for global comparisons but no longer used by OECD. Its main limitation is that the age range of the numerator does not correspond with that of the denominator. A striking features of contemporary patterns of enrolment in higher education, documented later, is the great variability in the age range of the student cohort. Hence, it is somewhat arbitrary to measure higher education enrolment with respect to the size of the immediate post-secondary school cohort. While acknowledging this lack of precision the availability of global data on crude enrolment ratios allows us to use this indicator to document the massive expansion in tertiary education enrolments. An important related statistic is the *Gender Parity Index* (GPI) which expresses the GER for females over the GER for males. Changes in this index, reflecting the major growth in the participation of women, is closely related to the massification process.

While in recent years the OECD has accumulated an impressive database on higher education enrolment which make it possible to calculate age specific enrolment rates, it does not routinely calculate any single summary enrolment indicator.[3] It has in the past used its data to calculate 'education expectancy', defined as the number of years of full- and part-time education in which a 5-year-old can expect to enrol over his or her lifetime, differentiated by level of education. It is estimated that based on 2011 enrolment patterns in OECD countries, a 5-year-old can expect to participate in full-time education for more than seventeen years of which 2.7 years will be in higher education with a

---

[2] Nine of the thirty-five OECD countries provide no data on overall graduation rates; three countries provide no data on graduation rates from general programmes.

[3] The OECD does publish enrolment rates by age group and some have taken the enrolment of the 20–9-year-old age group as a proxy for higher education enrolments. The National Centre for Education Statistics in the USA has used the higher education enrolments of all aged 20–9 in its comparison of G-8 countries (NCES, 2015). These measures seem to have little advantage over the GER discussed earlier.

further 1.2 years of part-time study mainly in higher education (OECD, 2013: 262). This calculation is based on the sum of age specific enrolment rates used later in this chapter: current enrolment levels by age are utilized to predict the likely future enrolment patterns of current entrants. The calculation of the sum of age specific enrolments aggregates the net rates of enrolment for each year for those aged 17 to 29 and the net rates of enrolment for those aged 30–4, 35–9, and those aged 40 plus.

Country level statistics for entry and enrolment are influenced by the international flow of students. In 2013 more than 4.1 million students went abroad to study, representing about 2 per cent of all tertiary enrolments. International students form a significant component of all enrolments in some countries, especially in Australia (18 per cent); Austria, Switzerland, and the United Kingdom (UK) (each 17 per cent); New Zealand (16 per cent); and Denmark, France, and the Netherlands (each 10 per cent).[4] Three-quarters of international students study in OECD countries, with seven countries hosting more than half of total mobile students; United States of America (USA) (19 per cent); UK (10 per cent); Australia and France (each 6 per cent); Germany (5 per cent); Russian Federation, Japan, and Canada (each 3 per cent). More than half of all international students come from Asia, with a further one-quarter coming from European countries. China is the country of origin of the largest percentage (17 per cent) of international higher education students followed by India (5 per cent), while Germany and Korea each contribute about 3 per cent (UNESCO, statistical data base; OECD, 2015).

The third set of indicators of participation relates to output from the higher education system and thus reflects previous enrolments. The most transparent measure of output is the graduation rate. However, as in respect of entry rates, this is bedevilled by measurement problems. Separate rates are collected by the OECD for short tertiary and Bachelor's level (previously, for tertiary Type A and Type B education) but these cannot be added to get an overall rate because of the problem of double counting, and while efforts are made to differentiate between first-time graduates and graduates from first degree programmes this is not always possible. Hence, for many countries there is no single overall measure of graduation rates.[5] Consequently, the indicator which is most frequently used is qualification level of the population. Data are available for all OECD countries on the percentage of the population that has attained higher education by age group. These data capture in an unambiguous way the scale of previous higher education enrolment and graduation levels.

---

[4] Luxembourg is a special case; while international students constitute 44 per cent of enrolments in its small higher education system outbound mobility is more than three times greater than this inward flow.

[5] The OECD (2015) estimates an average first-time graduation rate of 46 per cent (excluding international students) for the eighteen countries (excluding Luxembourg) for which these data are available; these range from 68 per cent for Japan to 35 per cent for Germany and Sweden.

HPS as Measured by the Gross Enrolment Ratio

Between 1970 and the early 1990s, total students in 'tertiary education', equated here with higher education, increased faster than population but at about the same rate as world GDP. Then participation began to climb ahead of GDP, at an accelerating rate. Between 1970 and 2013 population multiplied by 1.93, GDP by 3.63, and enrolments in higher education by 6.12 (World Bank, 2016; UNESCO, 2016). Figure 2.1 captures the dynamic of growth at world level and in high participation regions. UNESCO's worldwide GER was 34.5 per cent in 2014 suggesting that about one-third of the young age cohort participate. The GER for women (36.2 per cent) exceeded that of men (32.7 per cent) (UNESCO, 2016). Nevertheless, it needs to be kept in mind that the global GER is an abstraction. There is no world system of higher education serving a single population. Rather, there are many national systems offering a mix of programmes, supervised, regulated, and part funded by states.

The upward leap in participation shows in the large number of systems affected. In 1992 only five national systems had GERs of 50 per cent. However, by 2013, fifty-seven higher education systems had passed the 50 per cent mark, classifying them in this book as HPS; and in fourteen further systems, the GER exceeded 40 per cent. This does not mean all students received a tertiary education of equivalent or adequate quality. Higher education is stratified, between and within countries; in resources, status, and the potency of learning (see Chapter 5).

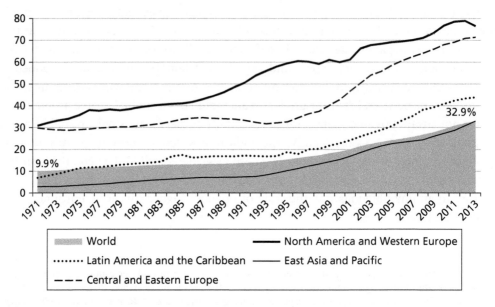

Figure 2.1. Gross enrolment ratio (%), world and high participation regions, 1971–2013

Source: Chart prepared by authors using data from UNESCO database, 2017.

Table 2.1. Gross enrolment ratio by world region: 1970, 1980, 1990, 2000, and 2014

Region	1970 %	1980 %	1990 %	2000 %	2010 %	2014 %
World	10.0	12.3	13.6	19.0	29.3	34.5
North America and Western Europe	30.6	38.5	48.6	60.0	76.9	76.4
Central and Eastern Europe	30.2	30.4	33.9	42.8	67.9	74.4
Latin American and the Caribbean	6.9	13.3	16.9	22.8	40.9	44.7
East Asia and the Pacific	2.9	5.1	7.3	15.4	27.3	39.1
Arab States	6.0	9.9	11.4	18.6	25.5	28.9
Central Asia	n.a.	24.4	25.3	22.0	26.7	25.7
South and West Asia	4.2	4.5	5.7	8.7	17.4	22.8
Sub-Saharan Africa	0.9	1.8	3.0	4.4	7.7	8.2

Note: n.a. = data not available.

Source: Table prepared by authors, using data from UNESCO (2016, 2017).

Figure 2.1 and Table 2.1 indicate that participation varies by region but the GER has risen sharply since 1990 in all regions except Central Asia, where the GER exceeded the world level until 2000 but is now below it. The whole of Europe and North America had attained a GER of about 75 per cent in 2014. The GER was nearing 50 per cent across Latin America and the Caribbean, with Venezuela, Chile, Cuba, and Argentina well above. In every East Asian system apart from China (39 per cent) the GER was over 50 per cent (UNESCO, 2016; World Bank, 2016). East Asia is marked by exceptional family and social commitment to education, with every student expected to be a high achiever (Marginson, 2013). This is manifest in the exceptional performance of East Asian school students at age 15 in the OECD's Program for International Student Assessment, PISA (OECD, 2014). Participation is low in sub-Saharan Africa and South Asia, except in India. In the rest of the world mass higher education is now normal—and it seems that HPS is becoming the new normal.

Table 2.2 lists all systems in which the 2013 GER exceeded Trow's 15 per cent mass higher education threshold, on the basis of GDP per head. All high-income and most middle-income countries are tending towards or have exceeded the 50 per cent mark. Almost two-thirds of all higher education systems for which GER data are available have reached 15 per cent, including thirteen systems in countries with GDP per head below US$5,000 per year.

HPS have spread well beyond the traditional zones of North America, Western Europe, Russia, and Japan. Systems with GERs above 50 per cent included Albania, Barbados, Bulgaria, Colombia, Costa Rica, Iran, Kazakhstan, Mongolia, Palau, Romania, Saudi Arabia, Serbia, and Thailand (World Bank, 2016). Further, when the GER reaches 50 per cent or more it keeps on rising. In 2013, it exceeded 90 per cent in South Korea

Table 2.2. Higher education systems with gross enrolment ratio of 15 per cent or more (by GDP per head in constant 2011 PPP prices (US$): 2013 or nearest year*)

GDP per head above US$30,000

System	GER %	US$
South Korea	97	32,684
Finland	91	38,867
USA	89	51,282
Spain	87	31,230
Australia	87	42,845
Puerto Rico	85	33,818
Iceland	82	40,975
Denmark	81	42,483
Austria	80	44,038
New Zealand	80	33,360
Netherlands	79	45,368
Norway	76	63,322
Ireland	73	46,182
Belgium	72	40,433
Hong Kong SAR	67	51,656
Israel	66	31,294
Italy	63	33,794
Sweden	63	43,430
Macau SAR	63	136,136
Japan	62	3,614
France	62	37,306
Germany	61	42,266
UK	57	37,309
Switzerland	56	54,912
Saudi Arabia	55	48,963
Cyprus	48	30,081
Aruba	38	36,015
Bahrain	36	41,932
Bermuda	30	50,669

GDP per head US$20,001–30,000

System	GER %	US$
Greece	110	24,198
Slovenia	85	27,350
Chile	84	21,801
St Kitts, Nevis	79	20,986
Russia	78	23,561
Estonia	73	25,775
Lithuania	72	24,813
Poland	71	23,175
Croatia	62	20,024
Latvia	67	21,329
Portugal	66	25,800
Czech R.	65	28,148
Hungary	57	22,821
Slovak R.	54	25,844
Kazakhstan	50	22,470
Malta	46	28,822
Malaysia	39	23,419
Antigua and B.	23	20,297

GDP per head US$10,001–20,000

System	GER %	US$
Belarus	91	17,085
Turkey	79	18,560
Bulgaria	67	16,022
Barbados	65	15,339
Cuba	64	19,950
Mongolia	62	10,757
Palau	62	13,152
Iran	58	16,023
Serbia	56	12,889

GDP per head US$5,001–10,000

System	GER %	US$
Ukraine	80	8,338
Albania	63	9,991
Armenia	45	7,473
Bolivia	38	6,091
Georgia	35	8,236
Philippines	34	6,365
Indonesia	31	9,375
El Salvador	29	7,838
Jamaica	27	8,430
Vietnam	25	5,122
Belize	24	7,921
India	24	5,132
Morocco	22	7,076
Cabo Verde	22	6,130
Guatemala	18	6,963

GDP per head US$5,000 or less

System	GER %	US$
Kyrgyz R.	47	3,121
Palestine	45	4,497
Marshall Islands	43	3,671
Moldova	41	4,542
Tajikistan	23	2,460
Honduras	21	4,608
Lao PDR	18	4,800
Timor Leste	18	2,039
Nepal	17	2,176
Sudan	17	3,847
Ghana	16	3,834
Cambodia	16	2,955

Country		GDP	Country		GDP	Country		GDP
Oman	29	36,855	Grenada	53	11,263	Benin	15	1,867
Kuwait	27	74,181	Romania	52	18,514			
Brunei	24	70,535	Thailand	51	14,943	**GDP data not available**		
Luxembourg	19	89,889	Colombia	50	12,304	Argentina	80	n.a.
UAE	19	62,056	Costa Rica	50	13,900	Liechtenstein	42	n.a.
Qatar	16	133,395	Jordan	48	11,405	Syrian Arab R.	35	n.a.
			Dominican R.	48	11,930	North Korea	30	n.a.
			Lebanon	46	16,527	Curacao	20	n.a.
			Ecuador	40	10,626			
			Mauritius	40	17,146			
			Macedonia	39	11,859			
			Panama	39	19,082			
			Tunisia	34	10,731			
			Algeria	34	13,301			
			Egypt	30	10,050			
			China	30	11,805			
			Mexico	29	16,141			
			Botswana	25	15,022			
			Azerbaijan	21	16,593			
			South Africa	20	12,454			
			Sri Lanka	19	10,242			
			St Lucia	17	10,268			

Notes: HPS, GER 50 per cent+in grey tone. n.a.=not available. SAR=Special Autonomous Region. R.=Republic. UAE=United Arab Emirates. Antigua and B. = Antigua and Barbuda. Palestine = West Bank and Gaza. PDR=People's Democratic Republic. *2014 GER for St Kitts and Nevis, Qatar, St Lucia, Ghana. 2012 GER for Iceland, Netherlands, Croatia, Cuba, Jordan, Dominican Republic, Marshall Islands, Aruba, Liechtenstein, San Marino, Antigua, Barbuda, Luxembourg. 2011 GER for Barbados, North Korea, Oman, Cambodia. 2010 GER for Timor-Leste. 2009 GER for Grenada. 2007 GER for Bolivia. GER data not available for 79 sovereign territories, of which half are small islands, including Bolivia, Brazil, Canada, Iraq, Kenya, Namibia, Oman, Paraguay, Peru, Sierra Leone, Somalia, South Sudan, Sudan, Suriname, Uruguay, Venezuela, Western Sahara, Zambia. 2011 GDP for Aruba.

Source: Author, drawing on data from World Bank (2016).

(97 per cent), Canada, Finland, and Belarus.[6] It was between 75 per cent and 90 per cent in sixteen higher education systems including Argentina, Australia, Austria, Chile, Denmark, Iceland, the Netherlands, New Zealand, Norway, Puerto Rico, Russia, Slovenia, Spain, Turkey, Ukraine, and the USA (World Bank, 2016). In many countries, there was a surge in the GER from the late 1990s. Some saw phenomenal growth. In Turkey, the GER rose from 25 to 69 per cent, an extraordinary increase of forty-four percentage points, between 2000 and 2012. Over the same period the GER in Albania jumped forty-two percentage points; Cuba by forty-one percentage points; Chile and Belarus both by thirty-seven percentage points; and Iran, Iceland, and the Czech Republic by thirty-six percentage points (UNESCO, 2016).

Emerging Countries

HPS proposition 1 states

As HPS spread to an increasing number of countries, equity in world society is enhanced.

This book mostly focuses on countries at HPS level, but educated populations are growing rapidly also in emerging countries below the 50 per cent mark.

In *The Haves and the Have Nots*, Milanovic (2011) imagines the global population as a single equity set. Worldwide income is becoming more equal: the global Gini coefficient is falling. The 'great convergence' (Mahbubani, 2013) is powered by emerging East and Southeast Asia, India, and Latin America, and economic progress in the Arab states, Central Asia, and sub-Saharan Africa. It signifies growth in the middle classes, people with discretionary income able to invest in self-improvement, including consumption, housing, and education. Defining a middle class person as someone with US$10–100 per day in purchasing power parity (PPP) terms, Kharas and Gertz (2010) identify 1.8 billion persons in 2009, 28 per cent of global population. They forecast growth to 4.9 billion persons in 2030, mostly in China and India. Using a more restricted definition of middle class, the World Bank expects it to double by 2030 (2016: 6). The new middle classes will want higher education for their children.

In middle-income nations, HPS higher education and research universities are signs and instruments of national emergence and modernization. Analyses of globalization often miss the evolution of a more plural map of power at world level, as indicated by the emerging HPS, as well as the growth of research science in many of these countries.

---

[6] Table 2.2 includes a GER for Greece at 110. This has been queried for possible double-counting. At the time of writing UNECSO was reviewing the country data and OECD participation statistics excluding Greece.

The growth of female participation is very significant (see later in this chapter). The HPS movement lifts the threshold of human capability and rights on a massive scale—always provided that the higher education really does augment people's capacity and social trajectory.

The surge in participation includes three of the world's four largest populations: China, India, and Indonesia. As noted in Chapter 1, all three are undergoing accelerated modernization, including population shift from the countryside to the cities where jobs and higher education are centred. In India, the GER rose from 6 to 26 per cent from 1990 to 2014; in Indonesia from 9 to 31 per cent. In China, it increased from 3 per cent in 1990 and 8 per cent in 2000 to 39 per cent in 2013 (UNESCO, 2016). The official target of 40 per cent by 2020 will be surpassed. However, there is pronounced regional variation in China. In 2010 the GER was at 60 per cent in Beijing and Shanghai regions but 18 per cent in Yunnan (Yang, 2014).

CAVEATS

The long progression to HPS across the world takes the form of combined but also uneven development, to draw on Leon Trotsky's formulation (Naidoo, 2014). The narrative of a more educated world must be qualified in three respects.

First, mass higher education is under-funded and under-supervised in many countries. There is a range of expedients for fostering cost-shared participation: tuition in public higher education institutions, notwithstanding effects on access; under-regulated private sectors, often with under-qualified staff, and poor upward transfer rates, as in India, Brazil, and the Philippines; official encouragement of for-profit providers, despite their poor completion and employability record in their American heartland (Mettler, 2014); and distance and online learning with low-intensity teaching, for example mass open online courseware (MOOCs) in place of on-site classes. Some governments under-fund mass higher education institutions because priority is given to building research-intensive universities capable of achieving 'World-Class University' (WCU) status in global university rankings, which further stratifies systems. The national elite and middle class dominate the research-intensive universities while other students find themselves locked into mass higher education institutions with limited cognitive and labour market value.

Second, some emerging countries exhibit startling social inequalities in access. Salmi and Bassett (2014) note that in Mexico the top income quintile enrols at eighteen times the rate of the bottom quintile. In francophone sub-Saharan Africa, children of the top quintile provide 80 per cent of tertiary enrolments; the bottom 40 per cent constitute 2 per cent (2014: 363). There are severe class and gender barriers in parts of South Asia. Gender patterns vary considerably in individual countries, and women's gains can be reversed. Given the historical social segmentation, it is possible that even in the HPS phase, higher education could reproduce caste barriers on a modernized basis by excluding a large uneducated underclass. In the long run the tendency to inclusive and universal systems is more likely to win.

Third, some states lack the administrative capacity, tax base, and time horizon to mount large-scale higher education, and the middle class is too small to place effective pressure on the state or to pay enough through taxation or tuition. Not all low-income countries have low GERs. However, of the forty-five higher education systems in countries where average GDP per head was below US$5,000 per year in PPP terms in 2013—this group was just over one-quarter of all systems—thirteen systems (29 per cent of the group) had achieved a GER of 15 per cent in 2013, while thirty-two systems had not. All but one of the systems located in countries with less than US$2,000 per person were below 15 per cent. (The exception was Benin, see Table 2.3.) On the other hand, of the 109 systems where average GDP per person exceeded US$5,000, ninety-nine of these (91 per cent) had at least 15 per cent age cohort enrolment. Many low participation systems were in sub-Saharan Africa, where the 2013 GER was below 15 per cent in all systems for which data were available except South Africa, Sudan, Ghana, Benin, the Atlantic islands of Cabo Verde, and Mauritius in the Indian Ocean.[7]

The 'hole' in participation in higher education in Africa has global ecological significance. In 2014 the world population projections were revised. For the previous twenty years it had been expected that world population would peak at nine billion in 2050. The revised projections state that total world population will keep increasing, reaching eleven billion in 2100, with no peak in sight. While fertility rates have come down in most countries, this is not the case in sub-Saharan Africa, and furthermore medicine and nutrition have reduced infant and other mortality. Africa's population is now expected to grow from one billion in 2010 to more than four billion in 2100. Nigeria alone is expected to grow from 200 to 900 million people. The average Nigerian woman has six children. Family size and birth rate are correlated to education levels, especially the education of women (Sen, 2000). When enough women reach tertiary education, population growth tends to slow. It seems that in the spread of the HPS tendency in sub-Saharan Africa, there is much at stake.

However, the GER is now climbing in that other zone of low participation and high population growth, South Asia. As noted, participation is increasing rapidly in India. The GER remains almost at sub-Saharan levels in Pakistan and Bangladesh as Table 1.1 in Chapter 1 showed, but is increasing in Pakistan at the worldwide rate (UNESCO, 2016).

---

[7] There were no World Bank/UNESCO participation data for Nigeria, Sierra Leone, and Zambia.

Table 2.3. Higher education systems with gross enrolment ratio below 15 per cent (by GDP per head in constant 2011 PPP prices (US$)), 2013 or nearest year

System	GER %	US$	System	GER %	US$
GDP per head above US$10,000			**GDP per head US$5,000 or less**		
Maldives	13	11,455	Bangladesh	13	2,843
Turkmenistan	8	13,555	Liberia	12	817
Seychelles	3	24,805	Cameroon	12	2,745
			Pakistan	10	4,476
GDP per head US$5,001–10,000			Lesotho	10	2,459
			Togo	10	1,324
Guyana	12	6,657	R. of Yemen	10	3,663
Bhutan	11	7,168	Sao Tome and Principe	10	2,963
Angola	10	6,949	Comoros	9	1,369
R. of Congo	10	5,749	Cote d'Ivoire	9	2,934
Namibia	9	9,143	Rwanda	8	1,516
Uzbekistan	9	5,002	Senegal	7	2,193
Swaziland	5	7,836	Haiti	7	1,630
			Congo Democratic R.	7	673
GDP data not available			Mali	6	1,466
			Ethiopia	6	1,330
Myanmar	14	n.a.	Zimbabwe	6	1,684
Turks and Caicos Islands	0	n.a.	Mauritania	5	3,595
			Mozambique	5	1,033
			Burkina Faso	5	1,530
			Djibouti	5	2,983
			Kenya	4	2,747
			Burundi	4	725
			Madagascar	4	1,367
			Tanzania	4	2,336
			Afghanistan	4	1,876
			Guinea-Bissau	3	1,321
			Central African R.	3	571
			Chad	3	2,005
			Eritrea	3	1,411
			Niger	2	871
			Malawi	1	765

Notes: n.a. = data not available. PPP = purchasing power parity. R. = Republic. GER 2014 Sao Tome and Principe, Turkmenistan, Haiti, Ethiopia, Chad, Eritrea. GER 2012 Myanmar, Bangladesh, Guyana, Liberia, Niger. GER 2011 Cameroon, Yemen, Uzbekistan, Djibouti, Afghanistan, Central African Republic, Malawi. GER 2010 Senegal, Mali. GER 2009 Namibia, Kenya. GER 2008 Maldives. GER 2006 Guinea-Bissau. GDP 2011 Angola, Eritrea. See Table 2.2 for a list of some countries for which GER data are unavailable.

Source: Authors using data from World Bank (2016).

GENDER PARITY INDEX

As noted, the high and rising level of participation has been partly driven by a dramatic increase in the participation of women. Traditionally women were seriously under-represented in higher education. Through the second half of the twentieth century this imbalance was progressively reduced and was eventually reversed in most Western

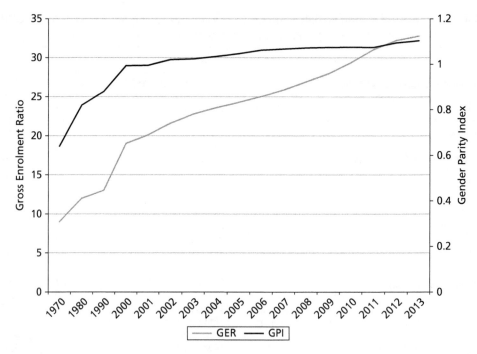

Figure 2.2. Gross enrolment ratio and gender parity index in higher education, all countries, 1970–2013

Source: Authors using data from UNESCO (2016).

countries. Figure 2.2 shows the parallels between the global pattern of growth in the GER and in the GPI since 1970. The GPI expresses the GER for females as a percentage of the GER for males. At a global level females first achieved parity with males in level of participation in higher education in 2002. In 1970 the female rate had been just 60 per cent of that of males.

The rise in female participation is highly differentiated across world regions (Table 2.4). Gender parity was achieved in North America and Western Europe by 1980 and while no aggregate data are available for the Central and Eastern Europe region prior to 2000, it is evident from country level data that the higher education systems in Russia and many of the former Communist countries had achieved a significant female majority prior to 1980. Latin America, the Caribbean, and Central Asia were the next regions to achieve gender parity. The Arab States achieved gender parity by 2005, followed by East Asia and the Pacific by 2010. While female participation is rising more rapidly than that of males in South and West Asia gender parity has not yet being achieved. The low level of higher education enrolments in sub-Saharan Africa is accompanied by no improvement in gender parity since 2000. Gender differentials in participation are closely linked to socio-economic conditions. At a global level, scores on GPI are directly related to the classification of countries by income. By 2013 all

Table 2.4. Higher education enrolment: Gender Parity Index for world regions, 1970–2010 and 2013

Region	1970	1980	1990	2000	2005	2010	2013
World	0.6	0.8	0.9	1.0	1.0	1.1	1.1
Arab States	0.3	0.5	0.6	0.9	1.0	1.0	1.0
Central and Eastern Europe	n.a.	n.a.	n.a.	1.2	1.3	1.3	1.2
Central Asia	n.a.	n.a.	n.a.	1.0	1.1	1.1	1.1
East Asia and the Pacific	0.5	0.6	0.7	0.8	0.9	1.0	1.1
Latin America and the Caribbean	0.5	0.8	0.9	1.2	1.2	1.3	1.3
North America and Western Europe	0.7	1.0	1.1	1.2	1.3	1.3	1.3
South and West Asia	0.3	0.4	0.5	0.7	0.7	0.8	0.9
Sub-Saharan Africa	0.3	0.3	0.5	0.7	0.7	0.7	0.7

Source: Authors using data from UNESCO (2016).

high-income, upper-middle-income, and middle-income countries, as defined by UNESCO, had achieved a female majority in participation with GPI score of 1.25, 1.16, and 1.07, respectively. In contrast, the low-income countries had a GPI of 0.53 while lower middle countries were approaching gender parity with a score of 0.97.

Comparative Measures of High Participation Systems

This section seeks to develop a more nuanced statistical measure of comparative trends in participation. This analysis is necessarily limited to OECD countries which provide more detailed comparative statistical data. Following an interrogation of the OECD database of statistics on higher education enrolment for 2013, two additional enrolment measures are calculated to complement the GER used above. There are also data on the output of higher education, on the percentage of the population, by age, with higher education. Data on five indicators are combined to develop a higher education participation index. The ranking of countries on this index and the scores on the individual indicators offer an important insight into the diversified pattern of participation in HPS.

One of the most striking features of the OECD database is the difference between countries in the age distribution of higher education students (Table 2.5). In all OECD countries except Israel the largest percentage of enrolments are from the 20–4 age group. The concentration of enrolments in this age group ranges from 62 per cent in Poland to less than 40 per cent in Israel, Austria, New Zealand, the USA, Australia, Iceland, and Finland. The main differences between countries are evident in the relative percentages of students aged under 20 and those 30 years or over. In three countries, Mexico, South Korea, and France, the percentage of student under 20 years of age exceeds 25 per cent,

Table 2.5. Percentage distribution of higher education enrolments by age group in OECD countries, 2013

Country	Age <20	Age 20–4	Age 25–9	Age 30–4	Age 35–9	Age 40+
Australia	17.4	39.0	15.5	8.7	6.1	13.2
Austria	17.0	38.0	22.4	10.0	4.7	7.8
Belgium	21.5	55.3	11.6	4.8	2.7	4.0
Canada	21.5	45.8	14.8	6.8	4.0	6.1
Chile	17.8	49.6	17.6	7.4	3.7	3.9
Czech Republic	7.0	57.5	16.3	5.9	4.6	4.9
Denmark	2.1	45.2	27.0	9.5	5.9	10.2
Estonia	9.3	48.8	20.2	9.6	5.7	6.4
Finland	3.9	39.5	24.3	12.8	7.4	12.1
France	27.7	53.9	10.2	1.7	1.7	4.8
Germany	6.0	46.6	30.2	10.1	3.4	3.3
Hungary	10.1	53.9	17.2	6.8	5.4	6.7
Iceland	1.2	39.3	22.5	12.9	8.2	15.9
Ireland	23.6	43.9	11.6	7.3	4.7	8.1
Israel	6.9	32.8	33.2	12.0	6.2	8.4
Italy	0.7	53.9	24.1	6.5	3.2	4.9
Latvia	9.8	54.6	17.3	7.1	4.7	6.6
Luxembourg	10.7	46.2	25.6	10.0	3.7	3.8
Mexico	29.4	54.1	10.1	3.1	1.5	1.8
Netherlands	19.8	55.7	15.9	3.7	1.6	3.2
New Zealand	18.6	38.4	13.3	8.1	6.0	15.5
Norway	4.5	44.7	20.0	9.6	6.9	14.2
Poland	6.3	61.7	17.3	3.2	3.0	8.3
Portugal	18.2	46.9	14.1	7.8	5.2	7.7
Slovak Republic	9.1	59.7	14.3	6.1	5.2	5.6
Slovenia	12.0	57.5	18.4	4.8	3.2	4.1
South Korea	28.6	53.6	10.1	2.8	1.6	3.3
Spain	17.4	44.6	17.0	8.4	5.3	7.2
Sweden	5.2	41.4	22.4	10.4	7.0	13.6
Switzerland	5.0	46.3	26.3	10.4	4.8	7.2
Turkey	17.0	47.0	19.4	8.7	4.2	3.7
UK	23.4	40.5	11.7	7.2	5.1	11.8
USA	20.0	38.7	15.8	8.9	5.5	11.1

Source: Authors using OECD data; data not available for Japan.

while it exceeds 20 per cent in four other countries (Ireland, UK, Belgium, and Canada). In contrast enrolments of the under 20 age groups are 5 per cent or less in Italy, Iceland, Denmark, Finland, and Norway. On average for all OECD countries about 20 per cent of higher education enrolments are aged 30 or over. This proportion exceed 30 per cent in Iceland, Finland, Norway, and Sweden. At the other end of the continuum three countries (Mexico, France, and South Korea) have fewer than 10 per cent of their enrolments aged 30 or over. Iceland, New Zealand, Norway, Sweden, and Australia have the highest percentage of students aged 40 or over.

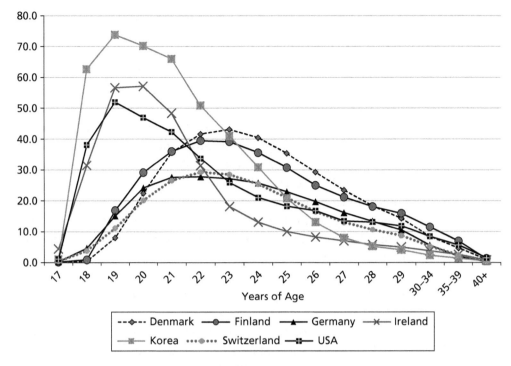

Figure 2.3. Age specific enrolment in higher education for selected countries, 2013

Source: Authors' calculations from OECD data.

The variability between countries in the age structure of higher education enrolments points to the arbitrary nature of the choice of any fixed age range for the population denominator in the calculation of enrolment rates. Hence, the calculation of age specific enrolment rates provides the optimum measure. As mentioned earlier in this chapter, using the OECD database age specific enrolments rates are calculated for those aged 17 and over. A graphic representation of these rates for selected countries offers an insight into country differences in enrolment patterns. This analysis replicates earlier work (Clancy, 2010), and the findings of Kaiser et al. (2005) which identified three general patterns regarding the age composition of participants in higher education. The first pattern is the early peak, followed by a flat tail; the second is also somewhat skewed to the left but the peak occurs later, is less high, and the participation of the older age group is more significant; the third pattern shows a more even distribution across the age spread. These patterns are clearly evident in Figure 2.3, which is based on a sample of selected countries drawn from the thirty-three-country analysis. South Korea, the USA, and Ireland exhibit early peaks; Finland and Denmark demonstrate later peaks; while Germany and Switzerland demonstrate lower peaks but a more even spread across the age ranges from age 20 years onwards. Variation in enrolment rates for the older age groups, as described above, is less easily identified in this graph, although it is clear that the two Nordic countries have higher enrolments among those aged over 30.

The data summarized in the graph represent the net rates of enrolments for each year of those aged 17 to 29 years and the net rates of enrolment for those aged 30–4, 35–9, and those aged 40+ years. This measure, the *sum of age specific enrolments*, which effectively calculates the area under the curves in the Figure 2.3, is clearly a comprehensive measure since it takes account of variability in the structure of higher education enrolments between countries, giving appropriate weight to all enrolments whether these are highly concentrated among younger students or whether enrolments are dispersed among a much wider age span (see Table 2.7 below, column b).

To complement this most comprehensive measure, which gives appropriate weight to all enrolments regardless of age, a third measure is included, *enrolment intensity*, based on the average enrolment rate for the two years of age with highest enrolment. This measure might be thought of as a proxy for entry rates since it takes particular account of all those who experience some higher education, many perhaps on short cycle programmes. It measures the two highest peaks in enrolment rates for each country as illustrated in Figure 2.3. For eleven countries, enrolment intensity is highest for those aged 20–1 years: this is the case for the Austria, Belgium, Czech Republic, Estonia, Hungary, Netherlands, Portugal, Slovakia, Slovenia, Spain, and Turkey. For ten countries enrolment intensity is highest for those aged 19–20 years; this is the case for Australia, Canada, Chile, France, Ireland, South Korea, Mexico, New Zealand, the UK, and USA. For six countries it is highest for those aged 21–2; for Germany, Italy, Latvia, Luxembourg, Norway, and Poland. In the case of Denmark, Finland, Iceland, Sweden, and Switzerland enrolment intensity is highest for the aged 22–3 years, while in the case of Israel enrolment intensity is highest for the 23–4 age group. Data on enrolment intensity is included in Table 2.7 (column c). Scores on enrolment intensity range from over 70 per cent for South Korea to less than 30 per cent for Mexico, Germany, and Sweden. Enrolment intensity in Slovenia, Ireland, and Belgium also exceed 50 per cent.

The impact of varying levels of enrolment is subsequently reflected in the education level of the adult population. Table 2.6 shows the percentage of the adult population who have attained higher education. A third of adults in OECD countries have done so. The rate is highest in Canada at 54 per cent and exceeds 40 per cent in ten other countries. It is lowest in Turkey and Italy at 17 per cent and below 25 per cent in a further seven countries. Reflecting the impact of recent expansion of higher education systems, the percentages which have attained higher education are significantly higher for the younger ages groups, averaging 41 and 38 per cent, respectively, for 25–34- and 35–44-year-olds. Differentials in the educational attainment levels of the age cohorts are especially striking in South Korea and Poland where the percentages of the 25–34 cohort with higher education are respectively four and three times those for the 55–64s. The higher education attainment of the younger cohort is more than double that of the older cohort in seven other countries; Turkey, France, Ireland, Slovak Republic, Slovenia,

Table 2.6. Percentage of the population that has attained higher education by age group, OECD countries, 2013

Country	25–34 years (%)	35–44 years (%)	45–54 years (%)	55–64 years (%)	25–64 years (%)
OECD average	*41*	*38*	*30*	*25*	*33*
Australia	48	46	38	33	43
Austria	38	33	27	21	23
Belgium	44	42	34	26	37
Canada	58	61	51	45	54
Chile	27	24	17	14	21
Czech Republic	30	21	20	15	22
Denmark	42	41	33	29	36
Estonia	40	39	35	36	38
Finland	40	50	44	34	42
France	44	39	26	20	32
Germany	28	29	26	25	27
Greece	39	27	26	21	28
Hungary	32	25	20	17	23
Iceland	41	42	36	29	37
Ireland	51	49	34	24	41
Israel	46	53	48	47	49
Italy	24	19	13	12	17
Japan	37*	29*	26*	21*	28*
Korea	68	56	33	17	45
Luxembourg	53	46	40	32	46
Mexico	25	17	16	13	19
Netherlands	44	38	30	27	34
New Zealand	40	41	32	29	36
Norway	49	49	36	32	42
Poland	43	32	18	14	27
Portugal	31	26	17	13	22
Slovak Republic	30	21	15	14	20
Slovenia	38	35	24	18	29
Spain	41	43	30	21	35
Sweden	46	46	32	30	39
Switzerland	46	45	38	31	40
Turkey	25	16	10	10	17
UK	49	46	38	35	42
USA	46	47	43	41	44

Note: *Data for Japan exclude those with short-cycle higher education only.
Source: Authors using data from OECD (2015).

Czech Republic, and Italy. In contrast, the earlier advent of mass higher education in several countries leaves more modest differential in educational attainment between the age cohorts. This is the case in Israel, the USA, Germany, Estonia, Finland, and Canada. Within this group of countries, Germany is something of an outlier. Higher education attainment has stabilized at a lower level, below 30 per cent of the age cohort.

It is clear from the foregoing analysis of entry rates, enrolment, and output measures that there is no single indicator which provides an adequate measure of participation in higher education. Following the logic developed in earlier analyses (Clancy, 2010, 2015) five indicators have been selected to develop a higher education participation index to facilitate a comparative analysis of participation. Ideally the optimum measure would include entry, enrolment, and output measures but as discussed above there is no comprehensive entry measure available. The index incorporates three enrolment measures: *GER*, the *sum of age specific enrolments*, and *enrolment intensity*. There are two output measures: the *percentage of the population aged 25–34 and 35–44 with higher education*. The inclusion of the second output measure is to take account of the situation in some countries with a late age of entry and those with relatively long first degree programmes. The distribution of scores on these indicators is shown in Table 2.7. To arrive at a single summary measure the scores on each of the five indicators out of a hundred have been standardized before adding. The resultant score is divided by five to give a score out of a hundred.

South Korea, the USA, Ireland, Australia, and Canada score highest on this index of participation. Six other countries, Finland, Slovenia, Spain, Belgium, Norway, and Denmark make up the top one-third of the distribution.[8] This top one-third is drawn from four continents, testifying to the pervasiveness of the phenomenon of HPS of higher education. The middle group of countries on this ranking include Netherlands, New Zealand, France, and the UK. It is no surprise that Mexico, which is the only OECD country which falls well short of the 50 per cent mark on the GER, used earlier as the crude measure of HPS, has the lowest score on the index. After Mexico, Italy, the Slovak Republic, Germany, and Hungary fall at the lower end of the distribution on this index. It is of interest to compare this ranking with an earlier analysis (Clancy, 2010) which included twenty-six of the same countries.[9] Overall there is a high level of consistency in the relative rankings. One exception is Ireland, which has improved its ranking, moving from twelfth to third. Otherwise all the other countries in the top third of the 2013 ranking were also within the top third of the 2003 ranking. Sweden has experienced the sharpest decline in its ranking, falling from fifth to twenty-second. Although less dramatic, Italy, Germany, and Hungry have also experienced a significant decline in their rankings.

A feature of Table 2.7 is that while the index provides an overall measure of participation, the scores on the separate indicators highlight distinctive features of the higher education system in different countries. To facilitate this analysis, the parenthesis in the table show the ranking of each country on each separate indicator, which can be compared with the overall ranking on the composite index. There is a good deal of consistency in the rankings on the separate indicators.[10] Of greater interest is where

---

[8] The eleventh ranking country in the top one-third of the thirty-one countries for which there are data is included because its score is almost identical to that of Norway.

[9] Canada, Slovenia, Israel, Estonia, and Chile were not included in the earlier analysis.

[10] The three enrolment measures are highly correlated (*r* values: 0.90, 0.82, and 0.62). The two output measures are also highly correlated (*r* = .92). The inter-correlation between the enrolment measures and the output measures were significantly lower. While the relationship between the percentage of the

Table 2.7. Selected indicators of participation in higher education for OECD countries, 2013 (country ranking in parenthesis)

Country	Gross enrolment rate a	Sum of age specific enrolments b	Enrolment intensity c	Percentage aged 25–34 with higher education d	Percentage aged 35–44 with higher education e	Higher Education Participation Index f
South Korea	95.3 (1)	451.9 (1)	72.0 (1)	68 (1)	56 (2)	98.4 (1)
USA	88.8 (3)	350.5 (4)	49.5 (5)	46 (10)	47 (7)	76.8 (2)
Ireland	73.2 (15)	303.9 (13)	56.9 (2)	51 (3)	49 (5)	75.7 (3)
Australia	86.6 (5)	323.8 (9)	43.1 (11)	48 (6)	46 (8)	73.7 (4)
Canada	63.1* (24)	269.4 (20)	38.4 (20)	58 (2)	61 (1)	72.9 (5)
Finland	91.1 (2)	328.2 (6)	39.4 (17)	40 (19)	50 (4)	72.7 (6)
Slovenia	85.2 (6)	370.9 (2)	56.5 (3)	38 (22)	35 (20)	72.6 (7)
Spain	87.1 (4)	325.2 (8)	44.5 (10)	41 (17)	43 (12)	71.2 (8)
Belgium	72.3 (17)	317.6 (11)	52.3 (4)	44 (11)	42 (13)	70.5 (9)
Norway	76.1 (14)	277.0 (18)	37.6 (21)	49 (4)	49 (6)	69.2 (10)
Denmark	81.2 (9)	326.9 (7)	42.4 (13)	42 (15)	41 (15)	69.1 (11)
Netherlands	78.5** (13)	299.1 (14)	41.3 (15)	44 (13)	38 (19)	66.6 (12)
New Zealand	79.7 (11)	293.7 (15)	41.7 (14)	40 (20)	41 (16)	66.5 (13)
Poland	71.2 (18)	304.6 (12)	48.7 (6)	43 (14)	32 (22)	65.1 (14)
Iceland	82.2 (8)	275.6 (19)	35.2 (24)	41 (16)	42 (14)	65.1 (15)
Israel	66.3 (19)	245.1 (24)	30.0 (27)	46 (7)	53 (3)	64.0 (16)
Estonia	72.9 (16)	291.4 (16)	40.0 (16)	40 (18)	39 (17)	63.9 (17)
France	62.1 (25)	277.4 (17)	46.0 (8)	44 (12)	39 (18)	63.8 (18)
UK	56.9 (28)	222.5 (30)	39.4 (18)	49 (5)	46 (10)	62.2 (19)
Chile	83.8 (7)	351.4 (3)	46.0 (7)	27 (28)	24 (26)	61.7 (20)
Austria	80.4 (10)	319.6 (10)	31.3 (26)	38 (21)	33 (21)	61.7 (21)
Sweden	63.4 (23)	246.9 (23)	28.8 (29)	46 (8)	46 (9)	60.8 (22)
Switzerland	56.3 (29)	223.1 (29)	28.9 (28)	46 (9)	45 (11)	58.0 (23)
Turkey	79.0 (12)	343.5 (5)	45.1 (9)	25 (30)	16 (16)	56.9 (24)
Portugal	66.2 (20)	263.4 (22)	39.1 (19)	31 (24)	26 (24)	54.1 (25)
Czech Rep.	65.4 (21)	266.5 (21)	42.6 (12)	30 (25)	21 (27)	53.1 (26)
Hungary	57.0 (27)	239.9 (27)	34.3 (25)	32 (23)	25 (25)	49.7 (27)
Germany	61.1 (26)	243.1 (25)	27.7 (30)	28 (27)	29 (23)	49.0 (28)
Slovak Rep.	54.4 (30)	229.8 (28)	36.4 (22)	30 (26)	21 (28)	47.4 (29)
Italy	63.5 (22)	241.2 (26)	36.0 (23)	24 (31)	19 (29)	47.3 (30)
Mexico	29.2 (31)	148.7 (31)	24.1 (31)	25 (29)	17 (30)	32.3 (31)

Notes: *Authors' calculations from OECD database: **data for 2012.

Source: Authors' compilation as follows: column a, adapted from UNESCO (2016); columns b, and c, authors' calculations from OECD database; columns d and e authors' from OECD database.

there are significant deviations between a country's ranking on an individual indicator and the overall index ranking. Such deviations reflect particular features of a country's

population aged 25–34 with higher education is significantly related to each of the enrolment measures (r values range from 0.45 to 0.39), the relationship between the second output measure and the enrolment measures are much weaker (r values: 0.39, 0.30, and 0.26) with only one of them being statistically significant. Each of the separate indicators is significantly correlated with the overall index (r values range from 0.83 to 0.75) higher education system. In several countries there is a noticeable discrepancy between the ranking on the enrolment scores and the scores on the educational attainment of people aged 25–44. Slovenia and Chile have much higher rankings on the enrolment indicators than on the educational attainment indicators, reflecting the recent expansion of their higher education systems. In contrast, the higher rankings for Canada, Norway, Israel, the UK, and Sweden on the educational attainment indicators reflect the impact of earlier expansion of these higher education systems.

Looking at the variability between the scores on the three enrolment indicators, some countries such as Ireland, Belgium, Poland, and France have much higher rankings on the enrolment intensity indicator, reflecting the relative extent to which enrolments are highly concentrated among particular age groups, typically the young. This is in contrast to the Nordic countries, Switzerland and Germany where enrolments are more widely dispersed among age groups. From a methodological point of view, an important implication of this analysis is that it demonstrates the risks attached to using any single enrolment indicator as a measure of participation. For example, both Chile and Austria have significantly higher rankings on the GER than Ireland, Canada,[11] or Belgium, although their rankings on several other indicators and on the overall index are reversed.

In a further exploration of how overall participation in higher education is related to other characteristics of systems, Table 2.8 presents additional correlates of participation. Three of the variables relate to the nature of the enrolment. The table shows the percentage part-time, where this distinction is observed, the percentage of undergraduate enrolments on short-cycle programmes and the graduation rate from advanced research degree programmes. The other correlates are the country scores on the GPI, the representation of foreign students as a percentage of total enrolments, the number of scientific publications per 1,000 population, the percentage of private expenditure on higher education institutions, and finally the country GDP per capita in US dollars using PPPs. Having ranked the countries in terms of their score on the higher education participation index, it is of interest to note how these characteristics are linked to the pattern of participation. For example, South Korea's leading position in terms of overall participation has been achieved with the highest level of dependence on private expenditure on higher education and the fourth highest percentage of undergraduate students on short-cycle programmes. It has the lowest OECD country score on the GPI and a low level of recruitment of international students. Its level of scientific publications per capita is below average while its output of higher research degrees and its GDP per capita are slightly below average.

Perhaps the most striking feature of this table is the absence of a uniform pattern of association of these variables with the overall levels of participation. The only correlate which is statistically significantly related to overall participation rates is GDP per capita

---

[11] The figure for Canada is based on the authors' own calculations from the OECD database.

Table 2.8. Some correlates of higher education participation, 2013

Country	Higher Education Participation Index a	Percentage part-time enrolments b	Percentage undergrads on short cycle c	Advanced research degrees grad. rate d	Scientific publications per 1,000 population e	Private percentage of spending on higher education f	Foreign students as percentage of all students g	GPI h	GDP per capita PPP US$ (000s) i
Australia	73.7	33		2.5	3.7	55.1	18	1.37	43.2
Austria	61.7		44	1.9	2.7	4.7	17	1.20	44.9
Belgium	70.5	30		0.5	2.8	10.1	10	1.30	41.7
Canada	72.9	20		1.3	2.8	45.1	9	1.27	42.6
Chile	61.7		46	0.2	0.5	65.4	0	1.11	21.3
Czech Rep.	53.1	3		1.6	1.9	20.7	9	1.43	28.7
Denmark	69.1		31	2.8	4.1		10	1.38	43.6
Estonia	63.9	15		1.3	2.0	21.8	3	1.48	24.7
Finland	72.7	44		2.5	3.4	3.8	7	1.21	40.2
France	63.8			1.7	1.8	20.2	10	1.25	37.3
Germany	49.0	14		2.7	2.0	14.1	7	0.93	42.7
Hungary	49.7	31	24	0.7	1.0	45.6	6	1.28	22.5
Iceland	65.1	29			4.3	9.4	7	1.72	40.5
Ireland	75.7	15	25	2.2	2.8	18.2	6	1.03	45.2
Israel	64.0	14	29	1.5	2.4	47.6		1.34	31.3
Italy	47.3			1.4	1.7	34.0	4	1.42	35.3
Mexico	32.3		8	0.3	0.2	30.3	0	0.96	16.8
Netherlands	66.6	9	2	2.1	3.3	29.5	10	1.10	46.1
New Zealand	66.5	44	34	2.2	3.2	47.6	16	1.45	32.2
Norway	69.2	37		1.9	3.7	3.9	4	1.50	51.4
Poland	65.1	47	1	0.6	1.0	22.4	1	1.55	22.9
Portugal	54.1	5	7	1.7	2.1	45.7	4	1.18	27.2
Slovak Rep.	47.4	31	2	2.5	1.2	26.2	5	1.54	25.7
Slovenia	72.6	23	26	3.6	2.9	13.9	3	1.46	28.5
South Korea	98.4		38	1.6	1.5	70.7	2	0.75	32.0
Spain	71.2	27	36	1.5	1.8	26.9	3	1.22	32.8
Sweden	60.8	47	16	2.7	3.8	10.7	6	1.56	43.9
Switzerland	58.0	24	8	3.2	5.2		17	1.01	55.6
Turkey	56.9		51	0.7	0.5	19.6	1	0.86	18.0
UK	62.2	31	13	3.0	2.9	43.1	17	1.35	37.2
USA	76.8	38		1.5	2.0	62.2	4	1.37	49.9

Source: Prepared by authors using data as follows: Column a from Table 2.7 above; columns b, d, f, g and i, using data from OECD (2015); column c, first-time entrants to undergraduate programmes, authors' calculations using data from OECD (2015); column e, authors' calculations. Scopus publication data from *SCImago Journal and Country Rank* (http://www.scimagojr.com). Population data taken from OECD database.

(r =.39, p < 0.03). However, even this relationship is relatively modest; there are many examples which run counter to expectations. Switzerland, the most affluent country included in the analysis has a moderate level of participation while, in addition to South Korea, Slovenia has also achieved very high levels of participation with a relatively modest level of GDP. The absence of a strong correlation illustrates the complexity of the relationships and raises the question of causality.

High levels of participation may ultimately contribute to economic growth but they may also reflect consumption decisions facilitated by affluence. Taking into account this latter finding and those reported in the first part of this chapter, it would seem that at a global level, where there are gross differences between countries in GDP, a relatively high income is a precondition for high level of participation in higher education.[12] However, for countries above a certain income threshold level other factors such as the nature of the welfare regimes (Esping-Anderson, 1990) and the extent of social demand may be more important in determining levels of participation. The relative prioritization of higher education has been linked to different welfare regimes. Liberal welfare regimes tend to spend more on higher education, reflecting a strong human capital philosophy, but spend less on social equity. Those who do not participate in higher education pay a higher price, as there is less spent on vocational education and social safety net policies. Conservative welfare regimes provide better conditions for those who do not attain higher education. The education system tends to be very highly streamed with early selection which is strongly class-based. The vocational training system provides an alternative route. Social democratic welfare regimes seem to avoid some of the tradeoffs faced by liberal and conservatives countries. The socially embedded human capital allows for expansion of higher education without neglecting those who do not participate (Andres and Pechar, 2013).

While the association falls short of being statistically significant, levels of participation appear linked to certain features of higher education systems. Countries with higher levels of participation tend to have higher levels of part-time enrolments, although these data are not available for eight of the thirty-one countries in this analysis.[13] Again there are many exceptions; Poland and Sweden, the two countries which report highest levels of part-time enrolments have medium to low levels of total enrolments. This trend is also evident for Hungary and the Slovak Republic, while in contrast both Ireland and Canada combine high participation rates with relatively low levels of part-time enrolments. While data are only available for a limited number of countries on the percentage of undergraduate enrolments on short-cycle programmes, this pattern of enrolment is

---

[12] Even at this global level large differences in income help to explain differences in participation; thus while these rates vary dramatically between 'low-income' and 'high-income' countries, differences in participation are more modest for 'lower-middle-', 'middle-', and 'upper-middle-income' countries (see Table 2.2).

[13] In some countries there is no acknowledgement of the part-time route even if very many students may in fact have a strong involvement in the labour market while being registered higher education students.

linked to overall participation rates. Countries with a high percentage of short-cycle enrolments tend to have higher overall participation rates. Again, there are many exceptions: Turkey, Austria, and Chile combine high levels of enrolment on short-cycle enrolments with more modest levels of overall enrolments.

Although it may seem counter-intuitive, the graduation rate from advanced research degrees is not linked to the overall level of higher education enrolment. Of the six countries with highest levels of graduation for Doctoral or equivalent level programmes, only two (Slovenia and Denmark) are in the top half of the distribution with respect to overall higher education enrolments. Switzerland, the UK, Sweden, and Germany combine high levels of graduation from such programmes with lower levels of total enrolments. While the output from Doctoral programmes is highly related to the level of scientific publications per 1,000 population ($r = 0.73$), the latter variable is more closely linked to overall participation levels ($r = 0.34$, $p < 0.06$). Countries with high levels of participation in higher education tend to have a higher output of scientific publications. Switzerland and Sweden, both with very high levels of scientific publications, are deviant cases, in addition to that of South Korea as noted earlier.

It was discussed earlier how national participation rates can be influenced by the levels of enrolment of international students. However, our analysis of these variables found that, for OECD countries, these variables are not statistically related. While it is clear that Australia's overall participation rate is strongly influenced by the fact that some 18 per cent of its enrolment is accounted for by international students, it is alone among the top four highest participation countries with a large international student component. In contrast the UK, Austria, and Switzerland, the countries with the next highest enrolment of international students, have more modest overall participation rates. There is a weak positive relationship between the extent of private expenditure on higher education and level of participation. Three of the four countries with highest levels of participation (South Korea, the USA, and Australia) have a very high reliance on private expenditure. However, several other countries with high levels of private expenditure on higher education (e.g. Chile, New Zealand, and the UK) have more modest levels of participation.

Further to our brief analysis above of the relationship between overall participation in higher education and the global rise in female participation, it is interesting to re-examine this relationship with respect to OECD countries. For this group of countries there is no statistical relationship between the overall score on the higher education participation index and the GPI ($r = -0.05$). While two of the three OECD countries (Turkey and Germany) which have yet to achieve gender parity are classified among the countries with lowest levels of participation, only four of the top ten participation countries have a gender parity score above the OECD median value (1.3). Iceland, the country with the highest gender parity score (1.7), has a participation level with is close to the OECD average, while as remarked above, South Korea, the country with the highest participation rate, has the lowest score on the GPI.

Table 2.9. Gender parity in participation in higher education for OECD countries, 1971–2013

Country	GPI 2013	Year gender parity was achieved	Changes in gender parity 1971–85	Changes in gender parity 1985–2000	Changes in gender parity 2000–10	Changes in gender parity 2010–13
Australia	1.41	1987	76	30	13	2
Austria	1.21	1998	96	29	8	3
Belgium	1.30	1994	46	30	13	3
Canada	1.33*	1990	n.a.	n.a.	n.a.	n.a.
Chile	1.13	2007	24	16	19	5
Czech Rep.	1.42	1999	28	39	35	2
Denmark	1.38	1981	66	33	6	− 5
Estonia	1.50	1992	n.a.	n.a.	12	− 10
Finland	1.21	1974	−2	24	1	− 1
France	1.23	1983	n.a.	18	3	− 3
Germany	0.92		n.a.	n.a.	n.a.	n.a.
Hungary	1.28	1977	52	4	11	− 5
Iceland	1.72*	1981	214	49	8	− 4
Ireland	1.06	1995	46	55	− 9	− 5
Israel	1.35	1991	10	53	− 7	2
Italy	1.40	1992	38	52	10	− 2
Mexico	1.01	2004	115	71	10	− 3
Netherlands	1.10**	1999	82	42	8	0
New Zealand	1.43	1989	23	65	1	− 2
Norway	1.50	1984	128	39	11	− 7
Poland	1.55	1973	40	9	7	3
Portugal	1.15	1983	54	18	− 12	− 2
Slovak Rep.	1.54	1997	n.a.	n.a.	46	− 0
Slovenia	1.45	<1981	n.a.	29	10	− 3
South Korea	0.75		47	28	20	2
Spain	1.20	1986	158	23	5	− 3
Sweden	1.55	1985	48	27	6	1
Switzerland	1.01	2013	n.a.	57	32	2
Turkey	0.86		102	53	17	6
UK	1.31	1993	64	42	14	− 3
USA	1.38	1978	67	17	5	− 2

Note: *Authors' calculations from OECD database: **2012 data.

Source: Calculations by the authors data from UNESCO (2016). Where data were not available for a single reference year, the values for the next year were taken in respect of Iceland, Israel, Mexico, and Turkey.

Table 2.9 shows the pattern of change in the GPI over the period 1971 to 2013. Most progress in respect of gender parity was achieved in the 1970s and early 1980s with especially striking breakthroughs evident in Iceland, Spain, Norway, and Mexico. Poland, Finland, Hungary, and the USA were the first to achieve gender parity. While the disproportionate rise in female participation continued through the late 1980s and 1990s the pace of change was noticeable slower in most countries. In many countries, the policy discourse had changed with increasing concern about the under-representation of males in higher education. The first decade of this century saw a reversal of the prevailing trend in three countries (Portugal, Ireland, and Israel) where the rise in male participation exceeded that of females. In the latest three-year period for which data were available (2010–13) more than half of OECD countries have experienced this reversal of the trend which has dominated developments for several decades. While it is possible to seek country specific explanations of the steeper rise in male participation, such as the declining employment for males associated with the steep recession in Portugal and Ireland, reducing the opportunity costs of attending college, it is significant that this trend reversal is now evident in many more countries. And while the scale of this reversal is modest it does mark a significant policy trend which has attracted very little attention.

Conclusions

This chapter has quantified the global phenomenon of rapidly expanding enrolments in higher education. More than a third, fifty-seven out of the 161 countries for which UNESCO has published enrolment data, have now achieved, and in most cases greatly surpassed, the 50 per cent GER which classifies them as HPS. A further one-third of countries have now surpassed the 15 per cent participation rate which Trow (1973) had earlier defined as the threshold for mass participation in higher education. While the phenomenon of HPS is most evident in high and medium income countries it is quickly spreading to countries with lower levels of GDP. Furthermore, while the incidence of HPS remains unevenly spread among world regions it is no longer confined to North America and Europe, the regions in which it first emerged. The rise in female participation has been a major factor in overall rising levels of participation. The traditional under-representation of females in higher education has been reversed over the past three decades. Females now form the majority of higher education enrolments in all major world regions, with the exception of sub-Saharan Africa where the gender parity ratio has remained at 0.7 for the past two decades, and in South and West Asia where it is approaching parity. A feature of developments in most OECD countries in very recent years is that male participation rates have risen faster than that of females, reversing the prevailing trend over previous decades.

Our analysis has pointed to significant limitations in existing data sources which inhibit more accurate measurement of comparative trends in participation in higher education. Much of the measurement difficulty is related to the growing heterogeneity of higher education. Participation in higher education is no longer a discrete sequential phase of the life-cycle which follows on directly after secondary school graduation. Less than half (49 per cent) of higher education enrolments in all OECD countries in 2013 belong to the five-year age cohort (19–23) which follows secondary school graduation; a further 26 per cent are aged 24–9 while 20 per cent are aged 30 or over.[14] The heterogeneity in the age structure of enrolments reflects the growing variability in modes of study which range from full-time to part-time to distance study and to the increasing variety of study programmes which are offered within higher education systems. A consequence of this heterogeneity is that no single currently used indicator provides a fully adequate measure of the comparative trends in participation. While ideally an optimum index of participation would combine indicators on entry, enrolments and graduation levels the index used in this chapter has been limited to indicators on enrolment and the education attainment levels of the population.

Exploration of the comprehensive OECD higher education database has documented the large differences between countries in the structural features of their higher education systems. While high levels of participation are a shared experience HPS have many manifestations. Countries with the same levels of participation can vary widely in the gender balance in enrolments, in the mix of private and public funding and in the level and direction of cross-border student flows. There are also large differences in the intensity of the study experience. Some countries have higher levels of part-time study and or higher enrolments in short cycle programmes; higher education may be experienced by a larger proportion of the population but may be a less intense and shorter term commitment. In other countries, with similar levels of overall enrolments, a smaller percentage of the population may participate in full-time programmes of longer duration with higher graduation levels from Doctoral programmes. While some of these differences may be related to levels of GDP per capita and to how recently very high participation was achieved, they also reflect more fundamental differences in social structure and national political culture. A major task for future researchers will be to explicate some of the causal factors accounting for these differences.

■ REFERENCES

Andres, L. and Pechar, H. (2013). Participation patterns in higher education: A comparative welfare and production regime perspective. *European Journal of Education* 48(2), 247–61.

Belich, J., Darwin, J., and Wickham, C. (2016). Introduction: The prospect of global history. *The Prospect of Global History*. Oxford: Oxford University Press.

Clancy, P. (2010). Measuring access and equity from a comparative perspective. In H. Eggins (ed.), *Access and Equity: Comparative Perspectives*. Rotterdam: Sense Publishers.

Clancy, P. (2015). *Irish Higher Education: A Comparative Perspective*. Dublin: Institute of Public Administration.

Esping-Andersen, G. (1990). *The Three Worlds of Welfare Capitalism*. Princeton: Princeton University Press.

---

[14] Authors' calculation from OECD database: The 19–23 population age cohort is that most commonly used to calculate the GER.

Kaiser, F., Hillegers, H., and Legro, I. (2005). *Lining Up Higher Education: Trends in Selected Statistics in Ten Western European Countries*. CHEPS International Higher Education Monitor. Enschede, NL: Centre for Higher Education Policy Studies.

Kharas, H. and Gertz, G. (2010). The new global middle class: A cross-over from West to East. In C. Liu (ed.), *China's Emerging Middle Class: Beyond Economic Transformation*. Washington, DC: Brookings Institution Press.

Mahbubani, K. (2013). *The Great Convergence: Asia, the West and the Logic of One World*. New York: Public Affairs.

Marginson, S. (2013). Emerging higher education in the Post-Confucian heritage zone. In D. Araya and P. Marber (eds), *Higher Education in the Global Age*. New York: Routledge, pp. 89–112.

Mettler, S. (2014). *Degrees of Inequality: How the Politics of Higher Education Sabotaged the American Dream*. New York: Basic Books.

Milanovic, B. (2011). *The Haves and the Have Nots: A Brief and Idiosyncratic History of Global Inequality*. New York: Basic Books.

Naidoo, R. (2014). Transnational higher education: Global wellbeing or new imperialism? Keynote presentation to the United Kingdom Forum for International Education Conference. London, UCL Institute of Education, 24 October.

NCES (National Center for Education Statistics) (2015). *Comparative Indicators of Education in the US and Other G-8 Countries 2015*. Washington, DC: NCES.

OECD (Organisation for Economic Co-operation and Development) (2004). *OECD Handbook for Internationally Comparative Education Statistics*. Paris: OECD.

OECD (Organisation for Economic Co-operation and Development) (2013). *Education at a Glance 2013*. Paris: OECD.

OECD (Organisation for Economic Co-operation and Development) (2014). *PISA 2012 Results in Focus: What 15 Year Olds Know and What They Can Do With What They Know*. Paris: OECD.

OECD (Organisation for Economic Co-operation and Development) (2015). *Education at a Glance 2015*. Paris: OECD.

Salmi, J. and Bassett, R. M. (2014). The equity imperative in tertiary education: Promoting fairness and efficiency. *International Review of Education* 60, 361–77.

Sen, A. (2000). *Development as Freedom*. New York: Basic Books.

Trow, M. (1973). *Problems in the Transition from Elite to Mass Higher Education*. Berkeley, CA: Carnegie Commission on Higher Education.

UNESCO (United Nations Educational, Social and Cultural Organization) (2005). *Global Education Digest 2005*. Montreal: UNESCO Institute for Statistics.

UNESCO (United Nations Educational, Social and Cultural Organization) (2012). *International Standard Classification of Education ISCED 2011*. Montreal: UNESCO Institute for Statistics.

UNESCO (United Nations Educational, Social and Cultural Organization) (2016). UNESCO Institute for Statistics database on education. http://data.uis.unesco.org/

World Bank (2016). Data and statistics. http://data.worldbank.org/indicator/all

Yang, P. (2014). Chinese higher education expansion. Paper presented at the Summer School on Higher Education Research, National Research University—Higher School of Economics, Institute of Education. Pushkin, St Petersburg, 13 June.

3 Governance

Brendan Cantwell, Rómulo Pinheiro, and Marek Kwiek

> The drift of authority for a quarter-century has been steadily upward, toward a growing web of multicampus administrations, coordinating boards of higher education, state legislative committees and executive offices, regional associations, and a large number of agencies of the national government.
>
> (Clark, 1983: 130)

Introduction

Assessing global tendency towards high participation involves better understanding the dynamics specific to high participation systems (HPS). This chapter takes up the question of governance, understood as the set of mechanisms by which individual higher education institutions are controlled and directed and by which higher education systems are coordinated. As the preceding statement implies, governance surely involves rationalization: 'It is the means by which order is created in the academy to achieve the goals of educating, researching, and providing service to multiple publics' (Austin and Jones, 2016: 2). Goal attainment, quality assurance, and mission (horizontal) differentiation are key elements of rationalized governance systems. Following interest articulation models (Baldridge, 1971), governance is understood as rational political processes in which multiple stakeholders negotiate goals and mechanisms of control. HPS governance, however, involves not only rational negotiation among stakeholders but also the exercise of power and social contest (Pusser, 2004). Establishing the goals of higher education, as well as the means by which goals are to be achieved, is the source of considerable political struggle and governance, and is at least partly the result of contest among social factions (Ordorika, 2003; Pusser, 2004).

Understanding governance as processes of stakeholder rationalization leads to a different sort of analysis than when governance is understood as social struggle. Yet both views are congruent with the claim that a variety of actors impose demands on individual departments and programs, higher education intuitions, and systems (Austin and Jones, 2016). High participation activates stakeholders, increases their number and variety, and softens the distinction between social relations within higher education and the wider socio-economic and cultural environment (Trow, 1974); hence, governance in HPS is characterized by active stakeholder engagement through multi-level coordination and accountability systems. This is not to say that higher education institutions are passively acted upon. The well-known articulation of higher education institutions as 'organized anarchies' (Cohen et al., 1972) suggests higher education institutions defy rationalization and resist collective action. The idea of higher education governance through organized anarchy must be registered as part of the story. After all, how does one standardize learning or plan for discovery? But the idea of university as collegium—self-organizing by the academic disciplines and without central authority—is confronted by the near universal observation that higher education institutions are increasingly managed enterprises. The tendency towards managerialism is both imposed upon higher education systems through new public management policies and is the product of gathering administrative capacity within higher education institutions. In the most general terms, higher education institutions are sites of individual and collective action, are capable of both self-regulation and action in the pursuit of self-interest, but are also subject to external influence, regulation, and control.

The central argument of this chapter is that HPS governance involves (a) multi-level control, coordination, and accountability; (b) the management of differentiation; and (c) corporatized self-governing capacities among higher education institutions. To be clear, HPS are not converging upon a single model. One needs look no further than to the differences between the market-oriented Anglophone systems and the egalitarian Nordic systems to conclude that HPS are governed heterogeneously. Nor is there a singular 'high participation governance' enacted automatically once participation levels cross some arbitrary threshold. A central claim of this book is that high participation is a contextually contingent process that qualitatively shifts higher education. In this regard, the argument advanced here departs from Trow's (1974) formulation. Shifts in system dynamics prompted by mass participation are context bound rather than regular, as implied by Trow. Increased participation interacts with system history and other contemporary developments to shape governance arrangements in ways that are unique to each system. This consideration entered, it is nonetheless possible to advance three propositions (4–6 in the list of propositions) about HPS governance:

- *HPS are governed by multi-level control, coordination, and accountability mechanisms.*
- *HPS governance tends to involve the management of horizontal differentiation.*
- *HPS complex multi-level accountability and coordination, coupled with system differentiation, result in higher education institutions adopting increasingly corporate forms and robust internal governance and management capacities.*

These propositions are not covering laws that operate predictably and can be applied to make explanations without consideration of context (see Chapter 1). Rather each proposition describes an observed tendency of HPS development, all of which are subject to contingencies. Comparative analysis permits analysis of the interaction between natural tenancies associated with HPS development and the situated socio-cultural and political economy of particular systems.

The remainder of this chapter considers each of the above-presented propositions and, in doing so, seeks to outline a general set of claims about the relationship between high participation and governance. Governance is, of course, not a singular concept. This chapter is simultaneously interested in the governance or control of individual higher education institutions as well as the coordination of higher education systems.

Multi-level Governance

The first governance proposition (Proposition 4) asserts that

HPS are governed by multi-level control, coordination, and accountability mechanisms.

The claim of multi-level governance is not original to the present analysis. According to a recent OECD commissioned report, advanced educational systems are coordinated by the interaction of individual and collective actors. Governance is the result of interaction between actors, whose behaviour is shaped by non-linear feedback mechanisms that operate at different time-scales (Burns and Köster, 2016). The contribution of this chapter is to analyse how high participation enacts and influences multi-level governance.

Governing higher education systems is a complicated business, especially when there is mass participation. High levels of participation introduce numerous governance-related challenges. Mass and universal systems are generally too large and complex to be governed through direct central coordination by a ministry of education or other governmental agency. In addition, higher education is considered by many actors to be too important to be left alone to the short-term agendas and shifting (political and economic) priorities of governments, or to market interests that prioritize short-term outcomes and special interests (e.g. industrially relevant R&D). HPS actors, operating both within (e.g. institutions) and outside the system (e.g. industry, regional actors, charities, social pressure groups), influence HPS. Multi-stakeholder participation means that higher education institutions face constraints that limit (full) autonomy—both substantive and procedural (Schmidtlein and Berdahl, 2005)—to set goals and go about their daily business. No system or individual university operates free of constraints. Consider the private university sector in the United States, which is not subject directly to the authority of any state agency. The range of goals these higher education institutions can seek is wide and subject to considerable discretion but there are still limits based on federal and state laws regulating the operation of non-for-profit organizations and norms that delineate legitimate behaviour. In mature systems cultures develop that establish the role and public responsibilities of universities. All of this is to say that higher education institutions are subject to multi-level systems of constrains and such constrains are assumed to become both more numerous and elaborate under the conditions of high participation in which more actors have a stake in higher education.

HPS governance is characterized by a fluid set of processes. Policymaking tends to occur in *waves* or phases (Gornitzka and Maassen, 2011; Pinheiro and Antonowicz, 2015a), and the salience of goals and centres of gravity surrounding the policymaking process both shift over time and are contextually contingent. The policymaking process in a country is likely to be different from one period to the next and is also likely to be different if one considers a research universities versus more regionally embedded higher education institutions (Pinheiro, 2013). While all HPS witness efforts to rationalize higher education governance, the rationales (motivation) and rationalizations (explanations) for governance efforts shift with time and across space.

Trow (1974) gives the seminal account of system transformation as a result of mass participation but offers few insights about governance. Tracing the complex multi-level governance structures of HPS presents a number of challenges. Elaborate descriptive accounts might be useful for detailing specific policies and for establishing the historical record, yet given the highly contingent and episodic nature of higher education policy, such accounts may also have limited comparative applicability. Perhaps with such a limitation in mind, those studying higher education policy and governance have often turned to models and heuristics to provide general frames of reference by which to *describe, compare,* and *explain* policymaking and governance. Clark's (1983) model of triangular coordination ranks among the most prominent and durable frameworks (see Jongbloed, 2003; Cloete et al., 2006; Salazar and Leihy, 2013; Pinheiro and Antonowics, 2015b; Austin and Jones, 2016). The value of Clark's model is that its minimalist elegance permits sophisticated comparative analysis that can be undertaken in a straightforward albeit fruitful manner. Another virtue of this heuristic is that it is more or less universally applicable. The coordinating triangle is best used to build typologies and locate systems among the tripartite poles. It is very useful for comparative analysis. For instance, one can place China in one position of the triangle, France in another, and Australia in the third, and one learns something about each of these systems by understanding their place on the triangle and their position relative to one and other.

Despite these considerable virtues, Clark's heuristic is limited in its analytic power. The triangle is implicitly zero-sum. Higher education in HPS has become increasingly more complex as waves of massification led to the substantial restructuring of domestic higher education systems (Trow and Burrage, 2010). Such processes can, for instances, simultaneously enhance state oversight and insert increased market competition into a system (Gornitzka and Maassen, 2000; Kwiek and Maassen, 2012). Contemporary higher education policymaking and governance encompasses a multiplicity of actors— non-governmental organizations (NGOs), industry, and civil society stakeholders, among others (Jongbloed et al., 2008), and occurs at multiple scales. Policy may be enacted at the local level, within sub-national regions, by nation states, through supra-national collaboration as is observed in the European Union (EU), and even globally when bodies such as the World Bank exert influence. This multi-actor, multi-scalar process, in turn, results in additional demands being placed on HE systems, ranging from access/equity dimensions (Tapper and Palfreyman, 2005), workforce development (Knapper and Cropley, 2000), community/regional engagement (Pinheiro et al., 2012), and innovation and local/national competitiveness (Benneworth et al., 2009). Such demands not only increase the complexity and ambiguity surrounding the governance of HPS, but also raise a number of new tensions that are both internally and externally initiated (Pinheiro et al., 2014).

Moreover, returning to Clark's heuristic model, it is sometimes difficult to separate the key actors composing the triangle of coordination. For instance, market-state dualism is particularly problematic in higher education because the sector is universally established and supported by the state (Marginson, 2013). Put simply, quasi-markets confound Clark's triangle. There are also often conflicting interests within the state, for example, through which the antagonistic goals of broadening access for social equity and developing world-class research capacity and elite higher education institutions are pursued simultaneously. The academic oligarchy is also increasingly fragmented (Kehm and Teichler, 2013), not only when it comes to the priorities held by specific knowledge communities (Trowler et al., 2012) and their strategic value to societal actors (Benneworth and Jongbloed, 2010), but also as it relates to the growing gap between university managers and the academic heartland (Amaral et al., 2003), as well as the fractioning of the academic profession itself (e.g. Jones, 2013).

Many have modified Clarks' triangle to address these and other limitations while maintaining the fruitful elements. Jongbloed (2003) expanded the heuristic by including stakeholders, while Marginson and Rhoades (2002) added a multi-dimensional element (global, national, local). Salazar and Leihy (2013) advanced a mode of interlocking 'dynamic domains', while others refined the points of the triangle. For example, some argue that given changing authority relations in HE, the 'academic estate' is a preferable term to the 'academic oligarchy' used by Clark (Pusser, 2008). Each of these efforts is useful. They add complexity and sophistication to the model, making important improvements to Clark's heuristic. All make the model applicable in more empirical cases and permit more complete and complex analysis. But none are complete insofar as is it will always be possible to find cases that are difficult to analyse and classify within the scope of the models. Moreover, when adding complexity to the models, there is a tradeoff between sophistication and ease of empirical application. In short, there may be diminishing returns to adding complexity to the heuristic.

For these reasons, this chapter neither relies on an existing governance model nor attempts to construct a new one. The overall argument is that there are fundamental commonalities in the governance of HPS but that these shared features are rather general and that governance arrangements vary substantially and are subject to contingencies.

CONTROL, COORDINATION, AND ACCOUNTABILITY THROUGH BOUNDARY DEACTIVATION AND MANAGEMENT

Many organized groups and civil society actors, along with state and market actors, have an interest in monitoring, and shaping activities within the HE sector. One necessary, but not sufficient, feature of governance in HPS is that the sector is subject to multi-level systems of control, coordination, and accountability. Many non-HPS also have complex and multi-level accountability and coordination systems. The presence of a multi-level accountability and coordination system does not automatically indicate high participation. But it is unlikely that any mature high participation system can operate without complex governance. Through the totality of exclusion, higher education institutions in elite systems could, at least in part (though town-gown questions are prominent from the founding of medieval universities), maintain cultures and internal social relations separate from the wider social-political environment. In elite systems a relatively small share of national income is devoted to higher education, the links between higher education and work are even more tenuous than in mass systems, and, most importantly, relatively few participate. These systems' primary function is the socialization of future economic, politic, and cultural elites (Castells, 2001). Homogeneity among the few who participate in elite systems facilitates the high consensus culture of universities as places for ascetic scholastic pursuits. This assertion is not ignorant of the long history of bawdy drunken behaviour that can be found in accounts of fifteenth century Oxford or nineteenth century Harvard but is simply stylized to draw a contrast between elite and mass social relations.

Elite system curricula were steeped in theology and the classics, the languages of antiquity were often used as the medium of instruction, and recitation rather than publication marked accomplishment. Here is the ideal of the cloistered, near monastic academy: the 'ivory tower'. But there are no ivory towers in modern mass systems. Even Oxbridge and the Ivy League are all science universities motivated at least as much by the pursuit scientific discovery, competition in quasi-markets, and returns on capital investment as by deep tradition (cf. Tapper and Palfreyman, 2011). Kerr (2001) introduced this modern organizational form as the multiversity. The multiversity is subject to multi-level accountability and coordination mechanisms and is part of a managed and differentiated system. Governance in HPS is, thus, shaped by social exposure (Amaral et al., 2009; Ramirez, 2010).

SOCIAL BOUNDARIES

Massification softens the distinctions between the social relations within the higher education system compared with relations in other social domains. Charles Tilly's specification of 'boundary de-activation' as a mechanism for social change helps to analyse these changes. In an abstract sense, governance establishes domain authority, or sets the boundaries that demarcate where and with whom the authority to make decisions lie. Because massification results in a new set of higher education / society relations, a 'social pact' (Gornitzka et al., 2007), mass-scale participation initiates a cascading set of boundary transgressions. 'Social boundaries interrupt, divide, circumscribe, or segregate distributions of population or activity within social fields' (Tilly, 2004: 214). Within stable social boundaries rules and norms of behaviour can be well established and even predictable—an observation shared by institutional theory. When boundaries are transgressed and deactivated, social ordering can be upended, making way for new, sometimes more complex orders.[1]

Massification deactivates the established boundaries of elite systems, and stimulates the sort of multi-actor, multi-temporal, multi-scalar governance and accountability systems descried above. How does this happen? The outcomes of these processes are dependent on contingencies located within particular systems and can only be specified through situated empirical analysis. To put another way, while boundary deactivation and social exposure are expected to rearrange the governance relations of all systems that experience mass participation, the processes and outcomes are not coincidental to any system but are rather historically specific. Borrowing from Tilly's insights and vocabulary, a partial inventory of general deactivation triggers are considered: (a) encounters, (b) impositions, (c) borrowing, (d) conversations, and (e) incentive shifts. High participation brings with it a tide of persons who had been considered 'outside' the system, such as female students, students from working class backgrounds, students from ethnic and religious minority groups, and mature aged students. *Encounters* between these students and traditional incumbents of the system can result in changed boundaries. Trow's (1970) essay in *Daedalus* details how encounters between new types of students and faculty were transforming the University of California, for example.

As more students participate in higher education, both public and private, are devoted to the sector, governments often *impose* new mandates that shift the boundaries of authority that govern higher education. Examples include regional policy that demands the extension of the higher education system into underserved regions, affirmative action polices that are designed to widen participation among historically excluded groups of

---

[1] It is important to acknowledge that boundary deactivation can occur without quantitative massification as measured by the gross enrolment ratio. In Latin America, for example, many systems have not achieved universal participation but the boundaries that distinguish universities from their environments are regularly deactivated, resulting sometimes in considerable social upheaval. In Mexico less than one-third of the age cohort participate in higher education, yet student movements are often at the centre of national political convolutions. When forty-two student activists from the state of Gurrero disappeared in 2014, the entire country was plunged into political turmoil as the public demanded accountability from the government both for specific questions into the fate of the missing students and for broader questions about state conduct in engagement with narcotics cartels and civil society groups.

students, or research ethics requirements that impose government determined standards for the responsible conduct of academic research. As the system expands both in terms of the size and scope of individual higher education institutions and in terms of the number of higher education institutions in the systems, new organizations (offices and entire universities) *borrow* from other, often successful, organizations for establishing governance structures (DiMaggio and Powell, 1983). Such instances of borrowed rationales include adoption of business-like human resource policies and the establishment of offices to standardize hiring practices (Ramirez and Christensen, 2013). Cross-boundary *conversations*, the result of increased cross-boundary encounters and new entrants to the system, lead to exchanges that change the relations amongst actors within the system. Examples from the USA and Northern Europe include 'articulation' agreements between universities and non-university colleges to define the rules of student transfer between sectors within the system (Pinheiro and Kyvik, 2009). Finally, *incentive shifts* can also deactivate 'traditional' boundaries that established university sectors in elite systems. Mass participation has been accompanied by new rewards and penalties for higher education institutions that change the rules governing within-boundary relations. Examples include celebration rather than stigmatization for those who engage in commercial activity, or the establishment of tuition fees that creates incentives for universities to recruit students. Informal distinctions between universities and other types of higher education institutions remain (e.g. as regards research capacity/excellence/ prestige), despite the gradual erosion of formal distinctions. Further, status and market position differentiates incentives within the same system. Universities that find themselves in the middle, rather than artisanal segments (see Chapter 5), may be incentivized to compete for students while those at the pinnacle of the system devote their efforts to turning aspirant students away. Similarly, some universities may enter the market once monopolized by non-university colleges by offering vocational degrees in the search of new students and associated resources.

MULTILATERAL AND TOP-DOWN CONTROL

Management is sometimes imagined as having absolute authority. Such claims are intensified in many HPS because administration is informed by new public management ideologies (Deem and Brehony, 2005) and quasi-market systems allocate scarce resources (Dill, 1997; Slaughter and Leslie, 1997). As HPS develop, with more multiple external relations connecting to complex formal and informal relationships in larger institutions, budget authority and management becomes the principal means of top-to-bottom coordination within institutions. A neoliberal ideology of market supremacy is the backdrop for the policy milieu especially in English-speaking countries.

The observed tendency to the rise of new public management (NPM) and quasi-market resource allocation in HPS is related to the coincident neoliberal policy turn, under which such policy approaches are favoured. Yet claiming neoliberalism as a singular 'cause' of managerial control may overlook both the specific contingencies that shape the ways managerial control may occur and the reality that higher education is subject to multiple, rather than singular, influences. Of particular interest here is the relationship between these governance techniques and high participation. While the cross-border diffusion of neoliberal policy regimes (Henisz et al., 2005) is independent of participation, it is plausible that greater social exposure and stakeholder activation of HPS simultaneously make traditional modes of top-down control, ministry fiat for example, difficult to maintain. As HPS develop, with more multiple external relations connecting to complex formal and informal relationships in larger institutions, budget authority and management becomes the principal means of top-to-bottom coordination within systems and individual higher education institutions.

Government regulation and oversight is probably the primary formal coordination and accountability mechanism. Such mechanisms are often (but not always) connected to funding. In many HPS countries, system wide regulation and oversight involves different ministries and/or governmental agencies. It is not uncommon, for example, for teaching and research functions to be overseen by different agencies, or for teaching places to be regulated by one agency within government bureaucracy and academic R&D and technology policy to be overseen by another. For example, across the Nordic countries public higher education institutions are often required to have a series of strategies in place that are aimed at enhancing gender equality across the board, including the training, tutoring, and selection of woman for senior management positions (Pinheiro et al., 2015).

Quality assurance and/or accreditation regimes constitute another set of formal coordinating and accountability mechanisms. The presence of a quality assurance regime is a near universal feature of higher education governance. As with direct oversight, there are often budgetary implications attached to the outcomes of quality audits. In HPS such regimes may assess quality ambiguously due to the complexity, size, and diversity of the system. This is a function of both the complexity of the system as a whole, largely due to size but also diversity, and the need to ascertain a certain degree of oversight or order by the state in the face of increasing decentralization. More often than not, quality assurance mechanism are themselves multi-level. Sometimes the state is the main entity responsible for devising and implementing such mechanisms, as is the case of emerging HPS in Southeast Asian countries such as Laos and Vietnam (SEAMEO, 2012). Direct state control of quality assurance is less common in larger and more complex systems. In well-established HPS like the UK and the Netherlands, quality assurance is the responsibility of government chartered independent bodies or foundations. In other mature HPSs, university networks and associations also play a leading role, as is the case of 'Universities New Zealand—Te Pōkai Tara', a body comprised of the Vice-Chancellors of the country's eight universities. Finally, there are also cases, like in the USA, where quality assurance is the charge of independent agencies without explicit government charter but that are nonetheless recognized by government and higher education institutions alike.

INFORMAL ACCOUNTABILITY MECHANISMS

HPS are subject to informal accountability mechanisms. University rankings are one obvious example of informal regulation. Rankings and league tables have been present in national systems for the past 30 years but their influence has waxed in the past decade with the introduction and proliferation of world university rankings. A central consideration is the extent to which rankings have become *more* important because of the global tendency towards high participation. As discussed in Chapters 4 and 5 on stratification and diversity, additional means of differentiation arise when systems expand and when many higher education institutions adopt missions similar to traditional universities. Rankings have been a part of the higher education landscape in the United States, the first HPS, for around 30 years, and the more recent development of world rankings differentiate between as well as within systems may reflect the globalization of high participation.

Rankings specifically shape HPS in a number of ways. They perform a quasi-quality assurance role by assessing higher education institutions' quality and status, and through measuring scientific outputs. While such measures are acknowledged to be limited, they are nonetheless influential among policymakers, higher education institutions' administrators, and the public. Thus, rankings indirectly coordinate systems by establishing benchmark type standards that are used by policymakers and institutional leaders for developing strategic priorities and by informing day-to-day decision making (Hazelkorn, 2011). The normative pull of rankings in shaping higher education institutions' strategy and management practices is powerful. But the governance pull of rankings may be felt most directly when efforts to compete in league tables are directly connected to financial allocations. In a number of European and Asian countries, governments have responded (at least indirectly) to rankings by enacting concerted policy efforts to develop 'World-Class' universities that might appear highly positioned in global league tables (Salmi, 2009).

Student markets may constitute another set of accountability/coordination mechanisms because students can 'vote with their feet'. Yet the influence of this mechanism with HPS is contingent upon other features of the system. Student markets are probably most powerful in shaping HPS dynamics in countries where students pay fees (e.g. Australia, the UK, France, Ireland), where fees are set at the institutional level (e.g. Croatia, Poland, Greece, Romania, USA), and in systems where public funding for higher education institutions is not allocated by block grant but on a per-enrolment basis (e.g. England and Spain) (Jongbloed, 2010). While non-HPS systems may have fees and use quasi-markets to allocate resources, there may simply not be enough higher education institutions in competition with one and other for enough students for market-like conditions to emerge. In HPS systems where participation is a universal entitlement furnished by the state—such as in Nordic and other on the European Continent—a market mentality may not develop among higher education institutions and students.

Interaction between system size and neoliberal policy conditions can produce market-like conditions that shape system dynamics. For example, in recent years markets have become formal coordination mechanisms in the UK, which is possible because the system is large both in terms of higher education institutions' numbers and participation levels. The system is run explicitly as a student consumer market, and instruments like the National Student Survey and the graduate outcomes survey are designed to feed information into the market, which is in turn intended to allocate resources. Student demand is essential for policy to effectively leverage market-like policy in higher education. Demand can and has played an important role in system expansion and marketization, for example across the BRICS—Brazil, Russia, India, China, and South Africa—countries (Schwartzman et al., 2015) and, presumably, ebbing of demand can also contribute to system contraction and retreat from the market, as the example of Poland demonstrates (Kwiek, 2016).

Beyond rankings and markets, many individual and collective stakeholders lobby higher education systems and seek to access levers of influence over the system. Student associations and/or unions exist in all HPS and have influence over individual higher education institutions and the entire system; however, the extent to which these bodies influence system dynamics varies based on historical trajectories, institutional arrangements, and critical events (e.g. crisis). As HPS develop, outside stakeholders, occupations and social movements have an increasing impact in shaping the contents of curricula and credentials. This is because high participation activates and energizes stakeholders while destabilizing central coordination among a closed set of interests (government, academic staff, institutional leaders, etc.).

Labour unions and organized interest groups straddle formal and informal domains. Teachers' unions and other professional organizations, which may be codified by law or contract or which may operate more spontaneously, exert influence over the system. At times—during contract negotiations, for example—the influential role of these entities might be immediate but at others their influence is indirect or so gradual that it only registers over time. For example, students and junior staff played a rather prominent role in the 'democratic revolutions' of the late 1960s and early 70s, both in the USA and throughout Europe (Pinheiro and Antonowicz, 2015b). Similarly, in emerging HPS like Brazil and Chile, NGOs and other grass-roots groups play an increasingly important role when it comes to equity-related issues such as access to higher education (e.g. the setting of quotas) by historically under-represented groups like racial minorities (Balbachevsky, 2015).

Managing System Differentiation

The second HPS proposition (5) on governance asserts that

HPS governance tends to involve the management of horizontal differentiation.

HPS generally exhibit high levels of differentiation. High Levels of differentiation occur along two overlapping tracks. First, many HPS are steeply stratified (vertically) in a prestige/resource type hierarchy (see Chapter 4). Second, HPS often exhibit horizontal diversity among higher education institutions in terms of mission, organizational scope, and culture. Some diversity persists even when there is a tendency towards the multiversity form because there are higher education institutions in different regions, of different sizes and with different (even if convening) missions. Horizontal diversity is especially important in the governing of HPS because massification partly transforms the meaning of 'university'. In elite systems there tends to be a strong binary division between the university and non-university sectors. Through system unification in some HPS (the UK for example) and through mission drift in nearly all HPS, many higher education institutions take on the name university and nominally adopt the university mission of research and advanced instruction. Yet not all universities play the same social role and governance maintains some differentiation within the tendency towards homogenization.

RATIONALIZING SYSTEMS

System rationalization is a key feature of HPS (Ramirez and Christensen, 2013). As systems enlarge both quantitatively through increased participation and qualitatively through expanded scope of operations, policymakers generally seek to control and make sense of higher education by subjecting the sector to modernist rationality. Policies that channel resources through defined criteria, geographic distribution of program offerings and instructions, and coordination of curriculum with perceived social needs are commonplace. Differentiation through rationalization is confronted by countervailing isomorphic pressures and the tendency towards mission drift (Bastedo and Gumport, 2003). Because higher education is a status-driven enterprise and because the goals of higher education institutions as well as the means for achieving these goals are both uncertain and contested by various stakeholders, higher education is famously subject to isomorphism (see DiMaggio and Powell, 1983) in which many higher education institutions nominally take up the missions and activities of the most successful organizations. As discussed in the chapters on stratification and diversity (5 and 4 respectively), while there is a strong tendency for higher education institutions strive for elite positions, with some exceptions systems are hieratically ordered and tend towards status bifurcation.

This is not to suggest that drift is without consequence to system dynamics. High participation may result in a shift in the very definition of the 'university,' whereby a much broader set of higher education institutions take on university identity. This occurs because more students want a place at 'university,' in response to the aspirations of academics and administrators, and through regulatory developments such as the unification of binary systems (Morphew and Huisman, 2002; for more discussion see Chapter 4). Because of absolute restraints in status position and the resources needed to support university activities it is common in HPS for higher education institutions that are ostensibly universities not to reflect more traditional markers of university status such as strict student selectivity and considerable volumes of research activity. Rationalization efforts, such as policies designed to avoid program duplication and regional distribution of higher education institutions further complicates the tendency of many higher education institutions adopting university-like identities. Rational differentiation and drift are in tension and efforts by states to rationalize system differentiation are counterbalanced by aspirational tendencies towards mission drift.

Funding mechanism prove to be prominent avenues by which states seek to rationalize HPS by distributing activities and consolidating strengths. Research funding allocations contribute to both concentration of resources (stratification) and to supporting the distribution of strength among different sub-sectors and individual higher education institutions (diversity). Systems like the Research Excellence Framework in the UK work to both promote diversity by distinguishing research-intensive universities from others and also distribute disciplinary field strengths by making research funding decisions based on department level strengths when allocating resources among higher education institutions. Centres of excellence and world-class university initiatives, which are used widely in Asia and Europe, are formal mechanisms that differentiate by concentrating resources, researchers, and overall research capacity in few higher education institutions. Germany's centres of excellence initiative supports specific programs within higher education institutions (Kehm and Pasternack, 2009), while other approaches involve broad system reform like China's 985 and 211 policies that target a modest number of institutions in order to support the development of an elite research university sub-sector (Mok and Yue, 2015). Generally speaking, funding mechanisms to support system diversity by targeting and distributing areas of strength throughout the system contribute to stratification by concentrating resources in particular higher education institutions and programmes.

Regional policy is another mechanism for rationalized system differentiation. Countries where the population is dispersed across considerable geographic areas, like Russia, Canada, Australia, and the Nordic countries, have traditionally put an emphasis on decentralization, for example, by allowing second-tier regional providers to cater for the needs of local student populations as well as external stakeholders like regional industry (Pinheiro et al., 2013). In federal systems like Australia, Canada, Germany, Russia, and the United States governance authority is (at least partly) devolved to sub-national administration though the federal government also plays in important role in funding and regulating higher education. Regional differences have long been central to under-standing governance in federal systems. Further, given the importance attributed to regional dynamics and imperatives, such as migration trends or socio-economic asym-metries amongst domestic regions, higher education and regionalization policy agendas have converged in some countries like Norway and Finland (Pinheiro, 2012). This phenomenon, in turn, has augmented the complexity linked to governance mechanisms and the need to articulate policy frameworks that span across governmental agencies. This agency-spanning is often referred to in political science research as domestic multi-level governance arrangements (Piattoni, 2010).

Rationalized system differentiation can also be a function of pre-determined efforts by government to increase higher education enrolments across specific fields considered to be of importance to the socio-economic well-being of the country. Many countries promote enrolments in Science, Technology, Education, and Mathematics (STEM)-related fields because it is assumed these fields contribute to the development of the knowledge economy and global economic competitiveness (Freeman et al., 2014). Governments have also long engaged in efforts aimed at enhancing the participation by particular student groups such as ethnic minorities, women, students from lower socio-economic family backgrounds, peripheral regions, among others.

Policy energies aimed at achieving rationalized system differentiation are confronted by social aspirations to attain elite status. Rankings provide a tangible vehicle for the expression of aspirations to the elite. They act both as informal coordination and accountability mechanisms and as informal mechanisms that contribute to system differentiation (Hazelkorn, 2009; Kehm and Stensaker, 2009). A good example is Russia where regional development policy is contradicted by federal world-class university policy (5-in-100 programme). Rankings trigger strong tendencies to establish status tiers rather than to promote horizontal diversity through specialization, binary systems, or regional bases. Rankings have the effect of distinguishing between elite and non-elite universities, for example, by distinguishing elite research universities (top 100, 200, 500, etc.) from the rest. However, because universities are also ranked by subject area, global rankings also help to further differentiate among top research universities by identifying their particular focus, or areas of strength. All participants want to be ranked highly and many try vigorously to achieve improved standing, even if such efforts are in conflict with rationalized differentiation. Rankings and efforts to attain world-class status illustrate the potential for internal contradiction within ostensibly rational policy. While differentiation efforts seek to promote and support heterogeneity within systems, world-class and excellence projects at least implicitly define a single preferred model for higher education institutions (promoting drift), and many HPS pursue both goals simultaneously.

Consortia, especially those established by elite higher education institutions, also work to establish the normative standards that other higher education institutions within a particular system might aspire. Bodies like the Russell group in the UK, American Association of Universities (AAU) in the USA and Canada, U15 in Canada, and the Group of Eight in Australia, act as the standard-bearers in their respective systems. These influential bodies continuously work to redefine what it means to be a 'top' university, often in direct alignment with their own historical trajectories, key assets, and strategic aspirations. Membership roles of these groups serve as de facto registries of elite higher education institutions, tacitly marking non-members as 'non-elite' or simply ordinary. In addition to serving as a shorthand marker of stratification, organizations like the AAU and the Russell Group help to shape institutional mission by (re-)defining the sorts of activities and goals that are legitimate for top universities to pursue. Equally important, these groups help shape the institutional (rules) and technical (resources) landscapes in which higher education institutions operate, through actively lobbying and advising the state to promote their collective interests relative to the sector as a whole. These are social associations established by strategic actors in order to concentration status and resources on a club basis, and to exclude other higher education institutions from the possibility of encroaching on their positions. In his comprehensive, comparative analysis of four major international higher education consortia across Europe and Southeast Asia, Beerkens (2004: 225) found that such strategic initiatives, directly associated with an increasingly competitive global higher education environment/market (for students, staff, and status) (see Marginson, 2004), are 'not so much driven by academics and professionals in specific fields, but more by the leaders of the member institutions'. This factor alone attests to the importance associated with strategic agency and the role played by formal leadership structures within higher education institutions (see also Pinheiro and Stensaker, 2014a). The aspirations to prevail in competition for social status proves to be a powerful force that resists system rationalization.

INSTITUTIONAL MERGERS AND SYSTEM CONSOLIDATION

In a 2011 article Malcolm Tight asks how many universities there are in the UK and how many there should be. This seemingly simple question is important to the governance of HPS. As noted above, when more higher education institutions become universities the meaning of 'university' as a social category can be hollowed out. It would seem intuitive that as systems develop to HPS they expand in terms of the number of higher education institutions and may even become fragmented. While it is almost certain that, all else the same, systems with high levels of participation will host more higher education institutions than systems that have lower participation levels. Yet observation does not fully support the notion of unbounded expansion. In fact, mergers and other forms of consolation are quite typical in HPS.

Differentiation through system rationalization appears to be a common element of governance among HPS. However, as HPS mature differentiation seems to be a less important goal and at least some government actions have the effect of lessening differentiation. In the late 1980s and early 1990s governments in the UK, Norway, and Australia took action to convert a binary system into a unitary one, dissolving the formal distinction between the university and polytechnic sectors, and resulting in a much larger pool of university higher education institutions. More recently in the USA some of the states have passed legislation allowing community colleges, previously restricted to awarding sub-university qualifications and facilitating transfer to the university sector, to award qualifications equivalent to university degrees.

Institutional mergers are also commonplace among HPS. Mergers often involve the amalgamation of smaller specialized institutions into comprehensive universities in order to facilitate increased access to the university sector. Typically such actions are government mandated or government encouraged. Norway is an example case. Up to 2005 there were only four public universities, a number that doubled since as a result of mergers and the attainment (some providers) of full university status. While voluntary, merges were encouraged by government policy. Partly as a (unintended) result of policy shifts in the late 1990s/early 2000s, the traditional binary divide has gradually been eroded—driven by academic drift processes. Beyond mergers encouraged by HPS governments some higher education institutions themselves elect to consolidate in order to achieve greater status and efficiency.

Post-Communist systems offer good insight into the ways HPS both expand and contract in terms of institutional numbers. The initial period of massification in the post-Communist period of the 1990s saw explosive growth of a private sector in Poland. Fuelled by deregulation and the system opening up, social aspirations for higher education, and a population spike, demand in the system was initially absorbed by a growing private sector. Some private sector higher education institutions in Poland came to be seen as lower quality and lower status than the public university sector. As this realization spread and demographic shifts softened demand, enrolments shifted back to the public sector and the number of private higher education institutions declined considerably (Kwiek, 2016).

Enhanced Corporate Capacity

The third governance proposition (6) asserts:

HPS complex multi-level accountability and coordination, coupled with system differentiation, result in higher education institutions adopting increasingly corporate forms and robust internal governance and management capacities.

Higher education institutions develop management capacities that allow them to (some more effectively than others) navigate the complex technical, resource, and normative environments in which they are embedded. In other words, a proposed third common feature of governance in HPS is that higher education institutions develop enhanced internal coordination and management capacity (see for example Clark, 1998; Marginson and Considine, 2000; Slaughter and Cantwell, 2012). Many higher education institutions come to resemble corporate organizations in terms of internal divisions and management, as well as engagement in strategic action. The aim is not profit making, although revenue generation is a growing concern for many higher education institutions (Slaughter and Leslie, 1997). Rather, enhanced corporate capacity refers to developing the capacity to manage internal complexity, to respond to and defend against external demands, and to engage in strategic activity. A consequence of robust corporate capacity may be an emboldened administration and weakened faculty.

INSTITUTIONAL IDENTITY

The concept of social boundary deactivation helps to explain why HPS are necessarily exposed to heightened stakeholder demands and multi-level governance arrangements. Attending entirely to boundary deactivation, however, points exclusively to external drivers. The environment clearly matters in shaping HPS governance, but can the control and coordination of higher education be attributed entirely to external conditions? The short answer is no. In writings from the 1970s and the start of twenty-first century, Trow (1974, 2000) argues the high participation was accompanied with changes in academic culture. Rather than understanding themselves as assemblages of disciplinary subjects bound together not by institutional affiliation but through common regard for disciplinary and occupational professional identities, in systems of mass participation higher education institutions tend to see themselves, at least partially, as corporate organizations with distinctive identities (cf. Fumasoli et al., 2015). Higher education institutions are sometimes even thought of as 'brands'. Internal divisions and multiple missions are not eliminated. In fact these may multiply among HPS institutions, but activities moving in multiple directions are held together by the centripetal force of institutional identity. As HPS develop, institutional (corporate) identity becomes increasingly important vis-à-vis disciplinary and occupational identities.

Weick (1976) identifies a tacit association between distinct parts as the 'glue' that binds educational organizations together. Although coordination is difficult in loosely coupled organizations, strategic capability may be enhanced when corporate identities are formalized as institutions. To put it another way, if 'governance is just a processes that permits people to work together' (Birnbaum, 1988: 229) a good measure of the togetherness that permits work to get done is achieved through the manufacture of a common institutional identity (Tierney, 1988). And as is often true of imagined communities (Anderson, 2006), the bulwark of identity is bureaucracy and administrative capacity. Consider the widely accepted notion that academics identify not only with their discipline but also with their department. The context of this observation is crucial. Direct writing on the topic comes from a study of the academic profession in the USA post-massification and is accompanied with observations about increased specialization and heightened division of labour (Clark, 1983). The verb 'divide' of course means to split asunder but as a noun—the multi-divisional firm, for instance—divisions are the building blocks of enterprise at scale.

Take for example three prominent studies on organization and systems transformation in high participation countries: Clark's (1998) *Creating Entrepreneurial Universities*, Marginson and Considine's (2000) *The Enterprise University*, and Slaughter and Leslie's (1997) *Academic Capitalism*. These books are not the same but in different ways each points to heightened organizational behaviour by higher education institutions, such as resource seeking and inter-organizational competition, and to the ascendance of a corporate identity and managerial capacity among institutions. The critiques are well-known. Clark's book is the most optimistic and was probably too sanguine about the possibility of preserving the academic heartland by empowering a management core. Revenue generation, competition, commercialization, university branding, and the like can and do draw higher education institutions into self-interested pursuits; can and do lead to the dilution of academic culture; can and do nip at academic freedom and scholarly independence; can and do open up the possibility to exploit students as consumers. But from Clark, one can pluck the reality of academic and corporate identities forming a hybrid identity that charters higher education institutions in mass systems. The administrative prerogative to define, even brand, higher education institutions generally seems to grow as HPS develop. Of course there is some variation. The faculties likely have more power, and academic cultures and identities are likely stronger among the most elite institutions within a given system. Moreover there is variably between systems as well. English-speaking countries as well as some Asian systems have adopted corporate institutional forms more fully than those in Continental Europe.

MANAGERIAL DEVOLUTION

The ways in which higher education institutions develop internal governance capacity varies based on system context and decisions made by individual institutions, as does the number and depth of administrative tasks directly regulated and controlled through policy. With that disclaimer entered, it appears mass participation leads to managerial devolution from policymakers and ministries to campus leaders. In the development of HPS, states move to lighten their political and administrative burden by both reducing the general policy issues for which they claim responsibility, and devolving management of institutions to the institutions, and sometimes sub-national levels.[2] By way of example, it is increasingly common to describe administrative decisions as 'policy' even though higher education institutions are not states. This tendency towards managerial devolution—even adopting state-like authority—may be both a response to the development of institutional identities as well as a driver of corporate institutions. This process of devolution is sometimes described as 'steering from a distance' whereby governments establish broad parameters to which higher education institutions are held accountable but allow individual institutions or sub-national regions (state or provincial governments) to specify specific goals and the means by which they are to be accomplished (Marginson, 1997).

Devolution of management of technical, strategic, and specialized operations to institutions is commonplace. Often this involves the development of specialized offices, staffed by non-academic professionals who are charged with control over a particular domain. Universities, especially those with a strong research mission, develop specialized, technical units to manage their research and development operations. In fact, many higher education institutions now host a number of specialized units to manage various aspects of the academic research enterprise. An extensive, but not exhaustive list of examples include units that aid researchers in securing research grants, units that manage intellectual property, and units that ensure ethical practices in research, units for managing the competition of data on various intuitional activities, units for facilitating students' transitions to the labor market, units that monitory and manage student engagement, and units that monitor and manage ranking positions. Some institutions have also developed sophisticated systems of internal research support as a means of targeting what is perceived to be strategic research areas (Rip, 2004; Pinheiro and Stensaker, 2014b). Many HPS higher education institutions have specialized units dedicated to human resource management, units charged with both managing student enrolments, but also that manage student social, health, and academic services (Seeman and O'Hara, 2006). Most institutions in HPS, especially those that are charged with generating part of their own operating budget, develop specialized accounting and financial management systems (Toma, 2010). Institutions in HPS develop specialized units for managing affairs with the government, industry, and other external stakeholders (Fisher and Atkinson-Grosjean, 2002; Vorley and Nelles, 2012). These units are involved in accountably and regulatory compliance, scan the environment to anticipate significant regulatory and resource flow changes, and lobby stakeholders in order to secure more favourable conditions for the sector and individual institutional position.

Managerial devolution tends also to include increased autonomy and responsibility for establishing and minting the 'image' and reputation of institutions. Hence, expanded

---

[2] Thanks to Simon Marginson for drawing out this idea.

administrative capacity and institutional identity development frequently involves 'branding' and public relations efforts. Higher education institutions in mass systems manage their identities, similar to corporate brands. Some institutions develop special-ized offices dedicated to communication, media-relations, branding, and marketing. Branding is partly related to broader efforts dedicated to achieving strategic advantage (through adaptation) in the market place. But branding and marking also signify a need to maintain institutional identity (stability) in a complex and cluttered field (Stensaker, 2007). Some aspects of image management involve things like logos, developing slogans, and mission statements, but part of it also involves demonstrating social responsiveness and accountability, through efforts like 'civic engagement' (Watson et al., 2011). The quest to manage image in HPS indicates that in complex systems higher education institutions cannot rely alone on the general social standing of the sector to secure and maintain external legitimacy, but instead must reinvigorate their individual identities to secure a competitive position within the system or organizational field (Stensaker, 2014; Fumasoli et al., 2015).

Summary and Conclusion

HPS, by their definition, reach a large segment of society. In many countries this also translates to relatively large systems in absolute terms, with many thousands and sometimes millions of students who participate among a large number of higher education institutions. These facts alone suggest that governing HPS is a complex matter. Because HPSs are found in a great variety of countries with different histories, cultures, governance structures, and resource levels it is inevitable that there can be no single model of governance among HPS.

What does all of this imply about the governance of HPSs in a general sense? All HPS are not governed in the same ways. And one cannot credibly claim that there is convergence into a single governance model. Nevertheless the main three propositions advanced in this chapter provide a useful generic starting point from which to conduct further conceptual and empirical analysis into the nature and function of HPS gov-ernance in specific contexts. While it is impossible to make specific predictions about what governance *should look like* within a particular HPS, or what governance *will look like* as participation continues to expand, it is reasonable—indented prudent—to approach the study of governance within HPS from a foundation on the broad elements that are likely present within these systems. Namely, that HPS involves some amount of multi-level coordination with a plurality of stakeholders (rather than singular state control); that governance involves both some mechanisms that differentiate the system as well as the tendency towards intuitional drift; and that, higher education institutions tend to develop institutional identities and corresponding corporate capacities. Attending to these propositions will help to avoid simplistic and flat accounts, for example, of total market control, of an omnipotent ministry/state, or of a static academic profession. Accounts of governance in HPS that do not attend to complexity, and nuance (even contradiction) should be approached sceptically.

▉ REFERENCES

Agasisti, T., Cappiello, G., and Catalano, G. (2008). The effects of vouchers in higher education: An Italian case study. *Tertiary Education and Management* 14(1), 27–42.

Amaral, A., Meek, V. L., and Larsen, I. M. (2003). *The Higher Education Managerial Revolution?* Dordrecht: Kluwer Academic Publishers.

Amaral, Neave, G. Musselin, C., and Maassen, P. (2009). *European Integration and the Governance of Higher Education and Research*. Dordrecht: Springer.

Anderson, B. (2006). *Imagined Communities: Reflections on the Origin and Spread of Nationalism*. London: Verso Books.

Austin, I. and Jones, G. A. (2016). *Governance of Higher Education: Global Perspectives, Theories, and Practices*. New York: Routledge.

Bailey, M. and Freedman, D. (2011). *The Assault on Universities: A Manifesto for Resistance*. London: Pluto.

Baldridge, J. V. (1971). *Power and Conflict in the University: Research in the Sociology of Complex Organizations*. New York: Wiley.

Balbachevsky, E. (2015). The role of internal and external stakeholders in Brazilian higher education. In S. Schwartzman, R. Pinheiro, and P. Pillay (eds), *Higher Education in the BRICS Countries*. Dordrecht: Springer, pp. 193–214.

Bastedo, M. N. and Gumport, P. J. (2003). Access to what? Mission differentiation and academic stratification in US public higher education. *Higher Education* 46(3), 341–59.

Beerkens, E. (2004). Global opportunities and institutional embeddedness: Higher education consortia in Europe and Southeast Asia. Unpublished Doctoral dissertation, University of Twente, Enschede.

Benneworth, P., Coenen, L., Moodysson, J., and Asheim, B. (2009). Exploring the multiple roles of Lund University in strengthening Scania's regional innovation system: Towards institutional learning? *European Planning Studies* 17(11), 1645–64.

Benneworth, P. and Jongbloed, B. (2010). Who matters to universities? A stakeholder perspective on humanities, arts and social sciences valorisation. *Higher Education* 59(5), 567–88.

Birnbaum, R. (1988). *How Colleges Work: The Cybernetics of Academic Organization and Leadership*. San Francisco: Jossey-Bass Publishers.

Bowman, N. A. and Bastedo, M. N. (2011). Anchoring effects in world university rankings: Exploring biases in reputation scores. *Higher Education* 61(4), 431–44.

Burns, T. and Köster, F. (2016). Modern governance challenges in education. In T. Burns, and F. Köster (eds), *Governing Education in a Complex World*. Paris: OECD Publishing, pp. 18–39.

Castells, M. (2001). Universities as dynamic systems of contradictory functions. In J. Muller, N. Cloete, and S. Badat (eds), *Challenges of Globalisation: South African Debates with Manuel Castells*. Cape Town: Maskew Miller Longman, pp. 206–33.

Clark, B. R. (1983). *The Higher Education System: Academic Organization in Cross-national Perspective*. Los Angeles, CA: University of California Press.

Clark, B. R. (1987). *The Academic Life: Small Worlds, Different Worlds*. A Carnegie Foundation Special Report. Princeton: Princeton University Press.

Clark, B. R. (1989). The academic life small worlds, different worlds. *Educational Researcher* 18(5), 4–8.

Clark, B. R. (1998). *Creating Entrepreneurial Universities: Organizational Pathways of Transformation*. New York: Elsevier Science Regional Sales.

Cloete, N., Maassen, P., Fehnel, R., Moja, T., Gibbon, T., and Perold, H. (2006). *Transformation in Higher Education: Global Pressures and Local Realities*. Dordrecht: Springer.

Cohen, M. D., March, J. G., and Olsen, J. P. (1972). A garbage can model of organizational choice. *Administrative science quarterly* 17, 1–25.

Deem, R. and Brehony, K. J. (2005). Management as ideology: The case of 'new managerialism' in higher education. *Oxford Review of Education* 31(2), 217–35.

Dill, D. D. (1997). Higher education markets and public policy. *Higher Education Policy* 10(3–4), 167–85.

DiMaggio, P. J. and Powell, W. W. (1983). The iron cage revisited: Institutional isomorphism and collective rationality in organizational fields. *American Sociological Review* 48, 147–60.

Fisher, D. and Atkinson-Grosjean, J. (2002). Brokers on the boundary: Academy-industry liaison in Canadian universities. *Higher Education* 44(3), 449–67.

Freeman, B., Marginson, S., and Tytler, R. (eds) (2014). *The Age of STEM: Educational Policy and Practice across the World in Science, Technology, Engineering and Mathematics*. London: Routledge.

Fumasoli, T., Pinheiro, R., and Stensaker, B. (2015). Handling uncertainty of strategic ambitions: The use of organizational identity as a risk-reducing device. *International Journal of Public Administration* 38(13–14), 1030–40.

Gornitzka, Å. and Maassen, P. A. M. (2000). Hybrid steering approaches with respect to European higher education. *Higher Education Policy* 13(3), 267–85.

Gornitzka, Å. and Maassen, P. (2011). University governance reforms, global scripts and the 'Nordic Model'. Accounting for policy change? In J. Schmid, K. Amos, and A. T. Schrader (eds), *Welten der Bildung? Vergleichende Analysen von Bildungspolitik und Bildungssystemen*. Baden-Baden: Nomos Verlagsgesellschaft, pp. 143–71.

Gornitzka, Å., Maassen, P., Olsen, J. P., and Stensaker, B. (2007). 'Europe of knowledge': Search for a new pact. In P. Maassen and J. P. Olsen (eds), *University Dynamics and European Integration*, vol. 19. Dordrecht: Springer, pp. 181–214.

Hazelkorn, H. (2009). Rankings and the battle for World-Class Excellence: Institutional strategies and policy choice. *Higher Education Management and Policy* 21(1), 1–22.

Hazelkorn, E. (2011). *Rankings and the Reshaping of Higher Education: The Battle for World-Class Excellence*. New York: Palgrave Macmillan.

Heller, D. E. and Callender, C. (2013). *Student Financing of Higher Education: A Comparative Perspective*. New York: Routledge.

Henisz, W. J., Zelner, B. A., and Guillén, M. F. (2005). The worldwide diffusion of market-oriented infrastructure reform, 1977–1999. *American Sociological Review* 70(6), 871–97.

Hillman, N., Tandberg, D., and Gross, J. K. (2014). Market-based higher education: Does Colorado's voucher model improve higher education access and efficiency? *Research in Higher Education* 55(6), 601–25.

Jones, G. A. (2013). The horizontal and vertical fragmentation of academic work and the challenge for academic governance and leadership. *Asia Pacific Education Review* 14(1), 75–83.

Jongbloed, B. (2003). Marketisation in higher education, Clark's triangle and the essential ingredients of markets. *Higher Education Quarterly* 57(2), 110–35.

Jongbloed, B. (2010). *Funding Higher Education: A View Across Europe.* Brussels: ESMU.

Jongbloed, B., Enders, J., and Salerno, C. (2008). Higher education and its communities: Interconnections, interdependencies and a research agenda. *Higher Education* 56(3), 303–24.

Kauppinen, I. and Kaidesoja, T. (2014). A shift towards academic capitalism in Finland. *Higher Education Policy* 27(1), 23–41.

Kehm, B. and Pasternack, P. (2009). The German 'excellence initiative' and its role in restructuring the national higher education landscape. In D. Palfreyman and T. Tapper (eds), *Structuring Mass Higher Education: The Role of Elite Institutions.* London: Routledge, pp. 113–28.

Kehm, B. M. and Stensaker, B. (2009). *University Rankings, Diversity, and the New Landscape of Higher Education.* Rotterdam: Sense Publishers.

Kehm, B. M. and Teichler, U. (2013). *The Academic Profession in Europe: New Tasks and New Challenges.* Dordrecht: Springer London, Limited.

Kerr, C. (2001). *The Uses of the University.* Cambridge, MA: Harvard University Press.

Knapper, C. and Cropley, A. J. (2000). *Lifelong Learning in Higher Education.* London: Kogan Page.

Kwiek, M. (2016). From privatization (of the expansion era) to de-privatization (of the contraction era): A national counter-trend in a global context. In S. Slaughter, and B. J. Taylor (eds), *Higher Education, Stratification, and Workforce Development.* Dordrecht: Springer, pp. 311–29).

Kwiek, M. and Maassen, P. (2012). *National Higher Education Reforms in a European Context: Comparative Reflections on Poland and Norway.* Berlin: Peter Lang.

Marginson, S. (1997). *Markets in Education.* St Leonards: Allen & Unwin.

Marginson, S. (2004). Competition and markets in higher education: A 'glonacal' analysis. *Policy Futures in Education* 2(2), 175–244.

Marginson, S. (2013). The impossibility of capitalist markets in higher education. *Journal of Education Policy* 28(3), 353–70.

Marginson, S. and Considine, M. (2000). *The Enterprise University: Power, Governance and Reinvention in Australia.* Cambridge: Cambridge University Press.

Marginson, S. and Rhoades, G. (2002). Beyond national states, markets, and systems of higher education: A glonacal agency heuristic. *Higher Education* 43(3), 281–309.

Mok, J. K. and Yue, K. (2015). Promoting entrepreneurship and innovation in China: Transformations in university curriculum and research capacity. In S. Schwartzman, R. Pinheiro, and P. Pillay (eds), *Higher Education in Three BRICS Countries.* Dordrecht: Springer.

Morphew, C. C. and Huisman, J. (2002). Using institutional theory to reframe research on academic drift. *Higher Education in Europe* 27(4), 491–506.

Morphew, C. C. and Swanson, C. (2011). On the efficacy of raising your university's rankings. *University Rankings*. Dordrecht: Springer, pp. 185–99.

Olssen, M. and Peters, M. A. (2005). Neoliberalism, higher education and the knowledge economy: From the free market to knowledge capitalism. *Journal of Education Policy* 20(3), 313–45.

Ordorika, I. (2003). *Power and Politics in University Governance: Organization and Change at the Universidad Nacional Autonoma de Mexico*. New York: RutledgeFalmer Press.

Piattoni, S. (2010). *The Theory of Multi-level Governance: Conceptual, Empirical, and Normative Challenges*. Oxford: Oxford University Press.

Pinheiro, R. (2012). Knowledge and the 'Europe of the Regions': The case of the High North. In M. Kwiek and P. Maassen (eds), *National Higher Education Reforms in a European Context: Comparative Reflections on Poland and Norway*. Frankfurt: Peter Lang Publishing Group, pp. 179–208.

Pinheiro, R. (2013). Bridging the local with the global: Building a new university on the fringes of Europe. *Tertiary Education and Management* 19(2), 144–60.

Pinheiro, R. and Antonowicz, D. (2015a). Opening the gates or coping with the flow? Governing access to higher education in Europe. *Higher Education* 70(3), 299–313.

Pinheiro, R. and Antonowicz, D. (2015b). I am tired of reading history: I want to make it! In M. Klemenčič, S. Bergan, and R. Primožič (eds), *Student Engagement in Europe: Society, Higher Education and Student Governance*. Strasbourg: Council of Europe Publishing.

Pinheiro, R. and Kyvik, S. (2009). Norway: Separate but connected. In N. Garrod and B. Macfarlane (eds), *Challenging Boundaries: Managing the Integration of Post-secondary Education*. New York: Routledge, pp. 47–58.

Pinheiro, R. and Stensaker, B. (2014a). Designing the entrepreneurial university: The interpretation of a global idea. *Public Organization Review* 14(4), 497–516.

Pinheiro, R. and Stensaker, B. (2014b). Strategic actor-hood and internal transformation: The rise of the quadruple-helix university? In J. Brankovik, M. Klemencik, P. Lazetic, and P. Zgaga (eds), *Global Challenges, Local Responses in Higher Education: The Contemporary Issues in National and Comparative Perspective*. Rotterdam: Sense, pp. 171–89.

Pinheiro, R., Benneworth, P., and Jones, G. A. (2012). *Universities and Regional Development: A Critical Assessment of Tensions and Contradictions*. New York: Routledge.

Pinheiro, R., Charles, D., and Jones, G. A. (2013). Equity, institutional diversity and regional development: A cross-country comparison. CHER Annual Conference, Lausanne.

Pinheiro, R., Geschwind, L., and Aarrevaara, T. (2014). Nested tensions and interwoven dilemmas in higher education: The view from the Nordic countries. *Cambridge Journal of Regions, Economy and Society* 7(2), 233–50.

Pinheiro, R., Geschwind, L., Hansen, H., and Pekkola, E. (2015). Academic leadership in the Nordic countries: Patterns of gender equality. In H. Syna and C. Costea (eds), *Women's Voices in Management: Identifying Innovative and Responsible Solutions*. London: Palgrave Macmillan.

Pusser, B. (2004). *Burning Down the House: Politics, Governance, and Affirmative Action at the University of California*. Albany: State University of New York Press.

Pusser, B. (2008). The state, the market and the institutional estate: Revisiting contemporary authority relations in higher education. In J. Smart (ed.), *Higher Education*. Dordrecht: Springer, pp. 105–39.

Ramirez, F. O. (2010). Accounting for excellence: Transforming universities into organizational actors. In L. Portnoi, V. Rust, and S. Bagely (eds), *Higher Education, Policy, and the Global Competition Phenomenon*. Basingstoke: Palgrave, pp. 43–58.

Ramirez, F. O. and Christensen, T. (2013). The formalization of the university: Rules, roots, and routes. *Higher Education* 65(6), 695–708.

Rip, A. (2004). Strategic research, post-modern universities and research training. *Higher Education Policy* 17(2), 153–66.

Rojas, F. (2007). *From Black Power to Black Studies: How a Radical Social Movement became an Academic Discipline*. London: JHU Press.

Salazar, J. and Leihy, P. (2013). Keeping up with coordination: From Clark's triangle to microcosmographia. *Studies in Higher Education* 38(1), 53–70.

Salmi, J. (2009). *The Challenge of Establishing World-Class Universities*. Washington, DC: World Bank Publications.

Schmidtlein, F. and Berdahl, R. (2005). Autonomy and accountability: Who controls academe? In P. Altbach, R. Berdahl, and P. Gumport (eds), *American Higher Education in the Twenty-first Century: Social, Political, and Economic Challenges*. Baltimore: Johns Hopkins University Press, pp. 71–90.

Schwartzman, S., Pinheiro, R., and Pillay, P. (2015). *Higher Education in the BRICS Countries*. Dordrecht: Springer.

SEAMEO (2012). *A Study on Quality Assurance Models in Southeast Asian Countries: Towards a Southeast Asian Quality Assurance Framework*. Bangkok: SEAMEO RIHED.

Seeman, E. D. and O'Hara, M. (2006). Customer relationship management in higher education: Using information systems to improve the student-school relationship. *Campus-Wide Information Systems* 23(1), 24–34.

Slaughter, S. and Cantwell, B. (2012). Transatlantic moves to the market: The United States and the European Union. *Higher Education* 63(5), 583–606.

Slaughter, S. and Leslies, L. (1997). *Academic Capitalism*. Baltimore, NJ: Johns Hopkins University Press.

Slaughter, S. and Rhoades, G. (2004). *Academic Capitalism and the New Economy: Markets, State, and Higher Education*. Baltimore, NJ: Johns Hopkins University Press.

Stensaker, B. (2007). The relationship between branding and organisational change. *Higher Education Management and Policy* 19(1), 13–30.

Stensaker, B. (2014). Organizational identity as a concept for understanding university dynamics. *Higher Education* 69(1), 103–15.

Tapper, T. and Palfreyman, D. (2005). *Understanding Mass Higher Education: Comparative Perspectives on Access*. Milton Park: RoutledgeFalmer.

Tapper, T. and Palfreyman, D. (2011). *Oxford, the Collegiate University: Conflict, Consensus and Continuity*. Dordrecht: Springer.

Taylor, B. J., Cantwell, B., and Slaughter, S. (2013). Quasi-markets in US higher education: The humanities and institutional revenues. *The Journal of Higher Education* 84(5), 675–707.

Tierney, W. G. (1988). Organizational culture in higher education: Defining the essentials. *The Journal of Higher Education* 59(1), 2–21.

Tight, M. (2011). How many universities are there in the United Kingdom? How many should there be? *Higher Education* 62(5), 649–63.

Tilly, C. (2004). Social boundary mechanisms. *Philosophy of the Social Sciences* 34(2), 211–36.

Toma, J. D. (2010). *Building Organizational Capacity: Strategic Management in Higher Education*. Baltimore: Johns Hopkins University Press.

Trow, M. (1970). Reflections on the transition from mass to universal higher education. *Daedalus* 99(1), 1–42.

Trow, M. (1974). Problems in the transition from elite to mass higher education. *The General Report on the Conference on the Future Structures of Post-secondary Education*. Paris: OECD, pp. 55–101.

Trow, M. (2000). From mass higher education to universal access: The American advantage. *Minerva* 37(4), 303–28.

Trow, M. and Burrage, M. (2010). *Twentieth-Century Higher Education: Elite to Mass to Universal*. Baltimore: Johns Hopkins University Press.

Trowler, P., Saunders, M., and Bamber, V. (2012). *Tribes and Territories in the 21st Century: Rethinking the Significance of Disciplines in Higher Education*. New York: Taylor & Francis.

Vorley, T. and Nelles, J. (2012). Scaling entrepreneurial architecture: The challenge of managing regional technology transfer in Hamburg. In R. Pinheiro, P. Benneworth, and G. A. Jones (eds), *Universities and Regional Development: A Critical Assessment of Tensions and Contradictions*. Milton Park: Routledge, pp. 181–98.

Watson, D., Hollister, R., Stround, S., and Babcok, E. (2011). *The Engaged University: International Perspectives on Civic Engagement*. London: Routledge.

Weick, K. E. (1976). Educational organizations as loosely coupled systems. *Administrative Science Quarterly* 21(1), 1–19.

4 Horizontal Diversity

*Dominik Antonowicz, Brendan Cantwell, Isak Froumin, Glen A. Jones,
Simon Marginson, and Rómulo Pinheiro*

> The 'Idea of a University' was a village with its priests. The 'Idea of a Modern University' was a town—a one-industry town—with its intellectual oligarchy. 'The Idea of a Multiversity' is a city of infinite variety.
>
> (Kerr 1963: 31)

Introduction

Burton R. Clark remarks that 'individual universities and colleges face the fateful decision of whether to strive for greater distinctiveness, and hence to differentiate oneself more from peers, or to find protection in similarity' (Clark, 1983: 223). System managers face a parallel question of whether to encourage or to regulate for more diversity, or less, or to step back and allow the play of resources and power to shape the mix of provision. In a larger system with a more complex social mix of students and stakeholders there is a natural tendency towards great variety of provision, is there not? But is that what actually happens? This chapter explores diversity in higher education in the context of high participation systems (HPS). What can we learn about HPS through the lens of diversity of mission and type of institution? Is diversity associated with more or less growth; and is growth associated with more or less diversity? What can the study of HPS tell us about the respective dynamics of inter-institutional (external) and intra-institutional (internal) diversity? How do patterns of diversity vary in different kinds of HPS?

Diversity in higher education has many aspects, and is itself subject to diverse understandings across the world. The focus here is largely on systemic diversity, meaning horizontal differences in institutional mission, form and type; and internal diversity within institutions. The chapter also notes structural diversity resulting from legal foundations or authority/governance, such as public/private sector variety. Vertical diversity in the social value and resources attached to institutions (stratification) is the topic of the next chapter.

COMPETITION AND DIVERSITY

Research and scholarship have failed to resolve the relation between growth and diversity. Given that massification is a strong and near universal tendency and has been central to higher education in North America, Europe, Russia, Australia, and Japan for half a century, it is surprising to find studies of diversity are largely decoupled from studies of growth, but there is some research at the intersection between the two (e.g. the comparative case studies in Shavit et al., 2007). One strand of work seeks to establish a one-to-one causal relation between diversity and growth. Two problems block this endeavour. First, diversity itself has many aspects and is not reducible to a single indicator. Second, there are too many contextual factors in play that can affect diversity, including policy contingency and the ongoing differences between systems, to derive a robust quantitative relation between expansion and diversity of provision that will hold up across time and space—that is, a generic equation. Comparative cross-country data studies face the problem that all is not equal in the different cases. For example, some HPS are more engaged in neoliberal marketization than are others and this affects the outcome. Such studies are inconclusive or unduly shaped by the selection of cases.

In the absence of clear-cut empirical tests of the relation between growth and diversity, there has been a continuing debate between advocates and sceptics of the market diversity myth. That is the claim that market competition and diversity necessarily go together. Here the diversity issue has been enlisted in a larger war. Advocates of the market diversity myth argue that when government steps back, allowing market competition free play, growth leads to diversity of provision, and diversity facilitates growth—as if higher education institutions emerge, evolve and specialize in response to diverse needs in the manner of retail services. Institutional diversity is said to increase the range of market choices available to students, better match their needs to educational programmes via a supply/demand conjunction, and respond to complex labour markets (e.g. Birnbaum, 1983). It is also argued that diversity allows elite and mass higher education to co-exist, facilitating growth (e.g. Palfreyman and Tapper, 2008). Empirical research in this tradition looks for a virtuous circle of competition, diversity, and growth. The virtuous circle's failure to appear is blamed on undue state intervention. The assumptions remain intact. On the other hand, in higher education studies for two decades there has been growing scepticism. Empirical studies persistently find that market competition enhances diversity in the sense of unequal status and resources, but is associated with less not more diversity of organizational type and mission (e.g. Meek, 2000). The sceptics note that higher education does not function like an orthodox economic market (e.g. Marginson, 2013). They point to the prevalence of isomorphic (imitative) institutional behaviour and institutional tendencies of upward academic 'drift' to the research role (Neave, 1979). This school argues that government can either foster and suppress diversity. It is a matter of policy choice.

The scepticism about marketization and diversity is well-placed. Competition does not always foster mimetic behaviour—take for example the competitive, successful, and original global strategy of the Singapore universities—but the tendency to mission convergence is too strong to ignore. Yet rejection of the market diversity myth is not enough for a theorization of HPS and diversity. The dominance of the market diversity debate indicates not its profound relevance to the diversity issue but the tenacious hold of marketization narratives on the policy imagination. Preoccupation with refuting (or defending) the market diversity myth has become unhelpful, blocking a more nuanced consideration of diversity in HPS. Likewise, to pose the problematic as 'what is the one-to-one causal relation between growth and diversification?' is another *cul de sac*, given that a definitive answer is impossible.

A better question is 'what systemic and institutional configurations are typical of higher education in the HPS era, and why?' What forms, homogenized or diversified, are present? With that answered, secular tendencies in the growth/diversity relation can be discussed.

PROPOSITIONS CONCERNING DIVERSITY IN HPS

Following this introduction, the chapter briefly reviews scholarship on diversity in higher education. It then discusses the institutional configurations, system designs and secular trends associated with HPS, including the 'multiversity' (Kerr, 1963), its internal diversity, and changes in other kinds of higher education institutions. The conclusion sums up the overall outcome of diversity in HPS and the intersection between neoliberal policies and diversity.

In the HPS era, the main features of the organizational environment that bear on diversity are threefold, as outlined in HPS Propositions 7–10. First, the rise of the multiversity, the large comprehensive research university, to a more dominant role, together with enlargement of the size and scope of individual multiversities. Second, reduction in the role of semi-horizontal binary distinctions, and single-purpose institutions, and decline in diversity in the horizontal sense overall, with the exception of online forms and in some countries the growing role for for-profit private sectors (see Proposition 10). Third, increased internal diversity within the comprehensive multi-purpose institutions. These three features of the landscape, or rather the extension and enhancement of these three features, can be understood as secular tendencies in HPS. Like other secular tendencies characteristic of the HPS era such as the bifurcation of the growing systems (Chapter 5) and greater inequality in access to elite institutions (Chapter 6), these three tendencies can be over-determined by policy and regulation. For example, governments in some countries do maintain binary systems despite the tide in favour of the academic research multiversity. However, the three secular tendencies show in any HPS where they can freely emerge. Despite the potentials of system managed diversity the three secular tendencies are sufficiently strong to be clearly apparent at world level.

- *In the HPS era, regardless of the political economy and culture of systems, an increasing proportion of higher education becomes centred on comprehensive multi-discipline and multi-function research universities, or 'multiversities'. The multiversity is increasingly dominant as the paradigmatic form of higher education.*
- *Regardless of the political economy and culture of the HPS, when participation expands there is no necessary increase in the overall diversity of institutional form and mission; and this has probably declined, except in relation to online provision.*
- *As participation expands the internal diversity of multiversities tends to increase. This affects some or all of the range of missions, business activities, institutional forms and internal structures, the discipline mix, research activities, levels of study and range of credentials, the heterogeneity of the student body, links to stakeholders, cross-border relations, and forms of academic and non-academic labour.*
- *All else being equal, the combination of expanding participation and enhanced competition in neoliberal quasi-markets is associated with specific effects in relation to diversity, including (1) increased vertical differentiation of higher education institutes (HEIs) (stratification); (2) reduced horizontal differentiation (diversification); (3) convergence of missions through isomorphistic imitation; and (4) growth in the role of private HEIs, especially for-profit institutions.*

Global university ranking further institutionalizes the multiversity form.

Diversity in Higher Education

How is institutional diversity within systems observed and measured? Birnbaum (1983) distinguishes between 'diversity', meaning difference in terms of specific characteristics of higher education institutions, and 'differentiation' or diversification, movement towards increasing diversity. He also distinguishes external diversity between institutions from internal diversity within them. Birnbaum uses several variables to record difference between institutions and establish categories: size, legal foundations, mode of control (state or private sector), disciplinary programme, degree level, services, procedural differences in teaching or research, climate and values, differences in the student body including age, sex, and ethnic origins. There is also reputational diversity, perceived differences in status or prestige. Birnbaum's simple measure of diversity is the number of types divided by the total number of higher education institutions. Wang and Zha (2015) identify three structural notions of diversity. Systems are more diverse if they include a greater number of institutional types, if the distribution of higher education institutions between the main institutional types is more evenly weighted, and if there is greater distance in kind between the institutional types.

Huisman and colleagues (2015) use five main indicators of difference: institutional size (student enrolments); forms of institutional control (public or private); disciplinary fields; types of degrees; and modes of study (full-time or part-time, short or long cycle, etc.). These indicators are used to compare a selection of Organisation for Economic Co-operation and Development (OECD) countries. The researchers find 'there is no textbook recipe for how to measure diversity . . . the selection of dimensions, variables and analytical methods' must be seen in terms of 'the goal of the study and its analytical framework', the characteristics of measures and variables, 'and their contextualization in the specific empirical setting' (p. 12). They also note that interpretations of diversity are diverse by context, a point made also in a report on diversity across five higher education systems commissioned by the European University Association (EUA) (Reichert, 2009: 122).

Nevertheless, generic concepts are within reach. An important distinction is that of vertical and horizontal diversity. For Teichler (1996: 118) vertical diversity distinguishes higher education institutions by 'quality, reputation and prospective status of graduates'. Horizontal diversity refers to 'the specific profile of knowledge, style of teaching and learning, problem-solving thrust'. Horizontal diversity can also include differences in mission, governance, or internal organizational culture. In this book the term 'diversity' refers to horizontal variety in higher education, the main subject of this chapter. 'Stratification' is used for the vertical dimension. Teichler also notes that the weightiest distinction between different higher education institutions derives from comparisons of research intensity. Research standing affects mission, and is so important in higher education and so readily measured—for example, in competitive funding rounds (Horta et al., 2008: 156) and most rankings (Marginson, 2014)—that the research/non-research distinction always has positional implications (Teichler, 2008: 351–2).

National HPS structures vary in the extent of horizontal diversity, vertical stratification, or both. The competitive unitary systems in the United Kingdom (UK) and Australia have little horizontal diversity and are ordered in a steep but informal hierarchy in which research and student selectivity play the differentiating role. Classically the Nordic and German-speaking systems used primarily horizontal diversity in binary systems though informal vertical differentiation and in Germany formal hierarchy has been gaining ground. Other systems such as the United States of America (USA), China, Russia, and parts of Latin America are vectored by both horizontal and vertical differentiation. Classifications in China and the USA order an explicit hierarchy, while they also manage mission differentiation with horizontal implications.

THE AMERICAN EXPERIENCE

Much of the scholarly literature on diversity in higher education derives from the US experience. This has had a shaping effect on the discussion. In the USA historical variations between states and in private sector institutions have produced a complex mix of research and Doctoral universities, liberal arts colleges largely used by elite families, lesser public universities, public community colleges, for-profit corporate colleges, vocational education arrangements, and on-the-job training. The Carnegie classifications hierarchy is also functional, with missions distinctions between tiers. Except for the distinction between Doctoral universities and liberal arts colleges, both elite sectors, the distinctions between tiers are steeper (less 'flat') than distinctions within tiers. However, same tier higher education institutions compete with each other and are routinely ranked. This plethora of types, which has become associated with the idea of a system-market, is seen (at least at home) as central to the virtues of American higher education. Institutional diversity is frequently positioned as an innate good based on a set of related assumptions:

it supposedly increases the range of choices for students, it opens higher education up to all of society, it matches education to the needs and abilities of individual students, it enables and protects specialization within the system, and it meets the demands of an increasingly complex social order.   (Goedegebuure et al., 1996: 9)

By fostering the access of diverse students with diverse needs, institutional diversity facilitates both universal opportunity and natural system growth. Given American geo-political preponderance, it is probably because in the USA diversity and market became associated in the first HPS that the narrative joining market, diversity, growth, and access became installed as a global policy norm. The geopolitical factor also helps to explain the central place of the work of Birnbaum (1983) in studies of diversity.

However, American institutional diversity preceded not just 50 per cent participation but 15 per cent mass participation and the ideology of the system market. Historically, diversity was not an outcome of either massification or market competition. This still leaves room for the alternate marketization narrative, that decentralized competition and diversity were the condition of growth. Nevertheless, growth to near universal levels has occurred in several systems without American style decentralized diversity—systems with closer government control over mission types, and less variety overall. Further, an American style multi-origin, multi-form, semi-decentralized system has evolved in other countries, such as Brazil and India, that did not exhibit a special tendency to growth until recently. This suggests that contextual factors other than diversity or market ideology, such as wealth and the burgeoning middle class, are needed to explain the emergence of high participation in the USA.

MARTIN TROW

Martin Trow (1973) was unsure whether growth to 50 per cent participation and beyond was associated with more diversity or less, though he was sure greater diversity was desirable. He saw two possible futures. One was 'systems planning', which would aim for 'a system of higher education marked by diversity and flexibility', responsive to both 'secular trends and unforeseen developments'. The other was 'prescriptive planning' by governments—though the future 'inevitably involves unforeseen developments', including technology, historical shifts, and changes in values, which negated prescription. Trow was pessimistic. He saw prescriptive planning as 'everywhere dominant', reinforced by demands for efficiency and accountability (p. 50) and 'uniformity or convergence associated with central governmental control' including building codes, research funding rules, equity policy and egalitarian values opposed to differences between public higher education institutions in 'functions, standards and support'. Prescriptive planning 'does not and perhaps cannot create genuine diversity in the forms and structures of higher education', though diversity was 'the major resource' of higher education in responding to both unforeseen and anticipated developments (p. 51).

In short, as Trow saw it the main problem was government, which typically suppressed diversity. He believed growth in itself triggered a natural variety of provision (p. 53), suggesting that unregulated institutions in a growing system would become more diverse over time. However, he also noted a second problem, previously identified by Reisman (1958), 'the tendency for institutions to converge towards the forms and practices of the most prestigious models of higher education, a tendency that operates independently of government control' (Trow, 1973: 51–2). In this respect, orthodox higher education was hostile to the subversive potentials of markets (p. 52). He concluded that taken together, 'the forces working against diversity in higher education'—government, and academic and institutional mimetics—'are very strong at a time when expansion increases the need for diversification of forms and functions beyond what presently exists' (p. 52). These factors worked against not just unregulated diversity but planned diversity, as in the British binary system (p. 53). But there were 'counter-forces' favouring diversity: multi-layered American government, multiple funding sources, educators' recognition of the benefits of diversity, the difficulty of standardizing education (pp. 52–3). Trow hoped 'planning for diversity' would foster variety in institutions, constituencies, and functions, and 'defend elite institutions in an emerging system of mass higher education' without imposing elite forms on other higher education institutions (p. 53).

Trow was handicapped by the difficulty of discerning a clear-cut empirical relationship between growth and diversity, and his touch in these passages was more normative and less sure than in other parts of the essay. The norms reflected the American system of his day: decentralized higher education institutions partly decoupled from state regulation, stratification in coherent tiers, market competition. He identified forces that were shaping diversity but did not understand how they were combined. The future did not evolve in terms of either his negative or positive scenario. Governments often homogenize higher education, yet in binary systems in countries such as Germany, states have defended variety better than have markets elsewhere. On the market side, Trow did not acknowledge that competition in higher education encouraged the habitual imitation of mission and form that he mistakenly saw to be an antiquated academic resistance to market forces. He also overstated the danger that elite higher education institutions would become standardized by mass higher education; understated the capacity of elite institutions to maintain their social power and indeed, to shape whole systems; and missed the significance of the multiplying functions inside higher education institutions. In relation to the last, Trow's prognosis was less complete than Clark Kerr's in *The Uses of the University* (1963) a decade earlier. Kerr saw the all-round aggregation of functions by the growing research 'multiversity', its horizontal and vertical spread across society, as a primary aspect of higher education.

AFTER TROW

Birnbaum (1983) researches changes in external diversity in higher education in the different American states from 1960 to 1980, a period of rapid enrolment growth. He finds that the number of institutional types has not increased and 'dediffereniation' may have occurred. In keeping with the assumption that spontaneous development would favour greater diversity of type, he hypothesizes that centralized state-level planning and the application of rigid criteria for the approval of new institutions and programmes has hampered differentiation. In contrast Rhoades (1990) finds that dedifferentiation resulted primarily from the capacity of academic professionals to block innovations by managers or lay governors of higher education institutions. This power of the professionals to conserve institutional mission is underpinned by government regulation. Like Rhoades, Morphew (2000: 58) identifies convergence in types of higher education provision in the different states of the USA, 'the tendency of diverse groups of institutions to grow more homogeneous over time as similar degree programmes are adopted by institutions with seemingly different missions and resources'. Morphew also notes that 'specific institutional types have become more prevalent (and systems have become more homogenous) even during periods of significant growth in resources and students'. Consistent with this, Eckel (2008) also finds in relation to the USA that institutions are converging in mission, while at the same time stratification has grown.

Johnstone (2010) notes that for the most part, in the process of system growth institutions do not come to specialize on the basis of sub-markets or niche markets, as the market diversity narrative would expect. 'Colleges and universities in the United

States...broaden or widen, rather than narrow or focus their positions' (p. 15). The American experience shows that diversity of institutions does not necessarily increase in direct relationship to growth in enrolment or participation rates. This finding seems to hold on the world scale.

REST OF THE WORLD

Outside the USA diversity of institutional type has been more explicitly policy driven. In the first stage of massification in the forty years after World War II many countries established binary systems in which the second non-university sector housed most of the growth in participation, for example in Central and Nordic Europe, the UK, and Australia. This cheapened the cost of growth, while protecting exclusive student selection and research in the traditional universities. Binary divisions derived from function. The universities prepared students for a different mix of professions to those serviced by non-university institutions. The former conducted research, the latter did not. However, some binary systems were sufficiently hierarchical to encourage non-university aspirations for upward mobility, sharpening the tensions between status distinction and functional distinction while tending to blur the difference between the two in practice. Research configurations also differed. The English-speaking countries developed research primarily within universities though public laboratories played a role. In Germany, France, Russia and China much funded research was conducted in academies and laboratories outside universities. A third area of horizontal variation was specialist higher education institutions. Many countries maintained small colleges in the visual and performing arts and music, specialist medical institutes were common, and some systems had many more single-purpose institutions. Russia and China attached specialist higher education institutions to specific ministries in domains such as health, defence and transport. Regional and local higher education institutions played varying roles in massifying systems, according to whether the country had a federal system, the degree of regional autonomy and the sources of funding.

Between the late 1980s and the early 1990s the binary line was abolished in Australia and the UK. Using mergers and the upgrading of non-university higher education institutions to university status, both nations established unitary university systems in which all instiutions competed with each other for students, research and other funding. Small higher education institutions tended to be absorbed into large universities, a process still happening in the UK. The UK system retains considerably more diversity than Australia's, but both systems are dominated by institutions with a common teaching/research mission ordered in a steep informal status hierarchy regulated by research intensity, resources and student selectivity (Fulton, 1996; Marginson and Considine, 2000), with low horizontal diversity (Marginson and Marshman, 2013). Meek

(2000) identifies isomorphistic convergence during a period of rapid growth in Australia. 'Institutions in direct competition with one another are more likely to emulate each other's teaching and research programmes than to diversify in order to capture a particular market niche'. As a 2000 editorial in *Higher Education Policy* stated:

Every official statement on higher education has stressed the need for a more diverse and responsive set of higher education institutions... But most of the evidence in Australia indicates that competition in a more market-like policy environment results in emulation of the research universities rather than functional diversity at the institutional level. Shattock (1996: 24) indicates a similar situation for the United Kingdom which too has abandoned the binary arrangement.

(Higher Education Policy, 2000: 2)

Likewise, in parts of continental Europe, with its historically varied structures, binary and specialist configurations have been reworked, a process continuing in the HPS era (see later). A cross-country study by Huisman and colleagues (2007) finds that system size, and whether a system is unitary or not, has little bearing on the extent of diversity (pp. 573–4). In some countries the incidence of large multi-purpose institutions has increased and that of small specialist institutions has diminished. Governments are capable of maintaining diverse structures (Huisman and Morphew, 1998), and also of reducing institutional diversity, for example through forced mergers. A 2009 EUA comparison on institutional diversity reaches similar conclusions. Policy and regulatory frameworks on the whole foster diversity, while quality assurance and internationalization encourage convergence. Financing encourages diversification in France, Norway and Switzerland while diminishing it in England and Slovakia (Reichert, 2009). Teichler (2008) finds that under the influence of American higher education and the 'World-Class Universities' movement shaped by global ranking, vertical diversity has become more important. When both stratification and horizontal diversity are included overall institutional diversity has increased but horizontal diversity on its own may have diminished (pp. 351–2).

Van Vught (2008) reviews the discussion. Combining Birnbaum (1983) and Rhoades (1990) he argues that two factors have a crucial impact on the extent of diversifying behaviour by higher education institutions: the level of uniformity in the systemic environment, especially state-driven homogenization; and the level of influence of academic norms and values, which also encourage homogenization (p. 162). He notes that government regulation can facilitate diversity on a planned basis, citing the Hong Kong case (p. 165). To explain tendencies to conformity in higher education, van Vught deploys Darwinian competition, resource dependency theory and the 'institutional isomorphism perspective' (DiMaggio and Powell, 1983: 153–4). 'The basic view of this perspective is that the survival and success of organizations depends upon taking account of other organizations in the environment' (p. 161). He finds that government expectations for marketization reform must be disappointed. Why is it that when free to determine their own strategies institutions prefer to imitate each other rather than innovate in response to the consumer-student? Because higher education is an 'experience good' students can only judge its quality after they have been enrolled (p. 167). Thus higher education institutions are driven not by consumers, but by competition with each other for institutional reputation and prestige. 'They compete among themselves for the best students, the best faculty, the largest research contracts, the highest endowments' (p. 168).

The dynamics of higher education are first and foremost a result of the competition for reputation. Higher education systems are characterized by a reputation race. In this race, higher education institutions are constantly trying to create the best possible images of themselves as highly regarded universities. And this race is expensive. Higher education institutions will spend all the resources they can find to try to capture an attractive position in the race. In this sense, Bowen's (1980: 20) famous law of higher education still holds: 'in quest of excellence, prestige and influence... each institution raises all the money it can... [and] spends all it raises'.

(van Vught, 2008: 169)

Reputation is by definition conservative. Higher education institutions maximize their position in a competition with each other for identical goals rather than by innovating in the form of difference.

While it is generally assumed that development of a mass system of higher education requires at least some institutional diversity, the role of diversity in HPS is less clear and more complex as growth continues in the HPS phase. Judging by most of the scholarly literature on diversity, it would seem that the dynamics of diversity in HPS are no different to those in systems with 15–20 per cent participation. One exception is Pinheiro et al. (2015), who suggest that in the last generation, the period in which HPS have spread across the world, systemic diversity may have declined. In many countries higher education institutions are pulled towards a single model, that of the comprehensive research university with an entrepreneurial bent. In some countries, such as Norway, the comprehensive model is facilitated by mergers and hybrid forms that combine previously separated missions, with policy borrowing and convergence across the joins. The comprehensive university model is also associated with upward drift of lower level institutions towards degree programmes, for example in Canada.

The Multiversity

At any time, systemic diversity is impacted by a range of local factors such as regional access and development; national factors such as government policies, funding mechanisms, research competition; and international factors such as cross-border competition and ranking. It is also affected by factors specific to HPS and in many countries, neoliberal policy and regulation. Chapter 5 discusses how in HPS there is a tendency to system bifurcation and stratification along hierarchical lines associated with growth. Market-based differentiation of higher education institutions has become steeper in many though not in all countries, reinforced by global ranking. Growth, the prestige of the research university form, and in marketized systems competition, all place pressure on binary systems, single mission higher education institutions and other regulated horizontality. In some systems there is a convergence of institutional type with a negative effect on external diversity. In other jurisdictions reforms have increased external diversity. In some cases new institutional forms have emerged to address new demands or roles within HPS, and mergers have established not just larger but different institutional types. Boundaries between sectors are blurred by hybrid institutional forms. Federal and regional arrangements continue to produce variations that cut across other developments (Carnoy et al., forthcoming).

In short, diversity within systems and institutions is vectored by an evolving mix of functional and hierarchical elements. However, main lines of development are apparent.

The first proposition on diversity, HPS Proposition 7, summarizes the most important development, the qualitative increase in the social role, the dominance, of the comprehensive multi-purpose research university in higher education. The term 'multiversity' describes this institution.

In the HPS era, regardless of the political economy and culture of systems, an increasing proportion of higher education becomes centred on comprehensive multi-discipline and multi-function research universities, or 'multiversities'. The multiversity is increasingly dominant as the paradigmatic form of higher education.

The dominance of the multiversity has a number of manifestations. The average size of research universities increases, often markedly, as systems grow. There is 'upward drift' to research university functions from higher education institutions positioned below, and a 'downward drift' of research universities to larger and more heterogeneous teaching and service missions. A range of combinatory forms develop the size and reach of multiversities, including mergers, multi-site and cross-border institutions, and hybrid structures. At the same time, the roles of non-research institutions in binary systems, and specialist disciplinary institutions, tends to decline in the HPS phase, and the multiversity increasingly absorbs research activities previously located outside higher education. In addition, the larger group of multiversities in the HPS era is subject to the growing stratification typical of that era. Multiversities are bifurcated into two broad tiers, with a relatively small number of Global Research Universities in Tier 1.

The rise of the multiversity and diminishing of the role of non-multiversity higher education institutions leads to the second diversity proposition (8).

Regardless of the political economy and culture of the HPS, when participation expands there is no necessary increase in the overall diversity of institutional form and mission; and this has probably declined, except in relation to online provision.

Note that the term 'university' carries increased prestige in HPS and is used more widely than the multiversity form. The term 'institute' provides alternate status only in a few unambiguously leading institutions such as MIT and Caltech in the USA, though one relatively new Canadian university attempted to cover all bases with the name University of Ontario Institute of Technology. Variant sectors and institutions now mostly carry designations such as 'applied science university' or 'university of technology'. Non-university designations such as 'polytechnic' are fading.

In an early summary of the emerging form in the USA, *The Uses of the University* (1963), Clark Kerr coined 'multiversity' to describe what the research university was becoming. Features of the multiversity are growth, aggregation of functions and activities, accumulation of social and economic status and resources, external extension and managed internal heterogeneity. It is powered by several normative principles, often pointing in different directions, including inquiry and knowledge creation, transmission of ideas and values, pastoral care, community service, collegial fellowship and managerial efficiency. It is replete with competing internal interests and external stakeholders. It becomes ever more 'multi' via additional disciplines, fields of training, research agendas and funding, functions, activities, constituencies and personnel. It engages with business, the professions, the arts, government, cities and local communities. Hence the expansion of HPS to include the bulk of society, as described in Chapter 3, is matched by expansion in the size, reach, complexity and connectedness of the central institution. '"The Idea of a Multiversity" is a city of infinite variety . . . . As against the village and the town, the "city" is more like the totality of civilization as it has evolved and more an integral part of it; and movement to and from the surrounding society has been greatly accelerated' (Kerr, 1963: 31).

Kerr wrote during a period of sustained growth in the size and research funding of the American 'flagship' public universities in each state, such as University of California (UC) Berkeley where he had served as Chancellor. As Trow remarked, 'the big state universities' carried out 'the autonomous and popular functions within the same institution', with these functions insulated from each other to protect elite tracks and high research activity (Trow, 1970: 5), thereby sustaining their prestige. These institutions above all came to epitomize the American 'multiversity' though Kerr later said that he also had Harvard in mind (Kerr, 2001: 106). Though some American private universities remained small, the multiversity dynamic of growth plus the multiplication of functions moved through other public Doctoral universities, much of the private sector and later many lesser tier higher education institutions in the USA. There is a limit to this augmentation of status and power through the expanse of operations. As Chapter 5 will discuss, few research intensive universities willingly dissolve the selectivity that makes them special. All multiversities must balance the time honoured fostering of demand by scarcity against the broad enthusiastic scope of their supply. The splintering of supply into variable sub-markets (by discipline, by campus) preserves a selective selectivity. But what is striking about the HPS era is that this moveable equilibrium between quality and quantity is fixed at a much larger scale.

Though it is often positioned in a larger network of institutions, Kerr's multiversity provides its own momentum. It is less a government department powered by the state than a self-actualizing organization like a business firm (though perhaps its institutional agency derives also from the clerical autonomy of the medieval university). The multiversity is responsive to both government and a larger definition of the public good that includes many stakeholders; and it moves beyond policy to create new social roles (and revenue sources) for itself. It fixes its own priorities. Here the American practices of Kerr's time were ahead of the global trend, but the quasi-corporate form of institutional autonomy has now become widely established (see Chapter 3), with governments supporting the downward transfer of responsibility and regulated autonomy within the constraints of funding, accountability and audit. This form of aggregative and externally engaged university, both enhanced and constrained by system management and market forces, is defined by Clark (1998) as the 'entrepreneurial university' and Marginson and Considine (2000) as the 'enterprise university'. Describing a later more international version nested in one world science and ranking, Mohrman et al. (2008) refer to the 'global research university' or GRU. Ma (2008) applies that term to Berkeley. The term 'World-Class University' (WCU) has also emerged, but is less explanatory, as it refers to relative rather than absolute qualities. (WCU status is measured by global ranking lists but if the number of universities with high research performance increases this does not change the number in the top 100.) Despite these lexical innovations, Kerr's concept of the multiversity, or perhaps the 'global research multiversity', retains its power. It highlights internal heterogeneity as well as reach; it is free of space, time and ideology; and it distinguishes the present institution from the smaller and narrower elite universities maintained by systems in the mass higher education era.

The multiversity has become more dominant in two sense: the large multi-purpose research university model has growing normative power, as the ideal form of higher education institution, and also its material weight within national systems has grown. The presence of the Anglo-American multiversity form was enhanced by the advent of credible global university comparisons in the Shanghai Academic Ranking of World Universities (ARWU) in 2003 (ARWU, 2015; Hazelkorn, 2015). The template used by the ARWU favours the large Anglo-American research university comprehensive of the science disciplines. This template underpins the state-fostered evolution of the 985 group in China, the 39 institutions being built as 'world-class', the excellence initiative in Germany, the merger programme in France, and reforms in Japan, Korea and other countries (Salmi, 2009). Rankings have driven investment in, and the concentration and expansion of, research firepower. In most rankings it is the quantity of research quality that lifts the overall position of an institution (Marginson, 2014).

Global ranking sustains an informal tier 1 of leading multiversities with research performance sufficient to position them in the world top 100 or 200. Tier 2 is much larger and ranges down from research universities with valued professional training in fields such as law and engineering, to primarily teaching-focused higher education institutions whose main status-building strategy is the name 'university'. Tier 2 carries most of multiversity's role in social inclusion. The bifurcation into research multiversity tiers 1 and 2 is driven by the essential opposition between selective and demand-responsive institutions in all systems (see Chapter 5). Below tier 2 are positioned the teaching-only conglomerates that share the multiversity's size, multiplicity and often the name 'university', but not its selectivity and research role.

THE SIZE FACTOR

The multiversity's share of enrolments within systems tends to grow, and the size of many individual multiversities also grows, though within the limits set by selectivity. In the case of both multiversities in systems and the size of individual institutions there were different starting points from country to country. The result is that while the common dynamic is one of a contained aggregation, the profile of the institution still varies across the world.

For example, at system level the multiversity commands the great bulk of enrolments in the UK but it has fewer than 45 per cent of higher education students in California and 10 per cent if only Doctoral institutions are included. At institution level, the variation in size is if anything increasing, as some multiversities remain small while the ceiling is going up. Among the small-and-hyperselective-is-beautiful higher education institutions are Princeton and Caltech in the American private sector. In 2016 Caltech, sixth in the world for the proportion of its research papers in the top 1 per cent by citation rate, had just 2,255 students, including 1,254 graduate students, 300 professorial faculty, and 600 research scholars (Leiden University, 2017; Caltech, 2016). The more typical pattern is one of marked expansion in the last generation that is coupled with continued selectivity, especially in elite professional training programmes such as medicine, law and perhaps finance. Some prestigious public research universities have achieved great size—in 2016 the University of Toronto in Canada enrolled 86,709 students, including 14,255 graduate students, and employed 20,658 faculty and staff (University of Toronto, 2016). In 2015 Monash University in Australia enrolled 70,071 students, including 20,976 at graduate level, and employed 6,709 faculty (Monash University, 2016). In the USA in 2016 Ohio State University (2016) with 63,964 students, and Michigan State University (2016) with 50,543 students, had populations large by historical standards.

The multi-purpose public university in the Latin American systems is bigger again: the Universidade de Sao Paulo (2016) in Brazil had 94,875 students in 2016, and

Universidad Nacional Autónoma de México (UNAM) (2016), enrolled a colossal 346,730 students and employed 39,500 faculty in 2015–16. While UNAM suffers in the research rankings because of the size of its non-research-intensive sections, the Latin American mega-university is not so far from Kerr's multiversity. The Latin American higher education institutions combine selective programmes in professional disciplines, and prestigious research concentrations, with access programmes and diverse regional centres, just as some of their North American counterparts. Both variations display the capacity to maintain within-organization separation and semi-independent missions under one umbrella that is a hallmark of the classical multiversity form. The type is flexible. The balance between the parts is continually tuned. The individual multiversity claims to be all missions to all people—while concentrating activity in areas of most capacity or opportunity.

One variant of the multiversity with mixed missions is that of prestigious global research multiversities in countries with a commercial international education industry, including the UK, Australia and New Zealand. In Australia the elite Group of Eight universities carry out two-thirds of funded research in the higher education system. Five of these eight institutions each enrol an exceptionally large number of international students by world standards (see Table 4.1). Australia's public funding of higher education at 0.9 per cent of GDP in 2012 was below the OECD average of 1.2 per cent (OECD, 2015: 235), and there is a regulated ceiling on the tuition that can be charged to local students. At the same time, there are no constraints on the maximum level of international student tuition or the number of fee-paying international students that can be

Table 4.1. Leading eight research universities, Australia: International student numbers and revenues, 2014

University	ARWU rank, 2015	International students, 2014		All students, 2014	International students as a share of total, 2014 %	Income from international education, 2014 US$ million
		onshore	offshore			
Melbourne	44	16,140	19	55,596	29.1	327
Queensland	77	12,195	0	50,749	24.0	234
Australian National	77	6,089	0	22,393	27.2	89
Western Australia	87	3,800	1,418	26,379	19.8	77
Monash	101–50	13,748	10,233	67,076	35.8	281
Sydney	101–50	13,710	198	55,975	24.8	293
New South Wales	101–50	13,603	30	53,481	25.5	173
Adelaide	101–50	6,594	679	27,167	26.8	111

Notes: ARWU = Academic Ranking of World Universities. Note that all international students are full-time while fewer than two-thirds of domestic student are full-time: the weight of international students is greater than the data for all students (full-time and part-time categories taken together) suggest.

Source: DET Australia (2016).

enrolled. International student tuition has become normalized as a core part of income and the main source of discretionary finance for research and infrastructure. The outcome of this mix of factors is that even high-status research universities find themselves having to build high international student volume. The academic threshold for international student entry is normally lower than for local students, sometimes much lower: oddly, these universities function as highly selective providers to local students and demand responsive providers to international students. They work the contradiction in their favour: local prestige and global rankings facilitate mass student recruitment in China, India, Malaysia, Singapore and elsewhere. In 2014 the University of Melbourne, 44th in the ARWU ranking, enrolled 16,140 full-time international students on its main campus, the largest onsite international student population in any research intensive university in the world, earning $327 million USD.

The expanded social weight of the multiversity is joined with two other systemic developments which follow from its rise. First, its growing internal diversity (Proposition 9). Second, the external 'multiversification' of HPS—the restructuring of systems to make room for a stronger multiversity, in part by folding non-university institutions into the multiversity form (Propositions 7 and 8). Before looking at these developments there is a question to answer. What powers the dynamic of the multiversity, above and beyond the growth of participation itself? Why has this form become qualitatively more important? What makes it so robust?

WHAT POWERS THE MULTIVERSITY?

The relative increase in demand for the multiversity is easy to explain. It is carried by the dynamic of growing participation, which tends to empty out the value of sub-university experience. But what of the supply side? What drives the institution? In some HPS the multiversity leverages its brand to generate revenues through profit-making activity. Yet this is not a corporation motored by profitability or shareholder value, though it wants to broaden its social power and reach in a manner akin to building market share. As van Vught (2008) states the multiversity is driven fundamentally by the accumulation of the social status or 'reputation', the basis of its social power. It wants position. Regardless of local history and common sense, there is no end to the ultimate dreaming of university leaders, until the level of Harvard is reached. In the multiversity, at every level of institutional status, the desire for betterment is universal. Thus the multiversity is driven also to acquire public and private resources for the research, infrastructure, teaching programmes and services that underpin status. The twin objectives, status and resources (quality and quantity)—which tend to produce each other—explain the multiversity's accumulative logic and hunger in quasi-markets. The more functions, students, land and buildings, and research glory it acquires, the stronger is the gravitational pull of its status. Every advance of status triggers possible further resources. There are opportunity costs in each pattern of activity. Periodically the multiversity reforms itself. But it rarely downsizes sharply. Though the mix of activity may be non-optimal, reductions of function trigger a difficult politics of management and can eat into status building capacity. Some inefficiencies are carried, routinely, in all multiversities. There is no natural size limit.

Of course, neither Harvard nor Berkeley can expand forever without impairing the exchange value of the credential, except in the attenuated form of mass open online courseware (MOOC) programmes, where vast numbers bring lustre to the elite university's global reputation without subtracting value from the exclusive onsite degree. (MOOCs are not so much a way into the prestige university whose brand they carry, as a space between inner and outer walls. The inner world protects the university's concentrated positional power.)

Hence the multiversity is shaped between two contrary and compelling logics: the logic of selectivity, which generates status by increasing unit value, and the logic of aggregation of functions, reach and power. It is striking that institutional status is generated through both means—on the one hand through accumulation/extension (quantity), and on the other hand through concentration/intensification (quality). These logics are not identical, yet at some level each needs the other. Selectivity without coverage is marginal. Selectivity multiplies the volume of status that accumulation provides. Broad social relations without zero-sum prestige turn the multiversity into mass higher education. Institution by institution the two drivers, selectivity and aggregation, are combined in varying ways. Some institutions take both pathways as far as they can. Others focus primarily on one alone. All follow selective or aggregative logics variously, in different parts of their operation. The multiversity form is sufficiently loose to permit that.

This same pull in two directions, towards quantity and towards quality, and this same matrix of strategic options, is apparent in both the high research intensive universities and in those struggling in the middle of the pack whose status is always in doubt (for the latter see the next chapter). The variation in strategies between selectivity and aggregation, with the different shadings of one into the other—along with variation in the contents of what is selective and aggregated—is key to the individual distinctiveness of each multiversity. Some higher education institutions are more selective than others or specialize in disciplines, levels or clientele. Some reach further than others or devise unusual combinations of roles or localities. There is much scope for strategic choice. Yet the choices are not arbitrary. Both the drive to institutional selectivity and the drive to aggregation of function are ultimately framed and constrained by the positional market in higher education. On the one hand, the role of positional competition in determining selectivity is obvious. On the other hand, the accumulation of status via the multiplication of social reach runs into one limit—the status of rival universities, which restricts the extent to which any institution can expand its role without becoming so non-selective as to lose status. If elite universities become predominantly demand-responsive they slip from the 'artisanal' category. One ambiguity of the multiversity is this invisible line dividing elite and non-elite status. This line is temporarily blurred by university marketing departments but never finally abolished, asserting itself continually in comparative judgements that weigh higher education institutions against each other. In the middle zone between elite artisanal and volume-building mass institutions, which in some HPS is a large group of institutions (Chapter 5), there is continual status tension.

More voluntary limits to the growth of the individual multiversity may be imposed by executive strategy or by government fiat. But the point is that like the growth of participation itself, the evolution of the multiversity is not governed by economic scarcity. It is driven by contrary logics of status intensification and status accumulation: quality and quantity.

WHAT BINDS THE MULTIVERSITY?

What then holds the multiversity together, despite its contrary 'animating principles' (Kerr, 1963: 15)? What prevents it from spinning off freely into centrifugal abandon, coming apart at seams it does not have? Here the economic argument blocks a plausible explanation. The economics of the firm suggests that the many specific functions and constituencies served by the multiversity are potentially separate lines of production, separate industries. Surely the clients could be served more effectively by commodity specialization? Yet the business model has so far failed to conceive de-bundled post-multiversity teaching, research and credentialing with the same social purchase as the combined institution. The multiversity follows precisely the opposite logic—aggregation, containment of great diversity, and also, at times, the blending of difference and opposition. Why? How? Clark Kerr was unclear about what binds the multiversity together. Though acutely conscious of the university president he made no overriding claim for presidential coordination and hints the multiversity could function without it. Instead he focused on the potency of the university's 'name':

This means a great deal more than it sounds as though it might. The name of the institution stands for a certain standard of performance, a certain degree of respect, a certain historical legacy, a characteristic quality of spirit. This is of the utmost importance to faculty, and to students, to the government agencies and the industries with which the institution deals. Protection and enhancement of the prestige of the name are central to the multiversity. How good is its reputation ... its 'institutional character'?   (Kerr, 1963: 15)

This brings Kerr's argument close to the claim of this book about the central role of social status building and competition in higher education. The different specialized functions of the university all gain something from the institutional brand ('name') in which they are housed. Often the main product is not the individual item of teaching, research or service—it is the institutional brand itself. Companies purchasing research gain not knowledge, but codified knowledge. What students access is not so much teaching, as credentialed learning. And while the rewards attached to the particular programme of study may be unclear, the status value of the multiversity, while fuzzy at the edges, is a matter of repute. The singular value of the multiversity both explains and is strengthened by league table ranking. Comparisons that eschew whole of institution ordering and focus on disaggregated functions, such as U-Multirank (2016), are more informative but less compelling. The different functions all feed into the common pool of status from which reputation derives. If these functions were de-bundled then the common pool would evaporate and the circular status-driven links between research, student selectivity and resource raising would be broken. The brand also protects the value of all the different functions in the multiversity. It conceals low selectiveness and low performing areas of activity, protecting their position while blocking their potential to corrode the social value of the institution as a whole. There is still something aristocratic in this power of a title to determine private virtue, and to turn private virtue into social value.

The multiversity is much larger than in Kerr's time, suggesting problems of coordination have increased. Yet it seems more robust a form than ever. If it has confounded the business model and orthodox policy imagining, the only plausible explanation is that the dynamics of social status are primary in relation to the economics of higher education. To repeat, what mediates relations between the institution and stakeholders is not the specific transactions in the specialist area, but brand value, the connection with the institution as a whole. Specialist production and narrowly framed higher education institutions exist but are an increasingly minor part of the sector. The multiversity continues to command the landscape. Even lower status multiversities add positional value *qua institution* to the use value of their programmes. The multiplicity of credentials, formative experiences, disciplinary knowledge and applications is expressed not as separated industries or firms but as internal diversity within the growing multiversity.

Diversity within the Multiversity

The third diversity proposition, HPS Proposition 9, states that

> *As participation expands the internal diversity of multiversities tends to increase. This affects some or all of the range of missions, business activities, institutional forms and internal structures, the discipline mix, research activities, levels of study and range of credentials, the*

heterogeneity of the student body, links to stakeholders, cross-border relations, and forms of academic and non-academic labour.

The growing internal diversity also extends to financing arrangements and research activities. Of these manifestations of diversity two are especially important: the structural diversity of organizational and academic (departments or schools) units, and the increasing heterogeneity of the student population.

Bastedo and Gumport (2003) suggest mission differentiation at system level might reduce the internal diversity of higher education institutions that become more focused on activities that embody and fulfil their missions. In Russia there are instances of regional mergers in which large differences between the merged parts continue, triggering pressures for de-merger and thus reduced internal diversity. However, mergers are more common than de-mergers; and the HPS era seems more associated with diverse missions inside multi-purpose higher education institutions, than specialist missions. In addition, growing external relations are associated with a proliferation of academic units, research centres, and programmes of study, including multi-disciplinary and trans-disciplinary units, links to industry and regional development roles.

Clark (1983) argues that the tendency for new branches of knowledge to become grounded in academic constituencies is the primary driver of diversification. As massification proceeds and more occupational areas are absorbed into multiversity credentialing, diversity in the workforce becomes one driver of the multiplication of knowledge and specialism. This is often associated with product differentiation via specialist credentials. However, there are two counter-tendencies. First, many higher education institutions reassert the role of the institutional brand by simplifying the proliferation of credentials using generic titles. Second, many if not most HPS experience growth in the proportionate role of generalist-vocational credentials, such as business studies and information technology programmes, designed to open a broad range of pathways in public and private sector employment. For example, in Russia much of the expansion of participation in lower tier institutions has taken this form, creating a bifurcation with specific professional preparation in more prestigious institutions (Konstantinovskiy, 2016).

A MORE DIVERSE STUDENT BODY

Arguably, in HPS the greater change in internal diversity is in the student body in individual higher education institutions. The larger multiversities often take in a more diverse clientele than their predecessors. Highly exclusive institutions are exceptions; but as noted, even top research universities in the North American and Australian public sectors may carry a heterogeneous student body through access programmes, multi-site locations or international recruitment. It is likely that in HPS student diversity increases in direct relation to the growth of institutional and system enrolment, although this needs empirical investigation. Though the growing diversity of students is partly the outcome of system level transformation that has expanded access (Carnoy et al., 2013; Pinheiro and Antonowicz, 2015), it not simply driven by demand from students and families or from the state as the proxy for students. On the supply side it also embodies institutional responses to expanding markets, and can be exacerbated by mergers, especially combinations of institutions with distinct missions.

In systems in which half or more of the age cohort enters higher education, and many students are not only the first generation in their family to enter a higher education institution (as happened also in the mass higher education era) but were only moderate achievers at school, new types of students are entering. They tend to concentrate in less exclusive and socially valued higher education institutions and programmes (Teichler, 2008: 353). The diversification of students is widely studied (Shah et al., 2016), with research focusing on fair opportunities for women, ethnic minorities, young people from socially disadvantaged families, older people and those with disabilities (e.g. Basit and Tomlinson, 2012). There is less on how individual institutions have changed in response to the educational needs of these groups (but see Thomas, 2016; Harvey, Burnheim, and Brett, 2016). However, many higher education institutions have developed specialized offices and services to support student success, and, in some cases, new relationships with communities in order to promote supportive pathways through high education (Jones et al., 2008).

As Trow remarked, the prevailing assumption in the era of elite higher education was that at point of entry, students were all academically prepared in much the same way. Wider access challenges that assumption. Historically, systems have used entrance examinations to differentiate students, matching well prepared students with elite higher education institutions. In large conglomerate multiversities this is no longer fully effective. The average entrance score at a higher education institution is not always sufficient guide to the character of highly heterogeneous student bodies. For example, in Russia more than two-thirds of all universities must deal with a wide distribution of individual entrance scores among incoming students (Aleskerov et al., 2014).

The How of 'Multiversitization'

In many (not all) countries the HPS era is associated with systemic reordering and new configurations. These changes have strengthened the multiversity form ('multiversification'), through merger and other combinatory forms (Pinheiro et al., 2016), while reducing the role of non-multiversity higher education institutions, including binary sectors and single purpose institutions, and/or drawing research formerly located in specialized research academies and institutes into multiversities.

COMBINATIONS

Johnstone (2010: 15) describes how the American multiversity has broadened its social coverage through both the upward drift of largely teaching institutions to the research function, and the downward drift of research institutions into market opportunities in mass teaching and applied research, 'sometimes at the expense of the more scholarly PhD programmes and basic research'.

Some public research flagship universities that are not part of comprehensive state systems will continue to diversify by creating new branch campuses that are more teaching-oriented and less research intensive, thus competing with, or actively pre-empting the expansion of, or creation of new public colleges in the non-research university systems.   (Johnstone, 2010: 15)

The spread in both directions is facilitated by the responsiveness of institutions to opportunity, the absence of a national system approach and in most states the lack of firm binary lines between research and non-research higher education institutions (Johnstone, 2010: 15). Another boundary-crossing trend is the upward movement of community colleges into degree programmes, though this is less frequent than upward drift by degree-granting institutions into research function (pp. 18–19). American community college degrees are paralleled in the UK and Australia by the growth of degree programmes in Further Education, and Vocational Education and Training, respectively, though again the incidence is localized and limited overall.

In some countries mergers entail heterogeneous combinations across sites, missions, and organizational forms. Consistent with the flexibility and diversity of the multiversity form, one feature of the HPS era is greater internal structural heterogeneity of higher education institutions. There are two kinds of combination—multiplicity, whereby heterogeneous functions share a common container without losing their distinctiveness; and hybridity, whereby formerly heterogeneous functions become partly or wholly blended. Hybridization takes time and is often incomplete. The abiding overall tendencies are growth in size and increased ambiguity. More agile and ambiguous formations have been facilitated in some countries by a shift from state administration to site governance, and everywhere by the evolution of multi-site and multi-level management, information systems, and devolved budgeting mechanisms.

New forms of multiversity in the last two decades include cross-border campuses, with the institution located in more than one policy, legal, educational, and financing environment. Global activity and internationalization are subject to much variation between higher education institutions and a primary source of distinctive organizational identity (King et al., 2011).

REDUCTIONS

Binary sectors have had mixed fortunes in the HPS era. On the whole the role of second national sectors paralleling the universities has diminished, with important exceptions. The German binary system of academic universities and universities of applied sciences (*fachhochschulen)* is unchanged. Strong binary systems have consolidated in Taiwan and South Korea. All three second sectors are embedded in and partly funded by a knowledge-intensive manufacturing sector. Austria and Switzerland retain stable binary divides. But binary lines have gone in Australia and the UK; and Ireland, Denmark, and Norway are closer to a unitary approach. Other boundaries are blurring. It can be difficult for policy and regulation to sustain inherited differences (Pinheiro et al., 2015).

In 2007 Danish universities were encouraged to merge with public research institutes, and the professional colleges also underwent mergers, leading to a smaller number (eighteen) of larger higher education institutions. In 2013 Aarhus University had 44,500 students after merging with Aarhus School of Engineering. In Norway after the government enabled colleges to apply for university status and offer PhDs, the number of universities increased from four to nine. In 2008 the definition of 'university' was broadened to encompass institutions not full research institutions. Amid both upward and downward drift, horizontal differentiation between the binary sectors has been partly eroded. There is competition among a larger group of higher education institutions for students and funding, policy emphasis on world-class excellence, and informal stratification of status is playing a growing role (Pinheiro, 2015). Ireland has opened a pathway for its second sector, the Institutes of Technology, to achieve designation as 'technological universities'. In the Netherlands a growing number of higher education institutions in the second sector, the *hogescholen,* carry the title 'university of applied sciences', have assumed a limited research role and are expanding their professional Master's programmes (Maassen, 2010).

In many countries local and provincial sectors continue, some at sub-university level, for example in Canada and Finland. These higher education institutions are more varied in character than are research-oriented universities. However, the role of local and provincial institutions may be ebbing, with a shift in the balance of enrolment to institutions with a national (and often global) mission. Some local higher education institutions have become absorbed into institutions with a larger reach, consistent with the regional mobility of educated employment, especially in Europe, and growth in the urban share of national populations. The longer term trajectory might be towards dual systems, in which multiversities are combined with short programme vocational schools (Pinheiro et al., 2015), but case by case empirical research is required to test this surmise.

Higher education in specialized higher education institutions is decreasing in proportional terms and probably in absolute numbers. Multiversity credentials are more potent. They carry not just specialist disciplinary value but generic brand value. Even elite specialist higher education institutions may gain from combination, such as those French *Grandes Ecoles* that have merged with research universities.

In the post-Soviet countries and China many specialist institutions have been repositioned as part of national higher education systems coordinated by a single ministry. The process has advanced further in China (Whang and Zha, 2015). In the quasi-market of Russian higher education since 1992, higher education institutions have expanded their boundaries to address new demands and market opportunities, opening new programmes and specialties within institutions to attract financial resources (Titova, 2008), often in new fields (Froumin et al., 2014). One analysis of the evolution of more than 200 Russian specialized universities between 1998–9 to 2013–14 (Semyonov and Platonova, 2014) finds that higher education institutions in fields such as agriculture, medicine, and applied engineering have become more comprehensive, opening departments of business, management, law, and communications to attract fee paying students and thereby generate revenue that cross-subsidize other university activities.

Beyond the Multiversity

The dominance of the multiversity is qualified in two respects: the growth of for-profit private sectors in some countries, and diversified online delivery. Each plays an important role in certain emerging countries. However, as separate forms of higher education both for-profit and online delivery are marginal to established HPS, though the margin has widened.

Online pedagogy and/or assessment are widely used inside and outside formal higher education. There is much technological potential for freewheeling diversity; and in policy circles online education is routinely seen as a mechanism for cheapening the unit cost of growing mass higher education provision. Yet solely online delivery has not established credentials with sufficient status to challenge onsite delivery—the most heavily subscribed MOOCs are those associated with Stanford, Harvard, and MIT. Many higher education institutions have folded these MOOC programmes into their own delivery. Online functions as a complement and supplement. Within classrooms or adjoining them, it has been effectively annexed by the multiversity.

In OECD countries the proportion of Bachelor's level enrolments in the private sector in 2013 varied from 88 per cent in Israel and 80 per cent in each of Chile and South Korea, to

2 per cent in Ireland, and 4 per cent in New Zealand. The overall OECD share was 31 per cent. The pattern was different at Doctoral level, with just 20 per cent of all students in private institutions and private sector components of more than one-quarter of students only in South Korea, Chile, Belgium, the USA, and Japan (OECD, 2015: 320). Sub-university private colleges play a major role in Japan and Korea. Many HPS have private multiversities. But non-profit private education has not changed fundamentally in the HPS era.

For-profit private higher education institutions are primarily revenue-driven not primarily status driven, and specialize rather than multiplying their functions. They play a larger role than a generation ago. Nevertheless, their growth is a contingent rather than necessary feature of HPS. They have grown from a negligible to a minor role where neoliberal government has fostered them. The USA (Mettler, 2014), the UK, and Australia all provide subsidized tuition loans in the private sector, pushing enrolments to about 10 per cent in each country, with the growth largely in for-profit institutions. However, in all three countries private degrees mostly lack prestige, and in the USA the subsidized for-profit sector has stopped growing. Low employer recognition and high tuition relative to public colleges have undermined the model.

Conclusions

Though the landscape varies by country, in the HPS era institutional higher education develops primarily by combination, including the gymnastic joining of heterogeneous parts, rather than de-bundled missions and nimble specialization. In the larger, more inclusive HPS there is greater stratification, on average less external diversity, horizontal merging into single higher education institutions (not always closely coupled), greater ambiguity—and more multiversity. Difference and specialization are contained within large multi-purpose institutions welded together by name-brands. The logics of system development and institutional development have converged. Both HPS and higher education institutions, except for the most exclusive, take in a growing portion of society, engage with more multiple stakeholders, and are more diverse within. System and institutional governance have become adept in holding difference within a common frame.

Regardless of the extent of neoliberal reform, the rules are the same: (1) selectivity and exclusion generate social status for institutions and for graduates; (2) size, combination, and inclusion also generate institutional status; (3) the 'commanding values' of an HPS, as in its smaller predecessor system, remain those of the leading research universities. This sustains a common hubris. Every multiversity wants social diction and the resources to finance it. This feeds its inexorable expansion: it moves upwards to the high research role and downwards to mass teaching and credentialing, and sideways to expand its social impact—while being nudged from underneath by sub-university institutions whose lower levels are losing value. There are more layers of multiversity. The title 'university' no longer carries the guarantees it once did. Yet status decline is not the whole of the story. The lower middle layer of large degree granting institutions offers some protection from the downward pressures on the value of mass education that have been unleashed by the dynamics of HPS.

As HPS Proposition 10 indicates, the neoliberal variant of HPS has specific implication for institutional configurations and diversity.

> *All else being equal, the combination of expanding participation and enhanced competition in neoliberal quasi-markets is associated with specific effects in relation to diversity, including (1) increased vertical differentiation of higher education institutions (stratification); (2) reduced horizontal differentiation (diversification); (3) convergence of missions through isomorphic imitation; and (4) growth in the role of private higher education institutions, especially for-profit institutions.*

When HPS are rendered more competitive in quasi-markets, horizontal distinctions of mission tend to become vertical. Formal market competition heightens the tendency to strategic imitation rather than innovation. Global competition via research rankings further undermines binary sectors and specialist institutions (which cannot figure in the rankings), and quickens mergers to concentrate research firepower. It is ironic that the markets expected to foster niche specialization have instead exacerbated the 'small is unbeautiful' syndrome and aggregation in order to create value. That is how positional competition works in this sector. This is not to say isomorphism is absent in social democratic systems.

In any system the decline in horizontal diversity expands the systemic costs of failure. 'Diversity permits low risk experimentation because failure is isolated in single institutions' (Brown, 1999: 5). Yet from an institution viewpoint the multiversity is shaped by the twin logics of aggregation and selectivity, innovations must comply with social reach and brand value, and new missions that may change reputation carry risks. Global strategy is one of the few options for executive-led innovation that does not risk institutional status or compromise the research role. This is one reason why many higher education institutions internationalize themselves despite the costs.

What is the overall verdict? Teichler's surmise that horizontal institutional diversity has declined, while vertical plus horizontal differentiation has increased, seems sound. What about the three structural forms of diversity identified by Wang and Zha (2015)? HPS are more diverse if they include more institutional types, if the distribution of institutions between the main types is more evenly weighted, and if there is a greater distance in kind between types. Though individual country patterns differ, it appears that overall in the HPS era the first two forms of diversity have decreased. The weakening of non-university sectors and specialist institutions suggests a reduction in types, and within the typology the large research multiversity is more dominant than before. On the other hand, the growth in for-profit higher education and diverse online provision, both of which in different ways vary sharply from convention, suggests greater diversity in the distance between institutional types. Does this matter? The exceptionalism of online and for-profits hints at subversive potentials. But neither has found a way to generate superior positional value—and the desire for social position is the essential driver of high participation higher education.

■ REFERENCES

Aleskerov, F., Frumin, I., Kardanova, E. et al. (2014). Heterogeneity of the educational system: An introduction to the problem. Working paper WP7/2014/03. Higher School of Economics Publ. House, Moscow.

ARWU (Academic Ranking of World Universities) (2015). *2015 Academic Ranking of World Universities*. Shanghai: Jiao Tong University. http://www.shanghairanking.com

Basit, T. and Tomlinson, S. (eds) (2012). *Social Inclusion and Higher Education*. Bristol: The Policy Press.

Bastedo, M. and Gumport, P. (2003). Access to what? Mission differentiation and academic stratification in U.S. public higher education. *Higher Education* 46, 341–59.

Birnbaum, R. (1983). *Maintaining Diversity in Higher Education*. San Francisco: Jossey-Bass.

Bowen, H. (1980). *The Cost of Higher Education*. San Francisco: Jossey-Bass.

Brown, R. (1999). Diversity in higher education: Has it been and gone? *Higher Education Review* 31(3), 3–16.

Caltech (California Institute of Technology) (2016). *Caltech at a Glance*. California: Caltech. https://www.caltech.edu/content/caltech-glance

Carnoy, M., Loyalka, P., Dobryakova, M., Dossani, R., Froumin, I., Kuhns, K., Tilak, J. B., and Rong, W. (2013). *University Expansion in a Changing Global Economy: Triumph of the BRICs?* Stanford: Stanford University Press.

Carnoy, M., Froumin, I., Leshukov, O., and Marginson, S. (forthcoming). *Federal Systems in Higher Education: A Comparative Perspective*. (Working title.)

Clark, B. R. (1983). *The Higher Education System: Academic Organization in Cross-national Perspective*. Los Angeles, CA: University of California Press.

Clark, B. R. (1998). *Creating Entrepreneurial Universities: Organizational Pathways of Transformation*. Oxford: Pergamon.

DET (Department of Employment and Training) Australia (2016). *Higher Education Statistics*. https://www.education.gov.au/higher-education-statistics

Di Maggio, P. J. and Powell, W. W. (1983). The iron cage revisited: Institutional isomorphism and collective rationality in organizational fields. *American Sociological Review* 48, 147–60.

Eckel, P. (2008). Mission diversity and the tension between prestige and effectiveness: An overview of U.S. higher education. *Higher Education Policy* 21, 175–92.

Froumin, I., Kouzminov, Y., and Semyonov, D. (2014). Institutional diversity in Russian higher education: Revolutions and evolution. *European Journal of Higher Education* 4(3), 209–34. DOI: 10.1080/21568235.2014.916532.

Fulton, O. (1996). Differentiation and diversity in a newly unitary system: The case of the UK. In V. L. Meek L. Goedegebuure, O. Kivinen, and R. Rinne (eds), *The Mockers and the Mocked: Comparative Perspectives on Differentiation, Convergence and Diversity in Higher Education*. Oxford: Pergamon, pp. 163–87.

Goedegebuure, L., Meek, V. L., Kivinen, O., and Rinne, R. (1996). On diversity, differentiation and convergence. In V. L. Meek, L. Goedegebuure, O. Kivinen, and R. Rinne (eds), *The Mockers and the Mocked: Comparative Perspectives on Differentiation, Convergence and Diversity in Higher Education*. Oxford: Pergamon, pp. 2–13.

Harvey, A., Burnheim, C., and Brett, M. (eds) (2016). *Student Equity in Australian Higher Education: Twenty-five years of a Fair Chance for All*. Singapore: Springer.

Hazelkorn, E. (2015). *Rankings and the Reshaping of Higher Education: The Battle for World-Class Excellence*, 2nd edn. Houndmills: Palgrave.

Higher Education Policy (2000). Understanding diversity and differentiation in higher education: An overview. Editorial. *Higher Education Policy* 13, 106.

Horta, H., Huisman, J., and Heitor, M. (2008). Does competitive research funding encourage diversity in higher education? *Science and Public Policy* 35(3), 146–58.

Huisman, J. and Morphew, C. C. (1998). Centralization and diversity: Evaluating the effects of government policies in U.S.A. and Dutch higher education. *Higher Education Policy* 11(1), 3–13.

Huisman, J., Meek, V. L., and Wood, F. (2007). Institutional diversity in higher education: A cross-national and longitudinal analysis. *Higher Education Quarterly* 61(4), 563–77.

Huisman, J., Lepori, B., Seeber, M., Frolich, N., and Scordato, L. (2015). Measuring institutional diversity across higher education systems. *Research Evaluation* 24(4), 369–79.

Johnstone, B. (2010). Higher educational diversification in the United States. In Research Institute for Higher Education (RIHE), Hiroshima University (ed.), *Diversifying Higher Education Systems in the International and Comparative Perspectives*. Hiroshima: RIHE, pp. 1–21.

Jones, G. A. (2009). Sectors, institutional types, and the challenges of shifting categories: A Canadian commentary. *Higher Education Quarterly* 63(4), 371–83.

Jones, G. A., Shanahan, T., Padure, L., Lamoureux, S., and Gregor, E. (2008). *Marshalling Resources for Change: System-level Initiatives to Increase Access and Success*. Montreal: Millennium Scholarship Foundation.

Kerr, C. (1963). *The Uses of the University*. Cambridge, MA: Harvard University Press, 5th edn, 2001.

Kerr, C. (2001). *The Gold and the Blue: A Personal Memoir of the University of California, 1949–1967*. Volume 1: *Academic Triumphs*. Berkeley: University of California Press.

King, R., Marginson, S., and Naidoo, R. (eds) (2011). *Handbook of Higher Education and Globalization*. Cheltenham: Edward Elgar.

Konstantinovskiy, D. (2016). HPS and social equity: Case of Russia. Paper prepared for High Participation Systems project.

Leiden University (2017). Centre for Work and Technology Studies. The Leiden Ranking 2016. http://www.leidenranking.com/ranking/2017/list

Ma, W. (2008). The University of California at Berkeley: An emerging global research university. *Higher Education Policy* 21(1), 65–81.

Maasen, P. (2010). Higher education diversification in Europe. In Research Institute for Higher Education (RIHE), Hiroshima University (ed.), *Diversifying Higher Education Systems in the International and Comparative Perspectives*. Hiroshima: RIHE, pp. 49–74.

Marginson, S. (2013). The impossibility of capitalist markets in higher education. *Higher Education Policy* 28(3), 353–70.

Marginson, S. (2014). University rankings and social science. *European Journal of Education* 49(1), 45–59.

Marginson, S. and Considine, M. (2000). The Enterprise University: Power, governance and reinvention in Australia. Cambridge: Cambridge University Press.

Marginson, S. and Marshman, I. (2013). System and structure. In G. Croucher, S. Marginson, A. Norton, and J. Wells (eds), *The Dawkins Revolution 25 Years On*. Melbourne: Melbourne University Publishing, pp. 56–74.

Meek, V. L. (2000). Diversity and marketisation of higher education: Incompatible concepts? *Higher Education Policy* 13(1), 23–39.

Mettler, S. (2014). *Degrees of Inequality: How the Politics of Higher Education Sabotaged the American Dream*. New York: Basic Books.

Michigan State University (2016). *MSU Facts*. https://msu.edu/about/thisismsu/facts.html

Mohrman, K., Ma, W., and Baker, D. (2008). The research university in transition: The emerging global mode. *Higher Education Policy* 21(1), 5–27.

Monash University (2016). *Monash at a Glance*. http://www.monash.edu/about/who/glance

Morphew, C. (2000). Institutional diversity, program acquisition and faculty members: Examining academic drift at a new level. *Higher Education Policy* 13, 55–77.

Neave, G. (1979). Academic drift: Some views from Europe. *Studies in Higher Education* 4(2), 143–59.

Ohio State University (2016). *High Points*. https://www.osu.edu/highpoints/

OECD (Organisation for Economic Co-operation and Development) (2015). *Education at a Glance 2015*. Paris: OECD.

Palfreyman, D. and Tapper, T. (2008). *Structuring Mass Higher Education: The Role of Elite Institutions*. New York: Routledge.

Pinheiro, R. (2015). HPS and diversity: The case of Norway. Paper prepared for High Participation Systems project.

Pinheiro, R. and Antonowicz, D. (2015). Opening the gates or coping with the flow? Governing access to higher education in Northern and Central Europe. *Higher Education* 70(3), 299–313.

Pinheiro, R., Charles, D., and Jones, G. (2015). Equity, institutional diversity and regional development: A cross-country comparison. *Higher Education*. DOI 10.1007/s10734-015-9958-7.

Pinheiro, R., Geschwind, L., and Aarrevaara, T. (2016). Mergers in higher education: The experience from Northern Europe. *Higher Education Dynamics*. New York: Springer.

Reichert, S. (2009). *Institutional Diversity in European Higher Education: Tensions and Challenges for Policy Makers and Institutional Leaders*. Brussels: European University Association.

Rhoades, G. (1990). Political competition and differentiation in higher education. In J. C. Alexander and P. Colony (eds), *Differentiation Theory and Social Change*. New York: Columbia University Press, pp. 187–221.

Riesman, D. (1958). *Constraint and Variety in American Education*. Lincoln: University of Nebraska Press.

Salmi, J. (2009). *The Challenge of Establishing World-Class Universities*. Washington, DC: World Bank.

Semyonov, D. and Platonova D. (2014). Program diversification and specialization in Russian higher education institutions. National Research University—Higher School of Economics. Series EDU Education No. 17/EDU/2014. https://publications.hse.ru/en/preprints/137664991

Shah, M., Bennett, A., and Southgate, E. (2016). *Widening Higher Education Participation*. London: Chandos Publishing, pp. xv.

Shattock, M. (1996). *The Creation of a University System*. London: Blackwell.

Shavit, Y., Arum, R., and Gamoran, A. (eds) (2007). *Stratification in Higher Education: A Comparative Study*. Stanford: Stanford University Press.

Teichler, U. (1996). Diversity in higher education in Germany: The two-type structure. In V. L. Meek, L. Goedegebuure, O. Kivinen, and R. Rinne (eds), *The Mockers and the Mocked: Comparative Perspectives on Differentiation, Convergence and Diversity in Higher Education*. Oxford: Pergamon, pp. 117–37.

Teichler, U. (2008). Diversification? Trends and explanations of the shape and size of higher education. *Higher Education* 56(3), 349–79.

Titova, N. (2008). *Put uspekha I neudach. Strategicheskoe razvitie rossiskikh vuzov [Way to Success and Failure. Strategic Development of the Russian Universities]*. Moscow: Higher School of Economics Press.

Thomas, L. (2016). Developing inclusive learning to improve the engagement, belonging, retention, and success of students from diverse groups. In M. Shah, A. Bennett, and E. Southgate (eds), *Widening Higher Education Participation*. London: Chandos Publishing, pp. 135–59.

Trow, M. (1973). *Problems in the Transition from Elite to Mass Higher Education*. Berkeley, CA: Carnegie Commission on Higher Education.

Trow, M. (1970). Reflections on the transition from mass to universal higher education. *Daedalus* 99(1), 1–42.

U-Multirank (2016). *U-Multirank*. http://www.umultirank.org/#!/home?trackType=home&section=entrance

Universidade de Sao Paulo (2016). http://www5.usp.br

Universidad Nacional Autónoma de México (2016). *La UNAM En Números, 2015–2016*. Mexico: Universidad Nacional Autónoma de México. http://www.estadistica.unam.mx/numeralia/

University of Toronto (2016). *Quick Facts*. https://www.utoronto.ca/about-u-of-t

van Vught, F. (2008). Mission diversity and reputation in higher education. *Higher Education Policy* 21(2), 151–74.

Wang, C. and Zha, Q. (2015). Measuring systematic diversity in Chinese higher education: A multiple methods approach. Paper presented to the 40th Annual Conference of Association for the Study of Higher Education (ASHE). Denver, CO, 4–7 November.

5 Vertical Stratification

Brendan Cantwell and Simon Marginson

> By positional competition is meant competition that is fundamentally for a higher place within some explicit or implicit hierarchy and that thereby yields gains for some only by dint of losses for others. Positional competition, in the language of game theory, is a zero-sum game: what winners win, losers lose.
>
> (F. Hirsch, 1976: 52)

Introduction

The entrance of millions of students into tertiary education clearly implies quantitative system expansion. All else being equal, more students require more places, additional academic and administrative staff, and greater overall investment in higher education from public and/or private sources. High and increasing levels of participation also entail important qualitative changes to the structural form and social character of higher education systems. As systems expand they necessarily involve a larger part of society and become entangled in a wider set of social relations. One consequence of such system expansion is a common tendency to increased vertical stratification. Vertical stratification includes: (1) differential value from participation; (2) segmentation of the student body on a hierarchical basis; and (3) institutional hierarchy. All three aspects are considered in this chapter and in other parts of this book, but the third type—the vertical stratification of institutions in a hierarchy—is the central focus here.

Vertical stratification in high participation systems (HPS) tends to take the form of *bifurcation*. A bifurcation is a binary division into separate and opposing sub-groups that together constitute an interdependent system. The first sub-group of higher education institutions is designated as the 'artisanal' sub-sector, consisting of high-demand, high-value institutions. The second group of higher education institutions is the 'demand-absorbing' sub-sector, consisting of lower demand, low value, and mass accessible educational opportunities.

Variation from the ideal types both within and between systems is expected. In the real world no system is fully bifurcated and, as discussed later, a middle layer is common. Some higher education institutions are close to pure examples of one ideal type or the other, while others possess elements of both types or even partially defy the division between exclusive and mass production. Some HPS are organized by a number of 'grades' of institution vertically arranged, for example through the device of a classification system, as in China and the United States of America (USA). Some HPS are not formally segmented but constitute a single market, and within it either steep, or more flat distinctions of value between institutions; for example, the UK and Australia (both also maintain additional further education/vocational education sectors). In other HPS, government protects a unitary research-oriented higher education system, sometimes protecting unitarianism in the universities by the device of running a subordinate local sector under the research universities (Netherlands); or maintains a second sector with formal parity on the basis of an academic/technical distinction (Germany). Other system arrangements are possible. The point is that while the tendency towards bifurcation is universal, there is no assumption that stratification will take the same form in all HPS.

The tendency to elite/non-elite bifurcation within systems is associated with the absolute scarcity of socially valued places. To put it another way, the zero-sum character of positional competition (M. W. Hirsch, 1976; Marginson, 1997) is the basis of bifurcation. In HPS some student places do not carry social distinctions and/or high economic value. As the rate of participation advances the proportion of relatively low value places tends to grow, so that the demand-absorbing segment of higher education grows in size relative to the artisanal segment. All tertiary places continue to confer advantages vis-à-vis non-participation. In that sense the ultimate structuring of combined participation/non-participation is ternary rather than binary (see Chapter 6 for a detailed treatment on equity and the returns to participation).

Social stratification occurs through two modalities: economic and cultural (Marginson, 2006). Economically, the levels of taxation required to offer universal access to research universities are prohibitive in most nations. Fiscal restraints often lead to institutional differentiation of the quality of higher education institutions based on resource levels, and access asymmetries based on cost. Universities need a certain level of resources to be able to compete effectively as research institutions. Some cannot achieve the threshold, imposing a binary structure. Culturally, following Bourdieu (1983, 1988), both student selection and competition for status among institutions tend to differentiation between, on the one hand, social-cultural elites, and, on the other, non-elites. Vertical social differentiation occurs among institutions, and there is competition among and differentiation between their student users. In addition to economic and social forces, stratification is also mediated by policy. Governments that adopt neoliberal polices rooted in quasi-markets and competition may extend system stratification whereas more egalitarian policy regimes that ensure the distribution of high quality and socially desirable places throughout the system may moderate the HPS tendency towards vertical differentiation.

Of course, bifurcation and stratification exhibit differing levels of intensity and take a variety of structural forms. These variations have implications not only for the structuring of HPS, but also for the role of higher education in shaping patterns of social equality/inequality. The forces driving the tendency towards bifurcation, along with the system-specific contingencies most prominent in shaping the quality and extent of stratification, are formalized in three general propositions (11–13):

- *The expansion of participation towards and beyond the HPS stage is associated with a tendency to bifurcation and stratification (vertical diversification) in the value of higher education, between elite (artisanal) institutions and mass (demand-absorbing) institutions.*
- *The tendency to institutional stratification is magnified by features common (though not universal) among HPS including (a) intensified social competition for the most valuable student places; (b) variable tuition charges; and/or (c) intensified competition between institutions.*
- *In stratified HPS, a middle layer of institutions tends to form, shaped by the combination of upward aspirations (drift) with systemic scarcity of resources and status.*

As is cautioned throughout this volume, propositions are not covering laws. Each proposition describes an observed secular tendency of HPS development, all of which are contingent. Comparative study permits analysis of the interaction between tendencies associated with HPS and the situated socio-cultural and political economy of particular systems.

System bifurcation

Analysis into vertical stratification is anchored by the first proposition on stratification (HPS Proposition 11):

> *The expansion of participation towards and beyond the HPS stage is associated with a tendency to bifurcation and stratification (vertical diversification) in the value of higher education, between elite (artisanal) institutions and mass (demand-absorbing) institutions.*

The logic of positional competition gives order to bifurcation but stratification is not fully driven by the logic of positional competition. Stratification is sustained also by the need for definition and identity in the face of what are large, open, and also opaque higher education systems (Marginson, 2016). Categories enable not only meanings but also uses. The different parts of a stratified system become fastened organically onto differentiated value, differentiated outcomes, stratified employer relations, and stratified client bases. Differentiated students become matched to differentiated institutions, resulting unequal social outcomes (Rivera, 2015; Marginson, 2016; see also Chapter 6). In other words, vertical stratification provides a social-cognitive roadmap of the high-ways and byways that link higher education institutions with social outcomes. Such a map not only gives order to the system but also helps to justify both the status of institutions and students outcomes.

BOURDIEU AND THE CHARACTER OF BINARY STRATIFICATION

HPS stratification is sustained outside formally regulated differentiation, which may or may not match the logics of the real social distinctions based on status, social power, and unequal resources. Bourdieu (1983, 1988) theorized the strong tendency of vertical social stratification within cultural and academic fields. He emphasizes that stratification takes binary form. In such systems, a minority of actors maintain high status through the possession of cultural and social resources (capital). Social distinction is attained through practice and, above all else, signed by exclusivity in taste and access. Elite actors (students and faculty) mutually select elite institutions, which expect culturally appropriate prac-tices among participants and exclude the great majority of would-be students and staff. This excess demand is not excluded from the system but is instead absorbed by subordinate institutions, which is why HPS feature a basic tendency towards splitting into elite and mass segments.

Institutional differentiation is a regulative technology capable of sorting the entire field (Foucault, 1977). Bifurcation is the master segmentation that creates the two poles of the field, and installs the felt experience of haves and have-nots, so legitimating all the other moments of hierarchy. Bifurcation is the product of persistent and reproduced stratification of status and reputation, resource asymmetries, technological innovations; and of policy demands for innovation in higher education. Most importantly, bifurcation is the product of the joint contests between families for social advantage and between institutions for social prestige.

Practice establishes field position and so higher education institutions are distin-guished not just by the exchange value of the things they produce—primarily knowledge and graduates—but also in the way academic production takes place. Production in the elite and non-elite sub-sectors take different forms. Elite production is at least partly separated from the economic necessities of cost minimization and compulsion for utilitarian applications. The field recognizes and normalizes the position of elite actors, as evidenced by the fact that elite graduates are selected for the best jobs based on their social practices rather than on the utility of their skills (Rivera, 2015). The qualities that establish elite status are seen as both legitimate and desirable to all, even while elite status remains inaccessible to almost everyone.

In the case of higher education, the top places are positional goods that confer social status (Marginson, 2006). For students and their families, elite institutions promise three kinds of benefit. First, winning a highly sought-after place is a lifetime achievement. It constitutes status in itself; claiming 'my daughter will attend Cambridge' is a badge of status. Second, elite institutions and programmes provide the certainty of gilt-edged mobile professional pathways, as in Harvard Law or Medicine. Third, there is an alternative offering, the larger and less defined freedom of the elite generalist, as in the liberal arts graduate. The more generic and symbolic the cultural form of elite positional goods, the less they are defined in terms of specific use, the more that their possessors have been freed for mobility across the upper layers of the whole society. Oxford philosophy graduates are welcomed to starting positions in the upper reaches of a great range of banks and management companies. Graduates of elite institutions overwhelmingly dominate access to the most socially and financially rewarding graduate jobs. Hiring firms select these students without special regard to their particular course of study or specialized knowledge, and their grades are much less important than their universities, though the specifically tailored forms of their cultural capital are into play (Rivera, 2015). The demand for liberally formed graduates from the community colleges is less compelling. Elite cultural goods are partly separated from economic logics yet, paradoxically, this is part of their mystic. As Bourdieu (1984) argues in *Distinction*, the social power of elite higher education institutions partly derives from their ability to distribute social and economic advantage using cultural criteria.

The Ideal Types

ARTISANAL

In all HPS the common sign of a social hierarchy of institutional value is the presence of institutions where large numbers of people—student, faculty, professional staff—*want to be*. This 'pull' factor is clearly greater than in relation to other higher education institutions. Many students and staff would 'upgrade' to elite institutions if they could. These flagship high-value higher education institutions create social position. Such institutions exist in almost every HPS, even in egalitarian Finland (the University of Helsinki) and Norway (the University of Oslo). These countries have just one unambiguously elite institution. In the HPS era that has become unusual. Whereas in pre-mass higher education systems there was often only one leading institution, in many cases simply designated 'the university', in the HPS era the number of elite institutions multiplies, though not necessarily in proportion to system growth. Even in tiny Singapore with five million people—albeit with a per capita income of close to US$80,000

(World Bank, 2017)—there are now two global research universities of the highest standing, which is the same number as in UK. Nevertheless, this passage from monopoly to oligopoly is a quantitative not qualitative change. It does not change the character of the elite sector.

Within the elite group there often continues to be a single national university that is lifted above all others. In Russia it is Moscow State University; in Japan the University of Tokyo. In ultra-high participation South Korea, Seoul National University is the place to graduate from. There are two supreme universities in China, one liberal and one more technical, side by side in Beijing: Peking University and Tsinghua. The UK has Oxford and Cambridge. In all the vast HPS that is US higher education, one unchallenged leader towers above all the others, both the private Ivy League and the top public universities. Harvard University is an awesome status-making colossus, publishing twice as many high citation papers as the world number two, Stanford (see Table 5.1).

Without positional competition and hierarchy, Harvard as we know it would cease to exist, because the value of capital, and resulting status orders, are relational and relative. No doubt its concentrated research capacity would be better distributed among US metropolises and regions, but that distribution would not yield the excitement of Harvard. Internet search volume demonstrates the absolute stature of Harvard. From 2010 through 2015 worldwide Google searches for 'Harvard University' were made at nearly double the volume as were searches for 'Yale University', 'University of Oxford', and 'University of Cambridge' (Figure 5.1). Though the relentless logic of zero-sum says that there can be only one Harvard, and university competition is largely closed, desires to be of Harvard (and, perhaps, university presidents' dream one day to be Harvard) are universal.

With Harvard set as the global prototype, the artisanal segment is primarily constituted by highly selective world-class research universities that compete among each other in national and global quasi-markets. It can be considered an 'artisanal' sector because research and teaching happen in a craft-like way and possession of a qualification from an artisanal institution can confer social distinction. The elite sector is distinguished by its research performance and prominence in objective research university rankings, by its student selectivity, and also by its position in those 'best university' league tables that are shaped less by precise performance metrics than by reputational surveys. Most institutions in this sector have long history. Some are pre-modern, drawing prestige from venerable origins and gothic spires. Yet elite higher education institutions are always also impeccably late-modern, temples of science, commanders of the future—not so much timeless (which would imply an inability to respond and change) as of all times, or eternal. This group includes super-incumbents at the very top of league tables like Harvard and Cambridge universities, but also national flagships like the University of Tokyo and world-class regional higher education institutions such as the University of British Columbia. These are globally networked universities, operating as an informal but recognizable world system in relation to the circulation of

Table 5.1. World top 50 universities in the production of high citation research papers (papers in top 10% of their field), 2009–12

University		Total research papers, 2012–15	Proportion of papers in top 10% of field by citation rate %	Number of papers in top 10% of field	Number of papers in top 1% of field
Harvard Univ	USA	31,678	22.5	7,134	1,072
Stanford Univ	USA	15,113	22.3	3,372	523
MIT	USA	10,277	25.0	2,565	437
Univ Calif—Berkeley	USA	12,116	21.7	2,628	349
Univ Oxford	UK	13,981	18.4	2,570	338
Univ Cambridge	UK	12,957	17.6	2,274	327
Univ Toronto	Canada	21,737	13.7	2,980	321
Johns Hopkins Univ	USA	16,368	16.2	2,649	316
Univ Michigan	USA	18,270	15.3	2,798	307
Univ Coll London	UK	13,743	17.1	2,357	306
Univ Washington—Seattle	USA	14 163	17.2	2,436	303
Univ Calif—Los Angeles	USA	13 898	17.3	2,398	297
Columbia Univ	USA	12 178	17.8	2,168	280
Univ Penn	USA	13,235	17.0	2,247	279
Univ Calif—San Diego	USA	12,092	18.3	2,217	270
Univ Calif—San Francisco	USA	9,989	19.7	1,967	267
Yale Univ	USA	11,071	19.2	2,130	265
Imperial Coll London	UK	11,230	16.7	1,871	227
Northwestern Univ	USA	10,375	17.5	1,813	209
Washington Univ—St Louis	USA	8760	16.7	1,467	199
Univ Minnesota—Twin Cities	USA	12,315	13.4	1,649	198
Duke Univ	USA	11,413	16.0	1,828	195
Univ British Columbia	Canada	12 453	13.9	1,730	195
Univ Wisconsin—Madison	USA	12,365	14.3	1,766	193
ETH Zurich	Switzerland	9075	17.6	1,596	191
Nanyang Technol Univ	Singapore	9,146	15.4	1,413	186
NYU	USA	8540	17.0	1,450	185
Tsinghua Univ	China	14,930	11.8	1,768	178
Cornell Univ	USA	9104	16.1	1,468	176
Univ Melbourne	Australia	11,571	13.1	1,518	171
Univ Pittsburgh	USA	12,047	13.5	1,629	171
Univ Texas—Austin	USA	9,332	15.5	1,451	171
Univ Queensland	Australia	11,258	12.8	1,443	166
National Univ Singapore	Singapore	11,657	13.7	1,597	163
Univ Chicago	USA	7,425	18.8	1,393	162
Princeton Univ	USA	5,312	22.0	1,170	160
Univ N Carolina—Chapel Hill	USA	9,931	15.5	1,543	156
Katholieke Univ Leuven	Belgium	10,374	14.1	1,459	155
McGill Univ	Canada	10,860	13.0	1,407	154
Caltech	USA	5,268	21.2	1,119	153
Ohio State Univ	USA	11,791	12.1	1,425	149

(*continued*)

Table 5.1. Continued

University		Total research papers, 2012–15	Proportion of papers in top 10% of field by citation rate %	Number of papers in top 10% of field	Number of papers in top 1% of field
Univ Manchester	UK	9,322	13.7	1,273	149
Univ Copenhagen	Denmark	11,090	12.9	1,432	145
Univ Edinburgh	UK	7,079	15.2	1,078	143
King's Coll London	UK	7,449	16.5	1,231	142
Univ Calif—Davis	USA	10,871	13.7	1,493	142
Univ Sydney	Australia	11,733	12.1	1,416	142
Ecole Polytech Fed Lausanne	Switzerland	5,573	18.2	1,013	138
Univ Southern Calif	USA	7,878	14.9	1,171	137

Source: Adapted by authors from various data series in Leiden University (2017).

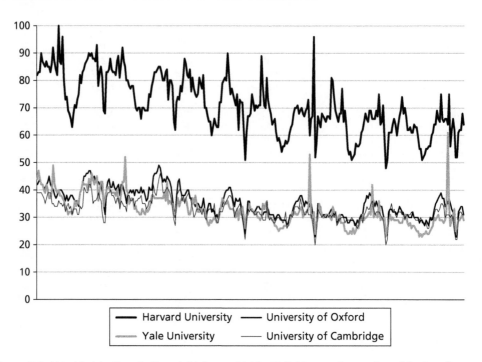

Figure 5.1. Worldwide Google Search Volume, 2010–15 (100 = peak search activity for all terms, all other values set relative to peak)

Source: Authors' analysis of Google search volume data, extracted from https://trends.google.com

knowledge, status-as-value, and human talent. Faculty and some students are sourced internationally, knowledge production occurs trans-nationally, and certain qualifications such as business, the elite professions, and science have exchange value on international labour markets. Academic production in this sub-sector, especially English-language research, is transnational and unbundled over time and space.

Claims to the global, and effective action at a distance, are essential to elite status and artisanal production. Yet artisanal higher education institutions are also rooted in national leadership and local power. Interestingly, in some nations (e.g. Malaysia, Russia) though not others (e.g. Netherlands, USA), building global reputation is a principal strategy for advancing national standing. For many artisanal institutions, if their presence within the circuits of global research is in decline their reputations will be affected. Yet their essential status, at least for the purposes of this analysis, is determined by relative position within national systems. In the strongest nations (and the most parochial), leading higher education institutions to focus solely on their position at home. Middle-tier US research universities try momentarily to signal their status at home by pointing to their top one hundred standing in the global rankings, but simply no one cares.

The US institutions are the global leaders. American power, which is also global power, is the end that they seek. In higher education, the most globally penetrated of social sectors, globalization is neither complete nor superior to within-nation competition between higher education institutions. Action in the global dimension is a primary means of stratification, widening the gap between artisanal and middle institutions; yet the HPS remains a national rather than universal form. 'Global participation' is an abstraction not a system. Global spaces are fictive, all action is taken in locales, and universities—even those with global status—remain nationally chartered. In the neoliberal imagination, universities are engines of competition, called into the service of individual and national competition while also competing among themselves, but all this effort generally fails to reshape existing status hierarchies. The artisanal sector remains financed primary on a national basis. Research funds and operating revenue are derived from mostly public and also private national sources. Nonetheless, it is not a clear-cut choice between national and global identity. Though teaching services are offered primarily within national or local markets, cross-border traffic is growing, and science is a global conversation—and the production of new knowledge and the generation of student credentials (which are the two pillars of academic production) occur simultaneously.

In most artisanal institutions teaching and research are unified in a Humboldtian manner, at least normatively. The normative practice of the 'teaching-research nexus' is a resilient feature of artisanal production and identity. It must be said that the nexus is more normative than empirical. Funded research concentrates activity, and combined teaching/research practice is never universal to faculty, even in research-strong universities. Star researchers often avoid teaching, perhaps with the exception of graduate supervision, altogether, and academics at leading research universities tend to spend less of their time teaching than do their counterparts with lower status positions. For aspirant middle-status universities (discussed later), whose missions and structures drift towards the artisanal sub-sector but find it hard to achieve artisanal status and lack a broad layer of research stars, the nexus is largely reduced to an ideology, at least when it comes to the instruction of undergraduate students.

Students in the artisanal sub-sector are educated by well-qualified academics, and rarely even by the professors who feature in mass open online courses (MOOCs), in the sort of labour and resource-intensive manner that typically cannot be efficiently scaled. This type of non-scalable production is characteristic of artistic performance and expert handicraft services like medicine as well as traditional higher education (Baumol, 1993). Baumol's example was the string quartet, which can neither be scaled to three players nor automated without something of the performance being lost. Artisanal character combines social status with cultural formation in a way that gives status to cultural practice itself. This economically inefficient production model does not demand efficiency or immediate utility from the sector. Yet there is an economic logic at the base of this; or at the least it does not undermine the economics of status. After all, who cares how much a Harvard degree costs? Most students are excluded from Harvard but not in the first instance by costs. For low-income students with high academic achievement there are scholarships and the lifetime returns will exceed the cost for nearly each student who reaches the starting gate at Harvard.

The differentiated value of elite higher education institutions is motored by research performance but it is directly expressed in student selectivity. The artisanal sub-sector produces global public goods and allocates valuable scarce positional goods on the basis of highly selective admissions. Artisanal institutions contribute to the reproduction of prior social stratification, while taking in a small measure of upward social mobility upon which the legitimacy of all depends. There are no iron laws here, just realpolitik. Social mobility never gets so out of hand as to transform the artisanal ambience or depopulate the social elite. It is hard to pin down the process of reproduction. Social advantage and academic performance are difficult to disentangle, socially and empirically. On an averaging basis, students from privileged social backgrounds are always more likely to excel in school. In most HPS, participants in the artisanal sector come primarily from middle and upper class families, and sustain a combination of ability and commitment to work that is sufficient to support high ambition. The artisanal sector also enrols students of pronounced academic achievement regardless of social background and in many HPS at the graduate level, regardless of nationality. The precise balance between on one hand social reproduction and on the other hand the distribution of merit and upward mobility to new places in society is contextually determined and system specific and can oscillate over time.[1]

DEMAND-ABSORBING

The demand-absorbing sub-sector is very large in comparison to the artisanal sub-sector and its institutions are not household names. Demand-absorbing refers to the social role

---

[1] Chapter 6 on HPS and equity compares the extent of social mobility in different HPS.

of this sub-sector. Like other mass goods, places at demand-absorbing institutions may have utilitarian value or, alternatively, little or no value at all, but tend not to denote social distinction. This sector can exhibit substantial in-sector stratification, featuring both higher quality institutions in teaching and services and lower quality and even (in some systems) fraudulent higher education institutions. The sector also features standardization, as degrees and parts of degrees, based on defined competencies, become increasingly comparable. Curricula are becoming more globally integrated and some cross-national standardization may occur.

As Bourdieu sees it, the demand-absorbing sector responds both to states and to (often state-sanctioned) market forces. Much of this sector is vocationally oriented and dedicated primarily to human capital production. It also covers preparatory and literacy-oriented courses, often pre-vocational in intent. It includes North American community colleges, and technical colleges across the world. Though some policymakers, such as those at the World Bank, imagine mass education as a commercial sector (or at least as a sector ripe for efficient commercialization), the demand-absorbing sector is inhabited also by large public institutions that offer state-shaped and state-induced mass higher education with limited positional value. The dynamic of mass public institutions parallels large-scale bureaucratically driven wartime mobilization by states, and systems of basic education or public health, rather than buyer/seller markets. Despite neoliberalism, public higher education institutions in this sub-sector are partly supply driven and are not yet always organized as quasi-markets. At the same time, the demand-absorbing sub-sector does include a growing for-profit component, especially in the global south and in the USA. The string of small for-profit institutions populate storefronts along Avenida de los Insurgentes in Mexico City, for example, reveals the presence of the commercial sector in the demand-absorbing segment. State-supplied education, it too is largely low quality in terms of both use value and positional value. This limits the ultimate scope for commodification. However, it still permits a good deal of commercial shadow play, as the for-profits manoeuvre to create precarious value through marketing, and there is no obstacle to their participation in state-regulated quasi-markets.

In the absence of a clear-cut institutional hierarchy of value in this sub-sector—there are no status indicators of any kind: no measures of research income or outputs, no global university rankings, no league tables of student entrance scores regulating comparative selectivity—labour market outcomes become the only means of defining social value. Yet defining educated value via labour market outcomes always comes close to fiction; and this is more so in the demand-absorbing sector, in which graduate outcomes have not been pre-set in terms of positional value by the institutional hierarchy. The visible relationship between higher education and the labour market is disrupted by graduate unemployment, the poor fit between field of training and allocation to specialist jobs at work, the vagaries of the job selection process itself (in which educated competence is only one of the factors that is taken into account). More generally, there is the profound social dislocation between education and work (Teichler, 2007). Though the human capital rhetoric binds the two great sites together, they are essentially different to each other, with heterogeneous purposes and cultures, as different as family and work, or education and government. Elite credentials can transmute in Bourdieu-ian fashion across the divide, but the exchange value of demand-absorbing higher education institutions never becomes clear. The clamour about 'standards' is therefore endemic, and independent of the quality of programmes. Educational standards in the artisanal sub-sector define themselves. Educational standards in the demand-absorbing sub-sector are a 'problem' that is never to be solved; a stick with which to beat demand-absorbing institutions, especially public sector ones, keeping them in their place.

Although there is no equivalent of the status indicators that are common to artisanal institutions, competition in the demand-absorbing sector occurs along at least three axes. The first is the perceived value of places. Higher education institutions differ in in quality and, in some HPS, price. The second axis of competition is market share. Some demand-absorbing institutions enrol few students and are hyper-local. Others have large numbers of students and are multi-national enterprises. The third axis is consumption status. In a more vocationally oriented sub-sector this is primarily regulated by standing in the labour market. Some demand-absorbing qualifications offer higher exchange values relative to the rest of the sector (such as qualifications from well-regarded polytechnics) and enjoy higher consumption status. A much larger number provide credentials with little exchange value and low status. In some HPS, competition is intense. However, true free-market competition is not to be found anywhere (Marginson, 2013). States maintain a keen interest in regulating and in most countries in subsiding the demand-absorbing sub-sector. Nor are all the higher education institutions in this sub-sector trying to grow or achieve larger market share. Many states still limit the enrolments of individual higher education institutions, and in some private sectors, for example the small colleges in India, the mode of production does not permit institutions to expand without limit.

Nevertheless, it is important for research to trace the growing role of state-sanctioned competition, and bona fide capitalist production, within the demand-absorbing group.

Social participation is varied in this sub-sector. Students come from a large swathe of society but few students from the highest rungs of the social ladder enrol in demand-absorbing institutions. Some students in this sector complete degree programmes within a single organization that look more or less like traditional higher education institutions. Others may enrol in new modalities that include credentials though online education but the precise possibilities are system and custom specific, being regulated by history, local quality assurance mechanisms, funding, and other factors. Some demand-absorbing higher education institutions engage in limited knowledge production but research is not a defining focus of the demand-absorbing sub-sector. Most research is technical in nature, and either in service to the sector itself (e.g. research about effective online pedagogy), or in service to the vocational sectors that graduates will enter (e.g. to make better websites, new accountancy techniques, improvement in nursing). Partial exceptions include those higher education institutions whose missions are drifting towards the artisanal pole but remain demand-absorbing in essence. Knowledge production and instruction in this sub-sector are almost fully distinct. In other words, there is no true teaching and research nexus in demand-absorbing institutions. The only demand-absorbing institutions that claim the nexus are those trying to reposition upwards.

Drivers of Bifurcation

Vertical stratification is near universal among HPS. Underlying social processes rather either economic laws of demand or worldwide institutionalization, which are often theorizing as spontaneously occurring, drives the secular tendency towards bifurcation of HPS. The second proposition on stratification, HPS Proposition 12, states:

> *The tendency to institutional stratification is magnified by features common (though not universal) among HPS including (a) intensified social competition for the most valuable student places; (b) variable tuition charges; and/or (c) intensified competition between institutions.*

The quality and extent of stratification is largely depended upon system specific conditions. The effects of drivers (a)–(c) are quickened under a number of conditions: For example, when economic recession enhances the importance of distinctions between graduates or when rankings enhance competition between intuitions. On the one hand, these drivers can be considered to be generic mechanisms. On the other hand, these drivers can be seen as arenas for action, points of effect, where dedicated policy efforts, and grounded system cultures can modify or even prevent the stratification of institutions, levelling upwards, and secure the equivalence of all students as citizens deserving of equal and socially valued opportunity.

INTENSE COMPETITION FOR VALUABLE PLACES

Economic growth does not alone explain expanded participation (Schofer and Meyer, 2005). In countries like China and India, which account for much of the global increase in participation, growth in tertiary participation outstrips even the impressive economic expansion (Marginson, 2016). Heightened aspirations for post-secondary education, both individual and social, underwrite system expansion. Aspirations also drive bifurcation, insofar as system expansion is associated with stratification. To put it another way, systems cannot at one and the same time accommodate aspirations for access and attainment, and exclusivity and zero-sum status, without generating unequal outcomes via segmentation.

Student and family aspirations are almost universally encaged by state policy, which presents education as a route for social mobility and secure livelihoods. For states it is far easier to peddle universal hopes and dreams through education than to guarantee all citizens with fecund conditions of life: easier, because the mechanisms of educational selection transfer the responsibility for social failure back to the individual (Clark, 1960). Nevertheless, educational/social aspirations *are* increasingly universal, and when aspirations heat up, public and private higher education institutions sooner or later must develop and expand to support the additional enrolment. HPS must provide additional spaces for new entrants by expanding existing institutions, and by establishing new ones. Increase in demand-absorbing institutions contributes to system bifurcation. Expansion contributes to bifurcation by simple virtue of the fact that newly formed higher education institutions cannot replicate the status of the established system leaders. With each additional student, elite institutions are further distinguished from the growing herd.

Competition for the most valuable places is perhaps the one driver of bifurcation common to all HPS. Put simply, as systems expand not all places retain the same social status or yield the same value of exchange in the labour market. In the post-Confusion systems of East Asia aspirations are universally high among families from all social classes (Wu and Bai, 2015) and large investments are made in shadow education to secure the most desirable spots. In the market-driven systems of the Anglo-American countries privileged students rely on both financial resources and social and cultural capital to secure an advantage in competition for the most desirable places, those forms of participation that offer the best chances to yield social and economic advantage (McDonough, 1997). Even in the most egalitarian systems students from professional classes exploit social advantage to secure seats in universities and specific programmes that have the greatest social return (Thomsen et al., 2013).

In most HPS institutional levels are patterned by social position, in that the institutions with the highest level of economic resources are the most sought after by students and this social desirability, in turn, enhances well-to-do institutions ability to garner even greater resources. Yet even absent profound resource asymmetries, competition to the most socially desirable places establishes vertical status dictions among intuitions. As noted, even in Finland and Norway, where parity of institutional esteem and the tradition of attending local institutions retard position-seeking mobility, many students (though more faculty) would like to be at Helsinki and Oslo. Such status dictions are endemic to HPS because few students are formally excluded. Competition among students is not to participate but to participate in a place that is socially desirable and valuable. Such competition is heated up, as argued earlier, when family aspirations for higher education, augmented by state policy, are high.

VARIABLE TUITION FEES

The relationship between fees and overall social stratification is not direct. Among Organisation for Economic Co-operation and Development (OECD) countries, as a general rule, those with lower levels of income inequality are less likely to charge tuition fees, but there are exceptions. In Mexico, public university fees are nominal and yet the distribution of incomes is highly unequal and in Korea tuition fees are relatively high but incomes are more equally distributed than the average among OECD countries. Variability in tuition fees within a system, however, is related to stratification among institutions. There are at least two different fee patterns that especially drive stratification.

First, fees accelerate system stratification when (a) they are set by institutions rather than the state, (b) vary by institution and are patterned by status, and (c) can be strategically discounted. The USA is the prototypal example. There both public and private universities rely on fees as a significant source of operating revenue. Subject to some restraints, institutions generally set fee levels and the most desirable intuitions charge the most. Elite research universities and liberal arts colleges tend to change the highest fees, whereas demand-absorbing community colleges charge fees that are lower, sometimes by a factor of ten or more. Further, it is a widespread practice for institutions in the USA to strategically discount tuition on an individual basis in order to woo desirable students (those with high test scores and the capacity to pay high tuition). Together, these features of the fee regime establish an up-market and down-market based on fee level and facilitate the concentration of both financial and social resources in a small set of intuitions. Fees that are universally high do not alone drive stratification to the same extent as does a system of fee variation. In the UK, for example, fees are high but are capped by the state and virtually all universities charge the same high tuition, which is financed by an income-contingent repayment scheme. While the introduction of high fees may have forced some students out of the university sector and thus extended bifurcation, fees are not a major driver of stratification among the large (and already stratified) unitary university sector because all places charge the same fees.

Second, variable fees also drive bifurcation when (a) the public supply is desirable, supply constrained, and charges low or zero fees, and (b) the demand-absorbing sector is comprised of fee charging, largely private institutions. This pattern is observed in some HPS in Eastern Europe and in many of the emerging HPS in Latin America. In these cases the public sector is typically higher quality, in high demand, and demand exceeds supply. Supply constraints often mean that public institutions are selective, and students who secure a scarce place are generally from middle and upper class families. Systems that follow this fee pattern may also have a private sector, typically comprised of small commercial institutions that provide access for a price. It is usual for there to be some differentiation within the private sector. Most will be demand-absorbing and explicitly commercial whose only entrance requirement is the ability to pay, and within this group quality may vary somewhat by price. A few may be elite private intuitions populated by wealthy students who have either been locked out of the public sector based on academic performance or have an ideological preference for private education; yet, even among these cases few enjoy the status of the leading public research universities.

While one of the two fee patterns listed earlier may generically describe the ways in which tuition charges drive bifurcation in many systems, these patterns are not absolute. A variation of the no fee/fee bifurcation is Russia where fee-paying students sit alongside higher achieving students in state-supported free places in the same higher education institutions and classrooms. In that case differential tuition is used to socially stratify students and graduates directly, rather than doing so via the stratification of institutions. Further, the absence of fees might be considered a third pattern. In the Nordic countries and parts of the European continent there are no fees assessed to domestic (or within the European Union where applicable) students (and in a few countries such as Finland most international students are even exempt from fees). All else equal, the absence of fees is a governor on stratification.

INTENSIFIED INTUITIONAL CONFLICT

Competition is endemic to higher education as a mass social enterprise. The actual incidence of competitive mechanisms, particularly state-fostered quasi markets, varies from system to system but the bedrock social competition is present in every HPS. Students compete for places. higher education institutions compete for students, resources, and status. Competitive forces, along with strategic actions devised to secure competitive advantage, drive bifurcation.

The quest for social distinction is the root of competition in higher education. As Bowen (1980) and others have observed, research-intensive universities seek to maximize prestige rather than profit. The pursuit of prestige drives universities to compete with one and other for resources that can be converted into academic capital, including financial resources as well as the most desirable students and academic staff. Universities that prevail in these competitions, such as Oxbridge and the Ivy League, tend to enjoy historical advantages and prevail consistently over time. Increasingly, over time, resources and status are concentrated in a small number of universities, normalizing and enhancing ongoing system bifurcation. Competition is heightened in every HPS, compared to pre-HPS configurations, in two senses. First, HPS is a contest of all comers. In a quantitative sense, there are more competitors so there is always more competition. Second, a larger number of actors are involved in a larger number of activities in the HPS (see the trend to multiversification), opening up multiple dimensions along which to compete and ever finer lines of distinction. Institutional contest within systems, and national competition between systems, both drive bifurcation. Key contingencies related to the extent to which inter-institutional competition drives bifurcation, then, include within system resource allocation mechanism and the ways in which systems compete on a global basis.

Neoliberal allocative regimes. The rise of neoliberal normative practices in government, especially the new public management (NPM) (Deem, 2001), has directly heightened competition among institutions within many HPS. Neoliberal ideology assumes that competition is virtuous and yields desirable outcomes. In systems with entranced neoliberal governance, especially the Anglo-American systems, competition has been installed as a central dynamic in system organization. While not all HPS have experienced the neoliberal turn, the use of NPM in HPS—and in all tertiary education systems—is more widespread; though the extent, intensity, and spread of competitive mechanism vary and should be traced system by system through empirical research. NPM asserts the authority of the state to evaluate university performance and to create incentives to promote competition among higher education institutions in order to optimize output. Competition is most intense in systems where resources are primarily allocated through competitions (Slaughter and Leslie, 1997). Competition-based governance intensifies, economizes, and in some cases formalizes competitive pressures already within higher education systems. On top of the social competition among families and students for position, the NPM layers on more specifically economic forms of contest between higher education institutions for resources and for students. This resulting hybrid seems to give substance to the NPM's imagining of higher education as an economy (for social competition in higher education is longstanding and very real). At the same time, the NPM modernizes the streaming of social rewards, renders the outcomes of competition a matter of individual choice (government can hardly be blamed, however socially unequal the resulting distribution of benefits) while providing government with more precise mechanisms for controlling the HPS. Techniques of economic policy have an unmatched capacity to both remake system relations and fine-tune allocations at the same time.

On the face of it market simulation is an odd project. No higher education system ever transforms into a laissez-faire capitalist market. The state is always there (Marginson, 2013). The state, at least indirectly, restricts new entrants in the higher education market by determining what constitutes a higher education institution and which organizations may provide tertiary services. Moreover, in most HPS, as in the smaller mass systems that preceded them, the state remains the primary source of funding, despite some pluralization of incomes. Yet as any number of observers have noted, higher education systems increasingly operate in market-like conditions wherein performance competitions are used to allocate resources. Resource allocation systems in public good sectors like health and education are best understood as welfare quasi-markets (LeGrand, 1991). Quasi-markets are not open exchanges governed by the invisible hand of a stateless market, but bounded competitive spaces with defined rules, installed and regulated by policymakers and other influential actors, with mostly predictable outcomes.

Quasi-market resource allocation exacerbates the tendency to unequal value between higher education institutions, so that in principle every institution can be individually ranked. Informal rankings are a regulatory technology that reflects the outcomes of competition, and they feed back into the reproduction of the competitively defined order. The underlying assumption that is possible to make meaningful assessments of where scarce public resources should be best dedicated, implies that it is possible to know the value and worth of each institution. Where even *some* resources are allocated through quasi-market mechanisms, competition can take hold fiercely even when other features of a market are absent. Government can manage a pure competition that ranks higher education institutions in terms of prestige, untroubled by economic markets with messy information asymmetries, dislocations between supply and demand, and subsidies that stymie profit-driven allocation. LeGrand outlines some of the conditions that define quasi-markets. These welfare quasi-markets thus differ from conventional markets in one or more of three ways: (1) not-for-profit organizations compete for public contracts, sometimes in competition with for-profit organizations; (2) consumer purchasing power in the form of vouchers rather than cash; and (3), in some cases, the consumers represented in the market by agents instead of operating by themselves (LeGrand, 1991: 1260).

One or more of the three conditions described earlier are present in most HPS, and each contributes to system bifurcation. In most HPS universities are primarily funded by the state for both teaching and research functions. Yet many systems are moving away from a block grant funding model towards a system in which institutions compete for funds between each other and sometimes with different types of organizations. For instance, the state may fund instruction on a per-student basis and higher education institutions compete to attract enough students to maximize their instructional allocation. In a few systems—but now including such influential global cases as the USA, UK, and Australia—not-for-profit and public universities even find themselves competing with for-profit institutions for state subsidies. Competition between universities and non-university entities for state research and development contracts is common in many HPS. Some leading institutions consistently prevail in competitions for state contracts, furthering the resource and status asymmetries within HPS. Here HPS behaviour can be understood largely as a quantitative extension of what happens in smaller systems, rather than a qualitative change occasioned by the fact of HPS. Nevertheless, quasi-market competition is an economical tool of system management that becomes increasingly attractive to states, as systems grow in size and reach.

Cross border competition. At the same time as many HPS have introduced NPM and quasi-market allocation regimes to increase competition within systems, globalization processes have accelerated competition between systems. Trow did not anticipate globalization processes but it is clear that these processes have had a substantive effect on all higher education systems, including HPS. Globalization neither caused mass participation nor are globalization processes only relevant for HPS. Instead, globalization processes interact with HPS dynamics, often in ways that accelerate stratification.

Standard economic rhetoric about globalization asserts the dissolution of borders and the opening up of a worldwide level plane in which all individuals and organizations compete. This is Friedman's (2006) 'flat' world. Following such an assumption to its logical conclusion—which would entail higher education institutions engaging in direct competition for resources with all other institutions in the world—quickly reveals the serious misapprehensions of a flat world theory. As noted, higher education institutions remain funded nationally, and despite increased international student mobility, most students study near their homes. Relatively few institutions can realistically claim to compete for status on a global basis. Yet, as Marginson (2011) explains: 'The story of globalization in higher education is about how changing space and enhanced mobility transform vision, imagining and the self' (p. 22). While the ways in which global higher education are imagined are many, policymakers and institutional leaders in many HPS tend to view globalization in the neoliberal economic terms that are dominant in policy. They understand globalization as intensifying the links between higher education and economic production, associate this with the importance of higher education to individual and national prosperity. As a follow-on assumption, higher education institutions must compete both within systems and on an international basis, in a constant state of readiness, to meet the demands imposed upon the sector.

Such global imaginings tend to reinforce policy mechanisms and instructional strategies that promote competition as a means of fulfilling institutional and sector missions. The imagined link between economic prosperity, globalization, and competition has become so strongly 'institutionalized' (Held et al., 1999) in HPS as to operate as a policy instinct, a managerial instinct, and a universal mantra for more or less every new situation. This construction of globalization is not modulated by the emergence of HPS but, as stated earlier, it is a condition in which contemporary HPS mostly operate, driving them towards enhanced competition and thus enhanced stratification.

Since the year 2000, when the World Bank announced it would pay increased attention to higher education, and the emergence of world university rankings soon after, many states have pursued policies designed to create or advance 'world-class universities' in order to compete on the global level. In many HPS, including Russia, Korea, and Japan (Salmi, 2009), this entails concentrating high budget scientific research in a small selected group of institutions. At the same time the successive UK research assessments, and the pattern of US national research grants, have de facto concentration effects, creating a layer of exceptional research universities, at the expense of a broad-based research capacity distributed equitably across every region and city.

World-class university strategies contribute to bifurcation in at least three ways. First, concentration of resources in a handful of higher education institutions provides an obvious advantage to those institutions over the rest of the field. Resource advantages permit a select group of institutions to engage in more high-status activities, and strengthen their attractive power in recruiting top students and faculty. Second, designation as a world-class university imparts a status distinction independent of resources. 'World-class' designation signifies a mission and status separation from the nation-bound field and establishes the standard of excellence that serves as a benchmark for other institutions within the system. Third, world-class status implies mobility, freedom, and opportunity, and is therefore sought after. Students want to be at top-ranked universities. For the elites who attend these institutions, the appearance of increased mobility furthers social distinction. For non-elites the possibility of attending a world-class higher education institution opens the door to increased mobility and a better life, creating incentives for the broad acceptance of rankings, and the legitimation of 'world-class' status and the zero-sum competition game on which it rests. In sum, the tendency towards global level competition between systems has intensified, and in some cases reshaped, competition and hierarchy within systems.

Imperfect Bifurcation and the Middle Strata

The tendency towards bifurcation in HPS is secular in that it occurs, to varying degrees, in all HPS. As with most conceptual models, even those strongly supported by observation, social reality is not fully conforming and in no HPS is there a perfect binary division. In all HPS there are now, and probably will continue to be, middle organizations that either lie in between these ideal type segments or operate in both at once. The third and final proposition (13) on stratification claims:

> *In stratified HPS, a middle layer of institutions tends to form, shaped by the combination of upward aspirations (drift) with systemic scarcity of resources and status.*

It is at least theoretically possible that artisanal and demand-absorbing sub-sectors can become parallel within any given HPS with very little mobility between them. Of course, there is also the possibility that innovators and entrepreneurs (organizational and individual) can jump sub-sector or bridge them. In rare cases unexpected events or coordinated efforts disrupt and reconfigure one or both sub-sectors. There is also intense competition and strategic action in a zone of middle organizations, and variation in the sizes of middle sub-sectors, as segmentation occurs and stratification shakes out. These variations, and their changing configurations over time, are one of the defining features of the different HPS. This middle zone is populated from both above and below.

Moving from above are those artisanal institutions for whom size and reach is one of their strategies of choice. As Chapter 4 discussed, social power in higher education is built via aggregation as well as through selectivity, providing that at the core, prestige is unquestionable. In the science power game, victory goes to those who can mobilize the quantity of quality. In all but a handful of the very strongest universities, size generates resources that underpin competitiveness. It is not the chosen path of Princeton, but it is one of the principal mechanisms deployed by Harvard. Hence the large research-intensive public universities that build volume in middle level professional training (accountants, teachers, nurses), or maintain regional campuses where entry is less selective than at the parent site. Inherited advantage, and the continuing prestige of the high research mission and elite training in medicine and law, are sufficient to ensure the brand protection of status in the outliers. In the UK and Australia several leading research universities, such as Manchester, University College London, Melbourne, and Sydney, also maintain high demand-responsive volume in the international student market, without, it seems, impairing precious reputation. In short, these are universities that play in the middle without becoming middle universities.

Moving into the middle zone from below are institutions whose status is much more precarious. There is always potential for colonization of the middle ground, in all but the smallest HPS. Upward aspiration is a universal truth of higher education. Mission drift—discussed also in Chapters 3 and 4—is a powerful force. Historically it has been very significant in systems like those of UK and Australia, which are not formally differen-tiated and are also highly competitive by temper and policy design. In both of these (similar) systems there is a strong tendency for institutional missions to cluster in the 'market middle', in an extraordinarily mimetic system dynamic. Market competition, regulatory requirements that designated universities should conduct research (in Australia), the need to sustain status in the global market for students (both countries), plus unchecked academic drift—all these factors drive degree-providing higher educa-tion institutions to aspire to be global top 500 research universities. Yet there is little real room at the top for newcomers. Amid the near ubiquitous mission drift, non-elite institutions may resemble elite universities in descriptive terms but they find that real elite status is more elusive. The genuine elite is readily identified, and there are now research metrics to confirm what is already known. Some of those that position them-selves in the middle belong in the open demand-absorbing sector below, and for some others the claim to a research role and elite status is weak.

The result in UK/Australian style systems is a strange shadow play, with gaps between on the one hand mission and marketing, on the other hand the social effects; and between the flattening policy discourse in the foreground and the jagged inequalities behind. Official institutional roles are uniform if not mono-cultural. Ostensibly, the higher education institutions are equivalent. Yet the reality is that research activity and positional status are steeply stratified, and everyone knows it. The artisanal sector continues to attract the bulk of student demand and the leading researchers. Stratification is enhanced over time by competition, which tends to reward those with prior advantages. Horizontal diversity of mission is preserved only to the extent that some public or non-profit private higher education institutions evade mission mimetics (see Chapter 4).

As depicted in Figure 5.2, middle higher education institutions are pulled between the contrary production and status logics of the two sub-sectors. Some have claims to be artisanal institutions (Quadrant A in Figure 5.2) and hope to expand research perform-ance while ideally, remaining smaller than their massifying peers. However, among many 'wannabes', the teaching-research nexus ideology has a hollow ring. Marketing can fake anything for a day but a lacuna in global research standings is hard to explain away. For pure demand-absorbing institutions (Quadrant D), the main line of develop-ment is volume building to secure market share, student demand so that some select into these institutions when first choices are off the table, and unit efficiencies through economies of scale. In that quadrant research is scarcely affordable, especially the big budget science that drives rankings.

A few middle higher education institutions attempt to provide a high quality learning experience in institutions in which modest size (Quadrant C) is part of the attraction. They may establish good programmes but in the absence of research and the status it brings, they never receive full credit for good teaching. Without substantial research they

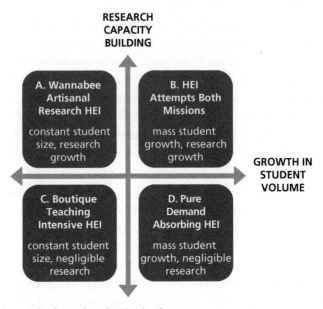

HEI = higher education institution

Figure 5.2. Strategies of middle higher education institutions with mixed missions and logics of production

Source: authors.

cannot pull themselves up very far. Essentially their mission can be neither demand-absorbing nor artisanal, except in the small number of HPS where there is an active sub-market of liberal arts colleges. Other institutions attempt to follow both artisanal and demand-absorbing pathways (Quadrant B), often in contrasting disciplines and sometimes on the basis of a division of labour in separated campus sites. It can be difficult for middle level multiversities with localized and partial research capacity to accept their limitations—and easy to begin believing the self-claims on the website. In national systems the tendency for too many higher education institutions to mimic the research-intensive university, despite the logic of bifurcation, is often strong. It is difficult to close off options, difficult to give up the dream. However, institutions that play it both ways are condemned to struggle with themselves. They try to use one mission to boost the other, but the relationship often flips into the negative. Some leverage government growth funding, and/or mass fee-paying students, to create economies of scale and use net surplus to subsidize research; but the more they bleed off for research the less they have for mass teaching, services, and facilities. Middle higher education institutions with the double mission may also attempt to compete by offering boutique credentials in niche areas, though their capacity to mount artisanal teaching is negligible, given their scale. In the long run, strong research outweighs moderate student demand, but moderate research in selected areas is not enough. As noted, only a small proportion of higher education institutions can be successfully artisanal, and those higher education institutions that have achieved self-reproducing artisanal status are hard to dislodge. These limits are irreducible.

Nevertheless, there are interesting, rare cases of higher education institutions that have moved sharply upwards by staying relatively small or small-medium, specializing in both teaching and research, and building research at a high level of quality (e.g. Hong Kong University of Science and Technology, Swinburne University in Australia).

Conclusions

In summary, all HPS are characterized by some level of vertical stratification, even though the height and slope of the mountain, and the space at the summit, have many possible permutations. Above all, the observed tendency towards bifurcation in HPS is universal. This tendency is primarily the outcome of positional competition among higher education institutions seeking status, and families seeking high-status places. As a result of this competition, which often takes zero-sum forms, an elite segment is distinguished from the rest of the system. The bifurcation tendency is only thinly disguised by mission drift, which has little purchase on the binary dynamic. However, in no system is bifurcation complete and in most systems the middle layer is extensive. The degree to which stratification occurs, and the precise configurations of artisanal, middle, and demand-absorbing higher education institutions are dependent upon system context. History often sets patterns that are hard to dislodge (Davis, 2017). Nevertheless, government policy and regulation, and social dynamics can either accelerate or buffer against the tendency towards bifurcation.

The significance of HPS lies in the fact that as the system expands bifurcation and stratification is enhanced unless they are deliberately corrected. It seems that every family has a stake in the HPS pecking order, even though most participants are not treated well. In HPS two processes of social stratification are brought together. Unequally ranked and valued students are matched with 'appropriate' unequally valued educational opportunity and the unequal social outcomes that follow. An imagined world of free choice and open possibilities is translated into a real world of social allocation and life closure.

This social system is rarely questioned, though there is much at stake. Here higher education plays its ultimate role in social order, as argued in Chapter 6, by fitting into an assemblage of family, the market, and the state that ultimately configures both individual social outcomes and the aggregated shape of the social system Not all forms of HPS need to feed into unequal societies, but unequalizing participation is the only HPS feature compatible with either state managed or free market capitalism. Here the HPS does not merely allocate, it 'manufactures consent' because all actors recognize and tacitly accept the resulting social hierarchy. Social selection and unequal outcomes would all seem manifestly unjust, if higher education and its production of academic merit did not legitimate binary social streaming. Academic merit operates as the formal basis of distinction between elite/non-elite positions. Not by coincidence, the same academic 'excellence', cloaked in the serendipity of research knowledge, is also the essential quality that high-demand elite universities possess. The mystique of 'quality' blurs the grim divide in social positioning, patterned in all-too-traditional a fashion along the line of domination/subordination. That slippery good, 'excellence' (Readings, 1996), so subjective in its educational operation and so chillingly objective in its social effects, confirms that the two parties, the elite student and the elite university, have fashioned themselves for each other.

■ REFERENCES

Baumol, W. J. (1993). Health care, education and the cost disease: A looming crisis for public choice. *The Next Twenty-five Years of Public Choice*. Amsterdam: Springer Netherlands, pp. 17–28.

Bourdieu, P. (1983). The field of cultural production, or: The economic world reversed. *Poetic* 12(4), 311–56.

Bourdieu, P. (1984). *Distinction*. Oxford: Routledge Kegan and Paul.

Bourdieu, P. (1988). *Homo Academicus*. Stanford: Stanford University Press.

Bowen, H. R. (1980). *The Costs of Higher Education: How Much Do Colleges and Universities Spend per Student and How Much Should They Spend?* San Francisco: Jossey-Bass.

Clark, B. R. (1960). The 'cooling-out' function in higher education. *American Journal of Sociology* 65(6), 569–76.

Davis, G. (2017). *The Australian Idea of a University*. Melbourne: Melbourne University Publishing.

Deem, R. (2001). Globalisation, new managerialism, academic capitalism and entrepreneurialism in universities: Is the local dimension still important? *Comparative Education* 37(1), 7–20.

Foucault, M. (1977). *Discipline and Punish: The Birth of the Prison*. London: Vintage.

Friedman, T. (2006). *The World is Flat: A Brief History of the Twenty-first Century*. New York: Macmillan.

Held, D., McGrew, A., Goldblatt, D., and Perraton, J. (1999). *Global Transformations: Politics, Economics and Culture*. Stanford: Stanford University Press.

Hirsch, F. (1976). *Social Limits to Growth*. Cambridge, MA: Harvard University Press.

Hirsch, M. W. (1976). *Differential Topology*. New York: Springer.

Leiden University (2017). The Leiden Ranking 2017. Centre for Science and Technology Studies. http://www.leidenranking.com/ranking/2017/list

Le Grand, J. (1991). Quasi-markets and social policy. *The Economic Journal* 101(408), 1256–67.

Marginson, S. (1997). *Educating Australia: Government, Economy and Citizen since 1960*. Cambridge: Cambridge University Press.

Marginson, S. (2006). Dynamics of national and global competition in higher education. *Higher Education* 52(1), 1–39.

Marginson, S. (2011). Imagining the global, in R. King, S. Marginson, and R. Naidoo (eds), *Handbook on Globalization and Higher Education*. Cheltenham: Edward Elgar.

Marginson, S. (2013). The impossibility of capitalist markets in higher education. *Journal of Education Policy* 28(3), 353–70.

Marginson, S. (2016). *The Dream is Over*. Berkeley, University of California Press.

McDonough, P. (1997). *Choosing Colleges: How Social Class and Schools Structure Opportunity*. New York: SUNY Press.

Readings, B. (1996). *The University in Ruins*. Cambridge, MA: Harvard University Press.

Rivera, L. (2015). *Pedigree: How Elite Students Get Elite Jobs*. Princeton, NJ: Princeton University Press.

Salmi, J. (2009). *The Challenge of Establishing World-class Universities*. Washington, DC: World Bank Publications.

Schofer, E. and Meyer, J. W. (2005). The worldwide expansion of higher education in the twentieth century. *American Sociological Review* 70(6), 898–920.

Slaughter, S. and Leslie, L. (1997). *Academic Capitalism: Politics, Policies, and the Entrepreneurial University*. Baltimore: Johns Hopkins University Press.

Teichler, U. (ed.) (2007). *Careers of University Graduates: Views and Experiences in Comparative Perspectives*, Vol. 17. Amsterdam: Springer Science & Business Media.

Thomsen, J. P., Munk, M. D., Eiberg-Madsen, M., and Hansen, G. I. (2013). The educational strategies of Danish university students from professional and working-class backgrounds. *Comparative Education Review* 57(3), 457–80.

World Bank (2017). Data and Statistics. Available from: http://data.worldbank.org

Wu, C.-L. and Bai, H. (2015). From early aspirations to actual attainment: the effects of economic status and educational expectations on university pursuit. *Higher Education* 69(3), 331–44.

6 Equity

Simon Marginson

> The question of the principles and processes of selection and admission to higher education is the crucial point where higher education touches most closely on the social structure.
>
> (Trow, 1973: 25)

Introduction

Extending the discussion of stratification in Chapter 5, this chapter is about social equity and equality in high participation systems (HPS).[1] Issues of equal rights, inclusion, and the distribution of outcomes go to the heart of higher education policy and the larger social role of higher education institutions. They affect every HPS whether accomplished or in formation. Here the potentials of HPS are ambiguous. Higher education is part of the circuits of social reproduction. It also opens a way to social mobility.

Much is expected of HPS; more because they take in the social majority. HPS maintain the promise of mass higher education, to foster inclusive, just, and productive societies in which everyone's learning is translated into skilled and professional work. However, HPS cannot expand the labour markets in line with enrolments, and find it difficult to redistribute opportunities. The hold of the middle class on places in elite institutions appears stronger, the value of mass higher education is more doubtful, and the state seems to have less scope to transform the opportunity structure. Government cannot intervene with the same targeted precision as in smaller systems, or secure ready consensus on the rearrangement of all outcomes. Families from low socio-economic status (SES) backgrounds find that although they are now inside the border of the HPS they face formidable barriers in accessing high-status higher education and turning degrees into careers. Societies vary in the extent of upward mobility, but prior social advantage makes a substantial difference to outcomes in all countries.

[1] Grateful thanks to Brendan Cantwell, David Konstantinovskiy, Marek Kwiek, Reetta Muhonen, Romulo Pinhiero, Anna Smolentseva, and Jussi Valimaa.

Yet in most countries, higher education still provides a better opportunity for the children of poor families to rise up the social ladder than does entrepreneurship or working the markets, or crime, or the military. Typically, first generation migrant families, regardless of the level of education of the parents, pin their hopes for their children's futures on schools and universities.

EQUITY, EQUALITY, AND SOCIAL MOBILITY

The term 'equity' is associated with notions of fairness and justice, whereas the term 'equality' refers to sameness or equivalence between persons (Espinoza, 2007: 345).

Equity in education is normative and custom-bound and varies according to the specific setting. It signifies an intention to justice, and a field of policy and educational practice, rather than a fixed quality comparable between social sites. Notions of equity vary according to the political culture, norms of conduct and entitlement, and prevailing expectations. Since the 1950s and 1960s, equity in higher education has moved from the assumption that all people with talent should have the opportunity to use it, to the assumption that because all people are potentially educable they should have educational opportunities. The two principal equity goals in higher education have become equity as universal social inclusion, and equity as the equal access of students from all social groups to opportunities in education (Husen, 1974). This can be extended to equal social access to opportunities in particular kinds of institutions, such as elite universities, or equal social access to careers and high incomes. Often the content of the second equity goals is supplied by measured equality, which enables comparison between cases.

Governments hesitate before taking the redistributive measures required to ensure equal measured social group access to high-status higher education institutions. This entails taking benefits from affluent and powerful families. Equity policy mostly focuses on equal access to higher education as a whole, consensual and easier to achieve. Unlike access to elite universities, access to bottom tier higher education is not a focus of social competition. The normative character of 'equity' allows policymakers to shift between its different meanings and to claim that in socially unequal systems, social justice at the margin is just enough.

Social equality has two dimensions. First, the extent to which social positions are equal or unequal in relation to each other—the degree of social stratification of wealth, power, and status. Second, the probability of inter-generational upward mobility, measured in terms of income, occupational status, educational level, or other social indicators. Social egalitarianism and social mobility are not identical. A society can have both relatively unequal incomes and high mobility from low- to high-income families, as was the case in the United States in the past, and happens now in China and other countries undergoing rapid development. However, all else equal, egalitarian societies facilitate upward social mobility, partly because there is less at stake in upward and downward movement; and highly unequal societies have more barriers to upward mobility. The cross-country comparison by Corak (2006, 2012) identifies a strong negative correlation between income inequality and upward mobility.

Higher education influences both the degree of equality/inequality, and potentials for upward mobility. More equal social distribution of educational outcomes facilitates a more egalitarian society, especially if all education is of high quality, as in the Nordic countries. Educational opportunities for students from poor backgrounds increase their probability of their upward mobility. At the same time, higher education is only one of the factors that determines stratification and mobility; and the prior extent of social inequality, and mobility, pre-structure the scope for higher education to function as a social evener.

SOCIAL CHARACTER OF HPS

In this book, HPS are conceived as social phenomena, not just educational phenomena or education-driven economic phenomena as imagined by human capital theory. Figure 6.1 contextualizes HPS in social terms. It highlights the interactive nature of relationships across the education/society distinction. The equality/inequality and

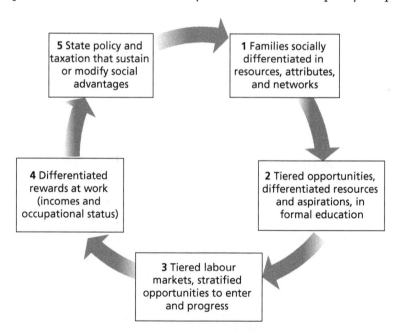

Figure 6.1. The family/state/education/economy assemblage

Source: author.

mobility of social groups in and through higher education are part of complex processes of social reproduction.

The interior world of higher education (part 2 in Figure 6.1) is only one part of the puzzle. Other factors at play include the social backgrounds of potential students (part 1), which for research purposes are mostly measured by parental or household levels of income, occupational status, or education; their gender and ethnicity; and their social capital or cultural capital. All of these factors shape student aspirations, and also outcomes in education and beyond, in interaction with each other (Britton et al., 2016). Then there are labour markets, occupations, workplaces, and systems of remuneration and progression at work (parts 3 and 4). A further dimension is that of government regulation, transfers, and social programmes, which impact social and economic inequality, and higher education provision, at many points (part 5).

Within higher education (part 2), student access and graduate outcomes are affected by the stratification of HPS in terms of institutional missions, prestige, and resources; and the student body is differentiated by fields of study, and by finance and tuition costs, and other elements. Social stratification and inequality arise in higher education regardless of the size of systems or the extent of participation. However, system expansion has specific implications for inequality, as will be discussed; and there are also reciprocal effects, in which social and economic inequalities shape the HPS, and feed back again into society and economy via higher education's role in social reproduction. Societies with high measured inequality and relatively low upward mobility are associated with more stratified higher education systems that foster unequal educational participation and achievement, enhancing larger social inequalities. More egalitarian societies tend to encourage a more egalitarian HPS, and vice versa.

Higher education is closely affected by governments/states (part 5). In many countries it is part of the formal state sector. States may either reduce or enhance competition, stratification, and unequal social outcomes in higher education. Nordic social democracies foster 'flat' HPS structures where access to high-quality public higher education institutions is a social right and part of the larger Nordic equality project. Formal competition between institutions is largely confined to research funding, where there is a moderate hierarchy. Neoliberal quasi-markets enhance the stratification of and competition between institutions, shaping higher education as a source of scarce private goods that confer individual advantage. Quasi-markets established by neoliberal policy intensify competition and educational stratification. But HPS and higher education institutions are not simply policy controlled in a top-down manner. The more robust are the educational technologies for academic training, assessment, and selection (part 2), the greater the potential of higher education itself to shape social outcomes, to make a difference to patterns of social mobility. One variable at play is the extent to which higher education itself, as a sector, reproduces existing social inequalities or changes them. Like all social sectors in Figure 6.1, higher education is a site of autonomous action. Does this potential for higher education-driven social effects grow or shrink in the HPS phase? This autonomous potency can be called the *social allocative power* of higher education.

PROPOSITIONS ABOUT HPS AND EQUITY

The chapter begins by reviewing the dynamics of competition for social position, where it intersects with higher education. It then explores four propositions about HPS and equity (HPS Propositions 14–17). The first two propositions on equity refer to secular tendencies that apply throughout the growth of an HPS. The third and fourth propositions (16 and 17) refer to characteristics of a fully developed HPS:

- *As participation expands in the HPS phase, equity in the form of social inclusion is enhanced.*
- *Because in the HPS phase the growth of participation is associated with enhanced stratification and intensified competition at key transition points, all else being equal (i.e. without compensatory state policy), the expansion of participation is associated with a secular tendency to greater social inequality in educational outcomes and, through that, social outcomes.*
- *Within a national system, as participation expands in the HPS phase, all else being equal, the positional structure of the higher education system increasingly resembles that of society (albeit with the caveat of Proposition 15). The HPS is increasingly implicated in the reproduction of existing patterns of social equality/inequality.*
- *As the HPS boundary of participation expands it becomes more difficult for the state and/or autonomous educational systems/institutions to secure a redistribution of educational opportunities, and, through that, of social opportunities.*

Though the HPS movement is associated with partial convergence between national systems, in each society the relations between the growth of participation, stratification of the HPS, and educational and social outcomes, are articulated via contextual and conjunctural elements (see Chapter 1). National variations are discussed in the final part of the chapter. The country chapters in Part II of the book further unpack equity at national level.

Social Competition in Higher Education

Though national HPS are subject to contextual variations, all are shaped by social competition. Education is a positional good (Hirsch, 1976; Marginson, 1997). Its sorting role is as important as the absolute opportunities it brings. It provides a stratified structure of opportunity, from elite universities and high-status professional degrees to the much larger number of mass education places with uncertain prospects. As every family knows, relative advantage is crucial, and students from affluent families dominate the high-value positions.

In HPS universal desires for social betterment are articulated through higher education systems themselves becoming universal. But the social opportunities that education is meant to bring are not universal—not in capitalist societies that, whether in low-, middle-, or high-income countries, are stratified by unequal earnings and hierarchical power; and where there is an absolute limit to the socially advantaged positions on offer. Konstantinvoskiy (2016) summarizes the problem succinctly: 'The increasing of a scarce resource cannot solve the problem of inequality in education.' The ultimate constraint on the equalizing capacity of HPS is the zero-sum nature of positional competition. The growth of HPS increases the pool of graduates faster than growth in the number of high-value social outcomes that are accessible to those graduates. The pattern of social rewards is determined by relations of power and equality/inequality beyond education. For graduates, growing scarcity is inevitable. Social power asserts itself, as it does routinely in all social sectors, capturing the main part of the scarce rewards on offer.

Here the point that the growth of HPS is driven by family aspirations for higher education as a positional good, not by state ordering or economic need (see Chapter 1), gains its full significance. HPS are populated by families that apply active agency in the contest for educational and social success, at every stage. Families experience higher education as a structure/agency dialectic. Each of agents and structure are differentiated: families by capacity, educational structures by value. Families strive for their children under conditions they cannot control. The strongest families handle those conditions best and tend to win. States and higher education institutions together structure higher education systems, stratifying the forms of provision and their cost and value, whether value is formally or informally determined. Though families have little scope to shape institutions, pathways, and means of differentiation, they work the structures facing them as well as possible in their own interests. Families with financial, social, cultural, or political capitals bring those capitals to bear on education and continue to do so in the transition to work and beyond into lifetime careers (Borgen, 2015).

INEQUALITIES IN FAMILY BACKGROUNDS

There are two fundamental limits to social equality of opportunity in higher education. These factors interact. Both are essential to the reproduction of social inequalities through education.

The first limit is the persistence of irreducible differences between families in the economic, social, and cultural resources that affect learning outcomes, access to selective higher education institutions and life trajectories (part 1 of Figure 6.1). Family inequality is inevitable. Policy can partly compensate for economic differences but cannot eliminate the potency of the family in cultural capital and social networks (Mountford-Zimdars and Sabbagh, 2013; OECD, 2014: 193). Families with prior social advantages are best placed to compete for those positions in higher education that offer the greatest private benefit, and best placed to translate educational achievement into career success. Oxfam (2014) refers to 'opportunity hoarding', the process whereby disparities become permanent. This occurs when certain defined groups take control of valuable resources and assets for their benefit and to 'seek to secure rewards from sequestered resources' (Oxfam, 2014: 20). Families with prior advantages do best in competitive settings and leverage that success to further elevate themselves. This is the logic of 'Matthew effects'[2] or cumulative advantage' (DiPrete and Eirich, 2006: 271–97).

Cumulative advantage becomes part of an explanation for growing inequality when current levels of accumulation have a direct causal relationship on future levels of accumulation ... small advantages or disadvantages at an early stage of a process grow larger over time.   (2006: 272, 280)

Research on social stratification persistently identifies the association between parental and familial inequality, and unequal educational-social outcomes. Though inequalities in social background are fundamental and limit social equality of opportunity everywhere, the extent of those inequalities varies by country. In a statistical comparison of eleven European countries, Triventi (2013b) finds that 'individuals with better educated parents have a higher probability of attaining a degree from a top institution, of a higher standard, and with better occupational returns' (p. 499). The strongest associations are in the Nordic countries and the UK (p. 495; Triventi, 2013a: 54). In the United States Soares (2007) reports that in 1988–2000, 64 per cent of students of Tier 1 American higher education institutions were from the top 10 per cent of households in terms of income. Tier 1 institutions are the leading private universities. There is similar social stratification in most academically prestigious institutions, with occasional exceptions (Marginson, 2016). In Russia, data on the education of students' parents show that top tier higher education institutions are overwhelmingly dominated by students whose parents received higher education (Table 6.1). Elite institutions are almost exclusively occupied by students from higher education families. It is significant that the gender gap in favour of women tends towards closure in the most prestigious higher education institutions.

Family income, social capital, and social networks also shape the later differentiation of careers (Marginson, 2016: 47). For Britton and colleagues (2016: 55), 'a main finding from this paper is that graduates' family background—specifically whether they come

---

[2] Christian New Testament, Matthew 25:29—'For unto every one that hath shall be given, and he shall have abundance.' Robert Merton originated the term 'Matthew effect' to describe the accumulation of reputation by research scientists.

Table 6.1. Proportion of students in Russian higher education institutions whose parents received higher education, by tier of institution, various years between 2004 and 2011

Category of higher education institution and data of survey	Proportion of students whose parents attended higher education	
	Mothers %	Fathers %
Tier 1 public 2011	66.5	57.5
Tier 2 public 2011	53.5	43.2
Tier 3 public 2011	45.6	29.9
All tiers public 2011	54.2	45.8
Elite public 2004	85.0	83.0
Elite public 2009	87.0	88.0
Proportion of 40–60 year age cohort with higher education, 2011*	24.8	19.2

Note: *Women and men in the 40–60 year-old population.

Sources: Adapted from Gasparishvili and Toumanov, 2006; Smolentseva, 2016. Original 2009 data from Higher School of Economics (HSE) survey, HSE Center for Institutional Research, 2009.

from a lower or higher income household—continues to influence graduates' earnings long after graduation'. In HPS with saturation participation by elite families there is intensified competition and crowding an entry into elite institutions and elite professions. Rivera (2015) shows that this leads to greater exclusivity in selection—elite law, banking, and consulting firms draw from a small group of top Ivy League universities. Candidates are also expected to demonstrate the cultural capital typical of a wealthy milieu, such as facility in elite sports and classical music. In their study of corporate networking activity among Oxford and Sciences Po students, Tholen and colleagues (2013) show that not all elite graduates are guaranteed elite employment, and again, social and cultural capital can be crucial. Corak notes that:

the differences between advantaged and disadvantaged children...have their roots in the more subtle advantages highly educated parents are able to pass on to their children: skills, beliefs and motivation arising from an advantaged family culture and parenting style. These non-monetary factors determine the strength of the relationship between a child's cognitive skills in adulthood and their parents' education, which in turn is also associated with the degree of generational mobility in a society.   (Corak, 2006: 31–2)

However, 'societies levelling these influences across the population display a higher degree of generational mobility' (Corak, 2006: 32).

DIFFERENCES OF VALUE IN HIGHER EDUCATION

The second fundamental factor limiting social equality is the hierarchies of value in higher education: of institutions, fields of study, credentials (part 2 of Figure 6.1). This is less absolutely inevitable than the effects of social background—the extent of value differentials varies by country more than does social background—but educational hierarchies have potent support. Differentiation of value protects the elite status of those 'born into privilege' (Arum et al., 2007: 5); and it provides other families with means to invest in favourable positions.

stratification of higher education refers to the degree of variation in selectivity, quality/prestige and labour market value of different courses, fields of study and institutions. All else being equal, the higher is the stratification of higher education, the more important is the role of social background in the occupational attainment process.

(Triventi, 2013a: 48–9; see also Lucas 2001, 2009; Triventi, 2013b: 499)

To repeat, families respond to the structures that face them. They may find themselves in an HPS that tightly limits access to educational and social success, and intensify competition, as in the Anglo-American countries—or in a Nordic HPS that values equality and upward social mobility. Between them states (especially) and institutions can change the structures to increase or decrease the equalizing effects. The point is that socially unequal agency can be reproduced as unequal outcomes only when it finds purchase in hierarchy-making structures.

Positional advantage is gained either via exclusive forms of participation at the same level (e.g. in high-status institutions), or in a new layer above the universal (e.g. postgraduate study) as participation grows. HPS are always moving and the site of policy contestation and social struggle. As HPS change the social hierarchy is continually rematched to the hierarchy of educational sectors, institutions, and programmes. Competition at the key points of transition and selection—especially entry to higher education and entry to professional occupations—enables fine-grained differentiation of the population and creates scope for self-differentiating investments. As Chapters 4 and 5 discussed, stratification is secured by institutional forms, including vertical and horizontal distinctions; field of study distinctions; institutional ordering such as ranking; and financial barriers. In turn these factors differentiate aspirations.

There is positional competition and some stratification in all HPS. However, the intensity of competition, extent of stratification, and modes of differentiation all vary. Different HPS are regulated by the degree and type of hierarchy and closure, within the regime of universal openness and inclusion. These variations are a primary distinction between HPS.

UNEQUALIZING INSTITUTIONS

Schooling. Some nations run comprehensive school systems with low stratification of quality. In others, selective private schooling provides for upper middle class investment.

In the UK spending per student in high-fee private schools is three times that in state schools; while quasi-market competition creates a state school hierarchy, which normalizes the role of private schooling (Cheung and Egerton, 2007: 218; Dorling, 2014: 28, 40–1). Boliver (2011) finds that over 1996 to 2006 in the UK, 53 per cent of students from fee-paying independent private schools entered Russell Group universities. Just 20 per cent of students from state schools did so (see Table 6.2). The majority of state school students entering higher education enrolled in the bottom tier post-1992 universities. In a later study Boliver shows that the social skew in favour of private school students is exacerbated by the university admissions process, which occurs before final school results are known. In the case of students *with equivalent qualifications* in the final school examinations, 'applying to a Russell Group university from a private school rather than a state school ... increases the odds of admission to a Russell Group university by at least as much as having an additional B-grade A-level' (Boliver, 2013: 358).

Higher education. In all HPS there is a formal or informal hierarchy of institutions led by higher education institutions with inherited prestige, most of which are research-intensive. Some systems such as those of the United States and China bed down their hierarchy with a formal classification system, but if there is no formal stratification of value and outcomes, informal proxies that enable differentiation tend to emerge, such as reputation. In the last decade many countries have emphasized the building of stronger research-intensive universities capable of 'world-class university' (WCU) status, meaning position in global university rankings (Salmi, 2009; Hazelkorn, 2015). Research-intensive universities are expected to generate not just economic innovation but global status, cross-border academic and student migration, and business and public support (Altbach and Salmi, 2011). Policies such as Germany's Excellence Initiative and state-induced mergers in Denmark, both departing from prior egalitarian HPS design; and China's 211 and 985 programmes contribute to the vertical 'stretching' of HPS. Where enhanced focus on research universities contributes to neglect of the quality of mass

Table 6.2. Rates of entry to UK university tiers, by social background and school background, combined entry data for 1996, 1998, 2000, 2002, 2004, and 2006

Entrants to higher education	Russell Group universities %	Other pre-1992 universities %	Post-1991 universities %
All entrants	22	20	58
Private school entrants	53	24	23
State school entrants	20	20	60

Note: n = 36,629 entrants.

Source: Adapted by the author from original data in Boliver (2011: 350).

higher education, stratification is enhanced from above and below at the same time. Research on institutional stratification ('college quality') focuses on the effects of this vertical 'stretching' on social outcomes. Though it is difficult to separate stratification effects from social background effects affecting student placement in tiers (Gerber and Cheung, 2008: 301), stratification effects appear greater in relation to occupational status than earnings (e.g. Triventi, 2013a: 54–7; Hu and Vargas, 2015: 19); and greater in lifetime earnings than immediate graduate earnings.

Private sectors. In some HPS diversification between public and private sectors feeds into stratification. In most countries national research universities are the focus of family ambition, but systems with elite private institutions include the United States (where the top private universities have the strongest research profiles), Korea, Japan, and Brazil.

Fields of study. Fields of study distinctions are also associated with differential social investments and outcomes, especially in relation to graduate income (e.g. Britton et al., 2016). In HPS that are relatively 'flat' in terms of stratification, fields of study become more important as private opportunities for self-differentiation. For example, in Finland, where social differences in higher education opportunities have narrowed, there is a continuing hierarchy in fields of study. This is where social competition occurs (see Chapter 13). In most countries medicine is the site of concentrated middle class ambition. More generally in realtion to the United States, Wozniak and colleagues (2008) find that the science, technology, engineering, and mathematics (STEM) disciplines reinforce prior family backgrounds, while business and education provide more scope to change inherited inequalities (p. 135).

In systems in which a high proportion of graduates have generic degrees without clear vocational pathways, the institutional hierarchy gains importance as a distinguishing factor. This happens in both the market-driven and highly stratified US system, and the publicly financed and relatively 'flat' Norwegian system (Borgen, 2015: 36). It is striking how, regardless of system settings, means of stratification emerge by one means or another.

Institutional ordering. Retiz (2017) discusses the proliferation of techniques for the rating and ordering of higher education institutions, such as publication and citation counts, rankings, research evaluation, measures of 'employability' via employment rates and starting salaries; and surveys of student satisfaction and engagement. In research-based measures, open source knowledge flows are 'vectored by a system of status production that assigns value to knowledge and arranges it in ordered patterns' (Marginson, 2008). Such mechanisms render more precise judgements about value and ordering, solidifying the existing university hierarchy, and guiding economic decisions on graduate hiring, valuation of expertise, and allocation of venture capital. 'These social technologies not only restructure the world of knowledge via status competitions, but also coordinate academic stratification with socio-economic inequality' (Retiz, 2017: 871).

ECONOMIC BARRIERS

Not all HPS charge tuition but all have private economic costs. Students must forgo earnings and be supported economically while studying. Only some systems provide universal living allowances in the form of grants or loans. Economic barriers stratify populations, along the line of prior economic and social inequalities, in relation to each of aspirations, access, choice of field of study, learning achievement and completion (Arum et al., 2007: 24–5).

Different HPS exhibit markedly varied levels of private tuition cost (OECD, 2014: 260–76). Tuition and living support are shaped by customs concerning the division of responsibility between family and state. Tuition is not a market price driven by supply, demand, production cost and profitability. It exceeds US$10,000 per year in the English-speaking countries, and in South Korea and Japan is again relatively high. In the last two countries most of the total cost of higher education is paid by households and there is also much investment in private tuition, though mostly prior to entry (Bray, 2007). In western and southern continental Europe, and public education in Latin America, no fee and low fee approaches prevail. In Nordic systems and Germany tuition is free and fully financed from general taxation. Average tuition is below US$2,000 in most of Europe, amid significant variations in systems; though mechanisms of 'social and cultural selection' can do the same work as financial selection (Piketty, 2014: 486).

In the pre-HPS era free tuition could be significant in widening identification with higher education and determining social inclusion. It eased and normalized participation by under-represented groups. When 15–20 per cent of the age group is enrolled, demand is more elastic and small financial changes at the margin determine enrolments. Once the desire for higher education reaches most families, tuition in itself is less of barrier; though it remains socially regressive, and can still block the participation of particular families.[3] Free tuition can be a powerful political issue and in the HPS phase it often still seen as *the* key to achieving social equality of opportunity. That is a hangover from the pre-HPS era. As noted, strategies to maximize inclusion do not necessarily enhance overall social equality in access, given that HPS are hierarchical and segmented in value. Stratification (especially) and competition are more important than tuition in determining the scope for a private goods rather than a common goods approach. While high fees block enrolment in elite private universities of the Ivy League type, the fundamental problem there is high stratification, not tuition per se. Tuition can be designed to exempt the most economically disadvantaged families and students, or levied in the form of government subsidized income contingent loans, as in the UK and Australia, where high

---

[3] In some countries tuition strongly affects cross-border mobility. The number of international students in Sweden dropped by 80 per cent when they had to pay tuition (Valimaa and Muhonen, 2016: 18).

tuition costs have little effect on demand, regardless of socio-economic origin, except for part-time students who pay during the year of study (Callender, 2013; Chapman, 2014).

UNEQUALIZED AGENCY

Structural inequalities in HPS do not just channel agents with differentiated capitals towards unequal destinations—they also differentiate agency itself, shaping unequal aspirations.

Brand and Xie (2010) note that although 'advantaged young people place a uniformly high value on college' (p. 291) they need higher education less than do poorer students. 'In the absence of a college degree ... [they] can still rely on their superior resources and abilities' such as family and social networks (p. 293). Students from poor backgrounds gain more from higher education credentials, relative to their compatriots who do not enrol (Borgen, 2015: 34). Yet upper middle class families habitually invest greater effort into securing maximum advantage within the HPS than a rational choice model would imply (Brand and Xie, 2010: 280); while students from poor backgrounds and/or remote location often invest less than suggested by rational choice: they are less likely to nurture high ambition, more likely to be deterred by cost, more likely to focus on secure and predictable employment-related paths rather than diffuse intellectual formation with uncertain generic potentials, more likely to believe they lack the cultural capital to survive and perform at university, and less familiar with performance and application strategies. Self-stratification and under-investment are found in all systems, including the Nordic countries (Arum et al., 2007: 31; Jonsson and Erikson, 2007: 137; Thomsen et al., 2013: 457, 471–4). There seems to be less social differentiation of aspirations in Post-Confucian systems than elsewhere (Marginson, 2013).

In a census-level study of all 2008 applicants to United States higher education, Hoxby and Avery (2013) track the applications of 'high-achieving' school students, ranked in the top 4 per cent by Scholastic Assessment Test (SAT) scores and grade point averages (p. 2). These students number 25,000–35,000 each year. In 2008, 17 per cent were in the bottom family income quartile (pp. 14–15). The vast majority of these low-income high achievers did not apply to a selective higher education institutions, though selective institutions charged lower tuition because of financial aid (pp. 5–6). Whereas high-income high achievers applied conventional advice by applying for a mix of highly selective and less selective higher education institutions, most low-income high achievers opted for uniformly safe choices. Typically, they were from districts too small to support selective public high schools or a mass of fellow high achievers, and/or unlikely to encounter a teacher, counsellor, or student who had attended a selective institution. These finding on the 'under-matching' of poor and remote students are replicated in Chankseliani's (2013) study of rural students in Georgia. In the UK, Boliver (2013) finds that 'applicants from lower class backgrounds and from state schools remained much less likely to apply to Russell Group universities than their comparably qualified counterparts from higher class backgrounds and private schools' (p. 344). There were widespread perceptions that prestige universities belonged to privately educated white upper middle class (p. 347), diminishing the aspirations and agency of other families.

Secular Tendency 1: Social Inclusion

The spread of HPS across the world enhances social inclusion in two ways. First, by narrowing the differences between high-, middle-, and some low-income countries, it leads to a more inclusive world society (see Chapter 1). Second, the formation of an HPS advances the boundary of inclusion in each country, moving down the socio-economic hierarchy and taking in geographical regions and members of ethnic groups previously under-represented or excluded. It is still possible to exclude designated groups, against the secular tendency to inclusion, but it takes a special effort of discrimination. The first proposition on equity (HPS Proposition 14) states:

> *As participation expands in the HPS phase, equity in the form of social inclusion is enhanced.*

However, this secular tendency to social inclusion is subject to two caveats. As participation expands in the HPS phase, the meanings of social inclusion change. Both caveats are present in all HPS, though they vary with context.

First, the social cost of non-participation increases. In all HPS the expansion of inclusion increases the social costs of exclusion, except in Nordic-type systems with robust alternate pathways and compensating mechanisms.[4] Those who do not participate, whether voluntary, circumstantial or imposed, are more unequal than before. As noted in Chapter 1, this is the dark side of the HPS movement. Even though with expansion the average value of credentials declines (see later) the lack of credentials, networks, social literacy, confidence, and credentials is a growing disadvantage. For example, in raw instrumental terms a shrinking proportion of labour market positions are accessible to those without qualifications. In high inequality societies, which typically exhibit high private returns to graduates relative to non-graduates (Corak, 2006, 2012), the penalties of exclusion are magnified. This is enough to explain the continuing expansion of HPS. Fears of exile run deeper than hopes of glory. Desires for higher education are desires not just for upward mobility but also to avoid demotion in the next generation (Triventi, 2013a: 47). HPS higher education is a defensive necessity, a hedge against both social exclusion and downward

---

[4] Thanks to Romulo Pinheiro for this point.

mobility. It is unclear that higher education provides security, or graduate skills will be used, but it is usually better to participate. Even in societies with shrinking middle classes becoming more unequal, higher education provides a better starting point, keeps more doors open, sets a floor on absolute decline, and promises enhanced possibilities of self-actualization, as it always has.[5]

Second, in an HPS the primary question of social equity in higher education shifts from access to higher education to the stratification of opportunities in higher education. As the gross enrolment ration (GER) approaches universality, equity as social inclusion meets equity as social group equality. When all social groups are fully included, under-representation appears to vanish. But that is only if inclusion is observed in terms of the system as a whole. The elephant in the room is that the higher education sector is stratified and places have unequal social value. In an expanding HPS, with most families entering higher education but with opportunities stratified by educational structure and family financial capacity, the primary question of social equity shifts from access to higher education to 'access to what kind of higher education?' In short, (a) populations are socially stratified, (b) socially inclusive HPS are stratified in terms of the value of participation, (c) access to high-value places is also stratified, (d) final social outcomes are stratified—and (a), (b), and (c) interact in complex ways to affect (d).

Secular Tendency 2: Social Inequality

What then are the effects of the expansion of higher education on the patterns of social equality of opportunity? This has been the subject of a number of research studies.

RESEARCH ON THE EFFECTS OF EXPANSION

In their theorization of maximally maintained inequality (MMI), Raftery and Hout (1993) find that until education at a given level is saturated for the upper classes, it remains selective; and social inequality as measured by odds ratios, meaning the comparative probability of social groups advancing to the next educational level, is constant (p. 41). In the alternate effectively maintained inequality (EMI) theory, Lucas (2001) finds that even when participation becomes universal at a given level, 'socioeconomically advantaged actors secure for themselves and their children some degree of advantage wherever advantages are commonly possible' (p. 1652); for example via selective secondary schools

---

[5] The last point is from Brendan Cantwell.

that confer advantage in entry to higher education, or by competing successfully at a higher non-universal level (Lucas, 2009: 460).

MMI states that policies to universalize a transition will reduce inequality, whereas EMI states that universalizing a transition may do nothing to reduce inequality because advantaged actors will discover or elaborate qualitative differences within the universalized transition and secure access to better quality. And, if better quality confers advantage, then qualitative differences will effectively maintain inequality...if EMI is correct, would-be egalitarian reformers face a much more difficult challenge than they would were MMI correct. (Lucas, 2009: 500)

Whether growth of participation is accompanied by enhanced stratification within universal enrolment, or additional layers of stratification at higher educational levels, is a case-by-case matter determined by contextual factors. The EMI notion emerged in Lucas's United States where the near universal transition from high school to college is accompanied by high institutional and financial stratification, and many families invest in education as a private good. In the Ireland of Raftery and Hout, participation was both less universal and less stratified in value. Mapping long-term social access to higher education in the UK, Boliver (2011) confirms both MMI and EMI. 'Quantitative inequalities between social classes in the odds of higher education enrolment proved remarkably persistent' from 1960 to 1995 and declined only during the early 1990s when the enrolment rate for the most advantaged social class reached saturation point. Meanwhile inequalities between classes in the odds of enrolment in higher status degree programmes and 'Old' universities remained fundamentally unchanged' (p. 229). Much of the expansion took place 'in a growing second tier of less prestigious higher education programmes and institutions' (p. 231). On the other hand, Nordic societies are less stratified than Ireland. When graduate returns are more modest, and less stratified between different higher education institutions and different fields of study, so higher education functions more as a common good, and when the cultural attributes that support educability are well-distributed in the population, there is less incentive for affluent families to invest so as to capture unequal outcomes.

In *Stratification in Higher Education*, Shavit, Arum, and Gamoran (2007) provide a multi-country study of the social effects of expansion. The summary chapter by Arum and colleagues (2007) attempts to identify general patterns. They find that growth is unequivocally associated with improved access to women, especially in fast growing systems (p. 26). The findings on socio-economic access are less clear-cut. The authors note that expansion intersects with many variable elements in higher education, including the vertical stratification and segmentation of schooling and higher education; whether there is a binary system with part-horizontal distinctions; the size of the elite university sector; private schooling and private higher education institutions, and tuition barriers. They also note but do not fully explore the potential for concurrent variations in the larger national contexts. The problem here is that the relationships between context and higher system are not necessarily subject to a constant law (see later). Because Shavit, Arum, and Gamoran (2007) attempt to derive general laws from empirical data in a small number of cases—despite the worldwide heterogeneity of systems—their conclusions are inevitably governed by case selection.

The authors find that higher education has become more socially inclusive overall and identify variations between countries in the rate of this democratization. This leads them to suggest that marketized systems such as the United States grow more quickly because they can freely diversify downwards in quality. Private funding is associated with relaxed eligibility for enrolment. German-type binary systems with low private funding, unable to diversify down, grow more slowly, though Sweden is an exception. However, the study included three binary systems, Germany, Switzerland, and the Netherlands but just one Nordic system. The Nordic model joins near universal public provision and low private funding to high participation, social equality and mobility. This contrasts with the market-driven systems. A further problem with the study is its reliance on 1990s data. High growth HPS are now very broadly spread and it can no longer be asserted that one system structure favours growth, or markets provide opportunity while governments deny it, if that were ever true.[6]

Interestingly, there is greater clarity in the statistical findings about the effect of the expansion of participation on social access to elite institutions, despite potential contextual variations. While at a given level of education growth towards universal participation reduces social inequality in access to higher education as a whole, social inequality in access to elite higher education is little changed (pp. 18–19), with slight variations either way in different countries. Stratification effects are decisive. 'Qualitative differentiation replaces inequalities in the quantity of the education obtained' (Arum et al., 2007: 4). This is confirmed also in the country chapters. In no case was the growing HPS associated with opening up in the positional structure of society. As in Boliver's study, newly participating social layers tend to populate sub-elite higher education institutions (e.g. Shavit, Ayalon, Chachashvili-Bolotin, and Menahem, 2007: 61 on Israel). Cheung and Egerton (2007: 195) state that in the UK, while students from unskilled and semi-skilled parental backgrounds have made access gains, these are largely manifest in the second tier institutions, and 'class inequalities are especially persistent in the more selective forms of higher education.' The consistency across different countries is striking. There is a common failure to democratize the elite institutions during the massification process.

---

[6] In 1975 the two highest GERs were in the United States and the Soviet Union (UNESCO, 2016).

The HPS in Sweden and the United States have different social premises but in each case the effects of expansion on social access are those noted by Trow (1973: 24). Sweden has seen a dramatic expansion of total participation but only a modest improvement in the social equality of odds of enrolment, and little change in social access to the leading institutions. 'The reason for the limited effect is that new educational opportunities are to a large extent used by middle-class students with mediocre grades but high educational aspirations' (Arum et al., 2007: 31). Likewise, in the United States between 1979 and 1997, expanded opportunities were taken up by low ability students from affluent families to the point of saturation (Belley and Lochner, 2007). Everywhere the middle class goes to the top of the line.

TENDENCY TO GREATER SOCIAL INEQUALITY IN POSITIONAL OUTCOMES

Chapter 5 showed the expansion of participation in itself generates structural bifurcation and enhances stratification. All else being equal, expansion increases the potency of social background (Triventi, 2013a, 2013b). Growth in participation strengthens the relative position of middle class families in two mutually reinforcing ways: expansion generates stratification and it intensifies competition at the key points of transition and selection in education (Arum et al., 2007: 7–8). Because the number of scarce high-value positional outcomes grows more slowly than the number of competitors, HPS higher education is a fiercer all-in competition than were the smaller mass systems. Competition and stratification also feed each other, while each are subject to Matthew effects. Middle class family advantage accumulates, as do the hierarchical advantages of elite institutions. These tendencies have run furthest in the United States, where a highly unequal society nurtures a highly stratified HPS.

Triventi's research confirms the mutual formation of expansion, stratification, and competition. 'All else being equal, countries with a mass higher education system may be characterised by stronger competition among graduates in the transition to the labour market and, thus, by a larger effect of social background on occupational returns' (Triventi, 2013a: 48). His eleven-country study concludes that 'social background matters more in those systems characterized by stronger competition among tertiary graduates in the transition to the labour market, and where the best educational alternatives lead to greater advantages in occupational outcomes' (Triventi, 2013b: 499). On the other hand, when competition diminishes there is potential for more equal outcomes. 'Those with tertiary educated parents are more likely to have a highly rewarded occupation in all the countries except Germany', because there, social selection takes place at earlier stages of education, there are strong institutional connections between higher education and the labour market, and there is a low intensity of competition between graduates in transition to the labour market (Triventi, 2013a: 58).

The second HPS proposition (15) on equity states that in addition to the secular tendency to inclusion, the growth of participation in HPS generates a second secular tendency, to more unequal social outcomes.

Because in the HPS phase the growth of participation is associated with enhanced stratification and intensified competition at key transition points, all else being equal (i.e. without compensatory state policy), the expansion of participation is associated with a secular tendency to greater social inequality in educational outcomes and, through that, social outcomes.

This important proposition has a number of aspects. As participation expands, additional opportunities are more likely to be taken up by families with superior capacity and resources to compete. Further, as participation expands in the HPS phase there is no improvement is social access to selective higher education institutions, especially highly selective institutions, and there may be a regression. The social elite becomes more dominant vis-à-vis the others, but it does not have an easier life—in HPS competition becomes tougher not just at the point of entry to the top echelons but inside them. Saturation participation by socially advantaged families leads to elite crowding of professional job markets (Rivera, 2015). But this crowding effect further weakens the social access of non-elite graduates to career opportunities.

The proposition that expansion leads to more not less social inequality is counter-intuitive. Surely, does making higher education more socially inclusive not bring more people from under-represented social groups to the starting gate, enabling them to compete, achieve educational merit, and climb the social ladder? But this common sense assumption misses the social dynamics of HPS. The upper rungs of the ladder become harder to climb from below. As Chapter 5 showed, the key to the social distributional character of HPS is what happens when competition and stratification intersect with growth. This then is the paradox of equity in HPS—all else being equal, the greater the social inclusion, the stronger the secular tendency to social inequality in the powerful upper parts of the education system. In the absence of state intervention the natural social dynamic of HPS is not neutral but regressive. Positional competition tends towards a shell structure of universal inclusion populated by increasingly unequal subjects and a modernized aristocracy peeling away from the rest. Because the social effects of growth, bifurcation/stratification, and competition compound, all else being equal, the generic secular tendency is to greater social inequality in educational outcomes over time. The tendency becomes stronger as social inclusion in the HPS approaches universality.

This does not mean that any given time all HPS are always heading towards greater distributional inequality, but it means that states and autonomous educational institutions must work harder to maintain a neutrally reproductive HPS, let alone one in which social equality of opportunity is advancing. Given the secular tendency, counter-tendencies will only flow from deliberate policy action. They will never spring naturally from the workings of the HPS. Regulation is always the key to greater equity but more so in the HPS phase. Deregulation can only enhance stratification and worsen socially unequal outcomes.

Reproduction of Society

Chapter 3 on governance stated that in the HPS era, higher education and society move closer together. The external/internal boundary is more porous. As Trow (1973) noted, HPS higher education becomes a common if fragmented social experience. It is almost as comprehensively inclusive as the law, polity, economy, money, and taxation; and likewise socially differentiated. The HPS engages with most families, employers, and public bodies. It is both more open to external influences and more fully implicated in social patterns, including equality/inequality. The opportunity structure of the HPS moves from being a simulacra of society, held accountable by the degree to which it represents (or improves on) society, to society itself.

Lifting participation near to universal levels does not provide all students with equivalent educational (let alone social) opportunities. Nor does it in itself render countries more open and mobile, or socially and economically egalitarian. In the elite phase every student place has clear-cut status. As mass participation advances and countries move through to the HPS phase, the middle and lower levels of higher education are not the ladder they were. The *average* place in the HPS no longer provides the social opportunities typical of higher education in the elite and mass phases. Average positional value, for example as measured by average graduate unemployment rates and earnings, declines relative to the social mean. As Chapter 5 on stratification discussed, peak institutions continue to provide places in higher education that confer clear-cut social advantage, but these shrink as a proportion of total places. Graduates retain their advantages over non-graduates in earnings and employment (OECD, 2015a: 125, 147–8) because non-graduates are also losing ground. However, many graduates find themselves working in non-professional occupations (Green and Henseke, 2016).

At the same time, in HPS average graduate returns have reduced meaning, as earnings and career paths are increasingly dispersed (Green and Zhu, 2010; Britton et al., 2016), mirroring the overall differentiation of social and labour market outcomes. Regression to the mean is partly disguised by the minority of graduates with high incomes (e.g. Britton, et al., 2016: 21–43), many of whom owe their position more to inherited advantages and social networks than to educated merit. In a study of high mobility in Denmark and Canada, Bingley et al. (2011) note that in both countries 30–40 per cent of young adults are employed by a firm that also employed their fathers, mostly early in working life. The employer-driven association between parent and child earnings is similar in Denmark and Canada, 'rising distinctly and sharply at the very top of the earnings distribution' (pp. 3, 7, 12).

Implications for social participation and equity are summarized in the third proposition on equity (HPS proposition 16):

> Within a national system, as participation expands in the HPS phase, all else being equal the positional structure of the higher education system increasingly resembles that of society (albeit with the caveat of Proposition 15). The HPS is increasingly implicated in the reproduction of existing patterns of social equality/inequality.

Increased social inequality tends to be associated with greater social stratification of value, opportunity, and outcomes in the HPS of higher education. Correspondingly, an increase in social equality provides favourable conditions for reduced stratification of value, opportunity, and outcomes in the HPS.

If mass higher education was a potential engine of redistribution, the mature HPS naturally settles into reproduction mode and is only reluctantly disturbed, while the secular tendency to greater inequality slowly erodes the position. In countries with high inter-generational social mobility, such as Nordic Europe, there is much shifting between origins and destinations, and in the political culture social equality is continually promoted—but even there HPS primarily reproduce existing mobility rather than enlarging it (Piketty, 2014: 484).

For a growing proportion of participants in the HPS, expectations of higher education as a ladder are disappointed. There is not enough room on the upper rungs of society to take in 50–80 per cent of the age cohort. Despite this a participation illusion typical of positional competition (Hirsch, 1976) lingers in the HPS phase. People assume zero-sum barriers do not apply to them. Research consistently finds that families and students are more optimistic about their prospects than the odds justify (Arum and Roksa, 2014; Borgen, 2015: 85, 105). This is accentuated by institutional marketing (Hansen, 2011: 80–1). The participation illusion, a form of edu-centrism, is functional for states, maintaining policy focus on the extension of the benefits of participation at the margin, though arguably the more important forms of inequality and exclusion derive from the internal stratification within. Meanwhile as Lucas (2009) notes the task of the reformer has been rendered more difficult. Large reproductive HPS have increasing inertia and are harder to shift than smaller mass systems.

STATE POTENTIALS IN THE HPS ERA

The fourth proposition on equity (HPS proposition 17) states that

As the HPS boundary of participation expands it becomes more difficult for the state and/or autonomous educational systems/institutions to secure a redistribution of educational opportunities, and, through that, of social opportunities.

As the HPS converges with society as a whole, this institutionalizes the existing social distribution as educational distribution. First, there is the size factor. HPS are like battleships. It is more difficult to turn a larger ship around. Reforms are diluted by the size of the system through which they pass. Second, an HPS is more open to pressure from, and manoeuvres by, powerful stakeholders. Third, changing the distribution is more politically fraught than before.

The shrinking gap between the total population and the participant population reduces the scope for state intervention. In smaller mass-scale sectors with GERs of 15–20 per cent, states readily intervene at the margin to create selective opportunities for under-represented groups, without removing existing place holders. Growth strategies can be used as a Trojan horse for redistributive programmes. During the process of expansion in early massifying systems everyone seems to benefit; or at least, no one is worse off. All increases in participation are potentially equalizing: sub-elite higher education has clear positional value, and elite places are less crucial and less contested than in the later HPS phase. However, when the GER is at 60–90 per cent in a socially reproductive HPS a much larger numbers of places have to be moved to improve distributional equality. Most importantly, there are losers as well as winners. The number of potential losers grows as participation approaches universality. Equity policy can be Pareto optimal only in smaller systems. In capitalist democracies there is more support from reforms that provide new opportunities for the middle class in mass higher education, than reforms that redistribute middle class benefits down the social scale at the HPS stage—and the fiscal cost of universal benefits via high-quality provision for all, as in Nordic systems, is high. In HPS, distributional social reform is more expensive for states in terms of both economic and political capital.

This does not mean equalization is impossible, just that the obstacles are greater. Under the more difficult conditions of HPS a state's capacity to advance social equality depends on the social consensus about its role, the policy instruments at its disposal, and its political will.

THE AUTONOMOUS HIGHER EDUCATION INSTITUTIONS

Under what conditions do higher education systems and their institutions autonomously make a difference to social equality in opportunity and mobility? States are the essential backbone for education as a social allocator. An autonomous higher education system is like an independent legal system: it cannot exist without state support. However, state support for the independent allocative role of higher education is not guaranteed. At worst, states (and higher education institutions themselves) subvert the autonomy of the sector, tying higher education more closely to elite families. Over time in a socially reproductive HPS the strongest families become more adept at working the state, the higher education institutions, and the mechanisms of formal stratification and selection.

The foregoing argument suggests that the autonomous potential of higher education in social allocation is increased when there is greater scope for higher education institutions to themselves make change-inducing decisions affecting individuals (e.g. when high social mobility is normal) and decreased when social background effects are stronger (e.g. when stratification steepens). Also, the greater the professional independence and determining power of institutions in the core educational functions of student preparation, assessment, and selection, the greater the scope for educational practices, not family finance, social networks, and educational stratification, to shape the pattern of outcomes. Emphases on cognitive formation and progress via hard work are especially important for students who lack economic wealth and social networks, though a strict focus on academic criteria tends to maximize the determining effects of family cultural capital. United States' research suggests that positioning students as consumers, and emphases on extra-curricular peer networking, in which integration into a middle class world becomes an explicit objective of the learning programme, are undermining cognitive formation (Arum and Roksa, 2014: 11–12, 21, 37–8, 42–4). In addition, the veracity of selection into Ivy League universities is stymied by the use of non-academic criteria and informal quotas limiting Asian-American entrants, despite superior performance and in many cases the required extra-curricular attributes as well (Unz, 2012). It is a good example of the way higher education can become captured as a mechanism for reproducing the position of powerful families.

Historical conditions also determine the extent to which growing participation can become associated with higher social mobility. Piketty (2014) remarks that in the United States in the first three decades after World War II, after the evacuation of private fortunes amid depression and war, and amid a sustained period of growth in the economy, professional employment, class, education, and earnings were more important than property and financial capital in determining incomes and wealth. This meritocratic setting was strengthened by progressive taxation of earned incomes and wealth (Stiglitz, 2013). It was possible to advance both social inclusion and social equality of outcomes. Today the emerging HPS-to-be in China, India, and Indonesia exhibit the 1960s American dynamic of rapid middle class growth, an active state, and fast growing social demand for higher education. In China in 2002 the party-state committed to making the majority of people middle class (Goodman, 2014: 26–7). Higher education defines social status in China (p. 183). The lesson of the American experience for policymakers in China, India, and Indonesia is that if they want an educational order that supports citizen equality, now is the time to put a 'flat' high-quality higher education system into place. It will be more difficult to do so when middle class and HPS growth have stabilized.

National Variations

This chapter has identified two secular tendencies pertaining to the relationship between the expansion of participation and social equity—to overall social inclusion and to greater social inequality in access to elite higher education—and argued that a fully developed HPS tends to reproduce pre-given social relations in higher education, more so as participation advances. These three generic factors rest on the condition 'providing all else is held equal'. However, a secular tendency is not the same as an empirically verified trend. While all three generic factors contribute to the observable pattern of social outcomes in higher education, other more contextual factors also contribute. For example, the extent of stratification in higher education varies according to both the inheritance from past higher education systems and the extent of the implementation of neoliberal marketization reform. In the real world all else is not equal. The same secular tendency can be associated with a range of outcomes.

This is why it is impossible to derive a general empirical explanation of HPS by 'reverse engineering' from combined national statistical trends as Shavit, Arum, and Gamoran (2007) try to do. The problem is not one of removing 'noise' in the context to identify the underlying essential sound. Statistically based attempts to discern a universal relationship (always the holy grail of social science) between expansion and social access assume that waiting to be found is a relationship between system size, social composition, and all other factors that is regular not context-bound, and is fixed over time. But these core relations themselves can vary according to the national political economy, political culture, and historical conjuncture. If there are social 'laws of motion' in operation here, then they differ from case to case.

VARIATIONS IN THE SOCIAL ASSEMBLAGE

How then to understand variations in HPS? Chapter 1 suggested that each HPS-in-context is nested in its own relational environment, the family/state/education/economy assemblage (see Figure 6.1). It was also argued that these assemblages can be grouped on a regional basis, with differing political economies and cultures. Such variations affect patterns of social equality and mobility, including social background influences in educational attainment (OECD, 2014: 193). State regulatory frameworks and policies, and the social allocative potentials of autonomous higher education institutions also vary between HPS. Given regional variation, it is striking that the pattern of growth towards and beyond the 50 per cent GER level is almost universal. At the same time, regional and national factors are essential to explaining the growth trajectory of each particular HPS.

Comparing Germany, Norway, Italy, and Spain, Triventi finds the effects of social background on graduates' occupational outcomes varies by '(i) the social selectivity of education system, (ii) the level of higher education expansion, (iii) the degree of institutional connections between higher education and labor market, and (iv) the degree of institutional stratification in higher education' (Triventi, 2013a: 47–8). Other factors include social inequality and mobility, the intensity of competition, and state policy.

One important area of difference is the extent of state redistribution. Like positional competition in education, market transactions in the economy generate inequalities between individuals. Table 6.3 summarizes the tax/spend redistributive role of OECD

Table 6.3. Market-generated income inequality and state equalization, OED countries, 2012

Country	Gini coefficient for market incomes	State discounting of inequality by tax/transfers* %	Country	Gini coefficient for market incomes	State discounting of inequality by tax/transfers* %
NORDIC			FRANCE AND SOUTHERN EUROPE		
Finland	0.488	46.7	France	0.518	40.9
Denmark	0.436	42.9	Greece	0.569	40.2
Norway	0.410	38.3	Portugal	0.536	36.9
Sweden	0.431	36.4	Italy	0.509	35.8
Iceland	0.399	35.6	Spain	0.511	34.4
LOW COUNTRIES/GERMAN SPEAKING			ANGLOPHONE AND IRELAND		
Belgium	0.488	45.1	Ireland	0.582	47.8
Austria	0.495	44.2	Australia	0.463	29.6
Germany	0.501	42.3	Canada	0.438	28.1
Luxembourg	0.502	39.8	New Zealand	0.461	27.8
Netherlands	0.402	30.1	United States	0.513	24.0
Switzerland	0.368	22.6	United Kingdom	n.a.	n.a.
OTHER CENTRAL AND EASTERN EUROPE			EAST ASIA		
Slovenia	0.466	46.4	South Korea	0.338	9.2
Czech Republic	0.455	43.7	Japan	n.a.	n.a.
Hungary	0.485	40.4	OTHER		
Slovak Republic	0.412	39.3	Israel	0.481	22.9
Poland	0.465	35.9	Turkey	0.424	5.2
Estonia	0.489	30.9	Mexico	0.472	3.2

Notes: *This table measures the impact of state action to reduce income inequality. Discounting factor transforms Gini coefficient for market income (i.e. prior to tax and transfers), to Gini coefficient after tax and transfers (see Table 6.4). The higher the discounting factor, the larger the impact of state taxes and transfers in equalizing incomes. Data for Canada only are 2011.

Source: Author, drawing on data from OECD (2015b).

member states (OECD, 2015b). The countries are grouped on a regional basis. To varying degrees, states modify prior income inequalities using progressive taxation, transfer payments, and public goods. In egalitarian Denmark the Gini coefficient for market incomes is 0.436 but this falls to 0.249 after taxation and transfers (see Table 6.4). The state discounts market income inequality by 42.9 per cent. State-driven equalization is high in the Nordic world, Germany, and central Europe; low in English-speaking

Table 6.4. Income inequality (2012), and two indicators of social mobility (2000s and 2012), OECD countries with available data

	Gini coefficient after tax/transfers (2012)	Ratio between incomes after tax/transfers at 90/ 10 percentile (2012)	Social mobility 1: IIE, Corak study (2000s)	Social mobility 2: Odds ratios, OECD (2012)
Denmark	0.249	2.8	0.15	3.0
Slovak Republic	0.250	3.2	–	–
Norway	0.253	3.0	0.17	2.0
Czech Republic	0.256	3.0	–	–
Finland	0.260	3.1	0.18	1.4
Sweden	0.274	3.3	0.27	2.3
Austria	0.276	3.5	–	5.1
Netherlands	0.281	3.3	–	2.8
Switzerland	0.285	3.5	–	–
Germany	0.289	3.5	0.32	5.1
Poland	0.298	3.9	–	9.5
Ireland	0.304	3.8	–	3.3
France	0.306	3.6	0.41	6.0
South Korea	0.307	–	–	1.1
Canada	0.315	4.2	0.19	2.6
Australia	0.326	4.4	0.26	4.3
Italy	0.327	4.4	0.50	9.5
Spain	0.335	4.9	0.40	3.9
Estonia	0.338	4.7	–	4.7
United Kingdom	0.350	4.2	0.50	6.4*
United States	0.390	6.2	0.47	6.8
Japan	–	–	0.34	5.1
Chile	–	–	0.52	–

Notes: OECD countries with available data. – = data not available
*England and Northern Ireland only. IIE = Inter-generational elasticity in earnings, the percentage difference in earnings in the child's generation associated with the percentage difference in the parental generation. An intergenerational elasticity in earnings of 0.6 tells us that if one father makes 100 per cent more than another then the son of the high-income father will, as an adult, earn 60 per cent more than the son of the relatively lower income father (Corak, 2012: 2). 'Odds ratios' compare the odds of enrolling in tertiary education for two groups of 20–34-year-olds–those with one parent who attended tertiary education (the numerator), and those neither of whose parents attended tertiary education (the denominator) (OECD, 2014: 93).
Sources: Table prepared by author, using data from Corak (2012); OECD (2014: 93, 232, 2015a).

countries; and very low in Mexico. It is also low in egalitarian South Korea, where market-driven inequality is low: the state has less to do.

The capacity of the state to act as equaliser is affected by the robustness of taxation, public spending and wage regulation, and the economic size of the state in the economy. In 1980–2000, taxation stabilized at about 30 per cent of national income in USA, 40 per cent in the UK, 45 per cent in Germany, 50 per cent in France, and 55 per cent in Sweden (Piketty, 2014: 476). Equalization policy is also affected by the social distribution of public goods, and whether these are open to private capture by affluent families, such as places in the leading universities.

Table 6.4 provides comparative data on social inequality and social mobility. The Nordic countries are relatively equal, while the English-speaking countries are in the lower 40 per cent of the table. In Denmark, a high-income person, 90 per cent above the bottom of the income distribution, has a net income 2.8 times that of the low-income person at 10 per cent. In the United States that ratio is 6.2. Israel, Turkey, and Mexico are also very unequal (OECD, 2015b).

Corak finds inter-generational income elasticity is low and thus mobility high in the Nordic countries and also in Canada, but relatively low in France (0.41), the USA (0.47), and the UK (0.50) (Corak, 2006: 42). The OECD measures inter-generational social mobility by comparing the odds of enrolling in tertiary education for students whose parents did or did not access tertiary education. On this measure, inter-generational mobility is low in the United States, and especially high in Nordic Finland and South Korea (OECD, 2014: 93).

The differences between nations and regions, in their political and educational cultures, are not fully explored here (but see the national cases in Chapters 8–15). One important distinction is the extent to which the state has implemented neoliberal competition and marketization in higher education. States also vary in the extent to which they operate autonomously in education, with politicians and state officials able to confront rich and powerful interests. In societies where equality goals are not deeply embedded in social consensus as in the Nordic world, state commitment to a more equal society is unreliable. Higher education policy is like taxation and spending in general: the democratic mandate needs to be periodically renewed, or it is open to plutocratic capture.

Conclusions

Has the growth of participation 'caused' greater social inequality in higher education? No method, whether multi-variate statistical analysis or historical synthesis, can identify a one-to-one causal pattern. The real question is 'what are the potentials of HPS for social equality/ inequality?' The short answer is that under conditions of HPS, social inclusion via the extension of participation is more readily achieved, while an improved social mix in elite higher education institutions is more difficult to achieve. Why are HPS more reproductive, less readily redistributive, and more naturally unequal than their smaller predecessors? First there is the tendency to bifurcation and vertical 'stretch', enhancing the potential for private goods and heightening the effects of social background on educational opportunities and outcomes. Second, social competition is intensified at the junction of social stratification and stratification in education. Third, the potential counter-weight to the secular tendency to greater inequality, state policy, and regulation is increasingly restrained, because of the difficulty of moving a unit as large as an HPS. (This effect operates independently of neoliberal policies, though it is exacerbated by them.) A consensual redistribution is harder if not impossible to achieve.

Higher education still creates new prospects for many people from low SES backgrounds lacking family capital (though never enough of them). However, the dynamics of HPS disrupt the old assumptions, inherited from mass higher education, that higher education is a ladder for all and a social equalizer. It is no longer possible to argue that extending participation alone, without modifying the social relations driving inequality, can achieve greater equity. In the HPS era, expectations are increasingly out of touch with the conditions of possibility. Baker remarks that 'belief in equality of opportunity as social justice rises with the value of universalism in education' (2011: 11). The illusion also becomes more unsustainable over time—or at least, more vulnerable to exposure, to the cry that 'the emperor has no clothes'.

In addition, neoliberal policies and WCU strategy have enhanced stratification and competition in many countries. So this is the conundrum of HPS, at least in much of the world: as participation grows to majority level and beyond and social integration is advanced, larger numbers of young people have greater self-determining agency than before—but also have less opportunity for upward mobility.[7] More agency plus less opportunity. There is a deeper contradiction than before between the expectations nurtured in education and the personal capabilities it builds, and the social outcomes that follow. In the societies becoming more unequal this is not a stable arrangement. These issues are further discussed in Chapter 7.

The best antidote to the secular tendency to inequality is a broad spread of high-quality higher education institutions with none diminished by quasi-markets. Jonsson and Erikson (2007) state that in Sweden 'social forces' other than educational expansion have been more effective in reducing social inequalities in educational attainment, including 'developments towards greater equality of condition and reforms that made the Swedish educational system less stratified' (p. 138). A 'flatter' HPS does not guarantee greater social mobility through education, but does provide more favourable conditions

---

[7] The author is indebted to Brendan Cantwell for this point.

for mobility. Narrow value differentials mean less is at stake. Positionality is less fraught. Destinations are more open. The Nordic experience suggests that educational equality is a necessary but not sufficient condition for social equality, and vice versa. When higher education is used as a policy lever for reducing inequality, it should be understood as part of a larger set of policies, including tax/spending that redistribute incomes and public goods, and discourage private hoarding of social resources and opportunities. A consensus on egalitarian social values is also essential, including 'cross-class solidarity and high levels of generalised trust. Without them, the problems of free-riding and misuse of public goods would be insurmountable' and the middle class would revolt against public charges. However, if incomes are highly unequal the required level of trust is out of reach. 'Countries plagued by a very skewed income distribution are imprisoned in a vicious circle, an inequality trap, which frustrates all attempts to establish policies aiming at redistribution because social disparities breed mistrust' (Gärtner and Prado, 2012: 19).

There is also high social mobility in South Korea. The Korean HPS is more competitive and stratified than the Nordic, and tuition is charged. Korea also exhibits low stratification features. Income determination and regional economic growth are egalitarian (Lee et al., 2012). Confucian educational preparation in the family is common to all classes, and school achievement is high and near universal. Strong state regulation of the mass private sector ensures the lower tier is of relatively good quality, when compared with most other large private sectors. Canada combines high mobility with higher stratification and tuition than in Nordic Europe, but again the lower tier institutions have better quality and standing than their counterparts in most other countries, and there is a large number of high-quality research universities relative to country size. The Netherlands combine near Nordic levels of social mobility with well-spread high-quality research universities and a second sector in good social standing. In all these cases, positional value is relatively broadly spread and accessed, and vertical systemic differentiation is narrowed. That is the way forward in HPS, if they are to contribute to societies that are becoming more equal rather than more unequal.

■ REFERENCES

Altbach, P. and Salmi, J. (eds) (2011). *The Road to Academic Excellence: The Making of World-class Research Universities*. Washington, DC: World Bank.

Arum, R. and Roksa, J. (2014). *Aspiring Adults Adrift: Tentative Transitions of College Graduates*. Chicago: University of Chicago Press.

Arum, R., Gamoran, A., and Shavit, Y. (2007). More inclusion than diversion: Expansion, differentiation and market structures in higher education. In Y. Shavit, R. Arum, and A. Gamoran (eds), *Stratification in Higher Education: A Contemporary Study*. Stanford: Stanford University Press, pp. 1–35.

Baker, D. (2011). Forward and backward, horizontal and vertical: Transformation of occupational credentialing in the schooled society. *Research in Social Stratification and Mobility* 29, 5–29.

Belley, P. and Lochner, L. (2007). The changing role of family income and ability in determining educational achievement. NBER Working Paper 13527. Cambridge, MA: National Bureau of Economic Research.

Bingley, P., Corak, M., and Westergård-Nielsen, N. (2011). The intergenerational transmission of employers in Canada and Denmark. IZA Discussion Paper No. 5593. Bonn: Institute for the Study of Labor.

Boliver, V. (2011). Expansion, differentiation, and the persistence of social class inequalities in British higher education. *Higher Education* 61, 229–42.

Boliver, V. (2013). How fair is access to more prestigious UK universities? *The British Journal of Sociology* 64(2), 344–64.

Borgen, N. (2015). College quality and the positive selection hypothesis: The 'second filter' on family background in high-paid jobs. *Research in Social Stratification and Mobility* 39, 32–47.

Brand, J. and Xie, Y. (2010). Who benefits most from college? Evidence for negative selection in heterogeneous economic returns to higher education. *American Sociological Review* 75, 273–302.

Bray, M. (2007). *The Shadow Education System*, 2nd edn. New York: UNESCO. http://unesdoc.unesco.org/images/0011/001184/118486e.pdf

Britton, J., Dearden, L., Shephard, N., and Vignoles, A. (2016). *How English Domiciled Graduate Earnings Vary with Gender, Institution Attended, Subject and Socioeconomic Background*. London: Nuffield Foundation.

Callender, C. (2013). The funding of part-time students. In D. Heller and C. Callender (eds), *Student Financing of Higher Education: A comparative perspective*. London: Routledge, pp. 115–36.

Chankseliani, M. (2013). Rural disadvantage in Georgian higher education Admissions: A mixed-methods study. *Comparative Education Review* 57(3), 424–56.

Chapman, B. (2014). Income contingent loans: Background. In B. Chapman, T. Higgins, and J. Stiglitz (eds), *Income Contingent Loans: Theory, Practice and Prospects*. Basingstoke and New York: Palgrave Macmillan, pp. 12–28.

Cheung, S. and Egerton, R. (2007). Great Britain: Higher education expansion and reform—changing educational inequalities. In Y. Shavit, R. Arum, and A. Gamoran (eds), *Stratification in Higher Education: A Contemporary Study*. Stanford: Stanford University Press, pp. 195–219.

Corak, M. (2006). Do poor children become poor adults? Lessons from a cross country comparison of generational earnings mobility. IZA Discussion Paper No. 1993. Institute for the Study of Labor, Bonn.

Corak, M. (2012). *Inequality from Generation to Generation: The United States in Comparison*. Ottawa: Graduate School of Public and International Affairs, University of Ottawa.

DiPrete, T. and Eirich, G. (2006). Cumulative advantage as a mechanism for inequality: A review of theoretical and empirical developments. *Annual Review of Sociology*. 32, 271–97.

Dorling, D. (2014). *Inequality and the 1%*. London: Verso.

Espinoza, O. (2007). Solving the equity-equality conceptual dilemma: A new model for analysis of the educational process. *Educational Research* 49(4), 343–63.

Gärtner, S. and Prado, S. (2012). Inequality, trust and the welfare state: The Scandinavian model in the Swedish mirror. Högre seminar. Ekonomisk-historiska institutionen, Gothenburg University, 7 November.

Gasparishvili, A. and Toumanov, S. (2006). Moskovskii student sto let nazad i nyne (Moscow student 100 years ago and now). *Otechestvennye Zapiski* 3(30). http://www.strana-oz.ru/?numid=30&article=

Gerber, T. and Cheung, S. Y. (2008). Horizontal stratification in postsecondary education: Forms, explanations, and implications. *Annual Review of Sociology* 34, 299–318.

Goodman, D. (2014). *Class in Contemporary China*. Cambridge: Polity.

Green, F. and Henseke, G. (2016). Should governments of OECD countries worry about graduate overeducation? *Oxford Review of Economic Policy* 32(4), 514–37. https://doi.org/10.1093/oxrep/grw024

Green, F. and Zhu, Y. (2010). Overqualification, job dissatisfaction, and increasing dispersion in the returns to graduate education. *Oxford Economic Papers*. 62 (2), 740–63.

Hansen, H. (2011). Rethinking certification theory and the educational development of the United States and Germany. *Research in Social Stratification and Mobility* 29, 31–55.

Hazelkorn, E. (2015). *Rankings and the Reshaping of Higher Education: The Battle for World-class Excellence*, 2nd edn. Houndmills: Palgrave Macmillan.

Hirsch, F. (1976). *Social Limits to Growth*. Cambridge, MA: Harvard University Press.

Hoxby, C. and Avery, C. (2013). The missing 'one-offs': The hidden supply of high-achieving, low-income students. *Brookings Papers on Economic Activity*, Spring.

Hu, A. and Vargas, N. (2015). Horizontal stratification of higher education in urban China. *Higher Education*. DOI 10.1007/s10734-014-9833-y

Husen, T. (1974). *The Learning Society*. York: Methuen.

Jonsson, J. and Erikson, R. (2007). Sweden: Why educational expansion is not such a great strategy for equality—theory and evidence. In Y. Shavit, R. Arum, and A. Gamoran (eds), *Stratification in Higher Education: A Contemporary Study*. Stanford: Stanford University Press, pp. 113–39.

Konstantinovskiy, D. (2016). HPS and social equity: Case of Russia. Paper prepared for High Participation Systems project.

Lee, H., Lee, M., and Park, D. (2012). Growth policy and inequality in developing Asia: Lesson from Korea. ERIA Discussion Paper 2012–12.

Lucas, S. (2009). Stratification theory, socioeconomic background, and educational attainment: A formal analysis. *Rationality and Society* 21, 459–511.

Lucas, S. (2001). Effectively maintained inequality: Education transitions, track mobility, and social background effects. *American Journal of Sociology* 106(6), 1642–90.

Marginson, S. (1997). *Markets in Education*. Sydney: Allen and Unwin.

Marginson, S. (2008). A funny thing happened on the way to the K-economy: The new world order in higher education. Research rankings, outcome measures and institutional classifications. Paper for conference of the Institutional Management in Higher Education, OECD. Paris, 8–10 September.

Marginson, S. (2013). The changing geo-politics of creativity: Rise of the Post-Confucian University. In M. Peters and Tina Besley (eds), *The Creative University*. Rotterdam: Sense Publishers, pp. 9–32.

Marginson, S. (2016). *The Dream is Over: The Crisis of Clark Kerr's Californian Idea of Higher Education.* Berkeley: University of California Press.

Mountford-Zimdars, A. and Sabbagh, D. (2013). Fair access to higher education: A comparative perspective. *Comparative Education Review* 57(3), 359–68.

OECD (Organisation for Economic Cooperation and Development) (2014). *Education at a Glance, 2014.* Paris: OECD.

OECD (Organisation for Economic Cooperation and Development) (2015a). *Education at a Glance, 2015.* Paris: OECD.

OECD (Organisation for Economic Cooperation and Development) (2015b). Data on income distribution and poverty. http://stats.oecd.org/Index.aspx?DataSetCode=IDD

Oxfam (2014). *Even it Up: Time to End Extreme Inequality.* Oxford: Oxfam GB.

Piketty, T. (2014). *Capital in the Twenty-first Century.* Trans. A. Goldhammer. Cambridge, MA: Belknap Harvard University Press.

Raftery, A. and Hout, M. (1993). Maximally maintained inequality: Expansion, reform and opportunity in Irish education, 1921–75. *Sociology of Education* 66(1), 41–62.

Reitz, T. (2017). Academic hierarchies in neo-feudal capitalism: How status competition processes trust and facilitates the appropriation of knowledge. *Higher Education* 73(6), 871–86.

Rivera, L. (2015). *Pedigree: How Elite Students Get Elite Jobs.* Princeton, NJ: Princeton University Press.

Salmi, J. (2009). *The Challenge of Establishing World-Class Universities.* Washington, DC: World Bank.

Shavit, Y., Arum, R., and Gamoran, A. (eds) (2007). *Stratification in Higher Education: A Comparative Study.* Stanford: Stanford University Press.

Shavit, Y., Ayalon, H., Chachashvili-Bolotin, S., and Menahem, G. (2007). Israel: Diversification, expansion and inequality in higher education. In Y. Shavit, R. Arum, and A. Gamoran (eds), *Stratification in Higher Education: A Contemporary Study.* Stanford: Stanford University Press, pp. 39–62.

Smolentseva, A. (2016). Universal higher education and positional advantage: Soviet legacies and neoliberal transformations in Russia. *Higher Education.* DOI 10.1007/s10734-016-0009-9

Soares, J. (2007). *The Power of Privilege: Yale and America's Elite Colleges.* Stanford: Stanford University Press.

Stiglitz, J. (2013). *The Price of Inequality.* London: Penguin.

Tholen, G., Brown, P., Power, S., and Allouch, A. (2013). The role of networks and connections in educational elites' labour market entrance. *Research in Social Stratification and Mobility* 34, 142–54.

Thomsen, P., Munk, M., Eiberg-Madsen, M., and Hansen, G. (2013). The educational strategies of Danish university students from professional and working class backgrounds. *Comparative Education Review* 57(3), 457–80.

Triventi, M. (2013a). The role of higher education stratification in the reproduction of social inequality in the labor market. *Research in Social Stratification and Mobility* 32, 45–63.

Triventi, M. (2013b). Stratification in higher education and its relationship with social inequality: A comparative study of 11 European countries. *European Sociological Review* 29(3), 489–502.

Trow, M. (1973). *Problems in the Transition from Elite to Mass Higher Education*. Berkeley, CA: Carnegie Commission on Higher Education.

UNESCO (United Nations Educational, Social and Cultural Organization) (2016). UNESCO Institute for Statistics data on education. http://data.uis.unesco.org/

Unz, R. (2012). The myth of American meritocracy. *The American Conservative*, December, 14–51.

Valimaa, J. and Muhonen, R. (2016). High participation systems in Nordic countries: The case of Finland. Working paper. (Early draft of Chapter 13 of this book.)

Wolniak, G., Seifert, T., Reed, E., and Pascarella, E. (2008). College majors and social mobility. *Research in Social Stratification and Mobility* 26, 123–13.

7 High Participation Society

Anna Smolentseva

if the future were the product of the secular trends alone we could plan for it with some assurance, some sense of our capacity to master the future, first intellectually and then institutionally. But the future is not just the aggregate of secular trends. It is also full of unforeseen events and developments that sharply limit our power to anticipate...

(Trow, 1973: 47–8)

Introduction

This book maintains that the social aspirations of the population for a better life, which are the primary driver of participation in higher education, are not stoppable and not reversible.[1] Assuming that, the ultimate question for the present high participation systems (HPS) project has been to try to envision what will change in a society where a majority of the age group has experienced higher education. The countries considered in this book are approaching that frontier of participation, if by 'higher education' is meant tertiary education at degree level. The authors have tried to document and analyse the most important changes within high participation higher education systems while also taking into account larger societal changes (such as demographics, urbanization, income distribution, labour markets, economic contexts, political culture), which accompany the growth. The contours of future societies and their higher education systems are being formed now and can be observed at least to some extent. One development is the spread of capabilities in self-forming agency among a larger group of higher educated people. Another very visible development is the growing inequality that is shaping the social order. Online technologies, all forms of networks, and the shared economy via collaborative production, distribution, and consumption are all continually expanding.

It is difficult to provide a forecast. The future is being shaped by a great number of social and natural forces. High participation is not universal participation. Even when

---

[1] The author is very grateful to Brendan Cantwell, David Konstantinovskiy, and Simon Marginson for their helpful comments on the draft of this chapter.

half or more of the age cohort reach higher education, there will be another almost half who do not and a majority in the older age groups with the lower level of educational attainment. The demographic trends in most of HPS countries demonstrate ageing populations (in most of Europe, Russia, Japan) or low to medium population growth (USA, Canada, Australia, UK). In the proximal future, the next two decades or so, the higher educated population—not the tertiary educated, the higher educated population—will still not comprise the majority of the population even in most HPS countries. Among those who do enter tertiary education, not all participate at a high level. In the first high participation system, the United States of America (USA), where more than 85 per cent of the young age cohort reaches some kind of tertiary education, so far only about 40 per cent of that cohort graduate at degree level (UNESCO, 2017). It is possible that there will be some levelling and attainment rates will not grow much or grow slowly.

Still, in the longer run social aspirations will probably continue to drive up higher education attainment. The higher educated may become close to half of the total working population, and will be a larger proportion of young working adults. In such a society, the younger and middle generations will actively build their own lives in the workplace, family, politics, culture, and all other social dimensions. They will shape future job contents, labour market structures, family structures, political choice, and cultural tastes. They will address issues in climate change, migration, inequality, and automation, and make greater use of information and complex data, as well as other developments we cannot yet predict.

The Formation of Society (Including People)

In attempting to better understand the future, we can begin with what we already know about higher education and its role in society. We can also look at the external forces which affect higher education and might affect it in the future. Once we understand how education and society are inter-related, we can approach the question of the effects of education in society. All this can help us to contemplate the meaning of a society where half or more of the population reaches higher education. However, despite the fact that higher education has been in the focus of social research for several decades, its social role in a society, in social development, and its inter-relations with society have not been thoroughly studied.

Generally, sociology sees education as an institution with broad functions in society. It enables and promotes the acquisition of skills, knowledge, and the broadening of personal horizons (Giddens, 2009: 834). While education can take place in many different settings, the formal process of education, the delivery of certain types of knowledge and skills, in specialized settings, schools, is called schooling (p. 834). These definitions of education and schooling can be reprised in tertiary and higher education, which are also processes of acquisition of knowledge and skills within various settings. However, differing traditions in social science address the question of education and its social role in a variety of ways.

Functionalist approaches consider education an important social institution. It promotes the socialization of individuals: both in a broader sense, as the transmission of unifying social and cultural norms; and in the sense that it provides skills necessary for participation in increasingly specialized occupations (Collins, 1971; Giddens, 2009). Education is also seen as important in contributing to the social integration, solidarity, and stability of society through the creation and transmission of norms, through merit-based social placement, and by facilitating cultural and technological innovations (Macionis, 2012). This tradition derives mainly from early scholarship in the sociology of education, but the ideas are kept alive in the current discussions.

In the early 20th century in France, Emile Durkheim emphasized the key role of education in maintaining collective solidarity by fostering the internalization of social norms, rules, discipline, and respect for authority; through the selection and allocation of talents; and by teaching the skills needed to perform social and occupational roles in an industrial society (Durkheim, 1956; Izquierdo and Minguez, 2003; Giddens, 2009). Durkheim's work emphasizes an instrumental role of education. As he sees it, the individual and his or her interests is not the only, or main, purpose of education. Rather, education is mostly a means by which society constantly reproduces the conditions of its own existence (Durkheim, 1995). It does so by developing in each person certain physical, intellectual, and moral states required of him or her (Durkheim, 1956). Durkheim describes as utilitarian the individual-centered approach to education advocated by James Mill (the idea that the purpose of education is to make the person into an instrument of happiness for him- or herself and those close to him or her (1956)). Yet Durkheim himself provides a rather utilitarian account, in which the individual and education serve society.

In the early second half of the twentieth century a similar approach is taken by Talcott Parsons (1959) in the USA. He sees socialization and allocation as the main social functions of education. Education instils in students the internalization of commitment, defined in terms of values and specific types of roles in the social structure; and also capacities, competences, or skills to perform certain roles and the ability to perform those roles according to others' expectations. Education forms individual students who will perform required future roles and helps to allocate them within the role structure of society. Parsons assumes that in the American society of his time, social status and education attainment are inter-related, with both related to occupational status. Completion of a high school diploma has become a social norm. The main line of division in occupational status is between those who have gone to college and those who have not.

Later, Parsons and Platt (1970) discuss the rapid growth of age cohort participation in US higher education, which has increasingly affected society. Among the qualitative indicators on the impact of this change are the widespread belief that societal problems can be alleviated through education, the greater prestige of college degrees and the greater importance of the possession of college degrees in the population, the stratifying function of college degrees in distinguishing between the upper and lower middle class, and the influence of higher education in government and industry. Quantitatively, there is a growing number of higher educational institutions and professional schools, an increasing number and variety of individuals and groups involved in higher education, and prolongation of the time in which individuals are involved in the educational process. Despite the fact of growing social pressure to attend higher education institutions, socio-economic disparities in participation remain high. Participation continues to be dependent on a person's social status at birth. However, expectations of participation have moved downwards from the elite level and this stimulates the continuing growth in enrolments.

Parsons and Platt (1970) maintain that learning in higher education involves two basic processes: assimilation of the cognitive content of the subject matter, and the internalization of values and norms. They call the latter 'socialization.' The advent of mass higher education means that the period of student life becomes a new phase of socialization unfamiliar to most members of previous generations. It divides youth into those who undergo this new socialization process and those who do not. The socializing impact of being a student includes development of the capacity to accept higher levels of achievement as goals for self and others; and development of the capacity to participate in and to accept a more differentiated environment with a wide range of action. Being a less hierarchical organization than the school, the college enables students to perceive different social relations. The period of being a student ('studentry') is a modified extension of adolescence. The student continues to be protected from many external pressures, but at the price of not making their own living and with some inhibition of marriage.

In 'technical function theory' (defined by Collins, 1971), structural functionalism assumes that in an industrial society, due to technological change, the demand for skills increases. This requires populations to spend longer periods in education in order to obtain the general capacities or specific skills that are necessary for more highly skilled jobs (Collins, 1971, refers to Clark, 1962; Davis and Moore, 1945; Kerr et al., 1960). In that sense the functionalist approach accords with human capital theory. Developed by Jacob Mincer and systematized by Gary Becker, this considers human capital as a wide range of knowledge, skills, social and personal characteristics that have economic value on the labour market. Schooling enables individual students to accumulate human capital that leads to higher wage income, jobs, and status; while at the macro-level an aggregated human capital enhances productivity and economic growth. Education also increases the capacity to handle new technologies and innovations. Importantly, human capital theory considers education as an individual investment and prioritizes the private economic benefits associated with it, thus making educational funding an individual responsibility. In the last fifty years these ideas have been actively taken on board by many policy-makers around the world, partly because they present a simple and comprehensible narrative of the relations between individual, education and economy (Marginson, 1997, 2017).

Neo-institutional sociology emerged in 1970s as an attempt to bring into the focus of social science research the social meanings and roles of institutions. Neo-institutionalism sees higher education as a national and global cultural institution which links the role structure of society to universalized cultural knowledge, rather than preparing graduates to fill social roles (Meyer et al., 2007). This theory argues that its contribution is to consider education as a social institution which *directly shapes* society, rather than as a social institution that is merely *affected by* society, as functionalism maintains (Meyer et al., 2007; Baker, 2014). If traditionally education's role was seen mainly as the reproduction of society by training people for social positions and jobs created by other social institutions, the present larger scale of higher education (its institutionalization) allows it to be seen as a separate and enduring social institution, which in large part socially constructs modern society rather than simply reproducing it (Baker, 2014).

For neo-institutionalism, formal education, like other social institutions, create cultural meanings, including new ideas, new social statuses, and new human capacities which transform post-industrial reality (Baker, 2014). Higher education has always had an important cultural and civilizational mission, being linked to a universal cultural core. This mission can be distinguished from its particular economic or political functions, historical legacies, or contestations in relation to power (Meyer et al., 2007). In addition, education legitimizes certain knowledge, and certifies certain persons as having that legitimized knowledge and through it, authority (Meyer, 1977). Universities and knowledge-workers have special power in the modern world. The cultural impact of education is related to the concepts of merit-based achievement and knowledge: it is associated with the universalism of educational merit, the educational development of individuals as a collective good, academic achievement as a supreme form of achievement, the belief in academically derived knowledge, and cognition as the master human capability (Baker, 2014).

Emerging as one response to dissatisfaction with functionalism, neo-institutional sociology itself embraces functionalist ideas of unifying values and norms, but unlike the earlier functionalism, it considers these values and norms to be immanent to education/ higher education and deriving from their universal nature. Neo-institutionalism disregards social, historical, and cultural contexts, seeing the ideas behind schooling as largely similar around the world. It is true that the neo-institutionalism's idea of a transforming role of education extends education beyond the socially receiving and reflective role to which functionalism is confined. However, the universalistic normativism entailed in neo-institutionalism's idea of convergence towards a single world model reduces the transformative potential of education to an idealistic imaginary—and one that can be refuted by pointing to the empirical and conceptual limits of institutionalism.

Another sociological tradition, that of conflict theories, also considers education an important social institution. Here education is again seen to support society, but by reinforcing the power of certain social groups over others (Collins, 1971; Giddens, 2009. Here the role of education is predominantly to maintain the existing social order, partly through the structure of higher education-trained professional and occupational positions and the utilization of those positions to perpetuate the domination of certain social classes. This sociological tradition goes back to Max Weber's work on status groups. These can be defined by various criteria, including occupation, class and ethnicity. Education can be used in two ways: to provide social advancement through merit-based selection or to operate as a social barrier that keeps outsiders from desirable positions (Arum et al., 2015). Bowles and Gintis (1976) open up discussion of the hidden curriculum by arguing that schooling teaches discipline, hierarchy and passive acceptance of the social structure of society (Giddens, 2009). This insight is complemented by research on resilience and protest within educational environments (Giddens, 2009). Collins (1971) argues that it is competition among status groups, rather than technological change and demand for new skills, that raises the level of education required for various jobs. Different status groups impose their cultural standards on selection. The role of education is mainly to produce credentials, rather than to provide knowledge and skills that augment productivity as is argued by human capital theory.

Theories of cultural reproduction likewise maintain that society is not a harmonious unity moving towards solidarity and stability but is organized to reproduce social inequalities that are based on culture and class (Giddens, 2009). Basil Bernstein focuses on language codes which serve as a means of reproduction of social inequality at the school level (Bernstein, 1990). The more comprehensive theory of Pierre Bourdieu establishes relationships between on the one hand economic status, social power, and symbolic capital, and on the other hand cultural knowledge and skills. Education is deeply embedded in society, and reflects and reproduces the existing social structure and relations of power. Education primarily contributes to the formation of cultural capital, in the form of thinking, speaking, or moving, in the form of educational qualification/credentials, and in material form such as books or art objects. It might also play a role in the acquisition of networked social capital, and can be exchanged into economic capital. It shapes one's position in social structure and strengthens the position of privileged social groups in a society (Bourdieu, 1984; Giddens, 2009). The most important functions of the educational system are to inculcate the existing social order and to disguise the 'objective truth of its [educational system's] relationship to the structure of class relations' (Bourdieu and Passeron, 1977). In this book on HPS, the chapters on vertical stratification and inequality productively employ the cultural reproduction perspective, among others. This perspective helps in understanding social stratification at the individual, intra-institutional and inter-institutional levels, in higher education and in broader social contexts.

The above major theoretical perspectives developed in sociology—functionalism, conflict theories, neo-institutionalism, cultural reproduction—mostly establish connections between the educational system and the social structure of society. They agree that education, including higher education, is an important social institution. They maintain that education/schooling ascribes social position and transmits knowledge and skills, both of which are essential for future roles in society and the workplace, as well as for imparting values and norms. However, they start from different perspectives on society and emphasize different knowledge, skills, values, and norms that are transmitted by the educational system, and they have different endpoints in view. Education variously leads to more solidarity and stability (functionalism) or convergence and unification (neo-institutionalism) or power struggle and social inequalities (theories of conflict and cultural reproduction).

It can be argued that these grand social theories do not sufficiently embrace the specific nature and content of higher education, namely the knowledge that is produced and transmitted to students and society. This lacuna tends to block a better understanding of the relationships between higher education and society. Employing social networks theories in a mixed-method international comparative study, Hoffman and Välimaa (2016) develop the concept of the networked knowledge society. This is a society which needs and uses knowledge, uses information and communications technologies, and relies on the social network as one unit of social structure. Such a society implies non-hierarchical social organization and potentially sees universities as important nodes (more spaces than places) in the collective production, transmission, transfer, and application of knowledge via networks. Hierarchical and non-hierarchical (network, rhizome-like) relationships co-exist in modern higher education.

It is true that network relationship are becoming increasingly important in the era of global flow of knowledge and knowledge-workers. In this sense, universities are becoming significant actors in the shaping of networked knowledge society. Although there is no evidence of decreasing social inequalities, and often networks are organized according to perceived social status, this theoretical perspective enables scholars to think in a different way about the role of knowledge and imagine new potential ways of social organization. It also provides a practical approach to operationalizing the relationship between society and higher education—by focusing on the networks connecting the two (Hoffman and Välimaa, 2016). At the same time, we can see that the social potentials of networking are ambiguous. Inclusive networks and networked technologies have a 'flat' form within the network. They also enhance individual agency and create social status for those who share the network. At the same time, networked relationships can form social closures and hierarchies, and enhance inequalities, in relation to those who are left outside the network. Under some conditions higher education has parallel effects to online social networks in this regard.

Another approach to addressing the relationships between higher education and society is the concept of social pact, one widely used in higher education research. Ase Gornitzka and colleagues (2007) define this as a long-term cultural commitment with and by the university, as an institution with its own foundational rules of appropriate practices, causal and normative beliefs, and resources that is validated by the political and social system in which the university is embedded. The social pact is sometimes called a social contract, but more usually a social contract refers to a contract that is based on continuous strategic calculation of expected value by public authorities, organized external groups, university employees, and students, all of whom regularly monitor and assess the university on the basis of its usefulness for their self-interest, and act accordingly (Gornitzka et al., 2007). The concept of social pact engages with the idea of society and the mutual understanding, trust, expectations, responsibilities, and obligations of both parties, society and university (Maasen, 2014). But it largely focuses on higher education itself, on the university and its transformations under changing environments, addressing the effects of higher education on society only to a lesser extent. Nor does it provide a clear conceptual system for the analysis of the social pact between higher education and society.

The concept of public or common good is a further way of analysing the relationship between higher education and a broader social entity such as society and/or economy. The contribution of higher education to broader society is acknowledged and the concept is widely used, but interpretations of what is 'public' vary (Marginson, 2018). The lack of clarity is related to the different assumptions in regard to the location of activity (state sector or outside), source of funding (government or household/private organization), and the nature of the activity; and also different traditions in various political cultures across national contexts, as well as different disciplinary traditions in the social sciences (Marginson, 2018). The public good concept embraces multiple dimensions: the source of provision and the location of provision, as well as the identity of the beneficiaries (whose public goods? See Marginson, 2018), which makes it difficult to operationalize and develop a working analytical framework for empirical research. The beneficiary dimension brings the focus back to systems of statuses, the social structure of society and issues of social inequality. Public or common goods are certainly important aspects of the relationships between higher education and society. However, there are dimensions of public good which have an impact on society but are very hard to operationalize and measure, such as the transmission of norms and values, and whether they are unifying or diversifying.

The Formation of People (and Hence Society)

Overall, the social theories mentioned earlier do not tell us much about the content of education—*which* knowledge, skills, norms, and values are being created and transmitted. Both the institutional sociology and the networked knowledge society approaches emphasize the key importance of knowledge in general. Functionalism and institutionalism appeal to universal and unifying content; conflict theories discuss skills necessary for technical and economic progress; the cultural reproduction perspective emphasizes language codes and the culture of dominant social groups that create social exclusion. The social pact and public good concepts focus more on knowledge in relation to social equity.

The nature of education and its content have been extensively studied in the philosophy of education and in the field of pedagogy. There are two major lines of inquiry on the nature and purposes of education: the German concept of *Bildung*, which evolved within the European continental tradition, and the related concept of growth elaborated in Anglo-American tradition (Siljander et al., 2012). The roots of the *Bildung* idea can be traced back to Ancient Greek and Roman ideas of education, and the Enlightment and humanistic scholarship, and is related to the work of Johan Comenius, J. J. Rousseau, I. Kant, G. W. Hegel, J. G. Fichte, and W. von Humboldt, among others. *Bildung* is concerned with cultivation of the inner life of the educated individual, and the creative process of individual self-development. It points to the ability of the person to overcome external determination and immaturity (Biesta, 2002; Siljander et al., 2012). The concept of *Bildung* also has a social and political dimension. It is seen as one key to individual and societal progress because it enables individuals to better understand themselves, and to relate to, understand, and change their external contexts, life circumstances, and cultural environments. The outcomes and results of the learning process cannot be predefined; *Bildung* is a self-forming and self-cultivating process. However, *Bildung* needs a facilitating, emancipating mediator, a social infrastructure that provides conditions in which it happens, which is formal schooling.

The concept of growth was developed later, in progressive pedagogy and pragmatism, in the works of John Dewey, William James, Horace Mann, George Herbert Mead, and others. It was associated with the modernization of the USA and the Western world, and the search for explanations of change (Siljander et al., 2012). The tradition emerged in lively discussion with European continental scholarship and the two concepts have important similarities. The idea of growth implies the ability of humans to evolve and continuously change, in a creative manner, in order to adapt to their environment. Creativity developed through experience (in education it can be implemented through learning by doing) is seen as a key human capacity which has enabled people to make the transition from a biological organism to aware individuals able to act intelligently. In this school of thought growth is seen as an individual activity that enables a person to create a different reality. It is close to the concept of *Bildung* in relation to self-formation or self-cultivation (Siljander et al., 2012). The growth of self is not spontaneous, it is a function of the person's active experience in conjunction with her or his environment (Väkevä, 2012: 277). In both traditions education is seen as a medium for reconstructive growth that extends well beyond a simple transmission function.

Another line of inquiry and debate relates to the applicability of knowledge and skills: whether these are seen in utilitarian and instrumental terms, or in terms of the humanistic character of education. The humanistic agenda is partly derived from the *Bildung* discussion, but the terms are not always strictly defined and have various meanings. In different national contexts, the division between the two approaches plays out in contrasting ways. In some countries, it is embodied in the binary/sectoral division between comprehensive universities, seen as bearers of the humanistic mission, and institutions of applied sciences (specialist universities, institutes, colleges), which are understood in terms of the utilitarian mission. Often, a broad education designed to prepare a cultivated person—Weber (2015) refers to an education possessing '"more" cultural quality' versus 'specialized training for expertness'—has been an elitist type of education, as in the case of liberal education for gentlemen in the United Kingdom (UK), and the leading liberal arts colleges in the USA today.

Perhaps the tensions between the humanistic and instrumental aims of education have increased in recent years. In many countries, policy has followed a neoliberal path, accompanied by both the massification of higher education and cuts in public financing, which has been associated with the predominance of utilitarian or instrumental approaches with their focus on training for job placement, the employability of graduates, the private economic benefits associated with degrees, and the aggregate contribution of higher education to economic growth (Smolentseva, 2017). However, the humanistic mission of education, the notion of developing individuals to their highest potential, has been elaborated through time and across countries:

to foster both diversity and unity; to impart specific skills through training and to free creativity; to develop both individual ambition and the ability to live in harmony with others; to ensure continuity and legacy, while establishing the foundations for societal innovation; and to ensure the basis for lasting citizenship and participatory governance. (Carneiro, 2015)

Marginson (2014) refers to the process of self-formation, which highlights a student's self-determining agency, shaped partly in and through higher education, which facilitates successful self-formation and enhances the individual's agency freedom in the social environment.

In sociology, discussion on the content of education has been less prolific. Some research problematizes the transmission of knowledge and learning, suggesting that actual learning outcomes in higher education are often very limited (e.g. Arum and Roksa, 2010; Konstantinovskiy, 2017, on higher education institutions that are focused on 'socialization' rather than knowledge-intensive training). Generally, there is a lack of sociological research on the larger effects on society of the personal development of individuals. One line of inquiry is the life course studies approach, which traces the age-graded roles that structure, or create patterns in, biography (Shanahan et al., 2016: 3). This situates the individual in a larger picture, illuminating the bi-directional interplay between individuals and their contextual environments (Crosnoe and Benner, 2016). These studies give considerable attention to the various dimensions of inequality. This perspective, developed within various disciplines, might serve a link between individual development and its impact on the broader social structure. Anthony Giddens' theory of structuration (1984) is an interesting attempt to connect the individual (agency) and structure, whereby the structures consisting of rules and resources are employed in their everyday practices by individuals involved in the reproduction of those structural rules and resources. Here human beings are active agents of the social world who are able to influence social reality, rather than merely being shaped by it. Another approach, that of the concept of social resilience (e.g. Lamont, 2014) at individual and collective levels, also attempts to emphasize the dimension of individual agency, while acknowledging that individuals contribute to societal well-being. This work also addresses the role of higher education in the formation of agency.

Conclusion

The contribution of higher education to society is multi-dimensional. That is why it is difficult to analyse comprehensively. The foregoing overview of the existing approaches shows that none offer clear guidance on how we can think about societies in which the majority of the working age population has engaged in higher education. However, in the light of the above conceptual approaches, it is apparent that there are two especially important areas to consider when inquiring into the relationship between higher education and society:

- the social and occupational structure;
- socialization as human/personal development, higher education as self-formation (Marginson, 2014; Carneiro, 2015; derived from concept of *Bildung*).

We can think of high participation society along these two lines of inquiry: how high participation in higher education affects the social and occupational structure, and how high participation in higher education affects socialization/personal development. One line of inquiry pertains primarily to structure, the other pertains primarily to agency.

An aggregate construction of society in terms of culture, social solidarity, social cohesion, and the collective well-being are also essential ways in which higher education connects to society. This aggregate construction is deeply embedded in the existing social order, in terms of social structures, and in terms of socialization as the processes of interiorization of norms and values, as theories of functionalism, neo-insitutionalism and cultural reproduction suggest.

THE SOCIAL AND OCCUPATIONAL STRUCTURE

Perhaps in higher educated societies (HPS societies), disparities among social groups should decline as the share of the population with higher education increases. According to functionalism and neo-institutionalism, this might lead to interiorization of common social norms by the majority of the population. Alternately, depending on which of the two theories are accepted, this implies greater social solidarity (functionalism) or the triumph of world society (neo-institutionalism). However, as indicated in the preceding chapters on vertical stratification and inequality (Chapters 5–6) and in the country cases in Part II of this book, while educational participation has grown to the HPS level and beyond, social inequalities in most countries have been increasing. In addition, in some parts of the world higher education is a divisive factor in the political sense, as was shown in the 2016 patterns of voting for Trump in the USA and Brexit voting in the UK.

Social differentiation though higher education is not confined only to the distinction between groups with different levels of education. Differentiation can be observed also within the higher educated group. As Chapter 5 argues, there is increasing vertical stratification of the higher education sector and a corresponding differentiation of credentials, faculty and student contingents. Over time this can be expected to produce more divergent economic, occupational, and social outcomes, partly counter-balancing the tendencies to commonality that the spread of higher education brings, especially among the educated.

In many sociological traditions, social status (or class) is a key category in structuring the social fabric. Education has long been essential in the construction of social status. In HPS societies the construction of social status might be increasingly complex. Higher education in itself no longer maintains its previous positional advantage due to the near universality of participation. The vast majority of the higher educated cohort, proceeding from the lower middle and bottom tier higher education institutions, find the social value of their degrees to be relatively low, which affects their positions in the social and occupational structure. These factors mean that 'entering higher education' or 'holding a university degree' lose much of their previous meanings as traditional class descriptors in social science, problematizing the status concept and creating new challenges for social stratification research.

Employing Gerhard Lenski's (1954) concept of status inconsistency/crystallization, meaning that different dimensions of social status do not correspond to each other, we could argue that in HPS societies the incidence of social groups with poorly crystallized statuses—such as higher educated persons who lack a high income or a clearly advantaged position in an occupational hierarchy—will tend to increase and might also become a social norm. Taking into account the greater differentiation of the higher education system, one might expect to find the increasing marginalization of such social groups. Lenski saw such groups as subject to pressures from the social order, which could lead to the destabilization of society and generate a need for change. As compared to the functional tradition, this approach suggests an alternative to the notion of a unidimensional social hierarchy and suggests possible directions for the formation of future social structures. With the massification of higher education and higher educated social groups we can already see some forms of downward differentiation and marginalization. Consider the internal differentiation within large occupational groups such as teachers, faculty, doctors, or lawyers, groups whose individual members carry credentials with unequal social value and have differentiated positions within the hierarchical social structures of their countries.

At the same time, even low status graduates from these groups might be in a different position from people without the formative experience of higher education.

PERSONAL DEVELOPMENT AND HUMAN FORMATION

Aside for the social structure dimension, the personal development or human formation dimension is becoming increasingly important in HPS societies.

As participation becomes a social norm, many more people experience the time that is spent as a student within the higher education system as an important period of life. For generations further down the track it might become an obligatory experience, as Martin Trow forecast. One possibility is that participation in higher education will become a norm that operates right after the completion of secondary school, rather than being postponed in many cases. Another possibility is that the socio-economic conditions will change so that school leavers must be prepared to enter the labour market, while enrolling in a part-time programme sooner or later. Either way, higher education will have become crucial to the learning and personal development of the majority of the population.

To what extent is higher education ready to develop itself for this extended social mission given the present era of declining resources, unattractive faculty positions, and decreasing contact hours? And if higher education, or large parts of it, is not ready for the high participation era, what will be the effects of higher education on individual development? Will the effects of higher education be calibrated across the population, from profound and transformative in the best cases, to superficial, and then to non-existent in the worst cases, depending on the institutional forms and material quality of the higher education in which students engage? Will such a differentiated higher education be able to counter-balance inequalities in the social backgrounds of incoming students?

In this HPS project issues of the content of education and its potential for personal development were not included in the main theme Chapters 3-6, but this is an important area for further research and conceptual inquiry. Within a stratified HPS system with a varying value of degrees, emerging issues in relation to graduate (un)employment, and the growing stratification in society, are becoming more rather than less important. In this context, the non-utilitarian aims of higher education—where education is seen to enrich individual lives, enable self-development, creatively reconstruct students' experiences, and potentially enhance or create new areas for the application of their knowledge and skills—intersect with problems of social stratification and inequality.

It can be argued that in HPS societies, two simultaneous social tendencies might develop. First an increasing capacity for self-formation, self-determination, especially if higher education and society can ensure this is well distributed. Second, increasing social inequality. There will be more individual agency, more broadly spread, but also less opportunity for the educated person. The tensions between these two tendencies at an individual and societal level might significantly affect social reality and lead to solutions we cannot now foresee. One example of this tension, which we already can see, is the popularization of downshifting, usually observed in relation to the educated middle class as a way to escape traditional social structures and associated social pressures and to find a better individual work-life balance.

At the same time, the individual abilities developed by the humanistically oriented agenda in higher education might provide a way out of the trap of the individual's social position. As noted, all else being equal, that kind of education builds more agency. Educated people not only have greater agency in general, they find it easier to be geographically and culturally mobile. Inequality is less of an inescapable fate. Such a non-utilitarian education becomes even more important when the size and scope of the emerging mass sector is considered. To repeat the point, in an HPS system the vast majority of students and graduates *must* be located in the middle and bottom tier higher education institutions (with the exception of the small number of countries where vertical stratification, tiering, is quite modest, as in the Nordic world). So, much depends on the formative character of the education those students receive.

It might also be argued that the vertical stratification of institutions and differences in the respective cultures that they instil in students will be a divisive factor in the cultural differentiation of populations. There is more involved here than the stratification of credentials, and inconsistency in the status of graduates of higher education institutions below the top tier. If higher education is associated with different cultures, and the reproduction of those differences, this can create social tensions, as theories of cultural reproduction suggest.

So far, in the HPS systems observed in the present book, mass higher education remains largely immersed in non-humanistic, utilitarian, and low-quality higher education, measured by the technocratic notion of 'output' noted by Bourdieu and Passeron (1977). As Bourdieu and Passeron point out, that kind of notion of output assumes an impoverished model of education, while it also prevents a deeper analysis of the system of functions of an educational system. But the utilitarian bias should not prevent scholars from considering and studying the educational system and its roles in broader terms. The questions to consider, which are both normative and empirical, are: What can the HPS offer to students and society? What is its better potential? And how can this better potential be achieved?

The humanistic *Bildung* idea originates from the long-standing attempts of scholars to understand the respective positions of the (self)-reflective and self-transforming individual and the changing world, and the relations between the two. Here there is a permanent tension between the person's perception of her- or himself as a free self-determining subject, and that same person's awareness of being determined by the natural and social world. This creates an ongoing duality in modernity (Kivelä et al., 2012: 311). This duality opens for analysis an encounter between two different disciplinary traditions that are both directly relevant to HPS of higher education—the philosophical-pedagogical tradition that inquires into the self-formation of individuals, and the sociological tradition that focuses on how individuals are shaped by the social order. In this intellectual encounter, in this space, scholars of higher education and society can develop fruitful pathways for further areas of research.

■ REFERENCES

Arum, R. and Roksa, J. (2010). *Academically Adrift: Limited Learning on College Campuses*. Chicago: University of Chicago Press.

Arum, R., Beattie, I. R., and Ford, K. (2015). Introduction. In R. Arum, I. R. Beattie, and K. Ford (eds), *The Structure of Schooling: Readings in the Sociology of Education*. Los Angeles: Sage Publications, pp. 1–10.

Baker, D. P. (2014). *The Schooled Society: The Educational Transformation of Global Culture*. Stanford: Stanford University Press.

Bernstein, B. (1990). *Class, Codes and Control*: Vol. IV. *The Structuring of Pedagogic Discourse*. London: Routledge.

Biesta, G. (2002). Bildung and modernity: The future of Bildung in a world of difference. *Studies in Philosophy and Education* 21, 343–51.

Bourdieu, P. (1984). *Distinction: A Social Critique of the Judgement of Taste*. London: Routledge and Kegan Paul.

Bourdieu, P. and Passeron, J.-C. (1977). *Reproduction: In Education, Society, Culture*. London: Sage Publications.

Bowles, S. and Gintis, H. (1976). *Schooling in Capitalist America: Educational Reform and the Contradictions of Economic Life*. New York: Basic Books.

Carneiro, R. (2015). Learning: The treasure within—prospects for education in the 21st century. *European Journal of Education* 50(1). DOI: 10.1111/ejed.12110

Clark, B. R. (1962). *Educating the Expert Society*. San Francisco: Chandler.

Collins, R. (1971). Functional and conflict theories of educational stratification. *American Sociological Review*. 36, 1002–19.

Crosnoe, R. and Benner, A. D. (2016). Educational pathways, in M. J. Shanahan et al. (eds), *Handbook of the Life Course*. New York: Springer. DOI 10.1007/978-3-319-20880-0_8

Davis, K. and Moore, W. (1945). Some principles of stratification. *American Sociological Review* 10, 242–9.

Durkheim, E. (1956). Education and its role, in E. Durkheim (ed.), *Education and Sociology* London: The Free Press.

Durkheim, E. (1995). Pedagogika i Sociologia [Pedagogy and sociology]. *Sociologia [Sociology]* (in Russian, translated from French, Durkheim, E. (1922). *Education et sociologie*. Paris, pp. 104–33).

Giddens, A. (1984). *The Constitution of Society: Outline of the Theory of Structuration*. Berkeley: University of California Press.

Giddens, A. (2009). *Sociology*, 6th edn. Cambridge: Polity Press.

Gornitzka, Å., Maassen, P., Olsen, J. P., and Stensaker, B. (2007). 'Europe of knowledge': Search for a new pact, in P. Maassen and J. P. Olsen (eds), *University Dynamics and European Integration*. Dordrecht: Springer, pp. 181–215.

Hoffman, D. M. and Välimaa, J. (eds) (2016). *Re-becoming Universities? Critical Comparative Reflections on Higher Education Institutions in Networked Knowledge Societies*. Dordrecht: Springer.

Izquierdo, H. M. and Minguez, A. M. (2003). Sociological theory of education in the dialectical perspective, in C. A. Torres and A. Antikainen (eds), *The International Handbook on the Sociology of Education: An International Assessment of New Research and Theory*. Lanham: Rowman and Littlefield Publishers.

Kerr, C., Dunlop, J. T., Harbison, F. H., and Myers, C. A. (1960). *Industrialism and Industrial Man*. Cambridge, MA: Harvard University Press.

Kivelä, A., Siljander, P., and Sutinen, A. (2012). Between Bildung and growth—Connections and controversies, in P. Siljander, A. Kivelä, and A. Sutinen (eds), *Theories of Bildung and Growth*. Rotterdam: Sense Publishers, pp. 303–12.

Konstantinovskiy, D. (2017). Expansion of higher education and consequences for social inequality (the case of Russia). *Higher Education* 74(2), 201–20.

Lamont, M. (2014). How do university, higher education and research contribute to societal well-being?, in G. Goastellec and F. Picard (eds), *Higher Education in Societies: A Multi Scale Perspective*. Rotterdam: Sense Publishers, pp. 9–16.

Lenski, G. (1954). Status crystallization: A non-vertical dimension of social status. *American Sociological Review* 19(4), 405–13.

Maasen, P. (2014). A new social contract for higher education?, in G. Goastellec and F. Picard (eds), *Higher Education in Societies: A Multi Scale Perspective*. Rotterdam: Sense Publishers, pp. 32–50.

Macionis, J. J. (2012). *Sociology*. Boston: Pearson.

Marginson, S. (1997). *Markets in Education*. Sydney: Allen and Unwin.

Marginson, S. (2014). Student self-formation in international education. *Journal of Studies in International Education* 18(1), 6–22. DOI: 10.1177/1028315313513036

Marginson, S. (2017). Limitations of human capital theory. *Studies in Higher Education*. https://doi.org/10.1080/03075079.2017.1359823

Marginson, S. (2018). Public/private in higher education: A synthesis of economic and political approaches. *Studies in Higher Education* 43(2), 322–37. DOI: 10.1080/03075079.2016.1168797

Meyer, J. W. (1977). The effects of education as an institution. *American Journal of Sociology* 83(1), 55–77.

Meyer, J. W., Ramirez, F. O., Frank, D. J., and Schofer, E. (2007). Higher education as an institution, in P. Gumport (ed.), *Sociology of Higher Education*. Baltimore: Johns Hopkins University Press.

Parsons, T. (1959). The school class as a social system: Some of its functions in American Ssociety. *Harvard Educational Review* 29(4), 297–318.

Parsons, T. and Platt, G. M. (1970). Age, social structure, and socialization in higher education. *Sociology of Education* 43(1), 1–37.

Shanahan, M. J., Mortimer, J. T., and Kirkpatrick Johnson, M. (2016). Introduction: Life course studies—Trends, challenges, and future directions, in M. J. Shanahan et al. (eds), *Handbook of the Life Course*. New York: Springer. DOI 10.1007/978-3-319-20880-0_1

Siljander, P., Kivelä, A., and Sutinen, A. (eds) (2012). *Theories of Bildung and Growth*. Rotterdam: Sense Publishers.

Smolentseva, A. (2017). Where Soviet and neoliberal discourses meet: the transformation of the purposes of higher education in Soviet and Post-Soviet Russia. *Higher Education*. doi:10.1007/s10734-017-0111-7

Trow, M. (1973). *Problems in the Transition from Elite to Mass Higher Education*. Berkeley: Carnegie Commission on Higher Education.

UNESCO (2017). Gross graduation ratio by level of education. http://uis.unesco.org/indicator/edu-compl-cgr-ggr

Väkevä, L. (2012). Experiencing growth as a natural phenomenon: John Dewey's philosophy and the Bildung tradition, in P. Siljander, A. Kivelä, and A. Sutinen (eds), *Theories of Bildung and Growth*. Rotterdam: Sense Publishers, pp. 261–79.

Weber, Max (2015). 'Rationalization' of education and training, in R. Arum, I. R. Beattie, and K. Ford (eds), *The Structure of Schooling: Readings in the Sociology of Education*. Los Angeles: Sage Publications.

Part II
Country Cases

8 Decentralization, Provincial Systems, and the Challenge of Equity: High Participation Higher Education in Canada

Glen A. Jones

Introduction

Canada is the second largest country in the world by area, with a landmass that stretches from the eighty-third parallel in the Arctic to the forty-second parallel in the Great Lakes, and from the Atlantic to the Pacific. This vast area is administered through ten provinces and three territories. Most Canadians are English speaking, though French is an official language and the large province of Québec is majority Francophone. Canada's population of over thirty-six million inhabitants is largely urban. Around one-half is clustered in a corridor between Montreal and Toronto along the border with the United States of America (USA). The country was founded in 1867 and remains a member of the British Commonwealth with the British monarch and a government-appointed governor general as the nominal head of state. Canada is a federal parliamentary democracy with power split between the parliament and prime minister located in Ottawa (the nation's capital), and the provincial governments. Per capita income is US$46,200 (purchasing power parity (PPP)). With a Gini coefficient of about 32, income inequality in Canada is higher than in the egalitarian Nordic countries but more equal than in the USA and United Kingdom (UK). The country is rich in natural resources—Canada is the world's fourth largest producer of crude petroleum—and timber; but most of the nation's economic activity is in the service sector.

Martin Trow had already classified Canada as a mass system of higher education at the time he published his essay in 1973. In the Canadian context, the transition to a high participation higher education system had undoubtedly led to an increase in institutional diversity with the emergence of new types or categories of non-university post-secondary institutions, and also the gradual homogenization of the university sector with the emergence of a single model or institutional type (Skolnik, 1986; Jones, 1996a). This chapter starts by describing these earlier transitions as an important foundation for analysing how Canada's provincial systems of higher education evolved into high participation systems (HPS). The objective of the chapter is to analyse Canada's high participation 'system', giving explicit attention to the seventeen propositions that have emerged from this project.

From Mass System(s) to High Participation System(s)

Canada is a federation with ten provinces and three territories. When the nation gained its independent dominion status from Britain in 1867 there were less than 1,500 university students in the entire country. Most were enrolled in small, private denominational colleges. The educational institutions that emerged in Canada's early history were colonial in origin and purpose, and there was little respect for Indigenous knowledge, language, or educational traditions, a historical reality that is only today being slowly acknowledged within the higher education system (Stonechild, 2006).

The total undergraduate enrolment increased rapidly in every decade over the next century (see Table 8.1), reflecting both population growth through immigration, and the expansion of the country westward with the creation of new provinces and new provincial universities. While there was only modest growth in enrolment during the depression of the 1930s, the massification of higher education in Canada began immediately following World War II and the basic structural arrangements associated with the transition had emerged by 1970.

Under Canada's federal arrangement, responsibility for education was assigned to the provinces. By the middle of the twentieth century it had become clear that the provinces

Table 8.1. Undergraduate university enrolment in Canada, 1861–1970

Year	Student enrolment	Growth from previous period (%)
1861	1,176	–
1871	1,590	35
1880	3,006	89
1891	5,112	70
1901	6,641	20
1911	12,891	94
1920	22,791	77
1930	31 576	39
1940	34,817	10
1950	64,036	84
1960	107,211	67
1970	276,297	158

Source: Compiled by author using data from Statistics Canada, Historical Statistics of Canada, table W439–455.

had also assumed responsibility for higher education. While the post-World War II expansion of higher education had originally been supported through direct grants to universities by the federal government, the provinces moved to assert their constitutional role in the sector, and by the 1960s each province was taking steps to develop a provincial 'system' of higher education. There were significant differences in the structural and organizational arrangements associated with these provincial systems, but in all cases they involved the expansion of the university sector as well as the creation of one or more non-university institutional types (Jones, 1997).

In the move towards developing a provincial higher education system that would address the needs of the jurisdiction, most provinces moved to create a new type of institution that would complement the existing universities. The form and mission of these new institutional types, generally termed 'colleges', varied by province, in part to address the distinctive roles assigned to them within these very different systems, but they shared some common characteristics, such as an emphasis on accessibility, the provision of technical and vocational programming to address the needs of an increasingly complex labour market, and the authority to offer programmes leading to a diploma or certificate, but not a university-level degree. In Québec, the new Collège d'enseignement général et professionnel (CEGEP) was positioned as an intermediary institution between secondary school (which concludes at grade 11) and university. University-bound students are required to complete a two-year CEGEP programme following high school, but the colleges also offer a parallel stream of technical and vocational programming. In British Columbia and Alberta the colleges were, at least in part, modelled on the American community colleges and were assigned a university transfer function as well as offering technical/vocational programmes. Students could complete the first two-years of university-level study at a college before transferring to a university to complete a degree programme. The Ontario Colleges of Applied Arts and Technology (CAATs) were designed to operate in parallel to the university sector and they offered a comprehensive mix of technical, vocational, and adult education programmes ranging from very short-cycle skills development training to three-year diplomas and one-year post-diploma programmes (that required a diploma or university degree for admission), but they did not have an explicit transfer function. The emergence of colleges represented an important increase in institutional diversity within provincial higher education systems; they were clearly a mechanism for increasing access to higher education, offering short-cycle and extended technical vocational programmes preparing students for work, and providing students with an alternative educational pathway. The fact that there were major variations in institutional type by province meant that, from a pan-Canadian perspective looking across the provinces, there was a substantial increase in institutional diversity because nationally a much broader range of institutional forms were associated with the delivery of post-secondary programmes. The same was true for systemic diversity since the various provincial college sectors involved differences in mission, funding arrangements, and governance and accountability mechanisms.

In contrast, the transition to mass higher education had gradually led to the development of a relatively homogeneous university sector across provincial systems. While private denominational universities had once represented the most common institutional form within Canadian higher education, provincial regulation of expansion generally favoured secular institutions, and many private faith-based institutions either morphed into public secular institutions, or entered into affiliation arrangements with public, secular institutions. Major differences in institutional mission gradually dissolved as a function of mimetic isomorphism and by the early 1970s Canada's university sector was composed of public, highly autonomous secular universities that shared similar missions and governance arrangements. The vast majority of universities were comprehensive institutions offering some combination of undergraduate, professional, and graduate programmes. A common model of a Canadian university had emerged. New universities were largely modelled on the old (Jones, 1996a).

Access continued to be a key priority of every provincial government, and higher education enrolment and participation rates continued to increase. Higher education was defined inclusively to include both the college and university sectors, and expansion was accomplished by increasing enrolment in both sectors. Questions about the relationships between institutional types emerged in several provinces. In Ontario the lack of an explicit transfer function for colleges meant that college students frequently found it difficult to transfer to a university programme and have their college education recognized through transfer credits. In British Columbia there were concerns with the modest level of transfers between community college and universities in order to complete four-year degree programmes, and a growing recognition that provincial participation rates were not as high as some other provinces. Provincial systems struggled to find ways of increasing access as well as student success and completion, to find ways of increasing participation while also providing students with pathways to move efficiently between programmes and institutional types in order to address their needs.

The clear boundaries between the college and university sectors began to blur as some provincial governments moved to expand the number of institutions with the authority to grant degrees (Jones, 2009). The British Columbia government repositioned a number of community colleges as 'university colleges' with the authority to offer four-year degree programmes, and provided degree-granting authority to a number of other specialized institutions. The university colleges would later be reclassified as teaching-focused universities. Two Alberta colleges transitioned to become reclassified as universities. Ontario passed legislation that allowed colleges to offer degrees in applied fields of study, subject to a review of the quality of proposed degree programmes. By 2015, six provinces and the Yukon Territory had provided at least some limited form of degree-granting authority to their colleges.

DRIVERS OF GROWTH

Both of the general propositions in this HPS project that address growth in participation and access are supported by the Canadian case. The second general proposition (HPS Proposition 2) states:

> *In HPS there is no intrinsic limit to the spread of family aspirations for participation in higher education until universality is reached; and no intrinsic limit to the level of social position to which families/students may aspire.*

In Canada family aspirations for higher education have continued to increase over time, and this has led to increasing demands for higher education, and, in the context of provincial systems that have been relatively responsive to demand, increasing enrolment and participation rates. Data on full-time equivalent (FTE) enrolment growth is provided in Table 8.2. It shows the steady growth of university enrolment in the period from 2000 to 2013. Over this period, FTE enrolment grew by 55 per cent. As the size of the traditional university cohort reduces in some provinces and regions as a function of demographic trends, the level of enrolment at some institutions has stabilized or declined, but participation rates have continued to climb and there is no sense that there is any sort of upper limit on family aspirations for participation in higher education.

FTE enrolment data for the college sector is provided in Table 8.3 for 2000–13. Except for two years, there has been slow, steady growth in enrolment, though it is clear that in

Table 8.2. Full-time equivalent enrolment at Canadian universities, undergraduate and graduate, 2000–13

Year	FTE enrolment	Change from previous year (%)	Increase since 2000 (%)
2000–1	677,019	–	–
2001–2	705,503	+4.2	4.2
2002–3	751,451	+6.5	11.0
2003–4	811,167	+7.9	19.8
2004–5	834,021	+2.8	23.2
2005–6	857,458	+2.8	26.7
2006–7	870,948	+1.6	28.6
2007–8	875,327	+0.5	29.3
2008–9	910,955	+4.1	34.6
2009–10	974,323	+7.0	43.9
2010–11	1,005,023	+3.2	48.4
2011–12	1,031,584	+2.6	52.4
2012–13	1,049,605	+1.7	55.0

Note: FTE enrolment pro-rates part-time enrolment and is fewer than total students enrolled in universities (headcount). For example, in 2012–13 total full-time enrolment was 958,154 and total part-time enrolment was 327,078.

Source: Assembled by author, drawing on material in Canadian Association of University Teachers *Almanac*, table 3.3 (September 2016), compiling data from Statistics Canada.

Table 8.3. Full-time equivalent enrolment at Canadian colleges, 2000–13

Year	FTE enrolment	Change from previous year (%)	Increase since 2000 (%)
2000–1	469,437	–	0.0
2001–2	481,737	2.6	2.6
2002–3	491,396	2.0	4.7
2003–4	510,836	4.0	8.8
2004–5	511,836	0.2	9.0
2005–6	501,591	−2.0	6.9
2006–7	505,622	0.8	7.7
2007–8	525,028	3.8	11.8
2008–9	519,516	−1.1	10.7
2009–10	564,298	8.6	20.2
2010–11	576,919	2.2	22.9
2011–12	586,010	1.6	24.8
2012–13	592,406	1.1	26.2

Source: Assembled by author, drawing on material in Canadian Association of University Teachers *Almanac*, table 3.3 (September 2016), compiling data originally from Statistics Canada.

the twenty-first century, the university sector has been expanding at a faster pace that the college sector. FTE college enrolments have increased by 26 per cent since 2000 while university enrolments have increased by 55 per cent. Total higher education enrolment in Canada has always relied quite heavily on the college sector. The college sector's share of enrolment has been higher than many other Organisation for Economic Co-operation and Development (OECD) nations, but the balance between the sectors is gradually shifting as universities absorb a greater share of the enrolment.

The third general proposition (HPS Proposition 3) states:

Once transition from a primarily agricultural economy is achieved, the long-term growth of HPS is independent of political economic factors such as economic growth and patterns of labour market demand; patterns of public and private funding of higher education; the roles of public and private institutions; and system organization and modes of governance.

The Canadian case provides support for this proposition. As noted, higher education policy in Canada is highly decentralized. In many respects Canada is best understood as ten distinct provincial systems, each with different policy approaches and political and economic contexts. Despite these differences, access has been the core government priority for higher education policy across systems (see Jones 1996a; Fisher et al., 2014), and participation rates have increased across almost all provinces despite significant differences in tuition fee policies, system organization, and governance by province.

There have been differences in the growth in participation by province (Frenette, 2017), which will be discussed in more detail later, but with the exception of Saskatchewan, where participation rates have remained relatively stable since 2001, participation has been increasing across the country.

At the same time, the Canadian case also illustrates that while a juridiction may be considered an HPS, there can be important and even dramatic differences in participation by region within that jurisdiction. There are no universities located in the three northern territories, and so university programme access is limited to online programming available through southern institutions, and some customized collaborative programmes linking territorial colleges and provincial universities to offer degree programmes in the north. There are immense challenges associated with providing access to higher education in these huge, sparsely populated regions. Nunavut Territory, with a population of approximately 37,000 in 2017, is roughly three times the size of France, or four times the size of California in the USA. In short, there continue to be geographic and economic barriers to participation within regions of a country that has, on a national basis, very high levels of participation.

Governance

Canada has a federal system of governance operating under a constitution that delegates authority for education to the provinces. The responsibility for higher education was less clear until the post-World War II period, and it was the federal government that played a key role in supporting the initial stages of massification through direct grants to universities to fund new higher education opportunities for veterans, and later continuing the expansion in response to increasing demand. As noted earlier, the provinces, especially Québec and Ontario, asserted their constitutional responsibility for the sector, and federal funding to support higher education evolved into transfers to the provinces which, by the 1960s, clearly assumed responsibility for coordinating and funding provincial systems. Federal funding of university operating costs continued to be an important element in the political discourse of higher education policy in the transition from a mass to a HPS. This funding was largely formulaic and unconditional from the mid-1970s until the 1990s, though unilateral tinkering with the formula on the part of the federal government became a source of tension in federal-provincial relations. These tensions reached an apex with federal budget reforms in the mid-1990s designed to eliminate the federal budget deficit, when provincial transfer funding arrangements were substantially revised and reduced (Fisher et al., 2006).

Higher education policy can therefore be seen as highly decentralized, with policy and funding in the hands of provincial governments. There is no federal ministry with responsibility for education or higher education, and there is no federal higher education policy directly regulating the educational activities of universities or colleges (Jones, 1997).

Given the dramatic differences in size of provincial systems, there are also differences by system in terms of policy and coordination capacity, and successful policy initiatives in one system are not uncommonly adopted by others.

At the same time, the federal government plays an important role in a variety of policy areas that have direct impact on the university sector, including research and student financial assistance. The federal government is a major funder of university research and, more recently, applied research in the college sector. Most of these funds are distributed on the basis of competitive peer-reviewed assessments of professor-initiated research proposals coordinated by three federal granting councils (engineering and science; health; and the social sciences and humanities), with support for research infrastructure provided by the Canadian Foundation for Innovation. In addition to the federal government, support for university research is provided by several provinces.

The federal government is also involved in student financial assistance (through the Canada Student Loans programme which is coordinated through provincial student support systems, as well as tax credits, graduate scholarships, and other forms of aid), support for arts and culture (Canada Council for the Arts), infrastructure (periodic investments in major capital projects), and Indigenous education (under the terms of the draconian Indian Act, but with responsibilities often shared with the provinces). In short, there are a patchwork quilt of federal government programmes and initiatives that directly or indirectly support university activities (Fisher et al., 2006).

Generalizing about provincial government coordination of higher education is challenging since there are major differences in system structures and governance mechanisms by jurisdiction. Higher education is traditionally defined as synonymous with tertiary education and governance involves a single ministry in each province with responsibility for both the public college (with institutional types that vary by province) and university sectors. Generally speaking, Canadian universities have relatively high levels of autonomy, and government coordination mechanisms tend to focus on conditions associated with operating grant funding, student financial assistance, and, to a far lesser extent, quality. Accountability mechanisms tend to focus on funding and enrolment, though there are more extensive accountability and reporting arrangements in some provinces than others.

Universities are established as independent corporations, and each has its own governance structure. Universities in British Columbia and Alberta operate under system-level legislation (the Universities Act in British Columbia, and the Post-Secondary Learning Act in Alberta) that defines institutional mission and governance arrangements for all universities, while most other universities are established by individual pieces of legislation that create the university as a not-for-profit corporation and define university-specific governance arrangements. Québec has a collection of universities with individual charters, but there is also a University of Québec system of universities that operate under a University of Québec governance apparatus, but where increasing autonomy is provided to university-level governance structures. Most universities have bicameral governance structures where charter legislation creates both a senate, with responsibility for academic policy, and a board, with responsibility for financial and administrative matters. There are faculty and student members on almost all boards, and internal members dominate the composition of senates. University presidents are usually appointed by the board, often on the advice of a search committee with members from various constituencies, though rectors are elected at some Francophone universities, and there are distinctive governance arrangements within the University of Québec system.

Colleges have generally had less autonomy than universities and have been viewed as instruments of provincial policy, though, once again, governance arrangements vary by province. Colleges are more frequently created under omnibus provincial legislation, rather than institution-specific legislation, with governance structures that place considerable authority in the hands of senior management, and less authority in the hands of academic councils, than in the university sector (Dennison and Gallagher, 1986; Dennison, 1995).

MULTI-LEVEL GOVERNANCE

The first proposition focusing on governance (HPS Proposition 4) is:

HPS are governed by multi-level control, coordination, and accountability mechanisms.

This claim is certainly true in the Canadian case, though it pre-dates growth to the HPS stage. Governance is clearly multi-level in structure, with a division of responsibility between federal and provincial levels of government, and, in the university sector, considerable autonomy at the level of the institution. In addition, there are a number of intermediary bodies that play a role in regional (the Maritimes Provinces Higher Education Commission plays a coordinating role for higher education institutions in Nova Scotia, New Brunswick, and Prince Edward Island) and provincial coordination (such as councils on admissions and transfer operating in British Columbia, Alberta, and Ontario). Once again, there are significant variations in the complexity and structure of these coordinating structures by province; the province of Newfoundland and Labrador, for example, has only one university and one college, and coordinating and accountability arrangements are modest compared with some other jurisdictions.

The second proposition on governance (HPS Proposition 5) is that

HPS governance tends to involve the management of horizontal differentiation.

If the frame of analysis is a broad definition of higher education, that is, including the college and institutes sector that provides short-cycle vocational/occupation programmes, then clearly the management of horizontal differentiation plays a role in provincial system-level governance. While they are coordinated by a single ministry in each province, government policies generally treat these two sectors quite differently, with greater autonomy provided to the university sector and stronger provincial coordination of the colleges sectors. Historically, the two sectors have been clearly differentiated by the levels of credentials that each sector can award, with colleges limited to short-cycle programmes leading to diplomas and certificates (or associate degrees in the case of British Columbia community colleges) and universities free to offer a wide range of undergraduate, graduate, and professional degree programmes. These clear boundaries between the two sectors have blurred in the last few decades in some provinces with the provision of at least some limited form of degree-granting to the college sector, but government policies continue to treat the two sectors quite differently.

If the frame is narrowed to focus only on the university sector in each province, then the answer becomes more nuanced. The management of horizontal diversity within the public university sector can certainly be observed in the provinces of British Columbia, Alberta, and Québec. In the expansion of degree-granting, British Columbia elevated a number of special purpose institutions to university status, and a number of community colleges have evolved into teaching-intensive universities with somewhat different mandates than their traditional university peers. In the transition to mass higher education, the government of Québec created the University of Québec as a distinct university system in order to address the needs of a large, under-served Francophone population, and this new system operated in parallel to a less coordinated collection of independent French and English language-of-instruction universities (such as Laval, Montreal, and McGill). The province of Alberta has moved farthest in the development of an integrated, coordinated system of post-secondary education; the province's Post-Secondary Learning Act establishes six sectors or institutional categories, including two categories of universities (comprehensive academic and research institutions; and baccalaureate and applied studies institutions) within the broad system framework of Campus Alberta. This framework is clearly designed to manage diversity, and the province has created a number of structures and mechanisms designed to facilitate coordination between distinct institutional types within this system.

The history of higher education in Nova Scotia illuminates a different form of managed diversity. This small province has a population of less than one million people, but currently has ten public universities. Attempts to rationalize the system in terms of reducing the number of institutions and/or stimulating greater specialization has been politically challenging; managing diversity has been far more a goal than a reality, in fact several distinctive institutions with specialized missions have evolved into universities and operate under the same regulatory and funding arrangements as the existing institutions (Cape Breton University and the Nova Scotia College of Art and Design University, though the latter has retained a quite specialized mission). However, some attempts at rationalization have been more successful, for example two formerly independent universities (the Technical University of Nova Scotia and the Nova Scotia Agricultural College) have become component parts of Dalhousie University through mergers mandated by government. These initiatives have reduced the level of horizontal diversity within the higher education system, a subject that will receive greater attention in the next section.

Examples of managed horizontal diversity in the university sector in other provinces are more difficult to discern. Generally speaking, the expansion of university enrolment in these provinces was largely accomplished by supporting the growth of existing institutions, and, in some provinces, creating new universities that closely resembled their established peers. Newfoundland has only one university and one college, while Prince Edward Island has one university and two colleges (one English, one French), and so expansion took place by increasing enrolment in these institutions. In Ontario, Canada's largest higher education system, expansion took place in an environment where the universities were largely treated as equals. Each of Ontario's twenty universities received funding under a common allocative formula that focuses on enrolment and there has been no attempt to develop distinct university categories or institutional types. Only in the last few years has institutional differentiation within the university sector become a policy goal, though a number of task forces have recommended this policy direction over the last four decades, and the initial policy approach has focused on the development of strategic mandate agreements for each institution, and, beginning in 2016, the development of a new funding approach, with both initiatives designed to simulate and support modest elements of diversity. Managing diversity within the university sector is an extremely new, and still emergent, policy direction within this large higher education system (see Jones, 2013b; Piche and Jones, 2016).

The third proposition on governance (HPS Proposition 6) states that

HPS complex multi-level accountability and coordination, coupled with system differentiation, resulting in higher education institutions adopting increasingly corporate forms and robust internal governance and management capacities.

Again, the Canadian case provides support for the proposition. Most Canadian universities have always been independent, relatively autonomous, not-for-profit corporations and have had to develop governance and management practices designed to support the needs of self-governing, independently managed institutions (Jones, 1996a). Governance structures generally distinguish between the roles associated with academic self-governance (the senate, faculty councils, and participatory academic decision structures), corporate governance (the board), and management (the president and other senior

administrators). These governance structures are specified under the provincial legislation that creates each university, and most universities have bicameral structures with
authority divided between a board and senate. At most universities the president,
sometimes referred to as rector or principal, is appointed by the board following an
external search process (though the rector is elected in some Québec universities) and
leads a central administrative structure that develops the strategic direction of the
institution and manages its day-to-day operations. Given the increasing complexity of
these institutions, some of which are literally billion dollar corporations, and the need to
respond to increasing government regulation related to the broad range of activities that
universities undertake, universities have developed strong governance and management
systems. Universities have considerable financial autonomy: they employ professors and
other staff, often under the terms established under institution-specific collective bar-
gaining agreements, they own property, construct buildings, enter into agreements with
industry, and raise funds through advancement. They have developed the necessary
governance and management capacities. While university senates continue to have final
authority over many major academic policy areas, there are concerns that the balance
of authority within university governance has shifted in favour of strong administrative
authority and corporate governance processes (Jones et al., 2002; Pennock et al., 2015).

Horizontal Diversity

While institutional diversity was closely linked to accessibility and regarded as a key
characteristic of the massification of higher education in the USA (Trow, 1973; Birnbaum,
1983), the massification of Canadian higher education was largely accomplished through
the creation of new non-university tertiary institutions (the college sector), and the emergence and expansion of a common model of the university. Scholars have generally noted
that lack of diversity within the Canadian university sector, and observed that institutional
diversity within provincial systems is primarily associated with the emergence of non-degree
college sector institutions (Skolnik, 1986; Jones, 1996b).

Four propositions related to horizontal diversity have emerged from this HPS project.
The first (HPS Proposition 7) is that

> In the HPS era, regardless of the political economy and culture of systems, an increasing
> proportion of higher education becomes centred on comprehensive multi-discipline and
> multi-function research universities, or 'multiversities'.

This is certainly true in the Canadian case. The common model of the university that
emerged in the post-war period was the multiversity. While universities vary dramatically in size, programme mix, and comprehensiveness, almost all universities offer some

combination of undergraduate, graduate, and professional programmes. Research is regarded as an important function of all universities, and while a commonly used categorization of universities emerged in the 1990s as part of the rankings system produced by *Macleans*, a national magazine, the boundaries between the three categories (primarily undergraduate, comprehensive, and medical/Doctoral universities) are porous. Many of the universities categorized as primarily undergraduate offer graduate and frequently Doctoral programmes, and many of the comprehensive universities have very large graduate and Doctoral programmes. It is certainly true that the vast majority of Canadian university students are enrolled in institutions that are 'multiversities'.

The college sector has played a significant role in higher education participation. The share of higher education students enrolled in the college sector is higher than in many OECD nations. In Québec, colleges are the pathway to university from secondary school, as well as the primary provider of technical/vocational education, and so partipation rates are very high. In Ontario, the largest higher education system in Canada, the colleges are far more than the short-cycle technical/vocational institutions that you might find in the UK in that they provide a comprehensive range of programmes of one to four years in duration, including university-level degree programmes. In British Columbia and Alberta, the colleges play an important role in geographic access in that students can obtain the first few years of a university education at a local institution before transferring to a university to complete their studies, as well as providing important technical and vocational programming. At the same time, it is important to note that the balance between the two sectors appears to be shifting as enrolment in the university sector increases at a faster pace than in the colleges (see Tables 8.2 and 8.3).

The second proposition on diversity (HPS Proposition 8) states:

Regardless of the political economy and culture of the HPS, when participation expands there is no necessary increase in the overall diversity of institutional form and mission; and this has probably declined, except in relation to online provision.

This claim enjoys general support from the Canadian case, though there are important differences between provinces. In the case of the provinces of British Columbia and Alberta, increasing institutional diversity has been viewed as a key policy element supporting the expansion of participation. British Columbia expanded the number of institutions that could offer university-level degrees, and created new forms of institutional diversity within the public university sector, including special-purpose universities (Emily Carr, Royal Roads) and teaching-intensive universities (such as Vancouver Island University). Under the umbrella of Campus Alberta, the government of Alberta has moved towards the development of an integrated system of post-secondary education with six institutional categories, mechanisms for coordination, and pathways to promote student mobility between institutions and programmes (Jones, 2009). In these two provinces, increasing institutional diversity has been viewed as a key element in the transition from a mass to a HPS. However, this is not true in other provinces.

While the creation of the University of Québec system was a key element in expanding higher education in Québec in the 1960s, especially in terms of providing geographic access to higher education throughout this large province (Trottier et al., 2014), over time each of the constituent campuses has acquired greater autonomy and increasingly taken on the characteristics of the more traditional universities. In Ontario, Canada's largest provincial system, institutional diversity is a very new policy aspiration; the province has a long history of using a common enrolment-based allocative formula to distribute government funding and treating each of the twenty universities as equals in terms of policy (Piché and Jones, 2016). The level of institutional diversity in other provinces has either remained stable, or modestly decreased (as in Nova Scotia where two specialized autonomous institutions have merged to become faculties of Dalhouse University).

It is important to note that a small private university sector has emerged in several provinces, and that this can be seen as a modest increase in institutional diversity within these systems. While private denominational institutions played a large role in Canadian higher education at the beginning of the twentieth century, provincial government policies supported the secularization of public higher education. Provincial governments also tightly controlled the authority to grant degrees or the use of the name 'university', but in recent years several provinces have supported the creation of new private universities, the vast majority of which are faith-based institutions. In addition, there are now several secular, private, not-for-profit universities, and several private, for-profit universities. While Statistics Canada does not collect data on private higher education, the total enrolment associated with this sector is estimated to be quite small, and private higher education has not played a major role in participation. The private sector is largely marginalized and invisible. Statistics Canada does not collect data on private sector institutions or their enrolments (Li and Jones, 2015).

In summary, institutional differentiation is not a necessary condition for the expansion of participation in most Canadian provinces, though it is a system-level policy strategy to increase access to university-level programmes in several provinces.

The third proposition on horizontal diversity (HPS Proposition 9) states:

As participation expands the internal diversity of multiversities tends to increase. This affects some or all of the range of missions, business activities, institutional forms and internal structures, the discipline mix, research activities, levels of study and range of credentials, the heterogeneity of the student body, links to stakeholders, cross-border relations, and forms of academic and non-academic labour.

While there have been no systematic studies of the internal diversity of Canadian universities, it is generally assumed that these institutions have become more internally diverse over time (Jones, 1996b), and there is considerable evidence suggesting an increase in certain forms of diversity. For example, there has been a major growth in graduate education programmes across the country (Looker, 2015), an increase in overall university research activities (and funded research activities), and a horizontal and vertical fragmentation of academic work associated with increasing specialization and a growth in new types of academic workers (such as sessional faculty, teaching-stream faculty, specialized research staff, etc.) (Jones, 2013a), all of which contribute to increasing institutional complexity and diversity.

The fourth diversity proposition (HPS Proposition 10) is that

All else being equal, the combination of expanding participation and enhanced competition in neoliberal quasi-markets is associated with specific effects in relation to diversity, including (1) increased vertical differentiation of higher education institutions (stratification); (2) reduced horizontal differentiation (diversification); (3) convergence of missions through isomorphistic imitation; and (4) growth in the role of private higher education institutions, especially for-profit institutions.

Some of these effects are true for Canada's provincial systems, while others are not. As will be discussed in more detail later, there has been an increasing vertical stratification of Canadian universities, especially in terms of research activity and status (as a function of rankings and selectivity). One could also argue that there has been a convergence of missions as a function of isomorphism; as already noted, the expansion of participation has largely been accomplished by the adoption of a relatively common model of the university, and this model has provided a template for the development of new universities. At the same time, as noted, several provincial governments, especially British Columbia and Alberta, have taken steps to protect or expand horizontal differentiation by creating different institutional sectors (Alberta) or by creating distinctive institutional types by expanding the range of institutions that can award degrees (British Columbia). Horizontal diversity within the university sector has not been an important component of system-level policy in other provinces (though it is now receiving considerable attention in Ontario), but there is little evidence that the level of horizontal differentiation has reduced. Finally, a modest private university sector has emerged in recent decades, but this has largely been a function of the growing tolerance of private denominational institutions on the part of select provincial government (in sharp contrast to the desire to create a public, secular university system during the post-World War II massification period). Most of these institutions have quite small enrolments and address the needs of niche markets, either as faith-based institutions or as secular institutions offering distinctive educational offerings or pedagogies. There are now several for-profit institutions, but the entire private sector has largely been invisible in policy discussions in Canadian higher education (Li and Jones, 2015).

Vertical Stratification

The first proposition related to vertical stratification (HPS Proposition 11) is that:

> *The expansion of participation towards and beyond the HPS stage is associated with a tendency to bifurcation and stratification (vertical diversification) in the value of higher education, between elite (artisanal) institutions and mass (demand-absorbing) institutions.*

There has been an increase in vertical stratification within the Canadian university sector, but this stratification is primarily associated with competition for research and prestige. In terms of enrolment, there is certainly competition for the best domestic students, but this stratification is more clearly seen in terms of graduate enrolment (which is of course tied to research activity) than to undergraduate enrolment. There is also competition for international students, since foreign student fees represent an increasingly important souce of income.

While there are different provincial mechanisms for providing government grants to universities, the level of government funding is frequently tied directly or indirectly to enrolment. Given that access is a key policy objective across the country, universities have generally expanded to address demand and increase revenue. This has generally meant that the most research intensive and prestigious universities in the country also have large enrolments; for example, the two highest internationally ranked universities are also the largest universities in the county (the University of Toronto and the University of British Columbia). In terms of undergraduate education, Canadian universities generally treat each other as equals and assume roughly comparable standards; for example, admission to graduate education is generally based on grades awarded by the undergraduate university (regardless of the Canadian university) rather than using a standardized graduate admissions test. It is also important to note that universities treat secondary schools as relatively equivalent; universities generally use secondary school grades, rather than some form of national standardized test, as the major criteria for admission to most undergraduate programmes. There are variations in average PISA scores by province, but scores suggest that school quality is relatively equitable within provinces. In other words, while universities compete for the best students, this is taking place in an environment where the perceived quality of secondary education is relatively equitable across the education system, and where governments generally limit the competitive nature of the undergraduate market by maintaining relatively equitable tuition fee levels within provinces and funding mechanisms that have generally incentivized access. Vertical stratification, therefore, has relatively little to do with assumptions about the quality of undergraduate education, and much to do with differences in research and prestige; high undergraduate enrolments become a mechanism for cross-subsidizing, prestige-bearing research and graduate programming.

There are approximately ninety universities in Canada, but approximately 80 per cent of all competitive research grants are awarded to investigators associated with fifteen universities. These institutions have branded themselves as the 'U15' universities[1] and, through the work of a small secretariat, they share information and lobby the federal government on research funding and related policies. Data on research funding and enrolment for the U15 universities is presented in Table 8.4. There are major differences in the level of research funding and research intensity (dollars per faculty member) by institution, and the breakpoint between U15 membership and the 'other' universities is somewhat arbitrary: the University of Guelph has a higher level of total research funding than Dalhousie, and there are four additional universities with over US$100 million in sponsored research funding per year.

Table 8.4. The U15 universities: Research funding, enrolment, and teaching language (language of instruction)

	University	Funded research 2015 (CA $ million)	Research funding / faculty (CA$s)	Full-time undergrad. enrolment (2016)	Full-time graduate enrolment (2016)	Teaching language	Province
1	Toronto	998.519	383,000	64,700	16,900	E	Ontario
2	British Columbia	541.553	229,500	35,070	7,800	E	British Columbia
3	Montreal	530.858	282,500	26,210	10,150	F	Quebec
4	McGill	473.107	277,000	23,410	7,140	E	Quebec
5	Alberta	470.690	231,800	24,420	6,720	E	Alberta
6	Calgary	358.298	240,800	23,320	6,690	E	Alberta
7	Laval	331.792	215,900	25,290	8,640	F	Quebec
8	McMaster	324.624	358,300	26,000	3,700	E	Ontario
9	Ottawa	294.215	235,400	31,100	5,500	E&F	Ontario
10	Western Ontario	229.821	168,600	29,700	5,600	E	Ontario
11	Queen's	187.338	242 400	19,500	4,200	E	Ontario
12	Waterloo	180.929	162 300	31,000	4,200	E	Ontario
13	Saskatchewan	168.947	158 600	15,850	2,780	E	Saskatchewan
14	Manitoba	162.948	135,200	21,670	2,940	E	Manitoba
15	Dalhousie	141.927	193,800	13,330	3,250	E	Nova Scotia

Notes: CA$ = Canadian dollars. undergrad. = undergraduate. E = English; F = French. Part-time undergraduate and graduate students are excluded from these figures.

Source: Author, using sponsored research funding and funding per faculty data from Research Infosource (2016). Enrolment data from Universities Canada.

---

[1] The size of the groups has expanded over time. The group began with conversations among the five top research universities in Ontario, and then expanded to become the national 'Group of Ten' universities in 1991. The group expanded to become the 'Group of Thirteen' in 2006, and became the 'U15' in 2011. A secretariat was established in 2012.

None of the U15 universities can be considered small, elite universities in the traditional sense of that term. The University of Toronto enrols more than 80,000 students. Nine of the fifteen universities have enrolments of over 30,000. In terms of their undergraduate programmes, these institutions primarily serve local, provincial populations; the vast majority of the undergraduate students attending the University of Toronto are from the greater Toronto area and the majority of students attending the University of British Columbia are from the Vancouver area. These universities may be somewhat more selective than some local peers, but they are essentially demand-absorbing institutions in a national environment where most students attend a university that is close to where their parents live. Distance from a university is a factor in the decision to participate (Frenette, 2002).

There is considerable vertical stratification within the Canadian university sector, but this stratification is largely understood in terms of the level of research activity, research funding, graduate/Doctoral education, research impact, and other indicators of traditional academic prestige. In some ways the U15 research universities can be seen as operating a comprehensive range of relatively accessible undergraduate programmes (especially in the humanities, social sciences, and sciences) that provide the financial foundation for a collection of more selective and elite graduate and professional programmes and support faculty who are productive researchers.

STUDENT COMPETITION AND TUITION REGIMES

The second proposition related to vertical stratification (HPS Proposition 12) is that

> The tendency to institutional stratification is magnified by features common (though not universal) among HPS including (a) intensified social competition for the most valuable student places; (b) variable tuition charges; and/or (c) intensified competition between institutions.

There is certainly competition within Canadian higher education. While general undergraduate degrees in the social sciences, humanities, and sciences are relatively accessible, there are differences between institutions in terms of the level of selectivity, and students compete for admission into the more selective institutions. The competition for entry into certain professional programmes such as engineering, law, and medicine can be immense. The same is true for many graduate programmes, though this may vary by area of specialization within the same university. Student competition clearly plays a role in vertical stratification. There is also increasing competition between institutions, especially for research funding, and this is a key factor in how vertical stratification is understood within the Canadian university sector.

The role of tuition fees in vertical stratification is a bit more complex given that there are major differences in tuition fee policies by province. Generally speaking, the provincial governments have regulated or controlled tuition, and this has served to moderate the role of market forces. As noted, tuition fee levels vary by province, with the lowest fees found in Québec, Newfoundland, and Labrador, and the highest fees in Ontario and Nova Scotia. However, since the vast majority of students attend a university that is close to their parental home, there is no real national market for higher education, and there is little evidence that differences in fees by province have an impact on choice of institution. There are generally only modest variations in fees between institutions in the same province, given government regulation, so the University of Toronto charges roughly the same fees for most (though not all) programmes as the other universities in the province. In short, government regulation of fees generally limits their impact on vertical stratification.

The third proposition on vertical stratification (HPS Proposition 13) claims that:

In stratified HPS, a middle layer of institutions tends to form, shaped by the combination of upward aspirations (drift) with systemic scarcity of resources and status.

As noted, the Canadian university sector is vertically stratified based on research activity, funding, and graduate, especially Doctoral, education. The U15 universities have branded themselves as the nation's elite research universities. While the boundaries of this group are somewhat arbitrary, there is clearly a middle category of institutions that offer a comprehensive range of programmes that aspire to become more research intensive and to increase their status within the sector.

Equity

The first HPS proposition on equity (HPS Proposition 14) states that:

As participation expands in the HPS phase, equity in the form of social inclusion is enhanced.

As noted, access to higher education has long been a key component of provincial policies, and equity of opportunity has been a key objective underscoring these policies. There is little doubt that in the process of post-war massification, issues of equity were largely understood in terms of socio-economic status. It was recognized that students from wealthy families were far more likely to attend university than those from other backgrounds. As participation rates have increased, the discussion of equity has moved far beyond the issue of income to include a broad range of frequently intersecting categories, including but not limited to language, cultural or racial background, gender especially in certain programmes, and first-generation status (students from families where there is no history of participation in higher education).

Inequities in terms of access to higher education programmes in the French language, for example, underscored many of the higher education reforms in Québec in the 1960s. The Francophone majority had less access to higher education than the Anglophone minority, and so the restructuring of the higher education sytem was designed to expand overall participation, but the creation of the University of Québec system, for example, was principally aimed at addressing the needs of French-speaking citizens, and language and socio-economic status have played significant roles in discussions of participation in Québec. The same is true, though to a lesser extent, in several other provinces: access to university programmes in both English and French played a large role in the design of the New Brunswick system, for example, and Ontario supports several French-language colleges and bilingual (where both French and English are languages of instruction) universities.

The general assumption underscoring the current discussion of access is that the Canadian provinces have done a good job at expanding participation, but that certain groups (such as black students; and some recent immigrant populations) have been left behind. Perhaps the clearest example is Canada's Indigenous peoples, where participation and completion rates are much lower than for other Canadians. There is a growing recognition that Canadian society, including its education systems, were built by colonizing settlers who had little respect for Indigenous peoples, knowledge, and language. There is a need for reconciliation between settlers and Indigenous peoples, and higher education becomes a key element in a much broader and very challenging conversation.

However, evidence-based discussions of equity and participation are frequently stymied by the reality that Canada's national data on higher education is inadequate and in decline. There is no national and little provincial data on higher education participation by groups, other than by gender and socio-economic status (SES; frequently defined in terms of parental income), and so while equity receives considerable attention in public discussions of higher education, there is relatively little empirical data to support a nuanced analysis of participation issues (Jones, 2014; Gallagher-Mackay, 2017).

EDUCATIONAL AND SOCIAL INEQUITIES

The second, third, and fourth propositions on equity (HPS Propositions 15–17) are as follows:

• *Because in the HPS phase the growth of participation is associated with enhanced stratification and intensified competition at key transition points, all else being equal (i.e. without compensatory state policy), the expansion of participation is associated with a secular tendency to greater social inequality in educational outcomes and, through that, social outcomes.*

* *Within a national system, as participation expands in the HPS phase, all else being equal, the positional structure of the higher education system increasingly resembles that of society (albeit with the caveat of Proposition 15). The HPS is increasingly implicated in the reproduction of existing patterns of social equality/inequality.*

* *As the HPS boundary of participation expands it becomes more difficult for the state and/or autonomous educational systems/institutions to secure a redistribution of educational opportunities, and, through that, of social opportunities.*

The Canadian case provides support for all three propositions, though with two important caveats. There is considerable evidence that access to higher education is inequitable, and given the relationship between higher education and future earnings, higher education plays a role in reproducing social inequities. Students from middle and upper income families are far more likely to attend universities than students from lower SES backgrounds. This is less true in the college sector, where the profile of participants tends to more closely resemble the characteristics of the population as a whole. Trying to address these inequities by providing need-based financial support and other initiatives designed to increase participation from under-represented populations has been a key element of provincial government policies across the country.

The first caveat, however, is that the lack of national data makes it impossible to provide the sort of nuanced analysis that is needed in order to actually understand who is being left behind in terms of access, the magnitude of the problem, and whether specific policy initiatives are being successful in addressing these problems (Jones, 2014; Gallagher-Mackay, 2017). Observers of Canadian higher education recognize that equity is a problem, but the lack of data on, for example, race, disability, or sexual orientation is a significant barrier to advancing the conversation.

The second caveat is that there is at least some recent data suggesting that the participation of students from low SES backgrounds is improving. A recent report from Statistics Canada on the higher education (community college and university) enrolment of 19-year-olds suggests that the provincial systems have been relatively successful at increasing participation rates over the last decade, and it also looked at participation in relation to parental income by province (Frenette, 2017). Frenette found that the greatest gains in participation rates between 2001 and 2014 involved those in the lowest income groups. The overall participation rate of 19-year-olds increased from 53 per cent in 2001 to 64 per cent by 2014. Rates for those in the top (after tax) income quintile rose from 73 per cent to 79 per cent while the participation rates of those in the lowest income quintile rose from 38 per cent to 47 per cent. The participation of students from high-income families increased by 8.3 per cent, while the growth in participation of students from low-income families was almost 25 per cent. Additional research is certainly required, but these findings suggest that as participation rates continue to increase, those who have been left behind may begin to catch up. Of course, improvements to student financial assistance and other initiatives have played a large role in supporting increasing participation from lower-income families.

The study also notes important variations by province. The eastern provinces appear to have been more successful at increasing access than those in the western provinces. The greatest participation gains were in the provinces of Newfoundland and Labrador (19 per cent) and Ontario (16 per cent) while Prince Edward Island, New Brunswick and Québec all had increases over 10 per cent. The greatest gains in the western provinces were found in British Columbia (6 per cent and Alberta 4 per cent), while participation rates in Saskatchewan remained relatively stable during this period. In terms of the participation of students from low-income families, there were large increases in Ontario and New Brunswick, while participation of low-income students declined in Saskatchewan.

Additional research is needed in order to understand the relationship between differences in participation rates by provinces and different provincial policies and system structures for higher education. Other important factors that need to be considered are the availability of low-skill, high-salary employment opportunities in natural resource industries in some regions, shifting demographics which vary by province, and immigration patterns which also vary by province and region.

Conclusion

The Canadian case provides support for most of the propositions that have emerged from our analysis of HPS systems.

Canadian higher education policy is highly decentralized, and in many respects is composed of thirteen quite distinct provincial and territorial systems. This decentralization has allowed for the development of high levels of institutional diversity within the non-university college sector, with significant variations in the role, structure, and governance arrangements of institutions by province. Massification led to the development of a relatively homogeneous university sector, though the expansion of degree-granting in some provinces has led to the emergence of somewhat distinctive university forms. The university sector is stratified, primarily by major differences in research activity, and levels of graduate/Doctoral education. At the same time, this stratification has relatively little to do with perceptions of quality in undergraduate education; relatively equitable secondary school outcomes means that the huge variations in university preparation that one might see in some systems are less present in Canada's provincial school systems and students attend a local university, rather than participating in a national, competitive market for places in high-status institutions. Government regulated tuition fees and enrolment-based funding systems serves to level the playing field in terms of undergraduate education. Most of Canada's high-status universities have very large undergraduate enrolments, where scale allows for the cross-subsidization of more elite professional and graduate programmes and the infrastructure required for research. Higher education governance is multi-level, complex and increasingly corporate in orientation, though the roles of academic senates continue to be protected by legislation, and institution-based level faculty unions have played a role in limiting certain forms of administrative discretion within corporate governance. Equity has been a key concern in provincial policies supporting increasing participation, and there appears to have been some success in the last decade in terms of increasing the participation of students from low-income families. On the other hand, there are serious concerns that some populations are being left behind, especially Canada's Indigenous peoples. Addressing these needs will require a much more nuanced, community-focused approach that recognizes the very different needs and aspirations of different groups and communities.

■ REFERENCES

Birnbaum, R. (1983). *Maintaining Diversity in Higher Education*. San Francisco: Jossey-Bass.

Dennison, J. D. (ed.) (1995). *Challenge and Opportunity: Canada's Community Colleges at the Crossroads*. Vancouver: UBC Press.

Dennison, J. D. and Gallagher, P. (1986). *Canada's Community Colleges: A Critical Analysis*. Vancouver: UBC Press.

Fisher, D., Rubenson, K., Bernatchez, J., Clift, R., Jones, G., Lee, J., MacIvor, M., Meredith, J., Shanahan, T., and Trottier, C. (2006). *Canadian Federal Policy and Post-Secondary Education*. Vancouver, BC: Centre for Policy Studies in Higher Education and Training, University of British Columbia.

Fisher, D., Rubenson, K., Shanahan, T., and Trottier, C. (eds) (2014). *The Development of Postsecondary Education Systems in Canada: A Comparison between British Columbia, Ontario and Quebec*. Montreal: McGill-Queen's.

Frenette, M. (2002). Too far to go on? Distance to school and university participation. Research Paper. Catalogue No. 11F0019MIE—No. 191. Ottawa, Statistics Canada.

Frenette, M. (2017). Postsecondary enrolment by parental income: Recent national and provincial trends. *Economic Insights* 070, April, 1–10. Statistics Canada Catalogue 11–626–X.

Gallagher-Mackay, K. (2017). *Data Infrastructure for Studying Equity of Access to Postsecondary Education in Ontario*. Toronto, Higher Education Quality Council of Ontario.

Jones, G. A. (1996a). Governments, governance, and Canadian universities, in J. C. Smart (ed.), *Higher Education: Handbook of Theory and Research*, Vol. XI. New York, NY: Agathon Press, pp. 337–71.

Jones, G. A. (1996b). Diversity within a decentralized higher education system: The case of Canada, in V. L. Meek, L. Goedegebuure, O. Kivinen, and R. Rinne (eds), *The Mockers and the*

Mocked: Comparative Perspectives on Differentiation, Convergence and Diversity in Higher Education. Oxford: Pergamon, pp. 79–94.

Jones, G. A. (1997). *Higher Education in Canada: Different Systems, Different Perspectives.* New York: Garland.

Jones, G. A. (2009). Sectors, institutional types, and the challenges of shifting categories: A Canadian commentary. *Higher Education Quarterly* 63(4), 371–83.

Jones, G. A. (2013a). The horizontal and vertical fragmentation of academic work and the challenge for academic governance and leadership. *Asia Pacific Education Review* 14(1), 75–83.

Jones, G. A. (2013b). Lineation and lobbying: Policy networks and higher education policy in Ontario, in P. Axelrod, R. D. Trilokekar, T. Shanahan, and R. Wellen (eds), *Making Policy in Turbulent Times: Challenges and Prospects for Higher Education.* Montreal/Kingston: McGill-Queen's University Press, pp. 99–116.

Jones, G. A. (2014). Building and strengthening policy research capacity: Key issues in Canadian higher education. *Studies in Higher Education* 39(8), 1332–42.

Jones, G. A., Shanahan, T., and Goyan, P. (2002). Traditional governance structures—Current policy pressures: The academic senate and Canadian universities. *Tertiary Education and Management* 8(1), 29–45.

Li, S. X. and Jones, G. A. (2015). The 'invisible' sector: Private higher education in Canada, in J. M. Joshi and S. Paivandi (eds), *Private Higher Education Across Nations.* Delhi: B. R. Publishing Corporation, pp. 1–33.

Looker, E. D. (2015). *Canadian Association for Graduate Studies 41st Statistical Report.* Ottawa: Canadian Association for Graduate Studies.

Pennock, L., Jones, G. A., Leclerc, J. M., and Li, S. X. (2015). Assessing the role and structure of academic senates in Canadian universities, 2000–2012. *Higher Education* 70(3), 503–18.

Piché, P. and Jones, G. A. (2016). Institutional diversity in Ontario's University Sector: A policy debate analysis. *Canadian Journal of Higher Education* 46(3), 1–17.

Research Infosource (2016). Canada's top fifty research universities 2016. https://www.researchinfosource.com/pdf/CIL%20Top%2050%20research%20universities%202016.pdf

Skolnik, M. (1986). Diversity in higher education: The Canadian case. *Higher Education in Europe* 11(2), 19–32.

Stonechild, B. (2006). *The New Buffalo: The Struggle for Aboriginal Post-secondary Education in Canada.* Winnipeg: University of Manitoba Press.

Trottier, C., Bernatchez, J., Fisher, D., and Rubenson, K. (2014). PSE policy in Quebec: A case study, in D. Fisher, K. Rubenson, T. Shanahan, and C. Trottier (eds), *The Development of Postsecondary Education Systems in Canada: A Comparison between British Columbia, Ontario, and Quebec, 1980–2010.* Montreal: McGill-Queen's University Press, pp. 200–91.

Trow, M. (1973). *Problems in the Transition from Elite to Mass Higher Education.* Berkeley: Carnegie Commission on Higher Education.

Weinrib, J. and Jones, G. A. (2014). Largely a matter of degrees: Quality assurance and Canadian universities. *Policy and Society* 33(3), 225–36.

9 Broad Access and Steep Stratification in the First Mass System: High Participation Higher Education in the United States of America

Brendan Cantwell

Introduction

The United States of America (USA) is the world's third largest population, 321.4 million people in 2015, occupies the fourth largest national land area of 9.5 million square kilometres, and produces the second largest national product. The USA is also the richest large nation and the most powerful in geo-political and military terms. Its total 2015 gross domestic product (GDP) of US$18,036.6 billion in purchasing power parity (PPP) trailed only China (US$19,815.1 billion). GDP PPP per capita of US$56,116 in 2015 was tenth, and first among countries with a population of over ten million (World Bank, 2017). Income and wealth are unequally distributed by region and by socio-economic status group. The USA has one of the highest Gini coefficients in the OECD (Piketty, 2014: ch. 6).

The USA was the first high participation system (HPS) of higher education, and since World War II has led the world in organizational models of higher education and in research-based science. Researchers in the USA produce almost half of the world's science papers that are ranked in the top 1 per cent of their field by citation rate (NSF, 2015), and in most global ranking tables, which are research-led, more than half the top twenty universities are located in the USA.

After the founding thirteen British colonies declared themselves an independent sovereign nation in 1776 the USA kept adding more parts to itself and the country is now a federation of fifty semi-autonomous states in which both national (federal) and state-level governments play a significant role in the higher education sector. The national level of government is responsible for underwriting the student loans system, public research funding, and legislation affecting a wide range of activities in the public and private sectors. Almost four-fifths of all higher education students in the USA are enrolled in public universities and colleges but the leading private Doctoral universities play a significant role in research and elite occupational preparation, alongside public sector Doctoral institutions.

Figure 9.1 illustrates the growth of mass higher education in the USA. The historical record of enrolments in the USA stretches to the late nineteenth century. In 1869–70 the newly established federal Office of Education collected data on participation. At that time 63,000 students enrolled in higher education (defined as ISCED 5–7), which was 1.3 per cent of the 18–24-year-old cohort. By 1900 enrolments rose to 238,000 but reached a cohort participation rate of only 2.3 per cent. During the twentieth century both total enrolments and the rate of participation exploded. Between 1900 and 1990 the number of students in higher education rose nearly fifty-eight times to a total of 13.7 million. The USA became a HPS in the 1940s or 1950s, a development that predates other systems.

Although participation remains very high, the USA is no longer exceptional in this regard. United Nations Educational and Cultural Organisation (UNESCO), which uses a different method of calculation than the US Department of Education, reported a 2013 gross tertiary enrolment ratio (GTER) of 89 per cent for the USA. This figure is high but fifteen other countries now also boast a GTER of 80 per cent or greater (UNESCO Institute for Statistics, 2016). Furthermore, qualification attainment in the USA has been stagnant over a generation. In 2011, 32 per cent of the population aged 25–64 years had attained a tertiary-type A qualification, a figure almost identical (33 per cent) for the

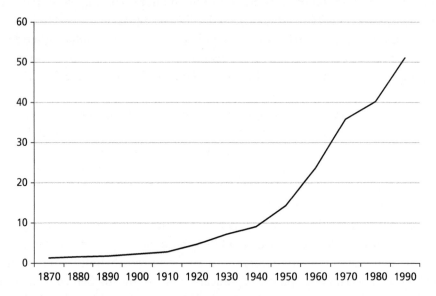

Figure 9.1. Higher education as a share of the 18–24-year-old cohort in the USA, 1870–1990

Source: Author's adaptation from Snyder (1993): table 23.

narrower 25–34 age band. Young people have not attained degrees at higher rates than did their parents. Among the 25–34 age group attainment levels are now greater in Australia, Canada, Ireland, Israel, Japan, Korea, Luxembourg, The Netherlands, New Zealand, Norway, the Russian Federation, and the United Kingdom (UK) (OECD, 2013).

The USA is sometimes regarded as the prototypical HPS (Marginson, 2016a). At the same time, it is wrong to assume that massification follows a single track and that the worldwide tendency towards HPS is a process of Americanization (Marginson, 2016b: see ch. 1). In fact, the US higher education system is atypical when compared to other HPS. As in the UK and Australia, quasi-markets are used extensively to coordinate and govern the system. As in Canada and Germany, higher education in the USA is a decentralized federal 'system of systems'. Like South Korea and the UK, private expenditures, largely though not exclusively from students' families, provide a bulk of the funding. Nearly twenty-one million students are enrolled at approximately 4,500 degree-granting institutions (NCES, 2014). Only China, whose population is roughly three times as large, exceeds the USA in total enrolments.

The control of higher education institutions is peculiarly arranged in the USA, which hosts a mix of public colleges and universities, private not-for-profit institutions that are run as independent charitable trusts, and a for-profit sector. The public sector is largest and is controlled formally by the states, though the steering power of the federal government has grown. Enrolment patterns vary somewhat from year to year but approximately 70 per cent of enrolments are in the public sector, 20 per cent in the private not-for-profit sector, and 10 per cent in the for-profit sector (NCES, 2014). Unlike more common unitary or binary systems, the higher education system in the USA is carved up into a complex quasi-formal set of 'institutional types' (see McCormick and Zhao, 2005) that classify higher education institutions by size, mission, degree granting patterns, research performance, location, and enrolment profiles. Two-year community colleges that award pre-baccalaureate qualifications are most numerous, there are currently over 1,000 of them, and these institutions enrol a plurality of students. Research universities that award Doctoral degrees are the most well-known higher education institutions both within and outside of the USA. These institutions host a large share of total enrolments, approximately 32 per cent, but are relatively few in number (only 335) (Center for Postsecondary Education, 2015). Research universities are the definition of peak status in most systems, but unlike any other system in the world private research universities lead the way in the USA. Although outsized in terms of resources and reputation (as well as output), the well-known private universities that dominate the system, including Harvard, Princeton, Stanford, Yale, MIT, and Caltech, enroll a tiny portion of all students.

Higher education in the USA is distinctive also in its simultaneous global reach and national insularity (a feature which is only likely to increase via Trumpism): the American model of higher education (Marginson, 2016a). Universities in the USA dominate the top echelon of world university rankings. More international students enrol in higher education institutions in the USA than any other country. And international graduate students and researchers both are attracted to American universities in large numbers and make extraordinary contributions to the academic research enterprise (Stephan, 2012). Even as higher education expands worldwide, and research power pluralizes with growing capacity in Asia and Europe, higher education leaders and policymakers in the USA remain remarkably inward-looking (Marginson, 2016a).

The USA is a special case. Given that the USA was the first HPS, that much of the most influential research on higher education has been based on the USA, and the enduring power of the system it necessary to consider not only the extent to which the USA affirms or challenges the general propositions outlined in the first section of this book, but also to consider (if only briefly) the historical development of the HPS in the USA. This may permit both a fuller understanding of HPS as a social phenomenon but also help to illuminate the perils of generalizing the USA beyond its territory.

Historical Development

The foundations of the American HPS predate national independence. Roger Geiger (2010) provides a useful shorthand history of higher education in the USA by dividing system development into ten generations. During the first five generations (1636–1850) the system grew from a handful of colonial colleges to a fledgling national system that included primarily private non-profit colleges alongside an emerging public sector. By 1870 there were 536 campuses in the USA, but each was small with an average of just 112 students (Snyder, 1993: 64). Generation six (1850–90) marked a point of departure in the history of American higher education (Geiger, 2010: 49–52). Just prior to, during, and in the decades immediately following the Civil War, higher education in the USA both saw marked quantitative expansion as well as a qualitative transformation towards the development of modern science-based research universities. Two developments in particular that helped to shape the system at that time have proven to be central to the system today. The first was the strengthening of academic professions following the German (Humboldtian) university model. The second was the passage of the first and second Morill Acts, through which the federal government granted the states large tracts of land. The sale of granted land provided funds for the establishment of seventy-five 'land-grant' colleges and universities. The seventh generation (1890–World War I) was defined by expansion and standardization of this newly developed system.

The inter-war period was another period of both quantitative growth and qualitative transformation. During the eighth generation (1919–38) the higher education system further expanded and became hierarchically differentiated. With more students entering the system, established higher education institutions sought to maintain social exclusion and cultural distinction. In the south Jim Crow policies formally blocked African Americans from enrolling beyond institutions designated for black people (historically Black Colleges and Universities), and in the north elite universities used informal quotas to suppress participation of Jewish and African American students. The result of differentiation, competition, and discrimination was the beginnings of mass system segmentation.

The ninth generation covered the post-World War II period (1945–75) when the USA enjoyed considerable growth and prosperity at the zenith of American hegemony. Fuelled first by wartime mobilization and huge demand by tuition paying (although modest by today's standards) students, American higher education institutions flourished. Jencks and Riesman (1968) called this period *The Academic Revolution*. Enrolments ballooned and the academic profession thrived as departments snapped up new PhDs into faculty posts as fast as graduate schools could produce them. The federal R&D grant system was institutionalized over this period and as Kerr noted, research universities quickly became dependent upon federal R&D money (Kerr, 2001: 35–58). This was also a progressive period in American history and access also became somewhat more equitable. The Civil Rights Act of 1964 formally prohibited racial discrimination, the Higher Education Act of 1965 established the first universal system of federal financial aid, and affirmative action admission programmes (following President Johnson's 1965 executive order) worked to partly redress historical patterns of exclusion. As a result, participation expanded not only at the growing number of community colleges and comprehensive universities but also at elite research universities (mostly public, but also private). Most emblematic of this period was the establishment of the California Master Plan and the development of the multiversity. Both projects were planned by the state but became social phenomena beyond the direct control of state planning (Marginson, 2016a).[1]

The tenth generation (1975–present) is marked by competition, privatization, and commercialization (Geiger, 2010). Student competition for places at elite universities intensified. A reactionary backlash to affirmative action, prompted primarily by the objections of white middle and upper class families who felt threatened by a perceived advantage enjoyed by minority students in the admission sweepstakes, led to a continuous stream of legal challenges and set in motion processes in which the contest over access to public research universities became an important plank in American social politics (Pusser, 2004). To buttress these legal and political efforts, well-to-do families invested in private schooling and high-cost college admission consultation programmes that include exam preparation and applicant grooming in order to give their children an edge (McDonough, 1997).

---

[1] Simon Marginson further notes the phenomenon of 'quasi-public civic intuitions' that are either created by the state and then privatized or are private foundations that are taken up with public support, constitute a distinctive feature of the US higher education system.

Competition for resources and status has intensified since the 1980s. Universities compete for students because their status is partially dependent on the types of students they attract and because student tuition fees play an increasingly important role in institutional finances (Winston, 1999). Private institutions have long relied on tuition. State appropriations have declined as a share of public higher education institutions' operating budgets and now public colleges and universities secure a majority of their resources from private sources (Desrochers and Hurlburt, 2016). Competition for research funds is now more intense both because higher education institutions seek grants to replace appropriations and because external revenue generation has become an important criterion in evaluating faculty careers (Bok, 2004).

Knowledge economy discourse also elevates the public and social importance of higher education in the USA (Slaughter and Cantwell, 2012). Participation has become a social, even moral, obligation for individuals. Human capital theory, which had become policy orthodoxy in justifying participation, assumes people entitled to a good life are those who 'earn' a degree (Slaughter et al., 2015). Since the Kennedy administration, though amplified since the Reagan era, succession of policy positions issued by both the Departments of Defense and Education establish academic research and student participation as vital to economic growth, national defence, and overall well-being (Teitelbaum, 2014).

Expenditures on tertiary education equal 2.6 per cent of GDP, a full percentage point higher than the GDP average (OECD, 2016). Higher education institutions collectively expend over US$500 billion per year (NCES, 2014). Participation is open to just about every student who completes secondary school (and some who do not) but patterned disparities in access and outcomes persist. This is the starting point from which we can begin to evaluate the several propositions related to governance, horizontal diversity, vertical stratification, and equity that are advanced in part one of the book.

Governance

There is not now, nor has there ever been, a singular central coordinating force that organizes higher education in the USA. In fact, higher education in the USA is not so much a 'system' (though that world is often used, including here, for convenience) as it is a 'system of systems'. The first governance proposition (HPS Proposition 4) states:

> *HPS are governed by multi-level control, coordination, and accountability mechanisms.*

and the US case supports the claim. Most institutions in the USA (excluding for-profits) retain some level of autonomy. This is classically described as a system of shared governance. Yet the presence of multiple stakeholders limits autonomy both in terms of goal specification and operational independence. The federalized organization of the system alone affirms the multi-level nature. State governments establish and support public institutions, the federal government has regulatory powers, independent accreditation agencies are responsible for quality assurance, and philanthropic organizations have influenced the system since its colonial establishment. Add to that the coexistence of public, private-not-for-profit, and for-profit higher education institutions and the multi-level nature of control would seem obvious.

Power of the purse is one mechanism of control. All higher education institutions generate income from a variety of sources. Public higher education institutions, which receive a state subsidy, are either mandated or expected as a condition of their appropriation to serve mostly within district (usually the state) students. Increasingly performance-funding policies are used by the states in order to directly tie the state appropriation to specific activities and outcomes. Such measures may be designed to improve coordination within the state and accountability to the public but necessarily increase government control and somewhat limit institutional autonomy (Dougherty et al., 2016). But government funding also includes, among other things, grants to conduct research. The federal government is the largest sponsor of academic research, providing about 60 per cent of all academic R&D funds (NSB, 2015). Federal research grants increase the autonomy of public higher education institutions insofar as grant funding make institutions less dependent on state appropriations and tuition. With federal funding comes accountability measures. More significantly, full participation in the federal grant economy demands that much of universities' activities are oriented to funding agency priorities (Slaughter and Leslie, 1997; Geiger, 2004).

Tuition fees are a significant source of revenue for all control types (NCES, 2016). It is often assumed that reliance on user fees introduces market-controls to higher education. Consumer choice, exercised by students who can 'vote with their feet', imposes a governing discipline by which higher education institutions compete on price and services. There is some evidence of this in the American system. Enrolments are better predicted by campus-level spending on amenities than by academic spending (Jacob et al., 2013), and expenditures on campus amenities is growing.

'The market', however, is not simply one layer of governance but is itself a reflection of multi-level coordination. Nowhere in the world, including the USA, is there a fully free market for higher education (Marginson, 2013). More accurately, quasi-markets that promote competition and market-like exchange are established by policy. The student market in the USA is an example of a policy created quasi-market. Important changes were made to federal financial aid programmes from the 1970s through the 1990s. Aid reforms first channelled grants away from institutions and to individual students who could use grants at any college or university of their choosing, and shifted from a system based primarily on grants to a mixed aid system of grants only for the neediest students, subsidized loans for a wider swath of students, and tax credits that primarily benefit students from middle income families (Hearn, 2001).

Even the notion that the market governs for-profit higher education institutions overlooks the reality of multi-level governance. It is no accident that for-profit institutions, which are either stand-alone business or owned by corporations, earn 90 per cent of their revenue from student fees. Through what is known as the 90/10 rule, the Department of Education requires higher education institutions to limit the share of revenue derived from federal financial student aid in the form of grants and loans to 90 per cent of total income. The for-profit industry often presents the 90/10 as an example of regulatory burden; the government getting in the way of free enterprise. In fact, however, allowing nearly all revenue for for-profit higher education institutions to flow from federal policy mechanisms is the result of successful corporate lobbying of Congress, which has shown considerable bipartisan support for for-profit higher education (Mettler, 2014), and has expanded the for-profit sector.

Participation, though more or less universal, does not occur on equal footing. Some places are socially valuable and desired, but these places are scarce. Other places accommodate all-comers and are abundant. As theorized in Chapter 3, high participation deactivates boundaries that governed access to desired places in elite systems. In HPS, not only do more students participate but social demand for the most desirable places in the system broadens. Determining how access to desirable places should be governed, especially at flagship public universities, has become an ongoing and important social contest in the USA. In *Burning Down the House*, Pusser (2004) demonstrates that the battle to eliminate affirmative action at the University of California was a multi-level political struggle involving campus activism and strategic management of the University of California board of regents, and was the proving grounds for a national debate over interventionist polices intended to promote social equity. The problem of how to select students to elite higher education institutions and who has the authority to decide remains disputed in the USA. While particular to the US context, this example of contested multi-level governance is a direct consequence of high participation. Absent the conditions of demand for elite places exceeding supply, and broad participation by different social groups that consider themselves rivals for political goods, it is unlikely that access to universities would have become a question of political and legal importance.

MANAGING DIFFERENTIATION

The second governance proposition (HPS Proposition 5) asserts:

> *HPS governance tends to involve the management of horizontal differentiation.*

On the face of things, this proposition seems to hold true in the USA. Higher education in the USA is differentiated. The Carnegie Foundation for the Advancement of Teaching, which has a long history of involvement in system design, generates an institutional classification system that has become a quasi-formal mechanism for segmenting the

Table 9.1. Basic Carnegie Classifications by number of institutions and share of all total, 2015

Type	Number	Per cent of all higher education institutions
Doctoral universities	335	7
Master's universities	741	16
Baccalaureate colleges	583	13
Baccalaureate/associates	408	9
Associate's colleges	1,113	24
Special focus: two-year	444	10
Special focus: four-year	1,005	22
Tribal colleges	35	1

Source: Author's adaptation of Carnegie Classification data, extracted from http://carnegieclassifications.iu.edu/downloads/CCIHE2015-FactsFigures.pdf

system based on higher education institution mission and activities. A list of the basic Carnegie classification along with the number of higher education institutions and share of the system that belong to each category are presented in Table 9.1.

The Carnegie categories show high levels of differentiation. Doctoral universities offer undergraduate programmes and terminal degrees (ISCED 6–8) in a wide variety of fields and conduct a programme of research alongside advanced education. Master's institutions are primarily involved in undergraduate education but also offer graduate programmes (ISCED 6–7), typically in vocationally oriented fields such as business, education, and nursing. Baccalaureate colleges offer only first degrees (ISCED 6), both academic and vocational, whereas baccalaureate/associates institutions offer a mix of both short-term and four-year degrees (ISCED 5–6). Special focus higher education institutions (both at the ISCED 5 and 6 levels) offer narrow, typically vocationally oriented, programmes. Tribal colleges, some of which are two-year and some of which are four-year institutions, are controlled by the sovereign nations of Native American tribes. Add to this list other minority serving institutions. Historically Black Colleges and Universities were established during the period of formal segregation to educate African Americans and maintain this historical mission. Hispanic Serving Institutions and Asian American and Native American Pacific Islander Serving Institutions are Department of Education designations that entitle higher education institutions enrolling a high share of particular groups access to some types of federal funding.

Perhaps the best evidence for rationalized differentiation as a means of managing high participation can be found in the design of state systems (e.g. Hearn et al., 1996). Particularly evident is the extent to which planners sought to establish a rational division of labour among institutional types as systems expanded in the mid-twentieth century. Designers of differentiation reasoned: not all students could or would want to participate in the same way; providing access to research universities to all comers would be cost-inefficient; and thus, a distributed set of higher education institutional types could best meet the parameters of social demand, cost effectiveness, and system coherence. The 'California Idea', which under-girded the Master Plan, is the prototype for rationalized differentiation (Marginson, 2016a). Planned differentiation, enforced by policy and funding mechanisms, provided the operating rationale for the development of a mass system.

The California story also brings into question the claim that mass participation demands the maintenance of rational differentiation through formal governance. The prototype for managed differentiation that established a rational division of labour among higher education institutions while providing a cohered system that permitted full upward mobility for those who are able is broken (Marginson, 2016b). Chapter 3 posits that a counterbalance to rational differentiation is the tendency for isomorphic drift; the draw of research university status pulls other higher education institution types to adopt research university-like missions. Delivering aspirations to achieve next level status becomes a central objective of academic leaders (Toma, 2010) and the literature is replete with accounts of how striving institutions operationalize their goal to become a tier one university (see Gonzales, 2012). The federal research grant economy may stimulate aspirations. Although a relative few research universities are awarded the majority of all federal R&D funds, all accreted higher education institutions are eligible for research grant funding. The (mostly hypothetical) possibility for research income tempts many institutions to pursue research objectives, though state policy makes this drift variable (Geiger, 2004).

Funding polices further defy the differentiation governance imperative. State divestment has proved to be a major drag on system performance among public higher education institutions in the USA. The tax revolt and anti-welfare politics have led to systematic under-funding in California (Marginson, 2016b) and around the country. As a result, the system lacks coherence and fails to deliver on the promise of access and mobility through a rationalized (and well-supported) differentiated system. The same observation applies to many of the states. Without sufficient funding effective vertical differentiation is difficult to maintain because no sector of the system is able to achieve its mission and crisp lines of differentiation wither with neglect. Some governance developments, such as performance-based funding (Dougherty et al., 2016), seem to promote homogenization, rather than differentiation.

ROBUST MANAGERIAL CAPACITIES

The final governance proposition (HPS Proposition 6) claims:

> *HPS complex multi-level accountability and coordination, coupled with system differentiation, result in higher education institutions adopting increasingly corporate forms and robust internal governance and management capacities.*

Observations of higher education in the USA supports this proposition. Corporate-like branding is ubiquitous among colleges and universities in the USA. Rooksby and Collins (2016) analysed trademark registration, college and university arbitration actions over trademark infringement, and relevant news stories and press releases in order to understand branding trends among higher education institutions in the USA. Rooksby and Collins (2016) explain: 'As sensitivity to brand creates brand opportunity, brands come to reflect markets' (p. 58). Brand sensitivity coincided with plausible growth. Attention to brand could be a response by higher education institutions who seek enrolment growth. Although it is also possible that this is related to neoliberal marketization and independent of participation levels.

Higher education institutions in the USA are subject to stakeholder demands and regulatory and accountability compliance. Offices for alumni relations, governmental affairs, institutional research and effectiveness, technology transfer, community relations, legal compliance, accreditation, and communications and brand management, among others, are commonplace. Most higher education institutions also have offices to manage institutional human resources, offices to support faculty, offices to manage information and instructional technology, offices to manage grants and research, and large student support services operations. Simply put, managing all of the external and internal demands placed on contemporary higher education institutions demands an extensive administrative infrastructure (Zemsky and Massy, 1990).

Gathering administrative power does not only reflect the technical demands placed on higher education. Slaughter and Rhoades (2004) identify expanded managerial capacity as a key plank in establishing the cooperate university. They argue that by claiming warranty over a variety of technical activates, administrators have expanded power in steering higher education institutions like corporate entities, including wielding greater control over faculty work (see also Rhoades, 2014). Enhancing the corporate capacity involves developing a professionalized layer of middle management, or 'managerial professionals' (see Rhoades and Sporn, 2002), with expertise in specialized administrative tasks. Staff employment patters at higher education institutions in the USA show the professionalized managers. For example, between 1990 and 2012 the number of professional non-faculty staff grew from fifty to eighty-three per 1,000 students at public research universities and from fifty-six to 102 per 1,000 students at private research universities (Desrochers and Kirshstein, 2014). Over this period the share of all faculty members who are part-time and who are not eligible for tenure has ballooned. Shifting staff ratios from securely employed faculty to professional administrators is both symptom and cause of intuitional control moving away from academic shared governances and towards corporate-like management (Rhoades, 2014).

Horizontal Diversity

Chapter 4 observes that system diversity commonly assumed to increase as participation grows but also that increased diversity is appropriate for meeting social needs.

The first diversity proposition (HPS Proposition 7) states:

> *In the HPS era, regardless of the political economy and culture of systems, an increasing proportion of higher education becomes centred on comprehensive multi-discipline and multi-function research universities, or 'multiversities'. The multiversity is increasingly dominant as the paradigmatic form of higher education.*

One part of the proposition claims that HPS are centred on the multiversity. If it is correct that the multiversity is the measuring stick for system diversity, then this proposition is not only upheld in the USA but is almost a tautology. Indeed, in the USA developed multiversities as part and parcel of the massification project (see Marginson, 2016a).

Another part of the proposition offers that over time multiversities become an increasing proportion of the higher education system. One way to assess the prospect of the increasing centrality of multiverses is to examine enrolments over time. Multiversities attend closely to research but multi-purpose research universities count in the low hundreds in the USA and by any measure constitute about 10 per cent of all higher education institutions. Because both research universities and community colleges are multi-purpose a liberal interpretation of this question could lead one to consider enrolments at both research universities and community colleges. Table 9.2 shows the share of total enrolments at community colleges and research universities over time. Community colleges and research universities clearly hold a dominant position in terms of enrolments. Together they hosted 66 to 69 per cent of enrolments over the period considered. It is remarkable that so relatively few research universities enrol so many students. However, this share remained more or less steady from 1990 to 2014. This may indicate that while the multiversity—and its junior counterpart, the American community college—are central to the system, the

Table 9.2. Share of total enrolment by sector

	1990 (%)	1995 (%)	2000 (%)	2005 (%)	2010 (%)	2014 (%)
Community colleges	37	36	37	38	40	36
Research universities	32	30	29	29	27	28

Source: Author's analysis of National Science Foundation data, extracted from https://www.nsf.gov/

centrality is not increasing. However, the American HPS was already a HPS by 1990 and the temporal frame may not be sufficient here to show consolidation towards multi-purpose institutions. In other words, there may both be a tendency towards increased centrality of multi-purpose higher education institutions and a limit to the share of students these institutions enrol. There will always be some demand for non-multi-purpose provision.

Overall it is clear that multiversities are a dominant and paradigmatic form of higher education in the USA. The literature is saturated with descriptive accounts and empirical studies of drift (see e.g. Morphew, 2002; Morphew and Huisman, 2002; Bastedo and Gumport, 2003; Toma, 2012; Gonzales, 2013; Jaquette, 2013).

STAGNANT DIVERSITY OF PROVISION

The second proposition in Chapter 4 (HPS Proposition 8) states:

Regardless of the political economy and culture of the HPS, when participation expands there is no necessary increase in the overall diversity of institutional form and mission; and this has probably declined, except in relation to online provision.

How does this proposition hold up to the US experience?

The US HPS *is* diverse in terms of modes of provision but it is not becoming *more* diverse, at least among traditional providers. Recent decades have seen drift towards multiversity form among many higher education institutions and evidence of contraction in the variation of provision among traditional institutions. One reasonable assessment, then, is that diversity of provision in the USA did accompany participation growth, but as the HPS became mature provision modalities contracted.

Consistent with the earlier proposition the one exception to a general movement towards multiversity-like provision throughout the system is growth in online higher education. Online teaching and learning is now commonplace in US higher education. It is estimated that 28 per cent of students take at least one online course (Allen et al., 2015). Expansion of online provision has advanced in in three ways. First, for-profit higher education institutions, such as the University of Phoenix and other non-traditional providers, like the Western Governors University, absorbed demand by offering flexible programmes that were fully or partially online. Second, traditional higher education institutions responded by offering individual courses and entire programmes online. These first two pathways partly fit the sort of 'disruption' model advanced by educational technology reformers. Mass open online courses (MOOCs), which originated with elite research universities, are the third form of online provision.

MOOCs have received perhaps the greatest attention but as of yet seem not to have challenged traditional delivery. Online provision has increased the diversity of the US higher education but has not fully disrupted the system as futurists predicted).

INTERNAL INSTITUTIONAL DIVERSITY

In Chapter 4, HPS Proposition 9 states:

As participation expands the internal diversity of multiversities tends to increase.

The US case largely, if not fully, supports this proposition. As multi-output and activity organizations, multiversities necessarily engage in wide sets of activities. Alongside traditional academic activities they host hospitals, technology parks, retail and residential operations, sports and performance halls (Weisbrod, 2009). More-over, traditional activities are increasingly undertaken through a complex and diverse set of networks. Slaughter and Rhodes (2004) describe 'new circuits of knowledge' that link universities with a variety of public, corporate, and non-profit sector entities, often through ties with intermediating and interstitial organizations, increase the scope and complexity of university activities far beyond traditional academic endeavours. Kauppinen and Cantwell (2014) extended this claim by further arguing that universities are becoming embedded in 'global production networks'. Multiversity activities are made more internally diverse not just because these organizations do many things, but because they become entangled in a set of ties with other organizations and social actors on local, national, and global scales (see Marginson and Rhoades, 2002).

Diversity of degree programmes, and the relative emphasis given to research and teaching in a variety of fields, is another way to measure the internal diversity of multiversities. Here the evidence for increased diversity among USA multiversities is mixed. In the initial stages of massification new fields of study and degree programmes were regularly added at US universities, typically without contraction of existing programmes. And as universities become more complex and diverse in both in terms of student body diversity and fields of study they also tend to host new inter-disciplinary programmes, adding to their internal diversity (Brint et al., 2009). Recent decades have seen growth in the number of university based cross-sectorial centres and institutes that link academia with government and industry. While inter-disciplinary fields and cross-sectorial fields may have increased, since the 1980s many academic fields, especially in the arts and humanities, have either shrunk or disappeared from US universities (Brint et al., 2012). One source of strain for arts and humanities programmes is quasi-market disfavour (Taylor et al., 2013). Multiversities are internally diverse in terms of their research and teaching activities but there is no universal trend towards increased diversity.

INTEGRATING HORIZONTAL DIVERSITY WITH OTHER ASPECTS OF SYSTEM DYNAMICS

The final proposition of the diversity chapter, HPS Proposition 10, advances four interlocking claims. It states:

> *All else being equal, the combination of expanding participation and enhanced competition in neoliberal quasi-markets is associated with specific effects in relation to diversity, including (1) increased vertical differentiation of higher education institutions (stratification); (2) reduced horizontal differentiation (diversification); (3) convergence of missions through isomorphistic imitation; and (4) growth in the role of private higher education institutions, especially for-profit institutions.*

Experience from the USA largely supports this set of claims. Higher education in the USA is strongly characterized by neoliberal competition, state divestment, and quasi-market resource allocation (Slaughter and Rhoades, 2004). As is discussed later, the US HPS is highly stratified and there is good reason to believe that stratification is extended by the conditions of high participation alongside neoliberal governance. Drift in the system towards multiversity form is strong and this phenomenon is associated with neo-liberal competition. The USA has seen substantial growth in the for-profit private sector. Much of the growth of this sector is directly attributable to quasi-market policies that channel public resources to for-profit providers (Mettler, 2014) but expansion is also underwritten by social demand that is not fully met by traditional providers.

Vertical Stratification

Some higher education intuitions—such as elite research universities—are enterprises that expend billions of dollars per year and hold billions more in reserve; others operate on a shoe-string, expend only what revenue is generated in a year and have few reserves. The divide between research universities, elite multi-purpose organizations, and community colleges, demand absorbing instructional workhorses, lends itself to the metaphor of a two-headed monster. But the Chimera metaphor is incomplete and overlooks the many sub-systems, points of differentiation, and most importantly the institutional stratification, and student segmentation that constitute steep vertical differentiation of the system.

The classification system devised by the Carnegie Foundation provides a somewhat more complete picture of vertical differentiation. The Carnegie categories are based on mission and function. Although Carnegie categories are not legal categories, they nonetheless have the codifying effect of hierarchically arranging all higher education institutions in the system in a pyramidal set of tiers (this despite the foundation's insistence that the classifications are value free descriptors that should not be used as a ranking or ordering scheme). The public/private divide is also an important line of division. Private research universities are the best-resourced higher education institutions in the country and there are also a handful of private liberal arts colleges that enjoy vast resources and high status (though most private colleges and universities are neither wealthy nor elite). Table 9.3 shows average revenue per student and level tuition dependence for various categories of public and private non-profit higher education institutions.

Community colleges are at the bottom of the hierarchy but enrol plurality of students, with approximately 40 per cent of all students at this type (College Board, 2014).[2] The

Table 9.3. Per-student operating revenue by institutional type

Average operating revenue per student (FTE) and percentage derived from tuition fees (constant 2010 US$)

	2000	2005	2010
Public research higher education institutions (US$)	32,962	36,225	38,755
(%)	17	20	22
Public Master's higher education institutions (US$)	17,155	17,477	18,413
(%)	24	31	35
Public Bachelor's higher education institutions (US$)	17,268	17,596	18,796
(%)	24	30	34
Public community colleges (US$)	12,440	12,281	12,160
(%)	19	23	27
Private non-profit research higher education institutions (US$)	91,519	83,824	79,600
(%)	19	23	26
Private Master's non-profit higher education institutions (US$)	22,625	22,885	23,555
(%)	54	60	64
Private non-profit Bachelor's higher education institutions (US$)	36,258	33,132	33,877
(%)	31	39	42

Notes: Held in constant 2010 US$. Tuition figures represent average net tuition paid on a per-student basis. Operating revenue on a per-student basis includes all sources including operating hospitals, auxiliary activates, research grants, and gifts, some of which does not directly contribute to instruction. Data not available for for-profit higher education institutions.

Source: Author's adaptation from the Delta Cost Project's *Trends In College Pricing, 2001–2011*, extracted from https://www.deltacostproject.org/sites/default/files/products/Delta%20Cost_Trends%20College%20Spending%202001-2011_071414_rev.pdf

[2] Most community college programmes at the ISCED 5 level. In many countries community colleges would not be considered higher education. They are in the USA in part because they hold a formal transfer-function into an ISCED 6 institution. The two-year community college degree can in many cases be converted into the first half a four-year (ISCED 6) degree.

Associates College group include for-profit higher education institutions and private non-profit higher education institutions but is dominated by the public community college sector, which enrols approximately 90 per cent of the students in the sub-sector (College Board, 2014: 32). Community colleges are typically lower priced and lower resourced higher education institutions that prepare students either for work or to transfer to a four-year college or university. They generally only offer tertiary-type B qualifications, though some are drifting into the four-year segment and offer Bachelor's degrees. As shown in Table 9.3, community colleges enjoy less revenue on a per student basis than do other types of higher education institutions. Community colleges are open access and do not offer high-value positional goods.

Baccalaureate Colleges make up approximately 17 per cent of all higher education institutions in the USA. This category includes a mix of public, private non-profit, and proprietary institutions, though private non-profits make up 66 per cent of the category (Center for Postsecondary Education, 2015). Although there are common features among these higher education institutions in that they only offer undergraduate degrees and engage in limited research, they are a heterogeneous group of institutions. For instance, this group includes both Amherst College, an elite liberal arts institution that admitted only 14 per cent of the 7,927 applications it received in 2012, and Alma College that admitted 68 per cent of its 2,699 applications that year (NCES, 2014). Non-profit private Bachelor's Colleges are, on average, modestly resourced and tuition dependent. However, the average value in this category has only minimal meaning as the distribution is likely very wide and includes a few elite liberal arts colleges with large endowments that are only somewhat dependent on tuition and higher education institutions operating by the skin-of-their teeth that have few reserves and depend heavily on tuition fees. Public and for-profit colleges each make up about 17 per cent of this group (CCIHE, 2015).

Master's Colleges are in many ways similar to Baccalaureate Colleges except that they offer some post-graduate degrees below the Doctoral level. The private non-profit sector is the largest within this category, accounting for 52 per cent of all higher education institutions in the group (CCIHE, 2015). Most private non-profit Master's Colleges are former low and moderate status liberal arts colleges that drifted by expanding in size and programmatic offering in order to stimulate student demand and increase revenue. Public colleges and universities make up 37 per cent of the higher education institutions in this category. They are primarily regional comprehensive universities with very small research operations that attract students from the local region. Public and private non-profit Master's institutions are middle resourced higher education institutions in terms of per-student revenue that tend to derive a high share of their income from tuition fees relative to other institutional types within the same control category. The specialized category includes a heterogeneous range of higher education institutions but most focus on specific occupations. Some are stand-alone professional schools (e.g. medicine, engineering, law) that offer adequate professional pathways but lack the status of their research university affiliated counterparts.

Research and Doctoral universities sit at the top of the institutional hierarchy. They are better-resourced and less tuition dependent than any other category of institution. They make up only approximately 7 per cent of all higher education institutions but enrol over one-quarter of all students (27 per cent). These are large universities in high demand by students who want to attend them, and by academics who want to work at them. Higher education institutions in this category are far-reaching and engage actively in all disciplines, scholarly and research pursuits, but it is clear that scientific research is paramount at most of these higher education institutions. Despite occupying a place at the top of the status hierarchy, this is not an undifferentiated group. The category includes some of the undisputed preeminent global research universities like Harvard, Stanford, and the Massachusetts Institute of Technology, as well as leading public flagships that are also global research universities such as the University of Michigan and the University of California at Berkeley, but the group also includes research universities struggling at the cusp of world-class status and higher education institutions that are research universities little more than in name only. To consider it another way, thirty-four of the top fifty universities in terms of paper production in the Leiden rankings are from the USA—a dominant showing indeed—yet these accounted only about 10 per cent of all research universities in the country.

The Carnegie classification includes three sub-groups of research universities, research universities with very high activity, research universities with high research activity, and Doctoral/research universities. Table 9.4 shows average research expenditures and PhD degree production in 2012 by sub-classification. At an average of US$440.7 million, very high research universities expended more than six times as much as high research universities, and about sixty-one times more than Doctoral/research universities. The gulf in PhD production is similarly wide. Even among the 108 research universities with very high activity there is considerable stratification; for example, the top fifty research performers accounted for 56 per cent of all academic R&D spending in 2012 (NSF, 2015). Consider these additional examples: Johns Hopkins

Table 9.4. Average R&D expenditures (in US$ millions) and PhD production by research university sub-group, 2012

Carnegie classification	Number of higher education institutions	R&D expenditures (US$)	PhDs awarded
Research universities—very high	108	440.7	309.3
Research universities—high	99	71.8	62.9
Doctoral/research universities	90	7.2	50.7

Source: Author's analysis of National Science Foundation data, extracted from https://www.nsf.gov

University, the Baltimore based biomedical research goliath, alone spent US$2.1 billion on R&D in 2012, nearly a billion more than the next largest performer (University of Michigan); Harvard University, which employs over 5,000 research post-docs, produces almost twice as many papers as the next highest (Stanford University).

Some universities play the research game (some well, some not so well), others want to be on the field but cannot keep up, and a few superstars dominate them all.

A final indicator of institutional stratification to consider is wealth. Most higher education institutions in the USA follow Bowen's (1980) rule and raise all the money they can and spend all they raise. A few, however, break the rule and amass enormous reserves. Endowment holdings are the clearest measure of higher education institution savings in the USA. Tax code permits colleges and universities to receive tax-exempt donations (donors can write off their gifts against income tax liability) and to invest in the capital markets without paying taxes on capital gains. Elite universities enjoy advantages because their wealthy alumni and other powerful social actors prefer donating to these institutions, and because they enjoy financial management expertise and are able to leverage consistently high returns (Cantwell, 2016). Over time enormous inequalities in endowment holdings have developed. An analysis of data from the National Association of College and University Business Officers (NACUBO) reveals just how unequally endowment resources are distributed (see Table 9.5). In 2013, the top 1 per cent, or just eight institutions held 30 per cent of all endowment assets, the 'middle' 2–10 per cent held 41 per cent of all reported assets, and the bottom 90 per cent, or 756 institutions, held just 25 per cent of all reported endowment assets. Even though these figures are not adjusted for institutional size they present a stark truth about resources available to different higher education institutions. Status and prestige are wrapped up in a reputation-resources complex so that those with the largest endowments also tend to enjoy the highest status and best social positions.

The first stratification proposition (HPS Proposition 11) states:

The expansion of participation towards and beyond the HPS stage is associated with a tendency to bifurcation and stratification (vertical diversification) in the value of higher education, between elite (artisanal) institutions and mass (demand-absorbing) institutions.

Table 9.5. Inequality in endowment asset holdings, 2013

	Number of institutions	Share of total endowment holdings (%)
Top 1%	8	30
Middle 2–10%	82	41
Bottom 90%	756	29

Source: Author's analysis of NACUBO data, adapted from Cantwell (2016).

Perhaps the best way to explore this tendency initially is to describe these oppositional sectors.

ARTISANAL

The higher education system in the USA unambiguously includes an artisanal sub-sector. The largest and most important component of the artisanal sector is a set of global research universities that not only rise above their national competitors but also stand among the leading research universities on a worldwide basis. Identifying the segment and its components, as well as describing key attributes, is a relatively uncomplicated task. The focus here is on elite research universities, which anchor the artisanal segment. Some research universities are publically controlled while others are controlled privately but there are no for-profit research universities. In total, there are 306 research universities in the USA but only a third or less of these can make a legitimate claim to artisanal status. While the remainder have multiversity missions and elite ambitions they simply cannot muster the resources, status, demand, and exclusivity to maintain artisanal production and, as a result, conduct a smaller volume of research and offer places of considerably less social value. The higher education institutions that make up the Association of American Universities (AAU) is a convenient grouping to set the boundary that circumscribes the research university component of the artisanal segment. The AAU was founded in 1900 and is an invitation-only membership association of thirty-four US public, twenty-six US private, and two Canadian research universities. The AAU is a lobby and policy coordination group and its members are widely viewed as the 'top' research universities in North America Lower status research universities have aspirations—sometimes expressed openly—to join the AAU and members who fail to keep up with research standards are asked to leave (Syracuse University and the University of Nebraska both lost AAU membership in 2010). The AAU contributes to bifurcation by lobbying for additional research funding that is in turn dominated by their members.

All AAU universities conduct a high volume of research, are science oriented, and host at least some prestigious graduate programmes; most are among the top hundred universities in the world according to ARWU and all are in the top 500. There is clear differentiation even among this group of ostensibly elite higher education institutions, and the primary dividing line is public/private.[3] Degrees from private AAU higher education institutions are in high demand and, as a result, these institutions can be choosey when selecting whom to

---

[3] Data presented in the AAU section come from the following sources: Sources: NSF, NCES (2012), and Leiden Rankings (2014).

admit and seem to be able to charge tuition fees as high as they please based on demand, though rarely change tuition as high as costs might justify. Public AAU higher education institutions tend to be in greater demand and more selective than lower status 'state schools', but only a few (e.g. University of California at Berkeley) enjoy the demand and selectivity levels of their private counterparts. Private AAU higher education institutions also tend to perform better in terms of research input and output metrics. The median private AAU fetches US$24,560 in federal R&D grants per student, produces a paper for approximately every two students, and 17.3 per cent of papers reach the top 10 per cent in their field by citation metrics. The median public AAU institution has only US$8,170 per student in federal R&D income, produces a paper for every five students, and 13.9 per cent of which are among the top 10 per cent. That only three of the twenty-six private higher education institutions in the AAU have per student federal research funding low enough to be in the bottom half of the public AAU distribution helps to demonstrate the bold financial line that separates these institutions. About half of the public higher education institutions in the AAU are in the ambiguous borderlands between the artisanal segment and what lies below (more on this soon). Quantitatively this position is measured by research expenditures and output. Qualitatively it is defined by a campus culture in which pockets of 'excellence' coexist with mass education.

The USA is unusual in that it has a small layer of high-demand teaching-only liberal arts colleges. Unlike research universities which have both national and international status, liberal arts colleges' status is derived almost exclusively on a national basis. Top liberal arts colleges can be considered artisanal even though they do not conduct an extraordinary amount of research because their production model is artisanal in character and resembles Baumol's account of the string quartet. Total enrolment is small at elite liberal arts colleges, below 3,000 students, and is limited to undergraduate education. Class sizes are also small at top liberal arts higher education institutions (no large lectures), contact between faculty members and their students is high (undergraduates have more contact with professors in this part of the sub-sector than at top research universities), and scholarship and teaching are produced simultaneously. Most faculty members have been trained at leading research universities and maintain a scholarly agenda, and undergraduate students often participate in faculty research projects. Demand for places at these institutions is high and student selectivity is also high with typically fewer than 20 per cent of applicants admitted. Graduates are often welcome in consulting, financial, and tech firms, and there are established pathways from top liberal arts colleges to leading professional graduate programmes (e.g. law, medicine). As with research universities, the boundary delineating artisanal liberal arts colleges from the rest is ambiguous, though a reasonable line is the twenty-fifth place on the *U.S. News* list of top national liberal arts colleges because the top-twenty-five enjoy 'front page' advantage that is associated with higher levels of resources, student demand, and selectivity (Bowman and Bastedo, 2009).

DEMAND ABSORBING

The demand-absorbing sub-sector is large in the USA—accounting for nearly 50 per cent of total enrolments—and includes community colleges and for-profit higher education institutions. Community colleges do not generally offer type-A qualifications but are instead focused on vocational and paraprofessional training or early preparation for a tertiary degree to be completed elsewhere. Since the 1970s community colleges have consistently enrolled between 35 and 40 per cent of all students (NCES, 2014). There has been some mission drift among community colleges, for example by adding residential dormitories and inter-collegiate sports teams to replicate the 'college' experience typical of four-year higher education institutions. But as a group, community colleges have maintained a consistent mission of providing access to post-secondary education, and have not pursued research-based strategies.

Community colleges are typically open access in that they enrol all students who have completed secondary school (and some who have not) and have few if any formal barriers to admission. Enrolments at community colleges wax and wane counter to the business cycle; in other words, when jobs are relatively scarce and entry-wages low, demand for tertiary education expands and community colleges have historically been the sector to accommodate this demand. Community colleges tend to have little social status attached and a weak organizational identity. The branding and sloganeering that is omnipresent among four-year institutions jockeying for social position is largely absent from community colleges. This is because community colleges adhere to an access mission that prioritizes processing students—by facilitating transfer to a four-year institution or by vocational training and labour market preparation—over seeking status. In this sector, operational efficiency is a goal.

The demand absorbing segment also includes proprietary, or for-profit, higher education institutions. For-profit higher education institutions have a particular type of mission: namely, to make money. The profit motivation separates these higher education institutions from all other parts of the system in the USA, including community colleges. Over the past forty years proprietary institutions have made substantial inroads into student markets. In 1970 for-profit higher education institutions were virtually non-existent, enrolling just 0.2 per cent of all students in the USA, in 1980 for-profits captured 1.1 per cent and crept up to 1.7 per cent by 1990. Over the course of the 1990s and the first decade of the twenty-first century enrolments at for-profit higher education institutions ballooned to 3.1 per cent of all enrolments in 2000 and 9.5 per cent in 2010 (NCES, 2014). For-profits have especially benefited from two features of the American system. The first is the generally slow movement to accommodate adult learners and students who work full-time. Until recently even community colleges have focused primarily on traditional students who are between 18 and 25, do not work full time, and do not have dependent children. For-profits have exploited this segment of the market by designing flexible, vocationally oriented programmes that meet these students' needs, thereby absorbing under-served demand in the market. In fact, the success of for-profit universities in catering to non-traditional students may have forced middle-sector higher education institutions to compete downward as well as up. Online offerings have expanded dramatically in recent years (Allen and Seaman, 2008), and along with the general development in information technology, competition from proprietary higher education institutions have prompted many traditional colleges and universities to adopt online offerings. The second feature of the USA HPS that benefits for-profit higher education institutions is a favourable policy environment (Mettler, 2014). Third-party accredited for-profits are eligible to collect up to 90 per cent of their revenue through federal financial aid and many operate almost exclusively on revenue derived from federal student aid grants and subsidized loans. In other words, favourable policy conditions as well as market strategies have aided the expansion of this segment.

Drivers of Bifurcation

Chapter 5 in HPS Proposition 12 posits two inter-related features common among HPS that contribute to stratification:

(a) intensified social competition for the most valuable student places; (b) variable tuition charges; and/or (c) intensified competition between institutions.

Each feature is present in the US system and each would seem to contribute to stratification.

COMPETITION FOR PLACES

Competition for valuable places is intense and has increased but not directly because of new segments of society who now participate. Lower income students are congregated in low resource segments of the system (more on this topic in the next section) and many of the highest performing low-income students never even apply to a selective higher education institution (Hoxby and Avery, 2012). The most intense competition for valuable places is among students from professional families, who aggressively deploy their financial, social, and cultural resources to secure admission at a desirable university.

Wise (2016) describes intense efforts undertaken by American students and their families—facilitated by secondary schools that encourage robust competition among students who seek to distinguish themselves through academic achievement and through athletic exploits and devotion to cultural and artistic endeavours—in order to secure a place at a top university. This competition is heated up by two macro-social conditions. The first is growing economic inequality in which the super-rich take a large share of all wealth. In this condition, the professional classes and even reasonably well-to-do families are not assured inter-generational transmission of status. This uncertainty, according to Wise, drives families to seek ever-finer distinction through higher education in order to improve the odds of social and economic success. The second macro-social condition is related to mass participation. Even though the majority of lower income students are not competing directly for coveted places and there is no absolute scarcity of places, expanded participation prompts families to seek qualitative advantage through a process describe as effectively maintained inequality (Lucas, 2001). As Wise explains 'the battle over qualitative distinction in educational opportunities can be expected to "heat up" as more generalized access to any given level of education is achieved' (Wise, 2016: 275). The 'heat up' in competition for the most valuable places drives system stratification and bifurcation insofar as the most elite segments of the system are able to capture an ever-larger share of the available social and economic resources.

VARIABLE TUITION FEES

Students pay fees in public, private non-profit, and proprietary sectors. Fees vary greatly. They tend to be highest at private universities and liberal arts colleges, ostensibly because these institutions do not receive a direct subsidy to provide education, and fees are generally lowest at public community colleges. But fees are also variable within sector and tend to follow selectivity. For example, as shown in Table 9.6, within the University of Wisconsin system the selective, desirable, and resource intensive Madison campus is the most expensive followed by the Milwaukee campus. Of note is the gap in non-Wisconsin fees between campus, which does represent market demand and does provide additional resources for the most desirable campuses. The ability to charge higher fees drives stratification because already better resources can generate revenue through tuition fees.

Market mechanisms may not be the primary way in which variable fees drive bifurcation. This is in part because students often do not pay the published fee rate because many enjoy tuition discounting. In fact, variable subsidies (rather than fees) may be a more profound driver of stratification. In higher education subsidy is equal to the cost of education net of fees (Taylor and Morphew, 2013). Students with the strongest academic performance, who disproportionally come from socially advantaged families, are concentrated in higher education institutions with both the highest fees and the highest subsidy (Winston, 1999; Taylor and Morphew, 2013). And high subsidy institutions are also the most selective and best resourced. The ability to offer a high

Table 9.6. University of Wisconsin per-semester tuition and fee rates, 2016–17 academic year

Campus	Wisconsin resident fees(US$)	Out of district fees (US$)
UW-Madison	5,208	14,833
UW-Milwaukee	4,715	9,801
UW-Oshkosh	3,744	7,530
UW-Parkside	3,671	7,665
UW-Platteville	3,744	7,669
UW-River Falls	3,969	7,755
UW-Stevens Point	3,836	7,970
UW-Stout	3,507	7,380
UW-Superior	4,018	7,805
UW-Whitewater	3,819	7,855

Source: Author's adaptation of University of Wisconsin system data, extracted from http://uwhelp. wisconsin.edu/paying/systemcosts.aspx

subsidy, even when fees are high, is a hallmark of artisanal production in the USA because it denotes a resource intensive education. By offering education that costs far beyond even high fees, elite higher education institutions are able to consolidate demand from the strongest students and put competition out of reach for would-be elites who may be able to increase revenue through higher fees but are unable to match quality through subsidy.

The Middle Segment

The final stratification proposition (HPS Proposition 13) states:

A middle layer of institutions tends to form, shaped by the combination of upward aspirations (drift) with systemic scarcity of resources and status.

In the USA, the middle segment is large and differentiated both in terms of function, mission, and strategy. Most of the public and non-profit private four-year colleges and universities occupy this middle sub-sector, many of which have obvious research aspirations, though not all pursue a strategy of mimicking top research universities. At the top of the middle sub-sector are a group of higher education institutions that are similar in many respects to incumbents of the artisanal sector. These 'wannabes' (quadrant A in Figure 4.1 of Chapter 4) constitute the borderlands of the artisanal sector and reasonable observers could describe some higher education institutions in this zone as artisanal. Quadrant A probably includes the bottom half of the AAU public universities, as well as the non-AAU research-extensive, and some research-very high and Doctoral/research universities.

These higher education institutions compete vigorously for research grants and contracts, especially from the federal government, invest their own funds into building research capacity (see Leslie et al., 2012), and seek to keep enrolments constant while increasing student selectivity. The University of Georgia is an example of a wannabe artisanal research university. Supported by a state scholarship programme that has increased both revenue and student selectivity, the University of Georgia is held in high esteem in the south. It seeks to expand its national and international reputation by investing in research activities without expanding enrolments but still falls well short of the top research universities in terms of research output (260 in the 2014 Leiden Rankings).

Not all pursue a strategy of expanding research while limiting size. A large number of non-elite research and comprehensive universities attempt both an artisanal and demand absorbing mission at once (quadrant B). These higher education institutions tend to articulate multiversity-like missions and claim to be points of access that are community responsive while at the same time offering access to high-end research. Such higher education institutions might, for example, simultaneously establish a medical school and enter into a partnership with community colleges or establish an online distance education programme—Central Michigan University is one example. Most that attempt this strategy remain largely in the business of absorbing demand and become 'little Harvard' only in motto, while placing stress on faculty who are burdened with new and mostly unrealistic expectations to conduct research and fetch external grants (Gonzalez, 2013). A few higher education institutions are able to more or less successfully attain both missions by internally bifurcating. Perhaps the best example of such a strategy is Arizona State University (ASU), whose main campus in Tempe has a research profile similar to many AAU publics but also includes many demand absorbing satellite campuses throughout the sprawling Phoenix metropolitan region, as well as an extensive network of online programmes and corporate education partnerships. It is reasonable to speculate that there are two ASUs, a traditional research university and a metropolitan demand absorber with global ambitions.

Just as the American system is unusual for having a non-research university set of artisanal higher education institutions it is also unusual in having a populated quadrant C, or middle higher education institutions that follow an undergraduate teaching mission. Some non-elite liberal arts colleges are mission adherent and focus on faculty-intensive undergraduate education in non-professional fields. Yet a growing number of these higher education institutions are drifting into professional and vocational-type education (Baker et al., 2012) and either acquire the research aspirations of quadrant B, or fall downward into the pure demand absorbing territory of quadrant D.

Equity

There are deep ideological commitments to higher education as a source of individual and social uplift in the USA (Marginson, 2016a). Along with hard work, education is a foundational plank in building the 'American dream' of progress though individual achievement. By providing a pathway to mobility it is believed that individuals and communities can improve their social station through participation in higher education. Yet there have always been cracks in this narrative. Burton Clark (1960) famously, and controversially, identified a 'cooling-out' function of American community colleges. Rather than being a pathway to mobility, Clark argued that community colleges absorbed demand and the aspirations that underwrite it while 'cooling-out' those aspirations by indirectly convincing those with aspirations that their goals are out of reach through exposure to educational bureaucracy. Astin and Oseguera (2004) offered a different critique. They document a declining equity of American higher education, noting that family income had become an increasingly important factor in shaping the status of higher education institutions students attended. Over time, higher education in the USA had become more stratified and the possibilities of higher education acting as a great equalizer eroded.

SOCIAL INCLUSION

The first equity proposition (HPS Proposition 14) states:

As participation expands in the HPS phase, equity in the form of social inclusion is enhanced.

The USA experience generally supports this proposition.

Gender equity of access has increased. Women now participate in higher education at a greater number than do men. Elite higher education was generally the province of men. While there have long been women's colleges in the USA until the twentieth century men participated in higher education at much higher rates than did women. By the mid-1990s around 60 per cent of both male and female high school graduates went on to college. However, by 2012 while 61 per cent of men attended college after high school 71 per cent of women did the same (Lopez and Gonzalez-Barrera, 2014).

As participation rates have expanded overall, they have also generally expanded by racial/ethnic group. Table 9.7 shows the percentage of high school graduates who immediately went on to higher education in selected years by racial/ethnic group. In 1980 fewer than 50 per cent all high school graduates attended college, including about 50 per cent of White high school graduates; about 50 per cent of Hispanic or Latino graduates; and 44 per cent of Black or African American high school graduates. By 2012 nearly 68.6 per cent of high school graduates directly went on to college, including 71.7 per cent of White students; 55.7 per cent of Black students; and 63.9 per cent of Hispanic students. All groups increased participation levels, but White students participate at the highest rate among considered groups (note: Asian Americans

Table 9.7. Proportion (%) of high school graduates who immediately thereafter participate in higher education

	Total (%)	White (%)	Black/African American (%)	Hispanic/ Latino (%)
1980	49.3	49.8	44.0	49.6
1990	60.1	63.0	48.9	52.5
2000	63.3	65.7	56.3	52.9
2008	68.6	71.7	55.7	63.9

Source: Author's adaptation from Auld, Fox, and Kewsal Ramni (2010): table 23.1.

are not included in this analysis) and show the greatest increase in participation rates. This same is generally true for low-income students. Students from families with low incomes have generally experienced increase in inclusion as participation grows. However, participation remains stratified by class. Students from the highest income quartile but lowest achievement quartile attend college at roughly the same rate as students from the highest achievement quartile but lowest income quartile (Heller, 2011).

STRATIFICATION OF OUTCOMES

Two facts stand together. The first is that participation in higher education has increased substantially in the USA over the past thirty years. The second is that inequality of incomes and wealth has increased over the same period (Piketty, 2014). Reconciling these facts should be a major task for higher education researchers. This chapter cannot fully take on the problem of what increased participation coupled with what increased inequality means, but it is addressed in relation to the second equity proposition (HPS Proposition 15); namely,

> *Because in the HPS phase the growth of participation is associated with enhanced stratification* [see earlier] *and intensified competition at key transition points* [also see earlier], *all else being equal (i.e. without compensatory state policy), the expansion of participation is associated with a secular tendency to greater social inequality in educational outcomes and, through that, social outcomes.*

Increased participation in higher education has coincided with increased inequality and decreased social mobility in the USA. Thomas Piketty's *Capital in the Twenty-First Century* has demonstrated growing inequality in the USA (and elsewhere) because the return to capital investment has outpaced total economic growth. While much of the wealth in the USA is derived from labour, because capital returns grow faster than labour wages, most workers are left behind while a few amass great wealth. These long term macro-economic processes can be understood in more concrete terms by examining the social mobility of individuals. A study by Raj Chetty and colleagues (2016) found that only 50 per cent of Americans born in the 1980s now have higher incomes than their parents at the same age. Approximately 90 per cent of Americans born in 1940 did better than their parents, as did 60 per cent born in 1970. Even though many Americans born in the 1980s were the first in their family to attend college, as a cohort they have even odds to do better or worse in terms of earned income.

Returning to the first part of the proposition: increased participation is associated with unequal outcomes. One driver of overall inequality is massive economic gains enjoyed by the top income earners (Piketty, 2014). Most of the highest income earners have college degrees but most college graduates do not enjoy top 1 per cent incomes. Selection into the best-compensated jobs is one mechanism that shapes differences in outcomes among college graduates. Lauren Rivera's (2015) ethnographic study about entry level hiring at investment banks, consulting firms, and top law firms, illuminates the selection processes into jobs with 1 per cent earning potential. Elite firms select nearly all of their applicants from elite private universities on the East Coast. Because these universities are overwhelmingly populated with students who are not only talented but also from privileged social backgrounds, the population of prospective candidates begins with the playing field tilted towards elite reproduction. Only a fraction of students at elite universities will be offered one of the most coveted entry-level job opportunities. Rivera finds the selection occurs through refined processes that rewards candidates who exhibit tastes, experiences, and cultural practices associated with an upper class upbringing. Merit as measured by academic performance and demonstrable skills prove less important than elite cultural presentation in determining which students enjoy extraordinary opportunity.

A Brookings Institution analysis found that the economic returns from attending college are smaller for students from poor families (Hershbein, 2016) and another study found that Black graduates of selective universities have, on average, lower incomes than their White counterparts, even when controlling for relevant variables (Gaddis, 2014). The accumulation of evidence about unequal economic outcomes from college graduation strongly suggest that growing participation has been associated with increased differences in graduate outcomes. Some variation in incomes can be explained by field of study (Carnevale, et al., 2015), which may be a reasonable approximation of skills profile. Yet characteristics such as cultural practice, social class, and race seem to be important variables in determining income potential, even when controlling for major and institutional status.

Inequality of outcomes is not only a function of graduate selection by employers. Many steps leading to graduate employment also contribute to stratification of outcomes by those who participate. Not all students who participate in higher education complete a degree. Although participation is near universal, participation in higher education does not guarantee educational success. Of those who attend a four-year institution, fewer than 60 per cent graduate within six years (NCES, 2016: table 326.10).

Sequential models of student stratification have generally given most emphasis to the transition to post-secondary education, with more recent models also considering the status of higher education institutions that students attend. A recently developed 'post-secondary resource trinity model' assumes students' socio-economic and academic resources interact with institutional resources in ways that accentuate the advantage of privileged students.

> This model has three main principles. The first is that all three postsecondary resources, namely socioeconomic, academic, and institutional resources, are positively related to student outcomes; high-SES students are more likely than their low-SES peers to participate in postsecondary and complete a degree, academic preparation is significantly related to postsecondary access and success, and there is a strong relationship between institutional selectivity and graduation rates.
> (Giani, 2015: 123)

Initial empirical evidence to support this model, which suggests that reproduction and extension of social inequality occurs not just in shaping who participates and where they participate, but also the quality of participation. Studies about learning in college (Arum and Roksa, 2011) and collegiate social experiences (Armstrong and Hamilton, 2013) further support the idea that within college unequal cognitive and social development likely furthers social inequity. Without making a claim about causality or the direction of the relationship, the US experience seems to support the claim that (a) high participation is associated with increased inequality of student outcomes; and (b) social inequality increases as inequality of post-secondary student socio-economic outcomes grows. These features of inequality appear self-reinforcing.

SOCIAL REPRODUCTION

The third proposition of the equity chapter (HPS Proposition 16) suggests that higher education becomes an ordinary part of social reproduction when systems reach the HPS stage. The proposition claims:

> *Within a national system, as participation expands in the HPS phase, all else being equal, the positional structure of the higher education system increasingly resembles that of society (albeit with the caveat of Proposition 15). The HPS is increasingly implicated in the reproduction of existing patterns of social equality/inequality.*

Continuing the theme from the previous sub-section, the question here is the extent to which higher education is a driver of social reproduction.

The ordinary and expected relationships between participating in higher education and social mobility are positive. This assumption is often demonstrated empirically by showing that individuals with a degree can expect substantially higher lifetime wages than those without a degree. Most often, these analyses do not consider the wage value added from a degree by controlling for the systematic pre-collegiate differences between degree holders and non-degree holders. But it is well-known that students are not randomly assigned to post-secondary places and that some places are more valuable than others in terms of conferring social and economic opportunity. For this reason, even some of the most strident advocates of college attendance as a vehicle for mobility express concern about the reproductive tendencies of US higher education. Anthony Carnevale of the Georgetown University Center for Higher Education and Work, for example, has identified the higher education system as an 'engine of inequality' (Carnevale and Strohl, 2010). Carnevale notes that White students are over-represented in selective institutions, which offer socially valuable places, whereas Black and Latino students are over-represented in open access, and low status institutions. Over time these enrolment patters have contributed to the widening wage gap between White Americans, and Black and Latino Americans.

Enrolment patterns, then, appear to more closely follow students' social station than their academic performance. What does this mean at the population level? One way to consider the question is by examining how degree holders do relative to all workers (with all levels of education), rather than just contrasting degree holders with non-degree holders. Figure 9.2 shows degree holders' median wage as a share of the median wage of all workers over time. In the early 1990s, the typical worker with a baccalaureate degree or above earned between 80 and 90 per cent more than the typical worker overall (median wage earner among all workers). By the mid-2010s the typical college-educated worker earned just under 70 per cent more than the typical worker overall. Over the fifteen years between 1990 and 2015 the typical college educated worker retained a wage advantage over the working population but that advantaged declined meaningfully. Workers who held a two-year associate degree saw an even more substantial decline in median wage advantage relative to the median wage of all workers. In 1990, the typical worker with an associate degree earned 30 per cent more than the typical worker overall. By 2015 that median associates degree wage advantage slipped to below 5 per cent. In other words, the typical wage for a worker with an associate degree is similar to the typical wage of all workers, including those in occupations that require no post-secondary training.

What does the decline in the median wage of college educated workers relative to all workers mean? As more workers hold degrees, of course, the median degree wage will necessarily move closer to the median wage overall. About four out of ten (42.3 per cent) adults 25 and older hold an associate degree or higher in the USA (Ryan and Bauman, 2016). Given the broad diffusion of degrees among the working population it is not

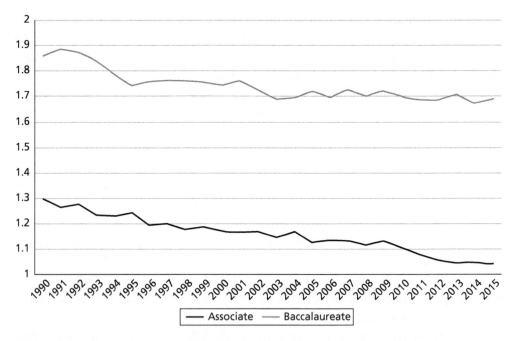

Figure 9.2. Median degree holder wage as share of overall median wage, 1990–2015

Source: Author's analysis of US Census Bureau data, Table P16.

surprising that the typical wage for college graduates is approaching the typical wage overall. For the typical worker with an associate degree, going to and completing a college degree appears to result in 'keeping up' rather than 'getting ahead'. This does not mean the economic value of attending college is hollowed out. Participation and completion may be a backstop against downward mobility for the middle class who are able to convert their financial and social resources into a college degree but unable to amass inter-generational wealth sufficient to allow children to live well without earned income. To put it another way, it seems plausible that college in the USA more often reproduces social status rather than propels mobility.

CAN THE STATE REDISTRIBUTE OPPORTUNITIES?

The final proposition of the equity chapter (HPS Proposition 17) considers the potential for state intervention in the distribution of educational and social opportunities. The proposition claims:

> *As the HPS boundary of participation expands it becomes more difficult for the state and/or autonomous educational systems/institutions to secure a redistribution of educational opportunities, and, through that, of social opportunities.*

Again, the US experience is broadly in line with this assessment. For decades, the USA has implemented policy goals at the federal and state levels designed to increase participation in higher education. Few of these policies explicitly sought to redistribute educational opportunities and in total they appeared not to have resulted in greater equity of educational outcomes.

Affirmative action had been the main mechanism to redistribute educational opportunities. At the Federal level, affirmative action was first adopted in the 1960s as a policy for hiring more women and racial and ethnic minorities into government jobs. In the following decades, most states implemented affirmative action policies designed to give some preference to women and minority groups that had been under-represented in higher education. However, affirmative action, while narrowly upheld by the Supreme Court as a lawful procedure in admission practices, has come under intense political resistance. Eight states (including California), making up nearly a third of the US population, have official bans on affirmative action at public colleges and universities (Potter, 2014).

At the federal level, efforts to expand college access have done little to redistribute opportunities. In fact, attention to aid through the tax credit, loans, and support for for-profit institutions may have had the effect of biasing opportunities downward for disadvantaged students (Mettler, 2014). By expanding access through tax credits the federal government has privileged families with incomes sufficient to have a substantial tax obligation. By expanding financial aid primarily through loans while cutting grants the federal government has exposed lower income students to a substantial debt burden. By allowing federal aid to flow to for-profit providers the federal government has encouraged enrolment in higher education institutions that have high tuition fees and offer credentials of dubious value. These policies—supported by both Democrats and Republicans—have helped to expand participation, but have done nothing to progressively redistribute educational opportunities. Mettler (2014) shows that there is strong political support for access, but very little support for policies that support a form of participation that will promote upward social mobility. In other words, a short analysis of government policy in the USA supports the proposition that governments have a difficult time—or little will—to redistribute educational opportunities.

Conclusion

As stated at the outset of this chapter, the USA is the prototypical HPS. For that reason alone it may not be surprising that the US case largely affirms the propositions advanced in the first part of this book. This does not, however, mean that the US case is typical or that other HPS are likely to converge on the US model. But the analysis presented in this chapter should offer additional support for the overall supposition that HPS share social features. Since the purpose of this chapter was to evaluate the extent to which the US case supports or refutes the propositions advanced in this volume, the chapter will conclude by way of summary rather than coda.

Analysis of the USA strongly confirms the three propositions advanced about governance. The US system is subject to multi-level control, coordination, and accountability. Governance addresses the management of horizontal differentiation and internal managerial capacity has grown. Propositions from the vertical diversity chapter are largely affirmed, but with more qualifications. Multiversities become central during the massification period and although there is drift towards the multiversity form, the share of enrolments to multiversities has not continued to increase; however, provision has generally become less rather than more diverse as predicted. If diversity between higher education institutions in the USA is not growing, diversity within, as suggested by the general chapter, does seem to be increasing in some ways (more divisions and inter-disciplinary) but not universally.

The case of the USA is largely supportive of the volume's claims about system stratification. There is a general tendency towards bifurcation into an elite, 'artisanal', and demand absorbing segments. This process is driven by intensified competition among students for the best seats in the system, variable tuition fees, and intensified competition among higher education institutions. The processes of bifurcation are not complete and a large middle layer has developed.

Similarly, the US case substantially supports the book's overall claims about the role of HPS in fostering and limiting social equity. In absolute terms participation has expanded and a wider breadth of society has access to higher education. With increased access, however, there is also greater inequality of outcomes as some graduates are much more likely to enjoy privileged social positions than others. As a result, higher education is a mechanism that generally contributes to social reproduction and government efforts to intervene in order to promote greater equity have had but modest effect.

In the end, the higher education system in the USA is part and parcel of American social life and political economy. Like the US healthcare system, the higher education system is massive, expensive, and broadly but unequally accessible. The system is defined both by excellence and by questionable providers and access to these segments is shaped by social position, which means that value added outcomes are predicted by how one participates. Higher education is a social institution that both reflects and constitutes society.

■ REFERENCES

Allen, I. E. and Seaman, J. (2008). *Staying the Course: Online Education in the United States, 2008*. Newburyport, MA: Sloan Consortium.

Allen, I. E., Seaman, J., Poulin, R., and Straut, T. T. (2015). *Online Report Card: Tracking Online Education in the United States*. Newburyport, MA: Sloan Foundation. http://onlinelearningsurvey. com/reports/onlinereportcard.pdf

Armstrong, E. A. and Hamilton, L. T. (2013). *Paying for the Party*. Cambridge, MA: Harvard University Press.

Arum, R. and Roksa, J. (2011). *Academically Adrift: Limited Learning on College Campuses*. Chicago: University of Chicago Press.

Astin, A. W. and Oseguera, L. (2004). The declining 'equity' of American higher education. *The Review of Higher Education* 27(3), 321–41.

Baker, V. L., Baldwin, R. G., and Makker, S. (2012). Where are they now? Revisiting Breneman's study of liberal arts colleges. *Liberal Education* 98(3), 48–53.

Bastedo, M. N. (2009). Convergent institutional logics in public higher education: State policy-making and governing board activism. *The Review of Higher Education* 32(2), 209–34.

Bastedo, M. N. and Gumport, P. J. (2003). Access to what? Mission differentiation and academic stratification in US public higher education. *Higher Education* 46(3), 341–59.

Bok, D. (2004). *Universities in the Marketplace: The Commercialization of Higher Education*. Princeton: Princeton University Press.

Bowen, H. R. (1980). *The Costs of Higher Education: How Much Do Colleges and Universities Spend per Student and How Much Should They Spend?* San Francisco, CA: Jossey-Bass.

Bowman, N. A. and Bastedo, M. N. (2009). Getting on the front page: Organizational reputation, status signals, and the impact of US News and World Report on student decisions. *Research in Higher Education* 50(5), 415–36.

Brint, S., Proctor, K., Murphy, S. P., Turk-Bicakci, L., and Hanneman, R. A. (2009). General education models: Continuity and change in the US undergraduate curriculum, 1975–2000. *The Journal of Higher Education* 80(6), 605–42.

Brint, S., Cantwell, A. M., and Saxena, P. (2012). Disciplinary categories, majors, and under-graduate academic experiences: Rethinking Bok's 'underachieving colleges' thesis. *Research in Higher Education* 53(1), 1–25.

CCIHE (Carnegie Classification of Institutions of Higher Education) (2015). 2015 update facts and figures. http://carnegieclassifications.iu.edu/downloads/CCIHE2015-FactsFigures.pdf

Cantwell, B. (2016). The new prudent man: Financial-academic capitalism and inequality in higher education. *Higher Education, Stratification, and Workforce Development*. Dordrecht: Springer International Publishing, pp. 173–92.

Carey, K. (2016). *The End of College: Creating the Future of Learning and the University of Everywhere*. New York: Riverhead Books.

Carnevale, A. P. and Strohl, J. (2010). How increasing college access is increasing inequality, and what to do about it, in R. Kahlenberg (ed.), *Rewarding Strivers: Helping Low-income Students Succeed in College*. New York: Century Foundation Books, pp. 1–231.

Carnevale, A. P., Cheah, B., and Hanson, A. R. (2015). *The Economic Value of College Majors*. Georgetown: Georgetown University Center on Education and the Workforce.

Center for Postsecondary Education (2015). Carnegie Classification of Institutions of Higher Education: 2015 update facts and figures. http://carnegieclassifications.iu.edu/downloads/ CCIHE2015-FactsFigures.pdf

Chetty, R., Grusky, D., Hell, M., Hendren, N., Manduca, R., and Narang, J. (2016). *The Fading American Dream: Trends in Absolute Income Mobility Since 1940* (No. w22910). New York: National Bureau of Economic Research.

Clark, B. R. (1960). The 'cooling-out' function in higher education. *American Journal of Sociology* LXV(May), 569–76.

College Board (2014). *Trends in College Pricing, 2014*. New York: College Board.

Derochers, D. M. and Hurlburt, S. (2016). *Trends in College Spending: 2003–2013*. Washington, DC: American Institutions of Research.

Desrochers, D. M. and Kirshstein, R. (2014). Labor intensive or labor expensive? Changing staffing and compensation patterns in higher education. Issue brief. Delta Cost Project at American Institutes for Research.

Dougherty, K. J., Jones, S. M., Lahr, H., Natow, R. S., Pheatt, L., and Reddy, V. (2016). Looking inside the black box of performance funding for higher education: Policy instruments, organizational obstacles, and intended and unintended impacts. *RSF: The Russell Sage Foundation Journal of the Social Sciences* 2(1), 147–73.

Gaddis, S. M. (2014). Discrimination in the credential society: An audit study of race and college selectivity in the labor market. *Social Forces* 93(4), 1451–79.

Garces, L. M. (2012). Racial diversity, legitimacy, and the citizenry: The impact of affirmative action bans on graduate school enrollment. *The Review of Higher Education* 36(1), 93–132.

Geiger, R. L. (2004). *Knowledge and Money: Research Universities and the Paradox of the Marketplace*. Stanford: Stanford University Press.

Geiger, R. (2010). The ten generations of American higher education, in P. G. Altbach, R. O. Berdahl, and P. J. Gumport (eds), *American Higher Education in the Twenty-First Century: Social, Political, and Economic Challenges*. New York: Johns Hopkins University Press.

Gerald, D. and Haycock, K. (2006). *Engines of Inequality: Diminishing Equity in the Nation's Premier Public Universities*. Washington, DC: Education Trust.

Giani, M. S. (2015). The postsecondary resource trinity model: Exploring the interaction between socioeconomic, academic, and institutional resources. *Research in Higher Education* 56(2), 105–26.

Gonzales, L. D. (2012). Responding to mission creep: Faculty members as cosmopolitan agents. *Higher Education* 64(3), 337–53.

Gonzales, L. D. (2013). Faculty sensemaking and mission creep: Interrogating institutionalized ways of knowing and doing legitimacy. *The Review of Higher Education* 36(2), 179–209.

Gumport, P. (2011). In *American Higher Education in the Twenty-First Century*.

Hearn, J. C. (2001). Access to postsecondary education: Financing equity in an evolving context, in M. B. Paulsen and J. C. Smart (eds), *The Finance of Higher Education: Theory, Research, Policy, and Practice*. New York: Agathon Press, 439–60.

Hearn, J. C., Griswold, C. P., and Marine, G. M. (1996). Region, resources, and reason: A contextual analysis of state tuition and student aid policies. *Research in Higher Education* 37(3), 141–78.

Heller, D. E. (2011). Trends in the affordability of public colleges and universities. In D. E. Heller, *The States and Public Higher Education Policy: Affordability, Access, and Accountability*. Baltimore: Johns Hopkins University Press, pp. 13–35.

Hershbein, B. (2016). A college degree is worth less if you are raised poor. Brookings Social Mobility Memos. https://www.brookings.edu/blog/social-mobility-memos/2016/02/19/a-college-degree-is-worth-less-if-you-are-raised-poor/

Hoxby, C. M. and Avery, C. (2012). The missing 'one-offs': The hidden supply of high-achieving, low income students. No. w18586, National Bureau of Economic Research.

Jacob, B., McCall, B., and Stange, K. M. (2013). College as country club: Do colleges cater to students' preferences for consumption? No. w18745, National Bureau of Economic Research.

Jaquette, O. (2013). Why do colleges become universities? Mission drift and the enrollment economy. *Research in Higher Education* 54(5), 514–43.

Jencks, C. and Riesman, D. (1968). *The Academic Revolution*. Garden City, NY: Doubleday.

Kauppinen, I. and Cantwell, B. (2014). Transnationalization of academic capitalism through global production networks, in B. Cantwell and I. Kauppinen (eds), *Academic Capitalism in the Age of Globalization*. Baltimore, MD: Johns Hopkins University Press, pp. 147–65.

Kerr, C. (2001). *The Uses of the University*. Cambridge, MA: Harvard University. (Originally published 1963.)

Leslie, L. L., Slaughter, S., Taylor, B. J., and Zhang, L. (2012). How do revenue variations affect expenditures within US research universities? *Research in Higher Education* 53(6), 614–39.

Lopez, M. and Gonzalez-Barrera, A. (2014). Women's college enrollment gains leave men behind. Pew Research Center. http://www.pewresearch.org/fact-tank/2014/03/06/womens-college-enrollment-gains-leave-men-behind/

Lucas, S. R. (2001). Effectively maintained inequality: Education transitions, track mobility, and social background effects. *American Journal of Sociology* 106(6), 1642–90.

Marginson, S. (2006). Dynamics of national and global competition in higher education. *Higher Education* 52(1), 1–39.

Marginson, S. (2013). The impossibility of capitalist markets in higher education. *Journal of Education Policy* 28(3), 353–70.

Marginson, S. (2016a). *The Dream is Over*. Berkeley, CA: University of California Press.

Marginson, S. (2016b). High participation systems of higher education. *The Journal of Higher Education* 87(2), 243–71.

Marginson, S. (2016c). The worldwide trend to high participation higher education: Dynamics of social stratification in inclusive systems. *Higher Education* 72(4), 413–34.

Marginson, S. and Rhoades, G. (2002). Beyond national states, markets, and systems of higher education: A glonacal agency heuristic. *Higher education* 43(3), 281–309.

Mathies, C. and Slaughter, S. (2013). University trustees as channels between academe and industry: Toward an understanding of the executive science network. *Research Policy* 42(6), 1286–300.

McCormick, A. C. and Zhao, C. M. (2005). Rethinking and reframing the Carnegie classification. *Change: The Magazine of Higher Learning* 37(5), 51–7.

McDonough, P. M. (1997). *Choosing Colleges: How Social Class and Schools Structure Opportunity*. New York: Suny Press.

Mettler, S. (2014). *Degrees of Inequality: How the Politics of Higher Education Sabotaged the American Dream*. New York: Basic Books.

Morphew, C. C. (2002). 'A rose by any other name': Which colleges became universities. *The Review of Higher Education* 25(2), 207–23.

Morphew, C. C. and Huisman, J. (2002). Using institutional theory to reframe research on academic drift. *Higher education in Europe* 27(4), 491–506.

NCES (National Center for Education Statistics) (2012). *Integrated Postsecondary Education Data System (IPEDS)*. https://nces.ed.gov/ipeds

NCES (National Center for Education Statistics) (2014). *Integrated Postsecondary Education Data System (IPEDS)*. https://nces.ed.gov/ipeds

NCES (National Center for Education Statistics) (2016). *Integrated Postsecondary Education Data System (IPEDS)*. https://nces.ed.gov/ipeds

NSF (National Science Foundation) (2015). *Science and Engineering Indicators*. Arlington, VA: NSF. http://www.pewresearch.org/daily-number/most-parents-expect-their-children-to-attend-college/

OECD (Organisation for Economic Co-operation and Development) (2013). *Education at a Glance*. Paris: OECD.

OECD (Organisation for Economic Co-operation and Development) (2016). *Education at a Glance*. Paris: OECD.

Piketty, T. (2014). *Capital in the Twenty-first Century*. Cambridge, MA: The Belknap Press.

Potter (2014). What can we learn from states with affirmative action bans? New York: New Century Foundation. https://www.census.gov/content/dam/Census/library/publications/2016/demo/p20-578.pdf

Pusser, B. (2004). *Burning Down the House: Politics, Governance, and Affirmative Action at the University of California*. Albany, NY: State University of New York Press.

Pusser, B., Slaughter, S., and Thomas, S. L. (2006). Playing the board game: An empirical analysis of university trustee and corporate board interlocks. *The Journal of Higher Education* 77(5), 747–75.

Rhoades, G. (2014). The higher education we choose, collectively: Reembodying and repoliticizing choice. *The Journal of Higher Education* 85(6), 917–30.

Rhoades, G. and Sporn, B. (2002). New models of management and shifting modes and costs of production: Europe and the United States. *Tertiary Education & Management* 8(1), 3–28.

Rivera, L. A. (2015). *Pedigree: How Elite Students Get Elite Jobs*. Princeton, NJ: Princeton University.

Rooksby, J. H. and Collins, C. S. (2016). Trademark trends and brand activity in higher education. *The Review of Higher Education* 40(1), 33–61.

Ryan, C. L. and Bauman, K. (2016). Educational attainment in the United States: 2015. https://www.census.gov/content/dam/Census/library/publications/2016/demo/p20-578.pdf

Slaughter, S. (1990). *The Higher Learning and High Technology: Dynamics of Higher Education Policy Formation*. New York: SUNY Press.

Slaughter, S. and Cantwell, B. (2012). Transatlantic moves to the market: The United States and the European Union. *Higher Education* 63(5), 583–606.

Slaughter, S. and Leslie, L. L. (1997). *Academic Capitalism: Politics, Policies, and the Entrepreneurial University*. Baltimore, MD: Johns Hopkins University Press.

Slaughter, S. and Rhoades, G. (2004). *Academic Capitalism and the New Economy: Markets, State, and Higher Education*. Baltimore, MD: Johns Hopkins University Press.

Slaughter, S., Thomas, S. L., Johnson, D. R., and Barringer, S. N. (2014). Institutional conflict of interest: The role of interlocking directorates in the scientific relationships between universities and the corporate sector. *The Journal of Higher Education* 85(1), 1–35.

Slaughter, S., Taylor, B. J., and Rosinger, K. O. (2015). A critical reframing of human capital theory in US higher education, in A.M. Martinez-Aleman, E. M. Bensimon, and B. Pusser (eds), *Critical Approaches to the Study of Higher Education: A Practical Introduction*. Baltimore: Johns Hopkins University Press, 80–102.

Snyder, T. D. (1993). *120 Years of American Education: A Statistical Portrait*. New York: DIANE National Center for Educational Statistics/Publishing.

Stephan, P. E. (2012). *How Economics Shapes Science*. Cambridge, MA: Harvard University Press.

Taylor, B. J. and Morphew, C. C. (2013). Institutional contributions to financing students: Trends in general subsidies, 1987–2007, in D. E. Heller and C. Callender (eds), *Student Financing of Higher Education: A Comparative Perspective*. New York: Routledge, pp. 225–51.

Taylor, B. J., Cantwell, B., and Slaughter, S. (2013). Quasi-markets in US higher education: The humanities and institutional revenues. *The Journal of Higher Education*, 84(5), 675–707.

Teitelbaum, M. S. (2014). *Falling Behind? Boom, Bust, and the Global Race for Scientific Talent*. Princeton: Princeton University Press.

Toma, J. D. (2010). *Building Organizational Capacity: Strategic Management in Higher Education*. New York: JHU Press.

Toma, J. D. (2012). Institutional strategy: Position for prestige, in M. N. Bastedo (ed.), *The Organization of Higher Education: Managing Colleges for a New Era*. Baltimore, MA: Johns Hopkins University Press, pp. 118–59.

UNESCO (United Nations Educational and Cultural Organisation) Institute for Statistics (2016). Education: Gross enrolment ratio by level of education. Data query. http://data.uis.unesco.org/?queryid=142

Weisbrod, B. A. (2009). *The Nonprofit Economy*. Cambridge, MA: Harvard University Press.

Winston, G. C. (1999). Subsidies, hierarchy and peers: The awkward economics of higher education. *The Journal of Economic Perspectives* 13(1), 13–36.

Wise, L. (2016). Positioning for elite and quasi-elite colleges and universities in the United States: Parent and student strategies for 'maintaining advantage' in new economic and postsecondary context, in S. Slaughter and B. J. Taylor (eds), *Higher Education, Stratification, and Workforce Development: Competitive Advantage in Europe, the US, and Canada*. New York: Springer, pp. 271–90.

World Bank (2017). Data and statistics. http://data.worldbank.org

Zemsky, R. and Massy, W. F. (1990). Cost containment: Committing to a new economic reality. *Change: The Magazine of Higher Learning* 22(6), 16–22.

10 Regulated Isomorphic Competition and the Middle Layer of Institutions: High Participation Higher Education in Australia

Simon Marginson

Introduction

Australia occupies a large island-continent of 7.7 million square kilometres located off the southeast end of Asia between the Indian, Pacific, and Southern Oceans with the 8,844 islands of the Indonesian archipelago immediately to the north. Australia is the world's sixth largest country by area, four-fifths the size of the United States of America (USA) but relatively sparsely populated. The interior is arid and most of the nation's 24.6 million people, as estimated in July 2017, and most of the forty-three Australian universities and other higher education institutions are concentrated in a small number of coastal cities, principally Sydney, Melbourne, and Brisbane/Gold Coast in the east of the continent. A British settler state that was first proclaimed as a colonial possession in 1788 and achieved formal nationhood in 1901, Australia continues to be shaped by its distinctive combination of British history and Asia-proximate geography and economy. The Indigenous population of Australia suffered badly at the hands of the British invader through land displacement, massacre, and disease, and was fragmented by policies of forced resettlement and the selective removal of children but is now increasing more rapidly than the settler population and reached 669,900 in the 2011 census, 3 per cent of the total (ABS, 2016b).

The nation retains the British monarch as the nominal head of state, its flag includes the imperial British ensign, and it follows British norms in government, policy, business, professions, education, and science. It is also influenced by the USA, like other English-speaking nations. Demography is increasingly mixed, reflecting the heterogeneity of Australia's history and geography. There is large-scale annual migration from on the one hand East and South Asia, on the other hand United Kingdom (UK)/Ireland and Europe. In March 2016, 28 per cent of the population was foreign born which was the highest level recorded since the colonial 1890s. The 2011 census recorded 39 per cent foreign born in Sydney and 35 per cent in Melbourne (ABS, 2014, 2016a). International students, four-fifths of whom are from Asia, now constitute 30 per cent of all onshore higher education students enrolled in HEIs and have become a primary source of high-skill migrants.

POLITICAL ECONOMY AND POLITICAL CULTURE

Australia is a large producer of energy and minerals with most exports going to China, South Korea, and Japan. Manufacturing is weak but services strong with education the third largest export, after coal and iron ore. In 2015 Australia's gross domestic product (GDP) per head in current US dollars and purchasing power parity (PPP) was US$45,501, falling between Denmark and Canada, compared to US$56,116 in the USA, US$14,450 in China, and a world average of US$15,546. Total 2015 GDP was US$1,082 billion, twenty-first of all countries (World Bank, 2017). National unemployment was at 5.9 per cent in October 2015 with an adult labour force participation rate of 65 per cent (ABS, 2015). Youth unemployment is lower than in most of Western Europe.

Australia has strongly meritocratic public values. There is little patience for inherited claims—wealth and status are only legitimated by competition—and equality of opportunity, including educational opportunity, is a central principle. A spare sense of entitlement and inclusion, and rejection of extremes of top or bottom, are pervasive characteristics of Australian life and of higher education. Equality of treatment, though not equality of condition or outcomes, is routinely expected. Economic inequality in Australia is more pronounced than in most of Europe but less than in the USA and UK (Piketty, 2014: 316). Australia lacks inherited wealth and great fortunes on the Anglo-American imperial scale. The mega-rich group is smaller. Low-income earners are better off. Nevertheless, Australia shares the common (though not universal) worldwide trend to greater work-based income inequality. In 1980, the top 1 per cent of income earners received 5 per cent of all income but by 2010 this had risen to 9 per cent, the highest since the early 1950s. The top 0.1 per cent moved from 1 to 3 per cent (Leigh, 2013: 50–1). In comparison, the top 1 per cent the USA saw its share rise from 10 to 20 per cent from 1980–2010. There has been a more dramatic shift in wealth distribution in Australia. Since the 1980s the richest 0.001 per cent have seen a sharp growth of wealth-holding in their favour (p. 57). Inter-generational social mobility in Australia is higher than in the USA and UK but in the bottom half of the OECD table, below Canada and well below northern and central Europe (Corak, 2006, 2012). The main reason for this is public policy. In 2012 Australia's Gini coefficient for market-generated incomes was 0.463, below inequality in Finland (0.488) and Germany (0.501) in Germany, but government taxes and public transfers reduced market-generated inequalities by only 29.6 per cent in Australia, similar to the level of redistribution in Canada but well below the effects of taxes and public transfers in securing greater equality in Finland (46.7 per cent) and Germany (42.3 per cent). The respective Gini coefficients for after-tax income were Australia 0.326, Finland 0.260, Germany 0.289 (OECD, 2015). Tax revenue as a proportion of GDP was just 27 per cent in 2013–14, limiting the scope for redistribution.

As this suggests Australia has an Anglo-American political culture, in which the state is strong but operates across a relatively narrow domain. There is a limited potential for publicly financed and/or provided goods, especially high quality public goods delivered free on a universal basis as in the Nordic world. Though the state played a larger role in the past (e.g. see Macintyre, 2015), since the 1980s Australia has been enthusiastic about neoliberal business modelling, cost recovery, and competition in quasi-markets, in higher education and elsewhere. Unlike the USA, Australia combines a neoliberal financial logic with targeted welfare to maintain social inclusion. The minimum wage and public safety net provide some protection for the unemployed, sick, and disabled. However, taken together, targeting and quasi-markets tend to suppress expectations about common economic and social rights.

HIGHER EDUCATION

In Australia most tertiary students are enrolled in degree programmes of three years or more. In all 99.5 per cent of degree places and more than two-thirds of all tertiary places at two-year diploma level are provided in designated HEIs, the vast majority in the thirty-seven public universities. There are three domestic private universities, two small foreign private universities and ninety-eight other private institutions, but all private institutions command just 8.0 per cent of the national total of 1,410,133 higher education students (2015). Alongside higher education are vocational education and training (VET) institutions, which enrolled 3.9 million students in 2014, mostly part-time, with 13.5 per cent at tertiary level and 0.2 per cent in degree-length programmes (NCVER, 2015; DET, n.d.). This chapter will focus primarily on the nation's HEIs which constitute a discrete and hegemonic system.

In Australian higher education, high levels of mission homogeneity and transparency on the basis of data collection make the system dynamics especially visible. Policy frameworks and internal organizational cultures resemble those of the UK. Both countries have treasury-led political systems integrated with a financial services sector that dominates the economy. Australia, unlike the UK, is a federation in which the states are in a strong constitutional position but since World War II national government has monopolized income-taxing power. This economically centralized federalism underpinned the takeover of higher education policy by the national government in the half century after 1960 (Carnoy et al., 2018). Like their British counterparts Australian HEIs underwent comprehensive neoliberal system reform at an early stage, orchestrated in 1987–92 by the national minister for education, the Labor Party's John Dawkins (Marginson and Considine 2000; Crowther, Marginson, Norton, and Wells, 2013). In both nations HEIs are led by executive presidents and shaped by financial imperatives. Both claim a general research culture and fulfil it in the top half of the institutional hierarchy. The systems have been cut from the same cloth, though perhaps UK intellectual life is more robust (in the leading institutions at least) and Australian HEIs more instrumental. There has been much policy borrowing between the two polities. Both developed a unitary system by abolishing a state-created second sector; both charge high tuition but soften it with income-contingent tuition loans, whereby repayment is delayed and subject to the capacity to pay; both provide large-scale commercial international education. As in other limited-liberal polities, university autonomy in Australia is vigorously asserted and also over-determined by state control. Academic agency is fostered so as to be proactive and productive and is also regulated in detail. Yet while boxed and bound by economic framings, it often leaks out from under them in uncontrolled ways.

For despite the policy rhetoric Australian higher education is more than the living clone of an abstract neoliberal formula. As in all university-led systems, competition between institutions and within disciplinary communities is fundamentally driven by status (prestige) rather than revenues or profitability, even though revenues are an important secondary objective as a means to the realization of mission. The economic imaginary does not fully explain system dynamics (Marginson, 2016b: ch. 7). Moreover, as is the case everywhere neoliberal norms are implemented in the context of a distinctive national history and political culture.

Australian higher education combines high participation, a mission template in which all HEIs are nominally equivalent and there is scepticism about status claims of the leading universities, with modelling of the sector as a competitive market and an investment in private goods. In the neoliberal era only two unambiguous public goods are expected from higher education and research: contributions to the national economy, and to individual opportunity. Opportunity is understood in human capital terms, as employability and rates of return; and the individual private benefits, summed together, are the sector's contribution to the economy—or so it seems. Other personal and collective benefits receive little policy attention, except the contribution of basic research to economic innovation. The position and prospects of individual HEIs are seen as determined in an American style education market in which, nominally, they earn their outcomes. Yet this market is framed by the state; and equity as social inclusion and equal opportunity are deeply felt. Though little is done about the living conditions of Indigenous families in Australia, there is much effort to open paths for Indigenous students into university. The state defines the performance measures, sustains the global viability of multiversity instituitions, sets tuition arrangements that protect access and limit market revenues to the top institutions, and helps middle institutions to become more competitive.

Growth of Higher Education

The general HPS Proposition 3 states that

> *Once transition from a primarily agricultural economy is achieved, the long-term growth of HPS is independent of political economic factors such as economic growth and patterns of labour market demand; patterns of public and private funding of higher education; the roles of public and private institutions; and system organization and modes of governance.*

The ultimate driver of growth is not state largesse but rising social demand for opportunities, rooted in family desires for social position. These desires are open-ended and spread and elevate over time, as aspirations for education extend to formerly under-represented groups, the cost of non-participation is more evident, and families find they must prolong education simply to maintain position.

> *In HPS there is no intrinsic limit to the spread of family aspirations for participation in higher education until universality is reached; and no intrinsic limit to the level of social position to which families/students may aspire.* (HPS Proposition 2)

Both propositions are wholly consistent with the Australian experience. In the 1960s Australia reached the point where degrees were so necessary in the middle class that growing demand for higher education was self-sustaining. As in the USA (Marginson, 2016a: ch. 2) but at a lower level of participation, the period between the late 1950s and the late 1970s was a time of rapidly rising expectations, when popular demand for secondary and higher education was matched by expanding public funding (Marginson, 1997). There was a brief downward fluctuation in demand amid recession in the late 1970s but since then nothing has interrupted the progress towards universal participation. Whether in boom or recession, and regardless of the many changes in tuition, each time national government has expanded the number of funded places, the opportunities have been fully taken up (Figure 10.1). In this gender equalization has played a significant role. Between 1965 and 1975 the proportion of students who were women increased from 24.0 to 40.6 per cent, partly boosted by including all teachers' college students in the data, and then rose to 55.2 per cent by 2000 (DET, n.d.).

Political parties, especially the Labor Party, have consistently drawn support by promising to expand higher education. Australian higher education's neoliberal moment, the Dawkins system reorganization in 1988, was premised on 60 per cent enrolment growth, part financed by income-contingent tuition loans. The enrolment

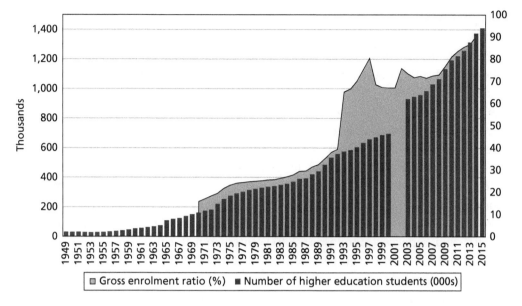

Figure 10.1. Higher education enrolments, Australia, 1949–2015 (thousands); and gross enrolment ratio, Australia, 1970–2015 (%)

Sources: For higher education enrolments DET (2017). Student inclusion expanded in 1965 (colleges of advanced education were added), 1973 (government teachers' colleges), 1974 (private teachers' colleges). Until 2000 data were collected annually for 31 March enrolment. From 2003 data include all enrolments during the calendar year, and all private providers. Expansion of data coverage in 1993 and data changes in 1998 and 2002 stymie comparability. For GER, UNESCO (2017).

target was achieved seven years ahead of schedule. There was a smaller growth surge in the early 2000s; and in 2009, Labor lifted the cap on publicly subsidized places for domestic students, allowing the social desire for opportunity to be fully matched by the supply of places: in what became called the 'demand-driven system', enrolments grew by a quarter between 2008 and 2014 (DET, n.d.). The generic status of higher education explains why demand for degrees is consistently more robust than demand for VET. Each jump in higher education participation has undermined the scope of VET to become a strong choice on the basis of its vocational mission. While VET has been severely under-funded since the 1990s, no government has sought to reduce higher education enrolments or substantially reduce total public outlays despite the low tax/spend political culture. Successive regimes have allowed per student public funding to fall as growth has proceeded, transferring more of the financing to students, whose regulated tuition now constitutes almost half the average cost of provision, though student contributions vary markedly by discipline. Under income-contingent loan repayment arrangements, variations in price have negligible effects on demand, except for part-timers who pay in the year of study (Chapman et al., 2014). Between the surges in domestic student numbers the system has continued to expand, as full-fee international student enrolments, deregulated in 1985, grew at an annual average rate of 14 per cent a year until the late 2000s.

Corporate Governance

In his system reorganization minister Dawkins abolished the binary system and the colleges of advanced education, creating a unitary university sector, the Unified National System, in which institutions competed for private funding, a growing proportion of public funds and the status underpinning competitive position. Dawkins encouraged strategic and entrepreneurial leaders who had new freedoms to raise non-government revenues and expand their scope via site acquisition and off shore ventures. With grants per student reduced by 8 per cent in 1988 (Burke, 1988), survival and development rested on growth in domestic students via merger and expansion, and international education. Full-fee international students, often managed by commercial university companies, became the main source of discretionary funding for research and for sites, facilities and services (Marginson, 2007). International education grew to become Australia's third largest export sector and institutionalized the entrepreneurial mindset within higher education. By 2015 the international student share of student load was 26.3 per cent, the highest in the OECD nations aside from Luxembourg; the export of higher education services generated US$10.2 billion in 2015–16 (ICEF Monitor, 2016), and international student fees provided almost one-fifth of the income of HEIs (DET, n.d.). At the same time, performance regimes became installed in non-profit academic operations.

HPS Propositions 4 and 5 on governance state that

- *HPS are governed by multi-level control, coordination, and accountability mechanisms*; and
- *HPS governance tends to involve the management of horizontal differentiation.*

The propositions are only partly true of Australian higher education. In folding up the colleges of advanced education Dawkins—whose first goal in national system redesign was to facilitate growth—completed the process of national takeover of erstwhile state government functions. If this was 'management' of horizontal differentiation, it was management by eliminating mission diversity (see later) and eliminating the old form of multi-level governance. Since Dawkins, despite ever-present legal potentials for a renewed state government role (Marginson, 2018) there has been no dilution of this national control. Yet the proposition about multi-level governance is true, at another level of governance. In the reform three poorly delineated levels of governance (national government, state government, institutional), whereby institutions could slip between national government and the states, were replaced by on the one hand tighter national control, on the other hand devolution of certain control and coordination functions downwards to university leaders, reimagined as quasi-business executives. The new system was governed in classic neoliberal fashion by state steering from a distance via rules, incentives, and formulae. Corporate autonomy took the form of 'responsibilization' (Rose, 1999), in which the duty of the central state for outcomes and quality was transferred down within the framework of the market to interacting managers and 'customers'. Managers' choices were regulated by government, with compliance secured as much by incentives as by prohibitions. For example, in the context of scarce public monies the state could use small parcels of funds subject to competitive bidding to shape institutional innovations at the margin. In the larger and more complex institutions of the HPS era, with their multiple sites and accountability to a larger and more varied group of stakeholders, and reformed to insert additional layers with corresponding performance management systems (teaching or research group, department, faculty, academic school, administrative division, site), internal institutional *'multi-level coordination and accountability'*, eased by electronic communications and data systems, positioned each university president as a mini-minister within the institution.

In other words, the first proposition on governance should be read alongside the third proposition (HPS Proposition 6):

> *HPS complex multi-level accountability and coordination, coupled with system differentiation, result in higher education institutions adopting increasingly corporate forms and robust internal governance and management capacities.*

Australia exemplifies this third proposition to a marked degree. The extent to which corporatization was driven by growth, or market ideology and neoliberal blueprints, is open to debate. However, during the reforms institutional leaders testified that new business systems facilitated their management of size and complexity (Marginson and Considine, 2000).

The transition to an executive mode of internal governance was complete within a decade of the Dawkins reforms. Central leader groups expanded in size and functions and over-shadowed faculty boards. Executive deans with budgetary control came to lead fields of study and eclipsed faculty assemblies. Quasi-business strategic planning, quality assurance systems, performance targets, customer focus, risk management, and executive salaries are now general to the sector, though the vast majority of academic leaders come from academic ranks; the business culture jars with the sector-specific language of shared learning, personal development, and scholarly creativity; and in parts of the stronger research universities a residual collegial power remains. In institutional governance Dawkins and his ministerial successors have encouraged the reform of governing councils along the lines of corporate boards, with less members, mostly external to the institution, and the reduction or elimination of representatives of staff and students. Here national government has been less uniformly successful—state governments still control the legislation constituting public universities, including their councils—but a common mission of corporate oversight has been established.

Horizontal Diversity

The central mechanism of the Dawkins reform, which entrenched a new model of HEI that could be transformed internally along corporate lines, was the imposition of new norms for institutional mission. Dawkins stated that a HEI would need 5,000 effective full-time students (EFTS) to maintain a 'broad teaching profile' and specialized research, and 8,000 EFTS for research 'across a significant proportion of its profile'. Institutions below these benchmarks had to achieve them via growth or merger. Smaller universities could combine with colleges (Dawkins, 1988: 29, 45–6). This generated a flurry of consolidation in which sixty-four separate institutions soon became thirty-six, often with new leaders. Small specialist institutions almost disappeared and the average size of public institutions, 4,700 in 1987, jumped dramatically and continued to climb, reaching 35,060 by 2014. The Dawkins reforms, together with mimetic institutional practices, established the dominant research university template, subsequently refined and stream-lined by federal administration and the conditions attached to grants. Top-down regulation by the minister enforced the 'multiversification' of institutions.

The first HPS proposition on horizontal diversity (HPS Proposition 7) states:

In the HPS era, regardless of the political economy and culture of systems, an increasing proportion of higher education becomes centred on comprehensive multi-discipline and multi-function research universities, or 'multiversities'. The multiversity is increasingly dominant as the paradigmatic form of higher education.

It is hard to think of any national system that more completely epitomises this proposition, than that of Australia. The state has relentlessly entrenched the logics of economy of scale and scope.

The Dawkins template of large, multi-disciplinary, multi-function institutions excluded small specialist HEIs from the public sector, and made life difficult for multi-disciplinary teaching institutions. Though Dawkins (1988) did not specify that all public HEIs had to be research universities, that was the outcome of the competition created. Even though some institutions had little faculty capacity for funded research projects at scale, all adopted the research role. Research was the common and definitive mission of universities while comparative teaching was invisible, and research conferred status essential in attracting students and faculty. In the global market, especially, a 'teaching-only' mission was a fatal handicap. New universities upgraded staff to PhD level, designated academic positions as 'teaching and research', drew surplus from applied projects and consultancy for research infrastructure capacity-building and maximized Doctoral enrolments, sometimes ahead of the capacity to service them. The government allocated some funding for research infrastructure and postgraduate scholarships to all HEIs on a non-merit basis, though never enough to enable post-Dawkins research universities to compete on equal terms. Research quickly became the high-status means of stratifying the whole sector. Within a decade the research multiversity was made official. In 2000 it was agreed by national and state governments, and the public universities, that to be a designated as a 'university' an HEI must conduct research and Doctoral education in at least three fields (Australian Government, 2014).

Competition has also favoured the multi-function multiversity form. Scale helps HEIs to be globally active. They cut a larger figure in the world and maintain corporate specialisms like marketing, recruitment, and financial management. The greater the range of sites, services, and stakeholders, the more scope there is to advance the institution in one or another sub-market with potential for status or revenues, and to move quickly to take advantage of new opportunities. The inevitable corollary of the spread of the conglomerate multiversity form is internal diversity. Since the mergers most Australian HEIs have used multi-site presence to broaden geographic coverage, augment scope, and manage discipline mix. Information systems enable structure and content to be varied without losing transparency. The third HPS proposition on diversity (Proposition 9) states:

As participation expands the internal diversity of multiversities tends to increase. This affects some or all of the range of missions, business activities, institutional forms and internal structures, the discipline mix, research activities, levels of study and range of credentials, the heterogeneity of the student body, links to stakeholders, cross-border relations, and forms of academic and non-academic labour.

Australian HEIs, even more so than most institutions elsewhere, happily position themselves as all things to all people.

The second HPS proposition on horizontal diversity (HPS Proposition 8) states that

Regardless of the political economy and culture of the HPS, when participation expands there is no necessary increase in the overall diversity of institutional form and mission; and this has probably declined, except in relation to online provision.

This again describes the Australian system. Public HEIs, which as noted enrol 92 per cent of students, are a unitary sector in which all but two small institutions are classified as comprehensive teaching and research oriented. All are self-accrediting, with degree-awarding powers. All receive federal subsidies for teaching places and for research projects and infrastructure. All are active in the global market in cross-border students. All can enrol as many students as they wish and are subsidized for each first-degree place. All compete for first-degree students, fee-paying international students, and scholarship-bearing Doctoral students; for research monies from public and private sources; and in markets for consultancy and commercial services. All are global research universities providing global competences and employability, all are socially engaged, all are student-centred, etc. The important word is 'all'. Mission, realization, and projection are all homogeneous. Across the sector website language and images converge. Temporary flourishes from the marketing department are soon homogenized again because the underlying strategies are common and no one is an outlier for long. It often seems there is one 'brand Australia', the term used in governmental promotion in the international market.

The Dawkins settings made small specialist institutions non-viable even when they did not aspire to research. Given diseconomies of scale, quality could be sustained only by a higher level of per capita resources than the standard funding formula allowed. Programmes in the arts, film and media, forestry, and agriculture, often inherited from state governments, were forced into larger HEIs or wound down. This created challenges for universities when they found the high per capita costs of teaching arts and music did not disappear in the larger institution; while at the same time, standard formulae for measuring academic workloads or computing 'research' scarcely applied. For their part, the arts schools, drama colleges, and conservatoriums of music found their old mission were often compromised. A policy designed to eliminate antiquated schools became a barrier to global excellence. From a cost-effectiveness perspective it made sense, but the loss of the small specialist colleges, with their focused and distinctive cultures joined to corresponding professional communities, constituted a significant loss of diversity.

Other kinds of non-market diversity have also withered. In the 1960s and early 1970s La Trobe, Flinders, Newcastle, Deakin, Griffith, and Murdoch Universities dared to be different. They experimented with inter-disciplinary programmes, social and ecological responsibility, flat decision-making, and participatory governance. Risk-taking of this kind, with long lead times and uncertain effects in resources and status, was possible only under conditions of strong and stable national public funding and the absence of supply-side competition. Success varied, but at best (e.g. at Griffith) these universities supplied new ideas and talented innovators that enriched the whole Australian system. In the 1970s it often seemed the newer universities were making the running. However, not all the new staff they recruited from the older universities bought into the innovations; reductions in per capita funding undercut the scope for initiative; and the competitive and isomorphistic pressures installed by Dawkins pulled them back towards the system norms. They had few resources outside public funding, such as the donations or consultancies accessed by older institutions, and, once they were competing for prestige and resources and were measured using standard research indicators, they had to maximize their position on the same basis as other HEIs. The scope for experiment shrank dramatically. Their profiles converged with the mainstream.

Instead of competition fostering diverse submarkets and de-bundled specialist products, as the retail sector, Australia's multi-purpose multiversities jostle for broad market coverage at the centre of large demand pools in each state capital, like free-to-air commercial television. The Australian experience undermines the belief that markets foster diversity; confirming, as argued in Chapter 4, that supply-led competition is consistent with uniformity (Meek, 2000; van Vught, 2008). This is not only because states would rather administer homogeneity than difference. It is generated by the isomorphistic game-logic of competition itself. If an initiative fails, risk-taking university leaders lose ground vis-à-vis their competitors. Intuition says it is safer to imitate others, to follow common and predictable paths. If all HEIs fail together, no one loses. While state intervention can secure either diversity or homogeneity, depending on the design of policy and regulation, supply-side competition always tends to foster homogeneity—unless the state holds down diverse missions in a stable binary system.

The one domain characterized by genuine inter-institutional diversity is offshore activity. All public HEIs educate international students, all foster academic mobility (though outward mobility of local students is modest, as in other English-speaking countries), and most engage in extensive cross-border research. Many are members of international consortia; some have deep long-term partnerships. Other practices vary. Some build stand-alone campuses in other countries, others maintain offshore campuses via franchising. Some provide specialist centres for student exchange, scholars and symposia, distance delivery, or research. Some invest heavily in online delivery or external Doctoral education; many engage in mass open online courseware (MOOC). These diverse activities are financed by autonomous market revenues and there are few historical norms to which to conform. But diverse offshore education is largely segmented and does not transform domestic teaching, facilities, and research. The education of onshore international students remains much the same as the education of local students, with little spill-over from cross-cultural insights abroad. Globally sourced potentials for diversity are contained.

Vertical Stratification

The first HPS proposition on vertical stratification (HPS Proposition 11) states that:

> *The expansion of participation towards and beyond the HPS stage is associated with a tendency to bifurcation and stratification (vertical diversification) in the value of higher education, between elite (artisanal) institutions and mass (demand-absorbing) institutions.*

In a competitive unitary system with a single mission, the stratification engendered by elite/mass bifurcation is readily calibrated in quantitative terms, for example by comparing volumes of funded research and high citation papers (Table 10.1), or student selectivity in programmes common to all institutions. HEIs become arranged as inferior imitators of the leaders, in a long vertical continuum in descending order of research-intensity, selectivity, and prestige. The further one moves down the list the more the social role morphs from selecting university to selected, the thinner the research, the

Table 10.1. Calibration of Australian universities in terms of competitively measured research

	Competitive funding for research 2014 (US$ million)	Top 10% papers by cite rate 2011–14		Competitive funding for research 2014 (US$ million)	Top 10% papers by cite rate 2011–14
ARTISANAL			**MIDDLE LAYER**		
Melbourne	165.2	1,442	Tasmania	30.3	197
Queensland	153.2	1,318	Queensland UT	29.8	252
Sydney	148.8	1,308	Newcastle	29.2	307
Monash	145.1	1,057	Macquarie	28.9	235
New South Wales	118.8	1,025	Curtin	25.2	289
Western Australia	80.7	582	Griffith	21.6	297
Australian NU	78.2	644	South Australia	21.3	199
Adelaide	70.8	541	Wollongong	21.0	273
			Deakin	19.5	253
DEMAND-ABSORBING			James Cook	19.2	239
Aust. Catholic	5.6	n.a.	Flinders	15.1	189
Charles Sturt	5.4	n.a.	RMIT	13.3	166
Canberra	4.3	n.a.	Charles Darwin	13.3	n.a.
Edith Cowan	4.2	n.a.	UT Sydney	12.4	227
Sunshine Coast	3.4	n.a.	La Trobe	11.4	156
Southern Qld.	2.7	n.a.	Western Sydney	11.2	170
Victoria	2.5	n.a.	Swinburne	9.9	136
Southern Cross	2.4	n.a.	New England	9.5	n.a.
Bond	2.3	n.a.	Murdoch	8.8	n.a.
Federation	1.1	n.a.			
Central Qld.	1.0	n.a.			
Notre Dame Aust.	0.3	n.a.			
Bachelor Institute	0.01	n.a.			

Notes: NU = National University. Aust. = Australia. Qld. = Queensland. UT = University of Technology. RMIT = Royal Melbourne Institute of Technology. AU$1.000000 = US$0.748864.

Sources: Author's compilation and adaptation using Australian DE, 2017b; Leiden University, 2017. The Leiden data are confined to the 842 HEIs that published more than 1,000 papers in Web of Knowledge in 2011–14.

more that claims to be a 'little Oxford' are merely normative. The appendages of scholarly life, academic gowns, and degree ceremonies are not enough. Marketing takes over. It is cheaper to claim excellence than to practice it. Rankings become more fraught and anxious. Attention shifts from research league tables to rankings like quality statistics that are manipulated by survey, then rankings are discarded altogether. So it is in Australia. Competition pulls the hierarchy up and down at the same time, though some vertical stretching is modified by government.

While calibration blurs the dynamics of the binary opposition between artisanal and demand-absorbing behaviours it does illustrate the institutions at the extremes of Bourdieu's polarity. Australia has well defined demand-absorbing HEIs (Table 10.1) with little competitively funded research and in the first eight institutions, more than 8,000 EFTS. Opposing these institutions are the unambiguously artisanal HEI (Tables 10.1 and 10.2). Calibration also throws some light on the ambiguous position of those HEIs

Table 10.2. Australia's artisanal institutions: The eight leading research universities and two comparators

University	ARWU ranking position 2017	ARWU ranking position 2004	Number of research papers 2011–14	Top 10% papers by cite rate 2011–14	Australian research block grant 2017 US$ million	ATAR for Arts and Engineering 2017		Total EFT student load 2015	International students proportion 2015 %
						Arts	Eng.		
Melbourne	39	82	11,026	1,442	143.2	89	85	45,431	33.5
Queensland	55	101–52	10,443	1,318	138.2	73	89	40,029	25.5
Monash	78	202–301	8,693	1,057	123.9	81	91	55,788	39.0
Sydney	83	101–52	11,142	1,308	138.2	80	90	45,054	28.4
Western Aust.	91	153–201	5,395	582	71.1	80	80	19,675	19.5
Australian NU	97	53	4,782	644	86.5	80	90	16,055	30.5
NSW	101–50	153–201	8,705	1,025	126.6	81	91	40,156	28.3
Adelaide	101–50	202–301	4,641	541	66.8	65	81	21,241	26.1
Illinois Urbana	30	25	9,549	1,346	–	–	–	*44,087	27.4
NU Singapore	83	101–52	11,514	1,489	–	–	–	*34,715	28.9

Notes: *Total students not EFT students at U Illinois, NU Singapore, for year 2015–16. AUD $1.000000 = US$ $0.748864. NSW = New South Wales. EFT = effective full-time. ATAR refer to the percentile rank for school leaver entry into the programme named. An ATAR of 90 for engineering means that students ranked in the top 10 per cent of the cohort, in the final year school examination, in the Australian state in which the university is located, gained entry into the first degree in engineering.

Sources: Author's compilation and adaptation using ARWU, 2017; Leiden University, 2017; Australian DE, 2017a; DET, n.d.; Unireviews, 2017.

that combine features of both polar types and pulled hither and thither by the contrary dynamics. Between the two Bourdieu-ian groups lies a middle layer of semi-intensive research universities, in various ways combining research and selected student selectivity with demand absorption. Arguably, the large middle layer in Table 10.1 is the most distinctive feature of the system design.

HPS proposition 2 on stratification (HPS Proposition 12) states:

The tendency to institutional stratification is magnified by features common (though not universal) among HPS including (a) intensified social competition for the most valuable student places; (b) variable tuition charges; and/or (c) intensified competition between institutions.

Since Dawkins institutional competitiveness has intensified, especially via research assessment and ranking. High demand institutions and programmes have become more socially selective as their proportion of total enrolments has shrunk. However, domestic tuition is fixed by the state and does not augment stratification. Tuition varies by field of study but not institution. Artisanal institutions in the Group of Eight agitate for variable tuition charges to financially realize the positional value of their degrees. This would widen their resource advantage and increase their global research competiveness. Like-wise, some middle institutions see variable tuition as an opening for upward mobility. In 2014, the government prepared a proposal for the tuition deregulation. In public there was little appetite for this and the reform was defeated in the Australian Senate, the upper house of parliament. Variable tuition breached notions of fair competition in the nominally egalitarian system. Australians were accustomed to a quasi-market which the state was accountable for conducting the game on a nominally level playing field. A more complete marketization, in which top HEIs set their prices (and called the shots), would depart from the consensus. State controlled standard tuition remains an import-ant constraint on stratification in Australia.

The secular dynamics of bifurcation and stratification are modified by two other factors. First, the status-averse Australian state, unlike many other states, does not identify and fund 'world-class universities' or use American-style classifications that would elevate leading research universities. Second, as noted in Chapter 5, five elite universities exhibit a strong growth trajectory in the international student market. Given the modest public outlay on higher education in Australia—0.7 per cent of GDP in 2013, below the OECD average of 1.1 per cent (OECD, 2016: 207)—and the inability of HEIs to lift their domestic student income because tuition is fixed, all depend on large-scale revenues from full fee-paying international students. The recruitment strategies of artisanal, middle layer, and demand-absorbing institutions are broadly similar, except artisanal institutions can use their status to recruit at exceptional volumes if they choose that strategy. Some do (see Tables 4.1 and 10.2). Often the marginal academic quality of their international intakes is well below that of the domestic students. They are artisanal institutions in the domestic market and demand-absorbers in the global market. Still, these factors modify rather than cancel the stratification of resources, value, and power. It is masked by policy ideology and considered to be in bad taste to discuss it, but bifurcation drives the Australian sector like all others.

ARTISANAL SUB-SECTOR

Table 10.2 lists the research-intensive universities in the self-proclaimed 'Group of Eight'. The University of Illinois and National University of Singapore provide comparisons. As Table 10.1 suggested in relation to competitive research funds, there is a clear large gap in status, resources, and research between the Group of Eight and the nearest contenders.

The primacy of the group derives from its historical position, augmented by cumulative advantage. In higher education the race is mostly won by those who start at the front row of the grid. These eight were among the first ten universities founded in Australia (the other two, Tasmania and New England in rural New South Wales, are in more marginal locations). They entered the Dawkins competitive system with most of the research infrastructure and reputational primacy and the gap has probably widened since 1988. All eight are in the top 150 in the Shanghai Academic Ranking of World Universities; seven having lifted since 2004 (ARWU, 2017). Queensland, Sydney and New South Wales, Melbourne, Adelaide, and Western Australia attract the great majority of high scoring school students in their cities. Percentile entrance scores of 80–90 (Unireviews, 2017) in large intake arts and engineering are not especially high but typical minimum scores for law and medicine are from 98 to 99 plus.

In 2014, these eight universities had a quarter of university student load but received 71.3 per cent of research funds distributed by merit and published most of the high citation papers. Though enrolling half the PhD students in 2017 the artisanal sub-sector received 63.2 per cent of block grants for research, based on research income, PhD students, and publications. They also receive the great bulk of monies in the form of bequests, endowments, scholarships, and prizes, although these forms of income do not play a marked role in Australia.

These elements are common. The group also manifests variable strategies. Five are large by international standards, though akin to some American public universities. In 2014, the University of Melbourne had a student load of 42,637, including an international student load of 13,200, securing US$327 million from the latter. Monash had an international student load of 19,634 (DET, n.d.). On the other hand, Table 10.2 shows that Australian National University (ANU), Western Australia and Adelaide are half the size of the other five, though Adelaide has entered a growth trajectory. Because they have smaller regional demographic catchments than the other five artisanals, these three universities build status more by concentration than volume (see Chapter 4). If citations are a measure of quality, ANU, which began in 1946 as a specialist research and Doctoral institution, has the highest average quality of research output. In 2011–14, 13.5 per cent of its papers were in the top 10 per cent of their field by citation rate, compared to 13.1 per cent at Melbourne (Leiden University, 2017). ANU leaders from time to time talk of a Caltech strategy, but Australia lacks defence science funding on the US scale—and tuition is fixed. Downsizing the undergraduate intake is not a prospect. Australian artisanal trajectories span the spectrum from high growth to moderate growth. Pure Caltech-style concentration is out of reach.

DEMAND-ABSORBING SUB-SECTOR

All the demand-absorbing institutions in Table 10.1 apart from the University of the Sunshine Coast, the most recent, began in colleges of advanced education and gained university status though the Dawkins reforms. They include the large multi-disciplinary Australian Catholic, Canberra, Central Queensland, Charles Sturt, Edith Cowan, Southern Cross, Southern Queensland, and Victoria Universities. The others are smaller teaching-focused institutions, including two private HEIs funded on a similar basis to public institutions (as is the case also with the Australian Catholic University). While demand-absorbing institutions all conduct research and are funded on a modest basis for research training, knowledge-building is confined to isolated units within high volume teaching settings. For example, in 2014 the Australian Catholic University enrolled a student load of 21,519 and received US$5.6 million in competitive research grants, US$261 per student unit. Research funding at the artisanal ANU, with student load of 15,587, averaged US$5016 per student unit (DET, n.d.).

Several HEIs in the demand-absorbing group expanded markedly when the cap on enrolments came off in 2009. Between 2008 and 2011, student load at Edith Cowan University jumped from 11,766 to 17,934 units (52.4 per cent), and grew at the University of Canberra by 45.7 per cent, Australian Catholic University by 44.5 per cent, Victoria University by 21.2 per cent, and Charles Sturt University by 20.2 per cent. By 2015, the Australian Catholic University was at 23,547 units, double the 11,547 of 2008. This funded growth offered demand-absorbing institutions not just economies of scale but prospects of a permanent increase in market share, cementing their social role. But as one government inquiry found (Lomax-Smith, 2011), in half of the disciplines provided to students in Australian HEIs the funding rate is below the average cost of provision. Lacking supplementary funds, demand-absorbing public institutions must endure a low ceiling on their teaching resources that sets material limits to quality.

The Australian system also includes ninety-eight private institutions not designated as universities. They do not conduct research. Nearly all are demand-absorbing institutions (none are akin to elite American liberal arts colleges, despite marketing claims) but they lack multi-disciplinary scale, with an average load of just over 800 units. Specializations include business studies, theology, and the arts. Although eligible for public tuition funding via income-contingent loans, and free to grow in scope and scale, new providers find it difficult to compete with multiversity credentials. Underpinned by their historical reputation and their inclusion in the primary system, even the demand-absorbing public HEIs in Table 10.1 enjoy a decisive advantage over the new private challengers.

THE MIDDLE LAYER

The third HPS proposition on stratification (HPS Proposition 13) states:

In stratified HPS, a middle layer of institutions tends to form, shaped by the combination of upward aspirations (drift) with systemic scarcity of resources and status.

This is central to the HPS in Australia. The secular dynamics of the HPS are modified by state policy and regulation so as to enhance the middle group and reduce the concentration at top and bottom. More than half of the Australian public universities appear in the Shanghai ARWU (Academic Ranking of World Universities, Shanghai Jiao Tong University) ranking and the Leiden ranking for research. Only the top eight institutions are clearly artisanal. Though the middle layer HEIs routinely claim elite status, they are decisively over-shadowed by the Group of Eight in each major city.

The proof of the bifurcation idea lies not in whether ideal types are manifest holistically in real institutions but whether the tensions between them shape the field and explain the vicissitudes of strategy and trajectory. This is most obvious in the middle HEIs, which oscillate freely and eclectically between building student volume and building research performance. Middle institutions are both powered and destabilized by their contradictory character. With each newly appointed university president there is the possibility of a sudden lurch in the reserve direction to that of her or his predecessor.

In all Australian multiversities the two principal missions, mass teaching and research, are intertwined. Each is a resource for the other. Status earned via research, real or simulated, sustains reputation that underpins the teaching of domestic and international students at home and in campuses abroad. Mass teaching in the global market finances the research that feeds status accumulation at home, and so on. This is the true teaching–research nexus, articulated through positional competition, and the accumulation and exchange of institutional status. However, the virtuous circle works fully only in artisanal HEIs. Status is a zero-sum game, and artisanals are best placed in contests over resources. The need for a continuous symbiosis between research, reputation, and money explains the always-provisional dynamic of middle institutions. Their potential to generate resources for research through prestige teaching is limited by the ceiling on domestic tuition and the fact that unlike artisanal institutions they cannot charge premium international prices. Their teaching, despite managed selectivity in boutique areas, is not highly selective overall and cannot generate a long-term reputational edge. In the middle group percentile entrance scores for arts are at 60–70 and engineering at 60–80, compared to 85–90 in most of the artisanals. Middle institutions' percentile entrance scores for business are 60–70 compared to 89–97 in the top five (Unireviews, 2017).

Australia's middle HEIs are stronger in research output than student selectivity, boosting their global rankings which are largely research-based. They cannot conduct world-leading research on a scale that would lift them into the artisanal institutions. The inherited gap is too great. In middle HEIs, research blossoms in tailored fields, though of these universities are nominally committed to the comprehensive approach. Some isolate their research from the rest of the operation, fostering stars and research-only positions to scramble more kudos. Moving down the middle group, world-class research becomes more scattered or episodic. Mostly, comparative citation rates, the quality measure, are weaker than are paper volumes (University of Leiden, 2017).

Though the middle institutions are typical multiversities, in that they all things to all people, their ambiguity is not constant. In some, when all the rhetoric is stripped away, mass teaching dominates, Quadrant D in Figure 5.2. Others are more chameleon-like, craftier, and maybe more conflicted. The middle sector is traditional and modern, selective and open, mass and elite; although the 'elite' status is always in doubt while the demand responsive character is obvious. Consistent with the national emphasis on growth, most middle institutions are large and are readily presented as social inclusion and democratic access to the professions. Since Dawkins the Australian state, mindful of educational opportunity and still more of apparent mobility, has favoured this group. It sustains them with policies that restrain the artisanal HEIs, especially the ceiling on tuition; and policies that sustain minimum research infrastructure and higher degrees, and government trade promotion in which all universities are equivalent in the global market. Yet these expedients are nowhere near enough to bridge the capacity gap between the lowest artisanal Adelaide, and the leading middle institutions: Tasmania, Curtin, Queensland University of Technology, Newcastle, Wollongong. Middle institutions bend themselves to the task. The top eight are out of reach.

Middle HEIs in Australia have two kinds of histories. One group were the second wave research universities founded between 1960 and 1975 at the high point of public funding, such as Macquarie, Newcastle, Wollongong, Griffith, Flinders, La Trobe. They began as comprehensive research universities but once funding levelled off, struggled to compete with the first mover artisanals. The second group, once colleges of advanced education, includes large universities of technology (UTs) such as Queensland, Curtin, UT Sydney,

Table 10.3. Growth oriented middle higher education institutions, Australia

Institution	Student load 2014	International student load 2014 (%)	Number of research papers 2011–14	Papers in top 10% of field 2011–14 (%)	Top 10% papers by cite rate 2011–14	Top 10% papers per 100 students 2014*	Fields of research strength 2011–14
RMIT	45,475	44.1	1,739	9.5	166	0.365	PSE
Curtin	35,310	32.7	2,770	10.4	289	0.818	LifeE, PSE
Deakin	35,272	17.0	2,432	10.4	253	0.717	Med, PSE
QUT	34,740	17.6	2,776	9.1	252	0.725	–
Griffith	33,058	19.8	2,821	10.5	297	0.898	LifeE, PSE

Notes: *Number of top 10 per cent papers by citation rate in 2011–14 for every 100 units of student load in 2014. Fields of research strength have at least forty high citation papers and 10 per cent of all papers are in this category. Med = biomedical and health sciences, LifeE = life and earth sciences, MathC = mathematics and computer science, PSE = physical sciences and engineering. Using earlier definition of research strengths none of these institutions have such strengths in social sciences and humanities. RMIT = Royal Melbourne Institute of Technology. QUT = Queensland University of Technology. West. = Western.

Sources: DET, n.d.; Leiden University, 2017.

the Royal Melbourne Institute of Technology (RMIT), and South Australia. Under the Dawkins funding formula, they were never fully supported for the development of research capacity but built research by creaming off surplus from domestic teaching, entrepreneurial international education (especially), and applied research. It is difficult to build large-scale basic research infrastructure this way, though sometimes whole teams are bought in from the artisanal sub-sector. All UT have vigorously pursued research development, massive domestic student growth, and major commercial international recruitment at different times, and sometimes at the same time. It is in these HEIs above all that the contrary dynamics of the middle layer play out.

Table 10.3 lists middle HEIs for whom volume-building has been especially important. Some have grown consistently, others in spurts. Here sustained growth is a frank strategy of demand absorption, drawing on academically marginal students but it also fosters economies, modernized services and facilities and facilitates internal restructuring. However, while the financial flows generated by student numbers can be taxed for research they also invoke mission dilemmas. A bigger teaching staff has larger gaps in research capacity that weaken average performance (the ARWU has a per faculty performance indicator) and standing. Yet comprehensive research-building, in institutions lacking stellar faculty across the board, lacks depth and generates a patchwork of high/low citation areas. The UT went different ways. Curtin became much the largest HEI in Perth, built international student load to one-third and moved into many research areas, feeding extra resources into those that did best. In Figure 5.2 terms this was a Quadrant B strategy. Curtin eventually consolidated as an ARWU top 500 research university, though its output of high citation research, 0.818 papers per hundred units of student load in 2014, was well below Melbourne (3.174) and the University of Western Australia in

Perth (2.958). Of other UTs, Queensland UT grew rapidly, fashioned a pristine inner-city site, worked every policy opportunity to advantage and invested selectively in research. Then it slowed domestic growth and shifted to a comprehensive research profile, positioning itself as quasi-artisanal in a long struggle with the rising star of the University of Queensland. RMIT likewise struggled to compete for talent with Melbourne and Monash but achieved scale, especially in international education, and like Queensland UT eventually bulldozed its way into the top 500 with a modest performance in high citation research.

The alternate strategy was to concentrate quality. UT Sydney (Table 10.4) remained smaller and invested in high value niche teaching and deep narrow research specializations. It achieved world-level strength in mathematics and computing—Australia's fourth biggest output of high citation work in 2011–14 and 19.3 per cent of papers in the high citation category, twelfth in the world, one place above University of California, Berkeley—and small high quality nodes in the physical sciences and engineering, biomedical and life sciences. It too reached the ARWU top 500, but its overall research intensity at 0.818 high citation papers was the same as that of Curtin with high growth and comprehensive research (ARWU, 2016; Leiden University, 2017). Regardless of starting strategy, all UT have hit a similar upper barrier, blocked by the talent and reputational weight of artisanal universities in the tier above. They are regularly out-recruited by prestigious rivals. Middle level HEIs have to run hard to achieve slow small gains.

The pre-1987 second wave universities had more options via their inherited research capacity. Provincial Newcastle and Wollongong, smaller than the metropolitan HEIs,

Table 10.4. Selective research concentration middle higher education institutions of smaller size, Australia

Institution	Student load 2014	International student load 2014 (%)	Number of research papers 2011–14	Papers in top 10% of field 2011–14 (%)	Top 10% papers by cite rate 2011–14	Top 10% papers per 100 students 2014*	Fields of research strength 2011–14
James Cook	16,471	35.7	1,835	13.0	239	1.451	LifeE,
Swinburne	22,131	29.4	1,107	12.3	136	0.615	PSE
Newcastle	25,582	15.8	2,622	11.7	307	1.200	Med
Wollongong	23,502	39.2	2,494	10.9	273	1.162	LifeE, PSE
UT Sydney	27,747	27.4	1,826	12.4	227	0.818	Med, MathC, PSE

Notes: *Number of top 10 per cent papers by citation rate in 2011–14 for every hundred units of student load in 2014. Fields of research strength have at least forty high citation papers and 10 per cent of all papers in this category. Med = biomedical and health sciences, LifeE = life and earth sciences, MathC = mathematics and computer science, PSE = physical sciences and engineering. None of these institutions have strengths in social sciences and humanities UT = University of Technology.

Sources: DET, n.d.; Leiden University, 2017.

grew moderately and fostered research in medicine (Newcastle), selected engineering, physical sciences, and mathematics (both), and life and earth sciences (Wollongong) (Table 10.4). Quality was respectable, especially at Newcastle with 11.7 per cent of papers in the top 10 per cent. The intensity of high citation papers per unit of student load was at the top of the middle group but only one-third that of artisanal institutions.

Griffith (Table 10.3) acquired new sites, and despite areas of leading research its prioritization of growth left it with overall numbers on research quality similar to a university of technology. Deakin, starting from a weaker research base, grew at the same rate as Griffith and then struck it lucky, securing a medical faculty. The associated research lifted it close to Griffith's position. No middle HEI in Australia stayed moderate in size while pursuing comprehensive research, like artisanal universities ANU and Western Australia. One pre-1987 second wave institution, Murdoch, tried this but failed. Both resources and comparative research performance deteriorated. Murdoch was ranked in the world top 500 in the early years of the ARWU but dropped out after 2007. To survive it belatedly switched tack, focusing on the global market, the card all Australian institutions can play. By 2015 international student load was 44.6 per cent of the total (DET, n.d.).

The other strategic option was to combine small size and specialized research. Two HEIs did this (Table 10.4). A decade after Dawkins, James Cook, a regional university with modest growth potential, had a student load of only 10,200 (2004) but outstanding capacity in tropical marine biology. In 2011–14 it was fifth largest Australian producer of high citation work in life and earth sciences, with 168 papers at an excellent high citation paper rate of 16.3 per cent—though negligible presence in other scientific fields, with just twelve highly cited papers in physical sciences and engineering and one in mathematics and computing. Student load rose to 16,471 in 2014—the need for income pushed international student load from 1,348 in 2004 to 7,164 in 2014—but size remained relatively modest. Swinburne UT began in similar fashion. Led by a corporate benefactor who chaired its council it stayed small at first (10,613 in 2004) while, in the ultimate hobby strategy, establishing a top astrophysics department. Of its 136 high citation papers published in 2011–14, ninety-one were in physical sciences and engineering, 14.8 per cent of all its papers in that field; higher field citation quality than the artisanal universities, but only in astrophysics. Their specializations lifted James Cook and Swinburne into the ARWU top 500 (ARWU, 2016; Leiden University, 2017) but there was little flow-on to student demand. James Cook's 2017 percentile entrance scores in arts was 52; Swinburne's was 60 (Unireviews, 2017). This is the closest Australia has come to a pure Quadrant A approach. It is significant this strategy has been used much more rarely than large-scale growth, and that Swinburne has now abandoned the small size approach, having more than doubled its student load since 2004.

The outcomes for HEIs determined to grow both massive student numbers and high quality research suggest the tensions between the two strategies cannot be resolved. Even the top artisanal institutions allocate too much income to teaching, site, facilities and services to reach the world top thirty. Yet of the twenty-three Australian HEIs in the ARWU 500, all but two are in the 400. It is a strong result for a nation of Australia's size and maximizes the global market position. Australia is remarkable in the extent to which the system and many of its individual institutions keep both balls in the air at once, the artisanal and demand-absorbing functions. All public universities carry visible traces of each Bourdieu-ian type. Loosely coupled multiversities, with varying emphases in different sites, allow presidents and research vice-presidents to mix and match. Though there is a common zeal in performance cultures the quality/quantity trade-offs vary between disciplines. Nevertheless, sooner or later every Australian HEI grows sharply. Even the small ones are large in global eyes. At times every Australian multi-purpose multiversity seem to be part of one gigantic middle layer.

It is not so. This system is more elite, less meritocratic, and more conservative than it appears. Like elsewhere the artisanal sector is unchallengeable, despite limited levelling by government. The state in Australia understands bifurcation and plays with it, using the two ends to fashion a large tense dualistic middle that is ultimately no threat to the top. Officially, policy never acknowledges bifurcation or any status distinction, peddling the contrary happy fictions that all HEIs can be elite institutions, and there are no elite institutions, and everyone is a contender in a grey contested zone where the choice-making consumer can upend the order of things tomorrow. The state pretends that competition revolves around teaching quality and student satisfaction, not history or positional status or even research. No one believes this. The artisanal sector mediates value as it always has, and research is the trump card that it always plays. The Australian HPS shows that regulation can moderate bifurcation, and frame its institutional manifestations in differing ways, but bifurcation governs the strategies used to manage it. The size and robustness of the middle layer, embodying the characteristic Australian idea of an equitable competition game, illustrates the theoretical point that in HPS secular tendencies common to all systems can be over-determined in nationally variant ways by state action.

Social Equity

The first HPS proposition on equity (HPS Proposition 14) states that:

> As participation expands in the HPS phase, equity in the form of social inclusion is enhanced.

Equity as inclusion, participation, and completion has been a core policy goal since the landmark social democratic report *Schools in Australia* (Karmel, 1973). But the policy framework established by that report legitimated the class-stratified public/private school system (Marginson, 1997), setting a decisive limit on equity. Since 1973 the policy approach to equity has been Pareto optimal, extending higher education to under-represented social groups at the margin of participation rather than redistributing social access to elite universities, much as in the colonial parent system in the UK (Harvey et al., 2016).

The second equity proposition (HPS Proposition 15) states that:

Because in the HPS phase the growth of participation is associated with enhanced stratification and intensified competition at key transition points, all else being equal (i.e. without compensatory state policy), the expansion of participation is associated with a secular tendency to greater social inequality in educational outcomes and, through that, social outcomes.

The fourth proposition (HPS Proposition 17) states that:

As the HPS boundary of participation expands it becomes more difficult for the state and/or autonomous educational systems/institutions to secure a redistribution of educational opportunities, and through that, of social opportunities.

Both of these propositions are consistent with Australian experience. In the context of educational competition for social position, the additional opportunities created by expansion are disproportionately captured by the middle class. It has been difficult to move the whole HPS closer to proportional inclusion of low socio-economic status (SES) and Indigenous students, let alone move the artisanal sub-sector towards those outcomes.

After 2009 the demand-driven system led to major total growth but triggered only a modest change in the proportion of all students drawn from the bottom SES quartile, from 16.2 per cent in 2007 to 17.9 per cent in 2014. The bottom SES quartile comprised 11.0 per cent of students in the artisanal Group of Eight, but 29.8 per cent in the regional HEIs where Indigenous students are concentrated. However, Indigenous students enrol at half the level of their population share. In 2011, the apparent Indigenous retention rate to the end of secondary school was 48.7 per cent compared to 79.3 per cent for all young persons (ABS, 2012). This remains the largest social equity issue in the Australian HPS.

Social inequality in access to the artisanal sector and the associated earnings and career pathways is readily explained. Privatized and stratified schooling, feeding into stratified higher education, provides extensive opportunities for family investment in education as a private good. In total 40 per cent of secondary students are enrolled in non-comprehensive private schools, with one quarter of these in high fee private schools dominated by affluent families. These schools play a similar social role to their counterparts in the UK in placing students on high value pathways. Like British private schools and Ivy League American colleges they sustain lifelong social capital networks. Low-income families are concentrated in the public sector. Analysis of entrance to higher education shows that of all variables, school sector is most strongly associated with entrance scores. Allowing for family income, students from independent private schools enjoy a 6–8 per cent advantage compared to public school students (Gemici, et al., 2014; Marks, 2015)—though once at university, on average independent school graduates perform less well than those from public schools (e.g. of many Birch and Miller, 2007). Independent schools have decisively blocked all policy strategies designed to equalise the school experience and this helps to shape the social character of artisanal universities.

However, to test the proposition concerning a secular increase in social inequality would require a finer level of analysis than Australian data permit. In measuring social trends in entry to higher education, the government uses not individualised data collected by census or sample survey but an aggregated residence-based measure of SES in which whole postcode districts share the same SES classification. Little is known in detail about social trends in participation in the artisanal institutions, and in work and career outcomes for graduates from differing social groups and differing kinds of institution, despite much research elsewhere (e.g. of many, Boliver, 2013 in the UK; Rivera, 2015 in the USA). The lack of rigorous social group-based data on final outcomes and of close scrutiny of social inequalities in the artisanal sector is symptomatic of a political culture in which equity is defined as inclusion, not equality of condition; the goal is equal treatment and fair process not equal outcomes for all social groups; and open competition is seen as sufficient for fair process. Policy adopts the apparently egalitarian norm that all students and all HEIs are equivalent. This blocks from view the real hierarchy in status and resources (in social power) between the different secondary schools, and the parallel differences between HEIs. Thus social competition in education is freely pre-structured so as to reproduce inequalities.

Conclusions

The fourth proposition on horizontal diversity (HPS Proposition 10) states that:

> *All else being equal, the combination of expanding participation and enhanced competition in neoliberal quasi-markets is associated with specific effects in relation to diversity, including (1) increased vertical differentiation of higher education institutions (stratification); (2) reduced horizontal differentiation (diversification); (3) convergence of missions through isomorphistic imitation; and (4) growth in the role of private higher education institutions, especially for-profit institutions.*

This could have been specifically tailored for Australia (though for-profit colleges are a relatively minor and recent development).

The state in Australia has created a symbiotic relationship between the growth of participation and neoliberal competition. HEIs of all types within this highly stratified system are impelled to grow, facilitating and legitimating expanding social demand for places. Though half of the disciplines are under-funded, in the last generation most Australian multiversities, including five of the eight artisanal HEIs, have leveraged domestic growth for economies of scale, development income, and/or market share. All, without exception, have expanded international enrolments to levels unheard of in most other countries. The global market is the material source of discretionary income, new research capacity, and additional status. This is not to say that growth and HPS would not exist without neoliberal policy. Participation has expanded beyond 50 per cent in other policy frameworks, for example in the Nordic world. It merely means that in Australia—though not everywhere—marketization and growth have come to form a single system. One cannot be changed without altering the other.

Yet the state is never far away in Australia, though clothed in limited liberal disguise. The unified national system is a state regulated quasi market in which public universities carry out commercial activity, not a producer-driven commercial market. Social competition between families has been modified by universal tuition charges and especially by income-contingent loans (Chapman et al., 2014). On the provider side, regulation does not flatten the hierarchy between artisanal and demand-responsive institutions so much as change the implications of that hierarchy for local market share and global status, while subtly tinkering with the capacity of autonomous institutions to do things for themselves. The strong HEIs are held back yet they continually enlarge their quantity and quality. The middle players are lifted and likewise freed to act, though they are never free from the driving, all-consuming anxiety about their position and prospects. The weak HEIs are nurtured enough to survive.

The third proposition on equity (HPS Proposition 16) states that:

Within a national system, as participation expands in the HPS phase, all else being equal, the positional structure of the higher education system increasingly resembles that of society... The HPS is increasingly implicated in the reproduction of existing patterns of social equality/inequality.

So it is in Australia. The HPS is steeply unequal (in research products, some resources, status), steeply equal (in research identity and global markets), and all so very homogeneous in form and mission. Higher education institutions are competitive, but within the terms of a highly structured competition-game. It is like the national football competitions, which use American-style rules on drafting talent and paying players so as to ensure that last year's low performing teams have some prospects of lifting themselves in future. Players move between one team and the other in the jostling for advantage, while on-field strategies tend to converge over time. As with national league football teams, universities never go bankrupt and disappear—and it is normally impossible for new entrants to join the main competition. It is all very nationally specific, and it also says something of higher education everywhere.

After three decades of partial marketization the Australian HPS still largely consists of the public HEIs, with the same artisanals leading the list despite occasional minor changes in the order. The rock-steady stability at the top of the quasi-market in universities demonstrates that, in the end, the neoliberal imaginary is conservative. The quasi-market in higher education is the instrument of a social/institutional hierarchy that long predates the neoliberal policies that began in Australia in the 1980s. No doubt, when neoliberalism has reached its use-by-date, that hierarchy will still expect to run the show.

▨ REFERENCES

ABS (Australian Bureau of Statistics) (2012). *Australian Social Trends*. Series Number 4102.0. http://www.abs.gov.au/socialtrends

ABS (Australian Bureau of Statistics) (2014). *Australian Social Trends*. Series Number 4102.0. http://www.abs.gov.au/ausstats/abs@.nsf/Lookup/4102.0main+features102014

ABS (Australian Bureau of Statistics) (2015). *Labour Force, Australia, Detailed, Quarterly*. Series Number 6291.0.55.003. http://www.abs.gov.au/ausstats/abs@.nsf/mf/6291.0.55.003

ABS (Australian Bureau of Statistics) (2016a). *Migration, Australia, 2014–15*. Series Number 3412.0. http://www.abs.gov.au/ausstats/abs@.nsf/lookup/3412.0Media%20Release12014-15

ABS (Australian Bureau of Statistics) (2016b). *Estimates of Aboriginal and Torres Strait Islander Australians, June 2011*. Series Number 3238.0.55.001. http://www.abs.gov.au/ausstats/abs@.nsf/mf/3238.0.55.001

ARWU (Academic Ranking of World Universities) (2017). Shanghai Jiao Tong University Graduate School of Education. www.shanghairanking.com

Australian Government (2014). National protocols for higher education. www.industry.gov.au/highereducation/StudentSupport/NationalProtocolsForHigherEducationApprovalProcesses/Pages/default.aspx

Australian Department of Education (2017a). *Research Block Grant Allocations for 2017*. https://docs.education.gov.au/node/42311

Australian Department of Education (2017b). *Higher Education Research Data Collection Research Income for 2014*. https://docs.education.gov.au/node/42326

Birch, E. and Miller, P. (2007). Tertiary entrance scores: Can we do better? *Education Research and Perspectives* 34(2), 1–23.

Boliver, V. (2013). How fair is access to more prestigious UK universities? *British Journal of Sociology* 64(2), 344–64.

Burke, G. (1988). How large are the cuts in operating grants per student? *Australian Universities Review* 31(2), 42–3.

Carnoy, M., Froumin, I., Leshukov, O., and Marginson, S. (eds) (2018). *Federalism in Higher Education: A Comparative Study*. New Delhi: Sage.

Chapman, B., Higgins, T., and Stiglitz, J. (eds) (2014). *Income Contingent Loans: Theory, Practice and Prospects*. Basingstoke and New York, Palgrave Macmillan.

Corak, M. (2012). *Inequality from Generation to Generation: The United States in Comparison.* Ottawa: Graduate School of Public and International Affairs, University of Ottawa.

Corak, M. (2006). Do poor children become poor adults? Lessons from a cross-country comparison of generational earnings mobility. IZA Discussion Paper No. 1993. Institute for the Study of Labor, Bonn.

Croucher, G., Marginson, S., Norton, A., and Wells, J. (eds) (2013). *The Dawkins Revolution 25 Years On.* Melbourne: Melbourne University Publishing.

Dawkins, J. (Australian Government Minister for Employment, Education and Training) (1988). *Higher Education: A Policy Statement.* Canberra: Australian Government Publishing Service.

DET (Department of Education and Training, Australia) (n.d.). Higher Education Statistics. https://www.education.gov.au/higher-education-statistics

Gemici, S., Lim, P., and Karmel, T. (2014). Can school characteristics influence university entrance scores? *Australian Economic Review* 47(1), 86–99.

Harvey, A., Burnheim, C., and Brett, M. (2016). *Student Equity in Australian Higher Education.* Singapore: Springer.

ICEF Monitor (2016). Australia's education exports surpass AUS$20 billion. *ICEF Monitor,* 28 November. http://monitor.icef.com/2016/11/australias-education-exports-surpass-aus20-billion/

Karmel, P. (Chair of Government Committee of Inquiry) (1973). *Schools in Australia.* Canberra: Australian Government Publishing Service.

Leiden University (2017). *CWTS Leiden Ranking 2016.* Centre for Science and Technology Studies (CWTS). www.leidenranking.com

Leigh, A. (2013). *Battlers and Billionaires: The Story of Inequality in Australia.* Collingwood, Vic: Redback.

Lomax-Smith, J. (Chair of Government Committee of Inquiry) (2011). *Higher Education Base Funding Review. Final Report.* Canberra: Commonwealth of Australia.

Macintyre, S. (2015). *Australia's Boldest Experiment: War and Reconstruction in the 1940s.* Sydney: NewSouth Publishing.

Marginson, S. (1997). *Educating Australia: Government, Economy and Citizen since 1960.* Cambridge: Cambridge University Press.

Marginson, S. (2007). Global position and position-taking: The case of Australia. *Journal of Studies in International Education* 11(1), 5–32.

Marginson, S. (2016a). *The Dream is Over: The Crisis of Clark Kerr's California Idea of Higher Education.* Berkeley: University of California Press.

Marginson, S. (2016b). *Higher Education and the Common Good.* Melbourne: Melbourne University Publishing.

Marginson, S. (2018). Federalism and higher education in Australia, in M. Carnoy, I. Froumin, O. Leshukov, and S. Marginson (eds) (2018). *Federalism in Higher Education: A Comparative Study.* New Delhi: Sage.

Marginson, S. and Considine, M. (2000). *The Enterprise University: Power, Governance and Reinvention in Australia.* Cambridge: Cambridge University Press.

Marks, G. (2015). Do Catholic and independent schools 'add-value' to students' tertiary entrance performance? Evidence from longitudinal population data. *Australian Journal of Education* 59(2), 133–57. doi:DOI: 10.1177/0004944115586658

Meek, L. (2000). Diversity and marketisation of higher education: Incompatible concepts? *Higher Education Policy* 13(1), 23–39.

NCVER (National Centre for Vocational Education Research) (2015). *Total VET Students and Courses 2014*. Adelaide: NCVER.

OECD (Organisation for Economic Co-operation and Development) (2015). Data on income distribution and poverty. http://stats.oecd.org/Index.aspx?DataSetCode=IDD

OECD (Organisation for Economic Co-operation and Development) (2016). *Education at a Glance, 2016*. Paris: OECD.

Piketty, T. (2014). *Capital in the Twenty-First Century*. Trans. A. Goldhammer. Cambridge, MA: Belknap Harvard University Press.

Rivera, L. (2015). *Pedigree: How Elite Students Get Elite Jobs*. Princeton, NJ: Princeton University Press.

Rose, N. (1999). *Powers of Freedom*. Cambridge: Cambridge University Press.

Trow, M. (1973). *Problems in the Transition from Elite to Mass Higher Education*. Berkeley, CA: Carnegie Commission on Higher Education.

Unireviews (2017). ATAR Scores for Australian Universities. https://universityreviews.com.au/atar-course-entry-scores/

UNESCO (United Nations Educational, Social and Cultural Organization) (2017). UNESCO Institute for Statistics data on education. http://data.uis.unesco.org

van Vught, F. (2008). Mission diversity and reputation in higher education. *Higher Education Policy* 21(2), 151–74.

World Bank (2017). Data and statistics. http://data.worldbank.org

11 Stratification by the State and the Market: High Participation Higher Education in Russia

Anna Smolentseva, Isak Froumin, David L. Konstantinovskiy, and Mikhail Lisyutkin

Introduction

The Russian Federation is the biggest country in world by area, with 17,098 million square kilometres (11 per cent of the global land area) stretched across eleven time zone and ranging from the Arctic to the forty-first parallel. It is a major producer of minerals and the location of large oil and gas reserves; in 2012 more than two-thirds of Russian exports were petroleum products. Russia is the world's ninth largest country by population with 144 million people in 2016. More than three-quarters of its people live in the more urbanized European part of Russia located west of the Ural mountains. The country is comprised of about 180 ethnicities, though 81 per cent of people are Russians with the second largest group, Tartars, constituting less than 4 per cent. Its eighty-five formal regions function under the auspices of a largely centralized political and administrative system. Russia is currently a middle-income country. Its gross domestic product (GDP) per capita in purchasing power parity (PPP) terms in 2016 was US$23,163, having declined by more than US$1,000 in real terms since 2013 due to the downturn of the economy in the wake of international sanctions. GDP in PPP terms in 2016 was US$3397.4 billion, the six largest in the world, 84 per cent of Germany and 18 per cent that of the United States (World Bank, 2017).

The contemporary Russian Federation is the heartland of the former Union of Soviet Socialist Republics (USSR), which for almost two generations after World War II was the world's second largest economy, science and technology system, and military power. The Russian Federation was formally constituted as an electoral democracy after the dissolution of the Soviet Union in 1991. While much has changed since 1991, with immense dislocation in the first decade, there are also significant cultural, political, and educational commonalities from the Soviet time. The remarkable leap to a high participation system (HPS) of higher education in the 1990s was facilitated by the transition to a market economy, implemented by inconsistent 'shock therapy', ineffective privatization and highly inflationary monetary policies, with little public participation in the reform agenda (Izyumov, 2010). As in some other parts of the former USSR the transition had a high human cost, higher than in the Soviet-dominated zone in Central and Eastern Europe. In the 1990s Russia's aggregate GDP and GDP per capita dropped dramatically, while the increase in the Gini coefficient was equally dramatic. High inequality has persisted; in 2012 the Gini was 41.6. In the absence of supportive governmental policies various private initiatives to cope with the transformation took destructive forms, with the explosive growth of the informal economy, corruption, crime and drug use (Izyumov, 2010).

But the neoliberal agenda, which asserted a limited role of the state and the responsibility of individuals and families for their own well-being, was also timely in a country that was trying to overcome the legacies of total state control in the Soviet era.

Writing in the 1970s Martin Trow did not consider the USSR as a mass higher education system, probably because he did not know much about it. The nation had achieved Trow's (1973) mass stage of higher education participation, 15 per cent of the age cohort, in the 1960s. Soviet policy towards higher education expansion laid a solid foundation for the exceptionally high growth that followed. In proportional terms Russia was a high participation country by 2000. In the later 2000s the rate of participation kept increasing but actual student enrolments began to drop sharply due to the decline of the birth rate in the 1990s. The number of students fell from a peak of 7.5 million in 2008 to just 4.4 million in 2016. Despite this 42 per cent contraction, Russia still has one of the biggest higher education systems in the world. According to the national micro-census of 2015, 40.5 per cent of the 25–34 age cohort held degrees, though there was a surprising gap between men (33.7 per cent) and women (47.2 per cent) (Indikatory obrazovania, 2017). Coupled with adults still working towards their degrees, it is apparent that Russia has achieved Trow's definition of 'universal' participation, meaning the HPS level of 50 per cent.

Higher education in Russia is called 'higher professional education' and includes public and private institutions of higher professional education awarding degrees mainly at ISCED-2011 Levels 6–8. Vocational education of ISCED Level 5 is considered a separate sector of educational system ('secondary vocational/professional education').

This chapter analyses the distinctive Russian path to high participation and the main characteristics of the Russian HPS in relation to governance, horizontal diversity, vertical stratification, and equity, discussing these areas in the light of the HPS project propositions.

The Russian Path to HPS: History and Drivers

After the 1917 revolution mass education at all levels was a priority of the new Soviet state. Educational attainment, especially in higher education, was far lower than in early twentieth century USA, Europe (Kuraev, 2014) and also Japan. Building a new social order and rapid industrialization required educated citizens and qualified workers. This

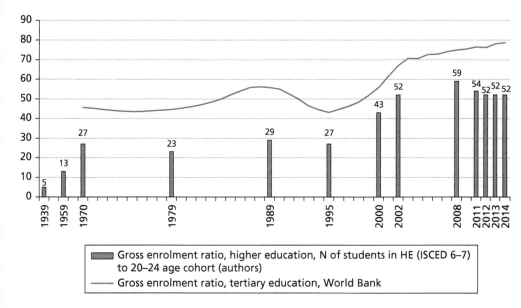

Figure 11.1. Gross enrolment ratio, Russian Soviet Federative Socialist Republic and Russian Federation, proportion (%) of age cohort

Source: Authors using data from World Bank (2017), Federal Statistics Service.

was achieved in little more than a generation. The need to rebuild the country after World War II, and the beginning of the Cold War, further stimulated economic and technical development and resulted in an increasing expansion of participation in and the size of higher education system (Figure 11.1).

In the 1960s the enrolment rose from 1.5 to 2.7 million (Figure 11.2). Building socialism was a political, social, and cultural project where education had a central role in the formation of a new Soviet man and transformation of the country, including economic and technological progress (Smolentseva, 2017b). The social prestige of higher education and higher educated people—more specifically, non-manual work (Konstantinovskiy, 2017)—was expected to increase on the path to communism. Highly qualified professions like engineers and doctors were supported socially and culturally despite strictly fixed Soviet salaries that reflected the hegemonic predominance of the working class. These factors shaped social aspirations and contributed to the continuing growth of participation in higher education. Enrolment in higher education was free of tuition costs except in the period 1940 to 1956.

In the next two decades of the 1970s and 1980s, until the disintegration of the USSR, age cohort participation remained at about the same level (see Figure 11.1) with the enrolment slipping a little in the 1980s. A low of 2.6 million was reached in 1993 but then numbers began to expand again until the demographic downturn in 2008 (Figure 11.2). The 'educational boom' was widely discussed in the 1990s. It was a puzzle for a nation

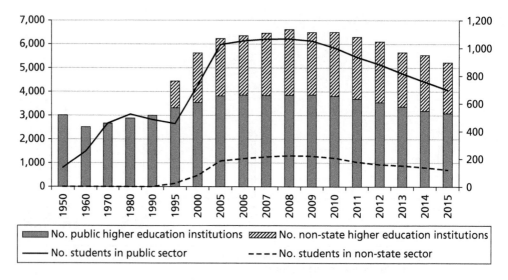

Figure 11.2. The expansion of public and non-state sectors of higher education: Number of higher education institutions and enrolments, Russia, 1950–2015

Source: Authors using data from Federal Statistics Service.

drowning in the debris of the Soviet political, social, and economic structure. The central planning which underpinned economic activities no longer existed. Jobs were no longer assigned to graduates by the state. No industry was thriving and demanding a highly skilled workforce, except for some new business services. Graduate salaries had little value due to hyper-inflation. None of the established social trajectories for status attainment, or social well-being, were meaningful given that the old social system was being deconstructed. The prevailing rhetoric was about breaking with the authoritarianism, centralization, paternalism, and collectivism of the Soviet past and replacing it by democracy, market economy, private property, and greater individual responsibility for one's own well-being. The 1990s were marked by economic decline and impoverishment of the population. GDP per capita dropped from US$3,100 (current US$) in 1992 to US$1,800 in 2000.

In the transition from mass to high participation several factors compounded to generate continuous growth. For the Russian case the second general HPS Proposition 2 holds true:

In HPS there is no intrinsic limit to the spread of family aspirations for participation in higher education until universality is reached; and no intrinsic limit to the level of social position to which families/students may aspire.

First, the Soviet time laid a solid structural and agential foundation for further expansion by having created large institutional systems of secondary and higher education (see Figure 11.2 and Table 11.1) and development of a high social value of higher education. By the end of the Soviet period participation had started to become a social

Table 11.1. Number of students, institutions, and faculty in Russian higher education, 1991–2016

Year	Total students (000s)	Students public (000s)	Students non-state (000s)	Students public (%)	Students non-state (%)	Total instit.	Instit. public	Instit. non-state	Total faculty (000s)	Faculty public (000s)	Faculty non-state (000s)
1991	2,762	2,762	–	100	–	519	519	–	235.5	233.5	–
1995	2,790	2,655	136	95.1	4.9	762	569	193	252.2	239.2	13.0
2000	4,741	4,271	471	90.1	9.9	965	607	358	279.6	265.2	14.4
2005	7,065	5,985	1,079	84.8	15.2	1,068	655	413	358.9	322.1	36.7
2006	7,310	6,133	1,177	83.9	16.1	1,090	660	430	378.4	334.0	44.4
2007	7,461	6,208	1,253	83.2	16.8	1,108	658	450	388.2	340.4	47.7
2008	7,513	6,215	1,298	82.8	17.2	1,134	660	474	377.8	342.7	35.1
2009	7,419	6,136	1,283	82.7	17.3	1,114	662	452	377.8	342.7	35.1
2010	7,050	5,849	1,201	83.0	17.0	1,115	653	462	356.8	324.8	32.0
2011	6,490	5,454	1,036	84.0	16.0	1,080	634	446	348.2	319.0	29.2
2012	6,074	5,144	930	84.7	15.3	1,046	609	437	342.0	312.8	29.2
2013	5,647	4,762	885	84.3	15.7	969	578	391	319.3	288.2	31.1
2014	5,209	4,406	804	84.6	15.4	950	548	402	299.8	271.5	28.2
2015	4,767	4,061	705	85.2	14.8	896	530	366	279.8	255.8	23.9
2016	4,379	n.a.	n.a.	n.a.	n.a.	817	n.a.	n.a.	n.a.	n.a.	n.a.

Notes: instit. = institutions. '—' = non-applicable, as private sector did not exist. n.a. = data not available.
Source: Authors using data from Federal Statistics Service.

norm for some social groups (Konstantinovskiy 2008). Second, the gradual structural transformation of the planned economy into a market economy required a new map of occupations, skills, and knowledge. Retraining, obtaining second and different higher education qualification, became popular. Third, economic returns to higher education were relatively high, especially for women, compared to the OECD countries (Gimpelson and Kapelyushnikov, 2011). Higher education facilitated better labour market outcomes including protection from unemployment, working conditions, and incomes; and as in some other countries a university degree was an increasing advantage when compared to secondary vocational qualifications (ISCED 5 (2011)) programmes (Kember, 2010; Parry, 2012). Fourth, the break-up of the old social structures reinforced the need to maintain or strengthen one's status and life chances. By the early 2000s, sociologists observed that higher education had become a social norm for many, including the groups that traditionally had shown less interest in obtaining higher education, such as rural population (Konstantinovskiy, 1999; Shishkin, 2004).

In short, during the period of major social transformation in Russia, higher education offered high positional value (Hirsch, 1976; Marginson, 1997) as a means of advancing, securing, or hedging status and income (Smolentseva, 2017a) and for some, supporting geographic as well as social mobility. Likewise, the significant expansion of Doctoral education in the 1990s–2000s may indicate the need for still higher positional value at a time when mass first degree education was growing very rapidly (Smolentseva, 2007).

Finally, noting that in higher education quasi-markets the incremental growth of student places is driven more by supply than by demand (Marginson, 1997), the massification of the 1990s and after was also fostered by the need of higher education institutions to survive by expanding the only product that they had to offer, which was student places.

In 1990s public funds were extremely scarce, and the new quasi-market funding mechanisms facilitated massification by creating places additional to publicly funded public sector places: (a) fee-based public places for those who did not score well enough to access state-funded free places; and (b) a fee-based non-state sector. Quasi-market mechanisms were urged by international experts, who considered Russia to be lagging behind in participation and access (Heyneman, 2010). It was also argued that the non-state sector would bring greater freedom and flexibility to the structure and content of education (Smolentseva, 2017b). The new system created conditions for the spread of low cost provision via territorial expansion of institutional branches of higher education institutions, and growth in part-time (distance) programmes.

MARKET MECHANISMS, GROWTH, AND QUALITY

Over the ten years from 1995 to 2005, government budgeted enrolments increased by only 20 per cent and the largest increase in students was associated with the growth of the fee-paying strand in public higher education (Figure 11.3). From 1995 to 2005,

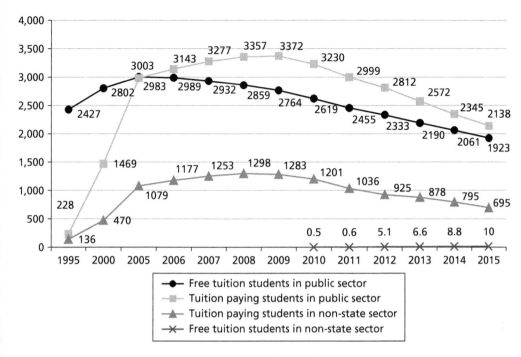

Figure 11.3. How the privatization of costs facilitated massification in Russian higher education: The number of tuition free and tuition paying students in public and private sectors, 1995–2013, thousands of people

Source: Authors using data from Federal Statistics Service, Indikatory obrazovania 2017 (2017).

tuition paying students in public institutions increased by 92 per cent. Though non-state enrolments also nearly doubled, increasing by 87 per cent, the emerging non-state sector was less competitive, at one third the size of tuition charging programmes in public institutions. It never exceeded 17 per cent of total enrolments.

From the mid-2000s onwards over half the students in the public sector paid tuition and this has kept increasing. Despite the demographic contraction, by the mid 2010s only 40 per cent of total higher education students were enrolled in places free of tuition (Figure 11.3).

The number of higher education institutions has been growing. In sector it increased from 514 in 1990 to 662 in 2009, the peak year in terms of number of institutions, complemented by almost 500 non-state institutions, mostly small scale social science, business, law studies establishments (see Figure 11.2; Table 11.1). New public institutions were established across all regions of the country during the two first post-Soviet decades (Table 11.2), delivering education free or on a tuition basis, full-time or part-time, to over six million students at the peak. The non-state sector also grown in all regions, reaching a peak total of 1.3 million students.

The establishment of affiliated branches delivering full-time and part-time programmes became a successful strategy for recruiting students outside the direct reach of the core

Table 11.2. Territorial expansion of public higher education, by federal districts, 1990–2014

Federal districts	1990	1995	2000	2005	2010	2014
Central	152	167	183	204	209	172
North Western	63	68	72	75	78	60
Southern	39	45	46	50	47	37
North Caucasian	21	26	28	29	30	27
Volga	93	103	111	123	118	96
Urals	37	43	48	51	51	42
Siberian	77	82	84	85	83	70
Far Eastern	32	35	35	38	37	30
Crimean						14
Total	2,504	2,564	2,607	2,660	2,663	2,562

Source: Authors using data from Federal Statistics Service.

Table 11.3. Expansion of the branches of higher educational institutions, number of branches, and the ratio of the number of branch campuses to the number of main campuses, 2002–15

	2002	2005	2010	2011	2012	2013	2014	2015
Public sector, branches	1,371	1,102	1,069	1,045	1,013	949	843	727
Non-state sector, branches	326	519	599	594	590	533	476	352
Total, branches	1,697	1,621	1,668	1,639	1,603	1,482	1,319	1,079
Public sector, ratio	2.1	1.7	1.7	1.6	1.6	1.5	1.7	1.6
Non-state sector, ratio	0.8	1.3	1.2	1.3	1.3	1.3	1.4	1.4
Total, ratio	1.6	1.5	1.5	1.5	1.5	1.5	1.5	1.5

Source: Authors using data from Federal Statistics Service.

institution (Table 11.3). Major city institutions stretched out to other regions, while other institutions were more location bound in the sense that they operated mostly within their own and neighbouring regions. Overall, bigger territorial reach helped higher education institutions to increase their funding through governmental subsidies and tuitions fees while making higher education more accessible for those living outside of major cities. That worked for many people, whose drastically declined living standards in the 1990s–2000s reduced their geographical mobility. The establishment of branches in small towns also served an important social mission, keeping some young people in the regions who otherwise may have left for larger cities with more opportunities.

Expansion was also facilitated by the proliferation of the part-time (distance) segment of higher education (Figure 11.4). In the Soviet period, the part-time sector was large, with 42 per cent of enrolments in 1990. Combining work and study was considered an effective way of improving the qualifications of the working population and was officially encouraged. In the post-Soviet period, it became a way for higher education institutions to deliver low cost education to a wider audience, generally with little regard for quality. For the population it became an opportunity to obtain higher education credential at

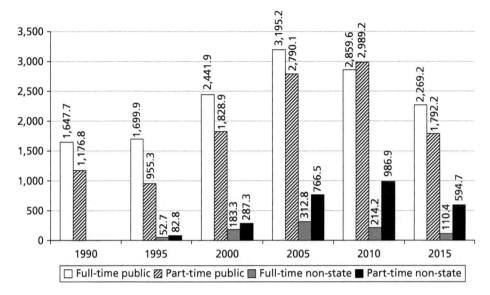

Figure 11.4. Expansion of full-time and part-time programmes, public and non-state sector, number of students, 1990–2015

Source: Authors using Federal Statistics Service.

lower cost, without interrupting their ongoing careers and income. As a result, from 1995 to 2008, while the full-time enrolments doubled, part-time enrolments quadrupled, growing to 54 per cent of total enrolments by 2008. The vast majority of the part-time students were (and are) enrolled into 'correspondence' programmes, which essentially means largely distance learning with very few contact hours.

In the mid-2000s onwards the government began to address issues arising from the expansion. It was obvious that the resources of the system bore little relation to its expanded size and this had to affect the quality of provision. In UNESCO comparisons of per capita GDP per tertiary student for 2007–10, Russia was in the bottom ten countries (UNESCO, n.d.). Between 1995 and 2005 full-time faculty in public sector institutions increased by only 17 per cent despite the 153 per cent growth in student numbers. As the result of successive government interventions designed to eliminate instances of poor provision, the number of public institutions and of public institutions' branches has now declined notably.

The third general HPS Proposition 3 is also supported:

Once transition from a primarily agricultural economy is achieved, the long-term growth of HPS is independent of political economic factors such as economic growth and patterns of labour market demand; patterns of public and private funding of higher education; the roles of public and private institutions; and system organization and modes of governance.

The dynamic of expansion embraced economic downturn and economic recovery; both graduates heading for old state-driven industries and graduates employed in new market-driven industries; both state funding and private funding; and both the period of growth of the non-state sector and the period of its shrinkage in the demographic decline after 2008.

However, the intention to participate varies between groups of students. Among secondary students in 2014, 96 per cent of those studying advanced subjects at school wanted to go on to higher or tertiary education; 89 per cent of regular secondary school students; and 55 per cent of those enrolled in secondary vocational institutions (Indikatory obrazovania, 2017).

Marketization indeed had a major role in the massification process and was implemented on a much larger scale than in Eastern European countries undergoing similar transformations. Like in Poland, marketization of higher education was dual: both internal to the public sector (through tuition) and external (through the emergence of non-state providers) (Kwiek 2008, 2011). But unlike in Poland, where internal privatization in the public sector was limited to part-time programmes, 'creeping marketization' in Russia penetrated all higher education system: to both full-time and part-time programmes. That shift was enabled by new political and economic course towards liberalization which implied diminished role of the state. Lack of governmental regulation was also an outcome of the economic and political turbulence of the time when higher education was not a priority among others and public resources were very scarce. This lack of political determination (Tomusk, 1998; Kwiek, 2008) or 'policy of non-policy' (Kwiek, 2008) contributed to the privatization of costs. The 'solution' to loosen governmental control and give institutions freedoms enabled higher education institutions to survive by raising their own money. That window of opportunities was used by the institutional administration to consolidate their control over the institutions, and supplement their vanishing budgets. It might have contributed to the subsequent growth of informal economy in the higher education sector. Marketization 'worked' quite well both for the state and higher education institutions at this time, but, perhaps, did not work so well for higher education as one of the key social institutions of society.

Governance

Unlike the system of financing of universities and of student participation, the governance system of Russian higher education has not radically changed since the Soviet time. It remains highly centralized at the federal level. The first governance proposition, HPS Proposition 4

HPS are governed by multi-level control, coordination, and accountability mechanisms

is not fully applicable to the Russian case.

ABSENCE OF MULTI-LEVEL GOVERNANCE

The Ministry of Education retains its regulatory functions over the system as a whole. The Federal Service of Control in Education performs the function of accreditation, licensing, and institutional quality assurance for both the public and private sectors. The public funding of higher education is from the federal level. The number of tuition-free places per field of study and the financing of each institution are negotiated and approved by the federal ministry each year. The majority of public institutions are under federal authorities, whether the Ministry of Education or sectoral ministries such as health, transportation, and culture, in the Russian government.

This essential structure is in direct lineage from the highly centralized, centrally planned, and top-down command methods of administration used in Soviet time (Froumin et al., 2014; Kuraev, 2016). The Soviet higher education system was built into a larger economic planning system and reflected the political and economic logic of the Soviet state. In the Stalin era in the 1930s, most institutions were transferred from the ministry of education to various sectoral ministries. These ministries were positioned as employing authorities in the planned economy. Each industry/ministry managed the development of its own capacity and cadre. This was considered the way to link the training of a qualified workforce with industrialization and military mobilization (Smolentseva et al., 2018). However, in the absence of centrally planned industrial production and labour allocation this system of organization of higher education no longer has its founding rationale.

In the early post-Soviet period the centralization of higher education governance and the multi-sectoral coordination of the sector were widely criticized, especially by international experts (Heyneman, 2010). After the disintegration of the USSR some institutions were transferred from sectoral control to Ministry of Education control, and more than half of the public institutions, enrolling two-thirds of public sector students, are now subject to the Ministry of Education. The remaining 40 per cent of higher education institutions still belong to other federal sectoral agencies including the Ministry of Healthcare, the Ministry of Agriculture, the Federal Agency for Railways Transportation, the Ministry of Culture, and the Supreme Court. These are various specialist institutions in training fields such as medicine, agriculture, transport, and others. This part of the sector is largely in continuity from the Soviet period (Table 11.4).

The old horizontal assignment of institutions to different ministries implied if not multi-level governance, then multi-site governance. In the consolidation of control and coordination of public higher education under one ministry, centralization has been enhanced. It has not been accompanied by a substantial delegation of power to regional and/or institutional level. This is the opposite tendency to that in the HPS proposition. Here the authority structure in higher education reflects the broader structure of the Russian comprehensive state.

Table 11.4. Distribution of public higher education institutions by subordination, 2015

	Number of institutions, main campuses	Share of institutions, main campuses, (%)	Number of institutions, main and branch campuses	Number and share of students in total number of students (million)
Ministry of Education and Science	261	50.8	668	2.6 (66.7%)
Regional and municipal authorities	49	9.5	63	0.1 (2.6%)
Various federal ministries and agencies, including the government of the Russian Federation	204	39.7	405	1.2 (30.7%)
Total	514	100.0	1,136	2.9 (100%)

Note: Data of Monitoring of Performance and Federal Statistics Service may differ slightly.

Sources: Authors using data of Monitoring of Performance, 2016.

Table 11.5. The proportional (%) funding higher education institutions by source, Russia, 2015

Sources of funding	Public institutions (%)	Non-state institutions (%)
Public/budget, total	60.8	2.9
Federal	*57.8*	*2.4*
Regional	*2.8*	*0.3*
Local/municipal	*0.2*	*0.2*
Industries	12.1	14.6
Individuals	24.1	79.3
Off-budget	1.7	0.8
Foreign	1.4	2.3
Total	100.0	100.0

Source: Authors using data Federal Statistics Service.

In Table 11.4 only forty-nine institutions, one-tenth of the public sector, are subordinated to regional authorities and very few belong to the municipal or local level. The data in Table 11.5 show that public sector institutions are largely dependent on federal funding, with 57.8 per cent of their budgets from federal ministries and 3.0 per cent from regional and local level. The other two important sources for public institutions are industries (12.1 per cent) and individuals (24.1 per cent). In the non-state sector these last two numbers are much higher (14.6 per cent and 79.3 per cent, respectively) with very little governmental contribution. Only in early 2010s were non-state institutions granted eligibility for governmental funding. It is likely that the funding from industry mostly refers to payment of tuition fees rather than R&D and consulting.

Despite this formally low level of regional subordination, for most public institutions located outside Moscow and St Petersburg, a high level of engagement with regional authorities, industries and communities is essential, as they are financially dependent on the influx of local students, contracts with local business and governments and the overall social and economic environment created by local authorities (Smolentseva, 2016). In the absence of direct mechanisms regional authorities still have some control over institutions in their respective regions by influencing rector appointments, membership of institutional supervising boards, negotiating with institutions the number of tuition free places, funding some students places, facilitating development of physical infrastructure (e.g. lending buildings), and through specific higher education and R&D activities (Froumin and Leshukov, 2015).

Generally, institutional autonomy has been low. The 1992 Law on Education granted some freedoms to universities which for a time were more readily exercised because higher education institutions were not tightly overseen by the weakened state. This empowered rectors, now elected by academic councils, and the rectors' union became a strong agent in promoting or blocking governmental policies and transformative reforms. After 2000 there was a political shift back towards centralization and institutional autonomy shrank. Candidates for rector positions are negotiated and the final appointment has to be approved by the authority that established the institution. The rectors of the Moscow and St Petersburg State Universities are appointed and dismissed by the president of the Russian Federation, while rectors of federal universities are subject to the government. Higher education curricula are shaped on the basis of unified educational standards developed at the federal level. Since 2008 certain institutions have been granted the right to develop their own educational standards, while at the same time ensuring those standards are not lower than the federal ones. These are those with statuses of federal universities, national research universities, and twelve other top institutions including Moscow and St Petersburg State Universities, and Bauman Moscow State Polytechnic University.

MANAGEMENT OF HORIZONTAL DIVERSITY

Despite (or because of) the absence of multi-level coordination, central federal governance is fractured, reflecting the horizontal field-specific and sectoral differentiation of higher education. Horizontal diversity is built into the system and its coordination. The second proposition on governance (HPS Proposition 5),

HPS governance tends to involve the management of horizontal differentiation

fits relatively well. Horizontal diversity is discussed in the next section.

CORPORATIZATION

Under conditions that combine centralized state control with market competition for students and funding (the post-Soviet HP is largely a quasi-market), institutions tend to employ corporate forms to maximize economic efficiency. The third proposition on governance (HPS Proposition 6),

> HPS complex multi-level accountability and coordination, coupled with system differentiation, result in higher education institutions adopting increasingly corporate forms and robust internal governance and management capacities

applies well to the Russian HPS.

The model of the 'entrepreneurial university' (Clark, 1998) proved timely and popular in Russia as it provided an idea and rationale for commercial self-financing institutions necessarily undergoing organizational transformation. The associated changes in structure and process included growth in financial management and marketing offices, branding, quality assurance and strategic planning. Higher education institutions learned to manage and expand revenues though increases in student numbers, the sales of educational and research services, and renting out facilities. From the 1990s onwards total quality control standards were actively implemented by institutions. Later, institutions established supervisory and governing boards focused on strategic institutional governance. Much has been invested in retraining university leaders to navigate the changing socio-economic environments. For example, during 2015–16 the Ministry of Education spent almost US$10 million on retraining programmes at one leading Russian business school.

New accountability mechanisms further entrenched competition and corporatization. For the first two post-Soviet decades, quality control and accountability were based on traditional individually oriented licensing and accreditation by the Federal Service of Control in Education. This did not facilitate performance and quality improvement or prevent expansion of low-quality institutions. In 2012 the government introduced annual performance monitoring of higher education institutions with fifty performance indicators. Using five of these indicators, relating to the quality of incoming students, research, and financial outputs, the Ministry divided the universities into two groups, 'normally performing' and 'low performing'. The bar positioned 15 per cent of universities in the 'low performing' group, and was later raised further. 'Low performing' institutions were expected to develop an 'improvement plan'. Failure to comply with requirements meant enforced reorganization, closure or merger with a stronger institution. With institutions employing all possible means to achieve the targets, the major global consultancy companies have been active in developing business models and strategies for Russian higher education sector.

In sum, despite the seemingly radical transition from planned economy to market, and from authoritarianism to democracy (albeit with limitations), higher education governance reflects the old Soviet control pattern of a centralized top-down federal system. After a relatively short period of non-policy the state regained comprehensive control. The timely development of the new public management facilitated 'steering from the distance'. The current policy goals are efficiency, excellence, matching higher education to the labour market, and enhanced international visibility. Regulation is reducing the number of higher education institutions. Government-devised indicators, graduate employment, and international rankings have added to the existing control mechanisms. The centralized management of an expanded higher education system has created many pressures and tensions in the distribution of limited public resources, the results of which are discussed in the next sections.

Horizontal Diversity

As noted, Soviet higher education was largely oriented towards vocational needs (Kuraev, 2016) and the prevailing type of higher education institutions was specialist institutes or academies that prepared the labour force for particular industries. A 'university' was a designated type of institutions with a wide range of fields of study and generally had higher prestige. In 1992 there were forty-two universities (8 per cent of all institutions) with 328,000 students (12 per cent of the student population).

MULTIVERSITIES AND THE DECLINE OF DIVERSITY

After 1992 popular demand, the growth of the service sector of the economy and the growing role of research and international activities encouraged the transformation of many traditional institutions into multi-purpose, multi-disciplinary 'multiversities'. This was partly consistent with the first proposition on horizontal diversity (HPS Proposition 7), which states that:

> *In the HPS era, regardless of the political economy and culture of systems, an increasing proportion of higher education becomes centred on comprehensive multi-discipline and multi-function research universities, or 'multiversities'. The multiversity is increasingly dominant as the paradigmatic form of higher education.*

However, in Russia the research dimension of the multiversity is less developed than the proposition suggests, due to the Soviet legacies of organization of research. In the Soviet period research was largely allocated to the academies of sciences and sectoral ministries. Even now only about 10 per cent of R&D takes place in higher education sector.

Table 11.6. Enrolments by field of study, higher education, Russia, 2005–13

	2005 (000)	(%)	2010 (000)	(%)	2013 (000)	(%)
Mathematics and physics	99	1.4	81	1.1	76	1.3
Sciences	93	1.3	86	1.2	86	1.5
Humanities	1,324	18.7	1,366	19.4	1,104	19.6
Social sciences	90	1.3	89	1.3	67	1.2
Education	748	10.6	557	7.9	456	8.1
Health	201	2.8	219	3.1	244	4.3
Culture and art	123	1.7	134	1.9	114	2.0
Economics and management	2,427	34.4	2,573	36.5	1,739	30.8
Services	80	1.1	106	1.5	114	2.0
Agriculture and fishery	214	3.0	200	2.8	171	3.0
Information security and IT	179	2.5	185	2.6	198	3.5
Other engineering	1,487	21.0	1,454	20.6	1,277	22.6
Total	7,065	100.0	7,050	100.0	5,647	100.0

Source: Authors using data from Federal Statistics Service.

In the 1990s the main mechanism of rapid growth of higher education institutions was via upgrading to the comprehensive university function. Using fee-based places individual institutions expanded their range of fields of study into economics, management, law, humanities, and social sciences, enabling them to change legal title from institute/academy to university. Many engineering, agricultural, and other specialist institutions opened new departments and schools. By 2010 enrolments in economics and management comprised 36 per cent and enrolments in services even increased in absolute numbers after 2008 despite the demographic decline (see Table 11.6). Many specialist universities lost or weakened their original focus. In the early 2010s, in agricultural higher education institutions, only 45 per cent of students enrolled in agriculture related programmes; at engineering institutions just 60 per cent studied in engineering related programmes (Froumin et al., 2014). In other cases, existing comprehensive universities further expanded by adding fields such as medicine and engineering (particularly in IT) once the province of specialist institutions. The restructuring of vocational education allowed higher education institutions to establish short-cycle vocational education programmes or include vocational colleges. By 2015 about 500,000 students in Russian public higher education institutions studied in vocational (ISCED 5) programmes (but they are not considered as higher education students) (Monitoring of Performance, 2016).

As noted, student demand for training in the new professions in Russia was initially enabled by the abolition of compulsory graduate job placement and sustained by the changing profile of the economy and labour markets. The interest in 'soft' fields can also be partly explained by their low provision in the Soviet system where engineering and related fields were dominant. The market demand for new fields of study, plus the introduction of quasi-market mechanisms, simulated the gradual transition of specialist institutions towards the multiversity model. The evolution of system and institutional configurations in the HPS in Russian higher education was a function of the socio-economic and political environment.

Nevertheless, there was some resistance to the diversification of formerly specialized universities. There were also doubts about the quality of training in the new fields. The government tried to stop or limit the diversification process. Specialized universities still under the sectoral ministries were forced to cut 'non-core' programmes. The Ministry of Health was successful—very few medical universities offer non-medical courses—while Ministry of Agriculture had the opposite outcome. At the same time, the Ministry of Education promoted the multiversity, providing incentives and administrative pressure to secure higher education institutional mergers. Between 2008 and 2012 almost one hundred mergers were registered. The most prominent was the formation of federal universities, very large institutions established by merging several regional institutions: usually a comprehensive university with specialized institutions with the objective of developing a leading role in higher education in their respective regions.

As a result of these developments the multi-subject university is now the most common type of a higher education institution in Russia. However, the research-intensive multiversity norm has yet to spread broad roots. Platonova and Semyonov (2018) show that large universities with a significant research activity in a variety of fields comprise only 3 per cent of higher education institutions and enrolling 5 per cent of students (see Table 11.7). The closest next type is public regional universities such as the federal universities, very large, selective, and engaged in some research (11 per cent of institutions and 38 per cent of students). The most common type of institutions is the public mass university, characterized by a mix of fields, relatively selective in admission, focused on part-time teaching, but with little research (32 per cent of institutions and 42 per cent of students).

Chapter 4 argues that the multiversity is characterized by size and power. In Russia those characteristics are yet to fully emerge. The group of large universities, products of historic eminence, higher education mergers, and social expansion is eclectic and diverse. It includes very prestigious Moscow State University (30,300 students) and St Petersburg Polytechnic University (29,4000), federal universities such as Urals Federal University (32,700), Siberian Federal University (29,800), Kazan Federal University (29,500), South Federal University (26,800), and merged middle-tier institutions like Moscow State University of Railways (30,300) On the whole the size of leading institutions exceeds the overall average public university of 5,800 students—for example St Petersburg University (19,000 students), the national research universities (13,500), the participants of global excellence programme 5/100 (17,000) and federal universities (21,000) (Monitoring of Performance, 2016).[1]

---

[1] The data here refer to enrolments on main campuses only.

Table 11.7. Diversity of institutional mission and type in Russian higher education, 2015

Type	Features	Share of institutions (%)	Number of institutions	Share of students (%)
Public research universities	Diversified fields, research-productive, selective, MA level, attract fee-paying students, mostly Moscow, St Petersburg	3	22	4
Public regional universities	Very large, diversified subject mix, selective, large part-time, large state support, some R&D	11	84	32
Public specialized institutions	Small, highly selective, highly specialized, full-time, mostly medical	11	88	8
Public mass universities	Diversified subject mix, selective, large part-time, large state support, do not attract fee-paying students	32	248	36
Non-state specialized	Specialization in popular programmes	22	167	5
Non-state diversified	Diversified subject mix	12	95	5
Non-state part-time institutions	Only part-time fee-paying students, very small, specialization in popular programmes	9	68	10
Totals		100	772	100

Source: Adapted by authors from Platonova and Semyonov (2018); data from Monitoring of Performance (2015).

The Russian case confirms that the overall diversity of the system has decreased, the traditional boundaries between comprehensive and specialist institutions are now more blurred, and the system is converging towards the multi-subject university as the dominant form, though that process has a way to run. The use of common performance indicators in all institutions also stimulates convergence. The government's focus on research as status might also move leading Russian higher education institutions closer to the multiversity. The Russian case illustrates the second diversity proposition (HPS Proposition 8) that:

> *Regardless of the political economy and culture of the HPS, when participation expands there is no necessary increase in the overall diversity of institutional form and mission; and this has probably declined, except in relation to online provision.*

INTERNAL (INTRA-UNIVERSITY) DIVERSITY

The large socio-economic transformations, governmental policy, and policy of non-policy (Kwiek, 2008), have together resulted in Russian higher education institutions with a broad spectrum of training fields, different delivery mechanisms, vocational and continuing education programmes, and branches in different cities. Dependent on the environment, higher education institutions have adapted markedly and this can lead to substantial heterogeneity for example Smolentseva's (2016) account of the launch of automobile and tractor construction programmes in a regional classic university, invoking tensions between vocational and academic missions. The academic level of incoming students as measured by the national university entrance exam is also very heterogeneous within institutions, generating pedagogical and social challenges (Aleskerov et al., 2014). Internal institutional diversity has become an important phenomenon in Russian higher education, corresponding to the third diversity proposition (HPS Proposition 9):

> *As participation expands the internal diversity of multiversities tends to increase. This affects some or all of the range of missions, business activities, institutional forms and internal structures, the discipline mix, research activities, levels of study and range of credentials, the heterogeneity of the student body, links to stakeholders, cross-border relations, and forms of academic and non-academic labour.*

There are also other forms of internal institutional diversity, such as social polarization. In the top fifty universities the salaries of top administrators vary from the highest of 196 million roubles (US$2,900,000) to the lowest of twelve million roubles (US$179,000). The average annual salary of academic staff is 660,000 roubles (US$9,900), so the ratio of top leaders' income to those of academic staff is up to 300 times (RBC, 2017).[2]

QUASI-MARKETS AND DIVERSITY

As the earlier account suggests the fourth diversity proposition (HPS Proposition 10) is agreed in relation to Russia:

> *The combination of expanding participation and enhanced competition in neoliberal quasi-markets is associated with specific effects in relation to diversity, including (1) increased vertical differentiation of higher education institutions (stratification); (2) reduced horizontal differentiation (diversification); (3) convergence of missions through isomorphistic imitation; and (4) growth in the role of private higher education institutions, especially for-profit institutions.*

Imitation of successful forms of higher education institutions able to survive in changing environment has contributed to the decline of diversity. The need for shared learning

---

[2] Rectors' salaries data from RBC, 2017. Ratio with faculty salaries from authors' calculations using Monitoring of Performance. Annual average exchange rate for 2016 was about 67 roubles = 1 US$.

Table 11.8. Average higher education institutions in public and non-state sectors, main campuses, 2015

Indicators	Average public higher education institution	Average non-state higher education institution
Number of students	6,740	1,445
Number of full-time teaching staff	453	44
National test admission score (state-funded full-time students)	63.78	47.31
Income from all sources (000 roubles)	1,310,688	131,480
Publications indexed by Web of Science per 100 faculty	8.25	7.64
Publications indexed by Scopus per 100 faculty	12.12	11.91
R&D income (000 roubles)	169,316	8,471

Source: Authors using data from the Monitoring of Performance by the Ministry of Education and Science (2016).

and solidarity (or at least shelter) prompted Russian higher education institutions to establish associations of the like-minded and professional learning communities, which furthered the isomorphic tendency.

However, in contrast with point (4) in the proposition, the role of the private sector has been modest. It contributed to the expansion of higher education at the peak of growth but works mostly in the mass teaching sector with very little contribution to R&D. As Table 11.8 demonstrates, on average private institutions are much smaller in size, have few full-time teaching staff, low selectivity at admissions, much lower income, much lower research-related income suggesting less research intensity, though surprisingly not much lower in English-language global publication. Private institutions have made a series attempts to consolidate through an association but it does not play an essential role in Russian higher education policy.

Vertical Stratification

Vertical stratification is a profound characteristic of the Russian HPS. After more than a decade of the policy of non-policy, from the mid-2000s onwards the national government put much effort into achieving a steeper system stratification. It set out to concentrate the resources of the dramatically expanded system in a handful of intended 'World-class' universities to enable them to achieve better quality in education and research, contribute to the national economy, and strengthen the position of Russia in the global space. Global 'relativization' has become an important driver pushing forward the strategic development of higher education across the world (Marginson and van der Wende, 2009). Global referencing was critical in the USSR, in which global super-power competition was uppermost, but was neglected in the first post-Soviet decade. In the last fifteen years policymakers and stakeholders have begun again to relate the national system and its institutions to international standards.

BIFURCATION AND STRATIFICATION

Government-driven vertical stratification has occurred in waves. In 2006 two initiatives were launched. First, fifty-seven universities received on a competitive basis up to US$33 million to develop innovative programmes. This laid a foundation for later identifying a smaller group of leading higher education institutions. Second, the process of establishing federal universities began. Ten institutions received federal university status by merging comprehensive and specialized institutions to strengthen higher education in their regions. Federal universities were expected to provide workforce training and research support for regional development and for the country as a whole, involving higher education in regional development and involving regions in the development of higher education (Kontseptsia sozdania i gosudarstvennoi podderzhdki razvitia federal'nykh universitetov, 2009). They took the new economic form of 'autonomous organization', in contrast to 'budget organizations' which had more financial entitlements.

In 2009, the government granted special status to the two oldest universities, Moscow State and St Petersburg State, and announced a competition for 'national research university' status and related funding of up to US$60 million per institution. In the outcome twenty-nine universities were awarded this status including nine comprehensive (classical) universities, seventeen technical universities, a medical university, and an economic university, as well as the Academic Research and Education Centre of the Russian Academy of Sciences. Almost half of the new national research universities were concentrated in two capitals. In 2012, the government launched a global excellence initiative titled 'Project 5/100' aimed at investing in the global competitiveness of leading Russian universities with a view to leveraging them into the QS, Times Higher, or Shanghai ARWU top 100. Currently twenty-one competitively selected higher education institutions participate in the programme including five federal universities, seven comprehensive/classical, seven polytechnics, one medical universities, and the Higher School of Economics, predominantly in social science with some engineering and science. The most recent initiative is the selection of 'flagship' universities in the Russian regions. The mission of the regional flagship is expected to drive the socio-economic and cultural development of the regions. So far nineteen institutions have been designated flagship universities, receive the development grants of about US$3 million per year.

The full set of federal, national research, and global excellence programme universities, plus Moscow State and St Petersburg State, comprise forty-five higher education institutions (the first three categories overlap). In total this group has 723,000 students on their main campuses, about 18 per cent of public enrolments or 15 per cent of all enrolments (Monitoring of Performance, 2016). These policies have formally stratified the higher education landscape. Different groups of leading higher education institutions became stand-alone administration objects. Universities from this group have more curriculum autonomy and greater access to publicly funded development projects.

Competition in higher education systems always tends to favour institutions with already accumulated prestige and resources. It is not surprising that in Russia historically strong institutions are found in the top group. An increased scarcity of public funding, rendering competition more intensive, has improved their position. Overall funding for higher education declined from 651 billion roubles in 2013 to 619 billion in 2014 and 537 billion in 2015 (Lisyutkin, 2017). Public expenditures moved from 513 billion in 2013 to 520 billion in 2014 and then 517 billion in 2015. Between 2010 and 2015 higher education funding dropped from 0.8 to 0.6 per cent of GDP (Indikatory obrazovania, 2017). In this context the special programmes that have redistributed funding in favour of high status universities have sharper effects in enhancing stratification. In addition, this stratification is enhanced by the regular system of public funding: the funding formula includes indicators directly or indirectly derived from institutional prestige, such as the average national test admission scores, and international research publications.

As Figure 11.5 shows, in 2013, thirty-five national research universities and federal universities (this includes the fifteen global excellence higher education institutions) received 38.1 per cent of all funding of higher education institutions controlled by the Ministry of Education and Science. The other 260 institutions received 61.9 per cent. The elite group's share reached 42.5 per cent in 2015 (Abankina, Vinarik, and Filatova, 2016).

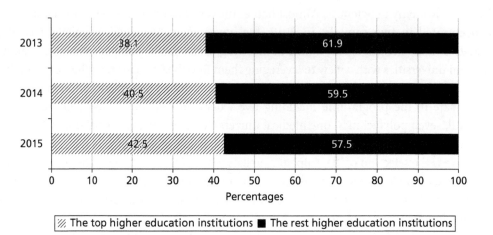

Figure 11.5. The allocation of the government subsidy for education to the higher education institutions under the Ministry of Education and Science (%)

Source: Adapted by authors from Abankina et al., 2016.

Table 11.9. Stratification of higher education institutions, by income and research, main campuses, public sector, 2016

	All leading (inc. federal, NRU, 5/100, MSU, StPSU)	National research (29)	5/100 group (21)	Federal (10)	Non-leading	Total public HEIs
Average income, million roubles	5,627	4,801	6,445	5,533	879	1,311
Overall income per number of students, roubles	544,000	612,000	531,000	361,000	307,000	329,000
Share of income from federal budget %	63	63	64	71	57	58
Share of income from regional and municipal budgets %	6	6	6	6	8	7
Share of income from off-budget sources %	36	36	35	28	35	35
Income from off-budget sources, million roubles	1,988	1,616	2,278	1,711	354	502
Average admission score, full-time, tuition free places	75	76	77	69	64	65
Share of income from educational activity %	56	53	52	61	78	76
Average amount of R&D, million roubles	1,153	1,218	1,205	662	71	169
Share of income from R&D %	22	26	21	11	8	9
Citations in Web of Science over 5 years per 100 academic staff	297	364	422	78	99	117
Citations in Scopus over 5 years per 100 academic staff	316	378	422	104	103	122
Citations in Russian citation system over 5 years per 100 academic staff	635	626	819	505	567	573
Publications indexed in Web of Science 5 years per 100 academic staff	35	44	54	17	6	8
Publications in Scopus over 5 years per 100 academic staff	46	55	67	27	9	12
Publications in Russian citation system 5 years per 100 academic staff	192	182	203	215	179	181

Note: HEI = higher education institution. MSU = Moscow State University; SPbSU = St Petersburg State University.

Source: Authors using data from Monitoring of Performance (2016).

More data on the vertical differentiation of public higher education are presented in the Table 11.9. There are significant differences between the leading universities in the table (federal, national research, 5/100, Moscow State, and St Petersburg State), and the rest. The total income of the elite group is five times higher than that of the non-elite strata, and income per student is double. The leading group is not homogeneous. In most respects, federal universities are similar to non-elite institutions, exceeding them only in size-related indicators. For example, federal universities are less selective than other leading universities in terms of admissions scores. Selectivity is usually a sign of the average prestige and popularity of the institution, which determines the social value of its degrees. The two special status institutions, Moscow State and St Petersburg State Universities are in a striking position, with overall average incomes one decimal point higher than other leading institutions (17,683 million roubles compared to 5,627 million roubles). Like federal universities they are especially dependent on federal funding. Non-leading institutions are more engaged with the regions, taking 8 per cent of their funding from regional and local budgets, compared to 0.6 per cent among the leading ones.

The most elite institutions are the State Universities in the two capitals, the national research group and the 5/100 universities. Despite policy expectations that leading institutions should be more entrepreneurial, leveraging their stronger human, material and reputational resources to raise more funding, they are more government dependent, leaving other higher education institutions with less resources. Amid economic decline, institutions of higher education are more reliant on government funding (Abankina, Vinarik, and Filatova, 2016).

Another important calibration is by research intensity. Non-leading higher institutions are much more dependent on educational provision than on research: the amount of research conducted in the leading institutions is sixteen times that of the non-elite group. R&D brings a fifth part of the budget (22 per cent) in the elite group and 8 per cent in the non-elite group. In the leading institutions international citation as measured by Web of Science and Scopus is at three times the rate in non-leading ones. In the number of publications indexed, the ratio is at least five to six times. Interestingly, in the Russian citation system the differences are not very great.

This data clarify the differentials between higher education institutions in linear terms. The first proposition on vertical stratification (HPS Proposition 11) is agreed:

> *The expansion of participation towards and beyond the HPS stage is associated with a tendency to bifurcation and stratification (vertical diversification) in the value of higher education, between elite (artisanal) institutions and mass (demand-absorbing) institutions.*

In Russia, the tendency to bifurcation was not only conditioned by the reputational and other differences inherited from Soviet time, which provided unequal starting positions in the quasi-market competition for government funding and tuition-paying students, but also shaped deliberately by policies designed to identify and additionally support a small group of leaders, in response to global relativism in the context of the expanded and now contracting system. It is also cheaper to fund higher quality in a few institutions than lift performance in all.

The second stratification proposition (HPS Proposition 12) is:

The tendency to institutional stratification is magnified by features common (though not universal) among HPS including (a) intensified social competition for the most valuable student places; (b) variable tuition charges; and/or (c) intensified competition between institutions.

All these features are found in the Russian system and they help to explain the intensity of stratification pressures.

The introduction of a nation-wide unified national test in 2009, replacing the former system of higher education admissions examinations, formalized in numeric form the competition among institutions for students. This is now another instrument of the quasi-market. The publication of comparative outcomes is seen to contribute to the transparency of education and increase in the information 'customers' receive. The list of higher education institutions that enrol the most top-scoring students has not changed much from year to year. It includes the institutions that have been the most prestigious since Soviet time, including Moscow State, St Petersburg State, Moscow State Institute of International Relations, and Moscow Institute of Physics and Technology. As measured by admissions scores the competition for entry into the elite universities and most prestigious fields of study is becoming stronger each year, while the large gap between average scores in the elite and non-elite institutions is widening. This is a neat indicator of the bifurcation process. For example, between 2015 and 2016, only two of the top twenty-five institutions, in terms of tuition free admissions, saw a small decrease in average test score. In the other twenty-three institutions average test score increased or was unchanged (Higher School of Economics, 2016b).

Differentiation in the prestige of institutions and the social value of the credential becomes transformed, as in Bourdieu's convertible capitals, into the differentiation of tuition fees. Annual tuition varies between 20,000 and 500,000 roubles. Elite institutions charge fees that in relative terms are very high. In the five institutions with the highest admissions of fee-paying students, fees vary from 200,000 roubles in Moscow Institute of Physics and Technology to 478,000 in the Moscow State Institute of International Relations (Higher School of Economics, 2016b). Few can pay: the average salary in Russia is about 35,000 roubles a month. This intensifies merit-based competition for publicly subsidized places.

THE MIDDLE LAYER

Non-elite public institutions and their students are not homogeneous. The third stratification proposition (HPS Proposition 13) maintains

In stratified HPS, a middle layer of institutions tends to form, shaped by the combination of upward aspirations (drift) with systemic scarcity of resources and status.

Table 11.10. Differentiation of higher education institutions by selectivity, main campuses, and number of higher education institutions

	Leading institutions	5/100	NRU	Federal	MSU, StPSU	Non-leading institutions	Total
Top (average score =84)	14	8	11	–	2	53	67
Middle (average score =69)	29	13	16	10	–	213	242
Bottom (average score =57)	2	–	2	–	–	173	175

Notes: NRU = National Research Universities. MSU = Moscow State University; SpBSU = St Petersburg State University.
Source: Authors using data from Monitoring of Performance (2016).

How are those institutions identified?

As noted, student selectivity is one way to calibrate higher education institutions. Simple clusterization creates three tiers of institutions (Table 11.10). The data show that the most selective institutions are not only those with formal elite status (fourteen out of sixty-seven institutions), but in large part are institutions not in that group (fifty-three). The latter include twenty-seven medical institutions and a number of other specialized ones in public administration, economics, law, arts and culture, and languages. Though those institutions have no special status from the government they have built on their reputation and status in their specific niche. In terms of student selectivity the middle tier (242 institutions) is the most densely populated and includes some 5/100, NRU and federal universities. These institutions have not concentrated all their resources on lifting reputation, though some of them are on their way to the top, having been named in the group of national research or 5/100 universities.

The classification study by Abankina, Aleskerov, Belousova, and colleagues (2016) identifies a middle layer. Using data on 219 public higher education institutions subject to the Ministry of Education, they cite several indicators: average national test score, proportion of younger academic staff with Doctoral qualifications, proportion of faculty with Doctorates, public funding per student, total students, share of all R&D funding from non-state sources, publication activity. Below two categories of leading institutions (25 per cent) there is an equally large group of institutions of medium and large scale in 'good standing' (25 per cent) (Table 11.11). These institutions maintain selective admissions but experience difficulties with raising the funding needed to sustain R&D. Unlike the sector leaders, all of their R&D support is sourced from government. On average their governmental funding is a little higher but it varies within the group. These are mostly classical universities and engineering institutions. The latter usually means a broad range of fields in Russia. However, the engineering institutions are also dependent on their respective industries, many of which have declined over last twenty-five years. Some of these institutions are long-standing and well-known. Their high reputation

Table 11.11. Institutional classification of Russian higher education institutions

Type of institutions	Characteristics	Cluster size, no. and % of institutions
potential and current R&D and education leaders	highest selectivity, highest funding per students, high R&D, over a half—technological	18 (8%)
market leaders	large, selective, higher R&D	37 (17%)
universities of good standing	medium-large, selective, good reputation, but less R&D, classical and technical universities	54 (25%)
indeterminate position universities	small-medium up to 10,000 students, non-selective, low per-student funding, low R&D	42 (19%)
niche universities	small, non-selective, low per student funding, low R&D, regional pedagogical, classical and technical institutions	68 (31%)

Source: Authors using data from Abankina, Aleskerov, Belousova, et al. (2016).

helps them to maintain highly skilled faculty, but this resource is not enough to succeed in the current competitive environment.

Platonova and Semyonov (2018) identify a large segment of public mass universities (Table 11.7). Half are public ones with programmes in multiple fields, relatively selective admissions, large governmental support and a high volume of part-time education.

Lisyutkin (2017) focuses on the institutional characteristics of 433 public institutions in the Monitoring of Performance database over 2011–15. About half experienced a decrease in total funding (50 per cent), R&D funding (46 per cent) and incoming student quality (56 per cent). Most (73 per cent) also experienced the ageing of academic staff; and 27 per cent deterioration of physical facilities. In total fifty-three institutions declined in all five dimensions. Most are comprehensive institutions, of average size (5,000–15,000 students), average income (601–2,000 million roubles) and average selectivity. This method identifies struggling universities. However, these are found not only at the bottom but among institutions slipping down from the middle tier. Overall, failure to succeed can be explained by various factors, often in combination: redistribution of government funding to elite groups; decline in industries with which institutions are linked (difficult for specialist institutions with no other role); local demographic decline with top students attracted to other cities or regions (Smolentseva, 2016); and intra-organizational factors such as flawed management, governance, or academic staff capacity.

The propositions on stratification help explain tensions between system size and the maintenance of hierarchy. Trow (1973) noted that elite sectors established in the previous stage maintain their advantage. In Russia, policy has helped to form a contemporary elite group built on older reputations and resources. A few elite higher education institutions maintain an advantage without being named in official programmes; these specialize in prestigious fields (e.g. medicine, international relations, economics). Less is known about the middle tier and bottom tier demand-absorbing higher education institutions that enrol most students. They should be more closely researched. Their position is weaker when funding cuts increase the gap between artisanal and demand-absorbing sectors.

Equity

When the majority of people are involved in higher education, issues of social equity affect all social groups. This highlights tensions between notions of equity based on the one hand on inclusion, on the other hand on equal distribution of opportunity, resources and outcomes.

In relation to equity, the unique aspect of the Russian HPS is that since the disintegration of the USSR, which had explicitly maintained and implemented principles of equality as they were understood politically, the idea of social equity in higher education has dropped almost entirely from the policy agenda. Discussion has been largely framed by economic rationales, being focused on ways to effectively distribute scarce public resources, rather than provision of opportunities. The 'over-education' of the population has become a popular theme. It is often simply assumed that in the dramatically expanded system everyone has an opportunity to participate, regardless of their level of academic achievement and future labour market outcomes. That assumption is further supported by the demographic decline.

The 2009 introduction of a compulsory unified national test (subject tests that serve as both final secondary school-leaver examination and higher education admissions test) was declared as a way to overcome corruption in the higher education admissions examinations, previously held separately at each institutions, and to enhance mobility by providing students with the opportunity to apply and study in another region. That has led to the brain drain of the best students from regions and smaller town to the capitals and major cities, which along with demographic decline and downward pressures on quality in a massifying system, tends to weaken the academic and social environment at regional institutions, all else being equal (Smolentseva, 2016).

Another important characteristic of the Russian situation, because of the low importance given to both large scale data collection in general and equity objectives in particular, is the lack of data and research that would describe in more detail issues of educational equity.

SOCIAL INCLUSION

The first proposition on equity (HPS Proposition 14) states:

As participation expands in the HPS phase, equity in the form of social inclusion is enhanced.

The Russian case illustrates this very well.

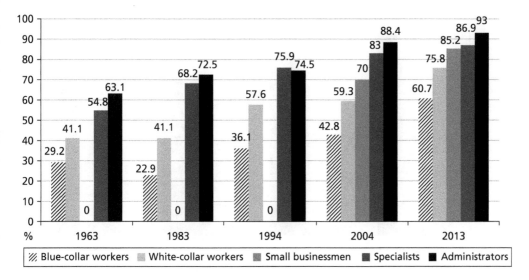

Figure 11.6. High school graduates' participation in higher education by parental occupation (those who became a student as percentage of total group), Novosibirsk Oblast, 1963–2013.

Source: Authors adapting from Konstantinovsky, 2017.

For several decades, aspirations of young people for higher education have been rising. The longitudal study by Konstantinovskiy (1999, 2008, 2017) in Novosibirsk oblast' identifies a drop in interest in 1980 due to social transformations which contributed to decline in the social value of higher education. Aside from that moment, intentions grew consistently, though at different levels by social group. Two stratifying factors are identified: parental occupation and place of residence (level of urbanization). From 1994 to 2013, the aspirations of high school students especially increased for those with blue collar parents (from 44.6 to 82.4 per cent), while always relatively high for those from administration and specialists families. Nevertheless, difference by social group continued. Although all social groups gained in social inclusion in the transition to HPS, and the participation rate increased by 30–40 per cent group (Figure 11.6), still students from blue collar working families demonstrate lesser representation (63.1 per cent in 2013 comparing to 88.4 and 93.0 per cent for students from families whose parents were specialists and administrators respectively).

Place of residence was another factor associated with inequality. Aspirations were higher in regional centres (moving from 89.1 per cent in 1963 to 95.3 per cent in 2013) than in smaller towns and especially rural area (reaching 64.5 and 84.8 per cent respectively in 2013). The social basis of participation has been expanding, as apparent from the change of time in Figure 11.7. But not all aspirations were realized, and the gap between aspiration and outcome was higher for rural people than those living in the cities and the regional centre.

These data show that Soviet society had inequalities in educational opportunity and those disparities have continued, with the gap between social groups maintained. They

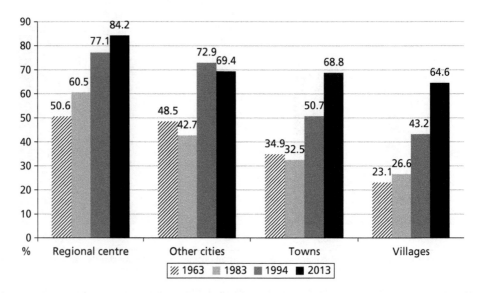

Figure 11.7. High school graduates' participation in higher education, by level of urbanization (those who became as student as percentage of total group), Novosibirsk Oblast, 1963–2013

Source: Authors adapting from Konstantinovsky, 2017.

also show that the social base of higher education has expanded during the massification process, so that overall social inclusiveness has been largely achieved. The elite to mass transition favoured the best positioned social groups such as specialists, administrators, residents of the regional centre. The 1990–2000s expansion saw much wider participation of less represented social groups.

INEQUALITIES IN PARTICIPATION

Data from a national survey provide more information about patterns of inequality within overall participation and importantly, within the different tiers of higher education institutions.

As apparent in Figure 11.8, while less than one-quarter of the people in the 40–59 age cohort (potential parents of current students) have experienced higher education, students from such families participate in higher education at twice the rate: 54.2 per cent of all students in higher education have mothers with higher education, and 45.8 per cent have fathers in that category. Employing the selectivity of higher education institutions, as measured by average admission test score, as a proxy for the institutional status (the higher the score, the higher the prestige), the data illustrate the social stratification of institutions and their student contingents. Students from higher educated families comprise over the half the student body in first tier institutions (66.5 and 57.5 per cent for mothers and

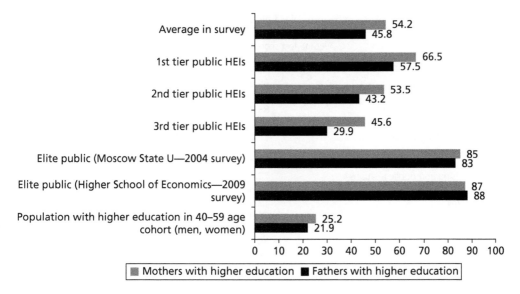

Figure 11.8. Parental education of higher education students by HEIs tiers (%)

Source: Adapted from Smolentseva, 2017a. Based on the data from Monitoring of Economics of Education data, 2011; for average in survey: public and private higher education institutions, full-time students; for 3 tiers: survey data, 2011; public institutions (N=37), 1288 full-time students. Population with higher education in 40–59 age cohort: National census 2010. Data on Moscow State University 2004: Gasparishvili and Toumanov 2006. Data on Higher School of Economics: Higher School of Economics Center for Institutional Research 2009.

fathers respectively), about half in second tier institutions (53.5 and 43.2 per cent) and notably less in the bottom tier (45.6 and 29.9 per cent) (Smolentseva, 2017a).

The composition of the most elite institutions is striking. At Moscow State and the Higher School of Economics, over 80 per cent of students are from higher educated families. The social reproduction of highly educated families is a long-standing pattern. A century ago, 26 per cent of students of Moscow (State) University had fathers with higher education (Gasparishvili and Toumanov, 2006). In 1994, among first-year Moscow State students, the ratios were 84 per cent of fathers and 83 per cent of mothers (Vasenina and Sorokina 2002).

This study (Smolentseva, 2017a) found no significant differences in parental education and occupation between tuition free and tuition paying students. This might be due to limitations of the sample. It might also indicate that families are universally committed to providing their children with higher education, even if they have to pay. This again confirms the general HPS proposition that in HPS social aspirations for higher education have no limit.

Another interesting characteristic of the Russian case that there are no data indicating that the introduction of the unified national test affected student mobility, as planned.

Table 11.12. The most selective/popular fields of study, higher education, Russia, 2015

Field of study	Average test score of students admitted	Number of first-year students admitted
International relations	85.5	919
Art theory	83.9	225
Oriental and African studies	83.1	496
Journalism and creative writing	79.9	1,234
Linguistics and foreign languages	79.8	2,858
Law	79.1	6,213
Advertising and public relations	78.8	879
Political science	78.6	936
Economics	77.5	7,913
Publishing	76.9	161
Design	76.6	1,467
Applied art (music)	75.7	239
History	75.3	1,746
Nuclear physics and technology	75.0	1,089
Business informatics	74.9	1,668
Healthcare/medicine	74.7	24,669
Philosophy	74.5	507
Philology	74.0	2,370
Cultural studies	73.7	354
Public administration	73.1	1,475
Applied art (painting, sculpture)	73.1	169
Architecture and construction	73.0	3,436
Management	72.3	7,786
Oil and gas	72.2	2,095
Choreography/dance	72.0	34
Information security	71.8	4,085
Physics	71.8	4,971
Sociology	71.7	1,924
Mathematics	70.4	9,710

Sources: Adapted by authors from Higher School of Economics (2016a) (Monitoring of quality of admissions).

In an international comparative perspective, the Russian HPS demonstrates a relatively high level of social inequality in participation. Comparing with the Eurostudent 2011 survey data, using parental educational and occupational status, Russia appears to have a higher level of inequality than most of the twenty-two European countries in the survey (Smolentseva, 2017a).

One of aspect of the inequality in participation is the inequality by the field of study: the data shows that the most prestigious fields are the most selective. Their exclusiveness might also be supported by the small number of public places. Among them international relations, arts, Oriental/Asian and African studies, journalism and creative writing, linguistics and foreign languages, and law (Table 11.12). But no representative data are available on students' background by the field of study.

Inequality of Outcomes

In 2015 the national government monitored graduate employment in 547 higher education institutions, including 376 public ones (Table 11.13). The level of employment in the first year after graduation was 75 per cent in the country but varied from 85 per cent in the Urals Federal District to 71 per cent in the Southern and 29 per cent in Sevastopol' in the Crimea; it also varies by institution. There are also significant differences in official ('white') income in the first year after graduation with a Bachelor's or Specialist degree, across the regions and institutions and fields of study. The Ministry website does not readily represent the full database. Here aggregated data on the regions, and examples of institutional differences are provided. The salary level in Moscow is much higher than in the rest of the country. Institutions with special status, or the most selective, also demonstrate higher level of salaries comparing to the national average. The data indicate differentiation within field of studies depending on the region and the prestige of the institution and also suggest differentiation within institutions by the field of study. The data do not show the later income of the graduates, but they represent a useful source of information and require further analysis.

This closer look at the disparities in participation and outcomes endorses the second proposition on equity (HPS Proposition 15):

Because in the HPS phase the growth of participation is associated with enhanced stratification and intensified competition at key transition points, all else being equal (i.e. without compensatory state policy), the expansion of participation is associated with a secular tendency to greater social inequality in educational outcomes and, through that, social outcomes.

In Russia selective admissions to the most prestigious fields and institutions require from students higher cultural, social, and economic capital; and in turn open opportunities to achieve higher salary and social status. Also, the higher the level of participation, the more social strata are involved, and the composition of the student body increasingly resembles the social composition of society. However, social justice does not become a reality. Following the concept of 'effectively maintained inequality' (Lucas, 2001; Ayalon and Shavit, 2004), when saturation is achieved at a given level of education, quantitative inequalities in the odds are replaced by qualitative inequalities in the odds of getting on the more selective track. Social inequality becomes increasingly associated with the stratification of higher education institutions and the differing positional value of their degrees.

Hence the third proposition on equity (HPS Proposition 16) is endorsed. This maintains that

Within a national system, as participation expands in the HPS phase, all else being equal, the positional structure of the higher education system increasingly resembles

Table 11.13. Graduate salaries in the first year (first degree full-time student graduates, roubles)

	Income
Average in Russia (Bachelor's, Master's, Specialists)	31,041
Public higher education institutions (Bachelor's, Master's, Specialists)	30,936
Cities and federal districts (first degrees)	
Moscow	45,969
St Petersburg	35,855
Far Eastern	31,757
Urals	29,389
Northern West	26,531
Siberian	25,803
Central	24,884
Volga	23,414
Sevastopol	23,071
Southern	22,496
Northern Caucasian	18,597
Some higher education institutions (first degrees):	
St Petersburg National Research University of Russian Academy of Sciences*	131,546
Vaganova Academy of Russian Ballet	82,746
Moscow Physics and Technics Institute	78,551
Moscow State Institute of International Relations	66,150
NRU Higher School of Economics	62,490
Gubkin Russian State Oil and Gas University (NRU)	60,097
Moscow State Technical University of Civil Aviation	57,707
Bauman Moscow State Technical University (NRU)	57,345
National Research Nuclear University 'MIFI'	57,080
Pirogov Russian National Research Medical University	50,435
St Petersburg National Research University ITMO	44,762
Russian People's Friendship University	43,467
Sechnov First Moscow State Medical University	42,679
St Petersburg State University	42,509
Tomsk Polytechnic State University (NRU)	35,700
Tomsk State University (NRU)	25,896

Note: *N of graduates in the database = 31.

Source: Authors using data from the Ministry of Education and Science (2015), Monitoring of Graduate Employment.

that of society (albeit with the caveat of Proposition 15). The HPS is increasingly implicated in the reproduction of existing patterns of social equality/inequality.

The more a society is higher educated, when the majority of people want to send their children to higher education, the stronger is the competition for a place in higher education in general and the more intensive the competition for the most prestigious positions in top institutions and those abroad.

Study abroad has become a new elite path to higher social position whereby economic capital accumulated in Russia is exchanged for cultural capital. Global education promises to open up more cultural, social, and economic opportunities. Though early in the post-Soviet period, the dramatic impoverishment of the population meant that few could study abroad, undergraduate and graduate study abroad were supported by Western foundations such as DAAD (German Academic Exchange Service), the Muskie programme, the Fulbright programme, the British Council, etc., and also through institutional scholarships. This provided a path for those most prepared and with foreign language skills, mostly from higher educated families. As wealth began to increase, along with income inequality, self-funded study abroad has increased. UNESCO estimates there are 56,000 Russian students abroad (UNESCO, n.d.). An international education is a positional good and in Russia its social value often exceeds that of national education.

The final equity proposition (HPS Proposition 17) states that:

As the HPS boundary of participation expands it becomes more difficult for the state and/or autonomous educational systems/institutions to secure a redistribution of educational opportunities, and, through that, of social opportunities.

As noted, Russian policymakers give little attention to equality. As Hirsch (1976) notes, to maintain the value of a positional good such as education it is necessary to restrict access to it, and to develop a vertical hierarchy to enhance the relative advantage associated with prestigious institutions. The Russian government tries to do both: limits the expansion of the system by cutting the number of publicly subsidised places in fields such as economics or law, and ideologically, by broadening the over-education discussion; and strengthens the hierarchy of credential value by increasing vertical institutional stratification and redistributing the resources towards the elite group.

Such a policy will increase the bifurcation of the system. Unless and until inequality is acknowledged as a policy challenge, there will be no attempts to counteract it. Policy executes counter-balancing measures for a few social groups such as orphans, and people with disabilities. But networked linkages with particular secondary schools tend to generate another layer of exclusion, at the secondary school level. The problem is not access per se, it is unequal social access to top tier higher education institutions.

Concluding Remarks

The Russian HPS is a broad social phenomenon at the intersection of many social, political, economic, demographic forces. The present HPS has been shaped first by the Soviet legacy, second by post-Soviet marketization and lack of state determination, and third by post-Soviet centralized state control. Along this pathway traditional institutional distinctions have become blurred, the old specialist institutional form has been diminished (though it is still a larger factor than in most other countries), and higher education institutions have converged towards a common model of multi-disciplinary multiversity. On top of that the state has layered a steeper institutional stratification, with consequences for the social stratification of both participation (who goes where) and outcomes (who gets what).

Most importantly, what has changed during this period is the idea of higher education, its role and purpose. The idea of education as a service and the educational system as a market of educational services, established in the early 1990s, has deeply penetrated into all levels of the higher education system, the academic community, and the larger society (Smolentseva, 2016). Instrumental, mostly economic aims of higher education dominate in public discourse and policies. That is a key transformation of a major and formative social sector which has led Russian society (as is the case in many other nations) away from the idea of education for personal development, the expansion of individual agency and self-formation (see Chapter 7).

In the passage to HPS there are signs of this changing role of higher education. Higher education in Russia has become a social norm for many social groups. It is an important part of the socialization process, an important period in life. As the average age of full-time enrolment is decreasing, it might become another obligatory stage of transition to adulthood. One empirical indicator of that is direct parental involvement in the higher education experience of their children, usually initiated by higher education institutions that are seeking parental support and engagement through meetings and phone calls. This pattern can be observed at some regional universities (Smolentseva, 2016). If earlier higher education was considered as an activity of adults, now it might be seen more as another pre-adulthood period.

That brings back into the foreground the role of higher education in modern society and the agency it is meant to make, and its quality and its resources. The bigger the system, and the larger the share of the population that shares the experience, the more important it is to understand, research, and discuss what higher education brings, and could bring, to individuals and society. And in the HPS in Russia there is an especially wide gap between what higher education is, and what it could be.

■ REFERENCES

Abankina, I., Vinarik, V., and Filatova, L. (2016). Gosudarstvennaia politila finansirovanis sektora vysshego obrazovania v usloviyakh biudzhetnykh organichenii [State policy of higher education sector financing under the budgetary constraints]. *Journal of the New Economic Association* 3(31), 111–42.

Abankina, I., Aleskerov, F., Belousova, V. et al. (2016). From equality to diversity: Classifying Russian universities in a performance oriented system. *Technological Forecasting & Social Change* 103, 228–39.

Aleskerov, F. T., Froumin, I., Kardanova, E., et al. (2014). Heterogeneity of the educational system: an introduction to the problem. Higher School of Economics. Working Paper WP7/2014/03, Series WP7.

Ayalon, H. and Shavit, Y. (2004). Educational reforms and inequalities in Israel: The MMI hypothesis revisited. *Sociology of Education* 77, 103–20.

Clark, B. (1998). *Creating Entrepreneurial Universities: Organizational Pathways of Transformation*. Bingley: Emerald Group Publishing Limited.

Froumin, I. and Leshukov, O. (2015). National-regional relationships in federal higher education systems: The case of Russian Federation. *Higher Education Forum Hiroshima University* 12, 77–94.

Froumin, I., Kouzminov, Y., and Semyonov, D. (2014). Institutional diversity in Russian higher education: revolutions and evolution. *European Journal of Higher Education*. DOI: 10.1080/21568235.2014.916532

Gasparishvili, A. and Toumanov, S. (2006). Moskovskii student sto let nazad i nyne [Moscow student 100 years ago and now]. Otechestvennye zapiski, 3(30). http://www.strana-oz.ru/?numid=30&article=1274

Gimpelson, V. and Kapeliushnikov, R. (eds) (2011). Rossisskii Rabotnik. Obrazovanie, Professia, Kvalifikatsia [Russian Worker: Education, Profession, Qualification]. Moscow: Higher School of Economics.

Heyneman, S. (2010). A comment on the changes in higher education in the former Soviet Union. *European Education*, 42(1), 76–87.

Higher School of Economics (2016a). Monitoring kachestva priema: Analitika 2011–2016 [Monitoring of quality of admissions: Analytics 2011–2016]. https://ege.hse.ru/stata#forth

Higher School of Economics (2016b). Spros na pedagogicheskoe obrazovanie rastet, differentsiatsia vuzov usilivaetsya [The demand for pedagogical education is growing, the differentiation of higher education institutions is increasing]. https://www.hse.ru/news/community/190201442.html

Hirsch, F. (1976). *Social Limits to Growth*. Cambridge, MA: Harvard University Press.

Indikatory obrazovania [Indicators of education] (2017). *Statistical Yearbook*. Moscow: Higher School of Economics.

Izyumov, A. (2010). Human costs of post-communist transition: Public policies and private response. *Review of Social Economy* 68(1), 93–125.

Kember, D. (2010). Opening up the road to nowhere: Problems with the path to mass higher education in Hong Kong. *Higher Education* 59(2), 167–79.

Konstantinovskiy, D. (1999). *Dinamika neravenstva* [*The Dynamics of Inequality*]. Moscow: Editoral URSS.

Konstantinovskiy, D. (2008). Neravenstvo i obrazovanie [Inequality and education]. Moscow.

Konstantinovskiy, D. (2017). Expansion of higher education and consequences for social inequality (the case of Russia). *Higher Education* 74(2), 201–20.

Kontseptsia Sozdania i Gosudarstvennoi Podderzhki Razvitia Federal'nykh Universitetov [Concept of establishing and governmental support of development of federal universities] (2009). http://mon.gov.ru/pro/pnpo/fed/09.09.22-fu.konc.pdf

Kuraev, A. (2014). Internationalization of higher education in Russia: Collapse or perpetuation of the Soviet System? A historical and conceptual study. PhD dissertation. Boston College.

Kuraev, A. (2016). Soviet higher education: An alternative construct to the Western university paradigm. *Higher Education* 71(2), 181–93. doi:10.1007/s10734-015-9895-5

Kwiek, M. (2008). Accessibility and equity, market forces and entrepreneurship: Developments in higher education in Central and Eastern Europe. *Higher Education Management and Policy* 20(1), 89–110.

Kwiek, M. (2011). Creeping marketization: Where Polish public and private higher education sectors meet, in R. Brown (ed.), *Higher Education and the Market*. New York: Routledge, pp. 135–45.

Lisyutkin, M. (2017). O vozmozhnykh prichinakh ukhudshenia resursnoi bazy vuzov [On possible causes of the declining resource base of higher education institutions]. *Voprosy obrazovania* [*Journal of Educational Studies*] 2, 74–94. DOI: 10.17323/1814-9545-2017-2-74-94

Lucas, S. (2001). Effectively maintained inequality: Education transitions, track mobility, and social background effects. *American Journal of Sociology* 106, 1642–90.

Marginson, S. (1997). *Markets in Education*. Sydney: Allen and Unwin.

Marginson, S. and van der Wende, M. (2009). The new global landscape of nations and institutions. *Organization for Economic Cooperation and Development, Centre for Educational Research and Innovation, Higher Education to 2030*. Volume 2: *Globalisation*. Paris: OECD, pp. 17–62.

Ministry of Education and Science (2015). Monitoring of graduate employment. http://graduate.edu.ru/

Parry, G. (2012). Higher education in further education colleges, *Perspectives: Policy and Practice in Higher Education* 16(4), 118–22.

Platonova, D. and Semyonov, D. (2018). Russia: The institutional landscape of Russian higher education, in J. Huisman, A. Smolentseva, and I. Froumin (eds), *25 Years of Transformations of Higher Education Systems in Post-Soviet Countries: Reform and Continuity*. London: Palgrave.

RBC (2017). Rector obednel na 85 mln [The rector got poorer at 85 mln], 13 June. http://www.rbc.ru/newspaper/2017/06/13/59393e299a794771fb28b93b

Shishkin, S. (ed.) (2004). *Dostupnost' vysshego obrazovania v Rossii* [*Accessibility of Higher Education in Russia*]. Moscow: Independent Institute for Social Policy.

Smolentseva, A. (2007). The changing status of the PhD degree in Russia: An academic attribute in the non-academic labor market. *European Education* 39(3), 81–101.

Smolentseva, A. (2016). Transformations in the knowledge transmission mission of Russian universities: Social vs economic instrumentalism, in D. M. Hoffman and J. Välimaa (eds), *Re-Becoming Universities? Critical Comparative Reflections on Higher Education Institutions in Networked Knowledge Societies*. Dordrecht: Springer, pp. 169–200.

Smolentseva, A. (2017a). Universal higher education and positional advantage: Soviet legacies and neoliberal transformations in Russia. *Higher Education*. DOI: 10.1007/s10734-016-0009-9

Smolentseva, A. (2017b). Where Soviet and neoliberal discourses meet: The transformation of the purposes of higher education in Soviet and Post-Soviet Russia. *Higher Education* 2017, 1–18. doi:10.1007/s10734-017-0111-7

Smolentseva, A., Huisman, J., and Froumin, I. (2018). Transformation of higher education institutional landscape in post-Soviet countries: From Soviet model to where?, in J. Huisman,

A. Smolentseva, and I. Froumin (eds), *25 Years of Transformations of Higher Education Systems in Post-Soviet Countries: Reform and Continuity*. London: Palgrave.

Tomusk, V. (1998). Market as metaphor in central and East European higher education. *International Studies in Sociology of Education* 8(2), 223–39. DOI: 10.1080/0962021980020026

Trow, M. (1973). *Problems in the Transition from Elite to Mass Higher Education*. London: Carnegie Commission on Higher Education.

UNESCO (United Nations Educational and Cultural Organisation) (n.d.). Global flow of tertiary level students. http://uis.unesco.org/en/uis-student-flow#slideoutmenu

Vasenina, I. and Sorokina, N. (2002). Vysshee obrazovanie v sovremennom mire [Higher Education in Contemporary World]. *Chelovek i sovremennyi mir [Man and Contemporary World]*. Moscow: Infra, pp. 418–40.

World Bank (2017). Data and statistics. http://data.worldbank.org

12 Building a New Society and Economy: High Participation Higher Education in Poland

Marek Kwiek

Introduction

Among the eight high participation systems (HPS) studied in this book, Poland is a high middle income country. Its 2015 GDP per capita on a PPP (purchasing power parity) basis was US$26,261, almost 69 per cent above the world average level but only 55 per cent of that in neighbouring Germany. Its total GDP in PPP terms in 2015 was US$1,020 billion, placing it in twenty-second place on the world scale (World Bank, 2017). Poland is one of the largest countries in Europe, with a land area of 311,888 square kilometres and a population of just under thirty-eight million in 2015 (World Bank, 2017). After breaking away from the Soviet system in Eastern Europe in 1989–90, Poland subsequently joined the North Atlantic Treaty Organisation (NATO) in 1999 and became a full member of the European Union (EU) in 2004. Poland is also a member nation in the Organisation for Economic Co-operation and Development (OECD).

Poland has experienced remarkable educational growth and contraction in the almost three decades since it left the Soviet bloc but throughout demographic ups and downs the rate of participation in tertiary education has increased. The leap in the gross tertiary enrolment ratio (GTER) in the last two decades was the highest among the eight systems under consideration in this book, from 32 per cent in 1995 to 71 per cent in 2013, almost 40 per cent in fewer than twenty years (see Chapter 1, Table 1.1). The changes in society and economy in Poland in the last two decades have been as fundamental as the changes in higher education participation. The two are strongly interrelated. The growth in the proportion of the population with completed higher education programmes, as illustrated by the difference between 25–34-year-olds (43 per cent) compared to 55–64-year-olds (14 per cent), was the highest in Poland of all the eight countries (see Chapter 1, Table 1.5). This substantial generational difference in the holding of qualifications shows the scale of change in tertiary educational opportunities between the pre-HPS communist era of the 1980s and the HPS era in the post 1989 period.

This Polish case study was prepared in the light of the generic findings about HPS presented in Part I of *High Participation Systems of Higher Education*. This case of a formerly communist country changing into a market economy and a liberal democracy, entering the NATO, the OECD and the EU, while at the same time changing from a low participation system to an HPS, constitutes an interesting testing ground for the HPS hypotheses outlined at the beginning of the book.

TRANSITION, GROWTH, AND DEMOGRAPHIC DECLINE

Poland has undergone change processes typical of Central and Eastern Europe. The communist legacy in higher education funding and organization generated similar challenges across the region. Polish higher education system stagnated in the 1970s and 1980s, being stable in both quantitative and qualitative terms. The numbers of institutions, students, and academics were relatively constant. The system was state-coordinated, binary in terms of university and non-university sectors with both located in the public sector, publicly governed, and publicly funded (Antonowicz, 2016; Pinheiro and Antonowicz, 2015; Kwiek, 2017). Prior to 1989 universities were conceived as major change agents designed to redress social inequality, while at the same time subject to strong political supervision and state coordination (Szczepański, 1974). The target was a change in the social composition of the educated social strata. Centrally planned higher education was also expected to serve the centrally planned economy. The principle of full employment combined with the principle of carefully planned supply of qualified workers to the closed, national labour market was a key factor limiting the massification of higher education. Massification was postponed for different reasons, including political ones: between mid-1970s and 1989, university academics were increasingly involved in anti-communist opposition movements, and research and technologies were developed in the research institutes sector and in the Polish Academy of Sciences, both without students. Access to higher education was heavily restricted.

One result was that when massification processes were finally set in motion in the 1990s, they could hardly be stopped (Siemieńska and Walczak, 2012). Increased social aspirations for higher education among the lower social classes, along with ever-present high aspirations of the former intelligentsia, now turned into the middle class, have fuelled growth ever since 1989.

According to the general HPS Proposition 3:

Once transition from a primarily agricultural economy is achieved, the long-term growth of HPS is independent of political economic factors such as economic growth and patterns of labour market demand; patterns of public and private funding of higher education; the roles of public and private institutions; and system organization and modes of governance.

In contrast to the OECD area as a whole, the Polish system has both massively expanded and is now heavily contracting (Kwiek, 2016d). This is rooted in a major decline in the birth rate in the early 1990s. Between 2013 and 2020–5, the number of people aged 20–4 decreases by 904,900 and by 2035–40 the decline will be 1.013 million (GUS, 2014: 152). Yet while the system shows the signs of saturation, the long-term growth of the participation rate seems inevitable.

In certain respects, the Polish system is exceptional from a global perspective. In the last generation it became dual in the sense of public-private, highly differentiated, strongly marketized, and hugely expanded. After that it came under exceptionally heavy pressure due to the declining demographics, Poland being the fastest ageing society in the EU. Total enrolments have fallen from 1.95 million in 2006 to 1.41 million in 2015 though the age group participation rate has continued to increase. The effects of the marked contraction in absolute student numbers (see Figure 12.1) have been to make the Polish system more public, less differentiated, and less marketized. The HPS in Poland seems to have found its own idiosyncratic way to develop. In the 1990s and 2000s it was a perfect example of privatization processes, with ever more private providers, more private funding, and more fee-paying students in both sectors. In contrast, in the last decade it has become a remarkable historic example of a de-privatization process, especially in financial terms (together with Romania, Bulgaria, and Estonia; Kwiek, 2016a; see also Marginson, 2016d and Szadkowski, 2017 on the operationalization of the public/private distinction).

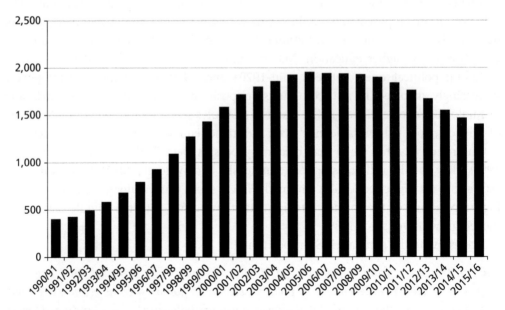

Figure 12.1. Higher education enrolment in Poland, 1990–2015

Source: Author, from GUS (2016) and previous editions.

The expansion of the Polish HPS, in terms of student numbers and growth in number of private institutions, was largely uncoordinated. At the end of the communist period in 1989 the gross enrolment rate in higher education (United Nations Educational and Cultural Organisation (UNESCO)/OECD tertiary type A education, only Bachelor's and Master's levels, distinct from post-secondary education) was about 10 per cent. Three years later in 1992 it was already 15.5 per cent and it reached 51.1 per cent by 2007. The drivers of this change included powerful social pressures, rising demographics, a new capitalist labour market with growing private sector employment and concurrent requirements for a more educated labour force, a laissez-faire public policy towards the quality of the emergent private sector in higher education, and the willingness of the academic profession to be directly involved in the institutional growth of both public and private sectors (Białecki and Dąbrowa-Szefler, 2009; Dobbins, 2011; Kogan et al., 2011; Kwiek, 2013; Antonowicz et al., 2017).

CHANGING ROLE OF THE STATE

The role of the state has also changed during the post-communist period and has done so twice. The explosive growth after 1989 was manifest in both an increase in size and an increase in the complexity of governance and funding. Massification created the need for new coordination mechanisms. There was a quarter of a century of large-scale structural changes intended to replace communist-period governance arrangements with new ones, mostly in an incremental manner. At this stage, no academic revolution occurred, but incremental changes gradually led to a new system based on new governing and funding principles. However, more far-reaching changes were introduced recently, in the 2009–12 wave of reforms (Kwiek, 2016b). These signalled the second change in the role of the state. When in the 1990s the Polish system became more market-driven and differentiated along public-private lines the role of the state was rendered weaker than in the communist era. Nevertheless, the state, through its Ministry of Science and Higher Education (MoSHE) has been gradually regaining power since 2005, when a new law on higher education was introduced, and especially since the 2009–12 reforms. Interestingly, 'de-privatization' has coincided with stronger central control, but state control has also taken a new form. The role of quasi-state intermediary agencies has grown, while at the same time, these agencies exercise a closer control over academic work than did the earlier direct state administration (Antonowicz et al., 2017).

At the level of the institution, while overall enrolments and the role of government have fluctuated, there has been a long-term trend to consolidation and strengthening of the position of the large multi-disciplinary public research universities or 'multiversities' (Kerr, 2001) in the Polish system. There are currently eighteen universities and polytechnics with enrolments exceeding 20,000, including three universities with about

40,000 students (University of Warsaw, Jagiellonian University in Cracow, and University of Poznan). The Polish system in 2015 consisted of 415 institutions (132 public and 283 private): nineteen universities, twenty-three polytechnics, seven universities of life sciences, sixty-seven of economics, fourteen of education, nine of medicine, six of physical education, twenty-two of arts, fifteen of theology, and more than 200 other institutions. Recent demographic pressures reduce the number of private institutions (from 330 in 2009 to 265 in 2017; POL-ON, 2017), and national policies strongly support mergers of public institutions, with very limited success so far. The conversion of mission goes in several directions: polytechnics become more comprehensive by range of fields of study (seeking new students, especially females), and universities turn to applied research, apart from basic research (seeking new public funding).

Governance: Towards Multi-level Arrangements

The first governance proposition (HPS Proposition 4) states that:

HPS are governed by multi-level control, coordination, and accountability mechanisms.

After 2009, within the framework of the so-called Kudrycka reforms, the Polish system was reconfigured on the basis of multi-level governance, with new intermediary coordinating institutions situated between higher education institutions and the state. The new national bodies included two independent and publicly funded national research councils, one for fundamental research (Narodowe Centrum Nauki (NCN)) and another for applied research (Narodowe Centrum Badańi Rozwoju (NCBR)); the renewed Polish Accreditation Committee (Polska Komisja Akredytacyjna (PKA)); and the national Committee for the Evaluation of Scientific Units (Komitet Ewaluacji Jednostek Naukowych (KEJN)). In association with this change, an amendment to the law on higher education of 18 March 2011 introduced new rules of the academic game in both governance and funding. Financing of public higher education and academic research became more directly linked to measurable research productivity (Kwiek, 2015a).

In the wake of the 2009–12 reforms major aspects of funding and organization were moved from the level of the state to the intermediary level of the new agencies. The two national research councils allocate funding on a competitive basis to individual academics and research teams, as well as to companies in the case of the NCBR, for research in all areas. The accreditation committee (PKA) evaluates and accredits study programmes and institutions across the whole of the public and private sectors. The evaluation committee (KEJN) provides a large-scale, periodical assessment of the research output of all 963 basic academic units—these are usually situated at the level of faculty, in the case of higher education institutions—through sophisticated periodical 'parameterization' and 'categorization' exercises (Kulczycki, 2017). These exercises took place in 2013 and 2017. The new bodies either directly allocate public funding, in the case of both national research councils; or provide input to the MoSHE in the form of scores for study programmes and basic academic units which are then linked to public subsidy levels, as occurs with the two accreditation and evaluation committees, the PKA and KEJN.

The Polish system is coordinated, funded, organized, and governed in a homogenous way. All public sector institutions are funded centrally through subsidies by the state through MoSHE. Research in public institutions is funded centrally through subsidies based on the assessments of an intermediary agency, the KEJN, as well through grant funding as the results of national competitions for research funding available from the NCBR and the NCN. The mechanisms of coordination operate at one basic level, the state. There are national salary brackets, national teaching loads, a national student aid system, and a national system of academic titles and degrees. Full professorships are awarded centrally by the Central Committee on Academic Degrees and Titles and nominations are signed by the President of Poland. However, the state has diminishing power in organization and management of individual institutions and in allocating public funding. The role of the four intermediary peer-run agencies is heavily increasing, as is the role of students as consumers, with consumer rights guaranteed by the state. Institutions are becoming ever more accountable to the state, through the new intermediary agencies to which they report, and academics ever more accountable to both their own institutions and the research councils sponsoring their research.

Corporatization

The third governance proposition (HPS Proposition 6) states that

> HPS complex multi-level accountability and coordination, coupled with system differentiation, result in higher education institutions adopting increasingly corporate forms and robust internal governance and management capacities.

Until 2011 the state in Poland, through the MoSHE, was directly involved in coordinating higher education. In the new governance architecture, higher formal autonomy for self-managing institutions and academics is combined with higher levels of accountability. The new intermediary agencies are, in principle, independent from the state in that they are either directly managed by academics elected by the academic community at large or indirectly influenced by academics through their governing boards. Hence either directly or indirectly, the four new agencies are managed and/or governed by academics through their democratically elected representatives. There is, however, a substantial cost for the more autonomous institutions, in that various aspects of university functioning are subject to rigorous systems of reporting, while there is an increasing bureaucratization of the whole system. This has provided a framework for processes of corporatization parallel to those emerging in many countries. Though corporate reform is very high on the policy agenda, the traditional Polish academic collegiality has so far retarded the change process (Kwiek, 2015b). However, the corporatist direction of the reforms proposed in 2017, in the context of an increasingly competitive national system, is unmistakable.

Increasingly, academic outputs in both teaching and research are being assessed, benchmarked and linked to public funding levels, at the aggregate level in the case of basic academic units, and at an individual level in the case of project-based research funding. Not only have research grants been rendered competitive, public subsidies for each of teaching and research now depend on how academic units perform in comparison with other units. There is quasi-market resource allocation for academic units in which they compete for a stable amount of funding available on a yearly basis. Detailed bibliometric assessments of individual academics and academic units, performed through a point system linked to a ranking list of academic journals, increasingly determine the level of financial resources available (Kwiek 2018b).

Overall, Poland is gradually implementing a performance-based research funding system (Kulczycki et al., 2017). Funding levels are linked either directly to prior research outputs, through subsidies for research allocated to individual academic units rather than institutions as a whole; or indirectly in the form of grant-based competitive funding for academics. The core of the ongoing changes lies in competitive project-based funding from the two national research councils, especially the NCN for fundamental research. Amid the changing architecture of governance, the four new agencies located in the coordination system between the universities and the state are becoming ever more crucial. Putting it in simple terms, the state leaves most funding decisions to the competitive quasi-market institutionalized in new intermediary agencies. The state continues to define the global levels of public funding for both subsidies and research projects, national research priority areas, and the primary division of funds between the NCN and the NCBR. Decisions on how to allocate research funds are taken by the academics located in the research councils.

The KEJN, the new national 'research assessment exercise' body formed in 2010, has been crucial for the implementation of these reforms. Consisting of experts elected by the academic community and nominated by the Ministry, its role is a comprehensive assessment of research activities conducted in all 'basic academic units' (institutes of the Polish Academy of Sciences (PAS), research institutes, and mostly faculties in higher education institutions), with the assessment largely carried out through bibliometric tools. The assessment process is termed 'parameterization' and leads to the categorization of all academic units, with the final assessment is presented on a four-point scale: A+ (national leaders), A (very good level), B (acceptable level), and C (unsatisfactory level). For a given unit assessed by KEJN, the level of a state subsidy for research is directly linked to the final assessment. The Ministry publishes a list of units with their respective categorization. The successive rounds of parameterization, leading to official categorization by the Ministry, have proven to a powerful instrument of stratification of the Polish higher education sector. The assessment process also tends to be reproductive of the stratification it creates. Units with low categorization in 2013, and consequently lowered research funding through annual state subsidies in the years 2014 to 2017, had limited prospects of achieving higher categories in 2017. The categorization of individual academic units does not directly lead to classifications of the institutions in which those units are located, but institutional funding and status are affected indirectly. The top higher education institutions in Poland house mostly A-category and A+category faculties, together with varying numbers of B-category units. The PAS sector comprises sixty-eight institutes which are involved in Doctoral-level education only, 80 per cent of its institutes have A+ or A categories, and its staff of 3,720 is responsible for 14 per cent of Polish publications; the PAS sector competes with the higher education sector for research grants from the NCN and in 2011–16 it received 1.21 billion PLN (Polish currency: zloty) out of 3.33 billion PLN disbursed, or 36.34 per cent.

The new system of coordination is associated with new tensions within institutions and between institutions, intermediary agencies, and the state. Managerial-type reforms, such as an increase in the power of academic leaders, both rectors and deans, as well as the increased role of the periodic research assessment exercises and performance-based research funding systems, have been introduced into a traditionally collegial system in which there is a very strong tradition of universities as communities of scholars. Indeed, the Polish system is one of the most collegial systems in Europe, and one that comes closest to the ideal of the Ivory Tower. Links between higher education institution and the economy are weak, as are links to society (Fulton et al., 2007). The perceived 'index of collegiality' for Poland is one of the highest in Europe, and the 'index of academic entrepreneurialism' is one of the lowest. The majority of academics perceive themselves as very influential (and somewhat influential) in shaping key academic policies at department levels but not at all influential at institutional levels (Kwiek, 2015b), with significant cross-generational differences between highly influential full professors and powerless new entrants (Kwiek, 2017).

That said, the newly introduced governance modes have strengthened both university-enterprise partnerships and the rise of tracer studies and student and graduate satisfaction surveys. The relatively large public funding allocated for the commercialization of research, mostly sourced from EU Structural Funds, have introduced new lines of accountability to EU and national-level sponsors, with specific project reporting regimes. The new intermediary agencies in Poland are in the process of learning of not only how to allocate funding on a highly competitive basis, but also how to systematically audit and assess research results. The state demands ever more measurable outputs from institutions, and inevitably, these institutions in turn demand ever more outputs from their academics. In addition, students demand ever more high quality instruction from their institutions and academics, now that they are conceptualized by the state and the private sector as 'clients' and 'consumers'; overall, recent reforms construct universities as organizations rather than traditional academic institutions (Kwiek, 2016c).

Finally, the second governance proposition (HPS Proposition 5) states that:

HPS governance tends to involve the management of horizontal differentiation.

In the Polish case, horizontal differences in institutional mission, classification, type, and profile are still limited: apart from the major public/private sectoral distinction, all public institutions are involved in both teaching and research, all academics are employed according to a national system of academic posts based on academic degrees. However, with new competitive research funding, the traditional division between universities and polytechnics is being turned into a division between more research-focused and better publicly funded universities and polytechnics on the one hand and much more teaching-focused and specialist universities (e.g. of economics or education), still more reliant on student fees from part-timers.

Diversity: The Increasing Power of Comprehensive Universities

The fourth proposition on horizontal diversity (HPS Proposition 10) states that:

All else being equal, the combination of expanding participation and enhanced competition in neoliberal quasi-markets is associated with specific effects in relation to diversity, including (1) increased vertical differentiation of higher education institutions (stratification); (2) reduced horizontal differentiation (diversification); (3) convergence of missions through isomorphistic imitation; and (4) growth in the role of private higher education institutions, especially for-profit institutions.

The power of recent reforms in Poland lies in their ability to combine changes in governance with changes in funding (Kwiek, 2012). The heavy dependence of public universities on public funds, as elsewhere in continental Europe, leads them to gradually accommodate the new rules of the academic game. New monies come through new funding instruments. There was much more public funding available in 2011–15 for higher education and for the university sector (see Table 12.2 later in the chapter). Total operating budgets, total income from teaching, and total income from research all rose compared to the previous period. All institutions, through their academic units, now compete in the quasi-market of public subsidies for research, striving for higher KEJN scores in the parameterization and categorization exercise. However, as noted, greater financial autonomy has gone hand in hand with the emergent audit culture and the new accountability mechanisms. The state-sponsored agencies directly shape academic work rather than handing over every aspect of its management to autonomous institutions.

In the contest for increasingly competitive funding the institutional winners are mostly the research-oriented metropolitan universities, especially the two flagships, the University of Warsaw and the Jagiellonian University in Cracow, and several other comprehensive universities. The role of these multiversities has grown substantially. The institutional losers are mostly the regional, teaching-focused public institutions that cater for regional and local students, located away from the major academic centres, and also the private sector of higher education, which is unable to compete successfully within the new funding arrangements.

The first proposition on horizontal diversity (HPS Proposition 7) states that:

In the HPS era, regardless of the political economy and culture of systems, an increasing proportion of higher education becomes centred on comprehensive multi-discipline and multi-function research universities, or 'multiversities'. The multiversity is increasingly dominant as the paradigmatic form of higher education.

In Poland there has been a powerful concentration of all types of public funding and all types of public resources, and all national-level infrastructural investments, in research universities. In a disintegrated system structure deriving originally from the communist period, Poland's comprehensive universities are separate not only from the polytechnics but also from specialist universities of medicine (except in the case of Cracow), economics, life sciences, education, and the arts. For instance, in Poznań there are separate public institutions which developed out of faculties of the comprehensive University of Poznań in the 1950s–70s: University of Economics, of Life Sciences, of Fine Arts and of Physical Education. A trend toward multi-function multiversities involves current debates about within-city mergers of academic institutions.

The second proposition on horizontal diversity (HPS Proposition 8) states that:

Regardless of the political economy and culture of the HPS, when participation expands there is no necessary increase in the overall diversity of institutional form and mission; and this has probably declined, except in relation to online provision.

The concentration of enrolments in metropolitan academic centres has grown, with the eight biggest enrolling over 60 per cent of all students. There are seventy-six public and private higher education institutions located in Warsaw, with 243,000 students (GUS, 2016: 25–7). In the period between 2005 and 2015, in the midst of contraction, different institutional types in the system experienced different trajectories. Universities and polytechnics enrolled more than a half of all students in Poland in 2015, compared with 45 per cent in 2010. In 2015, 30.0 per cent of students were enrolled in universities,

21.4 per cent in polytechnics, 12.8 per cent in academies of economics, 5.1 per cent in agricultural academies, 4.3 per cent in medical universities, 3.3 per cent in pedagogical academies, and the rest in other institutions (GUS, 2016: 59). So far there has been no large-scale tendency to merge specialist universities into comprehensive multi-disciplinary institutions of the multiversity type, as was suggested in Chapter 3's discussion of diversity Propositions 1 and 2, but the total weight of the multi-disciplinary institutions increases. The overall diversity of institutional form, profile, type, and mission has certainly decreased in the last decade.

The third proposition on horizontal diversity (HPS Proposition 9) states that:

As participation expands the internal diversity of multiversities tend to increase.

Major Polish comprehensive universities seem to increasingly specialize internally in attracting ever more students and attracting ever more diversified national and international monies. Multiversities may include several highly ranked units accompanied by several lower ranked units. The heterogeneity of these multiversities has increased, with the separated measures of the research intensity and separate national benchmarks applied to their different constitutive elements. Flagships seem to need ever more of everything and expand in all directions simultaneously, and one natural consequence is that their units change at a variable pace. Expansion has its costs and draws on ever more quality and quantity of students, Doctoral students, postdocs, grants, and publications. In the different units of multiversities there are differing emphases on teaching and research roles, and these variations are associated with different patterns of funding sources.

Since 2010 the gradually changing formula for the distribution of research funding has led to the 'haves' receiving more competitive research funds and the 'have-nots' receiving proportionately less, illustrating the workings of the mechanisms of cumulative advantage and disadvantage at an institutional level (Merton, 1968; Cole and Cole, 1973). In other words, the new funding mechanisms are fuelling vertical stratification, gradually leading to the emergence of two opposing families of institutions: on the one hand, those that are strongly and moderately research-oriented; and on the other, those with no research mission and no research funding.

While the distribution of resources for research was always unequal, this can now be illustrated in detail, in terms of research funding allocated by the national research council. During its first six years of operation from 2011 to 2016, the NCN funded about 10,000 research grants, with budgets totalling 3.331 billion PLN (approximately US$830 million). The distribution of these funds indicates the new geography of knowledge production, and indicates the growing stratification of the Polish HPS, driven by competition in the research quasi-market and the regulation of 'quality' in terms of international scientific excellence (Kwiek, 2016b).

Vertical Stratification

The first proposition on vertical stratification (HPS Proposition 11) states that:

> *The expansion of participation towards and beyond the HPS stage is associated with a tendency to bifurcation and stratification (vertical diversification) in the value of higher education, between elite (artisanal) institutions and mass (demand-absorbing) institutions.*

In Poland the two largest national universities, the Jagiellonian University in Cracow (UJ) and University of Warsaw (UW), between 2011 and 2016 together received about 30 per cent of all research funding competitively available from the NCN, with 14.98 per cent allocated to UJ and 14.82 per cent to UW. These two institutions are well ahead of the other leading institutions in Poland. In 2011–16 the top five institutions were awarded 46.12 per cent of all grants and the top ten received 62.99 per cent (see Table 12.1); and the top twenty received 80.56 per cent. There were 410 institutions in 2016 in total, but only 115 institutions were awarded NCN funding.

What of the 300 institutional losers under the new research funding regime? These are public middle-level institutions, together with, and especially low-level public and private institutions, where knowledge production is only marginally competitive. Interestingly, out of the 963 units awarded any of the KEJN categories in 2013, only 533 received any funding from the NCN. According to the second governance proposition (HPS Proposition 5),

Table 12.1. The concentration of research funding—the Polish top ten institutions by the amount of project-based competitive research funding awarded by the National Research Council in its first six years of operation (2011–16)

Institution	Location	Funding awarded (in milion PLN)	% of total funding awarded
Jagiellonian University (UJ)	Cracow	498.839	14.98
University of Warsaw (UW)	Warsaw	493.696	14.82
University of Poznań (UAM)	Poznań	222.613	6.68
University of Wrocław (UWr)	Wrocław	167.238	5.02
University of Science and Technology (AGH)	Cracow	154.028	4.62
Wrocław Polytechnics (PWr)	Wrocław	128.850	3.87
Warsaw Polytechnics (PW)	Warsaw	126.760	3.81
University of Gdańsk (UG)	Gdańsk	124.911	3.75
Nicolaus Copernicus University (UMK)	Toruń	92.317	2.77
Łódź Polytechnics (PŁ)	Łódź	88.933	2.67

Note: US$1 = 4.00 PLN.

Source: Author's calculations based on NCN (2017) data.

HPS governance tends to involve the management of horizontal differentiation.

The combination of KEJN categories and NCN funding works as a tool for the management of horizontal differentiation, with the missions of institutions defined by the number of high and low categories they receive, while at the same time also strengthening vertical stratification. The level of research funding serves as a precise system for calibrating competitive standing.

The increasing concentration of funding in top national institutions, which is also associated with the growing concentration of research talents and opportunities, goes far beyond competitive research funding from the NCN, however. It includes all funding categories: competitive and non-competitive, project-based and subsidies, subsidies for research and subsidies for teaching, international funding, as well as income from fees from part-time students. The Polish multiversities increasingly attract higher proportions of monies from all possible sources, compared with lower tier institutions. All funding mechanisms seem to work to their advantage; and in a contracting system, the top tier institutions attract an ever-higher share of total students. Their nominal numbers are falling but their share grows. The institutional data for 2011 to 2015 in Table 12.2 show in detail the changing incomes of six major Polish universities. These are the university sector's representatives in the list of top ten institutions, the other four being polytechnics. Note that the average increase in funding for the six institutions in 2011–15 was higher than for the university sector as a whole, underlining the point that multiversities tend to attract more funds from all possible sources.

It is clear both informally and formally, through the dense system of several competing national rankings, which institutions are prestigious, and which are less so. The list of top ten public universities and polytechnics has been stable in the last ten years, with two national flagship universities in Warsaw and Cracow holding top place in the list from the very beginning of national rankings two decades ago. The effect of the recent reforms has been to render the Polish system even more vertically stratified than was the case in the past two decades, and more (quasi-)market driven in research, while also less market-driven in organizational terms, given the decreasing number of private institutions and the increase in public funding as a proportion of funding. The prestige hierarchy seems tighter and the position of the leading universities if anything seems less open to contestation from below.

The third proposition on stratification (HPS Proposition 13) states that:

In stratified HPS, a middle layer of institutions tends to form, shaped by the combination of upward aspirations (drift) with systemic scarcity of resources and status.

In Poland the middle layer institutions are those with their faculties rated predominantly B by KEJN. They aspire to move up the ladder of prestige and resources but the distinction between the top layer and the middle layer institutions is made on the

Table 12.2. Income of top six Polish universities, 2011–15

	University of Gdańsk (UGd)	University of Poznań (UAM)	Jagiellonian University in Cracow (UJ)	Nicolaus Copernicus University in Toruń (UMK)	University of Warsaw (UW)	University of Wrocław (UWr)	Total (the university sector only)
Total operating budget							
2011	296,1120	519,472	792,658	370,516	1,037,086	381,111	5,916,606
2012	313,219	549,031	850,264	374,386	1,071,155	384,769	6,090,464
2013	353,496	610,002	946,333	407,144	1,132,558	410,237	6,529,304
2014	369,545	660,414	1,036,744	436,288	1,248,786	448,637	7,110,253
2015	401,994	701,248	1,123,350	483,590	1,318,199	472,415	7,448,954
% change	**136%**	135%	**142%**	131%	127%	124%	126%
Total public subsidies for teaching							
2011	171,376	295,821	417,673	224,227	373,944	216,530	3,146,467
2012	181,697	308,740	440,262	230,645	391,457	225,319	3,263,197
2013	198,133	344,226	504,433	256,079	447,798	244,138	3,638,974
2014	223,017	383,145	570,841	283,690	517,401	268,342	4,058,839
2015	246,500	428,128	636,492	307,172	572,410	292,476	4,453,927
% change	144%	145%	**152%**	137%	**153%**	135%	142%
Total income from fees (part-time students only)							
2011	56,168	65,799	99,136	41,788	153,036	69,375	906,102
2012	50,013	58,478	107,383	39,775	137,975	60,557	783,767
2013	44,220	50,406	106,252	36,429	127,535	53,954	708,675
2014	45,314	38,577	100,648	34,972	117,583	49,200	640,356
2015	44,260	45,749	100,850	33,821	101,500	45,619	606,830
% change	**79%**	70%	**102%**	81%	67%	67%	67%
Total income from research							
2011	34,463	65,351	126,860	42,687	329,620	53,222	853,829
2012	43,406	78,481	159,420	45,687	354,603	47,862	951,224
2013	55,463	82,487	175,279	46,877	352,809	55,211	975,837
2014	56,673	92,180	194,890	49,233	386,757	59,249	1,070,913
2015	58,950	95,126	209,785	58,316	420,299	63,327	1,126 352
% change	**173%**	146%	**165%**	135%	127%	119%	132%
Total public subsidies for research							
2011	12,514	28,382	44,491	17,424	199,823	24,120	394,488
2012	16,651	30,266	46,369	19,310	225,999	23,781	444,786
2013	18,380	29,952	40,742	17,141	213,763	19,128	418,530
2014	14,918	30,337	38,906	18,660	223,380	17,749	426,644
2015	17,337	25,016	47,459	20,301	252,346	15,622	565,200
% change	**139%**	88%	107%	117%	**126%**	65%	143%

Notes: In million PLN (US$1 = 4.00 PLN). Growth leaders in bold.

Source: Author's calculations based on POL-ON (2016) data.

basis of easily measurable research intensity, and the vast majority of institutions are unsuccessful in the research-based competition for A and A+ categories and for NCN competitive research funding. The Polish case clearly testifies Marginson's (2016c: 2) claim that 'the research/non-research distinction always has positional implications' and that 'the weightiest distinction between higher education institutions derives from comparisons of research intensity'. At the very top of the academic ladder of prestige, there are two universities, the only two ranked in ARWU (in the ranks 400–500 in 2016), comprising half of all faculties highly categorized across the system, and jointly collecting about 30 per cent of all research grants from the national research council.

Equity: Social Aspirations as Driver of Social Inclusion

The first proposition on equity (HPS Proposition 14) states that:

> As participation expands in the HPS phase, equity in the form of social inclusion is enhanced.

The Polish HPS clearly follows the pattern. However, Poland is distinguished from the other HPS countries in this book in that historically speaking, the most significant aspect of social inclusion is the urban/rural divide (in 2015, 60.4 per cent of the population lived in cities, and 39.6 per cent in rural areas), as distinct from the internationally more common divide between parents with high and low level of education. The two divides do not coincide and therefore questions of social mobility in Poland are related to both.

URBAN/RURAL DIVIDE

In the pre-HPS period the social distribution of access to comprehensive universities favoured the children of the intelligentsia class. Between 1960 and 1990, of the three major social classes in the communist world, the rural class, worker class, and intelligentsia, the enrolment shares of the intelligentsia and worker classes steadily increased while the share of the rural class was decreasing (see Table 12.3). In the HPS period, the share of students from the rural areas has moved much closer to the share of the population living in the rural areas. About one-third of students in 2015 were of rural socio-economic origin (GUS, 2016: 26), compared to approximately 40 per cent of the population living in the rural areas. However, the social importance of the rural/urban

Table 12.3. The social composition of Polish students accepted to the first year of studies in 1960–88 (%)

Year	Rural (%)	Worker (%)	Intelligentsia (%)	Other (%)
1960	18.0	26.2	49.4	6.4
1970	15.5	29.9	50.3	3.5
1980	8.5	32.2	55.2	4.1
1988	6.2	31.7	59.3	2.8

Source: Author, data adapted from Wasielewski (2013).

divide continues. In 2013 the share of population with higher education credentials in cities was three times higher than in the rural areas, with 30.9 per cent in the cities and just 11.0 per cent in rural area. Four in every five graduates were living in cities, 82.6 per cent. The urban/rural divide also shows itself in current educational aspirations. While in the cities, 82.7 per cent of parents want higher education for their children, in rural areas that share is merely 64.6 per cent.

The third proposition on equity (HPS Proposition 16) states that:

> *Within a national system, as participation expands in the HPS phase, all else being equal the positional structure of the higher education system increasingly resembles that of society . . . The HPS is increasingly implicated in the reproduction of existing patterns of social equality/inequality.*

No matter which institutional type is selected, the share of rural students (to use the urban rural divide) has substantially increased: of the students in polytechnics, 32.8 per cent were from rural areas in 2015, compared to 18.2 per cent in 1960 and 6.8 per cent in 1980. In comprehensive universities in 2015, 29.0 per cent were from rural areas, compared to 16.8 per cent in 1960 and 7.7 per cent in 1980 (Wasielewski, 2013: 34).

Surprisingly, rural access to higher education of the various institutional types was relatively high in 1960, decreasing in the 1960s, 1970s, and 1980s, with the lowest point in 1990, and then increasing again in the HPS era. Cross-sectional OECD data related to parental education show that the proportion of 20–34-year-olds in higher education whose parents have low levels of education in 2009 was 20.6 per cent, above the OECD average of 16.9 per cent (OECD, 2012: 102). Institutional-level studies indicate relatively stable patterns of selection of fields of study over time, with the constant more and less 'ruralized' fields (Wasielewski, 2013: 112–24). As in other Central and Eastern European countries, young people from lower socio-economic strata tend to choose Bachelor's level studies, with a stronger market orientation, and in less demanding academic fields (Kogan et al., 2011: 336). In 2013, intergenerational social mobility in the urban/rural terms was much higher in Poland's cities than the rural areas. In the cities almost half of the children of fathers without primary education reached higher education (46.2 per cent), as opposed to 5.5 per cent in the rural areas (CBOS, 2013a: 29).

NO LIMIT TO ASPIRATIONS

The HPS general Proposition 2 states that:

> *In HPS there is no intrinsic limit to the spread of family aspirations for participation in higher education until universality is reached; and no intrinsic limit to the level of social position to which families/students may aspire.*

In the HPS era in Poland, the difference in educational aspirations between the highly educated and lower educated families has decreased substantially. Between 1993 and 2009, a period which saw the most rapid educational expansion, among parents with vocational education, the proportion of parents who wanted higher education for their sons increased by 29 per cent to reach 82 per cent (and the proportion of inhabitants of the rural areas increased by 26 per cent to reach 82 per cent). This partly closed the gap between vocational parents and parents with higher education (and between parents from the rural areas and big cities). Among parents with higher education, 97 per cent aspired to higher education for their sons, an increase of 5 per cent in 1993–2009 (and among parents from big cities, 93 per cent, an increase of 18 per cent, CBOS, 2009: 8). Positional competition in society tends to spread and total social demand for higher education is rising (Hirsch, 1976; Brown et al., 2011; Marginson, 2016a).

The tendency to HPS has a universal character and 'the ambition for higher education now appears unstoppable' (Marginson, 2016b: 266). It seems that also in Poland, higher education is increasingly important. Nevertheless, the last decade the share of population stating that it is 'definitely worth it' to 'achieve education, to learn' decreased radically, from 76 per cent in 2004 to 49 per cent in 2013 (see Table 12.4). This suggests possible educational disillusionment.

There is a significant difference between the pioneering HPS era of 1990s, when a growing labour market was open to all newly highly educated graduates, and the stable HPS era of the 2010s when the labour market was saturated with graduates. In the first decade of growth it seemed that anything was possible. Opportunities for those with higher education, combined with personal entrepreneurialism, were seen as unlimited. Since about 2000 there has been growing disillusionment in Poland as indicated by public opinion surveys. It also comes as a warning to the Polish HPS system that for 57 per cent of Poles surveyed in 2013, 'in general, the higher education diploma has low value in the labour market'. And 78 per cent of those people surveyed confirmed that higher education is 'mass, everyone can study' (CBOS, 2013a: 2–7). One reconciliation of this tension between access for all, and the perceived value of higher education credentials, is to increase the vertical

Table 12.4. The attractiveness of education, 1993–2013

Is it worth it currently in Poland to achieve education, to learn, or not?	Answers by year (in %)											
	1993		2002		2004		2007		2009		2013	
Definitely worth it	42	76	66	91	76	93	70	93	68	91	49	82
Rather worth it	34		25		17		23		23		33	
Rather not worth it	16	20	5	7	4	5	4	5	6	7	13	16
Definitely not worth it	4		2		1		1		1		3	
Hard to say	4	4	2	2	2	2	2	2	2	1	2	2

Source: Author, adapted from CBOS (2013b).

stratification of the system so that some credentials retain value. As discussed, the present reform agenda has a stratifying effect.

SELECTIVITY

Finally, the second proposition on stratification (HPS Proposition 12) states that:

> The tendency to institutional stratification is magnified by features common (though not universal) among HPS including (a) intensified social competition for the most valuable student places; (b) variable tuition charges; and/or (c) intensified competition between institutions.

In Poland, social competition for the most valuable student places in most prestigious institutions is clearly increasing. However, as elsewhere in HPS, the intensity of that competition (which occurs in full-time taxation-financed studies in the public sector only) is highest in the traditionally least accessible faculties of law and, outside of comprehensive universities, the faculties of medicine in specialist universities. For instance, in 2016 there were on average 16.8 candidates per vacancy in medical studies. There are no admission tests or interviews and the scores from standardized national secondary education final exams are used instead. In 2016, the highest number of applications were filled for computing, management, law and psychology, the highest number of applications per vacancy was in four polytechnics (in Warsaw, Poznań, Gdańsk, and Łódź), followed by University of Warsaw. Thus the most valuable student places are located in selected metropolitan universities and polytechnics, in selected study programmes within these institutions. High selectivity in some faculties goes hand in hand with almost open access in numerous faculties even in most prestigious institutions. Dozens of study programmes are fully accessible to first-year students every year at comprehensive universities, including the two flagships. In other words, the primary social stratification of opportunity in higher education in Poland is centred on disciplines, but disciplines that are provided in specific institutional contexts.

Final Thoughts

Taking account of the continually growing family aspirations for higher education, which have been expressed by all socioeconomic strata in the post-1989 HPS era, the further expansion of participation seems unlimited. Given that the HPS in Poland has become transformed into a demand-driven system that is also highly stratified in the vertical sense, there seems to be no political, social, or economic rationale to keep anyone out of it.

However, while indeed there may be no limits to growth of the Polish HPS, there are clear limits in other components of what Marginson terms in Chapter 6 as the 'specific social *assemblage* of family/state/education/economy with nationally distinctive features', especially limits in the economy. The number of 'bad jobs' still exceeds the number of 'good jobs'. For graduates this scarcity of middle class jobs seems still inevitable. Prestigious and well-paid jobs are limited in number in every society. As Brown and colleagues argue (2011: 135): 'There are simply too many people wanting to make the same life journeys that depend on educational and occupational success.' In Poland there is increasing social congestion in the competition for decent jobs. As the earlier cited public opinion surveys show, the HPS society is aware that new educational opportunities do not necessarily lead to new occupational opportunities, and the expectations from the 1990s cannot be met in the 2010s and beyond. In that respect, the Polish high participation society seems realistic.

Higher education on the one hand is a 'positional advantage' (Smolentseva, 2017) in a race for middle class jobs and lifestyles, and on the other a 'defensive necessity' (Hirsch, 1976: 51) in a competitive social environment. As Hirsch (p. 51) argues, 'as the average level of educational qualifications in the labour force rises, a kind of tax is imposed on those lacking such qualifications, while the bounty derived from possessing a given qualification is diminished' (p. 51). In the Polish case, the two approaches come together: the 'how to win the race' approach dominates when economy is good and the 'how not to lose in the race' approach applies when economy is bad. In the case of some jobs there is an internal competition between graduates, while in the case of other jobs there is an external competition between graduates and non-graduates, with the non-graduates inevitably losing out.

Middle class growth is probably the key to understand the evolution of the Polish HPS. The evolution of the middle class is in turn linked to the emergence of the post-industrial society and market economy, with a new distribution of jobs and prestige, totally unrelated to their once standard distribution under communism. Changes in the economy in the 1990s led to gradual changes in the social structure and, especially, in social aspirations, with not only the middle class but all social strata willing to do everything necessary to secure higher education credentials for their offspring. Every generation wants for its offspring at least the same level of affluence and prestige it has experienced, and higher education seems to be the best way to achieve these qualities, although not the only way. Arguably, a HPS in Poland was inevitable once the social structure became transformed by the 1990s' economic changes. For a quarter of a century, when there were ever more graduates, returns from higher education remained high and growing, and the system continued to expand. While in the early HPS era economic factors probably mattered more in shaping demand for higher education, in the current more stable HPS era prestige-related factors, powerful social aspirations, seem more important. The society is now realistic in its economic expectations from credentials.

SIGNIFICANCE OF THE POLISH CASE

Universities in Central and Eastern Europe have not been included in any of the major typologies of university governance and organization, such as those by Burton R. Clark (1983) and Robert Birnbaum (1988). The region, Poland included, finally seems to follow the global trend towards high participation. On the demand side, the advantage of participation over non-participation in higher education is becoming a social fact, social inclusion has expanded (even while educational and occupational competition for position has become harsher than ever before), and social demand and social aspirations for higher education are on the rise. All of this has been accompanied by changes on the supply side. There the elite universities are becoming more elite and, as Kerr's multiversities, they are garnering ever more prestige and ever more funding from all sources possible (Kwiek 2018a). They are the winners in emergent post-2011 quasi-market resource allocation; and, though it is more difficult to measure (the proxy is KEJN scores) in the allocation of prestige. As elsewhere in HPS, the steep vertical hierarchy is reinforced by a permanent state-imposed and peer-run comparison of institutional research intensity.

In sum, the HPS propositions fit the Polish case very well: specifically, all the general propositions, and those on governance, horizontal diversity, and vertical stratification propositions provide conceptual guidance. However, in some cases, specific reservations need to be emphasized. The propositions that work only partially are equity ones, due to the post-2006 processes of contraction and de-privatization of the Polish system (Kwiek, 2016a). In terms of general propositions, the HPS period in Poland is accompanied by enhanced equity (HPS Proposition 1). Family aspirations for participation in higher education have been growing steadily, and the aspirational gap between the highly educated and lower educated families, and between the urban and rural families, has been closing steadily (HPS Proposition 2). While the system shows the signs of saturation and some disillusionment with education is reported, the long-term growth of the participation rate seems inevitable (HPS Proposition 3).

In terms of the HPS governance propositions, after 2009 the system was reconfigured on the basis of multi-level governance, with new intermediary coordinating institutions (HPS Proposition 4). Horizontal differences in institutional mission are still limited but with the increasing role of competitive research funding (from NCN) and research assessment exercise (by KEJN), a salient division between a group of more research-focused comprehensive universities and polytechnics on the one hand and a group of more teaching-focused and specialist universities on the other is growing. The combination of high-to-low KEJN categories and ample-to-none NCN competitive research funding applied to faculties provide a new tool for the management of horizontal differentiation within both groups (HPS Proposition 5). New multi-level coordination through new intermediary bodies leads to enhanced horizontal differentiation. All institutions are increasingly subject to rigorous systems of reporting and the corporatist direction of reforms—in the context of a gradually implemented performance-based research funding system—is unmistakable (HPS Proposition 6).

Comprehensive multi-discipline and multi-function research universities tend to dominate in the Polish system: there has been a powerful concentration of public funding and infrastructural investments in major research universities, especially in the two national flagships (HPS Proposition 7). While the overall diversity of institutional profile and mission has decreased (HPS Proposition 8), the internal diversity of comprehensive universities has increased (HPS Proposition 9). Major comprehensive universities tend to attract ever more students in some faculties and ever more research funding in other faculties, with different faculties internally assuming different roles, leading to growing internal heterogeneity. All institutions compete in the newly created quasi-markets of public funding and strive for higher KEJN scores in the national parameterization and categorization exercise (HPS Proposition 10). However, the role of the private sector has been diminishing and its decline is linked to declining demographics, in sharp contrast to global trends (Kwiek, 2016d).

The bifurcation between traditionally elite research institutions and demand-absorbing mass institutions (HPS Proposition 11) is clear: research funding, research talents and opportunities, as well as all competitive and non-competitive funding categories, are concentrated in the former institutions, with two Polish flagships garnering about 30 per cent of all competitive research funding from the national research council (NCN) and comprising half of all exceptionally highly categorized (category A+) faculties in the system (KEJN). The most valuable student places are located in selected study programmes within elite metropolitan universities and polytechnics, and social competition for them intensifies (HPS Proposition 12). However, in contrast to global trends, there are no tuition fees and there is wide access to non-elite study programmes within elite institutions. In the Polish HPS, a middle layer of institutions tends to form (HPS Proposition 13), aspiring to move up the ladder of prestige and resources but with limited chances to join the first university league with entry tickets based purely on research intensity.

Poland also clearly follows the pattern of equity in the form of social inclusion being enhanced (HPS Proposition 14). The positional structure of the higher education system increasingly resembles that of society (HPS Proposition 16): the share of rural students (and of students from lower socio-economic classes) has substantially increased in the HPS period. However, a greater social inequality in educational outcomes and social outcomes (HPS Proposition 15) was not observed, perhaps due to deeper social changes in Poland in the last two decades compared with other HPS systems except for Russia; the redistribution of educational opportunities and social opportunities, against the (HPS Proposition 17) proposition, seems to be still secured, perhaps due to a combination of declining demographics and a tax-based system in which educational opportunities are not limited by fees or class-based fee-/debt-aversion.

A HPS became the reality in Poland much faster than almost anywhere else, with still unclear consequences for the society, as well as for academic institutions. The conceptual framework of HPS explains what has happened in higher education in Poland since 1989, what may happen in the next few years, and why.

■ ACKNOWLEDGEMENTS

The author gratefully acknowledges the support of the National Research Council (NCN) through its research grant (UMO-2013/10/M/HS6/00561). And he would like to thank Simon Marginson and Anna Smolentseva for their friendly intellectual guidance, from the Moscow 2013 seminar on 'high participation systems' to the revision of the draft chapter. All traditional disclaimers certainly apply.

■ REFERENCES

Antonowicz, D. (2016). Digital players in an analogue world: Higher education in Poland in the post-massification era, in B. Jongbloed and H. Vossensteyn (eds), *Access and Expansion Post-Massification. Opportunities and Barriers to Further Growth in Higher Education Participation.* London: Routledge, pp. 63–81.

Antonowicz, D., Kwiek, M., and Westerheijden, D. (2017). The government response to the private sector expansion in Poland, in H. de Boer et al. (eds), *Policy Analysis of Structural Reforms in Higher Education.* New York: Palgrave, pp. 119–38.

Białecki, I. and Dąbrowa-Szefler, M. (2009). Polish higher education in transition: Between policy making and autonomy, in D. Palfreyman and D. T. Tapper (eds), *Structuring Mass Higher Education: The Role of Elite Institutions.* London: Routledge.

Birnbaum, R. (1988). *How Colleges Work: The Cybernetics of Academic Organization and Leadership.* San Francisco: Jossey-Bass Publishers.

Brown, P., Lauder, H., and Ashton, D. (2011). *The Global Auction: The Broken Promises of Education, Jobs and Incomes.* New York: Oxford University Press.

CBOS (2013a). *Studia wyższe—dla kogo, po co i z jakim skutkiem.* BS/92/2013, Warsaw, July.

CBOS (2013b). *Wykształcenie ma znaczenie?* BS/96/2013, Warsaw, July.

CBOS (2009). *Aspiracje i motywacje edukacyjne Polaków w latach 1993–2009*. BS/70/2009, Warsaw, May.

Clark, B. R. (1983). *The Higher Education System. Academic Organization in Cross-National Perspective*. Berkeley: University of California Press.

Cole, J. R. and Cole, S. (1973). *Social Stratification in Science*: Chicago, The University of Chicago Press.

Dobbins, M. (2011). *Higher Education Policies in Central and Eastern Europe: Convergence Towards a Common Model?* London: Palgrave Macmillan.

Fulton, O., Santiago, P. Edquist, Ch., El-Khawas, E., and Hackl, E. (2007). *OECD Reviews of Tertiary Education*. Paris: OECD.

GUS (2014). *Population Projection 2014–2050*. Warsaw: GUS (Central Statistical Office).

GUS (2016). *Higher Education Institutions and Their Finances in 2015*. Warsaw: GUS (Central Statistical Office).

Hirsch, F. (1976). *Social Limits to Growth*. Cambridge, MA: Harvard University Press.

Kerr, C. (2001). *The Uses of the University*. 5th edn. Cambridge, MA: Harvard University Press.

Kogan, I., Noelke, C., and Gebel, M. (2011). Comparative analysis of social transformation, education systems, and school-to-work transitions in Central and Eastern Europe, in I. Kogan, C. Noelke, and M. Gebel (eds), *Making the Transition: Education and Labor Market Entry in Central and Eastern Europe*. Stanford: Stanford University Press, pp. 320–51.

Kulczycki, E. (2017). Assessing publications through a bibliometric indicator: The case of comprehensive evaluation of scientific units in Poland. *Research Evaluation* 16(1), 41–52.

Kulczycki, E., Korzeń, M., and Korytkowski, P. (2017). Toward an excellence-based research fuding system: Evidence from Poland. *Journal of Informetrics* 11(1), 282–98.

Kwiek, M. (2012). Changing higher education policies: From the deinstitutionalization to the reinstitutionalization of the research mission in Polish universities. *Science and Public Policy* 35(5), 641–54.

Kwiek, M. (2013). From system expansion to system contraction: Access to higher education in Poland. *Comparative Education Review* 56(3), 553–76.

Kwiek, M. (2015a). Academic generations and academic work: Patterns of attitudes, behaviors and research productivity of Polish academics after 1989. *Studies in Higher Education* 40(8), 1354–76.

Kwiek, M. (2015b). The unfading power of collegiality? University governance in Poland in a European comparative and quantitative perspective. *International Journal of Educational Development* 43, 77–89.

Kwiek, M. (2016a). De-privatization in higher education: A conceptual approach. *Higher Education* 1–21. DOI 10.1007/s10734-016-0047-3

Kwiek, M. (2016b). Constructing universities as organizations: University reforms in Poland in the light of institutional theory, in E. Samier (ed.), *Ideologies in Educational Administration and Leadership*. New York: Routledge, 193–216.

Kwiek, M. (2016c). The European research elite: A cross-national study of highly productive academics in 11 countries. *Higher Education* 71(3), 379–97.

Kwiek, M. (2016d). From privatization (of the expansion era) to de-privatization (of the contraction era): A national counter-trend in a global context, in S. Slaughter and B. J. Taylor (eds), *Higher Education, Stratification, and Workforce Development. Competitive Advantage in Europe, the US and Canada*. Dordrecht: Springer, pp. 311–29.

Kwiek, M. (2017). A generational divide in the Polish academic profession: A mixed quantitative and qualitative approach. *European Educational Research Journal* 17, 1–26.

Kwiek, M. (2018a). Academic top earners. Research productivity, prestige generation and salary patterns in European universities. *Science and Public Policy*. 45(1). February 2018, 1–13.

Kwiek, M. (2018b). High Research Productivity in Vertically Undifferentiated Higher Education Systems: Who Are the Top Performers?. *Scientometrics*. April 2018, 115(1), 415–62.

NCN (Narodowe Centrum Nauki [National Research Council]) (2017). Database. https://www.ncn.gov.pl/

OECD (Organisation for Economic Co-operation and Development) (2012). *Education at A Glance 2012: OECD Indicators*. Paris: OECD.

POL-ON (2017). Zintegrowany System Informacji o Nauce i Szkolnictwie Wyższym. https://polon.nauka.gov.pl/

Marginson, S. (2016a). The worldwide trend to high participation higher education: Dynamics of social stratification in inclusive systems. *Higher Education* 72, 413–34.

Marginson, S. (2016b). High participation systems of higher education. *The Journal of Higher Education* 87(2), 243–71.

Marginson, S. (2016c). Diversity within high participation systems of higher education. A speech at the University of Oxford, 31 October.

Marginson, S. (2016d). Public/private in higher education: A synthesis of economic and political approaches. *Studies in Higher Education*. http://dx.doi.org/10.1080/03075079.2016.1168797

Merton, R. K. (1968). The Matthew effect in science. *Science* 159(3810), 56–63.

Pinheiro, R. and Antonowicz, D. (2015). Opening the gates of coping with the flow? Governing access to higher education in Northern and Central Europe. *Higher Education* 70(3), 299–313.

Siemińska, R. and Walczak, D. (2012). Polish higher education: From state toward market, from elite to mass education. *Advances in Education in Diverse Communities: Research, Policy, and Praxis* 7, 197–224.

Smolentseva, A. (2017). Universal higher education and positional advantage: Soviet legacies and neoliberal transformation in Russia. *Higher Education* 73(2), 209–26.

Szadkowski, K. (2017). The university of the common: Beyond the contradictions of higher education subsumed under capital, in M. Izak, M. Kostera, and M. Zawadzki (eds), *The Future of University Education*. Cham: Palgrave Macmillan, pp. 39–62.

Szczepański, J. (1974). *Higher Education in Eastern Europe*. New York: International Council for Educational Development.

Wasielewski, K. (2013). *Młodzież wiejska na uniwersytecie. Droga na studia, mechanizmy alokacji, postawy wobec kształcenia*. Toruń: Wydawnictwo Naukowe UMK.

World Bank (2017). Data. http://data.worldbank.org/indicator

13 Reproducing Social Equality across the Generations: The Nordic Model of High Participation Higher Education in Finland

Jussi Välimaa and Reetta Muhonen

Introduction

Finnish higher education illustrates the dynamics of a high participation system (HPS) of higher education based on core values of equality and equity, as is also found in the Scandinavian countries of Norway, Sweden, and Denmark (these countries, Finland and Iceland are commonly grouped as 'Nordic'). Since World War II equal educational opportunities have been a central political goal of Finnish higher education, as will be discussed later.

In addition to focusing on Finnish higher education the chapter also discusses the other Nordic systems of higher education in more general terms, in order to context-ualize Finnish higher education in the distinctive social dynamics of the Nordic welfare societies. The chapter examines the interplay between HPS and higher education policies in Finland. Focusing especially on the nature of access to higher education and the relationship between the university sector and the Universities of Applied Sciences (UAS, the former polytechnics), from the perspective of equality and equity, it reflects on the general propositions about HPS throughout the text. The chapter has been drawn together from existing research literature and publicly available sources of information.

FINLAND

Finland is a medium sized European country of 303,890 square kilometres. It is almost the same size as Germany but with much of its land located above the Arctic Circle, Finland is more sparsely populated than most European countries. There were 5.4 million people in Finland in 2015, less than 7 per cent of the population of Germany. Finland is nevertheless a comparatively wealthy country, with a total gross domestic product (GDP) of US$222.6 billion in current price and purchasing power parity (PPP) terms. Its 2015 GDP per capita of US$42,309 located the Finnish economy just below Belgium and above the United Kingdom (UK) in international comparisons.

Though people in Finland speak a distinctive language that helps to define a common cultural zone, most of the country was part of Sweden until 1809 (a small minority of citizens of Finland have Swedish as their first language) and was then controlled by Russia until 1917. In its one hundred years as an independent country Finland has evolved its own social model, one resembling the other Nordic countries in many respects, and an education system that is especially well-regarded in world terms. Finland has been the best performing European country in the Organisation for Economic Co-operation and Development (OECD)'s regular comparisons of student achievement at age 15, the Programme of International Student Assessment (PISA); and like Denmark and Sweden is very successful in research on the basis of publications and citations per capita (Leiden University, 2017). However, the bald comparative data on demography, economy, education, and research do not capture the essential character of high partici-pation higher education in Finland, which is the product of the country's distinctive history, culture, and social values.

Finnish Higher Education

The current Finnish system of higher education consists of two public sectors under the Finnish Ministry of Education and Culture (MEC). There are fourteen universities focusing on research and education and twenty-three UAS which focus on higher vocational education and R&D activities. In addition, there are the National Defence Academy under the Ministry of Defence, the Police Academy under the Ministry of Interior Matters, and Ålands Yrkehögskola under the autonomous province of Åland. There also are six university centres typically located in areas lacking a university. These university centres are hybrid organizations consisting of teaching and research activities organized by a variety of UASs and universities. However, common to all higher education activities are the facts that they serve public needs, they are publicly funded and studying is free of charge for all Finnish and European students (Välimaa, 2012). The only exception to the provision of free education is the Finnish open university system. Most universities and UASs run their own open university where students pay a low and state regulated fee for their studies, about 15 euros per study credit. However, these open institutions do not award degrees even though they are run by higher education institutions. In principle, open university studies contradict the principle of free education. In practice the situation is not that clear-cut. Many of the students in open universities are over 25 years old and take studying as a hobby, or want to improve their position in the labour markets with extra education. Only 6 per cent of new older students (those over 25 years) enter university through this open university route. In 2004, about one-third of Finnish university students were older than 30 years (Rinne et al., 2008).

This distinctive system, with its comprehensive framework of provision, the absence of significant financial barriers, and the availability of multiple and second chance routes into degree programmes cannot be meaningfully separated from the society which it serves. That in turn has deep roots. Analysis of the development of a national system of higher education is most often seen from contemporary perspectives. This approach is both understandable and misleading. Higher education institutions are complex organizations because of their multi-disciplinarity and their historically developed traditions, practices and processes.

HISTORICAL LAYERS

Finnish higher education began with the establishment of the Royal Academy in Åbo in 1640 with the main aim of educating clergy for the Lutheran Church and civil servants for the Kingdom of Sweden, which then included Finland. This laid the basis for the first historical layer of Finnish higher education, a tradition which continues in the training of priests for the church and civil servants for the state. This function was strengthened during the nineteenth century when Finland was conquered by the Russian Empire during the Napoleonic wars. Finland's time as an autonomous Grand Duchy within the Russian Empire (1809–1917) added a new social function to higher education because the Imperial Alexander University (the former Royal Academy in Åbo) acted as one of the cradles of, and for, Finnish nationalism. The university began to be defined as a national institution and education became seen crucially important for the development of the nation. Technical and commercial institutions (from the 1850s onwards) and teacher training seminars (from the 1860s) were important as Finland developed towards an industrial society by the beginning of the twentieth century. Though there was still only one university in the country, this period saw the first expansion of higher education when Finnish speaking students, including an increasing number of female students, entered that university which had previously been dominated by Swedish speaking students and professors.

The third historical layer developed after Finland became a republic in 1917. This became manifest as the 'White Republic', ruled mainly by right wing and centre parties after a bloody civil war of Reds versus Whites in 1918. Universities continued to be elite institutions with the majority of their students from middle class and upper middle class families. There was a low student participation rate, about 5 per cent of the age group, and elite university fields such as medicine and law that were exclusive in terms of their students' socio-economic backgrounds. The capital city university, the University of Helsinki (the former Imperial Alexander University) had a hegemonic position among all Finnish higher education institutions. However, in the 1930s over 30 per cent of the students were female and 20 per cent of all students came from lower socio-economic groups. This showed that both working class and middle class families aspired to educate their sons and daughters, reflecting the high social status given to higher education in Finnish society. Higher education was seen as one of the main channels for upward social mobility. This conviction had emerged already during the nineteenth century and grew stronger between the two World Wars.

By the end of the 1930s social democrats, allied with centre parties, had formed a coalition government. There were three universities in Finland, two in the private sector, one technical university, and three business schools. State ideology rested on the conviction that universities were autonomous institutions that should not be subject to any kind of state intervention, except for funding of the national university, the University of Helsinki.

The development of the Nordic welfare society and high participation higher education began in Finland after World War II. The welfare society had older roots. Nordic definitions concerning the role of state, citizens, and government originated in the Reformation during the sixteenth century (Alestalo and Kuhnle, 1987). The welfare society and ideas of equality were also influenced by the structures of pre-industrial rural communities with strong traditions of the division of labour between men and women, by nineteenth century modernization, by the rise of socialism which emphasized socio-economic equity, and by the rise of nationalism which emphasized national unity. By the 1930s the different ideologies had become more or less combined in the Nordic versions of social democracy. Kettunen et al. (2014: 16) state that

instead of making a choice between these different proposals, it is reasonable to re-interpret the divergent 'origins' as temporal layers in the Nordic welfare state. Mediated through mentalities, traditions, values, epistemic practices and social movements, these layers are present in the formal and informal rules and norms of the Nordic model.

The Finnish example is close to other Nordic countries in the creation of the welfare society. However, it differs from developments in Sweden and Denmark, the old imperial powers in the Nordic region, because of the strong nation-building function of higher education in Finland. Here the process in Finland has had something in common with the history of Norway, for example the parallel role of the capital city university (the University of Oslo) in building Norwegian national identity when Norway separated from the Swedish Kingdom at the beginning of the twentieth century (Vabo, 2000).

Eventually the evolution of the Nordic model in Finland became associated with a radical change in higher education that extended well beyond the role of the national university. The first national higher education policies, which began in the late 1950s, triggered a state-driven expansion of universities. Universities were established all over the country by the 1980s, followed by the creation of UAS in the 1990s. In this process, the metropolitan university lost its hegemony. The expansion was premised on the creation of equal educational opportunities for all citizens regardless of gender, socio-economic background or geographical location. Higher education was seen as an important instrument in creating an equal society. In addition, in the 1970s all private universities were made public universities and their administrative structures were standardized. This included three business schools, three universities, and two art academies.

Finnish higher education reached mass higher education level during the 1970s when more than 15 per cent of the relevant age cohort entered universities. The HPS level was achieved in the 1990s with the establishment of UASs. By the 2010s a starting place in higher education was being offered to over 70 per cent of the relevant age cohort. In 2015, there were 303,000 higher education students, including 161,000 in universities and 142,000 in UASs, as indicated in Figure 13.1) (Välimaa, 2018). However, these figures can be somewhat misleading in that access to universities is not automatic or easy for Finnish youngsters. As a rule, all higher education institutions use entrance examinations to select their students (see more discussion later).

This brief historical introduction shows that the values of equity and equality are part of the historical layers that are firmly positioned at the foundations of the Nordic welfare society in Finland. It also shows that contemporary Finnish higher education also incorporates a tradition of elitist academic fields, the legacy of a hegemonic state university, and the histories of the individual private universities. All of these historical

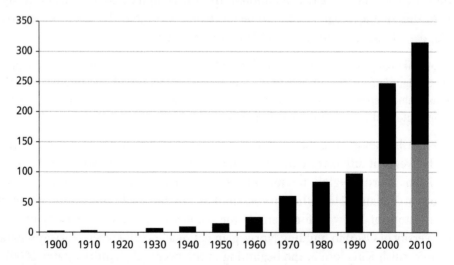

Figure 13.1. Number of students in Finnish higher education institutions, 1900–2010

Source: Adapted from Välimaa, 2017.

traditions and patterns live on and through families in Finland, even though from the 1950s to the 2010s national higher education policies have emphasized equity, equality, and the fair development of all higher education institutions, both universities and UASs. Having said all that, in addition, the last two decades have seen the increasing role of new public management policies which aim to utilize quasi-market mechanisms in steering higher education. This is creating tensions with policies rooted in the values of equity and equality. In addition, from the 1990s onwards higher education institutions have been seen by policymakers as crucially important for the development of a knowledge society and knowledge-based economy. National higher education and science policies aim to integrate higher education institutions better into the national innovation system while also encouraging variety in institutional missions and strategies. This policy approach is 'institutional profiling' (Välimaa, 2018; Rinne, 2010), as will be discussed further later.

EQUAL EDUCATIONAL OPPORTUNITIES AND EQUITY IN THE FINNISH CONTEXT

Chapter 1 in this book argues that family aspirations for social advancement and or maintenance of social position are the primary driver of the growth of higher education. The HPS Proposition 3 states that:

> Once transition from a primarily agricultural economy is achieved, the long-term growth of HPS is independent of political economic factors such as economic growth and patterns of labour market demand; patterns of public and private funding of higher education; the roles of public and private institutions; and system organization and modes of governance

and also Proposition 2 states that:

> In HPS there is no intrinsic limit to the spread of family aspirations for participation in higher education until universality is reached; and no intrinsic limit to the level of social position to which families/students may aspire.

These propositions do not fully apply in Finland. The drive for individual or family advancement is not without limit, it is modified by the consensus on equity and equality as social values. Further, the state as the instrument of these social values has been central in determining and shaping the expansion of higher education.

Ethically and politically, education, including higher education, is defined and normally understood as a public service and a civil right, not a consumer good. This understanding has many consequences. First, as already noted in relation to Finland, in all the Nordic countries education is free of charge for all citizens of European Union (EU) nations. Second, in Nordic countries the proportion of funding of higher education institutions that is from public sources is among the highest in the OECD. In both Finland and Norway in 2013 tertiary education was 96 per cent publicly funded, in Denmark the proportion was 94 per cent, and in Sweden 90 per cent. In Sweden the presence of private funding is larger mainly because of the strong role of private foundations in supporting Swedish research activities. When compared to the UK (with 57 per cent public funding), the USA (36 per cent public funding), and the OECD average (70 per cent) it is evident that Nordic countries are exceptional cases even in Europe (OECD, 2014: 218). Third, Nordic countries also invest heavily in public education, when compared with other countries. According to the OECD:

At the tertiary level, public expenditure per student on both public and private institutions averages US$9221 in OECD countries, but varies from about US$2000 in Chile to more than US$17 000 in Denmark, Finland, Norway and Sweden, four countries in which the share of private expenditure is small or negligible.   (OECD, 2014: 243)

Fourth, in Nordic countries education and research are seen as important in national identities and national economies and the well-being of societies.

As the above history in Finland shows, the strong emphasis put on education as a social instrument in making societies more equal is rooted in the Nordic understanding of welfare society. According to Esping-Andersen (1990) all Scandinavian countries belong to the same kind of welfare regime, in which all welfare benefits are provided to all citizens. These are 'universal' welfare regimes. Families and their aspirations are not recognized as a central driving force for higher education because state and society aim to take care of equality and equity in relation to gender, socio-economic status (SES), ethnicity, and geographical location.

In twenty-first century Finland it is commonly accepted that equality is based on the idea that society provides equal educational opportunities and helps to guarantee good educational outcomes for every citizen, regardless of gender, socio-economic background, or geographical location. Equity in the Finnish context is understood broadly in relation to each of equity for equal needs, equity for equal potential, and equity for equal achievement (Espinoza, 2007).

According to *equity for equal needs*, all students with the same needs are provided with the same amount of financial, social, and cultural resources. The principle of *equity for equal potential* is related to the broad idea that individuals should maximize their potential and therefore all individuals with similar abilities and skills should have access to higher education. The third approach, *equity for equal achievement*, is perhaps the most meritocratic approach because it ties students' past achievements to their access to higher education and their educational performance during their studies. The chapter will return to these perspectives when discussing the role of entrance examinations in Finnish higher education institutions.

According to the Development Plan for Finnish Education (2011–16):

Equal opportunity in education is the underpinning of Finnish welfare. For educational equality to be realised, it is imperative that everyone gains a solid basis for learning already in early childhood and in basic education and that pupils and students with special needs and at risk of exclusion have access to a diverse range of supportive action. Measures must also be taken to alleviate differences and heredity in post-compulsory education.   (MEC, 2012: 7)

The same value basis with different wordings can be found in other Nordic countries as well.

An important social basis for all Nordic welfare societies is trust. In social and economic life trust helps to save transaction costs because interpersonal relationships become easier. Trust also means that a smaller proportion of the resources of society are used to control citizens. There are two main hypotheses explaining the sources of trust in society. According to the institution-centred hypothesis, the role of the institutions of society is crucial in supporting trust. The society-centred hypothesis emphasizes the importance of civic engagement in associations and social interaction taking place at the grassroots level of society (see Kouvo, 2014). However, empirical evidence strongly supports the institution-centred hypothesis because it manages to explain better the nature of trust and why it is related to just and well-functioning public institutions. Impartial and objective taxation seems to be very important in reinforcing trust between fellow citizens. Universal welfare policies in the Nordic countries seem to be the key factor behind the high trust levels in these countries. In relation to higher education, the role of trust is apparent in Nordic ideas of evaluation, especially in Finland, which aim to use evaluation as an instrument of enhancement rather than an instrument of control and differentiation through the use of league tables (Hämäläinen et al., 2001). Trust is visible also in the Nordic conviction that universities are autonomous institutions which, however, are publicly funded and steered in and through national legislation and higher education policies.

Hence in the Finnish context it is natural to think that both autonomous universities and the beneficial state, through the MEC, want to make higher education institutions more efficient and relevant for state and society. However, Nordic values are now being tested by economic globalization, by reforms designed to make Finnish higher education more competitive on the global scale, and by debate on tuition fees for international students.

INTERNATIONAL STUDENT FEES

While there are no tuition fees for Finnish students or students coming from the EU or European Economic Area (EEA), the possibility of fees for international students from outside EU/EEA has been discussed, both as a potential source of revenue and from cultural and political perspectives (Weimer, 2013). This has become a contested policy issue with national debate in 2012–14. Weimer (2013) notes that the main actors opposing tuition fees for international students have been the powerful Finnish student organizations. They have feared that collecting tuition fees from international students would open the gate to tuition fees for national students as well. It has also been argued that free international education supports international social justice by providing students from developing countries with opportunities to participate in higher education; while to charge fees would undermine Finnish policies of internationalization in higher education by reducing the number of international students—as has already happened in Denmark and Sweden.

The promoters of tuition fees, including university managers, MEC, and business representatives, refer to neoliberal assumptions about education as a private good. It is also claimed that competition for international students would enhance the quality of teaching and make Finnish universities more competitive in the international marketplace; and that it is unfair for Finnish taxpayers to pay for the education and social welfare of international migrants in Finland, an argument that has gained special traction as a populist political view. Some also see international students as a new source of revenue for universities, a perspective not shared by university rectors who assumed the introduction of international student fees would lead to cuts in the higher education budget. The Finnish government has connected international students with migration policies, stating that it is fair for student immigrants to pay for their studies. Finnish higher education institutions will be obliged to collect tuition fees from international students from the beginning of the academic year 2017–18, at a minimum level of 1,500 euros per academic year. However, prior to the introduction of these international tuition fees only about 5 per cent of all higher education students in Finland were international students.

Governance: Coordination and Corporatization

The first governance proposition (HPS Proposition 4) states:

HPS are governed by multi-level control, coordination, and accountability mechanisms.

The most important factor in Finnish and Nordic approaches to higher education is the strong role the nation-state plays in shaping higher education through national legislation, ministerial steering, and funding. However, each university as an autonomous institution is free to internally allocate the funding it receives through the MEC's funding model, according to its own policies. In recent years the role of the Academy of Finland in coordinating research funding has increased through funding mechanisms, such as

University Profiling funding and Flagship programme funding, aimed at achieving national higher education policy goals. The Finnish case seems to confirm the HPS proposition. However, the Finnish case also challenges the proposition because higher education institutions have procedural autonomy in deciding how to meet national expectations. In this sense, the dynamics of the system confirm the multi-level aspect of the proposition but the mechanisms of system coordination are based more on Nordic-style trust than on control.

Nordic systems of higher and tertiary education share similar binary structures. They all have a university sector alongside a sector of vocationally oriented and more regional higher education institutions, which are called UAS in Finland and University Colleges in Denmark, Norway, and Sweden. The situation in Finland is distinctive in that before 2015 all UAS were run either by private foundations, or by public corporation owned by cities, or by an alliance of cities (Välimaa and Neuvonen-Rauhala, 2010). Now, all Finnish UAS are run, funded and regulated by the MEC; that is, by the Finnish state. The institutional autonomy of higher education institutions is regulated in national legislation and bylaws governing the universities (Universities Act 558/2009) and UAS (*Ammattikorkeakoululaki* 932/2014, see http://www.finlex.fi/en/). The second governance proposition (HPS Proposition 5) states that:

HPS governance tends to involve the management of horizontal differentiation.

This proposition is supported by Finnish experience. The state maintains and develops standardized legislative frameworks for all higher education institutions and has done so since the 1960s, beginning with the universities and now extending to the UAS, which are framed as a distinctive sector. State legislation regulates differing internal governance for the two sectors (Välimaa, 2018).

CORPORATIZATION REFORM

In response to the global challenges facing the Finnish HPS, from the mid-2000s onwards the government initiated a series of reforms under the label of 'the structural development of Finnish higher education system'. The official goals included diversification of the funding base of the universities, improvement in opportunities to compete for international research funding, more cooperation with foreign world-class universities, and ensuring the quality and effectiveness of university research and teaching. Two main strategies were implemented. First, the Universities Act (558/2009) separated universities from the state budget and turned them into public corporations subject to private law, able to make contracts and function as independent economic entities. Two universities decided to become foundation-based universities operating under foundation law, in order to increase their scope as employers to organize their workforce; while the remaining twelve universities became defined as independent legal entities. University governance became shaped by the ideals of corporate management. It was a radical transformation of the economic status of the universities—though their running costs continued to be financed from the MEC budget—and of their internal autonomy. The changes strengthened the executive powers of university rectors, streamlined university decision-making processes and increased the proportion of external members on university boards, the most important decision-making bodies in the universities, to a minimum of 40 per cent (Välimaa, 2012; Välimaa et al., 2014).

Governance proposition three (HPS Proposition 6) states that:

> *HPS complex multi-level accountability and coordination, coupled with system differentiation, result in higher education institutions adopting increasingly corporate forms and robust internal governance and management capacities.*

Here the Finnish case is consistent with the tendency to corporatization reforms, initiated by governments, evident in many HPS. However, it is less clear that this use of business models in Finland was driven by problems of coordination and systemic complexity that arose from growth, as the HPS proposition implies. In Finland the aim of the corporatization policy was to render the universities more efficient and competitive in the global educational market, using the world-class university as a policy tool. This instrumental policy reasoning was consistent with idea of making higher education institutions more economically useful for national innovation. It does not seem that the policy change was specifically driven by the growing level of participation in higher education. The most rapid expansion of higher education took place earlier and was completed by the end of 1990s, well before the reforms. If Finland had very high participation for some time before corporatization, then presumably the Finnish HPS could have continued to be coordinated by the state without the resort to business models.

Horizontal Diversity: The Binary System

A striking feature of the Finnish HPS is that the stratification of institutions is very modest when compared to most other HPS, though Finland has parallels in the other Nordic systems. As discussed later under 'Equity', the tendencies identified in the three HPS propositions on stratification can scarcely be detected in Finland. The social stratification of opportunity is articulated by a field of study hierarchy rather than an institutional hierarchy. Finland is also notable in that during the growth of the HPS horizontal diversity has remained central to the design of the higher education system. As with the modest institutional stratification, the key to horizontal diversity is the low intensity of competition between higher education institutions and the emphases on cooperation, solidarity, and parity of esteem between institutions, within and between the sectors.

As noted, the Finnish legislator supports a dual system with both vocationally oriented and academically oriented sectors of higher education. One principal difference between the universities and the UAS is related to degree structures. The majority of Finnish university students graduate with an Master's degree, whereas the UAS confer mainly Bachelor's level degrees. In addition, only universities are permitted to confer Doctoral degrees. Another difference is related to the respective research capacities. UAS are not assumed to conduct basic research but are expected to do applied research or the R&D type of research. The Finnish binary system could be described in terms of vertical (hierarchical) stratification with universities placed at the top of the system because of their better research capacities. However, it is more accurate to define the difference between universities and UAS in terms of a state-regulated and funded horizontal distribution of labour with differing tasks allocated to each sector.

The potential for the 'academic drift' of polytechnics and the 'vocational drift' of universities was discussed in the 1990s when the UAS sector was established (see Välimaa and Neuvonen-Rauhala, 2010). However, during the twenty years of the existence of the UAS the dividing line between universities and UAS has remained clear and accepted by both sectors. UAS have developed their role as professional training institutions in close cooperation with regional working life, very much like the *Fachhochschule* in Germany, whereas universities have emphasized their research functions. The MEC has strongly supported the binary pattern of development. Universities and UAS do not compete for the same public research and teaching resources. In relation to students, it might seem that universities and UAS are competitors, in that practically all students are qualified to enter both sectors at the end of their secondary education, and institutions in both sectors would like to enrol the best students. However, 'the best student' for universities means a student with an academic orientation, whereas for UASs it means a student with a more vocational orientation. For this reason the competition hypothesis is not strongly supported by empirical reality. Only about 20–30 per cent of the 18-year-old students know whether their preferences are academic or not; the remainder chooses their higher education institutions based on their general study orientation (academic or vocational); their interests in certain fields of work (e.g. social work, engineering, business, ICT), which often matter more than institution per se; or family traditions. Family traditions are naturally related to family cultural capital and social capital, but the influence of these factors varies according to the age of first year students. It is more significant with younger than older university students (Vuorinen and Valkonen, 2003; Rinne et al., 2008).

In principle and in practice UAS and universities are 'different, but equal'. They have different institutional profiles and resource bases—universities have more research funding—and different legal statuses. However, many universities and UAS cooperate, especially those located in the same cities (it is normal for cities to include both sectors). Students can move from a UAS to a university or vice versa through entrance examinations. In the fields that are found in both UAS and universities the transition is relatively easy. Nearly all academic leadership positions in both sectors are occupied by people with PhD degrees, and many teachers in UAS were trained in universities. It is possible to make a mixed career in universities and UAS especially in fields that are found in both sectors such as business, engineering, ICT, social work, music, and visual arts, or in management positions.

However, the binary system as inherited from the 1990s may change. The second proposition in relation to horizontal diversity (HPS Proposition 8) suggests that:

> *Regardless of the political economy and culture of the HPS, when participation expands there is no necessary increase in the overall diversity of institutional form and mission; and this has probably declined, except in relation to online provision.*

At the time of writing this proposition was under test in Finland. In the Tampere region there is an ongoing process which aims to merge one UAS with one multi-disciplinary university and one technical university. The MEC supports the merger and is willing to change national legislation to remove obstacles to it. If the merger is successfully implemented, it will probably lead to similar merger operations in other Finnish cities with UASs and universities. If so, that tendency would confirm the HPS proposition.

The first proposition under horizontal diversity (HPS Proposition 7) states that:

> *In the HPS era, regardless of the political economy and culture of systems, an increasing proportion of higher education becomes centred on comprehensive multi-discipline and multi-function research universities, or 'multiversities'. The multiversity is increasingly dominant as the paradigmatic form of higher education.*

This proposition will be confirmed if the merger process described above is implemented. However, a contrary process is also taking place in Finland. The MEC strongly supports the profiling of universities, meaning that universities should develop distinctive research profiles and focus on their research-based strengths, rather than every university trying to do everything in multiversity fashion. On the one hand, the policy motive is to save money by discontinuing overlapping activities; another case of the nation-state using its power to control and steer the higher education system. The profiling policy suggests that MEC has recognized the general HPS trend and wants to resist it. On the other hand, the profiling policy confirms diversity proposition three (HPS Proposition 9). By implementing a partly specialist approach in the research universities based on profiling, the state appears to be working against the common HPS tendency described in horizontal diversity proposition three, in which isomorphistic multiversities, adopting similar missions to each other, all become more comprehensive in function and thus also more internally diverse, with greater diversity of activities: *As participation expands the internal diversity of multiversities tends to increase.* It is another case of the strong state policy in Finland countering the normal secular tendency associated with the growth of HPS, in order to achieve a planned mix of horizontal outcomes.

Equity: Social Inclusion and Differentiation

The first proposition in relation to equity (HPS Proposition 14) states that: *As participation expands in the HPS phase, equity in the form of social inclusion is enhanced.* Data on the 'odds ratios' in OECD countries show that Finland's policy of providing equal educational opportunities for its citizens is effective in expanding the boundaries of social inclusion. The odds ratio 'reflects the relative likelihood of participating in tertiary education of individuals whose parents have upper secondary or tertiary education' (OECD, 2014: 93). In Finland, young people with one or more parent who attended tertiary education are 1.4 times as likely to themselves enter some form of tertiary education as young people from families where neither parent entered tertiary education, compared to an OECD average of 4.5. In Finland people from tertiary education families have some advantage but on the international scale this advantage is modest. Using this measure all Nordic countries perform better than the OECD average, including Norway (2.0), Sweden (2.3), and Denmark (3.0). In terms of the odds ratio Finland is the second most equitable country in the OECD, after South Korea.

In Finland social inclusion is facilitated by universal student financing. Not only is tuition free except in open university programmes, the nation provides a robust system of student support through grants and loans. Some even claim that this dampens policy discussion about widening access to provide equal educational opportunities (Melin et al., 2015: 10), because it looks at first sight that everybody already has equal opportunities to access higher education. In 2017, the Finnish government reformed student support to increase the proportion of financing provided as student loans guaranteed by the state and decrease the proportion covered by student grants. However, both secondary and tertiary students remain eligible for significant state support including a study grant for the duration of their studies. In tertiary education the maximum length of state support is forty-eight months. Monthly financial aid consists of the student grant (250 euros), the housing supplement (this covers 80 per cent of housing expenses, with a maximum of 275–405 euros per month depending on home town) and the student loan. Total monthly financial aid depends on the student's age, housing circumstances, marital status, and parents' income (Kela, 2017). However, coverage is not complete, as actual study times tend to be longer than the duration of state support. This increases the need for students to work during their studies.

According to Lindberg (2007) this is related to the Finnish tradition of access to labour market, which is similar to that in Germany. University graduates typically enter the labour market with an Master's degree, whereas in the British tradition graduates enter the labour market with a Bachelor's and at a lower level of job. Late labour market entry also further encourages work while studying and 57 per cent of Finnish students do so. Working while studying is not seen as an equality issue or a phenomenon connected to family background. The 2014 student survey found that the average monthly income of a Finnish student living independently was 800 euros: half from earned income, just under one-third from the student grant, 13 per cent from other sources, and 8 per cent from parental support (Student Survey, 2014: 28–9).

Students in Finland graduate later than in other OECD countries, their average duration of higher education studies is among the longest and they enter the labour market at a later age. Because of the shorter working careers this is seen as a national problem. The median time to complete a university Master's degree was 6.5 years in 2013 (OSF, 2013).

From the perspective of equality and equity, the Finnish system supports children from both lower and higher socio-economic groups in going to higher education, though UAS and university degrees lead to different jobs, working environments, and salaries. Statistics of Finland data on graduate outcomes after one year of the graduation indicate that employment rates are similar for both higher education sectors (OSF, 2018), as Figure 13.2 shows. The highest employment rate (84 per cent) was for persons who had

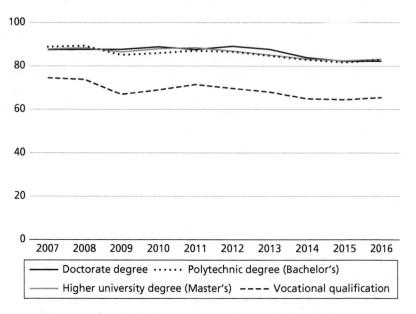

Figure 13.2. Employment of graduates (%) one year after graduation, by degree level, 2007–16

Source: Adapted by the authors from Official Statistics of Finland, 2018.

completed a Doctoral degree but the rate was almost as high (83 per cent) for graduates with a UAS Bachelor's or university Master's degree (83 per cent). However, persons with vocational qualifications had lower employment rates, with only 58 per cent of men and 72 per cent of women working.

Note that this figure does not provide the whole picture of the Finnish system because there are no dead ends for any citizen with any degree. The national policy principle of life-long learning encourages all citizens to continue studies at a higher level educational establishment. Empirical research indicates that middle-aged women with higher education degrees are the most active in using life-long education opportunities (Haltia et al., 2014).

EDUCATIONAL GROWTH AND SOCIAL INEQUALITY

As the HPS in Finland has grown, the differences in educational opportunities for children with academic and non-academic family backgrounds have narrowed. Figure 13.3 shows that in 1970, students with at least one parent who graduated from tertiary education were 19.1 times as likely to enrol as university students from non-tertiary education parents. By 2010, the odds ratio had fallen to 6.8. Educational opportunities have become more equal, though in the university sector (as distinct from higher education as a whole) there remain significant differences between tertiary education families and non-tertiary education families.

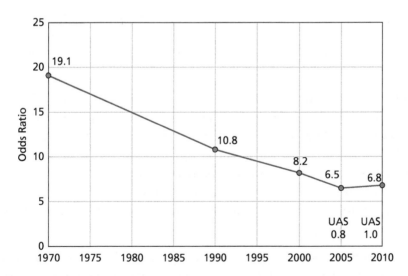

Figure 13.3. Gaining access to universities at age 24 or under, odds ratios, 1970–2010

Source: Adapted from Kivinen and Hedman, 2016, 93.

This trend line again confirms HPS Proposition 1:

As HPS expands... equity in world society is enhanced.

At the same time Finland's experience challenges equity proposition two (HPS Proposition 15), based on Bourdieu's notion of bifurcation between elite and mass higher education institutions:

Because in the HPS phase the growth of participation is associated with enhanced stratification and intensified competition at key transition points, all else being equal (i.e. without compensatory state policy), the expansion of participation is associated with a secular tendency to greater social inequality in educational outcomes and, through that, social outcomes.

While there is competition for entry to high-demand professional fields, it appears that access to universities has become more equal as the HPS has grown (Figure 13.3). That is, institutional stratification has reduced not increased. In order to fully test the proposition, it would be necessary to examine the evolution of social access to the most exclusive fields of study, alongside the evolution of social access in Finland overall. But it is clear that a principal source of growing inequality of outcomes in those HPS shaped by neoliberal competition, the increased stratification between institutions, is not such a factor in Finland. Moreover, in relation to access to the UASs, as distinct from the academic universities, there is no discernible difference between students from academic and non-academic families: the odds ratio was 0.8 in 2005 and 1.0 in 2010 (Kivinen and Hedman, 2016: 93–4).

The Finnish experience supports equity proposition three (HPS Proposition 16):

Within a national system, as participation expands in the HPS phase, all else being equal, the positional structure of the higher education system increasingly resembles that of society... The HPS is increasingly implicated in the reproduction of existing patterns of social equality/inequality.

Perhaps this proposition overemphasizes the role of higher education in the reproduction of social structures. Arguably, in Finland, the main impact of education is felt at the secondary level, where high quality education is provided to all citizens. Combined with the principle of lifelong learning, and flexible opportunities to move between universities and UAS, as noted, there are no structural barriers that prevent citizens from advancing to higher education. In that respect education helps to reproduce the equal social structures of Finnish society rather than being designed to change social structures. In that sense equity proposition four (HPS Proposition 17)

As... participation expands it becomes more difficult for the state and/or autonomous educational systems/institutions to secure a redistribution of educational opportunities, and, through that, of social opportunities.

does not really apply in Finland.

MECHANISMS OF SOCIAL STRATIFICATION

Despite the overall pattern of high and increasing social inclusion, and the apparent capacity of the Finnish state and society to maintain a comparatively high level of social equality in educational participation, access to tertiary education is not equal for everybody in Finland (Melin et al., 2015: 10). There is some social stratification in terms of sector of enrolment (universities and UAS), in terms of the starting age of students, and more so in terms of access to particular fields of study. These factors are inter-related, as will be shown. A feature of educational/social stratification in Finland is that parental cultural capital seems very important in shaping social differences in participation and graduate outcomes, while economic inequalities such as differences in parental income seem to be less important than in many other countries. This picture is consistent not only with the free education and moderate income inequality in Finland, but also with findings in certain studies of the Nordic countries concerning the reproduction of social segmentation (e.g. Thomsen et al., 2013).

Finland's relatively high level of access to students whose parents did not enter tertiary education has been noted. However, access in this respect is not uniformly equal across both sectors (Melin et al., 2015: 10). In 2014, 39 per cent of the university students came from families with at least one of the parents having completed at least a Master's degree, while family background was less determining in the UAS where 22 per cent of students had at least one parent with an Master's degree (Student Survey, 2014: 19). This difference between the sectors is shown also in the odds ratio in the universities of 6.8 in 2010 compared with the odds ratios of UASs of 1.0 in that year.

The median starting age of Finnish students in tertiary education is 20 years (Student Survey, 2014: 14). However, the starting age of students varies according to the parental level of education. Figure 13.4 demonstrates the relationship between social background, measured in terms of the educational achievement of parents, and the age of students. Half (51 per cent) of the students from higher education background families[1] are younger than 25 years old. The proportion of students from families without higher education degrees is the greatest in the oldest age group in Figure 13.4 students aged 30 years old and above. According to the 2014 Student Survey (Moisio, 2015), students whose parents lacked a higher education degree were on average four years older than students whose parents had a qualification. This four-year difference is noteworthy in the light of earlier research (Parker et al., 2015) which highlights the relation between gap-years and motivation to study. One gap-year between upper secondary school and

---

[1] Students with higher education background have parents of which at least one has attained a higher education degree (ISCED 1997 Levels 5–6). In terms of ISCED 2011, this means that at least one of these students' parents has successfully completed a short cycle tertiary degree (Level 5), a Bachelor's (Level 6) or Master's degree (Level 7), or a Doctorate (Level 8), or their national equivalent. Students without higher education background have parents whose highest educational degree is no higher than ISCED 1997/2011 Level 4 (post-secondary non-tertiary education) (Hauschildt et al., 2015).

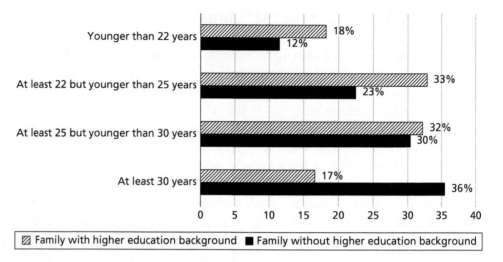

Figure 13.4. Age at the start of degrees and family education background: Proportion (%) of all students, with and without family higher education background, in each age group

Source: Authors, adapted from Eurostudent V 2012–15 Database.

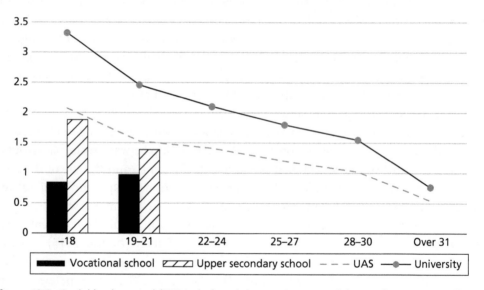

Figure 13.5. Social background (SES-index) and the starting age of the students in the different educational sectors, 2009–11

Source: Authors, adapted from Saari 2015, p. 36.

university has little effect on educational outcomes, but a larger number of gap-years tends to have a negative influence on studying.

Figure 13.5 sharpens the picture by demonstrating the relation between students' starting age in the different educational sectors, according to social background. Socio-economic background is measured by SES-index, which takes into account parents' level of income, education and position in the labour market (Saari, 2015: 14). The most significant transition occurs at the end of compulsory education in comprehensive schools, when pupils choose between an academic track (general upper secondary) and vocational track (vocational schools). Both are three years in duration. Most students who take the academic track continue their studies in universities or UAS. There is a notable difference in the social backgrounds of students in the four education sectors in Figure 13.5. In the case of each of universities, UAS, and the upper secondary schools that prepare students for higher education, the lower the student's starting age the higher the status of the student's family, as measured by SES-index. In vocational schools the relationship is reversed. On average, among students moving straight from comprehensive secondary school to vocational school, their social background status is lower than is the case for those students who enter vocational schools at a later age. Associated with these data, Figure 13.5 shows how families' cultural capital tends to influence students' choices when they are choosing between the academic and vocational tracks. Here the sorting role of education is as evident as the opportunities it brings (see Chapter 6).

In countries with HPS, social background has a larger impact on occupational returns (Triventi, 2013: 48). All else being equal, in Finland students with educated parents tend to study in more prestigious fields with better occupational returns, and they also tend to study in the capital area. Over half (59 per cent) of all university students in the field of arts and just under half (49 per cent) of students in medicine have at least one parent with at least tertiary level education, whereas only 18 per cent of students in sport and health sciences had such parents (Student Survey 2014: 19). Here also social differentiation based on institution intersects with social differentiation based on disciplines/occupations. Universities located in the capital area, the Aalto University and the University of Helsinki, are the most prestigious in terms of students' social backgrounds (Nori, 2011: 161). This role is grounded in historical tradition as Helsinki was the first university in Finland. The two capital area universities also rank well in global university league tables. However, this is largely because of their disciplinary composition. The University of Helsinki covers all disciplines and Aalto is strong in sciences and technology, which form the main component of global rankings. In contrast the majority of the Finnish universities are strong in humanities, social sciences, education and business.

The most strongly inheriting fields in Finland are architecture and biological sciences, as Table 13.1 shows (Kivinen and Hedman, 2016). In 2010, students coming from academic homes studied as architects 13.3 times more often than those coming from non-academic homes. However, students' study choices are influenced not only by socio-economic background but also by family traditions. Sciences are among the most strongly inheriting fields in Finland, especially from fathers to sons (Saari, 2015: 52). Natural sciences demonstrate not only the influence of cultural capital of the family but also the importance of familiarity of the field, rather than economic capital. Biologists' salaries are

Table 13.1. Social background and the probability of starting university studies by the age of 24: Top ten most strongly inheriting fields in Finland as measured by odds ratios, 2010

University graduates by 24 years of age, by discipline	Odds ratio
Architecture	13.3
Biological sciences	12.4
Communications engineering	10.9
Medicine	10.9
Construction engineering	10.8
Physics	10.6
Veterinary medicine	10.4
Electronics and automation	10.1
Psychology	9.9
Law	9.7

Note: The odds ratio is the ratio between students of parents of which at least one has attained a higher education Master's degree and students from non-tertiary education background families.

Source: Authors, adapting data from Kivinen and Hedman (2016).

modest. The most elitist field in Finland is still medicine, which enjoys top position in the disciplinary status hierarchy (Kivinen et al., 2012). Doctors also have the highest salaries.

In family strategies for securing access to the most favoured disciplines the key moment is the university entrance examination. New students are normally accepted by higher education institutions on the basis of a combination of three criteria: 1) the school leaving certificate; 2) the matriculation examination; and 3) higher education institutions' own entrance examinations. In sciences and mathematics high performance at matriculation is usually sufficient for entry into university. But it is different in high demand professional fields where competition is intense, with three times or more the number of applicants to university as starting places. Competition is rendered more intense because applicants to universities consist of new graduates from secondary education, applicants who failed to reach their preferred university course in previous years, and mature aged applicants who may have no matriculation and entirely depend on their performance in the higher education institutions' own tests. The entrance examinations for UAS are easier in academic terms.

With the university examination so decisive, a market in preparatory courses has developed. Preparatory courses are provided by private enterprise, with prices varying from 500–6,500 euros depending on the subject, the length of the course and the size of the student groups. These courses are taken most often by those preparing to apply to study law studies (55 per cent of candidates in 2014), medicine (50 per cent), and (economics 38 per cent) (Student Survey, 2014: 18). However, only one in five regular university applicants and one in ten applicants for the UAS participates in preparatory courses. Preparatory courses help relatively wealthy students to gain access to the higher education they want. This continues and strengthens the historically elitist nature of medicine and law. However, and typical of Finland, this market-driven activity for securing private advantage is seen as a problem by Finnish politicians, the MEC, and Finnish higher education institutions. Universities want to change their entrance examinations to provide fair chances to all. Further, there has been a recent attempt by government to decrease the importance of preparatory courses by changing the criteria for admission to higher education institutions.

INSTITUTIONAL AND DISCIPLINARY STRATIFICATION

In sum, Finland has elitist disciplines in higher education populated by students from advantaged socio-economic backgrounds despite the national policy of equal educational opportunities. In relatively 'flat' HPS, fields of study typically become the most important pathways to private opportunities for self-differentiation (see Chapter 6). In the Bourdieuian framework, in which families apply active agency in the competition for educational and social success (Chapter 6) the upper class strives always to find a way to distinguish itself from lower groups. In Finland these distinctions are not so clearly connected to institutional status because unlike the situation in the United States where graduation from an Ivy League university is in itself a sufficient passport to the elite echelons of the labour market, in Finland differential jobs and salaries derive not from institutional reputation but mostly from the differences between disciplines and professions.

Hence the Finnish case is one of the exceptions suggested in stratification proposition two (HPS Proposition 12):

> *The tendency to institutional stratification is magnified by features common (though not universal) among HPS including (a) intensified social competition for the most valuable student places; (b) variable tuition charges; and/or (c) intensified competition between institutions.*

If there is intensified social competition for places, it does not translate into institutional stratification. The other elements in the proposition, intensified inter-institutional competition and tuition fees, are absent from the Finnish context (except for students coming outside the EU or EEA starting on the academic year 2017–18).

Conclusions

The Finnish system illustrates four ways in which the trajectory of the Nordic model HPS diverges from the trajectories of most other HPS. First, the economically egalitarian Nordic model, with its free tuition and relatively generous student support providing broad social access to higher education institutions of good material quality, modifies the stratifying effects of family economic inequalities on educational access. Higher education plays less of a role in reproducing family income inequalities down the generations than in some other HPS though the Nordic model is less effective in diminishing family inequalities based on cultural (and perhaps social) capital. Second, differentials between institutions, in terms of status and resources, are modest—even the differentials between universities and UAS—so that institutional 'brand' plays a comparatively limited role in shaping socially stratified outcomes. Third, the binary system is stable and maintains an educational division of labour with a horizontal element. Fourth, and related to the other points, the investment of middle class families in private advantage is centred especially on prestigious professional fields of study, more than on the higher education institutions attended.

SYSTEM AND STRUCTURE

Higher education degrees are needed in credential societies, but credentialism in Nordic welfare society sorts individuals into good positions on the basis of the professional or occupational field rather than the reputation of the institution. Finland has both academic and vocational tracks which distribute students with different orientations (academic or professional/occupational) and from different socio-economic backgrounds to different higher education institutions. Institution and sector distinctions are primarily horizontal and have only slight or modest implications for social position. All higher education institutions have good resources and provide education of equally good academic quality, supported and controlled by the state.

In some countries binary systems have been associated with status competition across the sector divide. In Finland the state is dominant in policy and manages higher education as a single system. This is assisted by the fact that all Finnish higher education institutions are public institutions, publicly funded and serving public needs: there have been attempts to establish private higher education institutions or branches of private universities but they have failed. Finnish governments emphasize the specific missions of each sector, steering horizontal differentiation (diversity) between them, rather than a status hierarchy, vertical differentiation (stratification). There is isomorphistic imitation inside both sectors but not necessarily across the sector boundary. National steering primarily encourages cooperation rather than competition between sectors. In addition, the MEC has strongly supported in institution-specific institutional profiles and orientations among both UAS and universities. The policy support for a merger between one UAS and two universities is consistent with emphasis on cross-sector cooperation. If there are further mergers of universities and UAS in the future, it is intended to maintain diversity. The aim of the systemic change would be to make studying more flexible and thus more efficient.

The facts that the higher education system sorts students into district segments by social backgrounds, that students in universities have different educational background profiles to those in UAS, and universities select their students more than do

UAS, could be seen as driving system bifurcation between artisanal and demand-absorbing higher education institutions and a vertical calibration of higher education institutions (see Chapter 5, this volume). However, the picture is not that straightforward. Differences between individual higher education institutions in the same sector, and differences between fields of study, cut across the binary division. UAS in remote areas are the least popular higher education institutions but UAS in cities do much better. In universities, the level of student demand is determined by a complex combination of disciplines and location. Normally, large city metropolitan universities are the strongest attractors but it is not uniformly so. Instead of making university and UAS students compete for the same higher education programmes, jobs, and qualifications, the state follows the principle of 'equal but different' by producing both a skilled vocational labour force and a high quality academic labour force. Together with the policy principle of life-long learning this is seen to serve better the needs of knowledge-based society than a single system of higher education based on vertical stratification of institutions.

Finland's recent policy initiative to create a national student admission system is consistent with horizontal systemic differentiation. New access and admission rules are designed to favour first-time applicants to higher education in order to improve system efficiency and speed the transition from higher education to the labour markets (MEC, 2016). They are also consistent with the distinctive Finnish approach to HPS. MEC is forcing all higher education institutions to use the same national higher education institutions student admissions database. Students can now choose only a limited number of study options, in contrast to the previous practice where there were no limitations. The nation-state wants to distribute students fairly between all higher education institutions in the name of system efficiency, limiting the power of student choices as a market force.

In governance, Finland maintains a centralized system of control, coordination, and accountability that is implemented and executed through national legislation and the national funding formula, and steered by the MEC. The dynamics of the system are based on trust, consistent with procedural autonomy of higher education institutions. For example, quality assurance system are created and managed by the institutions while also being regulated by national norms. The nation-state through the MEC is the most important actor in the formation and implementation of higher education policies as well as the main funder of the system.

CULTURAL AND FINANCIAL CAPITAL

Neoliberal arguments for tuition fees for international students are part of the discussion in Finland. However, Finland differs from the Anglo-American world in that there are strong counter arguments rooted in the values of Nordic welfare societies which see higher education primarily as an equality issue. The common high level of education is seen to be beneficial for the development of society, including business and industry. Equality is understood more as a collective economic issue than an individual consumer choice. Students are not defined as consumers of education but as citizens with the right to high-quality education.

Though ensuring equal educational opportunities to higher education has been a long-standing and deep-seated goal in the Finnish system, it is clear that parental background still matters in Finland. However, a recent study (Erola et al., 2016) underlines the relatively small importance of family income levels in explaining children's achievement. When the relationship between achievement of children and parental education, income, and class was scrutinized, it became apparent that parental education mattered the most and parental income mattered the least. Policy in the welfare state in Finland has been able to diminish economic differences between students but cannot eliminate the potency of the cultural capital of families (see also Corak, 2006; Mountford-Zimdars and Sabbagh, 2013).

When families in Finland invest time, energy and money into their children's access to professional fields, the reproduction of social stratification through education can be understood primarily as the reproduction of (unequal) cultural capital and differing social status. In Nordic societies with their universal social security, money is not necessarily the only or even the main driving force for individuals and families. Citizens can afford to aspire other forms of capital. Professional education sustains a way of life which is an end in itself. Indeed, social status has a subjective element and different families may give status to differing occupations—like the binary system of higher education in Finland, the country's occupational differentiation has horizontal as well as vertical aspects.

The family-driven reproduction of occupations does have a downside for equity when it creates partial closure of those occupations. This constrains horizontal and vertical social mobility by making it more difficult for new families to enter. This might be more important than the effects of partial occupational closure based on economic inequality. The two forms of social differentiation—the occupational-cultural and the economic—do overlap in particular cases such as medicine. However, because equality and equity are core values of Nordic societies it is rational to study fields which prepare students for occupations that are close to these societal core values, for example in teaching, social work, and the caring professions.

▉ REFERENCES

Alestalo, M. and Kuhnle, S. (1987). The Scandinavian route: Economic, social and political developments in Denmark, Finland, Norway and Sweden, R. Erikson et al. (eds), *The Scandinavian Model: Welfare States and Welfare Research*. New York: Sharper, pp. 3–38.

Corak, M. (2006). Do poor children become poor adults? Lessons from a cross country comparison of generational earnings mobility. IZA Discussion Paper No. 1993. Bonn, Institute for the Study of Labor.

Erola, J., Jalonen, S., and Lehti, H. (2016). Parental education, class and income over early life course and children's achievement. *Research in Social Stratification and Mobility (2016)*. http://dx.doi.org/10.1016/j.rssm.2016.01.003

Esping-Andersen, G. (1990). *The Three Worlds of Welfare Capitalism*. New Jersey: Princeton University Press.

Espinoza, O. (2007). Solving the equity-equality conceptual dilemma: A new model for analysis of the educational process. *Educational Research* 49(4), 343–63.

Eurostudent, V. (2012–15). Database. http://database.eurostudent.eu/

Haltia, N., Leskinen, L., and Rahiala, E. (2014). Avoimen korkeakoulun opiskelijan muotokuva 2010-luvulla. Opiskelijoiden taustojen, motiivien ja koettujen hyötyjen tarkastelua. [The portrait of the student in adult education: The analysis of backgrounds, motives and experienced benefits]. *Aikuiskasvatus* 34(4), 244–58.

Hämäläinen, K., Haakstad, J., Kangasniemi, J., Lindeberg, T., and Sjölund, M. (2001). *Quality Assurance in the Nordic Higher Education*. Helsinki: ENQA Occasional Papers 2.

Hauschildt, K., Gwosć, C., Netz, N., and Mishra, S. (2015). Eurostudent V 2012–2015: Social and economic conditions of student life in Europe. Synopsis of indicators. http://www.eurostudent.eu/results/reports

Kela (2017). Student grant: The social insurance institution of Finland. http://www.kela.fi/web/en/financial-aid-for-students_study-grant

Kettunen, P., Kuhnle, S., and Ren, Y. (eds) (2014). Reshaping welfare institutions in China and in the Nordic countries: NordWel Studies in Historical Welfare State Research 7. Helsinki.

Kivinen, O. and Hedman, J. (2016). Suomalaisen korkeakoulutuksen taso on väitettyä parempi. Mahdollisuuksien tasa-arvo ja korkea osaaminen. [The level of higher education is better than discussed]. *Yhteiskuntapolitiikka* 81(1), 87–96.

Kivinen, O. Hedman, J., and Kaipainen, P. (2012). Koulutusmahdollisuuksien yhdenvertaisuus Suomessa. Eriarvoisuuden uudet ja vanhat muodot. *Yhteiskuntapolitiikka* 77(5), 559–66.

Kouvo, A. (2014). Luottamuksen lähteet. Vertaileva tutkimus yleistynyttä luottamusta synnyttävistä mekanismeista. [The sources of generalized trust—A comparative study]. *Annales Universitatis Turkuensis*. Turku: Annales Universitatis Turkuensis, Ser. C, tom 381.

Lindberg, M. (2007). 'At the frontier of graduate surveys': Assessing participation and employability of graduates with Master's degree in nine European countries. *Higher Education* 53(5), 623–44.

Leiden University (2017). Centre for Work and Technology Studies. The Leiden Ranking 2017. http://www.leidenranking.com/ranking/2017/list

MEC (Ministry of Education and Culture) (2012). Education and research 2011–2016. A development plan. Reports of the Ministry of Education and Culture, Finland 2012: 3.

MEC (Ministry of Education and Culture) (2016). Opiskelijavalintojen uudistaminen. Ministry of Education and Culture. http://www.minedu.fi/OPM/Koulutus/koulutuspolitiikka/vireilla_koulutus/opiskelijavalinnat/index.html?lang=fi

Melin, G., Zuijdam, F., Good, B. et al. (eds) (2015). Towards a future proof system for higher education and research in Finland. Publications of the Ministry on Education and Culture, Finland 2015:11.

Moisio, J. (2015). Mitä Eurostudent kertoo opiskelijoista, opinnoista ja opiskelusta 2010-luvun Euroopassa? Esitelmä korkeakoulu- ja innovaatiotutkimuksen päivillä 28.4.2015, Helsinki.

http://blogs.helsinki.fi/hegompage/files/2015/02/Eurostudent-V-2012–2015-tuloksia-opiskelusta-ja-opiskelijoista.pdf

Mountford-Zimdars, A. and Sabbagh, D. (2013). Fair access to higher education: A comparative perspective. *Comparative Education Review* 57(3), 359–68.

Nori, H. (2011). *Keille yliopiston portit avautuvat? Tutkimus suomalaisiin yliopistoihin ja eri tieteenaloille valikoitumisesta 2000-luvun alussa.* Turku: Annales Universitatis Turkuensis, Ser. C, tom 309.

OECD (Organisation for Economic Co-operation and Development) (2014). *Education at a Glance 2014: OECD Indicators.* Paris: OECD Publishing. http://dx.doi.org/10.1787/eag-2014-en

OSF (Official Statistics of Finland) (2013). University education. University students 2012. Helsinki: Statistics Finland. http://www.stat.fi/til/yop/2012/02/yop_2012_02_2013-06-19_tie_001_en.html (last accessed: 10 May 2018).

OSF (Official Statistics of Finland) (2018). Appendix table 1: Main type of activity of graduates one year after graduation at the end of 2016. Transition from school to further education and work [e-publication]. ISSN=1798–9469. 2016. Helsinki: Statistics Finland (25 January). http://www.stat.fi/til/sijk/2016/sijk_2016_2018-01-25_tau_001_en.html

Parker, P. D., Thoemmes, F., Duineveld, J., and Salmela-Aro, K. (2015). I wish I had (not) taken a gap-year? The psychological and attainment outcomes of different post-school pathways. *Developmental Psychology* 51(3), 323–33.

Rinne, R. (2010). The Nordic university model from a comparative and historical perspective, in J. Kauko, R. Rinne, and H. Kyykänniemi (eds), *Restructuring the Truth of Schooling: Essays on Discursive Practices in the Sociology and Politics of Education.* Jyväskylä: FERA Research in Educational Sciences 48, pp. 85–112.

Rinne, R., Haltia, N., Nori, H., and Jauhiainen, A. (2008). Yliopiston porteilla. Nuoret hakijat ja sisäänpäässeet 2000-luvun alun Suomessa. Turku: Suomen Kasvatustieteellinen seura [Research in Educational Sciences], p. 36.

Saari, J. (2015). Koulutuksen valikoituvuus koulutuspolkujen nivelvaiheissa, in J. Saari, L. Aarnio, and M. Rytkönen (eds), *Kolme näkökulmaa koulutuksen valikoituvuuteen. Nuorten koulutus-valinnat tilastojen ja kertomusten valossa.* Helsinki: Opiskelun ja koulutuksen tutkimussäätiö Otus 51, 11–76.

Student Survey (2014). Higher education students' income and studies. Publications of the Ministry of Education and Culture, Finland 2014:10. Ministry of Education and Culture, Finland. http://www.minedu.fi/OPM/Julkaisut/2014/Opiskelijatutkimus_2014.html?lang=fi&extra_locale=en

Thomsen, J. P., Munk, M. D., Eiberg-Madsen, M., and Hansen, G. I. (2013). The educational strategies of Danish university students from professional and working-class backgrounds. *Comparative Education Review* 57(3), 457–80.

Triventi, M. (2013). The role of higher education stratification in the reproduction of social inequality in the labor market. *Research in Social Stratification and Mobility* 32, 45–63.

Vabo, A. (2000). Mytedannelser i endringsprosesser i akademiske institusjoner. [Making myths in the processes of change in academic institutions]. Academic Dissertation. University of Bergen.

Välimaa, J. (2012). The corporatization of national universities in Finland, in B. Pusser, K. Kempner, S. Marginson, and I. Ordorika (eds), *Universities and the Public Sphere: Knowledge Creation and State Building in the Era of Globalization.* New York: Routledge, pp. 101–20.

Välimaa, J. (2018). Opinteillä oppineita. Suomalainen korkeakoulutus keskiajalta 2000-luvulle [The History of Finnish Higher Education form 14th to the 21 century]. Jyväskylä: University Press of Eastern Finland.

Välimaa, J. and Neuvonen-Rauhala, M.-L. (2010). 'We are a training and development organisation'—Research and development in Finnish polytechnics, in S. Kyvik and B. Lepori (eds), *The Research Mission of Higher Education Institutions outside the University Sector: Striving for Differentiation.* Dordrecht: Springer, pp. 135–54.

Välimaa, J., Aittola, H., and Ursin, J. (2014). University mergers in Finland: Mediating global competition, in L. M. Portnoi and S. S. Bagley (ed.), *Critical Perspectives on Global Competition in Higher Education.* San Francisco: Jossey-Bass, pp. 41–53.

Vuorinen, P. and Valkonen, S. (2003). *Ammattikorkeakouluun vai yliopistoon? Korkeakoulutukseen hakeutumisen orientaatiot.* Jyväskylä: Koulutuksen tutkimuslaitos. Tutkimusselosteita 18.

Weimer, L. (2013). Tuition fees for international students in Finland: A case study analysis of collective action and social change. Unpublished dissertation, University of Georgia holdings.

14 Balancing Efficiency and Equity in a Welfare State Setting: High Participation Higher Education in Norway

Rómulo Pinheiro and Bjørn Stensaker

Introduction

This chapter provides a historical analysis of the higher education enrolment patterns in Norway going back to the beginning of the massification phase after World War II. In so doing, it highlights the key dynamics facing the system as well as the dominant policy logics and mechanisms according to the propositions regarding high participation systems (HPS) advanced earlier in this volume, from the perspective of the Norwegian case. The chapter concludes by providing some brief reflections on Norway as a HPS system that has attempted to combine equity with relevancy, efficiency, and accountability.

POLITICAL ECONOMY AND POLITICAL CULTURE

Due to sharply increasing national income from the oil and gas industry from the 1980s onwards, Norway is today one of the wealthiest countries in the world if measured in GDP per capita, which at the time of writing was US$74,481 per year (World Bank, 2017). Although income from the oil and gas industry has decreased during the latter years due to lower prices on the world market, this sector is still an important contributor to the national economy along with fish and mineral exports. The service sector is growing, and the financial sector has benefitted from the considerable investments that have been directed at the oil and gas industry, and from the surpluses from this industry to be re-invested abroad. Although the income per capita is among the highest in the world, Norway's economy is still relatively small due to its population of only 5.2 million people.

As part of the Nordic social welfare region, Norway has a long tradition of having a rather pro-active state which has maintained ownership in important sectors including energy, transport and banking. Although Norway has been strongly influenced by new public management ideas regarding the governance of the public sector, the country has been less exposed to ideas about privatization—although deregulation and the opening up for more competition have been key ideas behind several public sector reforms during the latter decades (Lægreid and Christensen, 2013). The political culture can be said to be (still) founded on the values of equality, inclusion, meritocracy and cooperation (Stensaker, 2014). Typically, governments are based on various coalitions between two or more political parties, and while reforms are frequently initiated in various sectors, they tend to be incremental in their content and implementation, at least seen in a historical perspective (Bleiklie et al., 2000).

The Norwegian economy is heavily based on exports and can be characterized as an open economy. The country is not part of the European Union (EU), but is closely linked due to being a member of the European Economic Area (EEA) which provides Norway with access to the EU market. During the latter decades and due to the considerable economic growth, the unemployment rate has been very low at around 2.5 per cent, although it has risen in recent years due to the reduced prices of oil and gas.

HIGHER EDUCATION

Currently, the higher education sector in Norway consists of nine universities, five specialized universities in areas such as sports and music, and a smaller number of university colleges, some a result of recent mergers and with ambitions of becoming universities within a few years. There are also nineteen private higher education institutions in the country, but with a few exceptions these are quite small and enrol only a small percentage of the student population. Currently, several private higher education institutions have initiated merger processes which most likely will reduce the total number of private institutions.

Norway signed the Bologna declaration, and reformed its higher education system accordingly in 2003 (Aamodt and Kyvik, 2005). This implied adapting to a 3+2 year Bachelor's–Master's degree cycle, the introduction of the European Credit Transfer System (ECTS), and the development of a national system of quality assurance, both regarding institutional accreditation and study programme accreditation (Stensaker, 2014). Most Norwegian students are enrolled in programmes adapted to the Bologna degree structure. As will be described in the following section, the Norwegian higher education system expanded rapidly after World War II, not least by building up and later consolidating a quite large vocational college sector responsible for undergraduate studies in areas such as teacher training, engineering, business administration, and nursing/social work. Today, the binary system that was developed in this period has been abandoned, and a more unified higher education system has developed where issues with respect to horizontal differentiation rank high on the policy agenda.

The state has been the key actor in translating social demands into specific policy initiatives driving the expansion of higher education, both as the key funder of the sector, and also with respect to how the sector has been developed institutionally and how it is governed (Pinheiro and Antomowics, 2015). Historically, Norway can be said to belong to the Humboldtian university tradition where much authority and power has been located at the shop floor, and where the institutional leadership, especially at universities, has been rather weak (Beliklie et al., 2000). Several decades after World War II, the Ministry of Education had quite detailed control over budget and personnel policy, and while later reforms have transferred much responsibility to institutions, the Norwegian higher educational system is still culturally influenced by the tradition of strong state steering, and the neoliberal influence is—in a comparative perspective—rather moderate (Stensaker, 2014). Politically, there is considerable agreement on the key objectives of higher education policy. Across the political spectrum it is currently expected that higher education is to stimulate a more knowledge driven economy, that educational offerings are provided efficiently and that they are relevant for the labor market (with priorities given to STEM (science, technology, engineering, and mathematics) subjects), and that outputs in research and education should be of high quality, as understood from an international perspective. There are no tuition fees in Norwegian higher education, although some conservative governments have, in the later years, suggested that this is an alternative source of funding that should be explored.

Growth of Higher Education

In the present study the general propositions about HPS include HPS Proposition 3:

> *Once transition from a primarily agricultural economy is achieved, the long-term growth of HPS is independent of political economic factors such as economic growth and patterns of labour market demand; patterns of public and private funding of higher education; the roles of public and private institutions; and system organization and modes of governance.*

This is a fairly valid description of the development of the Norwegian higher education system after World War II. Due to increases in student demand, the massification of Norwegian higher education rose sharply in the late 1960s and early 1970s, with the establishment of a regional college system throughout the entire country. In the mid-1990s, and due to consolidation pressures and efficiency-related dimensions, a series of forced (government-mandated) mergers led to the consolidation of the emerging binary system of higher education composed of public universities and university colleges. More recently, a new wave of mergers has reshaped the higher education landscape resulting in fewer and larger institutions. Although a forecasted (2015–25) decline in the 19–24 years age cohort can reduce participation rates in the long run, enrolments have continued to rise also in recent years. This development hints at high aspiration levels among the youth (Thomsen et al., 2016).

FIRST WAVE OF EXPANSION

In the period between the end of World War II and the mid-1950s there was no major change in the number of students entering Norwegian higher education, for two reasons. Firstly, Norway as a country spent considerable time and resources in re-building the nation after the conflict. Secondly, there was a relatively stable number of pupils seeking higher education, a consequence of the population stagnation (small birth cohorts) in the 1930s (Aamodt, 1995). As it was the case with other OECD countries, the growth in the numbers of youth entering university and non-university higher education in Norway initiated in the late 1950s. Between 1955 and 1966, enrolments quadrupled, from fewer than 8,000 students to close to 29,000 (OECD, 1971: 23) (see Table 14.1). This growth occurred across the entire system, with both university and non-university programmes receiving three and five times more students, respectively, by the end of the decade. However, the total share of enrolments by universities declined slightly from 75 to 67 per cent.[1]

By 1965, the proportion of all 20–24-year-olds enrolled in some type of higher education programme was 11.2 per cent, up from an estimated 3.6 per cent a decade earlier (OECD, 1971: 68).[2] It is generally acknowledged that the key drivers for the exponential increase in the number of pupils entering Norwegian higher education

Table 14.1. Students as a proportion of the population and labour force, 1955–65

Students per 1,000	1955	1960	1965	% growth
Inhabitants	2.2	3.5	7.8	+355%
Labour force	5.1	8.4	18.8	+369%

Source: Adapted by authors from original data in OECD (1971: 66).

[1] The average annual growth-rate (in enrolments) at universities, throughout the 1960s, was 12.5 per cent; reaching 15 per cent during the first half of the decade (OECD, 1971: 23–9).

[2] Insofar the demographic profile of the student population at Norwegian universities, by 1965, the bulk (62 per cent) was composed of 20–24-year-olds, followed by those 25 years or above (28 per cent). Less than 10 per cent of all university students were younger than 20 years old (OECD, 1971: 69).

Table 14.2. Transfer rates into higher education, as a percentage of secondary school graduates

1950–2	1954–6	1959–61	1964–6	Change over the period
35%	38%	51%	47%	+12%

Source: Adapted by authors from OECD (1971: 108).

during this period were the combination of emerging social demands, the shortage of qualified labour force (economic rationale), and a strong governmental focus given to equality of educational opportunity (socio-political rationale) across the entire population (Aamodt and Kyvik, 2005).[3] Transfer rates from secondary schooling advanced (see Table 14.2). Starting in the late 1950s, a clear governmental policy of expansion was articulated via the Norwegian research councils, which had been established in the late 1940s (Bleiklie et al., 2000: 84–5), but also heavily influenced by the OECD, and the role OECD economists gave to education and research (Eide, 1995). The prevalence of economic imperatives and 'man-power' type of arguments continued up to the early 1960s, gradually declining throughout the following two decades. In 1960, the first Commission ('Kleppekomitéen') with the mandate for recommending policy measures in light of the expansionist wave in higher education was established by the Norwegian government.[4] However, the Commission's mandate was limited to the university sector and its prevailing assumption was that, 'the manpower needs [of the country] were much lower than the demand by youngsters for university education' (Eide, 1995: 85). As a result, in the period 1965–70, student demand became *the* legitimating factor for the expansion of the higher education system, with scientific, cultural, and economic (policy) rationales seen as secondary priorities (Forland, 1996 in Bleiklie et al., 2000: 86).

Throughout the 1960s and 1970s, access to higher education expanded, inter alia, via a gradual increase in the size (capacity) of the university sector, both with respect to the number of institutions and total study-places. While the University of Oslo was the only university in Norway before World War II, three new universities were created during the period after the war and up to the 1970s. Structural measures were also taken into account as to enhance the development of a binary system of higher education, through the creation of new types of non-university institutions; the district colleges. The latter measure was partly a consequence of strong political resistance—both from students and academic staff in universities—against the proposed reforms at universities by the newly

[3] The Labour Party and its policies of equity dominated national politics after World War II, where the party possessed a single majority in Parliament between 1945 and 1965.

[4] Three of the five Commission members were associated with the Joint Committee of the Research Councils formed in the late 1950s, responsible for developing expansion policies in higher education (Bleiklie et al., 2000: 84).

formed (Ottosen) Commission (Stensaker, 1995). Among other things, the Commission proposed radical reforms in controversial areas like the degree structures at universities, plans for life-long education, and the creation of new, non-university institutions. It also advanced proposals aimed at moving the existing Norwegian degree structure towards the Anglo-Saxon model, as to reduce the normal period of studies (Aamodt, 1995). Longer study periods in the humanities, law, and sciences in tandem with high failure rates were seen as the main justifications driving these reforms. In this respect, the Commission proposed new (innovative) measures such as more frequent examinations, the introduction of a course credit system, and the forcing of underperformed students out of the system after the first two years of studies, in other words via the establishment of a policy of 'selectivity' (Bleiklie et al., 2000: 86). Notwithstanding the ambitions goals and to a great extent due to fierce resistance by internal stakeholders, the Norwegian government was forced to 'look outside the universities to reform higher education' (Aamodt, 1995: 65).

The new non-university institutions, emerging after 1970, were the result of the establishment of the new district (or regional) colleges, as well as the transformation of some existing post-secondary schools (of teacher training, engineering, nursing, etc.) into higher education institutions; a measure that helped boost the capacity of the system considerably. It is also worth stressing that the popularity of this policy measure within the country was aided by the fact that the latter led to an increasing geographic decentralization of Norwegian higher education, from the main cities to the periphery/ regions (Pinheiro et al., 2016). In turn, this measure led to the emergence of a regional college system, which was to become the cornerstone of a binary higher education system. Thus, in retrospect, 'the creation of new institutions, the *Regional Colleges*, became the symbol of the new policy on higher education' (Aamodt, 1995: 65; emphasis added).

With respect to *implementation efforts*, the policy measures initiated in the 1960s and 1970s, as a follow-up from the proposals by the Kleppe and Ottosen Commissions, and resulting in the creation of a binary system of higher education, led to a stronger involvement of the non-university sector in the reform process. As a result of strong reactions by students and academics, who accused policymakers of being too adaptive to OECD ideas, 'the government backed off and left the universities to themselves' (Bleiklie et al., 2000: 91; see also Eide, 1995). The way that the new decentralization policy was implemented, the creation of so-called district/regional colleges, was, for the most part, an effect of the infusion of regional policy into the government's education policy (Bleiklie et al., 2000: 92).

SECOND AND THIRD WAVES OF EXPANSION

The success derived from the policy of channelling students from the university to the college sector (mentioned earlier), led over time to a stagnation of new enrolments at universities, as will be discussed further below. A new governmental Commission ('Hernes Commission'), set in the late 1980s, drew attention towards the worrying decline in university enrolments in general, and the lack of new (future) entrants in the fields of the humanities and across (long-term) research-based programmes in particular (Aamodt, 1995: 65–6). This meant that universities moved to the fore of the higher education policy agenda. The new Commission highlighted the need for improving the quality and the research-dimension of higher education programmes based at the universities, among other things, through the reallocation of financial resources. Nonetheless, the proposals advanced by the Hernes Commission had many similarities (i.e. policy continuity) with those of its predecessor, the 1970s Ottosen Commission; for example, with regard to system *integration, flexibility,* and *efficiency* (Aamodt et al., 1991: 129; Bleiklie et al., 2000: 97). The central role played by universities in basic research and the training of future researchers within an international context were also highlighted in the Commission's recommendations. The Commission expressed interest in furthering inter-institutional cooperation, based on a clear division of roles and responsibilities, rather than opting for a strategy of further expansion/decentralization via the establishment of new higher education institutions.[5]

In contrast to the first expansionary period (mentioned earlier), this second wave, starting in the early 1990s, was neither planned by the authorities nor a result of ongoing policy efforts/reforms. The two main drivers for expansion seem to have been related to: (a) considerable high levels of unemployment among the Norwegian youth (16–24-year-olds) during this period; and (b) higher educational aspirations among the youth, an effect of their parents' educational attainment and the influence of peer groups (Aamodt and Kyvik, 2005).[6] Somehow instinctively, the Norwegian government attempted to match supply to demand by, among other things, redirecting public resources (e.g. from unemployment subsidies) into higher education, thus using the sector as a policy instrument for tackling (assimilating) nation-wide unemployment (Stensaker, 1995). Furthermore, public pressure to provide open access for all qualified seekers was intensified. Writing in the mid-1990s Aamodt (1995) commented:

Today [mid-1990s] there are lots of criticisms of the [Norwegian] Government's policy on higher education, mainly because it is not considered expansive enough. Thousands of young qualified people are standing outside the gates of higher education, and this is a political reality not to be overlooked. Public opinion is undoubtedly on the side of potential students, and warnings that expansion has gone too far are seldom heard.   (Aamodt, 1995: 79)

---

[5] The Commission advanced proposals for *mergers* among the colleges, with the aim of creating 'regional educational centres', and, *fusions* among smaller university-departments, as to increase their overall size and teaching/research capacity (Bleiklie et al., 2000: 101).

[6] Writing about the process, in the mid-1990s, Aamodt (1995: 77) clarifies: 'high unemployment perhaps does not force many young people into higher education, because they had intended to enrol anyway, however, it may cause some to want to enter just at the moment'.

The earlier statement re-enforces the notion that, within the Nordic welfare context, 'access to higher education constitutes a quite strong *political pressure*, and indeed results in *political action*' (Aamodt and Kyvik, 2005: 132; emphasis added).[7] Thus, in retrospect, the policy rationales associated with the second wave of expansion in Norwegian higher education were based on both, *socio-political* arguments (equality of opportunity) as well as *economic* (supply/demand match).

A thorough review of the outcomes brought about by the 1994 reform across upper secondary education reveals a slight improvement in the progression and completion of courses by students following vocational tracks (OECD, 2005b: 14). In relation to direct impacts on access patterns into higher education, this reform seems to have been successful in increasing the number of upper secondary pupils (directly) entering higher education (OECD, 2005a: 84). Other studies, however, suggest that the access structure established by the mid-1990s, based on a considerably high number of advanced courses, has had unintended negative effects on students' progression throughout upper secondary education (OECD, 2005a: 83).

In 1994 Norway saw the forced merger of ninety-eight former regional colleges into twenty-six (new) state colleges (*høgskoler*). The mergers were driven by two core drivers or goals; efficiency and quality (Kyvik, 2002: 53; OECD, 2005: 23). Although some criticism was directed at the corporate dimensions in the 1990 reform, the proposal was, by and large, 'received with general acclaim by leading academics and administrators' (Bleiklie et al., 2000: 98–9). Based on the available data, it is unclear how much of an impact (if any) the merger process across the college sector, and the establishment of a 'de-facto' binary system of higher education in Norway, have had, in terms of students' choice and mobility. Evaluation studies seem to suggest that the institutions were able to adapt well to the new demands posed by the market place, for example via the establishment of new study programmes (Kyvik, 2002). Reliable data on student mobility from the college to the university sector is scarce, but there is some evidence pointing to the fact that, in Norway, students are equally likely to move (transfer) their higher education studies from the university into the college level as the other way around (Stensaker, 1995; Kyvik, 2009). There also seems to be some evidence that, by and large, the college sector has been successful in attracting students from the immediate geographic surroundings. Between 1992 and 2002, the participation rate in higher education among students originated from rural areas doubled, to 22 per cent, whereas that of individuals from urban districts was kept relatively stable (OECD, 2005: 57).[8]

---

[7] The Norwegian educational system has been characterized by some as being rather 'soft' since it is based on the principle of adjusting capacity to existing demand (Teichler, 1988 cited in Aamodt, 1995).

[8] Decentralization and flexible provision exercised via distance education, off-campus lectures, the use of ICT, etc., also contributed to the balance of higher education participation rates across the country (OECD, 2005).

In 1994, the Norwegian authorities removed a series of structural barriers across upper secondary education. This policy measure aimed at facilitating access into higher education by students possessing non-traditional academic backgrounds (OECD, 2005: 83). The new reform ('Reform 94') provided students between the ages of 16 and 19 with a statutory right to three years of upper secondary education, leading either to higher education entrance qualifications or, instead, to vocational/partial qualifications. 'Reform 94' also resulted in a substantial reduction from 113 to 13 in the number of foundation (first year) courses in upper secondary education, and an increase in advanced courses (second year) as to provide a clearer/more straightforward path to formal upper secondary qualifications and, consequently, access into higher education.

Due to the exponential increase of 52 per cent in the number of registered students in higher education, between 1988 and 1996 (SSB, 2001: 183), partly as a consequence of the refusal by many (university) faculties to adopt a policy of 'limited admission' or *numerus clausus*, the government was forced to introduce stricter admission policies across the entire university sub-sector in 1990.[9] Due to the considerable number of students engaged in part-time work, which resulted, it was believed, in low academic performances and high drop-out rates, the Hernes Commission expressed a strong willingness to re-establish full-time (FTE) studies as the norm.[10] A key aspect in the recommendations was the need to improve both the *structure* and *supervision* of research-training at universities, which, along with other strategic aspects, was positively accepted by internal university stakeholders.[11]

By the mid-1990s, the shift towards the 'knowledge society/economy' paradigm (World Bank, 1999) raised new concerns in Norway. Concerns included meeting demands of future labour markets, retraining individual skills and competencies, as well as unfulfilled socio-economic and cultural needs of society. The higher education sector was, once again, seen as an important policy instrument for leveraging the country's capacity to compete regionally and internationally and a means of addressing remaining equity-related dilemmas like the under-representation of certain groups such as ethnic minorities, people with disabilities, mature students, and other untraditional student groups (OECD, 2004).

The second half of the 1990s was characterized by a period of continued, but less disruptive, growth in total student enrolments at Norwegian universities and colleges.

---

[9] This was mostly evident across the humanities, social and natural sciences. Professional fields like medicine and engineering at university/college levels had already adopted stricter admission criteria (Aamodt, 1995).

[10] By the late 1980s, the proportion of part-time working university students surpassed the 50 per cent mark. The average number of study hours, on a weekly basis, was twenty-seven (Berg and Aamodt, 1987, cited in Aamodt et al., 1991: 136).

[11] It is worth stressing that, many of the Commission's proposals originated either from the universities themselves or the main trade union in the sector (Bleiklie et al., 2000: 101).

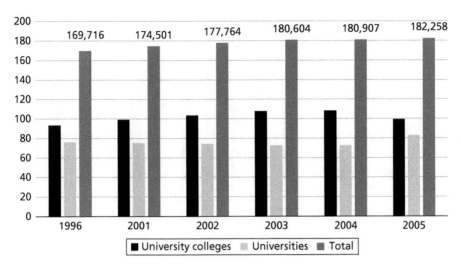

Figure 14.1. Enrolments in higher education, per type of institution, 1996–2005

Source: Data adapted by authors from SSB.

Between 1996 and 2001, the growth rate in enrolments did not surpass 6 per cent, totalling 23 per cent for the entire decade (Figure 14.1); way below the 58 per cent rate achieved in the previous period (see earlier). However, the data reveal substantial differences across the sector. Whereas the intake of new students at the colleges increased by 30 per cent during the decade, the growth at the universities was much smaller; around 7 per cent. The proportion of students enrolled at the colleges continued to grow, from 54 per cent in 1996 to 58 per cent of the total by 2005 (SSB, n.d.). This growth was, in part, the result of government measures in the mid-1990s aimed at facilitating access to higher education through the removal of a series of structural barriers across upper secondary education, as pointed out earlier.

As the 2000s proceeded, the dynamic of growth again gathered pace and there was a continuing shift in favour of universities. Between 1998 and 2006, there was an increase of 272 per cent in new entrants into higher education, despite the fact that the total number of registrations only grew by 20 per cent (Figure 14.2). In this eight-year period the number of applicants for higher education quadrupled, from fewer than 140,000 to more than 618,000 (NSD-DBH, n.d.). Universities increased in popularity during this period. Whereas in 2001, 71 per cent of all applications for higher education targeted either a public and/or private college, by 2006, this figure had declined to 54 per cent. Insofar the capacity of the system as whole, the number of students being offered a study place at a university and/or college grew by 56 per cent during the above period. In this context, no substantial changes as regards the host institution occurred, with the universities accepting an average of 36 per cent of all applicants. Between 1998 and 2006 the number of higher education graduates rose by more than 50 per cent, with the

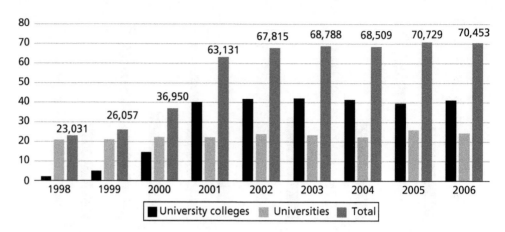

Figure 14.2. Newly registered students in higher education, 1998–2006

Source: Data adapted by authors from NSD-DBH.

relative share held by universities increasing by 10 per cent during the period, from 26 per cent to 36 per cent (NSD-DBH, n.d.).

From the mid-2000 and onwards, expansion has continued in what we might label as the third wave of expansion, with the number of applicants to Norwegian higher education institutions rising by 67 per cent; from about 612,000 in 2006 to over one million in 2016 (NSD-DBH, n.d.). Among universities, applications in absolute figures more than doubled, while university colleges saw a more modest rise of applicants (16 per cent). Although being a small part of the system, private higher education had the sharpest rise in the number of applicants (see Figure 14.3).

Governance

With respect to governance, HPS Propositions 4–6 all fit well with the Norwegian situation:

- *HPS systems are governed by multi-level control, coordination, and accountability mechanisms.*
- *HPS governance tends to involve the management of horizontal differentiation.*
- *HPS complex multi-level accountability and coordination, coupled with system differentiation, result in higher education institutions adopting increasingly corporate forms and robust internal governance and management capacities.*

Government-led reforms in the last three decades have changed the nature of coordination and control across the system. Higher education institutions are currently enjoying high degrees of procedural autonomy (see Schmidtlein and Berdahl, 2005) with respect to how they go about their daily businesses, especially insofar financial and organizational matters (Stensaker, 2014).

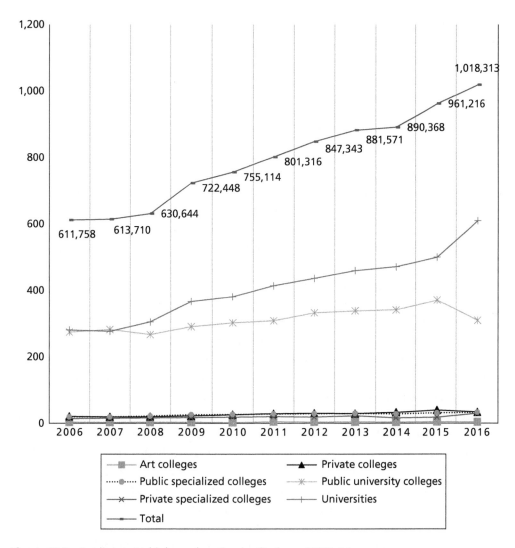

Figure 14.3. Applicants to higher education institutions, 2006–16

Source: Adapted by authors from NSB-DBH.

With strengthened autonomy came new mechanisms of control and accountability for all institutions, and the levels of discretion as regards more substantive issues ('the what') have declined as a direct result of the changing relation (from a trust- to a transactional-based one) between state and higher education institutions. Of particular relevance is that in the last decade, intermediate bodies such as quality assurance and funding agencies have played a prominent role.

With respect to horizontal differentiation, the Norwegian case provides interesting insights. Up to the late 1990s, the government established a clear demarcation between the university and the non-university sectors, but legal changes combined with institutional (and individual) aspirations led to a gradual drift towards a unitary university-based system. This shift also moved many students from the university college sector to the universities. The recent merger frenzy was an important driver in this respect. Yet, the state still adopts a dual criterion when it comes to quality assurance mechanisms, with universities enjoying a higher degree of discretion when compared to the university colleges.

In general, from the 1990s onwards a key ambition in governance reform has been to improve coordination of the system. For example, a new legal framework enabling the integration of the existing universities and colleges across the binary divide making governance rules and regulations homogeneous was introduced in 1990. Later reforms have also made the legal regulatory frameworks between public and private higher education institutions more coordinated, not least regarding institutional accreditation (Stensaker, 2014).

More corporate forms of governance have also been adopted. In relation to corporatisation, the Norwegian story reinforces the perspective that as systems grow in both size and complexity, and as institutions become increasingly accountable to external actors like the Ministry and funding agencies, there is a natural tendency for devising new internal structures aimed at professionalised management and internal governance. Recent reforms have promoted the notion of (stronger) appointed rather than elected leaders and the role of external actors in matters of strategic importance. It can be expected that the drive towards more managed and professional institutions will be further strengthened as institutions are becoming larger and are granted full university status. The most controversial measure associated with the 1990 law related to changes in the management/governance of higher education institutions, where a smaller board replaced the previous academic collegium (the senate) where all faculties used to be represented. The new executive body, headed by the rector, was constituted by elected representatives among employees and students. In addition, universities have become responsible for appointing their own professors, a task previously reserved to the government. The 1990 governmental white paper also launched the idea of a *Network Norway*. The latter was geared towards facilitating coordination across the entire higher education sector by, first and foremost, removing existing obstacles hindering institutional collaboration (OECD, 2005: 23).[12] As a means to achieve this goal, the Ministry devised measures in order to establish a stronger institutional basis for both teaching and research across the college sub-sector, and this fed the mergers of regional colleges and the creation of the new state colleges. The college sector mergers were undertaken in a highly effective way, but nevertheless as a 'top-down' exercise, with

---

[12] The Network aimed at facilitate student mobility, enhance institutional specialization and co-operation, and establish 'research academies' as a future framework for graduate education (Bleiklie et al., 2000: 75).

the governmental agencies (Ministry and Regional Boards) setting the agenda; despite the initial reluctance of various internal stakeholders (Kyvik, 2002: 69).

The governance changes started during the 1990s can be interpreted in light of the expansion of the system and the most significant aspect behind the governance reform was undoubtedly the exponential increase in total enrolments (system level), close to 60 per cent. According to Bleiklie et al. (2000), the 1980s and 1990s reforms marked a shift in the relationship between academic institutions and the government, in terms of 'a realignment of the co-ordinating forces, but not necessarily a fundamental shift regarding power distribution' (Bleiklie et al., 2000: 79). It can be questioned whether the latest wave of reforms (2003 onwards) have contributed to change this picture dramatically (Stensaker, 2014).

Horizontal Diversity

The propositions regarding horizontal stratification state that in HPS

an increasing proportion of higher education becomes centred on comprehensive multi-discipline and multi-function research universities, or 'multiversities'. The multiversity is increasingly dominant as the paradigmatic form of higher education. (HPS Proposition 7)

Further,

when participation expands there is no necessary increase in the overall diversity of institutional form and mission; and this has probably declined, except in relation to online provision (HPS Proposition 8)

though at the same time,

as participation expands the internal diversity of multiversities tends to increase. (HPS Proposition 9)

All these propositions can be said to be valid in the Norwegian context.

The fourth diversity proposition (HPS Proposition 10) states:

All else being equal, the combination of expanding participation and enhanced competition in neoliberal quasi-markets is associated with specific effects in relation to diversity, including (1) increased vertical differentiation of higher education institutions (stratification); (2) reduced horizontal differentiation (diversification); (3) convergence of missions through isomorphistic imitation; and (4) growth in the role of private higher education institutions, especially for-profit institutions.

While Norway has not adopted a neoliberal quasi market, certain elements outlined in this scenario have been apparent, to some degree, including reduced horizontal diversity, isomorphism and partial mission convergence.

THE BINARY SYSTEM

The building of a vocational system during the 1970s had implications for both horizontal diversity and vertical stratification. While it fostered the tiering of the national system, for a time it was also associated with a relative enhancement in the status of non-university pathways. This occurred though both the lifting of policy approval and social demand for higher education institutions other than universities, and a concurrent decline in the esteem of and demand for the universities. However, these trends were not to last.

The influx of students in the late 1960s and the sluggish economic growth across the Nordic region during the mid-1970s, as a direct result of the oil shocks, led to substantial cuts in public budgets and higher levels of unemployment. The fear of an over-supply of higher education graduates (especially from universities) combined with a climate of uncertainty led to a serious questioning of governmental plans for further higher education expansion. Higher education institutions were forced to respond to external calls for efficiency and flexibility (Aamodt and Kyvik, 2005). Shorter and more vocationally oriented education, usually provided at the college level, increased in popularity. In essence, the 'policy of vocationalism' was a technocratic attempt, by the government and its agencies, to manage higher education outputs in light of the economic needs of the country (Bleiklie et al., 2000: 96). The 1975 to 1985 period saw enrolment growth of 136 per cent across the non-university sector, in the colleges, while there was a gradual decline of the number of applicants for traditional university-based education, and university enrolments stagnated (Vabø and Aamodt, 2005: 17).

By 1987, the total number of higher education enrolments at Norwegian universities and colleges had reached 100,000; an increase of more than 40 per cent since the mid-1970s (Aamodt, 1995: 66). Between 1975 and 1987 the non-university sector,[13] of which the regional colleges were a key component, increased its market share from 39 per cent to 58 per cent of total higher education enrolments, making Norway in this respect a little unusual in international terms (Kyvik, 2009). As Figure 14.4 shows, the highest growth rates in student enrolments occurring at the regional colleges (close to 200 per cent) and other types of colleges (550 per cent), with smaller growth rates across the pedagogical (23 per cent) and engineering colleges (17 per cent). Overall, the non-university sector expanded its enrolments from fewer than 26,000 students in 1975 to 61,000 individuals by 1987, a 136 per cent rise.

The earlier political belief on universities as 'engines' for national economic development, prevalent in the 1950s and 1960s (Eide, 1995) was replaced by a new ideological

---

[13] In addition to the regional or district colleges, until the mid-1990s the non-university sector was composed by a wide variety of ('other') colleges; teacher training, engineering, health education, social work, military, as well as various other institutions offering a specialist range of teaching programmes.

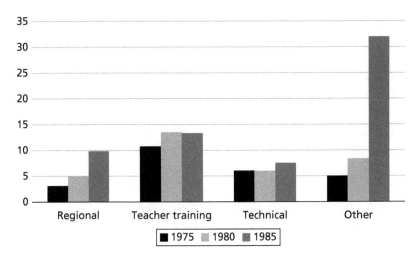

Figure 14.4. Non-university enrolments, per type of institution, 1975, 1980, and 1985
Source: Adapted by authors from Aamodt et al., 1991, p.131, SSB.

influence supporting the demand for socially-relevant universities (Stensaker, 1995). By the mid-1970s, universities 'were regarded as of hardly any practical use at all . . . blamed for being too involved in the social world [via their critical function] and yet, too secluded from it' (Forland, 1996, in Bleiklie et al., 2000: 95). Hence, the status and reputation of universities as elite institutions was not especially high, although there was an element of vertical stratification in the binary system. The successful policy of channelling students from the university to the college sector led to the stagnation of both student numbers and resource allocations at universities. Between 1975 and 1987, the expansion of the higher education system took place exclusively within the non-university sector (Aamodt, 1995: 65); with business administration and engineering at universities and few (selected) research fields, as exceptions (Bleiklie et al., 2000: 94–5). The challenge to the universities was most pronounced across the faculties of arts, sciences, and the social sciences, the disciplinary areas where the recently formed colleges expanded their influence (Bleiklie et al., 2000: 93). Some programmes in the college sector drew many more applications than did a significant number of programmes in the university sector.

Despite the importance attributed to vocational higher education, observers contended that the Norwegian government, by the mid-/late 1970s, 'had few specific preferences regarding what [HE] studies should promote' (Bleiklie et al., 2000: 94). The same observers argue that better articulate—that is, less vague—policies should have been implemented, emphasizing the importance of economic imperatives and the link between on the one hand higher education, on the other hand the labour markets and economy.

The decade 1975–85 was also characterized by a strong involvement of regional governance structures representing the non-university sector—helping to boost the regional relevance of those institutions—alongside a minor, almost negligible, role played by the universities. Towards the end of the period, as a result of the decline in the number of university students and the consequent stabilization of financial allocations, the response by universities became increasingly more local, with the latter expressing a sense of 'abandonment' by the national authorities. According to Bleiklie and colleagues: 'Supported by the power nexus of regional politics, where the district college leaders, local politicians and regional parliamentarians fraternize, this [HE] expansion went on unimpeded while the universities stagnated financially' (Bleiklie et al., 2000: 93).[14] Aamodt and colleagues state that: 'The strong focus on geographical decentralization of educational offerings pushed the universities somewhat into the background, and surprisingly enough, they [universities] were largely unable to defend their interests' (Aamodt, Kyvic and Skoie, 1991: 135). The Humboldtian inspired governance structures of the existing universities, securing considerable staff influence and power at department level yet with a rather weak central administrative leadership, may be part of the explanation (Stensaker, 1995).

As shown in Table 14.3, the largest and well-established universities like Oslo and Bergen suffered the most, partly due to the fact that Tromsø was a recently created institution and Trondheim acquired a new status through merger in the early 1970s.

Given the position of the universities at this time, it is perhaps not surprising that the hierarchical aspect of the binary system during the 1970s and the 1980s had little impact in elevating the social status of universities, although some specialized universities in business and economics and in engineering, and some study programmes in universities, such as medicine, did enjoy elite status (Eide, 1995)—a status these programmes

Table 14.3. University enrolments, 1975, 1980, and 1985

	1975	1980	1985	Change 1975–85(%)
University of Oslo	20,224	18,863	19,157	−5.2%
University of Bergen	7,888	7,588	8,028	+1.7%
University of Trondheim/NTNU	7,280	8,203	8,270	+13.6%
University of Tromsø	1,289	1,680	2,058	+60.0%
Others*	4,093	4,286	4,145	+1.3%
Total enrolments	40,774	40,620	41,658	+2.2%

Notes: Includes the specialized universities (*vitenskaplige høgskoler*) in the areas of; agriculture (Ås), business and administration (Bergen), sports (Oslo), music (Oslo), art (Oslo), religion (Oslo), and veterinary (Oslo).

Source: Authors, adapted from Vabø and Aamodt (2005: 17).

---

[14] For example, between 1977 and 1985, the teaching staff across the entire regional college sector increased by 20 per cent; the correspondent figure at the universities was 7 per cent (Bleiklie et al., 2000: 93).

have retained since (Hansen, 2010). However, as described below, there has been some tendency for the formation of a middle layer of institutions, as suggested by the propositions, though this has been affected by several factors.

MERGERS AND THE MULTIVERSITY FORM

As in Australia and the United Kingdom, for a time the binary system and social esteem for the non-university mission were important in expanding participation, but the full-blown binary system lasted only for a generation. In Norway the turn away from binarism began a decade or so later than was the case in the two English-speaking countries.

The comprehensive merger process, reducing the number of regional colleges from ninety-eight to twenty-six large university colleges in 1994, stimulated the development of more comprehensive 'multiversities' in Norway (Kyvik, 2009). The governmentally initiated mergers had several objectives, including the creation of a more robust and sustainable vocational sector bringing together formerly disciplinary specialized institutions in such fields as engineering and teacher training to larger more multi-disciplinary institutions. The government also set out to stop tendencies to academic drift among some regional colleges that aspired to attain university status (Kyvik, 2002). The amalgamation of quite distinct institutions under a more generic university college label drove considerable institutional convergence (Kyvik, 2009).

The last decade in Norwegian higher education has been marked by another major restructuring of the domestic landscape via voluntary mergers involving both universities and university-colleges (Kyvik and Stensaker, 2013; Pinheiro et al., 2016). These processes are, partly, a result of inefficiencies at the system level, combined with a projected decline of the regional student population (all areas but greater Oslo) between 2015 and 2025 (NOU, 2008). The number of registered students across the entire sector in the last decade grew by 30 per cent, from 206,000 to 269,000 (NSD-DBH, n.d.). Among universities (some of them much larger now due to the mergers) the figure grew by 73 per cent (from 82,000 to 141,000), while public university-colleges[15] (fewer than before due to mergers) suffered a 13 per cent decrease.[16] Interestingly, private higher education institutions (university college level) increased their enrolments substantially by 65 per cent, to about 40,000 students. The share of enrolments across the private sector rose by 3 per cent during the period, from 12 to 15 per cent between 2006 and 2016. This result can partly be explained by measures taken as part of the quality reform (see later) where the regulatory framework of public and private institutions became

---

[15] Includes both 'normal' university colleges and specialized university colleges.
[16] Prior to the recent wave of mergers in the period 2006–15, universities increased their enrolments by 40 per cent whereas enrolments at the public university colleges remained relatively stable over time.

more similar, providing the private sector with enhanced opportunities for educational expansion and market adaptation (Stensaker, 2014). The number of applicants to Norwegian higher education institutions in the last decade rose by 67 per cent from about 612,000 in 2006 to one million in 2016 (NSD-DBH, n.d.). Among universities, the absolute figures more than doubled whereas university colleges saw a more modest rise of 16 per cent. The number of applicants among private institutions rose by 83 per cent, the highest across the sector.

With the unfolding of the Bologna process as an important European context, in 2003–4, a major structural effort, known as the *quality reform*, was enacted.[17] This reform placed a strong focus on the international dimension (new degree structure, the introduction of the ECTS system, a national quality assurance system, etc.), and can be said to continue the strong emphasis put on the relevancy of Norway's tertiary educational system from an international perspective (OECD, 2005: 8). The reform also encompassed a wide variety of changes not directly related to the Bologna process as such, including higher education institutions' governance structures, new funding arrangements, and new forms of student guidance and financial support schemes (OECD, 2005; Vabø and Aamodt, 2005). The internationalization agenda, in tandem with the pressures for improving quality across teaching and research, were seen by the Ministry of Education and Research as vital conditions for securing political support necessary for the realization of the reform. During 2005, a new legal Act for universities and colleges was passed by Parliament, which, inter alia, stipulated a series of new regulations regarding students' admission into higher education. According to the 2005 Act: 'The Ministry may impose restriction of [higher education] admissions when found necessary following a total assessment of educational provision in Norway' (Norwegian Ministry of Education and Research, 2005: 10). Section 3.7 of the Act establishes the role of the Ministry in sector-wide regulations concerning the national coordination of admissions into higher education; the development of a separate admission process for higher degree courses; and the responsibility of the institutions regarding the placement of foreign students (Norwegian Ministry of Education and Research, 2005).

The quality reform allowed for a closer integration between universities and colleges, leading to a further erosion of the binary divide through an identical act for higher education, an accreditation allowing for academic drift, and a system of credit transfer between colleges and universities (Kyvik, 2009). The quality reform also gave higher

---

[17] The reform was initiated in 2001 via a governmental white paper, following-up on the recommendations of the Mjøs Commission (set in 1998). Legislative amendments followed (in 2002) and the reform was first implemented in the academic year 2003/4. It has been widely suggested that, in reality, the quality reform, implemented by the centre-right coalition government led by Kjell Magne Bundevik (2001–5), was an efficiency-enhancing measure.

education institutions new decentralized powers (e.g. as regards entry-regulations) with the Ministry of Education and Research exercising oversight; reserving itself the legal right for intervening (via *numerus clausus*) in case of need. Finally, when it comes to information diffusion and accountability, a new independent agency for quality assurance (NOKUT) was established in 2002, with both, students and employers as key audiences. Data on the number of applicants into higher education suggest that the 2003–4 quality reform did not have a major immediate impact. Figures for 2004–6 show the number of applicants for one student place remained stable at around two (SSB, n.d.). Interestingly, whereas the total number of study places in this period grew by 5 per cent, the absolute number of applicants declined by 200. However, the number of applicants to university-programmes increased substantially when compared to applications into the colleges. One explanation for this tendency is that institutions in urban areas had much higher application rates than those in rural areas. Universities are mostly located in the big cities and benefit from the increasing urbanization of Norwegian society (Michelsen and Aamodt, 2007: 8).

In short, Norway's horizontal story is about increased diversity in the early phases of high participation, followed by contraction and isomorphism in the later phases. This largely accords with the HPS propositions. Hence, Norway's story confirms the premise that expansion does not necessarily result in the diversification of missions. Rather, the search for particular institutional profiles (market niches) and international competitiveness have led higher education institutions to reduce, rather than enhance, diversity between institutions, in relation to both teaching programmes and research endeavours. Depth comes at the expense of breadth, with only a small set of leading old university players capable of realizing both; yet in this 'leading' group, also, the dynamics of concentration can be detected.

Vertical Stratification

The first proposition on vertical stratification (HPS Proposition 11) states that:

> *The expansion of participation towards and beyond the HPS stage is associated with a tendency to bifurcation and stratification (vertical diversification) in the value of higher education, between elite (artisanal) institutions and mass (demand-absorbing) institutions.*

It is also suggested in HPS Proposition 12 that:

> *The tendency to institutional stratification is magnified by features common (though not universal) among HPS including (a) intensified social competition for the most valuable student places; (b) variable tuition charges; and/or (c) intensified competition between institutions.*

In addition, HPS Proposition 13 states that:

In stratified HPS, a middle layer of institutions tends to form, shaped by the combination of upward aspirations (drift) with systemic scarcity of resources and status.

Some but not all of these scenarios are apparent in Norway.

There has been a strengthening of the relative position of the top universities, and a middle layer of higher education institutions can be detected, but overall the tendency to bifurcation is limited. In general, the national commitment to maintaining quality across higher education is a counterweight to competitively-driven tendencies to stratification. There is social competition for places, limited forms of selectivity (principally on the basis of field of study), and competition between higher education institutions for esteem, but no tuition fees are charged and equalising resource policies counterbalance the effects of competition. As noted, and as in common with other Nordic countries such as Finland, full-blown neoliberal stratification has not occurred.

It can be argued that in the evolution of Norway's higher education system, processes of horizontal diversity and vertical stratification have been tightly linked. As the binary divide eroded, both by design (policies emphasized effectiveness, efficiency, and quality) and strategically (institutions and academics wanted higher institutional status), horizontal diversity declined, as suggested in the HPS propositions. Currently, largely as a result of the new mergers, the Norwegian higher education landscape is populated by 'multiversities', with the rise of larger, comprehensive, hybrid universities that provide both research-intensive and vocational training. However, the heritage of the old binary system still has an impact. Many of the new universities have a distinct professional and vocational profile that builds on the key subject areas that dominated in the university colleges, such as nursing, business administration, engineering, and teacher training.

The Ministry has attempted to steer developments towards the maintenance of system diversity, despite policy pressures pushing institutions towards increasing differentiation in the form of institutional profiling. Individual mission and performance-based contracts between the Ministry and the institutions were initiated in 2016. That being said, largely as a result of existing funding structures and 'voluntary-forced' amalgamations, Norway is moving towards a system of regional universities, decreasing regional competition while attempting to boost international competitiveness. Funding-wise, this is resulting in increasing vertical differentiation with respect to resource allocation, empirically observed in the growing gap between 'haves' and 'have nots' in relation to competitive research funding, centers of excellence, and other factors (see also Geschwind and Pinheiro, 2017). Taking EU funding as an example, between 2004 and 2013 the total amount of funds generated by the three flagship universities (Oslo, Bergen, and NTNU) increased fourfold. In 2013 alone, 97 per cent of all EU funds were allocated to the eight existing universities, with the three leading universities commanding 86 per cent of the total (NSD-DBH, n.d.). Similarly, in 2015 the leading three universities generated

74 per cent of all publications across the university sector, with one institution (Oslo) commanding a third of all publications. Some of the younger universities increased their publication outputs at a higher rate than the old universities but their share of the total number of publications remains moderate. Thus the big difference between the old and the new universities is their resource base. For example, nine out of the current twenty-one highly competitive centres of excellence are based at a single institution, the University of Oslo.

It can be speculated that we are currently seeing the establishment of a new higher education system, consisting of three flagships able to compete internationally, a larger group of new regional universities with a strong professional profile and international ambitions, though their resource base will make it difficult to achieve those ambitions, and a smaller group of colleges that either have resisted mergers or ended up outside merger discussions. In the last respect we can indeed see the contours of a 'middle layer' of institutions emerging, as suggested by the HPS propositions.

From a regional perspective, a process that started in the early 1990s aimed at establishing more solid and robust regional institutions is slowly coming to an end. The steady build-up, expansion in, and merger of the regional institutions seems to have reduced social competition for the most valuable study places as more offerings have been established over the decades. Due to the lack of an established status hierarchy among domestic higher education institutions, it has been suggested that, in the Norwegian context, prestigious study programmes are more important than prestigious institutions (Thomsen et al., 2016; see also Chapter 13 on Finland).

As is the case in other countries, the vertical stratification story in Norway has been about the establishment of an elite cadre of research-intensive universities (Oslo, Bergen, and NTNU). However, in the case of Norway distinction among a few research universities has occurred in tandem with the maintenance of relative equality among the remaining institutions and the distance between the leading research universities and all other institutions is comparatively small. The tendency towards extreme bifurcation, then, observed especially in the Anglo systems, has, overall, been resisted. This is partly because of the overriding emphasis on equity as a key feature of the Nordic welfare model, and in part due to the gradual but steady move towards a unitary system centred on comprehensive universities as the dominant form for organizing activities across the sector.

Social Equity

According to the HPS equity propositions:

> *As participation expands in the HPS phase, equity in the form of social inclusion is enhanced.* (HPS Proposition 14)

As elsewhere, this happened in Norway.

More controversially, the propositions state:

> *Because in the HPS phase the growth of participation is associated with enhanced stratification and intensified competition at key transition points, all else being equal (i.e. without compensatory state policy), the expansion of participation is associated with a secular tendency to greater social inequality in educational outcomes and, through that, social outcomes.* (HPS Proposition 15)

The propositions go on to state that:

> *Within a national system, as participation expands in the HPS phase, all else being equal the positional structure of the higher education system increasingly resembles that of society (albeit with the caveat of Proposition 15). The HPS is increasingly implicated in the reproduction of existing patterns of social equality/inequality.* (HPS Proposition 16)

Consistent with this, the final equity proposition (HPS Proposition 17) states that:

> *As the HPS boundary of participation expands it becomes more difficult for the state and/or autonomous educational systems/institutions to secure a redistribution of educational opportunities, and, through that, of social opportunities.*

Much but not all of this holds true in Norway. As noted, Norway has avoided the enhanced inequalities associated with stratification in the United States (Chapter 9) and United Kingdom, partly via consistent government policies of reducing structural (including financial) barriers to entering higher education, promoting mobility across tiers of the domestic system, and supporting others in studying overseas, particularly within fields that are costly (e.g. medicine) and/or for which there is limited domestic supply. However, that does not mean there are no continuing social inequalities in higher education.

SOCIAL INCLUSION

Equity as social inclusion has been advanced in a number of ways. In 1999, the government devised a reform, the Competence Reform, with the objective of easing access into higher education by non-traditional student groups (OECD, 2005: 63).[18] A central aspect of the reform was the implementation of measures for documenting the

---

[18] In the spring of 1998, the government presented a white paper on 'Lifelong Learning' to Parliament (*Storting*), where, among other things, the participation of higher education institutions in continuing education and the retraining of adults were highlighted.

formal, non-formal, and informal qualifications of adults.[19] This assessment, in turn, was to be used as a basis for professional recognition and/or entry into further, formal education at university and/or college. A 2005 OECD report on Norwegian higher education suggests that, in principle, the Competence Reform and the quality reform (see earlier) were mutually supportive. For example, the modularization of study pro- grammes as part of the quality reform was thought to establish stronger linkages between higher education and continuing education by increasing the number of access points into higher education (OECD, 2005: 85).

It is important to highlight that, in the Norwegian national context, discussions around social inequalities in access into higher education are framed around specific notions of 'equity', in the way the latter is conceptualized and/or measured statistically. The traditional focus, as far as education (including higher education) policies are concerned, has been on equality of opportunity or access rather than equality of outcomes (OECD, 2005: 65). By and large, most higher education policies in Norway have been designed around mainstream issues, despite the fact that different student groups may indeed have different educational demands. For example, the competence reform seems to 'have increased access from people who normally would not have qualified for access to higher education. However, this is a policy on equity of access which does not necessarily imply equity of outcome' (OECD, 2005: 65), although recent research has suggested that Norway is among the countries within the OECD where a quite low income effect of higher education can be identified (Busemeyer, 2014). As such, there seems to be a general lack of specific policies and measures ensuring that particular student groups (e.g. adult learners) successfully complete their higher education studies, despite the fact that many higher education institu- tions monitor such developments (OECD, 2005: 65). On the whole, there is some evidence supporting the view that the student group targeted by the competence reform seems to perform relative well, although some institutions report slightly higher failure-rates for the adult learners when compared with the overall student average (OECD, 2005: 65).

Another important policy measure during this period was the adoption in 2003 of a strategic plan geared towards improving learning and participation by language minor- ities across the entire educational sector (day care, schools, higher education).[20] The main aim of the latter policy was to increase the percentage of minority language students, particularly first-generation immigrants, in higher education. In 2003, there

---

[19] In practical terms, the Norwegian higher education legal framework was amended so that applicants who are 25 years of age (or older) and do not meet the general matriculation standard, can be accepted on the basis of an individual assessment of their acquired ('real') competencies or *realkompetanse*.

[20] 'There are great differences between minority language and majority language pupils and students throughout the education system, as regards school achievement, as well as participation and completion rates. These differences are mostly found in stages prior to tertiary education' (OECD, 2005: 64).

were 7,500 students with immigrant background registered at Norwegian universities and colleges, the equivalent of 3.6 per cent of the student population. The majority were first generation immigrants, but the relative proportion of this group (19–24 age cohort) was much lower than for people born in Norway to immigrant parents (i.e. second generation immigrants); 18 per cent and 27 per cent, respectively (SSB, 2003). The corresponding 2003 figure for all 19–24-year-olds in Norway, irrespective of ethnic background, was 29 per cent (Pinheiro, 2005). In this respect, the strategic framework for 2004–9 that was advanced by the Ministry of Education and Research identified higher education recruitment and completion—that is, reduction of drop-out rates—as core aspects (OECD, 2005: 64). In practical terms this meant that the government's focus was to increase *equality of opportunity* in relation to access, as well as *equality of outcome* (see Deer, 2005: 29–30).

There has also been an important gender factor in the expansion of participation. In the fifteen years before 1985 there was a critical shift in the composition of the student population enrolled at Norwegian universities and colleges, with the stagnation of male enrolments and the continue rise of female representation in higher education. Whereas in the beginning of the 1970s females represented 29 per cent of all higher education enrolments, by 1980 this figure had increased to 40 per cent, with parity with males reached by the mid-1980s (SSB, n.d.). By the end of the 1980s, female enrolments in higher education had reached 54 per cent of the total, including 50 per cent at universities and 57 per cent at the colleges (SSB, n.d.). During the 1990s, policies continued to promote the participation of females across the entire higher education system. By the early 2000s, governmental policies insofar gender equity focused on three main objectives: to reduce the gender segregation across study fields; to increase female participation/completion at the graduate levels (Master's and PhD); and, to enlarge the share of female professors (OECD, 2005: 62). As a result, all Norwegian higher education institutions are currently required to develop a strategic plan of action in relation to gender equality.

A major qualitative development has been the end of male dominance of long-term higher education, degrees lasting over four years. In the academic year 2004/5, female postgraduate Master's students surpassed males, with 52 per cent of all degrees (SSB, 2005a). In Doctoral studies, males still dominate, but the gender gap has been shrinking, from 67 to 60 per cent since 1995. Finally, despite the fact that in 2004 close to one-third of all Norwegian students took twice as long to complete their higher education degrees, women, particularly in female-dominated fields like education and nursing, had the largest proportion of students finishing their studies within the normal timeframe (SSB, 2005b).[21]

---

[21] By 2005, 41 per cent of all the males who were first registered in higher education a decade earlier (1995) had not completed their higher education degrees. The respective figure for females was 30 per cent (SSB, 2005b).

All in all, the Norwegian data indicate that, in the last two decades, the gap in higher education participation rates across gender groups has increased. In 1982, 16 per cent of all 19–28-year-old males and 18 per cent of females were enrolled at higher education level. By 2002 the gap had increased: 20 per cent for males and 27 per cent for females (OECD, 2005: 57).

In relation to location, by 2002 differences in participation rates across upper secondary education along the rural/urban divide were almost non-existent. However, there was still socio-economic gap in participation, on the basis of the educational background of parents. In all 80 per cent of upper secondary pupils whose parents had experienced higher education themselves entered higher education, compared to 67 per cent of upper secondary pupils whose family members had only primary schooling (OECD, 2005b: 21). In relation to the geographic pattern of graduates, in 2002, 38 per cent of 30–34-year-olds living in urban areas had obtained some type of tertiary degree (short or long), whereas the corresponding figure for those living in the country side was 22 per cent; a 16 percentile gap (OECD, 2005a: 58).[22] All in all, the policy of expansion of Norwegian higher education into the regions, initiated in the late 1960, is considered by many has having been rather successful (Aamodt, 1995; Bleiklie et al., 2000; OECD, 2005a). Despite the regional decentralization of higher education enrolment and attainment rates, there has been no change in the high levels of (geographic) concentration in traditional research and development (R&D) activities, which are normally located in the surroundings of the big urban areas.

LIMITS TO IMPROVED SOCIAL EQUALITY

When one looks at the outcomes of the policy measures aimed at tackling socio-economic asymmetries in equality of opportunity, in light of the expansion in the number of higher education students and institutions in the last half decade, it is clear that such policies have fallen short of (governmental) expectations. There was a slight decline in social differences in access patterns in the period 1960–75 (Aamodt, 1982 in Aamodt and Kyvik, 2005). In the 1980s and 1990s there was no dramatic change in social inequality of access to universities and colleges (Knudsen et al., 1993 and Hansen, 1999, cited in Aamodt and Kyvik, 2005), but studies on the patterns of access/recruitment into Norwegian higher education suggest a slight reduction in social inequality throughout the 1990s (Hansen, 1999; SSB, 2003).

This positive development mainly took place within the non-university sector and in shorter educational programmes (two–four years) (Hansen, 2010). In universities, where

---

[22] Bearing in mind that urban areas tend to attract highly skilled individuals from the rest of the country, prior and/or after the completion of HE studies.

long-term and prestigious programmes (medicine, law, etc.) are located, in the last two decades the socio-economic profile of new entrants changed little (Hansen, 2010). As elsewhere, Norwegian pupils whose parents have higher education qualifications have a higher rate of participation in higher education than do pupils whose parents have no formal education beyond compulsory schooling. Whereas in 1992 the participation rates in higher education across the two reference groups were 36 per cent and 6 per cent, respectively (OECD, 2005: 57), ten years later in 2002 the figures for the two groups had remained stable in relation to each other. They both rose modestly, to 40 per cent and 8 per cent, respectively.[23]

Figure 14.5 makes a similar point, It illustrates the stratification of entry into tertiary education according to parental educational background. For example, for 1995–2005 students with one or more parents who had undergone a long tertiary education programme, 36 per cent had achieved a long tertiary degree, 32 per cent had achieved a short tertiary qualification while 28 per cent had no qualification. But for students whose parents left school at the early secondary stage, just 4 per cent had a long tertiary degree, while 52 per cent had a short tertiary qualification, and 39 per cent had no qualification. When the 1995–2005 student cohort is compared to the previous 1985–95 cohort, the relative educational achievement of the two groups of families had not significantly changed.

With respect to equity it is fair to say that overall, the expansion of the education in the last two decades combined with other policies such as geographic

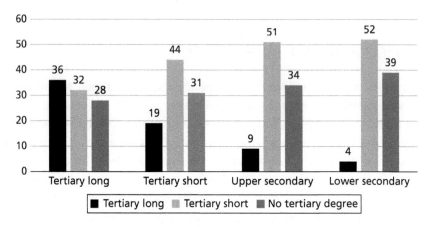

Figure 14.5. Awarded qualification by parents' level of education after ten years of entry, 1995–2005

Source: Authors, adapted from SSB (2007).

[23] While reflecting on the expansion of higher education in Norway, up to the mid-1990s, Aamodt (1995: 78) hypothesized that: 'changes in the class structure and the increasing educational level in the parent population are possible explanations for the long-term trends towards increasing demand for higher education'.

decentralization and a regulated system of scholarship and loans, has contributed to greater social access to educational opportunity. Policy and regulation, especially region-ally distributed access and broad consensus about the need to sustain institutions of good quality below the top research universities, and moderate the esteem given to the older universities, modify any secular tendency of expansion to generate bifurcation of Bourdieu's type. Demand-absorbing higher education institutions are not impoverished. Status and resource differentials remain moderate compared to many other systems and all graduate qualifications carry social value. One outcome is that along with growth Norway has seen a decrease in social inequality in recent decades with respect to recruit-ment to higher education (Thomsen et al., 2016).

CONTINUING CHALLENGES

That being said, challenges remain. In the last decade alone, the 66 per cent rise in higher education applicants has only partially been met, if one looks at enrolment patterns, where there has been a 30 per cent increase. A considerable number of applicants, particularly to universities, have not been able to secure a study seat: inclusion has fallen short of growing social demand. This, in turn, has created an opportunity for the private higher education market to grow; while many Norwegian students have continued to go overseas for optimizing their educational opportunities. While studying abroad was quite normal in a historical perspective, due to a lack of domestic opportunities, this phenomenon has continued to be a key characteristic of Norwegian students even after the expansion of the higher education system. As the domestic system for student funding, which is made available to those that go abroad, is generous in international terms, a high proportion of Norwegian students attend prestigious foreign study pro-grammes in, for example, medicine.

The available data for 2007–16 show that average entry grades across all types of higher education institutions have declined, perhaps influenced by high labour market demand and absorption into work of people who otherwise might have entered higher education. In that respect, and despite the fact that not everyone who applies is accepted, the sector has become less rather than more selective, particularly so across private providers and public specialized university colleges (NSD-DBH, n.d.). Interestingly, with respect to continuing education (an area of potential growth), enrolments declined by about 19 per cent in 2002–12. Other challenges to higher education in Norway include continuous high drop-out rates, especially within some subject areas in the universities, the long time to completion, and a concern about how education and research can assist Norway into the transition (economic diversification) to a knowledge intensive and services-based globally competitive economy, thus reducing its current dependence from natural resources (oil and gas). These are the main reasons why quality issues remain high on the policy agenda.

Conclusions

The Norwegian higher education system underwent continuous expansion from the 1950s onwards, in three distinct peaks or 'access waves'. The initial stage, from the mid-1950s to the mid-1980s, was characterized by a policy effort to expand higher education enrolments across the board, which has been described as a policy logic of 'more is better' (Pinheiro and Antonowicz, 2015). The second stage, initiated in the late 1980s and lasting until the mid-1990s, was characterized by the implementation of policy measures aimed at coping with the unplanned growth in the number of student applicants ('more is problem') (Pinheiro and Antonowicz, 2015). The third and current stage, from the mid-1990s onwards, reveals a policy environment in which preferential focus is given to the under-representation of certain constituencies, such as ethnic minorities and women/men in some fields, and implementation of systemic measures aimed at increasing quality, efficiency, and international inter-operability, particularly in a regional European context. This phase can be referred to as 'more but different' (Pinheiro and Antonowicz, 2015).

If this pattern of development is compared with the general HPS propositions about the growth and equity of higher education systems, we can indeed conclude that the expansion has reduced inequality in Norway in the form of social exclusion, and also that there are currently no signs that the demand for higher education is fading, neither from higher nor from lower economic strata. Governments belonging to different political ideologies have all continued to support the expansion of the higher education system, independently of the swings in the labour market in the decades after World War II, though continuing expansion has been combined with several attempts at the structural re-organization of the sector.

As described, the expansion has over time led to a series of challenges, most recently around institutional fragmentation and system diversity, against the backdrop of fiercer national and international competition and a forecasted decline in the age cohort in the period 2015–25. Governance has evolved as a means to cope with the complexity of the system while ensuring quality, efficiency and accessibility along the lines of the Nordic welfare tradition (Christiansen et al., 2005). Externally, a new set of mediating actors have come to the fore, with responsibility for overseeing teaching quality and accreditation as well as research funding. Internally, higher education institutions have become more centralized and their relationship with society, brokered via the state, has shifted from one based on *trust* towards a transactional approach more based on *results*. Recent developments in the form of mergers have led to a decline of horizontal differentiation and greater stratification among domestic higher education institutions, but it is still early to say what effects, if any, this will have in terms of equity-related issues such as access, choice, and transferability. However,

Hansen (2010) has demonstrated that much of the equality achieved in Norwegian higher education derives from the regional college system. It is interesting to consider what will be the consequences over time for equality, of a shift in institutional status and perhaps in educational offerings. In several comparative studies Busemeyer (2014) shows the importance of various forms of vocational education as a route towards equality. In the long run, the potential transformation of these types of institutions may turn out to have damaging unintended effects.

In the last decade an upswing in applicants combined with limited institutional capacity to host them, and new pressures on the public purse, partly resulting from low oil prices, have brought to the fore a new set of equity concerns. Excellence is no longer a taboo in Norwegian higher education (Geschwind and Pinheiro, 2017). A small sub-set of leading higher education institutions increasingly commands the bulk of research funds. Over time these institutions may attract the best and most motivated students, widening the gap between 'haves' and 'have nots' and putting new pressures on the traditionally egalitarian Norwegian higher education model.

To conclude, Norway follows the general pattern observed elsewhere—with slight local variations—in terms of the general process of expansion, and HPS governance and diversity. Yet it departs significantly from other national systems in terms of stratification and equity. This is to some degree the result of a political culture that prizes equity and state intervention in an attempt to find an adequate balance between social goals (equity of access/participation) and economic imperatives (global competitiveness within research).

REFERENCES

Aamodt, P. O. (1995). Floods, bottlenecks and backwaters: An analysis of expansion in higher education in Norway. *Higher Education* 30, 63–80.

Aamodt, P. O. and Kyvik, S. (2005). Access to higher education in the Nordic countries, in T. Tapper and D. Palfreyman (eds), *Understanding Mass Higher Education: Comparative Perspectives on Access*. London: Routledge.

Aamodt, P., Kyvik, S., and Skoie, H. (1991). Norway: Towards a more indirect model of governance?, in G. Neave and F. van Vught (eds), *Prometheus Bound: The Changing Relationship between Government and Higher Education in Europe*. Oxford: Pergamon Press.

Bleiklie, I., Høstaker, R., and Vabø, A. (eds) (2000). *Policy and Practice in Higher Education: Reforming Norwegian Universities*. London: Jessica Kingsley Publishers.

Busemeyer, M. R. (2014). *Skills and Inequality: Partisan Politics and the Political Economy of Education Reforms in Western Welfare States*. Cambridge: Cambridge University Press.

Christiansen, N. F., Petersen, K., Edling, N., and Haave, P. (2005). *The Nordic Model of Welfare: A Historical Reappraisal*. Copenhagen: Museum Tusculanum Press.

Deer, C. (2005). The politics of access to higher education in France, in T. Tapper and D. Palfreyman (eds), *Understandig Mass Higher Education: Comparative Perspectives on Access*. London: Routledge.

Eide, K. (1995). *OECD og norsk utdanningspolitikk. En studie av internasjonalt samspill*. Oslo: Utredningsinstituttet for forskning og høyere utdanning.

Geschwind, L. and Pinheiro, R. M. (2017). Raising the summit or flattening the agora? The Elitist Turn in Science Policy in Northern Europe. *Journal of Baltic Studies* 48(4), 513–28.

Hansen, M. N. (1999). Utdanningspolitikk og ulikhet. Rekruttering til høyere utdanning 1985–1996. *Tidskrift for Samfunnsforskning* 40, 173–203.

Hansen, M. N. (2010). Utdanningspolitikk og ulikhet. *Tidsskrift for samfunnsforskning* 51(1), 101–33.

Kyvik, S. (2002). The merger of non-university colleges in Norway. *Higher Education* 44, 53–72.

Kyvik, S. (2009). *The Dynamics of Change in Higher Education*. Dordrecht: Springer.

Kyvik, S. and Stensaker, B. (2013). Factors affecting the decision to merge: The case of strategic mergers in Norwegian higher education. *Tertiary Education and Management* 19(4), 323–37.

Lægreid, P. and Christensen, T. (eds) (2013). *Transcending New Public Management: The Transformation of Public Sector Reforms*. London: Ashgate Publishing, Ltd.

Michelsen, S. and Aamodt, P. O. (eds) (2007). *Evaluering av Kvalitetsreformen. Sluttrapport*. Oslo: Norges forskingsråd.

Norwegian Ministry of Education and Research (2005). Act relating to universities and university colleges (in English). Oslo: Norwegian Ministry of Education and Research.

NSD-DBH (n.d.). Database for higher education statistics. Norwegian Social Science Data Services. http://dbh.nsd.uib.no/

NOU (2008). Sett under ett: Ny struktur i høyere utdanning'. *Norges Offtenlige Utredninger*. Oslo: Statens forvaltningstjeneste.

OECD (Organisation for Economic Co-operation and Development) (1971). *Development of Higher Education: 1950–1967. Analytical Report*. Paris: OECD.

OECD (Organisation for Economic Co-operation and Development) (2004). *Equity in Education: Thematic Review. Norway*. Paris: OECD.

OECD (Organisation for Economic Co-operation and Development) (2005). *OECD Thematic Review of Tertiary Education: Country Background Report for Norway*. The Norwegian Ministry of Education and Research. Paris: OECD.

Pinheiro, R. (2005). *The Impacts of the Higher Education Experience in the Quality of Life: A Study Focusing on Individuals with an Ethnic Minority Background*. Oslo: University of Oslo.

Pinheiro, R. and Antonowicz, D. (2015). Opening the gates or coping with the flow? Governing access to higher education in Northern and Central Europe. *Higher Education* 70(3), 299–313.

Pinheiro, R., Charles, D., and Jones, G. (2016). Equity, institutional diversity and regional development: A cross-country comparison. *Higher Education* 72(3), 307–22.

Pinheiro, R., Geschwind, L., and Aarrevaara, T. (eds) (2016). *Mergers in Higher Education: The experiences from Northern Europe*. Dordrecht: Springer.

Schmidtlein, F. and Berdahl, R. (2005). Autonomy and accountability: Who controls academe? In P. Altbach, R. Berdahl, and P. Gumport (eds), *American Higher Education in the Twenty-first Century: Social, Political, and Economic Challenges*. Baltimore: Johns Hopkins University Press, pp. 71–90.

SSB (2001). Students at universities and colleges, by sex. 1 October' (table 190). *Statistical Yearbook of Norway*. Oslo: Statistics Norway.

SSB (2003). *Education Statistics: Pupils and Students. Immigrants Take Tertiary Education*. Oslo: Statistics Norway.

SSB (2005a). *Male Postgraduates Outnumbered by Females in 2004/05*. Oslo: Statistics Norway.

SSB (2005b). *Women closing education gap on men*. Oslo: Statistics Norway.

SSB (2007). *New Entrants to Tertiary Education in 1985 and 1995, by Parents' Level of Education and Awarded Qualification after 10 Years*. Oslo: Statistics Norway.

SSB (n.d.). Statistics Norway. http://ssb.no/en/ (in English).

Statistical Yearbook of Norway (1998). Oslo: Statistics Norway.

Statistical Yearbook of Norway (2000). Oslo: Statistics Norway.

Statistical Yearbook of Norway (2006). Oslo: Statistics Norway.

Stensaker, B. (1995). *Kunsten å vedlikeholde et universitet—Et opprop for det akademiske ansvar*. Spartacus pamfletter—politikk, polemikk og propaganda. Oslo: Spartacus/Tiden Forlag.

Stensaker, B. (2014). Troublesome institutional autonomy: Governance and the distribution of authority of Norwegian universities, in M. Shattock (ed.), *International Trends in University Governance: Autonomy, Self-government and the Distribution of Authority*. New York: Routledge, pp. 34–48.

Thomsen, J. P., Bertilsson, E., Dalberg, T., Hedman, J., and Helland, H. (2016). Higher education participation in the Nordic countries 1985–2010—A comparative perspective. *Eur Sociol Rev*. doi: 10.1093/esr/jcw051

UNESCO (Nations Educational, Scientific, and Cultural Organisation) (1977). *Access to Higher Education in Norway: A Study Prepared for the European Centre for Higher Education*. Paris: UNESCO.

Vabø, A. and Aamodt, P. O. (2005). Kvalitetsreformen og universitetene som masseutdanning-sinstitusjon. *NIFU skriftserie* nr 2/2005. Oslo: Norwegian Institute for Studies in Innovation, Research and Education.

World Bank (1999). *Knowledge for Development: World Development Report 1998/99*. New York: Oxford University Press.

World Bank (2017). Data and statistics. http://data.worldbank.org

15 Towards Universal Access Amid Demographic Decline: High Participation Higher Education in Japan

Akiyoshi Yonezawa and Futao Huang

Introduction

Japan is the fourth largest economy in the world after the United States of America (USA), China, and India in purchasing power parity (PPP) terms and third largest in nominal gross domestic product (GDP) (World Bank, 2017). In 2015 Japan's GDP in PPP terms was US$5,175.3 billion, 26 per cent the level of China and 29 per cent that of the USA. Japan's GDP per capita was US$41,470 in 2015, placing the nation between the United Kingdom (UK) and France (World Bank, 2017). Its 127 million inhabitants live in a relatively narrow area, slightly smaller than California, of 399,915 square kilometres. Japan's population has become more concentrated and urbanized because 73 per cent of the land is mountainous and sparsely peopled.

Historically, Japan evolved on the periphery of the tributary system of Chinese dynasties and was subject to Chinese cultural influence but maintained its political independence. The country had limited interactions with Western civilization and was largely closed to outsiders in the Edo (Tokugawa) period (1603–1868 CE). However, under the Meiji regime from 1868, Japan implemented a remarkable accelerated modernization by absorbing selected science, technology, industrial methods, and state organization from Europe and North America, joined to its own modes of organization and innovation. By the early twentieth century Japan had achieved primacy in East Asia, and military and industrial equivalence with leading European powers; and again after World War II it built a durable export economy and advanced modern society with remarkable speed. Japan is a leader at global level in a diverse range of fields including electronics, computing, communications, automobiles, transport systems, urban architecture, interior design, and branches of the arts, not to mention production systems in manufacturing and civic administration.

Japanese society is ethnically homogenous and culturally integrated. Shared identity is important and constitutes a form of equity. Within the nation, Japan used to be regarded (and regarded itself) as an egalitarian country. However, recent data indicate that Japan is no longer so equal in terms of income. The Gini coefficient after taxes and transfers was 0.33 in 2012. In 2014 market-generated income inequality was the highest since the 1980s. Along with the growth of inequality there has been decline in Japan's income per head compared to the Organisation for Economic Co-operation and Development (OECD) average, and the 2012 income poverty ratio (16.1 per cent of the population) was relatively high within the OECD. These developments can be partly attributed to neoliberal policies but have been mostly affected by the aging of the population.

HIGHER EDUCATION IN JAPAN

Japan's successive economic miracles were powered by the conjunction between high technology and well-trained human resources. In a society influenced by Confucian practices, families in Japan have long been committed to self-cultivation via education and perform strongly in the OECD's Programme of International Student Assessment (PISA) comparison of 15-year-olds. Japan has also built deep research cultures within its leading universities and is a major producer of high citation research, especially in the Physical Sciences. In all, twenty-four Japanese scientists have been awarded Nobel Prizes.

By the mid-1970s, Japan had realized the first mass higher education system in East Asia, relying heavily on demand-absorbing private institutions to sustain expansion. After that the government moved slowly into the higher education participation era, but from the mid-1990s, at time of accelerating growth in many countries, the participation ratio rose. Now the demographic decrease in the youth population and widening participation in higher education are transforming Japanese higher education into a universal access system (Altbach and Umakoshi, 2004). Japan is also an ageing society struggling to design a sustainable future amid a declining population and economy, and the pressures of globalization. Reworking the functional diversification among higher education institutions is one possible policy solution to the profound challenges facing Japan.

Japan has a fairly simple higher education system (Table 15.1) that mostly follows the US model, an outcome of the American occupation after World War II. Universities offer four-year undergraduate programmes (six years in medical, dentistry, veterinary, and pharmacy), two-year Master's, three-year Doctoral and postgraduate professional programmes. Junior colleges provide two-year associate degrees. Colleges of technology offer three-year upper secondary education plus two-year short cycle higher education leading to associate degrees. The professional training colleges, often classified as higher education, provide two- or three-year vocational and professional training diploma programmes.

Table 15.1. Number of higher and post-secondary institutions and students, 2016

Type of institution	Number of institutions			Number of students		
	National	Local public	Private	National	Local public	Private
University	86	91	600	610,401	150,513	2,112,710
Junior college	0	17	324	0	6,750	121,710
College of technology	51	3	3	51,623	3,740	2,295
Professional training colleges	9	186	2,622	2,622	25,251	563.490

Source: Authors adapting data from School Basic Survey (MEXT) (2016).

This chapter will describe the historical pathway towards high participation in higher education in Japan and reflect on the changes in governance, functional differentiation, diversification between institutions in the form of vertical stratification, and the challenges for social equality and equity, including the gender gap that is the most visible inequality issue. These issues are considered in the light of the propositions about high participation systems (HPS) of higher education that appear in Part I of this book.

From Mass System to High Participation

Japan realized basic education for all at an early stage. From its inception the Meiji Government set out to enrol all children in basic education, establishing primary schools all over the country in 1872. In 1907, compulsory education was expanded from four to six years; and after World War II it reached nine years, including three years of junior secondary education. By the mid-1970s, the gross enrolment rate in senior secondary schooling exceeded 90 per cent. Near universal enrolment in senior secondary education, which was not legally compulsory, was partly achieved by a social movement involving a wide variety of stakeholders (Institute for International Cooperation, 2004). This was the platform on which the early and rapid massification of higher education was built.

Figure 15.1 illustrates longitudinal trends in the participation ratio for 18-year-olds in Japan. In evolving from massification to post-massification and, now, to near universal access, the Japanese higher education system has experienced three different patterns of development. The shift from mass to universal participation did not occur as a steady and continuous expansion. Dramatic expansion up to the mid-1970s was followed by a period of slowing growth and decline between the mid-1970s and the early 1990s, which in turn gave way to a new period of continuing rise in participation, though the ratio plateaued in the half decade after 2010. Affected by various external factors, Japan's participation trajectory has not completely complied with Trow (1973; Huang, 2012b). At the same time, there has been continuous interplay between two system design principles that together shape higher education provision: on the one hand,

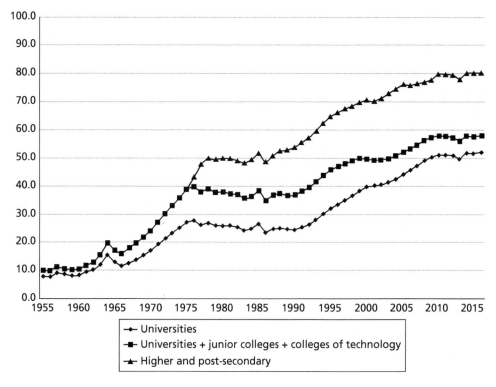

Figure 15.1. Participation ratio of 18-year-olds in Japan, 1955–2015

Source: Authors adapting data from *School Basic Survey* (MEXT) (2016).

differentiation; on the other hand, equivalence, equal treatment among universities and other institutions with differing characteristics (Yonezawa and Inenaga, 2017). In some moments differentiation is joined to equality of treatment, in other moments it is not. In Japan as other HPS, system relations are shaped by a distinctive combination of horizontal diversity and vertical stratification.

POST-WAR EXPANSION

Prior to World War II, the higher education system was influenced by European, especially German, models. There was a binary structure. Nine 'imperial universities' were established by the national government, comprehensive universities with high-level research that were not dissimilar to the American land grant institutions. The University of Tokyo, created in 1877, became the first imperial university. It integrated the school of engineering at a very early stage. (This school is now the largest school of the university.) Polytechnics were also established, for example the Tokyo Institute of Technology.

In addition to institutions established and operated directly by national government, prefectures and cities operated local public universities and other institutions to meet local demand additional to that catered for by the national sector. Private higher education institutions had origins separate from government—in fact Keio Gijuku, the ancestor of today's Keio University, opened in 1858 before the period of accelerated modernization began. Private institutions helped to absorb the growing demand for higher education triggered by economic and social development. Some formed comprehensive universities. After 1919 these received official authorization from the national government.

In the post-World War II reform, as noted, Japanese higher education system was transformed into a system compatible with American higher education. It also absorbed features of the pre-war system. The binary system was abolished and the pre-war polytechnics were upgraded and integrated into the new universities and junior colleges. Higher schools (gymnasiums) were also mostly integrated into the new universities as newly introduced general education divisions. At the same time, the national university system was remodelled in the form of flagship universities in the forty-seven Japanese prefectures. The imperial university system was included in the new university system and its institutions were treated as having equal status with others. Here the new national university system resembled the US state university system, though operation and budgets remained under the control of the national government. Local public and private universities and other institutions, which were still operated and funded by prefectural and city governments, were also included in the new system, with the role of national government largely confined to authorization of universities, schools, and programmes. Private universities were operated by non-profit school corporations with governing boards. Under this governance structure it was possible for the governing board to be chaired by the university president.

The national government used student enrolment quotas as a central instrument of control and quality assurance across all higher education institutions. In national universities and junior colleges it directly controlled funding for education and research and specified student numbers accordingly. The government also set enrolment quotas for local public and private universities, even though until the 1970s, when public financial support for private sector operating costs was introduced, it had no direct financial reason to exert control. Within this structure the government was free to determine where growth would occur and in the early decades had a financial incentive to channel that growth through the private sector.

In the 1960s and early 1970s there were strong pressures for expansion due to demographic demand from the baby boom generation born just after the World War II and growing industrial demand for high skilled workers in science and technology in Japan's globally competitive manufacturing sector. The national government was reluctant to expand the national higher education sector, preferring to maintain the quality of education. Instead it sanctioned new universities and junior colleges and increased enrolment quotas (Yonezawa, 2013), and positioned the private sector for growth. By the beginning of the 1970s, a mass higher education system had been achieved, supported by universal graduation from senior secondary education. In contrast to the USA and Europe, where most students were in state universities and colleges, the Japanese government expanded the system at limited public cost by using the private sector to absorb most of the demand. Some private universities diversified their fields of study so they became comprehensive universities. Many private universities, including prestigious ones, enrolled a larger number of students than was authorized. There was no effective sanction against excessive enrolment. Private institutions had legally assured academic autonomy and to close them was a measure of last resort. Hence while over enrolment posed problems for quality the national government had no means of preventing it.

The period of rapid growth was also associated with material and political tensions. Universities needed to upgrade their buildings and facilities, and inflation increased salary costs. Average private costs rose, as expansion was primarily located in the private sector. Tuition increases and inadequate provision generated student resistance which spilled over into far-reaching demands for democratic reforms. In the face of these problems the government issued a report proposing a system design based on functional differentiation, from research universities to vocationally oriented education and training. This was the first stage of national higher education planning but the classification scheme was not fully implemented. Instead policy focused on the evident problems of finance and quality in the private sector, which became more closely regulated. Later, in 1976, the government established a new sector, the professional training colleges, to absorb some demand for post-secondary education at sub-degree level (for more on the regulated private sector and professional training colleges see 'Governance'). In this manner, the government fostered a horizontal range of institutions with differing missions, to serve massification, but the mission distinctions also had implications for vertical stratification.

FROM QUANTITY TO QUALITY

During the second half of the 1980s there was a further increase in enrolment due to growing demand created by the children of the post-war baby boom generation, but in 1992 the 18-year-old population began to decline, mainly because of the low birth rate. The government's response was modest. First, it decreased undergraduate enrolment capacity in the national universities, shifting some places to the postgraduate level. Second, the junior colleges, most of which were short-term colleges for women, saw their enrolments frozen or reduced, or were transformed into four-year universities and colleges of co-education. The number of four-year Bachelor's students increased overall.

In the 1990s the 18-year-old population was expected to decrease from 2.05 million in 1992 to 1.51 million in 2000. After 1993 the government ceased to provide a target for enrolment, deciding instead to let the market decide (Amano, 1997). This led to a further increase in the gross enrolment ratio (GER). Japan exceeded 50 per cent in 2002 and exceeded 60 per cent in 2012. The government also switched the focus of regulation from quantity management to the quality of education programmes and to enhancing students' engagement in learning. Because of high graduation rates some students were relatively inactive (Kaneko, 2008). The mode of managing quality shifted from approval in advance by government, to encouraging self-monitoring and self-evaluation by institutions, to obligatory evaluation of all institutions by a government accredited third-party organization (Huang, 2006). From 2004 onwards all universities, junior colleges, and colleges of technology were regularly accredited every seven years and professional graduate education every five years (Yonezawa, 2002). The government and the Central Council for Education (CCE) also began to require faculty development, including training programmes to improve faculty teaching. There was also a growing emphasis on programmes to assist students under-prepared for university or college, and programmes to assist students with career design and job searching. However, there was little system-wide evidence as to the effects of these initiatives to lift quality (Huang, 2006).

In the last fifteen years the low birth rate and aging population have become associated with an economic disadvantage called 'demographic onus', in which the decrease in the proportion of the population that is working hampers national economic activity overall (Ogawa et al., 2005). To compound this problem, general governmental debt in Japan is the highest among the OECD member countries. It was estimated at 232.5 per cent of GDP in 2015 (OECD, 2015). In the outcome government spending on higher education has been very constrained, especially in the national universities, including the leading ones. Government support for the operational budgets of national universities declined since their incorporation in 2004, from 124,150 million JPY (Japanese yen) in 2004 to 109,450 million JPY in 2015. This is an annual reduction of about 1 per cent (Huang, 2018).

GENERAL HPS PROPOSITIONS CONCERNING GROWTH

The first general proposition in this project (HPS Proposition 1) states:

As HPS spread to an increasing number of countries, equity in world society is enhanced.

Japan as a country case, and the Asia Pacific as a regional case, both endorse this proposition.

After massification Japan became recognized as a model combination of rapid economic development and educational achievement. The United Nations Educational and Cultural Organisation (UNESCO) GER at tertiary level was 24.6 per cent in 1975. This placed Japan among the world leaders, after the USA (51.0 per cent), Canada (47.9 per cent in 1976), and Russia (43.6 per cent) but ahead of New Zealand (24.4 per cent), Italy (24.0 per cent), Netherlands (23.9 per cent), France (23.5 per cent), and Australia (23.2 per cent) (UNESCO, 2017). The 1990s-era shift towards a more deregulated market in higher education led to a further increase in the GER. Japan exceeded 50 per cent in 2002 and exceeded 60 per cent in 2012. Japan is no longer quite as strong as it was in comparative terms in the mid-1970s. With a GER of 63.4 per cent in 2014, in the Asia-Pacific it was behind South Korea (94.2 per cent), Australia (90.3 per cent), and New Zealand (80.9 per cent). However, Japan's GER was similar to Hong Kong (68.9 per cent) and Mongolia (64.3 per cent), and ahead of rising GERs in Thailand (52.5 per cent), China (39.4 per cent), the Philippines (37.8 per cent), Indonesia (31.0 per cent), Viet Nam (30.5 per cent), and Malaysia (27.6 per cent). The growth of participation in Japan and other Asia Pacific nations indicates that high participation has spread and become more equalized between countries.

The second general proposition (HPS Proposition 2) states:

In HPS there is no intrinsic limit to the spread of family aspirations for participation in higher education until universality is reached; and no intrinsic limit to the level of social position to which families/students may aspire.

In general terms, this also applies to the Japanese case.

Like the USA, Japan does not have a national examination system in the end of secondary education, such as the *Baccalauréat* in France or the *Abitur* in Germany. In theory all graduates of secondary education, both in academic and vocational tracks, are eligible to apply for universities and other higher and post-secondary education institutions (Yonezawa and Akiyama, 2015). Because the private rate of return to higher education has continued to exceed that for secondary education in Japan, and it is profitable for secondary school graduates to proceed to higher education, growth in participation has been likewise continuous, from elite to mass to high participation levels.

The UNESCO data may be underestimated because professional training colleges, two-year vocationally oriented post-secondary education, are not included in the GER. According to the Ministry of Education, Culture, Sports, Science and Technology (MEXT, the department of education) School Basic Survey in 2016, 54.8 per cent of 18-year-old youth enrolled in universities, junior colleges, and colleges of technology directly after secondary education. However, if professional training colleges are included, 71.1 per cent of 18-year-olds enrolled in some kind of higher or post-secondary education. Japan has a tradition of career promotion within internal labour markets.

Employers prefer to recruit fresh young graduates. The proportion of adult students at the undergraduate level is very limited. However, if newly enrolled students older than 18 years old (most are those who spent one or two more years for preparing for the university entrance examinations after graduating from secondary schools) are included, the proportion entering universities, junior colleges, and colleges of technology rises to 56.8 per cent and the total proportion entering all forms of post-secondary education, including professional training colleges, rises to 79.1 per cent. Hence on the fullest definition of participation in Japan the level has now risen to four persons in every five.

According to statistics from the Ministry of Health, Labour and Welfare, the proportion of all workers engaged in the agricultural and forestry sector decreased from 48.5 per cent in 1950 to 19.3 per cent in 1970, and then to 9.3 per cent in 1985.[1] The third general proposition (HPS Proposition 3) states:

> *Once transition from a primarily agricultural economy is achieved, the long-term growth of HPS is independent of political economic factors such as economic growth and patterns of labour market demand; patterns of public and private funding of higher education; the roles of public and private institutions; and system organization and modes of governance.*

This proposition can be applied basically to the Japanese case as well. However, changes in policies and socio-economic environment have accelerated or slowed down the growth of higher education, and participation patterns have often been influenced in a quite different manner among the various socio-economic groups. As noted, these environmental factors include the large role of private institutions, and substantial private financial contributions in the form of student tuition (Geiger, 1986), greater than in most countries that were early in establishing mass higher education. In addition, as noted the pace of expansion has been closely regulated by Japan's government, in part because the government is concerned to protect established relations between education and the labour markets in the highly embedded Japanese social context (Yano, 1997; Kaneko, 2014).

Governance

From the modernization process in the second half of the nineteenth century onwards, the challenge of governance in Japanese higher education has been to both meet the expanding demand for higher learning, and enhance its quality—at some times one

---

[1]   http://www.mhlw.go.jp/wp/hakusyo/roudou/08/dl/10.pdf

objective has been emphasized, and at other times both together. Governance has become more complex as the system has grown. The first proposition in relation to governance (HPS Proposition 4) is:

HPS are governed by multi-level control, coordination, and accountability mechanisms.

In Japan multi-level governance has worked mainly through differentiated management of the three higher education sectors—national, local public, and private—and has often developed through trial and error. The second proposition on governance (HPS Proposition 5) states:

HPS governance tends to involve the management of horizontal differentiation.

This is illustrated in Japan by the development of national higher education planning, and the use of multiple sectors of higher education to manage supply and demand while maintaining control over the quality of provision. More recently, the government has attempted to remake the map of functional diversity.

At the beginning of the 1970s the national government moved to address private sector quality by introducing public subsidies and regulating student numbers. This also gave the government a tool of control, through the sanction of reduced subsidies, and the scope to manage sector size and proportion. In the first higher education plan (1976–80) student enrolment at all universities and junior colleges and also the colleges of technology became strictly controlled, in the private sector as well as the public sector.

In addition, as noted, in 1976 the government launched the professional training college system. These were non-university post-secondary education institutions formally separated from higher education, including junior colleges and colleges of technology. MEXT set the professional training colleges not under the higher education bureau, but under the bureau of lifelong learning. The labour markets often treated graduates of two-year programmes in professional training colleges almost as equal as the graduates of two-year junior colleges. The training provided in professional training colleges was linked with specific professions, jobs, and qualifications. However, most professional training colleges were private and most of their classes were provided by part time instructors. Professional training colleges were not designed to meet the quality standards required of higher education institutions. Here again a horizontal distinction of mission was given a vertical edge.

In the last fifteen years the government has been especially active in promoting the differentiation and diversification of institutional forms and professional roles among the different sectors and types of higher education institutions, with both horizontal and vertical implications. It promulgated a succession of reports intended to shape the future of higher education, including *The Future of Higher Education in Japan* (2005), *The Basic Plan for Education Promotion* (2008), and *On Constructing Undergraduate Education* (2008). These reports suggested that higher education institutions should choose from one or some of the following functions in order to define their distinctive mission (Huang, 2014):

- A centre for research and education at an international level;
- The production of highly specialized professionals;
- The production of graduates with wide vocational knowledge and skills;
- A comprehensive liberal or general education;
- Education and research focused in specific fields (art, physical education, etc.);
- A centre for providing regional lifelong learning opportunities;
- Making specific contributions to society (regional contribution, academic-industry collaboration, and international exchange, etc.).

From the end of 2012 onwards, under the cabinet led by Shinzo Abe, the government opened a more detailed discussion about comprehensive reform. This included the creation of three vertical layers of national university (see under stratification). At the same time the government also created a new category of 'professional universities' to provide professional and vocational programmes. Some existing professional training colleges providing post-secondary-level vocational education were candidates for upgrades into this new type. It was also hoped that some existing universities would transform into professional universities, establishing a stronger binary structure, though the incentives for existing institutions to take this path were not made clear.

CORPORATIZATION

The third proposition on governance (HPS Proposition 6) states:

> *HPS complex multi-level accountability and coordination, coupled with system differ-entiation, result in higher education institutions adopting increasingly corporate forms and robust internal governance and management capacities.*

This partially fits the Japanese case, albeit in a complex manner.

The evolution of the private universities as the sector with the majority of institutions and students is one development of 'corporate forms and robust internal governance and management capacities'. In addition, from the 1980s on, ideas about governance drawn from neoliberalism and the new public management gained principal policy influence. National and local public higher education was transformed by the incorporation reform of 2004, and since then public higher education institutions have gradually built their capabilities in internal governance, finance, and personnel management. However, the incorporation of the public sector was introduced in conjunction with decline in the youth population, rather than being used to manage a growth process. At the same time, private universities achieved greater management autonomy, while being steered from the distance by the national government in neoliberal corporate fashion through quality assurance mechanisms.

Horizontal Diversity

The first proposition on horizontal diversity (HPS Proposition 7) states:

> *In the HPS era, regardless of the political economy and culture of systems, an increasing proportion of higher education becomes centred on comprehensive multi-discipline and multi-function research universities, or 'multiversities'. The multiversity is increasingly dominant as the paradigmatic form of higher education.*

In case of Japan, this proposition fits in general. The tendency was especially evident in the period of growth of private universities in the 1960s. Amid the then laissez-faire market conditions, private universities were relatively free to develop as 'multiversities' by absorbing growing demand. The formation of new comprehensive national universities in the forty-seven prefectures was another variation of this proposition. After the end of 1980s, the upgrade of junior colleges changed the pattern, so that the majority of designated 'universities' were very small-scale institutions. Moving in the reverse direction, amid demographic decline, are mergers among national, local public, and private universities, though the speed of these amalgamations is relatively slow. Also moving in the reverse direction are the effects of demographic decline on the non-multiversity sectors. In recent years, more than half of all four-year private universities have fallen short of official enrolment capacity and some of these universities have closed. Non-university professional training colleges have also been disadvantaged by the more intense competition for the smaller number of 18-year-olds leaving school.

The second proposition on diversity (HPS Proposition 8) states:

> *Regardless of the political economy and culture of the HPS, when participation expands there is no necessary increase in the overall diversity of institutional form and mission; and this has probably declined, except in relation to online provision.*

Likewise, this statement applies to the period of system growth prior to the mid-1970s. After that, as discussed, the government intentionally diversified institutional forms and mission. This makes it difficult to assess whether the secular tendency referred to in the proposition applies in Japan—it is unclear whether higher education institutions have become diversified voluntarily, or reluctantly under policy pressure.

HPS Proposition 9, the third proposition on horizontal diversity, states:

> *As participation expands the internal diversity of multiversities tends to increase. This affects some or all of the range of missions, business activities, institutional forms and*

internal structures, the discipline mix, research activities, levels of study and range of credentials, the heterogeneity of the student body, links to stakeholders, cross-border relations, and forms of academic and non-academic labour.

This proposition applies to Japanese 'multiversities' in general, and has become associated with increasing emphasis in both policy and management on the management of internal diversity, devolution, and shared governance.

The fourth proposition on horizontal diversity (HPS Proposition 10) states:

All else being equal, the combination of expanding participation and enhanced competition in neoliberal quasi-markets is associated with specific effects in relation to diversity, including (1) increased vertical differentiation of higher education institutions (stratification); (2) reduced horizontal differentiation (diversification); (3) convergence of missions through isomorphistic imitation; and (4) growth in the role of private higher education institutions, especially for-profit institutions.

All of the phenomena mentioned in this proposition apply in the Japanese case, especially the evolution of a highly hierarchical system, and a large private sector. In part, the government has pushed for functional differentiation of mission to counter the consistent tendency among higher education institutions towards mission convergence, in which isomorphistic imitation is driven by the desire to rise up the hierarchical ladder in the higher education system. As in other countries, only state intervention can counter the tendency of competition to drive stratification. However, in Japan some policy interventions and systems have also had stratifying effects.

Vertical Stratification

From the beginning of the modern higher education system the national government used budgetary concentration to maintain a limited number of elite research universities, a hierarchy that was generally accepted by faculty networks and by institutions as a whole. There was a parallel hierarchy among private universities. Some developed as prestigious and selective, like the multiversities Waseda and Keio. Most were demand-absorbing institutions. Government enrolment planning strengthened the selectivity of the elite private universities, lifting their capacity to compete with the public sector. However, the imperial universities were always dominant in funded research (as has continued up to the present).

The first proposition under stratification (HPS Proposition 11) states:

The expansion of participation towards and beyond the HPS stage is associated with a tendency to bifurcation and stratification (vertical diversification) in the value of higher education, between elite (artisanal) institutions and mass (demand-absorbing) institutions.

This proposition applies especially well in Japan. For example, the process of massification in the 1960s and 1970s was strongly linked to the tendency to bifurcation. The rapid expansion of mass private higher education widened the gap between the older elite-oriented university education understood by faculty, and the more democratic notion of mass education for career improvement, often in less prestigious institutions. Since then government policies and funding have maintained the position of the elite public research universities. If bifurcation between elite and demand-absorbing higher education institutions arises naturally in system evolution, it has also been deliberately enhanced by government policy and regulation in Japan.

First, under the neoliberal policies that began in the 1980s, the government increased the use of project-based funding, which benefitted the top universities that were best equipped to win resources in open competition. Second, the 1990s-era policy focus on the knowledge economy government drove public investment in science and technology, which benefitted the leading research universities. Third, at the beginning of the 2000s the government adopted a budgetary approach termed 'selection and concentration'. Through this process, the top national universities managed to maintain or increase their institutional income. Although annual budgets for basic operations did not increase—in fact they may have decreased—the top universities were the most successful in acquiring public and private research grants, joint project with industry, and project funds for the capacity development of graduate schools and key research units. The budgetary shift from operational funding to project funding started in 1980s, and was enhanced after the incorporation of national universities in 2004, further stratifying the national system. Fourth, an explicit focus on globalization and on enhancing the global competitiveness of the top universities through global programme funding has again lifted their relative position within the nation (though with no discernible improvement in their comparative global performance).

In Japan government believes that higher education should enhance the international openness and capabilities of Japanese graduates and industry. In 2008 the government established as a goal the recruitment 300,000 international students by 2020; and in 2013 it proposed to double the number of Japanese students studying abroad to reach 120,000 by 2020. However, this expected role in internationalization is not uniform across all institutions. While less prestigious higher education institutions focus on helping their students to acquire the generic skills needed for survival in the aging Japanese society, it is expected the top universities will lead the internationalization of both teaching and research. Hence national responses to globalization contribute further to bifurcation and stratification.

The reforms in 2004 and after, which had both horizontal and vertical implications, formalized stratification within the national university sector while linking this explicitly to global activity and competitiveness. In 2014 the government began a ten-year 'Top Global University Project', prioritizing thirteen Japanese universities that it wanted to see ranked in the world top 100, and selecting another twenty-four universities expected to further the internationalization of Japanese society (Yonezawa and Shimmi, 2015). The government also created three categories of national universities for additional funding purposes, to codify functional diversification of the eighty-six-strong national university sector. The functional categories, with both horizontal and vertical implications, were: (1) national universities competitive with top world universities in all areas and disciplines; (2) national universities serving national and international communities and competitive in education and research in specific fields; and (3) universities that mainly serve local communities in specific fields. In 2017 the government added a super-elite category of 'designated national universities' that were expected to be globally competitive, including in this group only the universities of Tokyo, Kyoto, and Tohoku.

The second proposition on vertical stratification (HPS Proposition 12) states:

> *The tendency to institutional stratification is magnified by features common (though not universal) among HPS including (a) intensified social competition for the most valuable student places; (b) variable tuition charges; and/or (c) intensified competition between institutions.*

As suggested in relation to both competition between institutions, and the growing selectivity, this proposition also mostly applies to the Japanese case. What is different in Japan compared to, say, the USA, is that in Japan the leading and most selective national universities have a relatively low level of standardized tuition. Demand-absorbing institutions often charge higher fees than selective universities. Even in the private sector, Waseda and Keio University maintain relatively low tuition to compete with the prestigious national universities for high scoring students. Student selectivity, not tuition price, is the primary element in stratifying participation. Because the graduation rate is very high even among mass universities, selectivity at the point of admission to the first degree is an important signalling device. Employers tend to assess the value of university graduates by the degree of selectivity of the universities that the graduates attended.

The third proposition on stratification (HPS Proposition 13) states:

> *In stratified HPS, a middle layer of institutions tends to form, shaped by the combination of upward aspirations (drift) with systemic scarcity of resources and status.*

This proposition fits Japan very well. National universities below the level of the top institutions are in the middle category. Many have strong aspirations for upward positioning, the source of not only status but also resources. In an over-supplied private sector, institutions strive for middle status in order to survive.

Equity

Regardless of fluctuations in the government's management of vertical and horizontal differentiation, the idea of meritocracy—equal access to higher education on the basis of talent and ability—has always been important in Japan (Kariya and Dore, 2006). Article 26 of the Constitution decrees that all people shall have the right to receive an equal education corresponding to their ability; and this applies also in the principle of equal access to prestigious universities regardless of the student's socio-economic background.

Throughout East Asia academic credentials are seen as tools for climbing the career ladder. This is rooted in China's long history of utilizing the national examination system to select and recruit senior government officials, which also influenced Korea and Japan. After the Meiji Restoration in 1868 Japan developed a modern higher education system that in theory was open to all social classes. After the development of a modern industrial sector, senior government service, with candidates selected on the basis of success in education and examinations, strengthened the powerful elite forming function of the leading universities. In Japan being admitted to universities, especially prestigious ones, was seen as a crucial indicator of career success and provided access to elite social networks (Kinmonth, 1981). Open and meritocratic education was cemented into place in society by elite reproduction.

The first proposition in relation to equity (HPS Proposition 14) states:

As participation expands in the HPS phase, equity in the form of social inclusion is enhanced.

If social inclusion means the access of all social groups to opportunities to enter higher education then the experience of Japan basically supports the proposition. As noted, nearly all students complete senior secondary education, and its graduates have an automatic right to apply upwards. There are several devices for enhancing the enrolment of disadvantaged socio-economic groups such as student loans, tuition exemptions at public universities, and evening programmes. On the supply side, the principle of access has been sustained by de facto open entry into the less prestigious parts of the private higher education sector.

In the 1990s the most significant change in the student body was the dramatic growth of female students (Huang, 2012a). As Figure 15.2 shows there has been a significant gender gap in participation in four-year university education, especially until 1980s. At the stage, most women enrolled in junior colleges and professional training colleges, but from the second half of the 1980s onwards there was rapid female enrolment growth in four-year universities. One driver of this tendency was a change in the law in 1986 to provide for equal employment opportunities between male and female workers. This allowed female university graduates to make better use of degrees. Figure 15.2 also shows that between the mid-1970s and the beginning of the 1990s there was a slight decrease in

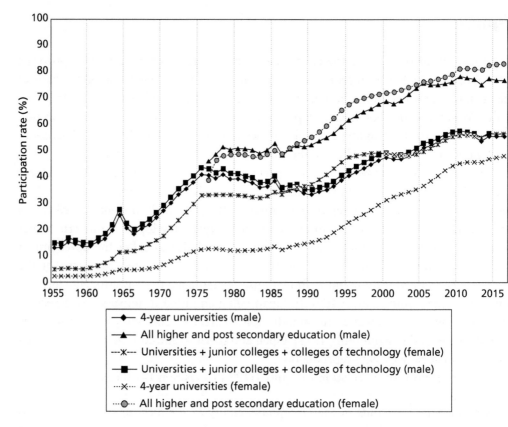

Figure 15.2. Trends of participation towards higher and post-secondary education, by gender, 1955–2015

Source: Authors adapting data from School Basic Survey (MEXT).

male enrolment in four-year universities and junior colleges. During this period, government controls over student numbers, coupled with the rise in female participation, squeezed out some male students on grounds of academic merit. The subsequent shift toward regulation of numbers using the market mechanism resulted in an increase in male participation.

The second proposition in relation to equity (HPS Proposition 15) states:

Because in the HPS phase the growth of participation is associated with enhanced stratification and intensified competition at key transition points, all else being equal (i.e. without compensatory state policy), the expansion of participation is associated with a secular tendency to greater social inequality in educational outcomes and, through that, social outcomes.

The growth of participation benefits the middle range socio-economic groups rather than lower range groups. Kondo (2002) examines the relationship between growth of higher education participation and socio-economic inequality, finding that the inequality expanded during the period of most significant growth in the 1960s and the first half of the 1970s, and diminished in the more stable period from the mid-1970s to the mid-1980s.

In Japan, the secular tendency to greater inequality amid growth is enhanced by the private cost of tuition. In recent years financial affordability has become a more serious social issue. Yano finds that economic factors, such as financial affordability, tuition level, and job expectations, are crucial in determining the level of enrolment in an higher education institution (Yano and Hamanaka, 2006; Yano, 2012). According to the *Student Life Survey*, from the Japan Student Service Organization (JASSO), in 2014, 51.3 per cent of full-time undergraduate students, 55.4 per cent at Master's level, and 62.7 per cent of Doctoral students had student loans or scholarships. While the government has strengthened financial support and wants to facilitate delayed repayments, for graduates with low incomes or unstable working conditions the repayment of governmental loans is a serious social problem.

The third proposition on equity (HPS Proposition 16) states:

Within a national system, as participation expands in the HPS phase, all else being equal, the positional structure of the higher education system increasingly resembles that of society... The HPS is increasingly implicated in the reproduction of existing patterns of social equality/inequality.

This proposition also applies in general to Japan, and has increasingly done so since the 1980s, when the pattern of a mature ageing society became entrenched, and female participation in higher education began to rise to a level more representative of society as a whole. The fourth and final proposition on equity (HPS Proposition 17) states:

As the HPS boundary of participation expands it becomes more difficult for the state and/or autonomous educational systems/institutions to secure a redistribution of educational opportunities, and, through that, of social opportunities.

This proposition also applies more or less to Japan.

Conclusion

Most of the propositions in this study concerning HPS apply well to the case of Japan during the transition from mass system to HPS. Higher education in Japan has also been shaped by factors specific to the national landscape, including policy.

The Japanese government has pursued a two-sided policy with both vertical and horizontal implications, often at the same time. On the one hand, it has fostered functional diversification among universities and other post-secondary institutions. On the other hand, it has concentrated public investment in selected universities. It has continued to foster an elite sector as it has done since the nineteenth century. This stratification has been enhanced by neoliberal competition policy and the positioning of the top universities as responding to globalization. The government believes that it has maintained the autonomy of higher education institutions, they set their own missions and can pursue financial options. It is a corporate autonomy. They are more tightly controlled than before through quality assessment and assurance, and the device of project-based funding.

The deliberate pursuit of functional diversification has modified the secular tendency to reduced diversity of institutional type but not eliminated it. In the evolution of the HPS, on the whole the vertical differentiation has been more dominant than the horizontal. The universities became more dominating as an institutional type—in that respect it appears that Japanese higher education has become more horizontally 'equalized'—but the universities themselves are more stratified than before. Their diversification in terms of governance structure, financial condition, curriculum, and instruction has strengthened.

As a society with a shrinking population and economy, Japan is struggling to design a sustainable future vision of higher education. However, recent history suggests that it is difficult to find a simple solution through a top-down approach at the level of national policies and plans. A high-participation society will be realized in Japan, where the government wants to provide higher education competitive in terms of both quality and size. But at present, the majority of university staff and students are not well-prepared to meet such high expectations. Japan needs to improve the capacities of individual faculty and students to make them more globally competitive, as well as the capacities of policymakers and university administration staff to work effectively with globally viable visions. Japanese society needs to combine high-level social capital based on its mature citizenship with the active intake of highly skilled human resources from other countries, and efforts to foster global literacy through its increasingly universal higher education.

◾ REFERENCES

Altbach, P. G. and Umakoshi, T. (eds) (2004). *Asian Universities: Historical Perspectives and Contemporary Challenges*. Baltimore: Johns Hopkins University Press.

Amano, I. (1997). Structural changes in Japan's higher education system-from a planning to a market model. *Higher Education* 34(2), 125–39.

Geiger, R. L. (1986). *Private Sectors in Higher Education: Structure, Function, and Change in Eight Countries*. Ann Arbor: University of Michigan Press.

Huang, F. (2006). Assuring and enhancing educational quality in universities: A perspective from Japan. *Higher Education Policy* 19(3), 343–60.

Huang, F. (2012a). Massification of higher education in China and Japan in the comparative perspective, in W. R. Allen, R. T. Teranishi, and M. Bonous-Hammarth (eds), *As the World Turns: Implications of Global Shifts in Higher Education for Theory, Research and Practice.* Volume 7: *Advances in Education in Diverse Communities: Research, Policy and Praxis.* Bingley: Emerald Group Publishing Limited, pp. 133–50.

Huang, F. (2012b). Higher education from massification to universal access: A perspective from Japan. *Higher Education* 63(2), 257–70.

Huang, F. (2014). Challenges for higher education and research: a perspective from Japan, *Studies in Higher Education* 39(8), 1428–38. DOI: 10.1080/03075079.2014.949535

Huang, F. (2018). Higher education financing in Japan: Trends and challenges. *International Journal of Educational Development* 58, 106–15. https://doi.org/10.1016/j.ijedudev.2016.12.010

Institute for International Cooperation (2004). *The History of Japan's Educational Development.* Tokyo: Japan International Cooperation Agency (JICA).

Kaneko, M. (2008). Beyond the politics of competence, balancing the social claim and the core of higher education. In presentation to the OECD-IMHE General Conference, September.

Kaneko, M. (2014). Higher education and work in Japan: Characteristics and challenges. *Japan Labor Review* 11(2), 5–22.

Kariya, T. and Dore, R. (2006). Japan at the meritocracy frontier: From here, where? *The Political Quarterly* 77(s1), 134–56.

Kinmonth, E. H. (1981). *The Self-made Man in Meiji Japanese Thought: From Samurai to Salary Man.* Berkeley: University of California Press.

Kondo, H. (2002). Gakureki Shugi to Kaiso Ryudo sei [Credentialism and the Mobility of Social Strafitication], in H. Junichi (ed.), *Ryudo sei to Shaki Kakusa [Mobility and Social Divide].* Kyoto: Minerva Shobo, pp. 59–87.

OECD (Organisation for Economic Co-operation and Development) (2015). *Economics: Key Tables from OECD.* Paris: OECD. DOI: 10.1787/2074384x

Ogawa, N., Kondo, M., and Matsukura, R. (2005). Japan's transition from the demographic bonus to demographic onus. *Asian Population Studies* 1(2), 207–26.

Trow, M. (1973). *Problems in the Transition from Elite to Mass Higher Education.* Berkeley: Carnegie Commission on Higher Education.

UNESCO (United Nations Educational, Social and Cultural Organization). (2017). UNESCO Institute for Statistics data on education. http://data.uis.unesco.org/

World Bank (2017). Data and statistics. http://data.worldbank.org/indicator/all

Yano, M. (1997). Higher education and employment. *Higher Education* 34(2), 199–214.

Yano, M. (2012). Gakuryoku, Seisaku, Sekinin (Student Achievement, Policy and Responsibility). *The Journal of Educational Sociology* 90, 65–81.

Yano, M. and Hamanaka, J. (2006). Naze Daigaku ni Shingaku Shinainoka? Kenzaiteki Juyo to Senzaiteki Juyo no Kettei Yoin [Why don't high school students go to university?: determinants of the demand for higher education]. *The Journal of Educational Sociology* 79, 85–104.

Yonezawa, A. (2002). The quality assurance system and market forces in Japanese higher education. *Higher Education* 43(1), 127–39.

Yonezawa, A. (2013). The development of private higher education in Japan since the 1960s: A reexamination of a center-periphery paradigm, in A. Maldonado-Maldonado and R. M. Bassett (eds), *The Forefront of International Higher Education: A Festschrift in Honor of Philip G. Altbach.* Dordrecht: Springer, pp. 183–94.

Yonezawa, A. and Akiyama, T. (2015). The transition from secondary education to higher education in Japan, in UNESCO (ed.), *The Transition from Secondary Education to Higher Education: Case Studies from Asia and the Pacific.* Bangkok: UNESCO Bangkok Office, pp. 67–80.

Yonezawa, A. and Inenaga, Y. (2017). The consequences of market-based mass postsecondary education: Japan's Challenges, in P. G. Altbach, L. Reisberg, and H. de Wit (eds), *Responding to Massification: Differentiation in Postsecondary Education Worldwide.* Boston: Boston College Center for International Higher Education, pp. 82–90.

Yonezawa, A. and Shimmi, Y. (2015). Transformation of university governance through internationalization: Challenges for top universities and government policies in Japan. *Higher Education* 70(2), 173–86.

16 Conclusions: High Participation Higher Education in the Post-Trow Era

Brendan Cantwell, Simon Marginson, and Anna Smolentseva

Observations are unavoidably position-based, but scientific reasoning need not, of course, be based on observational information from one specific position only. There is a need for what may be called 'trans-positional' assessment—drawing on but going beyond different positional observations. The constructed 'view from nowhere' would then be based on synthesizing different views from distinct positions. The positional objectivity of the respective observations would still remain important but not in itself adequate. A trans-positional scrutiny would also demand some kind of coherence between different positional views.

(Sen, 2002: 467)

Introduction

The countries discussed in Part II of this book are diverse in economic and political systems, cultural traditions and demographics but all have achieved high participation systems (HPS) of higher education. The United States of America (USA) was the first to reach a mass enrolment, Trow's 15 per cent of the age cohort, not long after World War II. Canada, Japan, and Russia achieved mass systems in the 1960s; Australia and Finland in the 1970s; and Poland in the 1990s. It took most of case study countries between two and four decades to move from 15 to 50 per cent, except for Poland where development was more compressed. The USA had an HPS by the end of the 1970s; Australia, Finland, Norway, and Canada achieved an HPS in the 1990s; Japan and Russia in the early 2000s; and Poland by the late 2000s.

This final chapter summarizes the findings of the country studies in Part II in relation to the seventeen propositions about HPS outlined in Part I. The country studies do not exhaustively explore the propositions. In some cases, data are lacking. In some cases, not all the questions are fully explored. Nevertheless, patterns can be discerned, to an extent that varies by proposition. The final section of the chapter compares the findings of this book to the earlier insights of Martin Trow (1973) and reflects on the study as a whole.

General Propositions

The first group of propositions focus on the character of increasing participation. Proposition 1 concerned the global landscape and was not tested in the national studies. The others (Propositions 2 and 3) stated:

- *In HPS there is no intrinsic limit to the spread of family aspirations for participation in higher education until universality is reached; and no intrinsic limit to the level of social position to which families/students may aspire.*
- *Once transition from a primarily agricultural economy is achieved, the long-term growth of HPS is independent of political economic factors such as economic growth and patterns of labour market demand; patterns of public and private funding of higher education; the roles of public and private institutions; and system organization and modes of governance.*

These propositions are generally endorsed in the country studies. The authors largely concur with the editors in understanding higher education as a positional social good and enrolment as primarily driven by family desires to maintain and improve position (Trow, 1973). Regardless of whether provision is mainly in the public sector, or the private sector as in Japan; regardless of the arrangements governing tuition and living costs; each increment of growth is sooner or later followed by the further expansion of demand and supply until universality is approached. Historically, participation growth begins on the supply side, with the foundations of mass systems, and increasingly switches to demand-drivers as populations pressure governments to expand provision and ease access. Correspondingly, governments support the extension of higher education to all regions and social groups: universal participation is functional for states because social inclusion furthers social order. Governments deploy human capital and international competitiveness rationales for expansion, as if it is grounded in rational economics, but participation always seems to go up and not down. Nowhere has economic recession or economic growth, political alternations or large-scale demographics triggered a lasting decline in the gross enrolment ratio. All the country chapters agree the growth to HPS-level participation is irreversible.

There are partial reservations about the propositions in relation to Japan, where policy halted the secular dynamic of growth for a decade or more, and Finland. The authors of the Finland chapter argue that individual family and student demand does not play a central role in the HPS trajectory. The state shapes participation collectively, on behalf of society.

Governance

The first proposition on governance is HPS Proposition 4:

HPS are governed by multi-level control, coordination, and accountability mechanisms.

The country studies find that control and coordination are shared between federal/central authorities, regions (states or provinces), institutions, public and non-public agencies, and professional bodies, though much of this infrastructure predates the HPS period. In Canada and the USA, governance is shared between provinces/states and autonomous universities but the federal government shapes research and student financing. Finland distributes governance between the central authorities and autonomous universities, primarily on a trust not control basis. Norway shares power between central authorities, intermediate bodies, and institutions. Trust as the basis of transactions may be giving ground to output regulation. In both Russia and Poland, the national state has reasserted itself after a hiatus in the 1990s, the early post-communist years. In Poland intermediary public bodies for allocation of research funding, accreditation, and evaluation have come to play a key role in higher education governance, buffering pressure on the national authorities. Russia is an exception to the proposition. Higher education remains centralized at the national level with little institutional autonomy or regional authority. Australia is a partial exception. The constitutional authority of the states is over-determined by the fiscal power of the national government, which directly regulates the universities. In place of state government, the national government has built market-focused institutions with strong corporate personalities.

The country cases illustrate the straightforward HPS Proposition 5 on managing horizontal diversity:

HPS governance tends to involve the management of horizontal differentiation.

The extent of systemic diversity varies. Some systems include vocational colleges that operate primarily at ISCED Level 5; in others ISCED is negligible or outside higher education (see Chapter 1). National government coordinates a traditional binary system in Finland, with academic universities alongside universities of applied sciences (UAS), and a larger range of public and private institutions in Norway. There is significant diversity of institutional mission and type in the USA, regulated by the Carnegie classifications; Japan, which evolved after World War II along American lines; and Canada, where there are distinctive provincial systems. State public education systems in the USA evolved mission differentiated provision that combines excellence in elite universities with high participation in lower tiers (Chapter 9). Mission differentiation was eliminated from Australia prior to the HPS, and is limited in Poland. Facing a mix of comprehensive, regional, and specialized higher education institutions, in partial transition from the Soviet era, central government in Russia is struggling to cohere 'its' system.

The third proposition on governance (Proposition 6) highlights corporatization and managerialism at the institutional level, larger administration and growing professional strata, and the weakening of academic power:

> *HPS complex multi-level accountability and coordination, coupled with system differentiation, result in higher education institutions adopting increasingly corporate forms and robust internal governance and management capacities.*

All case studies report these tendencies though they less pronounced in the Nordic countries. Corporatization is fostered not only by growing size and complexity, and the need for devolved authority to enable coordination and accountability, but by neoliberal ideologies, and by competition, commercialization and associated business practices. The new public management (NPM), sitting on the fault line between size-driven changes and neoliberal reshaping, has been taken furthest in the most marketized systems, the USA and Australia. But whenever institutions become more active agents in global and national quasi-markets, raising part of their revenue, this encourages executive strategy-making, efficiency drivers, and quality assurance. The case study on Finland describes how state policies to make universities more competitive at a global level triggered corporatization moves, two decades after the establishment of the HPS. It is notable that corporate forms of autonomy/accountability flourishes in systems with a classical tradition of university autonomy (Nordic, Anglo-American), and in centralized bureaucratic systems as in Russian higher education. Poland combine a thorough corporate devolution of the NPM type with ongoing central control. For all states, this is a functional template.

In sum, the cases largely confirm the phenomena described in the three propositions on HPS and governance. However, it is unclear whether (and to what extent) the identified developments are secular tendencies that have been triggered by the growth of higher education, or changes that would have occurred in the absence of growth.

Horizontal Diversity

In contrast to widespread assumptions that larger system size and expanding access result in higher institutional diversity, whereby more diverse students become matched to more diverse 'products' and institutional types, this book argues the opposite. If anything, on the whole in HPS there is a decline in diversity of institutional mission and type of education, and in most countries there are tendencies to convergence towards the form of the multiversity, the large, multi-level, multi-disciplinary, and multi-purpose research university, though the proportional role of the multiversity in enrolments varies by country.

The first proposition on horizontal diversity (HPS proposition 7) states:

In the HPS era, regardless of the political economy and culture of systems, an increasing proportion of higher education becomes centred on comprehensive multi-discipline and multi-function research universities, or 'multiversities'. The multiversity is increasingly dominant as the paradigmatic form of higher education.

The rise of the multiversity is driven by both institutional competition and government policy. In Australia, both drivers are apparent. In 1987–92, government established a single template of institution, the comprehensive university. It engineered mergers and eliminated specialist institutions. In the next decade, competitive pressures sealed the template and ensured that all universities would include research. These homogeneous institutions now enrol more than nine degree-level students in ten. In Canada, multiversities enrol a large majority. The USA resists the tendency to some extent. Its diversity is protected by classifications, and the prestigious multiversities command a minority of enrolments, though there is both upward and downward drift towards more comprehensive institutions. The Norwegian binary system has been modified by a comprehensive two-stage merger process leading to larger conglomerate institutions: the 1990s merger of regional colleges into university colleges, and voluntary mergers of universities and university colleges in the last decade. In Poland and Russia, the comprehensive university is now the majority form, though its research role is less well-developed than the proposition suggests. One-third of Russian institutions are still specialized in function, but mergers are being fostered by government. There has been no move to fold specialized Polish institutions into larger comprehensive universities, but the comprehensive research institutions are growing and more dominant.

The second horizontal diversity proposition (HPS Proposition 8) is:

Regardless of the political economy and culture of the HPS, when participation expands there is no necessary increase in the overall diversity of institutional form and mission; and this has probably declined, except in relation to online provision.

The proposition largely applies in most cases, especially Australia, Norway, and Russia where horizontal diversity have clearly declined. In Norway, regional mergers, and the drive for market niches and global competitiveness have all tended to reduce diversity. Firm state policy in Finland maintains a clear-cut binary system, though a merger of one university of applied sciences with a multi-disciplinary and technical university was in process while the book was being written. In the USA diversity has probably declined a little in the HPS era, except in for-profit and online provision. The Canadian provinces of British Columbia and Alberta have fostered diversity as a means of managing growth, but this has not happened in other provinces. Japan is a more important contrasting case. During massification the national government diversified institutional forms and missions; in the HPS era it has worked on institutional profiling.

The third horizontal diversity proposition (HPS Proposition 9) focuses on internal diversity:

> *As participation expands the internal diversity of multiversities tends to increase. This affects some or all of the range of missions, business activities, institutional forms and internal structures, the discipline mix, research activities, levels of study and range of credentials, the heterogeneity of the student body, links to stakeholders, cross-border relations, and forms of academic and non-academic labour.*

The proposition was agreed in all case studies but sparked only modest curiosity. A question here is how internal diversity might be measured, aside from calculations of the number and range of degree programmes at undergraduate and graduate levels. It can be surmised that in countries with a relatively weak tendency to the dominance of the multiversity, internal diversity might be lower, for example Finland.

HPS Proposition 10, the final horizontal diversity proposition, focuses on marketization policies, which affect some of the eight countries more than others:

> *All else being equal, the combination of expanding participation and enhanced competition in neoliberal quasi-markets is associated with specific effects in relation to diversity, including (1) increased vertical differentiation of higher education institutions (stratification); (2) reduced horizontal differentiation (diversification); (3) convergence of missions through isomorphistic imitation; and (4) growth in the role of private higher education institutions, especially for-profit institutions.*

The proposition applies most strongly in Australia, the USA, Russia, and Poland. Points (1) to (3) are discussed earlier and later in this chapter. In relation to (4), the private sector, federal loans, and legislation foster the American for-profit sector and small private sectors have grown in Australia and Canada. In both Poland (especially) and Russia the private sector expanded markedly in the 1990s but then shrank amid demographic decline. Japan has a majority private sector that predates neoliberalism. There is no private sector in Finland.

In sum, the argument of Chapter 4 on horizontal diversity is supported overall. Instead of triggering a pluralization of institutional types, growth to the HPS level has primarily stimulated an expansion in the size and scope and internal diversification of large multi-purpose universities. For government, this facilitates a more manageable expansion system, with fewer administrative units, and larger ones more apt to the downwards devolution of responsibility. For institutional leaders, greater scale and scope maximize status and resources. Significantly, these tendencies show in the eight HPS regardless of the extent to which NPM reforms and/or neoliberal quasi-market forms are introduced, though, as often the case, Finland is least affected by the secular tendencies.

Vertical Stratification

In Chapter 5, the first proposition on stratification (HPS Proposition 11) states that

> *The expansion of participation towards and beyond the HPS stage is associated with a tendency to bifurcation and stratification (vertical diversification) in the value of higher education, between elite (artisanal) institutions and mass (demand-absorbing) institutions.*

Growth drives bifurcation on a larger scale. There was an increase in vertical stratification in all countries except Finland. Less clearly—because it requires more testing than was applied in some chapters—most chapters identified the strengthening of an artisanal sector, identified by the calibrated outcomes of competition for national and global prestige, research funding, the best students, and in some countries, fee-paying international students. Research funding is especially important in defining the prestige groupings: the 'U15' in Canada, the Association of American Universities in the USA, the Group of Eight in Australia, institutions in the excellence programme in Russia, leading research universities in Poland, the top three in Norway, the national universities in Japan. In the steep American hierarchy, the artisanal sector is also demarcated by wealth, and includes liberal arts colleges focusing on elite student formation but not research. The cases highlight the diverse ways that elite sectors, adaptive and resourceful, are both self-sustaining and sustained by state policy. The chapters say less about the character and evolution of mass or demand-absorbing institutions.

Status in higher education is a zero-sum game. There are no routes into elite groups but no end of aspirants. The third stratification proposition on middle institutions (HPS Proposition 13) is the corollary of the first on bifurcation:

> *In stratified HPS, a middle layer of institutions tends to form, shaped by the combination of upward aspirations (drift) with systemic scarcity of resources and status.*

Australian policy sustains a large middle layer where corporate institutions energetically pursue contrary strategies: comprehensive research capacity, specialist research concentrations, boutique degrees, large teaching programmes pumped up for market share and economies of scale, inventive global ventures to secure a novel edge. None of it brings them close to the artisanal level. The other country cases acknowledge an unstable middle layer but there is little exploration of strategies and trajectories.

The second vertical stratification proposition (HPS Proposition12) highlights effects specific to marketization:

> *The tendency to institutional stratification is magnified by features common (though not universal) among HPS including (a) intensified social competition for the most valuable student places; (b) variable tuition charges; and/or (c) intensified competition between institutions.*

The USA exemplifies all three drivers. However, the cases do not exhaustively investigate the proposition. Most chapters do not examine student selectivity in data terms. Tuition fees exacerbate stratification in only some countries with pronounced differentiation. The most prestigious universities charge higher fees in the USA and Russia.) In Japan, as throughout East Asia, fees are lower at the most prestigious institutions, the subsidized national research universities. Their status is secured by student selectivity and research funding, not the 'sticker price'. Affordability plays a larger role in mediating access to the lower tiers. In Australia, the government sets uniform tuition, and the income contingent tuition loans system, whereby there are no financial disincentives at the point of entry, blocks price-based competition. In Canada, provincial regulation restricts fee-based strati-fication, and most students attend their home universities regardless of prices elsewhere. Finland has no fees for domestic and EU students, though foreign student fees apply.

The larger point about the stratifying effects of intensified competition applies in most cases. The country chapters also show that policy-induced stratification is often expressed directly through policies boosting the artisanal sector, rather than indirectly by tweaking market mechanisms. Between them the case study countries use project-based funding, selection, and concentration, profiling in Japan, Carnegie classifications in the USA, evaluation of scientific units in Poland, and excellence and global competitiveness programmes in Japan and Russia. Australia is unusual in the extent to which the state so valorizes market equity (the 'level playing field') that it eschews mission-based classifi-cations and extra world-class university (WCU) funding, ordering the system solely through regulated contests for research prestige and funds, high score domestic students and international student revenues. Even so, the artisanal sector retains its position without challenge, within a steeply calibrated system.

SEPARATING THE EFFECTS OF GROWTH AND NEOLIBERALISM

In considering the propositions on vertical stratification the question arises of how to disentangle the respective effects of growth in participation, government policy and regulation, and deregulated markets (in higher education systems, partly deregulated market forces constitute a specific regulatory regime, albeit one with endogenous effects). This separation is more readily made for some systems than others. In Australia and Russia, if there is a secular tendency to stratification driven by growth it is hard to identify given the many stratification effects engendered by neoliberal policy. Japan during the massification period was a textbook case of induced bifurcation. Mass growth was channelled through the self-expanding and user financed private sector, while Japan's artisanal sector was (as it still is) closely nurtured by government. The Japanese state exacerbates the secular tendency to bifurcation so as to work with it, using it to hold down total public costs. On the other hand, in the provincial Canadian systems, expansion has become joined to increased stratification amid competition in prestige and research, and to some extent for first degree students, in the absence of a national neoliberal reform agenda. This makes visible the secular tendency.

The Nordic systems, which have grown to HPS extent without strong evidence of vertical stratification, are the opposite case to Japan. This is especially helpful in clarifying the relations between states and stratification. In Norway and Finland, status and resource differences among higher education institutions are small, and social competition of families is primarily expressed in access to the most sought-after fields of study, not institutions. In the absence of fees, and given state finance for student living costs, there is little stratification via family capacity to pay. At the same time, in the case of Norway competitive research funding is enabling the top three research universities to strengthen their relative position, early signs of a WCU layer, and there seems to be an emerging middle layer of institutions pulled between the elite research mission and building student volume. This suggests two interpretations. First, where there is the firm Nordic social consensus about equal citizen rights to high quality higher education, and policy regulation and funding are governed by the corresponding social democratic norms, tendencies to vertical stratification, apparent elsewhere, do not show, despite a major expansion of participation. Second, the secular tendencies to bifurcation and stratification are present in Norway, albeit suppressed by policy and regulation, and become visible when the social democratic norms are modified. These interpretations have not been tested in Finland. A review of recent history in Nordic Denmark and Sweden, where the use of competitive mechanisms has increased, might be instructive.

As noted, it is also apparent that in systems where social and/or institutional competition become more intensive—whether induced by growth itself, by the effects of policy, or both—vertical stratification effects become more pronounced. The extent to which (a) growth drives stratification, or (b) neoliberal policy drives stratification, or (c) neoliberal competition is anyway more pronounced in HPS located in societies more prone to hierarchy and inequality, or (d) the secular tendency to bifurcation/stratification is itself subject to national-cultural variations, is yet to be clarified. However, it is clear that even in unambiguously marketized systems, governments manage the settings to shape stratification; as in Japan and Australia, with its policy constraints on artisanal universities and the large middle layer. This underlines the character of quasi-markets as instruments of state. Like the Nordic examples, it also emphasizes that *nations can modify the extent of stratification if they choose.* They can enhance it or reduce it. Given the underlying secular tendency towards steeper stratification, induced by growth, it is mostly easier for governments to go with the flow, given the political costs of confronting stratification—unless there is a Nordic-type social consensus on equity.

Equity

The equity propositions follow from those on stratification. The first equity proposition (HPS Proposition 14) states that

> *As participation expands in the HPS phase, equity in the form of social inclusion is enhanced.*

This straightforward achievement of HPS is confirmed in the cases. Growth been accompanied by diminished quantitative gaps in participation, in relation to gender (all countries), urban/rural (e.g. Poland), racial/ethnic (e.g. the USA), SES and income (e.g. the USA, Canada). All the same, in most countries, including relatively egalitarian Norway, there are continued social disparities in terms of urban/rural parental social background, ethnicity, language, and/or gender in some disciplines. In Japan gender disparities are more pervasive than elsewhere. Disparities vary by level of education (undergraduate, graduate, postgraduate). In Finland, social differences in participation have not disappeared but have decreased. There are limited differences between students in the universities and UAS sectors, but larger differences in the social background of students by fields of study. Differences in participation based on parental income have largely disappeared, but there are continued differences in the success of students on the basis of cultural capital.

The second proposition on equity is discussed later. The third proposition on equity (HPS Proposition 16), like the first proposition, follows from growth itself. It is confirmed by the cases, though not subjected to data-based tests:

> *Within a national system, as participation expands in the HPS phase, all else being equal, the positional structure of the higher education system increasingly resembles that of society (albeit with the caveat of Proposition 15). The HPS is increasingly implicated in the reproduction of existing patterns of social equality/inequality.*

Arguably, this proposition applies regardless of the degree of egalitarianism in the system. In Finland the HPS helps to reproduce the relatively equal opportunities of society; in the USA it reproduces family status more than it fosters social mobility, though these interpretations require further empirical investigation.

The fourth equity proposition (HPS Proposition 17), about the potentials of state, might follow from Proposition 3:

As the HPS boundary of participation expands it becomes more difficult for the state and/or autonomous educational systems/institutions to secure a redistribution of educational opportunities, and, through that, of social opportunities.

This is less relevant in Norway and Finland where educational opportunities are already relatively equal. Elsewhere, observation suggests that in the HPS era states find it difficult to advance a redistribution of opportunities, perhaps regardless of the extent to which they jump on the neoliberal bus. Politically, it is easier to expand the base of participation than to open up social access to the top of the pyramid, where every hopeful middle class family is already crowded around the points of entry. The proposition as worded requires historical tests beyond the scope of this study and has not generated much discussion in the chapters. Nevertheless, the case studies highlight the fact that *policy always matters*. The nation-state, and in some cases provincial/state governments, can increase or decrease the location and variety of provision, foster or impede institutional stratification, expand or restrict access, support or ignore under-represented groups, stimulate or impede reforms to extend equity.

SOCIAL INEQUALITY

The most important proposition on equity is the second (HPS Proposition 15). With the expansion of participation, plus greater institutional stratification and associated social competition in education, there is a secular tendency to social inequality:

Because in the HPS phase the growth of participation is associated with enhanced stratification and intensified competition at key transition points, all else being equal (i.e. without compensatory state policy), the expansion of participation is associated with a secular tendency to greater social inequality in educational outcomes and, through that, social outcomes.

This aims to explain why (1) high participation in higher education has not brought about greater social equality; and (2) in all HPS the most prestigious places tend to be dominated by families with higher socio-economic status. Students from families previously under-represented tend to slot into lower tier institutions—for example in Canada in community colleges; in Australia outside the top eight universities. The proposition is supported by some, though not all, the quantitative research literature (Chapter 6). It is not exhaustively tested by the syntheses in Chapters 8–15, and the chapters vary in the extent to which they express judgement on it.

Setting aside the Nordic systems with their low stratification and relatively equal societies, in five of the other cases, in the HPS era, sharper stratification and intensified competition for the most powerful places in higher education are combined with growing economic and social inequality. (The exception is Poland, where Chapter 12 finds that distributional equity in higher education has advanced.) This alignment of inequalities is most obvious in the USA, as explored in Chapter 9. However, it is more straightforward to show that social inequalities in access to the top universities have increased not diminished (while noting that longitudinal data are surprisingly thin, for example in Australia, Canada, and Russia), than to demonstrate that this form of educational inequality is causal in overall rising social inequality (*or* vice versa). The two kinds of inequality are not the same phenomenon. Nor it is clear whether one causes the other, they are reciprocal, or both are shaped by a third factor. Other factors affect social inequality, aside from educational allocation, such as taxation, public spending, and wage determination. Further, degrees from a prestigious university, even an Ivy League university, do not guarantee top jobs, which derive also from family economic, social, and cultural capital. *High Participation Systems of Higher Education* does not settle the question about the extent to which higher education is causal in social outcomes. It is likely that the relationship varies by country, and also varies by the historical conjuncture.

In sum, in most countries the propositions about growing social inclusion, greater social representativeness of HPS of higher education, and constraints on state redistribution appear as plausible descriptions of the actual HPS. The proposition about HPS generating a secular tendency to educational and hence social inequality, unless modified by regulation as in Nordic Europe, is again a plausible description; and it is consistent with the crucial bifurcation proposition, which is confirmed in most of the cases. But the social inequality thesis requires further research to pin down the social implications of inequality in higher education.

Compared to Trow

What is new about the outcomes of *High Participation Systems of Higher Education*? Its goals are to contribute to the theorization of massification and high participation, and to throw light on their empirical presence, especially in the case study countries. The starting point was Martin Trow's path breaking 1973 theorizing in *Problems in the Transition from Elite to Mass Higher Education*. National and global higher education have transformed radically since Trow's essay was published. This book has not addressed all the issues discussed by Trow, and it gives greater space to social equity. Yet the contemporary account of HPS in this book shares much with Trow—first, because

Trow conceived many of the terms in which discussion of growth in education is conducted; and, second, because this study, working independently of Trow on similar phenomena, has reached often similar findings.

High Participation Systems of Higher Education benefits from a richer base of experience, research, and theory. Yet Trow apprehended the social processes of his time. He matched close personal observations in the USA and Europe with intellectual adventurousness and rigour. His remains a remarkable achievement, a highpoint in higher education studies.

SOCIAL DRIVERS

The most meaningful agreement between Trow and this book is that both identify family aspirations as the micro-foundation of high participation. The secular tendency towards growth is a mutual duty between families/young people and society. As Trow explained:

As more students from an age cohort go to college or university each year, the meaning of college attendance changes—first from being a privilege to being a right, and then . . . to being something close to an obligation.   (Trow, 1973: 5)

System expansion becomes inevitable because failure to participate is 'increasingly a mark of some defect of mind or character' (p. 7). Trow understood that families demand access for their children to avoid social failure and to strive for advancement, even when participation becomes so common that graduates objectively lose most of the distinction they once enjoyed (p. 25). Like Trow this book de-emphasizes economic and labour market explanations. High participation is understood as a primarily social not economic phenomenon. Both Trow and this book find that once a threshold of development is reached, the secular tendency towards growth is likely to proceed without regard to prevailing economic conditions. In their institutionalist account Schofer and Meyer (2005) make a similar point about the tendency to expansion, regardless of the economic growth rate or the pattern of industrial development. *High Participation Systems of Higher Education* offers a different social explanation for massification to that of Schofer and Meyer, and a different method of theorizing, but shares with them the break with economic determinism.

At the same time, this book extends Trow's insights about family aspirations in two ways. Chapter 1 suggests why higher education has become a near-universal conduit for the expression of family aspirations. One reason is worldwide modernization, urbanization, and growth of the middle class. Societies have left the fields and congregated in cities and suburbs. Higher education fits the cultural and political economic demands of urbanization, which uses rationalization beyond kinship networks to allocate social opportunities. The second reason is zero-sum positional good competition, whereby higher education readily maps onto the universal human desire for betterment—the desire for something more. Trow understood the common demand for betterment but the zero-sum aspect partly escaped him. It was developed three years later by Fred Hirsch in *Social Limits to Growth* (1976).

Like Trow, *High Participation Systems of Higher Education* understands the secular trend to expanding participation as contributing to social 'democratization'. This book avoids the term because of its normative implications. Trow embraces the implied norms of 'democracy'. A point of departure from Trow is in relation to where democratization occurs. For Trow, expanded participation means increased representative plurality within the higher education sector and, by extension, within national societies, though he was sceptical about massification as a social equalizer, and also worried that egalitarian policy agendas might undermine the elite multiversities. This book is more interested than is Trow in the question 'what kind of human agency does HPS make possible?' It understands HPS as empowering individual agency on an expanded scale, and enhancing global equity between nation-states. Like Trow it identifies limits to higher education's capacity to equalize educational outcomes within nation-states. Unlike Trow it highlights the egalitarian potentials suggested by Nordic societies. Again unlike Trow, it is untroubled about the prospects of the elite universities.

SYSTEM GOVERNANCE

This book agrees with Trow that changing relations between higher education and society have implications for governance. Trow (1973) said that

higher education comes increasingly to the attention of large numbers of people, both in government and the general public, who have other, often quite legitimate ideas about where public funds should be spent, and, if given higher education, how they should be spent. (p. 4)

He said that government and society would hold higher education to account for the 'value' added (p. 13); and a predictable response would be 'the rationalization of university administration' (p. 15). Chapter 3 finds the boundaries between higher education and other social sectors are eroding, activating a web of interests and stakeholder claims that place on the sector ever-increasing demands and accountability standards. Higher education institutions—sometimes following government, sometimes leading—respond by developing their self-governing corporate capacity.

There are also underlying differences in the two accounts of governance. This book understands de-activation of the boundaries between higher education and the larger society to trigger a complex set of new social relations. While Trow does not exclude this possibility, he was primarily interested in shifting ties vis-à-vis government. He was most concerned with state regulation and erosion of institutional autonomy. He did not much consider engagement with non-governmental organizations and business, or anticipate globalization and the development of rankings and other post-state regulatory technologies (although it is difficult to imagine how he could have anticipated these developments!). This book also extends Trow on the corporate capacity of institutions. He knew the academic oligarchy would weaken but still considered the university to be run by professors. He failed to anticipate the diminishing or evacuation of academic governance that has since transpired. However, as noted, the extent to which this change has been triggered by high participation rather than coincident changes such as the neo-liberal turn in public administration is unclear.

DIVERSITY, STRATIFICATION, EQUITY

Both this book and Trow discuss tension between horizontal diversity of institutional mission and a tendency to convergence of organizational forms and missions, but they read the setting in different ways. Along with growth and democratization, Trow identifies diversification as one of the secular tendencies of HPS: 'Another broad trend in higher education that we might reasonably expect to continue is the diversification of the forms and function of higher education' (Trow, 1973: 46). Again, Trow saw student demand as driving this process, putting pressure on systems to 'reflect the diversity of students in a similar diversity of educational provision' (p. 46). Trow also noted mechanisms that had the potential to restrain the secular trend towards diversity. He gave most attention to the potential of government regulation to drive organizational convergence through bureaucratic standardization and the application of democratic and egalitarian norms in policy. A second mechanism was the tendency for institutions to emulate the most prestigious forms of higher education (p. 51).

Chapter 4 of this book notes that Trow's argument—diversity of provision results from diverse demand, by diverse students—accords with traditional market explanations of higher education. In the market vision the sector responds by offering niche provision corresponding to consumer preferences. Yet there is no empirical description of the concrete mechanisms that translate varied preferences into varied products. Findings throughout this book invite scepticism about the market explanation. First, students mostly demand not nuanced learning but more generic positional value. Fine tuning is inhibited by information asymmetry, but 'university' or 'profession' are readily under-stood. If there are nuanced choices they are mostly made at the level of discipline, not institutional type, though there is larger scope for fine-tuning once inside the compre-hensive institution. Second, on the provider side, powerful university exemplars are always competing, as Trow noted, and the logic of competition for prestige further drives mission convergence around research university norms. Third, in most systems, gov-ernment planners, far from being uniformly uniformist, often seek diverse provision as a means of rationalizing the system, at least in the early stages of an HPS.

Some regulation furthers convergence. For example, quality assessment and uniform compliance requirements both foster standardization. But the eight national case studies show that most policymakers also value diverse systems as a way of ensuring efficient, equitable, and socially responsive provision. This book also finds that planner's efforts to establish and maintain system diversity often fail over the medium- and long-term. Isomorphic tendencies are strong. The extent of convergence varies by country but this book finds extensive evidence of the growth of multiversity-like organizational forms. The multiversity offers institutions status and resources, and offers students recognizable and valuable places. So, in comparison with Trow, this book finds an opposite set of mechanisms shaping system diversity/convergence. Policy often supports horizontal differentiation as a means of rationalization whereas the dynamics of student demand encourage convergence.

In relation to vertical stratification, the book identifies a strong, though not universal, tendency to bifurcation between a small elite (artisanal) segment and a demand-absorbing segment. The attention to theorizing stratification marks an essential differ-ence between this book on HPS and Trow's account. Trow was aware of status differ-entials among institutions, and focused on the effects of massification on the status and function of elite universities. He concluded that the status of elite universities would likely remain intact and most new provision would be of lower social ordering. Hence Trow implied that system bifurcation—to the extent he discussed it—was an incremental outcome of system expansion. Newcomers simply lagged behind the established pace-makers in the sector. While he was right to assume that all else equal, established institutions enjoy competitive advantages, Trow was mostly indifferent to the ongoing processes that produce social status in higher education. For him status was performance merit and pedigree. He gave little attention to the underlying social relations, conflict, and inequality. The HPS theory in this book makes a different claim: stratification is shaped by social dynamics beyond expansion alone. Stratification results from status-seeking behaviour among individuals and institutions that compete with one each other in zero-sum positional contests. High participation exacerbates the competitive social dynamics that generate the vertical ordering of both new and legacy providers, and ensure that over time the elite sector becomes more elite, unless those dynamics are modified by policy. Bifurcation protects the social power of elite universities better than Trow knew. It permits them to grow and accumulate functions, clients, and stakeholders to an extent that he did not expect, while amassing rather than diluting status. The robust social power of elite research universities in the HPS era is one of the strongest findings from the eight case studies.

As with stratification, and as noted, Trow gives limited direct attention to problems of equity and his generation of scholars and policymakers have left HPS with difficult issues in that domain. Trow was aware that students from elite families were more likely to secure admission to the most valuable places. He also expected that expanded participation would reduce the social and economic returns of a degree, but that family demand for higher education would nonetheless remain strong.

While a detached observer might suggest that tripling or quadrupling the number of university graduates must reduce the special status and privileges accorded to the 'graduate,' it does not appear so at the time to participants in the process: For example, to the parents of the would-be university entrant.   (Trow, 1973: 25)

The egalitarian impulses that Trow understood as contributing to massive-scale participation could, according to him, democratize access and perhaps even approach equity of 'achievement'. But little was revealed about what larger social inclusion would do regarding socio-economic position beyond a general dissolution of the graduate advantage.

In some ways, Trow's thoughts on equity accord with the HPS findings presented in this book. Like Trow, Chapter 6 assumes both a decline in the distinctiveness of graduates and greater equity of inclusion. This book also identifies secular tendencies in HPS that intensify the stratification of student outcomes, and reproduce and extend inequalities, with limited potential for redistributive state interventions. These tendencies extend Trow's work. There is also a departure from Trow. The latter understood high participation to be part of an egalitarian and democratic social and political project. Although he is less explicit than contemporaries like Clark Kerr in acknowledging it, Trow presents massification as part of the twentieth-century welfare state-making project in North America and Europe. While the present book agrees that high participation is a form of state project, it differs from Trow in at least two ways. First, high participation is not limited to the OECD welfare state, and the associated secular effects in social equity are not tied to egalitarian and democratic norms familiar to readers in, say, France or Canada. Second, rather than growth in HPS merely diluting the social distinction associated with participation, and thereby attenuating the link between higher education and social position, this book finds that HPS also function actively to reproduce and accentuate social inequality. HPS socially stratify access to valuable places and generate inequitable graduate outcomes, and these tendencies worsen as participation expands—again, unless the system dynamics are modified by policy.

NATIONAL VARIATIONS

Both Trow and this book identify broad trends while acknowledging that no two systems evolve identically. Put simply, system development is contingent even when high participation presents similar social forces. An essential point of divergence between this book and Trow is the source of contingency in system development.

Trow was preoccupied with affect. The dispositions and attitudes of—as he put it—'academic men' were a paramount concern. He identified changes in academic departments. New faculty 'largely define the norms of academic graduate study', which 'increase the chances for academic innovation', but also 'weaken the forms and processes by which teachers and students are inducted into a community' (Trow, 1973: 2). University governance, in Trow's assessment, was also politicized by 'radical currents' because of a 'breakdown of the academic consensus' (Trow, 1973: 17). Trow theorized that all academics in mass systems belonged to one of four ideal-types: (1) Traditionalist Elitists; (2) Traditionalist Expansionists; (3) Elitist Reformers; and (4) Expansionist Reformers. Ultimately, the function and form of systems would depend, he theorized, on which of these orientations proved dominant and most influential. This book does not emphasize the dispositions and attitudes of faculty, students, administrators, and policymakers. Instead, this book finds history, political and civic culture, and political economy to be the primary sources of contingency and differences among national HPS. Governance, horizontal diversity, vertical stratification, as well as higher education's effect on social equity are all contingent upon national cultural, economic, and political contexts. This book finds no evidence that the secular tendencies among HPS are the result of or regulated by attitudinal changes.

This book also breaks with Trow's tendency to rely on American exceptionalism as an analytical device. Trow was not a jingoist and was well aware of differences between systems, but he provided an exceptionalist reading of the American sector (Marginson, 2016: 31), which becomes especially explicit in his later *Minerva* essay (Trow, 2000). High participation first occurred in the USA, and the American system was (and is) influential elsewhere. But high participation is now common to nearly every middle- and high-income country. Like much mid-century American social thought, Trow assumed (albeit more softly than most) that the USA was a locomotive pulling other countries along. By contrast, this book assumes a multi-centric process of system development propelled by secular social forces. The extent to which this book overcomes methodological nationalism is the result of contributions from a multi-national group of higher education scholars. One of the abiding lessons of this project, then, is that analysis of macro-tendencies in higher education may be best accomplished collaboratively through multi-positional research.

Concluding Thoughts

This study has sought to grasp the evolution of HPS of higher education at scale by observing and tracing overall patterns within and across national systems. Big picture work done well can be highly generative. It has a crash-through effect, punching holes in older paradigms and opening up new vistas. A newly theorized big picture brings into view detail that was previously unnoticed, while providing some insight into the future (always the talisman of social science). Whether *High Participation Systems of Higher Education* has done it well is for others to say. Certainly, the book focuses on tendencies that will continue into the foreseeable future. At the same time, the approach taken in this book has three limits.

First, as noted, it can be difficult to separate developments associated with the growth of participation from other changes, common to most countries in which educational expansion is taking place, such as partial global convergence, the spread of corporate forms of organization, and, in many countries, the intensification of quasi-economic competition between universities. When investigating the seventeen propositions about HPS, it was possible to separate effects associated with growth from effects associated with the NPM and marketization in relation to some propositions but not others.

Second, the significant variations between nations in the HPS era are only partly explored here. While the book was being prepared the national factor in politics and policy was being asserted more strongly in four of the case study countries—the USA, Russia, Poland, and perhaps Japan—and in others not part of the book, including China, India, and the UK. Nations operating autonomously can imitate each other, to be sure, but it can be surmised that if national identity (if not nativism) is looming larger, there will be more variation between HPS in future, in the forms of participation and perhaps in its intensity. This also raises the question of to what extent the patterning of national HPS owes itself to nation-bound dynamics, including the cascading processes of mutual rivalry, catch-up, and forging ahead to gain an advantage—national positional competition—or it is ultimately more social-cultural than political, and more bottom-up than top-down, taking the form of a broad tendency that is so common and irresistible that it seems to sweep across every border without a single point of origin, like the remarkable radiation of farming in the Neolithic era (Cunliffe, 2015).

Third, the book has sought to bridge the gap between theorization of the larger patterns and the empirical realities of higher education by the device of the seventeen propositions. These are a series of claims about effects associated with the growth of participation. The national case studies considered the relevance of the propositions to each national system. Essentially the national case study authors were asked, seventeen times: 'is this summative proposition a plausible description of what has happened or is happening in your national higher education system'. The limitations of this method are two-fold. One is that the case study chapters largely tested the propositions as broad descriptors, rather than collecting comprehensive empirical data on a national scale, and still less by applying data-based analytical tests. However, it is possible to subject most of the propositions to more systematic testing of empirically gathered data.

Table 16.1. Potential for testing the HPS propositions

Proposition group	
3 General	*Once base economic growth reached*, growth of participation is independent of other factors
4 Governance	Multi-level control, coordination, and accountability
6 Governance	Increasing incidence of corporate forms at institutional level
7 Diversity	Growing incidence and importance of the multiversity type of institution
8 Diversity	Decline in diversity of institutional form and mission, except for online provision
9 Diversity	Increased internal diversity of institutions
10 Diversity	*If neoliberal reform*, more convergence, less diversity, more stratification, privatization
11 Stratification	Enhanced tendency to bifurcation between 'artisanal' and 'demand-responsive' institutions
12 Stratification	*If more competition for places, competition between institutions, fees*, greater stratification
14 Equity	Enhanced social inclusion
15 Equity	*All else equal*, greater social inequality of educational outcomes
16 Equity	Positional structure of HPS increasingly resembles that of society as a whole

Source: Authors.

Table 16.1 identifies propositions that might be subject to comprehensive data collection that would identify whether the phenomena described in each proposition are present in growing HPS. Arguably, the majority of these propositions could be subjected to quantitative tests, of the associations between enrolment growth and the phenomena in the proposition. However, in certain of the seventeen propositions, it is difficult to hold the definition of observed phenomena constant across national systems, for example where phenomena (e.g. 'corporatization' or 'internal diversity') include arbitrary elements subject to local and national variations. Also, while it may be possible to establish a quantitative association between, on the one hand, growth and, on the other hand, phenomena described in the propositions, this does not necessarily settle the question of whether growth *caused* the phenomena in question. Quantitative tests help by identifying the presence of strong relations. They do not exhaustively explain those relations.

In the face of the difficulties of tracking all of the HPS tendencies discussed in this book, some scholar-researchers might lower their ambition, confining themselves to what is readily counted. But not all social tendencies (and causes) can be understood that way. This does not mean that they do not exist. To understand the times, it is essential to reserve a place for all of quantitative analysis, empirically based description, historically grounded contextualization *and* large, bold theorizing that seeks to join (and imagine) the dots as best as can be done.

Whereas quantitative explanations are especially helpful in isolating structural elements, they are less effective in the domain of agency. Martin Trow's account of massification was made possible by an act of bold theorization. He broke with the structural determinism common to social science and higher education policy in his time (and ours). He understood the social growth of higher education as driven not by abstracted economic demand for skills or the statistical residual in equations of national economic growth, but by human agents. He also understood that desires and expectations were not constant but rather were continually shaped by ongoing historical processes, and that the field was relational: as collective participation grew this fostered more individual desires, further participation, and so on. *High Participation Systems of Higher Education* also foregrounds agency. Human agents make decisions, though under conditions they do not control. Inherited structural constraints (class, location, gender, politics, discrimination, global inequalities) are real. Yet in higher participation systems of higher education, expanding agency—individual and collective—is itself one of the shaping conditions. It is the feedback loop entailed in the spread of knowledge-based higher education that makes HPS especially exciting in social terms. Over time, human agency and its possibilities become larger and, if the higher education is good enough, freer than before.

Higher education as self-formation (Marginson, 2018) has an expansionary open-ended potential. As the Confucian scholars in China, Immanuel Kant (1996) and the German *Bildung* theorists argued, educated self-formation provides people with the tools to continually enlarge themselves and their horizons, while remaking and improving relational society. Yet three factors tarnish this bright story of advancing mutual empowerment in HPS.

First, as noted in Chapter 1, the position of those without degrees and diplomas is increasingly weakened by the expansion of educated populations. In some countries this plays out in the fracturing of societies and polities. Second, the potential for self-formation is maximized in well-funded elite universities with knowledge-rich curricula, and reduced when higher education consists of shorter instrumental programmes in impoverished demand-absorbing institutions. In some forms of designated higher education, including certain offsite variants without organic relational contact, there is little self-formation at all. This underlines the virtues of those systems, such as the Nordic, where quality differentials are narrow and all higher education is cognitively and relationally rich. Third, in a political economy that is partly zero-sum, in which the growth of higher education outstrips the growth of paid, sustaining, and interesting work, the opportunities facing graduates are *not* open-ended. As Hirsch puts it, baldly: 'Education enjoyed in its own right is capable of infinite extension; as an instrument for entrée into top jobs, it is not' (Hirsch, 1976: 59). This is the paradox underlying the discussion of high participation society in Chapter 7. In societies continually being fed by HPS, the gap between human agency and human opportunity continually becomes wider.

The situation of worldwide higher education and society is without historical precedent. To what extent can the expanded agency of educated people act as a causal factor, breaking through the structural limits set by unequal societies, and economies that are now expanding under-employment? Or are many of the much larger number of graduates in future doomed to remain frustrated, lacking opportunities of the scale and scope that are needed? Doesn't something have to give? The next step in the sociological investigation of HPS is to more systematically test those of the seventeen propositions that can be tested. The next step in the investigation informed by political philosophy are to explore the positive collective potentials opened up by reflexive self-formation on the scale of HPS, and to understand the meaning of that growing gap between social agency and social opportunity.

■ REFERENCES

Cunliffe, B. (2015). *By Steppe, Desert and Ocean*. Oxford: Oxford University Press.

Hirsch, F. (1976). *Social Limits to Growth*. Cambridge, MA: Harvard University Press.

Kant, I. (1996). What is enlightenment?, in M. Gregor (ed.), *Immanuel Kant: Practical Philosophy*. Cambridge: Cambridge University Press.

Marginson, S. (2016). *The Dream is Over*. Berkeley, CA: University of California Press.

Marginson, S. (2018). *Higher Education as Self-formation*. London: Institute of Education, University College London. https://www.ucl-ioe-press.com/books/higher-education-and-lifelong-learning/higher-education-as-a-process-of-self-formation/

Schofer, E. and Meyer, J. (2005). The worldwide expansion of higher education in the twentieth century. *American Sociological Review* 70(6), 898–920.

Sen, A. (2002). *Rationality and Freedom*. Cambridge, MA: Harvard University Press.

Trow, M. (1973). *Problems in the Transition from Elite to Mass Higher Education*. Berkeley, CA: Carnegie Commission on Higher Education.

Trow, M. (2000). From mass higher education to universal access: The American advantage. *Minerva* 37(4), 303–28.

INDEX